IFIP Advances in Information and Communication Technology 370

IFIP – The International Federation for Information Processing

IFIP was founded in 1960 under the auspices of UNESCO, following the First World Computer Congress held in Paris the previous year. An umbrella organization for societies working in information processing, IFIP's aim is two-fold: to support information processing within ist member countries and to encourage technology transfer to developing nations. As ist mission statement clearly states,

> *IFIP's mission is to be the leading, truly international, apolitical organization which encourages and assists in the development, exploitation and application of information technology for the benefit of all people.*

IFIP is a non-profitmaking organization, run almost solely by 2500 volunteers. It operates through a number of technical committees, which organize events and publications. IFIP's events range from an international congress to local seminars, but the most important are:

- The IFIP World Computer Congress, held every second year;
- Open conferences;
- Working conferences.

The flagship event is the IFIP World Computer Congress, at which both invited and contributed papers are presented. Contributed papers are rigorously refereed and the rejection rate is high.

As with the Congress, participation in the open conferences is open to all and papers may be invited or submitted. Again, submitted papers are stringently refereed.

The working conferences are structured differently. They are usually run by a working group and attendance is small and by invitation only. Their purpose is to create an atmosphere conducive to innovation and development. Refereeing is less rigorous and papers are subjected to extensive group discussion.

Publications arising from IFIP events vary. The papers presented at the IFIP World Computer Congress and at open conferences are published as conference proceedings, while the results of the working conferences are often published as collections of selected and edited papers.

Any national society whose primary activity is in information may apply to become a full member of IFIP, although full membership is restricted to one society per country. Full members are entitled to vote at the annual General Assembly, National societies preferring a less committed involvement may apply for associate or corresponding membership. Associate members enjoy the same benefits as full members, but without voting rights. Corresponding members are not represented in IFIP bodies. Affiliated membership is open to non-national societies, and individual and honorary membership schemes are also offered.

Daoliang Li   Yingyi Chen (Eds.)

Computer and Computing Technologies in Agriculture V

5th IFIP TC 5/SIG 5.1 Conference, CCTA 2011
Beijing, China, October 29-31, 2011
Proceedings, Part III

 Springer

Volume Editors

Daoliang Li
Yingyi Chen
China Agricultural University
China-EU Center for Information & Communication Technologies (CICTA)
17 Tsinghua East Road, P.O. Box 121, Beijing, 100083, P.R. China
E-mail: {dliangl, chenyingyi}@cau.edu.cn

ISSN 1868-4238   e-ISSN 1868-422X
ISBN 978-3-642-43944-5   ISBN 978-3-642-27275-2 (eBook)
DOI 10.1007/978-3-642-27275-2
Springer Heidelberg Dordrecht London New York

CR Subject Classification (1998): I.2.11, H.3-4, C.3, I.4, C.2, D.2

Typesetting: Camera-ready by author, data conversion by Scientific Publishing Services, Chennai, India

Printed on acid-free paper

Springer is part of Springer Science+Business Media (www.springer.com)

Preface

I would like to express my sincere thanks to all authors who submitted research papers to support the 5th International Conference on Computer and Computing Technologies in Agriculture (CCTA 2011) held in Beijing, China, during October 29–31, 2011.

This conference was hosted by China Agricultural University; the IFIP TC5 Special Interest Group (SIG) on Advanced Information Processing for Agriculture (AIPA); National Natural Science Foundation of China; and China-EU Centre for Information and Communication Technologies (CICTA).

Proper scale management is not only a necessary approach in agro-modernization and agro-industrialization but also required for the development of agricultural productivity. Therefore, the application of different technologies in agriculture has become especially important. 'Informatized agriculture' and the 'Internet of Things' are hot research topics in many countries aiming to scientifically manage agriculture to yield high incomes with low costs. CICTA covers the research and development of advanced and practical technologies applied to agriculture and promotes international communication and cooperation; it has successfully held five International Conferences on Computer and Computing Technologies in Agriculture since 2007.

The topics of CCTA 2011 covered a wide range of the interesting theory and applications of all kinds of technology in agriculture, including the Internet of Things; simulation models and decision-support systems for agricultural production; agricultural product quality testing; traceability and e-commerce technology; the application of information and communication technology in agriculture; and universal information service technology and service system development in rural areas.

We selected the 189 best papers among all those submitted to CCTA 2011 for these proceedings. The papers are divided into three themes. It is always exciting to have experts, professionals and scholars with creative contributions getting together and sharing some inspiring ideas and hopefully accomplishing great developments in high-demand technologies.

Finally, I would like also to express my sincere thanks to all authors, speakers, Session Chairs and attendees, from home and abroad, for their active participation and support of this conference.

October 2011   Daoliang Li

Conference Organization

Sponsors

China Agricultural University
The IFIP TC5 Special Interest Group (SIG) on Advanced Information
  Processing for Agriculture(AIPA)
National Natural Science Foundation of China

Organizers

China-EU Center for Information and Communication Technologies in
  Agriculture (CICTA)

Chair

Daoliang Li

Conference Secretariat

Lingling Gao

Table of Contents – Part III

Simulation, Optimization, Monitoring and Control Technology

Discrimination and Prediction
of Pork Freshness by E-nose

Xuezhen Hong and Jun Wang[*]

Department of Biosystem Engineering, Zhejiang University, Hangzhou 310058, P.R. China
{xzhong,jwang}@zju.edu.cn

Abstract. An electronic nose (e-nose) was used to establish a freshness evaluation model for pork. A pre-experiment was performed to acquire optimum parameters (10 g sample mass with 5 min headspace-generation time in 500 mL vial) for later e-nose detection of pork. Responding signals of the e-nose were extracted and analyzed. Linear Discriminant Analysis (LDA) results showed that the e-nose could classify pork with different storage time (ST) well. Back Propagation Neural Network (BPNN) was performed to predict the ST, and the results showed that 97.14% of the predicting set (with 95.71% of the training set) was classified correctly; and Multiple Linear Regression (MLR) was used to predict the sensory scores, with the results showing that the correlation coefficients (R^2 = 0.9848) between the e-nose signals and the sensory scores was high. These results prove that e-nose has the potential of assessing pork freshness.

Keywords: Electronic nose, Pork freshness, Prediction, Back Propagation Neural Network, Multiple Linear Regression.

1 Introduction

Due to its high nutritional value and tasty taste, the consumption of pork has been increasing dramatically during the last decades. However, pork is highly susceptible to spoilage and contamination by micro-organisms. The main ingredients of pork are water, protein, fat and a small amount of carbohydrates. During the storage, the ingredients will be decomposed by enzymes and bacteria, producing odor: the protein will be decomposed into ammonia, hydrogen sulfide, ethyl mercaptan, etc.; the fat will be decomposed into aldehydes and aldehyde acids odor; the carbohydrates will be decomposed into alcohols, ketones, aldehydes, and carboxylic acid gases [1]. The odor gets more and more intense with the decrease of pork freshness. Consumption of spoilage pork could cause serious health hazards [2]. Thus, it is necessary that a rapid and accurate detection system be developed for microbiologically spoiled or contaminated pork [3-4].

At present, there are mainly three traditional methods in the meat industry to detect pork freshness: sensory evaluation based on the texture, color, organization

[*] Corresponding author.

D. Li and Y. Chen (Eds.): CCTA 2011, Part III, IFIP AICT 370, pp. 1–14, 2012.

status, viscidity and odor of the pork [5]; detection of the total volatile basic nitrogen (TVBN) [6]; and aerobic plate counts of the pork samples using standard protocols (FDA-US Food and Drugs Administration, 1998) [7]. The first method provides immediate quality information but suffers from some disadvantages, for example, the subjective nature of the assessment. Furthermore, errors may arise from fatigue of panelists and low threshold concentrations of stale odor compounds may not be perceived [8]; The latter two methods are objective, but destructive, complicated and time consuming. Moreover, they are just used to analyze one or two specialized components instead of giving the whole information of pork quality. Consequently, these traditional methods are unsuitable for fast and on-line application in pork industry.

Electronic nose (e-nose), also known as artificial olfactory, is a simulation of biological functions to identify some simple or complex odor [9-10]. A typical e-nose system contains a selective chemical sensor array, a signal processing subsystem and a pattern recognition subsystem. The sensors in the sensor array are sensitive to different substances. For example, some sensors can discern ammonia and some can discern aldehydes. Thus the whole sensor array can discern complex odor. Instead of detecting one or two components of the substances, the e-nose extracts the whole information for identification. In the last decade, a few researchers have been studying the potential of using e-nose as a non-destructive method for food detection. García et al. [11] used a metal oxide semiconductor thin-film sensors based electronic nose to characterize and classify four types of red wines of the same variety of grapes which came from the same cellar. Two pattern recognition methods: Principal Component Analysis (PCA) and Probabilistic Neuronal Network (PNN) were performed, and the results showed that electronic nose was able to identify the wine well; Torri, Sinelli, and Limbo [12] used a commercial electronic nose to monitor the freshness of minimally processed fruit (packaged pineapple slices) during storage. The samples were stored at three different temperatures (4-5, 7-8, and 15-16 °C) for 6-10 days. After a continuous monitoring of the headspace around the fruit, the result showed that the fruit freshness was maintained for about 5 days at 4 °C, 2 days at 7.6 °C and 1 day at 16 °C.

In the previous research, most sensor arrays used in e-nose are Metal-Oxide Semiconductors (MOS). However, seldom information about the quality assurance of the e-nose performance has been given regarding sensor drift and humidity (MOS sensors used in e-nose are water sensitive), so it is impossible to rule out the fact that their research results may be significantly affected by either a day to day sensor drift of the sensor system, or the fact that the temporal changes observed in the sensor reading is due to the fact that the sensors perceive increasingly proportions of humidity due to increase in water vapor during storage. Moreover, few papers have mentioned the study of optimum experimental parameters, and the recognition models used are just focused on discrimination rather than prediction. In most cases, only e-nose was used, with no other experiments carried out. So even if we could predict the storage time of the food, we still can't precisely identify its freshness degree, since we don't have other indexes for cross-reference.

In this research, two experiments were conducted: e-nose detection and sensory evaluation. The main objective of this research is to evaluate the capacity of an electronic nose to classify pork samples stored for different time, as well as to predict their storage time and sensory scores. As for the e-nose detection, the sensor drift and humidity problem were taken care of by controlling the environment parameters (temperature and humidity) and by choosing calibrated data as the initial data. A pre-experiment was conducted to study the effects of headspace-generation time and pork sample mass on the response of e-nose performance. The optimum experimental parameters of headspace-generation time and sample mass were determined after employing Multivariate Analysis of Variance (MANOVA) and One-Way Analysis of Variance (ANOVA), and the later e-nose experiment was taken under the optimum experimental parameters. Linear Discriminant Analysis (LDA) and Back Propagation Neural Network (BPNN) were employed to observe if the e-nose could classify the pork samples stored for 0-6 d well, as well as to predict the storage time; and Multiple Linear Regression (MLR) was employed to build the prediction model between e-nose data and sensory scores.

2 Materials and Method

2.1 Sample Preparation

Fresh lean pork samples were purchased twice: the first purchase was for the pre-experiment, and the second purchase was for the discrimination of pork samples stored for 0-6 d. For both of the time, all the samples were obtained from the same parts of pigs and the same supplier in the local farmers' market (30.26 N, 120.19 E, Zhejiang province, China) 4 h after been killed, and were minced immediately on the spot. All the samples were packaged immediately using polystyrene base trays and were covered with commercial food grade polymer wraps before being transported to the lab. The samples were stored at 10 °C in the fridge before detection, except the ones detected on the first day (marked as day 0).

2.2 Electronic Nose System

The experiment was performed with a portable electronic nose (PEN2, Airsense Analytics, GmBH, Schwerin, Germany) (Fig. 1), which is consisted of an auto-sampling apparatus that is exposed to the volatiles, a sensor array, and pattern recognition software that is ran on a computer. The sensor array is composed of ten MOS. A description of the ten MOS is given in Table 1.

The operating process is based on Win Muster V1.6 software. There are two kinds of data obtained from the e-nose, one is R (the resistance value of the sensors when the sample gas flow through them), the other is G/G_0, where G and G_0 are the conductivities of the sensor when exposed to the sample gas and the zero gas, respectively. The G/G_0 value is more reliability cause it could avoid sensor drift in some degree, so in this study, the G/G_0 value is chosen as the initial data.

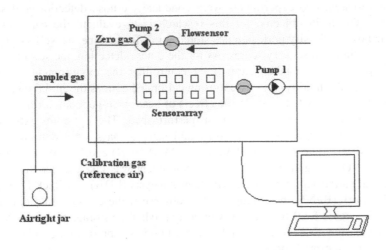

Fig. 1. Schematic diagram of the electronic nose (e-nose) measurements

Table 1. Sensors used and their object substances in PEN2

Array number	Sensor	Substances for Sensing
MOS 1	W1C	Aromatics
MOS 2	W5S	Nitrogen oxides
MOS 3	W3C	Ammonia, aromatic molecules
MOS 4	W6S	Hydrogen
MOS 5	W5C	Methane, propane, and aliphatic non-polar molecules
MOS 6	W1S	Methane
MOS 7	W1W	Sulfur-containing organics
MOS 8	W2S	Broad alcohols
MOS 9	W2W	Aromatics, sulfur- and chlorine-containing organics
MOS 10	W3S	Methane and aliphatics

2.3 Experimental Procedure

Sensory Evaluation. A sensory evaluation of pork is a method for description of the quality in an objective way. A descriptive method in accordance with GB/T 5009.44—2003 [13] was carried out at the Department of Biosystem Engineering and Food Science by a selected and trained sensory panel consisting of 8 assessors. All assessors were familiar with pork characters and descriptive analysis procedure. Scoring standard is given in Table 2.

Table 2. Sensory evaluation standards

Parameters	Scores		
	5	3	1
Color	Muscle: shiny, red, uniform Fat : white	Muscle: a little dark red Fat : lack of luster	Dark color with sign of depravity
Viscosity	Slightly dry or moist	Sticky or dry moist new cut section	High viscosity
Elasticity	Instantly and completely recover from acupressure	Slowly and incompletely recover from acupressure	Low elastic
Flavor	Normal	Ammonia or sour odor	Strong odor

E-nose Sampling Procedure. The concentration of the volatile gas is affected by the mass and headspace-generation time of the samples [14], so a set of pre-experiments were performed to determine the optimum experimental parameters. Three main factors were considered: mass of the pork samples (M: 10 and 25 g), storage time (ST: 0 and 1day) and headspace-generation time (HGT: 5, 15 and 25 min). The samples stored for 0 and 1 day were divided into six groups respectively, marked as 10-5, 10-15, 10-25, 25-5, 25-15, 25-25. The number format was mass – headspace-generation time, for example, the 10-5 group means 10 g sample mass with 5 min headspace-generation time. The multifactor pre-experiment was conducted with seven replicates of each group (Table 3). After acquiring the optimum experimental parameters, the pork samples stored for 0-6 d (15 replicates each day) were detected by e-nose under such parameters.

Each pork sample was placed in a 500 mL airtight glass vial that was sealed with plastic wrap. The glass vial was closed for a certain time (headspace-generation time) to collect the volatiles from the pork sample. During the measurement process, the headspace gaseous compounds were pumped into the sensor array at a constant flow rate of 50 mL min^{-1} through Teflon tubing connected to a needle in the plastic wrap, making the ratio of conductance of each sensor change. The measurement phase lasted for 65 s, which was long enough for the sensors to reach stable signal values. The signal data from the sensors were collected by the computer once per second during the measurements. When the measurement process was complete, the acquired data were stored for later mathematic analysis. After each measurement, zero gas (air filtered by active carbon) was pumped into the sample gas path from the other port of the instrument for 50 s (flush time). In case of sensor pollution which could cause sensor drift, after all the measurements were done every day, nitrogen gas was pumped into the sample gas path to clear the sensor array. All the measurements were carried out at a temperature of 20 °C ± 1 °C and 50% to 60% relative humidity (controlled by air-conditioning).

Table 3. Pre-experiment method

Storage time/ d	Mass/ g	Headspace-generation time/ min	Number of replications
0	15	5	7
0	15	15	7
0	15	25	7
0	25	5	7
0	25	15	7
0	25	25	7
1	15	5	7
1	15	15	7
1	15	25	7
1	25	5	7
1	25	15	7
1	25	25	7

2.4 Statistical Analysis Methods

LDA is a widely used statistic method. Similar to PCA, it is also a linear combination of the original variable to construct a discriminant function [15]. Compared with PCA, the LDA method can notice the distribution of points in the same category and the distance between them. It maximizes the variance between categories and minimizes the variance within categories to improve the resolution of classes [16]. The graphical view of LDA analysis is similar to a PCA display.

BPNN has been a widely-used method for e-nose [17-18]. BPNN can be described as a non-linear projection between the input vectors and output vectors. A typical BPNN model includes the input layer, the hidden layer (one layer or more) and the output layer. The dimensions of the input and output layer are usually decided by the dimensions of the input and output vectors, respectively, while the dimensions of the hidden layer is usually decided by try and error methodology. While determining the suitable network topology, the network processed the inputs and compared the resulting outputs against the desired outputs. Errors were then propagated back through the system, causing the system to adjust the weights that control the network [19]. This process continued over and over until the error matched the training goal error.

MLR analysis is a common method used in quantitative analysis. Equations relating the dependent variable behavior to the descriptors are developed with the following form: contribution, with numbers enclosed in parentheses and set on the right margin.

$$Y_i = \beta_0 + \beta_i X_i, \quad (i = 1, 2, 3, \ldots, N). \tag{1}$$

Where Y_i is an independent variable; β_0 is the intercept and β_i are the regression coefficients of the independent variables X_i; and N is the number of independent variables.

ANOVA is a method of portioning variability into identifiable sources of variation and the associated degree of freedom in an experiment. The frequency test (F-test) is utilized in statistics to analyze the significant effects of the parameters, which form the quality characteristics [20]. MANOVA is a generalized form of univariate ANOVA. It is used when there are two or more dependent variables. It helps to answer : 1. do changes in the independent variable(s) have significant effects on the dependent variables; 2. what are the interactions among the dependent variables and 3. among the independent variables [21].

The data processing method LDA was performed in WinMuster, which is combined in the e-nose software; (M)ANOVA and MLR were performed in SAS software, and BPNN was proceeded using the network toolbox in MATLAB R2008a.

3 Results and Discussions

3.1 Discussions of Sensory Evaluation Results

Sensory evaluation result is shown in Fig. 2. The sensory scores of color, elasticity, viscosity and odor attributes decreased as the storage time increased. It is also noticeable that both of the curves had declined quickly since the third day, while in the first 3 days, the total score curve only declined slightly, and the odor score nearly kept the same. This manifested that the pork sample didn't corrupt until the third day. So in the first 3 days, it remained fresh, with its appearance or odor change little.

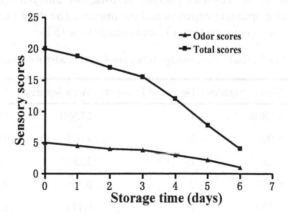

Fig. 2. Sensory evaluation result

3.2 Discussions of Pre-experiment Results

Responding Curves of E-nose. Fig. 3 shows two typical responding curves of the ten sensors during measurement of a pork sample in day 0 (Fig. 3a) and day 1 (Fig. 3b), respectively. Each curve represents a sensor's ratio of conductance (G/G_0), which increased in the first few seconds and finally stabilized at about the 60th s. Compare Fig. 3a and Fig. 3b, the ratio of conductance values of all the sensors increased with the storage time of pork. It is also noticeable that the sensor MOS 2, which is sensitive to nitrogen oxides (one of the main odor in pork putrefaction), increased most observably with storage time, with its G/G_0 value differing significantly by the storage time. This indicates that it is potential to monitor pork freshness by e-nose.

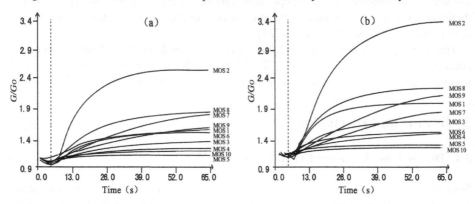

Fig. 3. Responding curves of sensors for fresh pork samples: (a): stored for 0 day; (b): stored for 1 day

Optimum Experimental Parameters.

Multivariate Analysis of Variance Result. A 3-factors analysis of variance was performed to acquire optimum experimental parameters. The three factors are sample mass (M), headspace-generation time (T) and storage time (ST).

Table 4. MANOVA (factors are storage time, mass, and headspace-generation time)

Different Source	Sum of Squares	Degree of Freedom	Mean Squares	F	Sig.
M	17.880	1	17.880	172.231	0.000
T	8.043	2	4.021	38.736	0.000
ST	22.875	1	22.875	220.338	0.000
M × T	0.890	2	0.445	4.288	0.017
M × ST	0.145	1	0.145	1.393	0.241
T × ST	0.217	2	0.108	1.044	0.357
M × T × ST	0.678	2	0.339	3.267	0.043

MANOVA was performed to see how these factors affected the response of e-nose. The MANOVA results are summarized in Table 4, where the magnitudes of the F-values indicate the relative importance of the factors to some extent. As is shown in Table 4, M, T, and ST all have very significant effect on the response of the e-nose respectively (Sig. < 0.001). The interaction of M × T, and M × T × ST also have a significant effect on the response of the e-nose (Sig. < 0.05). It can also be observed that the ST has the highest F-value, which means the e-nose signals are differed between samples with different storage time. This proves the feasibility of using the e-nose to distinguish pork freshness. The mass factor has the second highest F-value, next is the headspace-generation time, suggesting that it is very important to determine the sample mass and the headspace-generation time.

One-Way Analysis of Variance Result. ANOVA (the factor is storage time) was applied for group 10-5, 10-15, 10-25, 25-5, 25-15, 25-25 and got each group a F-value, respectively. The results of six groups are summarized in Table 5, which shows that all the groups have very significant effects on the response of e-nose, and the combination 10-5 has the highest F-value. This means that when the mass is 10 g and the headspace-generation time is 5 min, the e-nose has the most obvious difference in its responding values towards samples with different storage time.

Table 5. F-values of six combinations

Combinations	F-value	Sig.
10-5	209.883	0.000
10-15	44.131	0.000
10-25	66.676	0.000
25-5	89.451	0.000
25-15	159.226	0.000
25-25	55.049	0.000

Therefore, in this research, the optimum parameters are 10 g pork sample with 5 min headspace-generation time.

Discrimination Power (DP). DP is another index used to observe the magnitude of difference among samples [22]. All combinations with different mass and headspace-generation time (as was described before) were applied the DP analysis and got a value respectively (listed in Table 6). The number format is storage time − mass − headspace-generation time. For example, 0-10-5 means stored 0 day and 10 g sample mass with 5 min headspace-generation time. As is shown in Table 6, the combination 10-5 has the highest DP value, which means the e-nose response of this combination has the most obvious difference between day 0 and day 1. This result is the same with the ANOVA result.

Table 6. Results of DP test of six combinations

	1-10-5	1-10-15	1-10-25	1-25-5	1-25-15	1-25-25
0-10-5	0.967					
0-10-15		0.555				
0-10-25			0.753			
0-25-5				0.582		
0-25-15					0.852	
0-25-25						0.448

3.3   Discussion of E-nose Detection Results

The pork samples stored for 0-6 days (15 replications of each day) were detected by e-nose under the optimum experimental parameters, and the signals of e-nose were analyzed by multiple data analysis methods.

Linear Discriminant Analysis (LDA). For all 105 pork samples (7 storage time × 15 duplicates), the response signal values of the e-nose at the 60th s were extracted and analyzed by LDA. The results are shown in Fig. 4, which is a two-dimensional spatial plot defined by two discriminant functions. The first discriminant function (LD 1) explains 64.70% of the total variance, and the second discriminant function (LD 2) explains 23.72% of the total variance. The total contribution rate is 88.42%, which means these two reflect 88.42% of the original information.

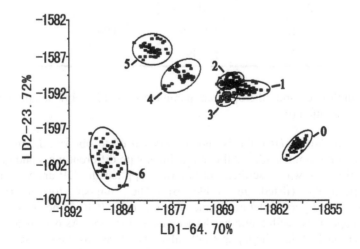

Fig. 4. LDA analysis of pork stored for 0-6 days

As is shown in Fig. 4, the samples stored for 1-3 days are very close to each other. This may be explained as follows: in the first 0-3 days, fresh pork stored at 10 °C in the fridge still remained fresh, and the change in their volatile gases was subtle so the e-nose could not notice the difference well. Thus, the data that e-nose extracted was similar to each other and concentrated. However, freeze & unfreeze could cause cell damage and affect the quality of pork, so the samples stored 0 day, which were taken for experiment directly without being stored in the fridge, are discriminated from those stored in fridge for 1-3 days. It is also noticeable that the samples stored 6 days are obviously discriminated. In general, except a little overlapped among the samples stored 1-3 days, all the samples can be clearly divided into seven regions according to their storage time.

Back Propagation Neural Network (BPNN). In this study, a 30-7-7-7 BPNN model was applied for the storage time prediction of the pork samples stored 0-6 days. Three eigenvalues (the 20th s, 40th s and 60th s value) of every sensor signal were adopted, and then all 30 (3 × 10) signal values were used as the input vector of the BPNN. The output vector was designed seven-dimensional in accordance with the seven storage days, and the training goal error was set as 0.001. After many trials, the hidden layer was decided and the network topology was designed as 30-7-7-7.

All the 105 samples were divided into two groups: 70 samples for the training set (10 samples of each group were randomly chosen), and 35 samples for the predicting set. So the input layer for the training set and the predicting set was a 70 × 30 matrix (3 eigenvalues of each sensor) and a 35 × 30 matrix, respectively. The results were shown in Table 7 and Table 8.

The total identification rate of the simulated results for the training set was 95.71%, and the total identification rate for the predicting set was 97.14%. It should be noticed that neither the predicting set nor the training set could correctly discriminate the samples stored between 2 and 3days.

Table 7. BP results of the original data in the training set

ST	NS	Recognition results							Identification rate of each day	Identification rate of all days
		0	1	2	3	4	5	6		
0	10	10							100%	
1	10		10						100%	
2	10			8	2				80%	
3	10			1	9				90%	95.71%
4	10					10			100%	
5	10						10		100%	
6	10							10	100%	

Table 8. BP results of the original data in the predicting set

ST	NS	Recognition results							Identification rate of each day	Identification rate of all days
		0	1	2	3	4	5	6		
0	5	5							100%	
1	5		5						100%	
2	5			4	1				80%	
3	5				5				100%	97.14%
4	5					5			100%	
5	5						5		100%	
6	5							5	100%	

Multiple Linear Regression (MLR). The MLR algorithm establishes the model that describes the relationship between sensor signals and odor scores. All variables used in the models are significant at the 0.01 level. The sample data (105 pork samples from 7 storage time) were separated randomly into two groups: one group for the calibration set was used to develop the calibration models (70 pork samples, 10 samples each day) and the other group containing the remaining samples was used for the prediction set (35 pork samples, 5 samples each day).

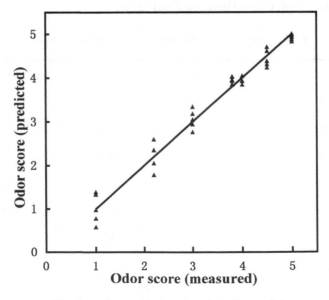

Fig. 5. Prediction of odor scores by MLR model

The predictive model for the odor score is given below.

$$S = 6.695285 + 1.314430X_1 - 0.552935X_2 + 2.401326X_3 - 4.553837X_4 +$$
$$3.023900X_5 - 2.250302X_6 - 6.150372X_7 - 1.827269X_8 - 1.609080X_9 + \quad (2)$$
$$8.197955X_{10},$$

where S is the odor score, while X_1, X_2, X_3, X_4, X_5, X_6, X_7, X_8, X_9 and X_{10} represent the 60th s signal data of the ten sensors MOS1 - MOS10, respectively. The R^2 of this model is 0.9848.

Fig. 5 shows the prediction ability of the e-nose, where each triangle represents the predicted values versus the real value of each measurement. The figures illustrate a linear correlation between the response of sensors and odor scores, indicating that the responses of sensors linearly correlated with the odor scores.

4 Conclusions

A PEN2 e-nose detection combined with sensory evaluation were conducted for discrimination and prediction of pork freshness. A pre-experiment was conducted to observe if the sample mass and headspace-generation time would affect the performance of e-nose, and the optimum experimental parameters (10 g sample mass with 5 min headspace-generation time in 500 mL vial volume) were determined by MANOVA and ANOVA. The later e-nose experiment was taken under such parameters. LDA, BPNN and MLR were employed to observe if the e-nose can classify the pork samples stored during 0-6 d well, as well as to predict the storage time and sensory scores. The results were good: The pork samples could be well discriminated by LDA; 97.14%% of the predicting set (with 95.71% of the training set) was classified correctly using BPNN model; and the MLR model also provided an accurate quality index model between e-nose signals and sensory scores with high correlation coefficients ($R^2 = 0.9848$). These results prove that the e-nose has the potential of being a reliable instrument for the assessment and prediction of pork freshness.

Acknowledgments. The authors acknowledge the financial support of the Chinese National Foundation of Nature and Science through Project 31071548, the Research Fund for the Doctoral Program of Chinese National Higher Education through Project 20100101110133, the Fundamental Research Funds for the Central Universities and the Seed Fund Project on Cross Research For Young Teachers of Zhejiang University.

References

1. Kong, B.H., Ma, L.Z.: Meat Science and Technology (肉品科学与技术). Chinese Light Industry Press, Beijing (2003)
2. Gram, L., Ravn, L., Rasch, M., Bruhn, J.B., Christensen, A.B., Givskov, M.: Food Spoilage-Interactions Between Food Spoilage Bacteria. Int. J. Food Microbiol. 78(1-2), 79–97 (2002)

3. Archer, D.L.: The Validation of Rapid Methods In Food Microbiology. Food Control 7, 3–4 (1996)
4. Ellis, D.I., Broadhurst, D., Goodacre, R.: Rapid and Quantitative Detection of The Microbial Spoilage of Beef by Fourier Transform Infrared Spectroscopy and Machine Learning. Anal. Chim. Acta. 514(2), 193–201 (2004)
5. Shirsat, N., Brunton, N.P., Lyng, J.G., McKenna, B., Scannell, A.: Texture, Colour and Sensory Evaluation of A Conventionally and Ohmically Cooked Meat Emulsion Batter. J. Sci. Food Agric. 84(14), 1861–1870 (2004)
6. Malle, P., Vanelle, A.M., Petit, A.: Total Volatile Basic Nitrogen Rates In Salt-Water Fish Muscle. Recueil de Med.Veterinaire 165(4), 395–402 (1989)
7. FDA-US Food & Drugs Administration: Bacteriological Analytical Manual, 8th edn. AOAC International, Gaithersburg (1998)
8. Limbo, S., Sinelli, N., Torri, L., Riva, M.: Freshness Decay and Shelf Life Predictive Modelling of European Sea Bass (Dicentrarchus Labrax) Applying Chemical Methods and Electronic Nose. LWT Food Sci. Technol. 42(5), 977–984 (2009)
9. Gardner, J.W., Bartlett, P.N.: A Brief History of Electronic Nose. Sens. Actuators, B 18(19), 211–220 (1994)
10. Yu, Y., Wang, J., Zhou, M.: Research Developments of Electronic Nose and Its Application in Processing of Agriculture Products. Journal of Zhejiang University: Agriculture & Life Science 29(5), 579–584 (2003) (in Chinese)
11. García, M., Aleixandre, M., Gutiérrez, J., Horrillo, M.C.: Electronic Nose For Wine Discrimination. Sens. Actuators, B 113(2), 911–916 (2006)
12. Torri, L., Sinelli, N., Limbo, S.: Shelf Life Evaluation of Fresh-Cut Pineapple by Using An Electronic Nose. Postharvest Biol. Technol. 56(3), 239–245 (2010)
13. Method for analysis of hygienic standard of meat and meat products. National Standard of the People's Republic of China: GB/T 5009.44-2003 (2003)
14. Olsson, J., Börjesson, T., Lundstedt, T., Schnürer, J.: Detection and Quantification of Ochratoxin A and Deoxynivalenol In Barley Grains by GC-MS and Electronic Nose. Int. J. Food Microbiol. 72, 203–214 (2002)
15. Buratti, S., Benedetti, S., Scampicchio, M., Pangerod, E.C.: Characterization and Classification of Italian Barbera Wines by Using An Electronic Nose and An Amperometric Electronic Tongue. Anal Chim Acta, 133–139 (2004)
16. Neely, K., Taylor, C., Prosser, O., Hamlyn, P.F.: Assessment of Cooked Alpaca and Llama Meats From the Statistical Analysis of Data Collected Using An Electronic Nose. Meat Sci. 58(1), 53–58 (2001)
17. Magana, N., Evans, P.: Volatiles As An Indicator of Fungal Activity and Differentiation Between Species, and The Potential Use of Electronic Nose Technology For Early Detection of Grain Spoilage. J. Stored Prod. Res. 36(4), 319–340 (2000)
18. Zhang, Q.Y., Zhang, S.P., Xie, C.S., Zeng, D.W., Fan, C.Q., Li, D.F., et al.: Characterization of Chinese Vinegars by Electronic Nose. Sens. Actuators, B 119(2), 538–546 (2006)
19. Pang, L.J., Wang, J., Lu, X., Yu, H.: Discrimination of Storage Age for Wheat by E-nose. Transactions of the ASABE 51(5), 1707–1712 (2008)
20. Muthukrishnan, N., Paulo Davim, J.: Optimization of Machining Parameters of Al/SiC-MMC with ANOVA and ANN Analysis. J. Mater. Process Tech. 209(1), 225–232 (2009)
21. Wikipedia, http://en.wikipedia.org/wiki/MANOVA#cite_note-0
22. Backhoff, E., Larrazolo, N., Rosas, M.: The Level of Difficulty and Discrimination Power of The Basic Knowledge and Skills Examination (EXHCOBA). Revista Electrónica de Investigación Educativa 2(1),
http://redie.uabc.mx/vol2no1/contents-backhoff.html

Nonlinear Optimization of GM(1,1) Model Based on Multi-parameter Background Value

Tangsen Zhan and Hongyan Xu

School of Information Engineering, Jingdezhen Ceramic Institute,
Jingdezhen, Jiangxi, China
ztangsen@yahoo.com.cn

Abstract. By studying the existing algorithms for background value in GM(1,1), a nonlinear optimization model of GM(1,1) based on multi-parameter background value is given. The paper uses the invertible matrix of the parameter to optimize and estimate the parameters $\hat{a}$; in addition, the parameter estimate $\hat{a}$ obtained from the multi-parameter background value has higher prediction accuracy, thus overcoming the restriction on the prediction based on the fixed average background value in other literatures. the simulated values obtained by the optimized model (NOGM(1,1)) are more precise, and the maximum error is reduced by 15%. The nonlinear optimization model of GM(1,1) based on multi-parameter background value provides algorithms for further study of GM(1,1) model.

Keywords: background value, parameter, nonlinear optimization, ratio.

1   Introduction

The grey model GM(1,1) is a forecast model in grey system. It is important to the application of grey system theory. Successful examples of using GM(1,1) for prediction can be found in many fields [1-2]. Much research has been done on this model, and a number of methods have been proposed to improve it [3-9]. Fundamentally, the effect of the change of the background value on the fitted value has been analyzed. However, when solving GM(1,1), the area is partitioned and the background value is obtained through approximate iteration, or the solution can be obtained through a parameter expression derived from a special background value model.

As for the background value, the $(1 - \delta : \delta)$ ratio established between the background value and the two endpoint prototype values restricts the expression and estimation of grey differential equation, which causes the estimated parameters to produce a greater prediction error. The model solution is probably imprecise. This paper discusses the GM(1,1) model of the background value with two or more parameters obtained through the extension of the background value, the nonlinear optimization of the analog value with parameters called the nonlinear optimization model of GM(1,1) based on the background value with multi-parameters (NOGM(1,1)).

D. Li and Y. Chen (Eds.): CCTA 2011, Part III, IFIP AICT 370, pp. 15–19, 2012.
© IFIP International Federation for Information Processing 2012

2   The Nonlinear Optimization Model of GM(1,1) Based on the Multi-parameter Background Value

2.1   The Grey Model GM(1,1) of Background Value with Two Parameters

Denote the original sequence by $X^{(0)} = (X_{(1)}^{(0)}, X_{(2)}^{(0)}, ..., X_{(N)}^{(0)})$, calculate an AGO $X_{(k)}^{(1)} = \sum_{i=1}^{k} X_{(i)}^{(0)}$, get the new sequence $X^{(1)} = (X_{(1)}^{(1)}, X_{(2)}^{(1)}, ..., X_{(N)}^{(1)})$, albinism differential form of GM(1,1) is

$$\frac{dX^{(1)}}{dt} + aX^{(1)} = b \qquad (1)$$

Difference form of GM(1,1) is

$$X_{(k)}^{(0)} + a * z_{(k)}^{(1)} = b \, (k=2, 3, 4, ..., N) \qquad (2)$$

There is $z_{(k+1)}^{(1)} = r_k * X_{(k)}^{(1)} + s_k * X_{(k+1)}^{(1)}$, solving (2) and getting parameter

$$\hat{a} = [a, b]^T = (B^T B)^{-1} B^T Y_N \qquad (3)$$

Where $Y_N = (X_{(2)}^{(0)}, X_{(3)}^{(0)}, ..., X_{(N)}^{(0)})$,

$$B = \begin{bmatrix} 1 & 1 & ... & 1 \\ -z_{(2)}^1 & -z_{(2)}^1 & ... & -z_{(N)}^1 \end{bmatrix}^T$$, the model of the background value $z_{(k+1)}^{(1)}$

with parameters r_k and s_k is obtained, and it is called the grey model GM(1,1) of the background value with two parameters.

2.2   The Nonlinear Optimization Model of GM(1,1) for the Multi-parameter Background Value

In order to achieve parameter estimation based on the multi-parameter background value, inverse matrix must be directly expressed by easy other matrix. The following is the process to get the parameter estimate through invertible matrix.

Theorem 1. If F= $\sum_{k=2}^{N} (z_{(k)}^{(1)})^2$, and C= $\sum_{k=2}^{n} z_{(k)}^{(1)}$,

$$(B^T B)^{-1} = \frac{1}{(N-1)F - C^2} \begin{bmatrix} N-1 & C \\ C & F \end{bmatrix}$$

Proof: Because $B^T B = \begin{bmatrix} \sum\limits_{k=2}^{N} (z_{(k)}^{(1)})^2 & -\sum\limits_{k=2}^{N} z_{(k)}^{(1)} \\ -\sum\limits_{k=2}^{N} z_{(k)}^{(1)} & N-1 \end{bmatrix} = \begin{bmatrix} F & -C \\ -C & N-1 \end{bmatrix}$,

$$(B^T B)^{-1} = \frac{(B^T B)^*}{|B^T B|} = \frac{1}{(N-1)F - C^2} \begin{bmatrix} N-1 & C \\ C & F \end{bmatrix}.$$

Theorem 2. If $D = \sum\limits_{k=2}^{N} X_{(k)}^{(0)}$ and $E = \sum\limits_{k=2}^{N} X_{(k)}^{(0)} \cdot z_{(k)}^{(1)}$, $B^T Y_N = \begin{bmatrix} -E \\ D \end{bmatrix}$

Theorem 2 is easily established.

Derived from Theorem 1and Theorem 2 is equation (3), the parameter estimate

$$\hat{a} = [a, b]^T = (B^T B)^{-1} B^T Y_N, \text{ where}$$

$$a = \frac{C*D - (N-1)E}{(N-1)*F - C^2}, \quad b = \frac{D*F - C*E}{(N-1)F - C^2} \tag{4}$$

Substituting a and b in the discrete responsive type

$$\hat{X}_{(k+1)}^{(1)} = (X_{(1)}^{(0)} - \frac{b}{a}) * e^{-a*k} + \frac{b}{a} \tag{5}$$

Because matrix B and estimation parameter $\hat{a}$ include parameters r_k and s_k , parameters a and b cannot be directly calculated by (3), but will be calculated by the nonlinear optimization model as follows:

Step 1: Get a and b with parameters r_k and s_k and the expression of the fitted value.

Get the fitted value $\hat{X}_{(k+1)}^{(0)}$ of the original data $X_{(k+1)}^{(0)}$ from form (5), and

$$\hat{X}_{(k+1)}^{(0)} = \hat{X}_{(k+1)}^{(1)} - \hat{X}_{(k)}^{(1)} \ (k = 0, 1, \ldots, N-1), \ \hat{X}_{(1)}^{(0)} = X_{(1)}^{(0)}$$

Step 2: Get and solve the expression of the minimum object function:

$$\min f(r_i, s_i) = \sum_{k=2}^{N} (\hat{X}_{(k)}^{(0)} - X_{(k)}^{(0)})^2 \tag{6}$$

Use MATLAB to program and calculate r_k and s_k.

Step 3: Substitute r and s in (3) to calculate a and b, substitute r_k and s_k in (4) to calculate the fitted value $\hat{X}_{(k+1)}^{(1)}$, and get the error values.

3   Application of the Nonlinear Optimization Model of GM(1,1) for the Background Value with Parameters

Use the GDPs of china from 1991 to 2003 to set background values with two parameters r and s in NOGM(1,1), and get r=0.0267, s=0.8945, but r+s $\neq$ 1 through (3), (4), and (5). The results show that the model that expresses the background value better is not based on the $(1 - \delta : \delta)$ ratio between the two endpoint values. The values simulated in the NOGM(1,1) are compared with those simulated in NGM(1,1)[7] in the following table 1.

Table 1. Comparison between values simulated in NOGM(1,1) and those in NGM(1,1)

year	Original data	Simulated data in DGM(1,1)	Simulated error in DGM(1,1) %	Simulated data in NOGM(1,1) with two parameters a=-0.1040,b=34468	Simulated error in NOGM(1,1) with two parameters %
1991	21617.8	21617.8	0	21617.8	0
1992	26638.1	40500	52.04	36548	37.21
1993	34634.4	44750	29.22	42754	23.4437
1994	46759.4	49450	5.76	47419	1.41063
1995	58478.1	54640	6.56	52594	10.0621
1996	67884.6	60380	11.05	58332	14.0718
1997	74462.6	66720	10.4	64697	13.1148
1998	78345.2	73720	5.9	71756	8.4107
1999	82067.5	81460	0.73	79586	3.02373
2000	89468.1	90020	0.61	88269	1.34025
2001	97314.8	99470	2.21	97901	0.602375
2002	105172.3	109910	4.51	108580	3.24011
2003	117251.9	121450	3.58	120430	2.71049
Average error			10.1977		9.167

4 Conclusion

GM(1,1) model has its adaptation range[6]. By optimizing and making background values parametric, the paper uses the invertible matrix of the parameter to optimize and estimate the parameters $\hat{a}$, the improved model overcomes the dependence of the background value on the $(1-\delta : \delta)$ ratio between the two endpoint values in other literatures. It provides a better prediction model for the conversion from a continual form to a discrete form. The examples indicate that the simulated value obtained by the model NOGM(1,1) is more precise, and the maximum error is reduced by 15%. However, because the simulated value is expressed by an exponential function, the simulating error is bigger at some points. Then, how to reduce the overall error will be a concern of the future study.

Acknowledgements. Supported by the National Natural Science Foundation of China under Grant No.61066003.

References

[1] Shui, N., Qin, Y.: On some theoretical problems of GM(1,1) model of grey systems. Systems Engineering—Theory & Practice 18(4), 59–63 (1998)

[2] Liu, S., Guo, T., Dang, Y.: Grey System Theory and Its Applica-tion. Science Press, Beijing (2004)

[3] Tan, G.-J.: The structure method and application of background value in grey system GM(1,1) model (I). Systems Engineering—Theory & Practice 4(4), 98–103 (2004)

[4] Wang, Y., Liu, G.: A step by step optimum direct modeling method of GM(1,1). Systems Engineering—Theory & Practice 9(6), 99–104 (2000)

[5] Xie, N., Liu, S.: Discrete GM(1,1) and mechanism of grey forecasting model. Systems Engineering—Theory & Practice 1(3), 93–99 (2005)

[6] Xu, H., Chen, Y., Fei, Z.: Discussion of the region suitable for GM(1,1) and its improving model. Mathematics in Practice and Theory 11(4), 58–63 (2008)

[7] Fei, Z., Xu, H., Jiang, Z.: Theoretical defect of GM(1,1) model and its optimum analysis based on time response function. Mathematics in Practice and Theory 5(10), 214–219 (2009)

[8] Liu, N., Sun, W., Yao, H.: Research on improving the fitting and prediction precision of the GM (1,1) Model. Mathematics in Practice and Theory 4(8), 33–39 (2008)

[9] Chen, S., Li, Z., Zhou, S.: Application of non-equal interval GM(1,1) model in oil monitoring of internal combustion engine. Journal of Central South University of Technology 12(6), 705–708 (2005)

Plant Leaf Water Detection Instrument
Based on Near Infrared Spectroscopy

Jiannan Jia and Haiyan Ji[*]

Key Laboratory of Modern Precision Agriculture System Integration Research,
Ministry of Education, China Agricultural University, Beijing, China 100083
instru@cau.edu.cn

Abstract. In the near infrared spectral region, a reflection plant water detection instrument was designed by using microcontroller STC12C5A60S2. The instrument consisted of signal acquisition system, microcontroller system, software system and calibration model. The signal acquisition system was composed of three LED of different wavelength and a light-to-frequency converter. Three LED of different wavelength were lighted by turns for avoiding interaction. Light-to-frequency converter was used as the receiving tube, thus simplifying the circuit structure greatly. This paper described the instrument's hardware design, software design, modeling of Forsythia leaf water content and forecasting. Predicted results were consistent with the true values of water, and the correlation coefficient between them was about 0.820. Advantages of this instrument were small, simple structure, low power consumption and so on. The experimental results showed that the instrument could detect plant water content rapidly on fieldwork.

Keywords: reflection measurement, water detection, leaves, portable instrument.

1   Introduction

Water is a major component of crop. Water deficit directly affect the plant's physiological and biochemical processes and morphology, thus affecting plant growth, yield and quality [1]. Getting plant water status rapidly is very important for agriculture, horticulture, forest water management and potential fire assessment [2].

Water absorption spectrum has five absorption bands, their central wavelength are located in near 760nm, 970nm, 1145nm, 1450nm and 1940nm. Based on this, the spectral information of this region has been widely used to analyze the water status in plants [3-6].

Several researchers have described relationships between leaf water content and infrared (700-2500nm) reflectance. Tucker [7] considered simulated leaf reflectance along with atmospheric transmission properties, and determined the spectral region between 1550 nm and 1750 nm was best suited for remotely measuring leaf water content. Carter et al [8] found that visible wavelengths (551nm) correlated best with the total water potential of loblolly pine needles. Hunt et al [9] and Hunt and Rock [10] described a liquid water content index that was used to estimate leaf relative water contents. Penuelas et al found that the water index WI ($WI=R_{900}/R_{970}$) or minimum of

---

[*] Corresponding author.

D. Li and Y. Chen (Eds.): CCTA 2011, Part III, IFIP AICT 370, pp. 20–27, 2012.

first derivative in the near infrared band can clearly indicate the change of water status [11]. The subsequent study of Penuelas and Inoue also showed that the ratio $WI/NDVI$ ($WI=R_{900}/R_{970}$, $NDVI=(R_{900}-R_{680})/(R_{900}+R_{680})$) not only could be used to predict the moisture content of leaves but also could be used to predict the water content of plant or canopy, and significantly improved the prediction accuracy [12,13]. By using derivative spectrum, Yan Shen established the water content model of monocots and dicots, it provided new ideas of remote sensing classification for identifying monocots and dicots [14]. By using principal component regression, Hanping Mao established the moisture content model of grape leaves based on spectral reflectance characteristics, and found that grape leaves dry-basis moisture content was significantly correlated with derivative spectra of 703nm [15]. By using spectral stepwise regression analysis and constructed spectral index method, Yong Yang analyzed the relationship between citrus leaf spectral reflectance and moisture content, and established the moisture content model of citrus leaves based on spectral reflectance [16]. These findings show that diagnosing plant water status by using spectral reflectance is feasible.

Near infrared water detection instrument generally has two measurement methods [17-19]: transmission method and reflection method. Reflection method, namely, determine the water content of samples by detecting the reflected light intensity from the sample surface. Near infrared water detection instrument designed by Xiaoying Lin [20], measured water by reflection method and used three beams of 1700nm, 1940nm and 2100nm. The instrument consisted of electronic circuit and complex optical probe, therefore its size was relatively large. The instrument in this paper is a battery-powered handheld device, so its Light source used LED. The system selected 970nm as measuring wavelength. In the band from 900nm to 680nm, the absorption of water is less and the curve of absorption tends to flat. Therefore, the system selected 900nm and 680nm as reference wavelength.

2   Instrument Design and Modeling

2.1   System Components

According to the logic function, the hardware circuit of this instrument was divided into several sub-modules. Modules could be divided into: microprocessor, light source, detector, LCD display unit, keyboard control unit and storage unit. System diagram of hardware is shown in Fig.1.

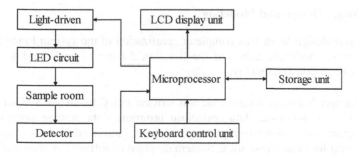

Fig. 1. System diagram of hardware

Microprocessor. The microcontroller used in this design was STC12C5A60S2. STC12C5A60S2 is an enhanced microcontroller of 8051 series, and its operating speed is faster. Its operating voltage is 5.5V to 3.3V. It has three kinds of operating mode, thus its CPU could be placed in power-saving mode firstly, then, waking up CPU by interruption to reducing power consumption as much as possible. It has the EEPROM function. And, it is very easy to develop, can download user program directly via the serial port.

Signal Acquisition Module. The Signal acquisition module of this hardware system included light source, sample room and detector. The incident light shined on the sample in the sample room, then, the detector detected the light intensity of reflected light. The detected results would be sent to microcontroller.

Light source consisted of three LED, and their central wavelengths located in 650nm, 880nm and 940nm. Each LED had adjustable constant current circuit to ensure the stability of light sources. Three monochromatic lights of different wavelengths under the control of the microprocessor shined leaves by turns, and the reflected light was received by detector. Whole device was located in a black-box to avoid the interference from outside light, and improve the measurement accuracy.

The system selected TSL230 as the detector. The TSL230 programmable light-to-frequency converters combine a configurable silicon photodiode and a current-to-frequency converter on single monolithic CMOS integrated circuits. The output can be either a pulse train or a square wave (50% duty cycle) with frequency directly proportional to light intensity. The sensitivity of the devices is selectable in three ranges, providing two decades of adjustment. The full-scale output frequency can be scaled by one of four preset values. All inputs and the output are TTL compatible, allowing direct two-way communication with a microcontroller for programming and output interface.

Interface Module. The system selected 1602 character LCD for displaying. Its displaying capacity is 16×2 characters. The system included six buttons, they were measuring the incident light intensity count, measuring the reflected light intensity count, showing water index and leaf water content, previous record, next record, deleting record. LCD and the six buttons achieved information input, output and display.

2.2   Software Design and Modeling

After hardware design work was completed, realization of the system function had to rely on software. Software achieved the function driving of each module, the data collection, calculation and display.

Software Design. Software source code was written with C language. Software system consisted of main program, data collection program, data storage program, LCD display program and button interrupt program. After initialization was completed, the program waited for button operation. System diagram of software is shown in Fig.2.

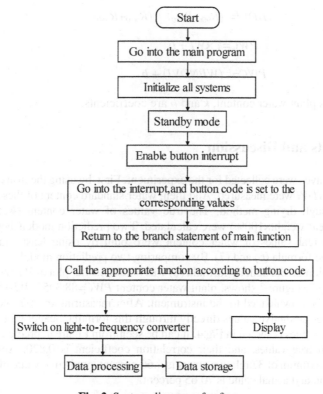

Fig. 2. System diagram of software

Modeling. The instrument measured some samples whose water content had been known. Three LED lights were lit by control of program, at the same time, switching on Light-to-frequency converter. Light-to-frequency converter would send pulse to the microcontroller. This frequency of pulse was gotten from incident light intensity I_0 and reflected light intensity I. Then, the time counter of microcontroller would record the corresponding frequency count value n_0 and n within a certain time. Therefore, light intensity and the count value are directly proportional. By the formula (1) to (3), we could calculate reflectivity R_{680}, R_{900} and R_{970}, and stored them in memory. The water index WI and $NDVI$ could be calculated by the formula (4) and (5). Then, we could build a mathematical model between the water index and water content by the formula (6) or (7), and downloaded it to the instrument. When measuring the same type of leaves again, as long as getting the reflectivity under three different wavelengths monochromatic light, the instrument can predict and display the water content.

$$R=I/I_0=f/f_0 \tag{1}$$

$$f \propto n \tag{2}$$

$$R=n/n_0 \tag{3}$$

$$WI=R_{900}/R_{970} \tag{4}$$

$$NDVI= (R_{900}-R_{680}) \, / \, (R_{900}+R_{680}) \tag{5}$$

$$PWC=k \times WI + b \tag{6}$$

$$PWC=k \, (WI/NDVI) + b \tag{7}$$

Where PWC is plant water content, k and b are coefficients.

3   Results and Discussion

37 Forsythia leaves were collected for the experiment. First, by using the instrument, water index WI and $NDVI$ were measured. And then, water standard content of these leaves was measured through drying method. The true values of water content (water standard content/fresh leaf weight×100%) were calculated. Two prediction models between water index and the real values of water content were built by using least square method according to the formula (6) and (7). By comparing two prediction models, we could find that the prediction model built by formula (6) was better. Scatter plot of WI and true values is shown in Fig.3. Figure 3 shows, plant water content PWC=88.3957×WI-11.3608. This formula could be downloaded to the instrument. After measuring the WI, the instrument can obtain water predictive values directly through this formula. Scatter plot of predicted values and true values is shown in Fig.4. It can be seen from Figure 4, predicted values are consistent with true values, and their correlation coefficient is 0.820. Among the 37 samples, the maximum of 37 relative errors is 4.66 percent, predictive value of this sample is 67.36 percent, and actual value is 70.65 percent.

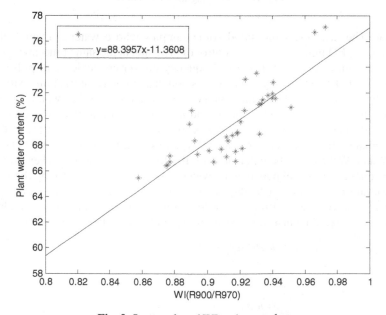

Fig. 3. Scatter plot of WI and true values

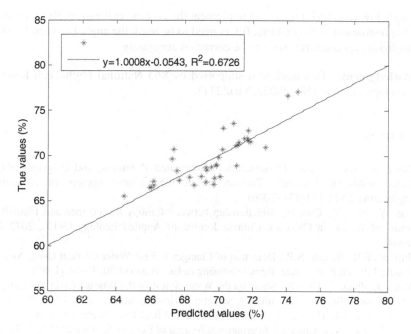

Fig. 4. Scatter plot of predicted values and true values

There were not filters in the sample room. Therefore, the collected light intensity signal was not a single wavelength, but light intensity count values in a bandwidth. Because the angle between LED and light-to-frequency converter could not be corrected accurately, so the size of leaves had some influence on the measurement result. These would affect the measurement result. In the experiment, because the range of water content was limited, so result would have a big error if it was used to forecast some water content outside this range. In order to expand the measuring range, segmentation modeling in different ranges of water content could be built. When Measuring leaves of different plants, different forecasting models need to be built.

4   Conclusions

In the near infrared spectral region, a water detection instrument based on the sensitive spectrum of water absorption was designed. Using near infrared light 650nm, 880nm and 940nm, microcontroller STC12C5A60S2 and a new type of light-to-frequency converter TSL230, initial design of the reflection plant water detection instrument and debugging were completed. Modeling and forecasting in water content of the experimental samples were finished, and got some satisfactory results. To different plant species, different forecasting models can be built to achieve the rapid measurement of leaf water. In the hardware design and software code writing process, features such as low power consumption and anti-interference were fully took into account. The instrument has good stability and good reproducibility, simple operation, small size, low cost, and it is easy to implement the commercialization. But, in order to using the instrument in the real life, filters need to be used, the angle between LED and light-to-frequency converter need to be corrected accurately.

Acknowledgments. This work was supported by 863 National High-Tech Research and Development Plan (No. 2007AA10Z211).

References

1. Zhang, J., Duan, A., Sun, J.: Advances in Automated Monitoring and Diagnosis of Crop Water Status (in Chinese). Transactions of the Chinese Society of Agricultural Engineering 22(1), 174–178 (2006)
2. Tian, Y., Zhu, Y., Cao, W.: Relationship between Canopy Reflectance and Plant Water Status of Wheat (in Chinese). Chinese Journal of Applied Ecology 15(11), 2072–2076 (2004)
3. Hunt Jr., E.R., Barrett, N.R.: Detection of Changes in Leaf Water Content Using Near-and Middle-Infrared Reflectance. Remote Sensing of Environment 30, 43–54 (1989)
4. Wang, J., Zhao, C., Guo, X.: Study on the Water Status of the Wheat Leaves Diagnosed by the Spectral Reflectance (in Chinese). Scientia Agricultura Sinica 34(1), 104–107 (2001)
5. Liu, L., Wang, J., Huang, W.: Estimating Winter Wheat Plant Water Content Using Red Edge Parameters (in Chinese). International Journal of Remote Sensing 25(17), 3331–3342 (2004)
6. Rollin, M.E., Milton, E.J.: Processing of High Spectral Resolution Reflectance Data for the Retrieval of Canopy Water Information. Remote Sensing of Environment 65, 86–92 (1998)
7. Tucker, C.J.: Remote Sensing of Leaf Water Content in the Near Infrared. Remote Sense Environ. 10, 23–32 (1980)
8. Carter, G.A., Paliwal, K., Pathre, U., Green, T.H., Mitchell, R.J., Gjerstad, D.H.: Effect of Competition and Leaf Age on Visible and Infrared Reflectance in Pine Foliage. Plant Cell Environ. 12, 309–315 (1989)
9. Hunt Jr., E.R., Rock, B.N., Nobel, P.S.: Measurement of Leaf Relative Water Content by Infrared Reflectance. Remote Sense Environ. 22, 429–435 (1987)
10. Hunt Jr., E.R., Rock, B.N.: Detection of Changes in Leaf Water Content Using Near and Middle Infrared Reflectance. Remote Sense Environ. (1990)
11. Penuelas, J., Filella, I., Biel, C.: The Reflectance at the 950-970nm Region as an Indicator of Plant Water Status. International Journal of Remote Sense 14, 1887–1905 (1993)
12. Penuelas, J., Inoue, Y.: Reflectance Indices Indicative of Changes in Water and Pigment Contents of Peanut and Wheat Leaves. Photosynthetica 36(3), 355–360 (1999)
13. Penuelas, J., Pinol, J., Ogaya, R.: Estimation of Plant Water Concentration by the Reflectance Water Index WI (R900/R970). International Journal of Remote Sense 18, 2869–2872 (1997)
14. Shen, Y., Niu, Z., Wang, W.: Establishment of Leaf Water Content Models Based on Derivative Spectrum Variables (in Chinese). Geography and Geo-Information Science 21(4), 16–19 (2005)
15. Mao, H., Zhang, X., Li, X.: Model Establishment for Grape Leaves Dry-Basis Moisture Content Based on Spectral Signature (in Chinese). Journal of Jiangsu University 29(5), 369–372 (2008)
16. Yang, Y., Zhang, D., Li, S., Hu, C.: Model for Citrus Leaves Water Content Based on Spectral Signature (in Chinese). Chinese Agricultural Science Bulletin 27(2), 180–184 (2011)

17. Li, J., Zhao, L., Lao, C.: Modern Near Infrared Spectral Analysis Technology of Farm Products (in Chinese). Modern Scientific Instruments 1, 17–19 (2005)
18. Yuan, H., Long, Y., Lu, W.: A New Infrared Spectrometer with Charge Coupled Device Detector (in Chinese). Chinese Journal of Analytical Chemistry 27(5), 608–614 (1999)
19. Zhou, X., Zhu, Y., Liu, X.: Instrument Technology and Applications of Modern Fourier Transform Near Infrared Spectrometer (in Chinese). Modern Instruments 8(4), 29–32 (2002)
20. Lin, X.: Develop on Near Infrared Moisture Instrument (in Chinese). China Instrumentation 2, 13–14 (2001)

Optimization Strategy on Cash Transportation Routing of Banks

Longjia Xiao[1] and Xin Wang[2]

[1] School of Automobile, Chang'an University, Xi'an, 710064
[2] Computer Network Center, China Agricultural University, Beijing 100083, PRC

Abstract. This paper studies the cost control strategy on cash transportation of China's banking industry under the context of the global financial crisis. It analyses the actual work law of the bank cash transportation profoundly and the impact factors at the transportation costs, and constructs the single- material vehicle routing optimization model with rigid time constraints. It uses the genetic algorithm to design a solution for the model. It establishes a practical example based on the actual data from the savings network of CCB and traffic information of Hohhot urban road network, and gets a satisfactory solution, which verifies the effectiveness of the optimization model.

Keywords: Cost control, Vehicle routing, Optimization model, Genetic algorithm.

1 Introduction

In March 2007, the U.S. subprime crisis outbreak formally, then evolved and deepened, which triggered the most serious financial crisis since 30 years of last century of American history and caused a big shock in global financial markets. It led to an international financial crisis. Lots of financial institutions had been closed down one after another, follow that the world's major stock markets fell sharply, investors suffered heavy losses, world economic growth in severe decline. According to incomplete statistics, the global stock market capitalization had suffered the loss of more than 27 trillion U.S. dollars since the beginning of 2008 to October 2008 [1].

Impact of the financial crisis is extensive and far-reaching, which also led to a range of effects on our economy. In response to the growing spread of financial crisis, in second half of 2008, our government adopted a series of decisive measures, the companies also made a variety of means to reduce costs. Meanwhile, the low-carbon economy with purpose that reduces the carbon emissions is developing rapidly worldwide. How to reduce emissions and pollution is which the scholars from various countries study actively. Number of savings outlets in the front line of banking services, which are most grassroots organizations in the entire banking system, also is the extremely important foundation institution. Because of their large number and wide distribution, the daily transportation costs to transport all savings of the savings outlets, which is a huge expenditure over many years. In the context of the global financial crisis, how to control the cost of transportation effectively has an important practical significance to the healthy development of China's banking industry.

D. Li and Y. Chen (Eds.): CCTA 2011, Part III, IFIP AICT 370, pp. 28–42, 2012.

2 The Decision of Armored Car Transportation Route Based on the Structure of Urban Road Network

Control of transportation costs has to use the means of optimization of transportation scheduling, which is based on the characteristics of transportation tasks, road network data, the condition of the vehicles that can be used, assigns the transport vehicles and determines driving routes, transports the monetary savings needed to be shipped to from the savings outlets to return the specified location within the limited time, which makes comprehensive evaluation index on transport costs and transport time best. The core issue is the selection of the shortest path.

2.1 Problem Description

The grassroots organizations of banking institutions are savings outlets, which are service window for the general customer, the contents of daily work fixes relatively. They need get the cashes daily from armored car from 8:00 to 8:40, and bags the day cashes then transport it back to treasury by the armored car when settlement is completed at 5:20-6:10. Also, if the day savings in a single savings outlet exceed the prescribed limits, you need to return the excess amount of units to treasury by the armored car. Therefore, the number of used armored car of banking Management is greater than or equal twice daily, the distance is long and the arrival time of the armored car has a strict limit. Considering the long term, lower cash-carrying transportation costs to improve transport efficiency have a great significance to costs control on the banking operation.

According to the actual work requiring, in the rigid time constraints, based on the key considerations of economic rationality of transport, it need to consider vehicle loading rate, the number of dispatched trucks, a reasonable line and other issues. Therefore, this research can be attributed to the optimization decision problem based on urban road network structure, that with single varieties of goods, fully loaded, through all outlets, time constrained, and to minimize the total transportation cost from the starting point of delivery to the receiving point, that a "vehicle routing with time windows problem" (Vehicle Routing Problem with Time Windows, VRPTW). In order to accurately establish the mathematical model of the problem, following assumptions are made particularly:

- Urban transport network is the complete network and no direction.

- The transport sector banks have sufficient and different load vehicles which can be scheduled using, and does not consider the problem of vehicle maintenance.

- The starting and finishing point of armored car is the same point, that is the starting point and the end of transportation.

- The savings outlets only be accessed each time in a activities of a particular cash-carrying, each armored car services only one route.

- A collection of savings outlets and monetary transportation route is known, and the time transformation weights associated with the path and transport costs transformation weights are known.

- All savings outlets have deadline constraints, but the sooner or later two deadline fixed, the extra conditions are determined by the status of deposits.

2.2 Model

2.2.1   The Idea of Modeling

To build a single variety of materials VRPTW model, it must focus on analyzing the factors and weight that affect the transport costs with strong time request, and try to simplify the model structure so as to solve easy. At the same time it adds the last time constraints to the model and quantifies the time period. Following, it focuses on the function construction with last time deadlines.

The VRPTW vehicle routing problems with time windows comply with the armored vehicle transport characteristics in the urban road network. The crux of the matter is to transfer the time function cost to the cost function so that it comply with the goal of economic unity, if it violates the time constraints, the cost function will tend to infinity. If the armored cars reach the savings outlets too early, its security will not be guaranteed. If it reaches too late, it will affect the efficiency and safety of whole system. Therefore, it sets $D_i^{'}$ to the first time deadlines and D_i to the latest time deadlines for cash-carrying of savings outlets, $M \to \infty$ is a large enough positive number, according to the actual time of point i T_i get the construction function with the last time deadlines constraint as follows:

$$G(T_i) = \begin{cases} 0 & D_i^{'} \leq T_i \leq D_i \\ M & T_i > D_i 或 T_i < D_i^{'} \end{cases} \tag{1}$$

2.2.2   Model Objective Function

$$\min Z = \sum_{i=0}^{k}\sum_{j=0}^{k}\sum_{v=1}^{n} \alpha_{ij} \cdot d_{ij} \cdot X_{ijv} + \sum_{v=1}^{n} C_v \tag{2}$$

Constraints:

$$\sum_{i=1}^{k} R_i \cdot Y_{iv} \leq Q_v, \quad \forall v \in V \tag{3}$$

$$\sum_{v=1}^{n} Y_{iv} = 1, \quad \forall v \in V, \ i = 1, 2, \cdots, k \tag{4}$$

$$\sum_{i=0}^{k} X_{ijv} = Y_{jv}, \quad \forall v \in V, \ j = 0, 1, 2, \cdots, k \tag{5}$$

$$\sum_{j=0}^{k} X_{ijv} = Y_{iv}, \quad \forall v \in V, \quad i = 0,1,2,\cdots,k \tag{6}$$

$$\exists X_{ijv} = 1, T_j = T_i + S_{iu} + S_{ijv} \Rightarrow$$

$$T_j = X_{ijv} \cdot \left(T_i + S_{iu} + S_{ijv} \right), \quad i = 0,1,2,\cdots,k, \quad j = 0,1,2,\cdots,k, \quad i \neq j \tag{7}$$

$$D_i' \leq T_i \leq D_i \Rightarrow$$

$$G(T_i) = \begin{cases} 0 & D_i' \leq T_i \leq D_i \\ M & T_i > D_i \, \vec{\mathfrak{R}} \, T_i < D_i' \end{cases} \tag{8}$$

Where:

i, j—the savings outlets, i = 0 point is the starting point of armored car, but also the end point, the treasury.

V—All vehicles armored car collection;

K—savings outlets collection;

d_{ij}—The distance from point i to point j;

α_{ij}—the economical weights per unit distance (transportation costs);

β_{ij}—the timeliness weights per unit distance (time consumption factor);

C_v—the fixed cost of vehicle v be used (average daily cost of hiring staff, routine maintenance costs, all taxes, etc.);

Q_v—The maximum load capacity of vehicle v;

T_i— the actual time of reaching point i , T_0 is the time from the starting point;

S_{ijv}—the time taking from point i to j;

S_{iu}—the cash-installation time at the point i;

M—large enough positive number;

R_i—the money supply of savings outlet i needed to transport (the multiple of defined volume) $i = 1,2,\cdots,k$;

D_i'—the earliest time when armored car arrived savings outlets;

D_i—the latest time when armored car arrived savings outlets;

$$X_{ijv} = \begin{cases} 1 & \text{when car } v \text{ drive } from \ i \ to \ j \\ 0 & \text{when car } v \text{ donot drive } from \ i \ to \ j \end{cases}$$

$$Y_{iv} = \begin{cases} 1 & \text{the cash } \sup ply \ of \ \text{point } i \ is \ served \ \text{by car } v \\ 0 & \text{the cash } \sup ply \ of \ \text{point } i \ is \ \text{not } served \ \text{by car } v \end{cases}$$

Objective function (2) makes the costs of armored vehicle transportation (the sum of total costs and fixed costs of vehicles) minimum. Constraint equation (3) is the load capacity constraint to ensure that the money supply responded by the vehicles v don't exceed the maximum capacity; Constraint (4) ensure that the cash to be sent in each savings outlets is delivered only by a single vehicle; Constraint (5) said that if the money to be delivered of savings outlets j is distributed by the vehicle v, the vehicle v must travel from the savings outlets i to j; Constraint (6) said that if the money to be delivered of savings outlets i is distributed by the vehicle v, then after the vehicle v has deposited the cashes of savings outlets I, it must go to another savings outlet; Constraint (7) is the service time expression, which reflects the arrival time relationship between the savings outlets j and the previous savings outlet serviced by the same truck, $T_j \geq T_i$; Equation (8)is the last time constraints, which ensures the timeliness of armored vehicles transportation. In order to facilitate solving the model calculation, it need to convert the directly constraints into the penalty function, which is well versed in the objective function, then there is:

$$\min Z = \sum_{i=0}^{k}\sum_{j=0}^{k}\sum_{v=1}^{n} \alpha_{ij} \cdot d_{ij} \cdot X_{ijv} + \sum_{v=1}^{n} C_v + M \cdot \max\left(\sum_{i=1}^{k} R_i \cdot Y_{iv} - Q_v, 0\right) + M \cdot \max\left(T_i - D_i, D_i' - T_i, 0\right) \qquad (9)$$

3   Model Algorithm

3.1 Model Algorithm

Genetic Algorithm is the mathematical model that imitation of genetic selection and survival of the fittest evolutionary, which was first proposed in 1975 by the professor J.H.Holland in University of Michigan. At the same time, he published the representative monographs <Adaptation in Natural and Artificial Systems>, the genetic algorithm proposed by Professor JH. Holland was often called simple genetic algorithm (SGA).

Genetic algorithms include: the creation of the initial population, evaluation of each chromosome, selection, crossover, mutation in the population and post-assessment procedures, and include encoding and decoding, initialization groups, fitness function, reproduction, crossover and mutation factors. Considering the nature of the research and model features, this paper selects the genetic algorithm to solve VRPTW model, solution procedure is as follows:

(1) chromosome structure design: Chromosome structural design is to determine the length and way of the chromosome encoding. Considering the specific circumstances of the vehicle path decision problem, it should use natural number encoding, which represents the starting point of armored car with "0" and a collection of savings outlets with "1,2, ..., k". For example, chromosomal "03450120670", represents that the vehicle assignment and route options is that the three cars start from the starting point of departure, to deliver the currency for seven savings outlets. "0" is the starting point; the middle of the "0" does not have to be expressed in the specific procedure code. As follows:

- The first armored car path: the starting point → dot3 →dot5 →dot 4 → the starting point;
- The second armored car path: the starting point outlets → dot2 →dot1 → the starting point;
- The third armored car path: the starting point for network → dot6 → dot7 → the starting point.
- Chromosome length = the total number of savings outlets + 1.

(2) Determination on the genetic control parameters: Genetic algorithm parameter settings has a large effect on the algorithm, so which needs to be selected carefully. The usually parameters include: population size N, crossover probability P_c , mutation probability P_m and the set of the end computing conditions. Groups of population size N is the number of solutions which realizes search in each generation, which usually is selected within 10 to 200; crossover probability P_c is the proportion that the offspring number by cross-algebra takes up individuals number of the total population, to ensure the expansion of the search space, it general values 0.5 ~ 1; mutation probability P_m is the ratio that the mutated gene number take up the total number of genes, which set the range of 0 ~ 0.05. When the genetic algorithm satisfies certain conditions, terminate the evolution cycle, and stop rules often are: the maximum number of failures (the iterations number when it can not get a better solution), the maternal chromosomes have reached the pre-set standards, achieved the goals set in advance and the setting maximum number of evolution generations MAXGEN and so on.

(3) To generate initial population: Genetic algorithm is a population-based search method, it must prepares for genetic operators with the N initial population composed of individuals, and each individual is representation of a solution. Therefore, the initial group is the groups at the beginning of "evolutionary" computation, is the initial solution set, it usually generated initial population with the

random method so as to reach all the states. To improve the convergence speed of the algorithm, it can generate the initial groups according to the following steps:

- Step1: Random sorting for the savings outlets.
- Step2: It calculates from left to right, if the capacity of first car is greater than the savings amount of first k saving outlets (per unit volume), and less than the savings amount of first k +1 saving outlets, which are the savings outlets substring 1: "1 2 ⋯ k" responsible by the first vehicles;
- Step3: Deleting the first k savings outlets in sort, with the same method determining the savings outlets substring 2: "k +1 k +2 ⋯ l" served by the second vehicle. Repeating that until all the armored car and savings vehicles are assigned completely;
- Step4: Connecting all the substrings after "0" is inserted between the two substrings, then it can get an initial chromosome after head and tail is added "0".
- Step5: Giving the savings outlets new order random, it can be another chromosome with the same steps. Calculation operation repeatedly until the number of chromosomes is equal to population size N.
- In order to avoid a large number of infeasible solutions generated in the initial population, it check on the chromosome with constraints (3) and (8), the chromosome corresponds to a feasible solution of the problem if satisfying the condition, which is added to the population; otherwise, chromosome corresponds to the feasible solution, which should be discarded.

(4) Fitness evaluation: Genetic algorithms need evaluate the fitness of chromosomes whether good or not through the size of chromosomes fitness function in the process of solution. Fitness is calculated by the (3.1), the fitness function is obtained by the transformation of the objective function, the variable value X_{ijv}, Y_{iv}, T_i in the objective function is obtained by selecting calculation of each chromosome codes.

$$f_h = \frac{Z_{\min}}{Z_h} \tag{3.1}$$

Where, f_h represents the fitness function of chromosome h, $Z_{\min}$ represents the transportation costs of best chromosome in the same group, Z_h represents the transportation costs of the chromosome h.

Aim at the problem on transportation route decision of the armored car, the chromosome whose fitness is large corresponds to the transportation routes options whose transportation cost is small, which have a larger probability of genetic to the next generation.

(5) The genetic operations: selection, crossover and mutation

1) The selection operator: In this paper designs the selection operator through the method with retaining the best chromosome combined with roulette.

2) The crossover operator: Crossover operator uses the parent genetic to generate a new chromosome, whose cross-process carry out in two steps: First, it pairs the chromosomes in father groups randomly; the second is that the paired parent chromosome gets genes cross-recombination and exchange the genetic information, which generates a progeny chromosome. The cross-operator happens in a certain probability, which is called crossover probability P_c. The convergence of genetic algorithm is mainly decided by the convergence of crossover operator [2].

For the path problem of the cash-carrying transportation network, it is disorder between the chromosome sub-paths and order within the sub-path, if it uses the past some crossover operator, which will not be able to maintain the excellent characteristics of the parent, and may even receive a large number of infeasible solutions. Therefore, it preserve good gene combinations from their parents, this paper structures the maximum special retained crossover.

3) The mutation operator: Mutation operation is to avoid the permanent loss of some genetic information caused by the cross-selection process, which can avoid the shortcomings of only getting local solutions. Exchange mutation operator is a local optimization technique, in essence, which is the exchange to the sections of feasible solution to improve the driving line of armored cars.

Because there are many 0 in the chromosomes of transport path decision-making program, normal crossover and mutation operators are not suitable for transport routes decision-making problem, so it need to construct a special bit-based exchange mutation operator. Such as chromosomes"01203450670", to identify the gene "5" and gene "6" to exchange, it gets a new chromosomal "01203460570" by the exchange of location [3].Variation as follows:

- Step1: to produce a random number r between [0,1];
- Step2: If $r \le P_m$,it selects a chromosome randomly, in which selects two non-zero genes arbitrarily; if $r > P_m$, it goes into the next step directly;
- Step3: After exchanging the location of the selected two non-zero genes, it constitutes a new chromosome.

(6) Genetic evaluation: The crossover and mutation operators do not produce better chromosomes necessarily. For that, it need to take the genetic evaluation in order to ensure that the convergence rate. It calculates the each fitness chromosome after crossover and mutation and compares with the fitness before the cross then chooses the largest fitness populations to enter the next generation.

3.2 Algorithm Flow

The flow of solving the path optimization decision model with genetic algorithm is shown in Fig.1.

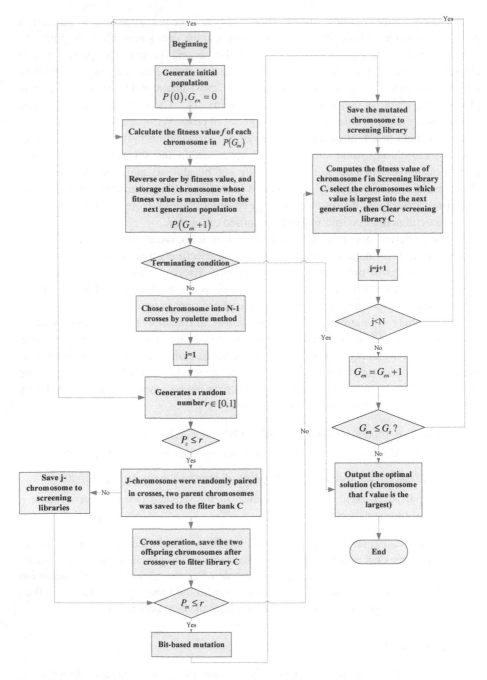

Fig. 1. The genetic algorithm solving process of path decision-making model in cash truck transportation network

Note: section of information from: zhang yi. Research on the method and decision theory of disaster relief supplies and logistics [D]. Doctorate thesis, Chang'an University, 2007

4   The Practical Examples

According to the actual data information of the savings outlets in Inner Mongolia Branch of China Construction Bank, the operating conditions on armored car department of Management units and traffic network data of Hohhot, it constructs the optimization model of the transport   routing of armored car based on the urban road network. The actual operational procedures: the CCB armored cars (normalized and owned by the operation and management section of Construction Bank) usually stops in the Construction Bank vault, it sends several armored cars within the time limit to perform the tasks of all saving outlets in Hohhot with the daily job requirements, and then shipped back the deposit to the vault of each saving outlets security.

In this case, the CCB vault is the starting point (point i = 0) of armored car and destination point after the transport task is completed. In the practice work, the CCB savings outlets requires that the armored cars arrive as early as 8:00-8:40 am and 4:40-5:30 pm, if not it will affect the normal operation of the savings outlets, which will take a security risk to the transportation.

The CCB Branch Office of Inner Mongolia in Hohhot has 52 savings outlets, due to the limited space of this article, from which it takes the data of 10 savings outlets and only considers the activities of cash transportation in afternoon to establish an example. If it needs to solve a greater number of network problems the actual work, just modify the input data of program. 10 savings outlets require to transport the 70 units of volume (special bag that loads models of bank), after the clearing the amount of money in the afternoon. The maximum capacity of a single armored car is 30 units of volume and the cost of vehicle operation is 100. It requires assigning the armored car to start from the treasury and selects transportation routes, which makes the transportation cost to minimize under the conditions of time requirements of the savings network.

Table 1. The actual name of the savings dots that grade points correspond to

Saving outlets	Saving outlets name
0	Treasury (starting point)
1	Iron road savings bank
2	Station west street Branch
3	Xi lin north road Branch
4	Unity Community Branch
5	Dong da Square Branch
6	Tian qu Square savings bank

Table 1. (*continued*)

7	Hu lun south road Branch
8	Ulanqab west street Branch
9	New city south street Branch
10	Chang' an Golden Block Branch

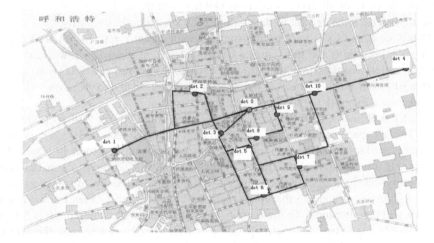

Fig. 2. The distribution map of savings network of Construction Bank in Hohhot area and its shortest path

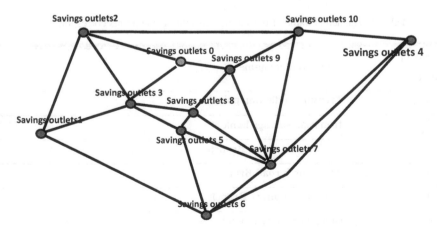

Fig. 3. The network topology of savings network and its shortest distance between points

Table 2. The cost matrix of pots in inter-network transformed from the distance

Saving outlets	1	2	3	4	5	6	7	8	9	10
0	3.650	1.780	1.414	2.973	1.821	2.891	2.164	1.038	0.519	1.763
1	0	3.149	3.018	6.598	4.932	5.418	6.829	4.205	4.263	5.278
2	3.149	0	1.331	4.983	2.896	3.651	4.216	2.407	2.533	3.742
3	3.018	1.331	0	4.270	1.387	2.390	2.904	1.133	1.812	3.034
4	6.598	4.983	4.270	0	5.290	5.778	4.528	4.029	2.880	1.219
5	4.932	2.896	1.387	5.290	0	1.342	1.774	0.418	1.543	3.226
6	5.418	3.651	2.390	5.778	1.342	0	1.269	1.778	2.892	4.554
7	6.829	4.216	2.904	4.528	1.774	1.269	0	1.780	1.635	3.306
8	4.205	2.407	1.133	4.029	0.418	1.778	1.780	0	1.106	2.824
9	4.263	2.533	1.812	2.880	1.543	2.892	1.635	1.106	0	1.672
10	5.278	3.742	3.034	1.219	3.226	4.554	3.306	2.824	1.672	0

Table 3. The time-consuming matrix of pots in inter-network transformed from the distance (min)

Saving outlets	1	2	3	4	5	6	7	8	9	10
0	3.650	1.780	1.414	2.973	1.821	2.891	2.164	1.038	0.519	1.763
1	0	3.149	3.018	6.598	4.932	5.418	6.829	4.205	4.263	5.278
2	3.149	0	1.331	4.983	2.896	3.651	4.216	2.407	2.533	3.742
3	3.018	1.331	0	4.270	1.387	2.390	2.904	1.133	1.812	3.034
4	6.598	4.983	4.270	0	5.290	5.778	4.528	4.029	2.880	1.219
5	4.932	2.896	1.387	5.290	0	1.342	1.774	0.418	1.543	3.226
6	5.418	3.651	2.390	5.778	1.342	0	1.269	1.778	2.892	4.554
7	6.829	4.216	2.904	4.528	1.774	1.269	0	1.780	1.635	3.306
8	4.205	2.407	1.133	4.029	0.418	1.778	1.780	0	1.106	2.824
9	4.263	2.533	1.812	2.880	1.543	2.892	1.635	1.106	0	1.672
10	5.278	3.742	3.034	1.219	3.226	4.554	3.306	2.824	1.672	0

According to the r the armored car's average speed in the city, this paper takes 60km / h (1km/min), which can sets different values in practical applications at different cities according to traffic conditions. Here comes the time consumption matrix between the saving outlets.

Table 4. The deposits needed to transport in every savings pots (unit volume)

Transportation Materials \ Saving Outlets	1	2	3	4	5	6	7	8	9	10
savings	6	8	7	8	6	7	8	6	7	7

Because the title design is known , they take the Treasury to be the starting point, at between 5:20-6:10 pm daily, arriving 10 savings outlets to perform models transportation tasks; the volume capacity of each armored car is 30 units, a total of cash that should be transported of 10 savings Outlets is 70 units volume, so it first determines to arrange more or equal to 3 armored car to perform the transportation task of models to 10 savings outlets; according to the general models of armored car, which gets the actual city driving Hundred kilometers to 16L/100km and the 93 # gasoline the average price of the 3,4month in 2009 of Hohhot is 5.3RMB / L, which obtain the cost of actual fuel consumption per kilometer that 0.832RMB/km.

The chromosome length is 10 +1 = 11, it takes the population size N = 150 and according to the nature, type and experience of this example takes the crossover probability $P_c = 0.5$, mutation rate $P_m = 0.02$, M = 99999. Algorithm termination condition is set to meet: genetic evolution generations reach 100 generations, that is $G_s = 100$.

According to the known data, the parameters listed in Table 1, Table 2, Table 3 and Table 4, Table 5 below. Using of algorithm design and the above process, based on the AMD Athlon (tm) 64 X2 Dual Core Processor 3600 + processor, 1.91Ghz, 1.50GB RAM, Window xp computer system, through the preparation of C + + program, using VC + + operators it gets the results shown in Figure 4.

Operation Results:

The best chromosome 0-6-7-8-2-0-9-3-1-5-0-4-10-0, the optimal distance 53.4491km. The specific arrangements for transport path are shown in Table 5.

In the conditions that the transport equipment is adequate and meet the time requirements, in order to reduce the total mileage to save the cost of the emergency distribution, in principle, the different needs of the same point should be responsible by one car (or team) to transport as far as possible from. In addition, the numerical example of solutions is the global satisfaction solution, which distributes in strict time limit. And the penalty cost is zero. It solved the decision problem of cash distribution path.

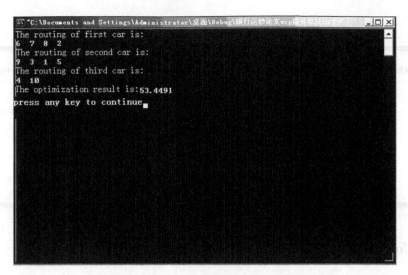

Fig. 4. The running results of example program

Table 5. The number of deposits needed to transport, time of loading cash, time interval

Saving outlets i	the number of deposits needed to transport R_i	time of loading cash S_{iu} (min)	time interval $D_i' \sim D_i$
1	6	4.5	4:40~5:30
2	8	5.4	4:40~5:30
3	7	4.8	4:40~5:30
4	8	5.7	4:40~5:30
5	6	4.2	4:40~5:30
6	7	5.1	4:40~5:30
7	8	5.4	4:40~5:30
8	6	4.2	4:40~5:30
9	7	5.1	4:40~5:30
10	7	5.1	4:40~5:30

Table 6. The results of the path decision-making of cash transportation

Vehicle	Loading	The Sorts of Distribution by site	Transportation costs	The truck-setting out costs
1	29	0-6-7-8-2-0	8. 426	10
2	26	0-9-3-1-5-0	10. 069	10
3	15	0-4-10-0	4. 955	10

5 Conclusion

It outbreaks the global financial crisis in 2008, which cause a great extent to the countries in the world, national economists and government put together a large number of human and financial resources to research the strategy. China's economy also suffered a certain degree of influence. In the backdrop of the world financial crisis, it is particularly important to study the control strategy on the transport costs of China's banking shall.

This paper focuses on constructing the optimization model of single- material vehicles routing with rigid time constraints and establish a practical example based on that the actual network data of Construction Bank savings outlets and Hohhot urban traffic network data, which obtains a satisfactory result and verified the validity of the optimization model. It plays an important role at the bank's real cash-carrying transport work of grass-roots institutions. Meanwhile, the decision research on cash-carrying transport path in the case of complexity traffic is the contents needed to continue to study in the next step.

References

1. Research Department of China Construction Bank. U.S. sub prime mortgage crisis triggers the global financial crisis: Causes and strong potential. Research on Investment, 1 (2009)
2. Bai, Z.: Research on the fuzzy systems based on genetic algorithm. PhD thesis, East China Normal University (2005)
3. Zhang, Y.: Research on the method and decision theory of disaster relief supplies and logistics. Doctorate thesis, Chang'an University (2007)
4. Luo, Y.: Research on Optimization of Vehicle Routing and Scheduling. Dalian Maritime University, Dalian (2003)
5. Xie, B.L., Li, J.: The genetic algorithms on non-loaded Vehicle Routing Problem with a time window. Systems Engineering Journal (September 2000)

Drought Monitoring Based on the Vegetation Temperature Condition Index by IDL Language Processing Method

WenHao Ou, Wei Su[*], Chen Wu, ZhongZheng Zhu, YanMin Li, and Shi Shen

College of Information and Electrical Engineering,
China Agricultural University, Beijing, 100083
suwei@cau.edu.cn

Abstract. Landsat TM5 images are used to calculate and retrieve normalized difference vegetation index (NDVI) and land surface temperature (LST). Combining with two index mentioned, vegetation temperature condition index (VTCI) can be retrieved for drought monitoring indicator applied in Junchuan farm of Heilongjiang Province in Northeast China. With well performance in matrix operation of IDL language, retrieving VTCI in a short time, fast batch calculation and mapping work as well, to a great extent, saving time and laborites, also providing real-time data for the government's macroeconomic regulatory policy.

Keywords: VTCI, Drought Monitoring, Batch Processing, IDL.

1   Introduction

Drought, which happens periodically with complex procedure, has been a kind of natural catastrophe that mankind has to deal with of all time. It takes place in all kinds of climate zones and is listed as one of the main natural catastrophes around the world. Of all kinds of natural catastrophes, drought has the strongest impact on agriculture. According to conservative statistics, drought takes 61% percent of the disaster-affected area in China, while flood takes 24%, hail takes 9%, and frost takes 6%[1-2]. Traditional method to monitor a drought is by using meteorological data to decide the level and range and it is only restrict to monitoring on a certain spot. However, in order to monitor a large area of drought condition, remote sensing should be used as the main method [3-4].

With the development of remote sensing techniques, available data have been increasing all the time. To monitor drought, vegetation index (NDVI) and land surface temperature (LST) are often used to retrieve. NDVI is to express the condition of vegetation by using the spectral character of red light, near infrared band or their simple combination or linear combination, based on the strong absorbing property that chlorophyll has on lights [5]. There are many indexes to show the drought condition, for example, Anomaly Vegetation Index (AVI), Vegetation Condition Index (VCI), Land Surface Temperature (LST), Vegetation Temperature Condition Index (VTC) etc.

---

[*] Corresponding author.

D. Li and Y. Chen (Eds.): CCTA 2011, Part III, IFIP AICT 370, pp. 43–49, 2012.

VTCI is based on the triangle composed of scatter diagram (feature space) of Normalized Difference Vegetation Index (NDVI) and LST and is used to study the drought level and its variance of a certain area during a certain period of a year. It takes the variance of NDVI into consideration and at the same time, the variance of LST under the same NDVI, that is, the harm that high temperature can have on plants [6]. This method, which is put forward by Pengxing Wang, is now used to monitor the drought in Shanxi Province (China), Texas and Oklahoma (USA). Results show that it is an effective way and can be a real-time procession [7].

In order to provide data faster and better, VTCI by IDL language processing method, combined with remote sensing image, should be used. IDL is a simple matrix-oriented and cross-platform language and it has the ability to process a large amount of data in high speed. Therefore, IDL language is an ideal tool to process remote sensing image [8]. This paper is mainly discussing drought monitoring based on the vegetation temperature condition index by IDL language processing method.

2   Basic Information about Research Area and Data Resource

In 2007, Heilongjiang Province suffered from the most serious drought in 50 years and then the importance of drought monitor emerged. Take the Junchuan farm (115/027 in TM5) for example. It is a temperate continental climate place located at 131 °02' to 131 °30'east longitude, 47°20' to 47°40' northern latitude in Luobei and Suibin. We analyse the drought condition on the farm to capture the level of the drought. This paper use VTCI, combined with LandSat TM5 remote sensing data to monitor the drought, providing the support for some decisions on the farm.

Fig. 1. Landsat TM5 image of study area (Red: Band7, Green: Band4, Blue: Band3)

In the process of pre-processing original TM remote sensing image, radiative correction and geometrical correction are usually carried out. Radiative correction is the first setp, followed by atmospheric correction. Then geometrical correction is carried out to pick some control point on the image by polynomial method. Gauss-Kruger projection is used to do the geometrical correction. All the steps above is processed by ENVI 4.7.

3   Results and Analysis of Drought Monitor by IDL

3.1   Extraction of VTCI

1) Normalized vegetation index is calculated by Landsat TM5, band 3 and band 4. The formula is as below:

$$NDVI = \frac{\rho_4 - \rho_3}{\rho_4 + \rho_3}$$

(Formula 1)

ρ_4 refers to reflectivity of band 4, and ρ_3 refers to that of band 3.

2) The calculation of land surface bright temperature

$$BT = \frac{K_2}{\ln(\frac{K_1}{L_\lambda} + 1)}$$

(Formula 2)

L_λ refers to radiance of thermal infrared band. K_1 and K_2 are calibration constants. K_1 equals 607.76 and K_2 equals to 1260.56 because of the empirical model of Landsat-5 data.

3) The calculation of land surface temperature

Land surface temperature is calculated by Landsat TM5, band 6, mainly the surface thermal infrared radiation [9].

$$LST = \frac{BT}{\varepsilon^{1/4}}$$

(Formula 3)

$\varepsilon = 1.009 + 0.047 \ln NDVI$, BT refers to the spectrum radioactive brightness.

4) The calculation of VTCI

$$VTCI = \frac{LST_{NDVI_i \max} - LST_{NDVI_i}}{LST_{NDVI_i \max} - LST_{NDVI_i \min}}$$

(Formula 4)

$LST_{NDVI_i} = a + b * NDVI$; $LST_{NDVI_i \min} = a' + b'* NDVI$. a, b, a', b' are undetermined coefficient and need to be determined by linear fitting on borderline of scatter diagram.

3.2   Export VTCI Image with ENVI/IDL

According to requirements above, we designed a reasonable scheme, which can be processed spontaneously.

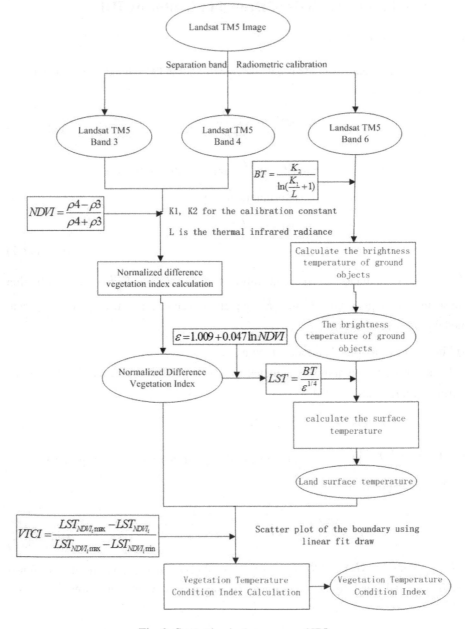

Fig. 2. Computing in the process of IDL

According to figure 2, firstly, wave band separation and radioactive calibration are carried out on TM5 image. Secondly, extracted band 3, band 4 and band 6 are calculated in NDVI, BT AND LST. At last, calculate VTCI and output VTCI image by fitting hot and cold borderline.

1) TM5 Band3 radiation calibration calculation method (DegreeToRad for custom Angle turn radian function name):

```
function compute_l, origin
    result = float(origin) * 1.039880 - 1.17
    e = 1554 ; According to the atmosphere of solar spectrum top average irradiance
    d = 1 ; d to the distance for the day
    result = !pi * l * d * d / e / cos(DegreeToRad(25)) ; For radiation correction
    return, result
end
```

2) According to TM5 band 3 and band 4 the calculation method of NDVI (according to the above Formula 1) :

```
function compute_ndvi, b1, b2, check = check
    den = float(b1) + float(b2)
    if(keyword_set(check)) then ptr = where(den eq 0., count) $
    else count = 0
    if (count gt 0) then den[ptr] = 1.0
    result = (float(b1) - float(b2)) / den +0.00001 ; In order to avoid value, plus 0.00001
    if (count gt 0) then result[ptr] = 0.0
    return, (float(b1)-float(b2))/(float(b1)+float(b2)+0.001)
end
```

3) Inversion of LST (Formula 3):

```
function compute_lst, bt, ndvi
    result = fltarr(n_elements(ndvi[*,0]),n_elements(ndvi[0,*]))
    e = 1.009 + 0.047 * alog(ndvi) ; Calculate e
    result = float(bt]) / e^(0.25)
    return, result
end
```

4) Calculation VTCI according to the results of NDVI and LST:

```
function compute_vtci, ndvi, lst, aw, bw, ac, bc
    lstmax = bw + ndvi * aw ; Warm boundary
    lstmin = bc + ndvi * ac ; Cold boundary
    vtci = (lstmax - lst) / (lstmax - lstmin) ; Export image
    return, vtci
end
```

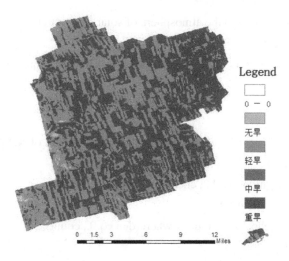

Fig. 3. Result of VTCI monitored in JunChuan farm

In the program above, ";" is a sign of comment. We can see that IDL is a language of simple grammar. It processes the matrix as a whole without pixels by pixels and it saves a lot of time when processing large matrixes. By using the method above, it took 18.658 seconds to process this image of Junchuan farm on September 25th, which saves much time than hand operation, and there's no need to wait in front of the computer for the next step. Figure 3 is the resulting VTCI image. From it we can see that the area is in middling drought or severe drought, which is exactly the same with the real condition.

4   Conclusion

This paper uses spontaneous and time-saving method to retrieve VTCI based on IDL language as an example to put forward a way to process large amount of remote sensing data also spontaneously and automatically to monitor drought condition. By using IDL, we can realize that:

1) Modularization of the process and the ability to be transplanted through different operating systems.

2) All-day automatic work, which can output real-time VTCI result, and make it easier for government to know the drought and take emergency measurement.
3) Once successfully set, there's no need to interfere or guard it with labor, which is time and labor saving. Computers can make automatic procession and save result as the settings, file names and path, which can avoid mistakes.

Acknowledgments. This research is funded by the Natural Science Foundation of China entitled *Estimation of tree height using LIDAR data and QuickBird imagery* (40801128). All of the authors appreciate the co-operation and support of many experts from the Research Institute of Forest Resource Information Techniques of Chinese Academy of Forestry, and we all would like to thank Professor Liu Qinfu of the College of Geoscience and Surveying Engineering, China University of Mining & Technology (Beijing), for his support with human resources.

References

[1] Wang, P., Wan, Z., Gong, J., et al.: Drought monitoring mode based on vegetation index and land surface temperature. Earth Science Progress 8(18), 527–533 (2003)
[2] Wang, X., Guo, N.: Progress of drought monitoring and the research methods of remote sensing. Arid Meteorological, 77–80 (2003)
[3] Lambin, E.F., Ehrlich, D.: The surface temperature-vegetation index for land cover and land cover change analysis. International Journal of Remote Sensing 17, 463–487 (1996)
[4] Liu, W., Kogan, F.N.: Monitoring regional drought using the vegetation condition index. International Journal of Remote Sensing 17, 2761–2782 (1996)
[5] Chen, S., Tong, Q., Guo, H.: Reaserch of remote sensing information. Beijing Science Press (1998)
[6] Wang, P., Gong, J., Li, X.: The application of drought monitoring with vegetation temperature condition index. Journal of WuHan University, Information Science Edition 10(26), 412–418 (2001)
[7] Wan, Z., Wang, P., Li, X.: Using MODIS land surface temperatureand normalized difference vegetation index products for monitoring drought in the southern Great Plains, USA. International Journal of Remote Sensing 25(1), 61–72 (2004)
[8] Quan, T., Zheng, N.: Remote sensing systems development methods based on the secondary devel-opment with ENVI/IDL. Computer Application 6(28), 270–276 (2008)
[9] Liu, Z., Lei, Z., Dang, A., et al.: Remote sensing technology and SEBAL model in the application of arid evaporation estimation. Journal of Tsinghua University (Natural Science Edition) 44(3), 279–679 (2004)

A Kind of Rice Nitrogen Status Rapid Diagnostic Tool

Jin-heng Zhang, Xin Yu, Yongliang Lv, Zhenxuan Yao,
Dapeng Li, and Chao Han

Institute of Eco-environment & Agriculture Information,
School of Environment and Safety Engineering,
Qingdao University of Science and Technology,
Qingdao, Shandong 266042, China

Abstract. Using data from three deformation positions (680 nm, 730 nm, and 765 nm) of spectral reflectance and derivative spectra curves from red to near infrared spectral bands, red edge reflectance spectra index was developed. Nitrogen contents of rice canopy leaves were found to be significantly correlated with the red edge reflectance spectra index values at 0.01 probability level for different rice growth stages and genotypes studied. Four models established - for four rice growth stages were used to predict the nitrogen content of canopy leaves. Significant correlations were found between measured nitrogen contents and predicted nitrogen contents with high coefficient of determination (R2 = 0.97) at 0.01 probability level. Based on the four field experiments, we developed a new rice nitrogen status rapid diagnostic meter. The working principle of the meter was introduced, and the measuring accuracy of the meter was analyzed. Results showed that the precision of nitrogen status rapid diagnostic meter for predicting nitrogen content was more than 80% at tiller stage and more than 90% at booting stage at 0.01 probability level. The nitrogen status rapid diagnostic meter appears to be a promising tool for rapid, on-farm analysis of rice nitrogen status.

Keywords: Rice Nitrogen Content, Vegetation Index, Reflectance, Meter.

Introduction

Synthetic fertilizers especially nitrogen fertilizer have acquired a bad reputation in recent decades for causing serious ecological damage when farmers use them excessively. Nitrogen status of various crops is an very important factor which can reflect the nitrogen apply level. In agricultural research, organic chemical constituents have been successfully measured by using multiple linear regression to relate the constituents of interest to the reflectance spectra of dried ground samples. Approximately 42 minor absorption features in the visible and near-infrared portions of the spectrum have been successfully correlated with foliar chemical contents, including those of nitrogen, protein, and lignin as demonstated [1]. Nitrogen status of various crops has been related to reflectance at certain wavelength, and various reflectance ratios and indices have been used to detect nitrogen deficiencies in plants as demonstrated [2-4]. Many

D. Li and Y. Chen (Eds.): CCTA 2011, Part III, IFIP AICT 370, pp. 50–61, 2012.

relationships between the spectral response of crops and growth factors have been elucidated, based on reflectance obtained from handheld and aircraft-mounted sensors providing images in visible and other parts of the electromagnetic spectrum. More recently these procedures have been extended to the laboratory analysis of dried ground foliage as demonstrated [5] and fresh forest foliage as demonstrated [6]. Spectral determination has been proved to be an automatic, quick, and nondestructive method for assessment of nutrients.

Spectroscopy can provide information about a substance by relating its interaction with electromagnetic radiation as a function of wavelength to its chemical composition and physical properties. Spectral bands in the visible and near-infrared regions of the spectrum have been used to develop a number of indices for estimating nitrogen content. Vegetation index is a simple, effective, and experiential measurement of terrestrial vegetation activity, and plays a very important role in qualitative and quantitative remote sensing. Most of the indices based on reflectance spectrum including single band spectral reflectance and reflectance band ratios or difference have been used as indicators of nitrogen content.

Some studies have been conducted to measure nitrogen content of crops using field spectrometry. The nitrogen status of various crops has been related to reflectance at specific wavelength, and various reflectance ratios and indices have been used as indicators of nitrogen deficiencies in plants as demonstrated [2-4] [7-13]. Spectral determinations can provide an automatic, quick, and nondestructive method for estimating crop nutrient status.

As a fundamental research tool for the application of current and future hyperspectral and even multi-spectral sensing systems, a field spectroradiometer was used to collect reflectance data. But, until now, there is no report on predicting the nitrogen content of rice using handheld spectral meter. Therefore, the purpose of this study was to verify the feasibility and effectiveness of a newly developed RERI Nitrogen Meter to diagnose rice nitrogen nutrient content.

1   Materials and Methods

1.1   Experimental Description

Four field experiments were conducted in 2002, 2009, and 2010.The first experiment was conducted in a ploughed field of 3.02 hm2 near JiaShan County of Zhejiang Province (Latitude 30.84°, Longitude 120.92°). The field was divided into three N supply areas: an area of 0.47 hm2 did not receive any N fertilizer, an area of 0.23 hm2 received half of the recommended rate, and the remainder of the field received the recommended rate. The recommended N application rates were 135 kg urea hm-2, 202.5 kg urea hm-2, and 120 kg urea hm-2 for tiller, booting, and heading stage, respectively. Three genotypes of rice (Oryza sativa L) were used: late rice 101, late rice C-67, and late rice 004.

The second field experiment was laid out in a split-plot design with three replications at Yuhang Town, Hangzhou City, Zhejiang Province (Latitude 30.43°, Longitude 120.3°). The main plots were arranged in a randomized complete block and consisted of six basal N rates: 0, 150, 225, 300, 375, and 450 kg N hm-2. Subplots were seeded with two genotypes of late rice, Bing 9363 and Bing 9652, which had the same growth cycles and different foliar colors (dark and bright, respectively). The main plot size was 5.0 m × 3.6 m with four repeats.

The third field experiment was extended over 0.7 hm2 at Chengyang Qingdao of Shandong Province (Latitude 36.07°, Longitude 120.33°). It was designed in a randomized complete block with three replications, using three varieties of rice, Shengdao 13, Lindao 11, and Yangguang 200, with similar growth stages. Four basal nitrogen (N) rates were used: 0 kg urea hm-2, 270 kg urea hm-2, 585 kg urea hm-2, and 750 kg urea hm-2.

The fourth field experiment was laid out in a split-plot design with three replications at Yutai town, Jining city (Latitude 35°, Longitude 116.65°), Shandong province. The main plots were arranged in a randomized complete block and consisted of 4 basal N rates: 0, 156, 310, and 403 kg N hm-2. Subplots were seeded with three genotypes of rice (Zhendao88, Shengdao16, and Shengdao15), which had similar growth cycles. The main plot size was 5.0 m × 8 m with three repeats.

For the 1st, 2nd and 3rd field experiments, 50%, 40%, and 10% N fertilizer was applied before transplanting, at tillering, and at heading, respectively. But for the 4th field experiments, N fertilizer was applied according to the following ratio: 20% before transplanting, 55% at tillering, and 20% at heading.

1.2   Canopy Reflectance Spectrum Measurements and Plant Sampling

In the first and second field experiments, rice canopy reflectance at 350-2500 nm in 1-nm–wide wavebands were measured using the portable spectroradiometer FieldSpec FR held 70 cm above the canopy top. In the third and fourth field experiments, the reflectance spectrum was measured at 350-1100 nm in 2.4-nm-wide waveband by the portable spectroradiometer AvaSpec-2048FT-SPU held 100 cm above the canopy top using the controllable field spectral measurement device (China patent of invention 200810180572.7) (see figure 1). All canopy reflectance spectra were measured under cloudless conditions and as close to solar noon as possible.

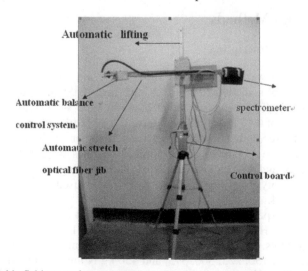

Fig. 1. Controllable field spectral measurement device (China patent of invention 200810180572.7)

After measuring the reflectance spectra, several rice clumps were obtained and their leaves were used as subsamples. Total N was determined for the subsamples based on the Kjeldahl method. Total N was expressed in g N kg-1 dry weight.

2   Results and Analysis

2.1   The Feasibility and Effectiveness of Vegetation Index and Prediction Models

The RERI standard bands were selected according to Figure 2. The following equation was developed to estimate the canopy leaf N content [14]

$$ RERI = \frac{R_{765} - R_{730}}{R_{730} - R_{680}} \tag{1} $$

Where, Ri indicates the rice canopy reflectance at the band i (nm).

According to the reference [14], the RERI increased with increasing N levels (the 1st, 2nd and 3rd experiments). Correlation coefficients between RERI and the N content were significant at 0.01 probability level for eight rice genotypes in the 1st, 2nd and 3rd experiments.

The relationship between RERI and the canopy N content can best be described by linear regression models of the form y = ax + b. Data from the third experiment were used in canopy leaf N content prediction models (Table 1) [14].

The models described in Table 1 were tested using two validation data sets from the first and second experiments. The canopy reflectance spectra of the validation samples were used to calculate RERI, and the algorithm equations were used to predict canopy leaf N content. We observed good agreement between the predicted and measured values (Table 2). A high positive correlation was observed between the predicted and actual N contents [14].

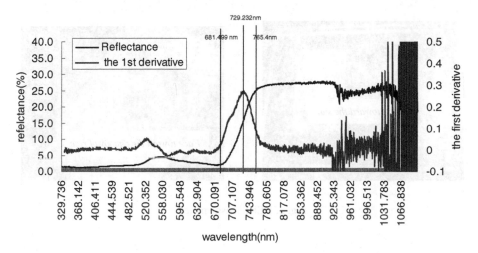

Fig. 2. Special wavebands of the first derivative and reflectance spectrum curves of rice canopy

Analysis of the visible/NIR canopy reflectance and canopy leaf N content for a wide range of rice experiments allows the development of better algorithms for quantifying the N content from canopy reflectance spectra. With better algorithms, new (satellite) sensors of remote sensing can be developed. The RERI developed in the present study could be used to accurately estimate the N fertilizer level and canopy leaves' N contents. Regression analysis indicated that RERI was a better indicator of the canopy leaves' N contents. The power of predictors and prediction models was tested using two validation datasets, and revealed good agreement between the predicted and measured canopy leaves' N contents. We concluded that satisfactory results were obtained using the new vegetation index RERI to predict the rice N nutrient status.

2.2   Introduction of RERI Nitrogen Meter

According to the research described above, the meter (figure3, figure4) only records three wavelengths of rice canopy spectral reflectance. Recording speed for testing and spectral reflectance can reach millisecond timescale. The meter accomplishes data rectification, processing, and recording functions automatically and intelligently. The meter performs simply and fast, without requiring manual intervention which can avoid the influence of human factors. The micro processing system will record canopy spectral reflectance at wavelengths of 680 nm, 730 nm, and 765 nm. RERI values are calculated using the following formulas:

$$\Re_{680} = k_1 \frac{\lambda_{680}}{\eta_{680}} , \qquad \Re_{730} = k_2 \frac{\lambda_{730}}{\eta_{730}} \quad \text{and} \quad \Re_{765} = k_3 \frac{\lambda_{765}}{\eta_{765}}$$

(k_1 , k_2 , k_3 *are the corresponding error correction coefficients*).

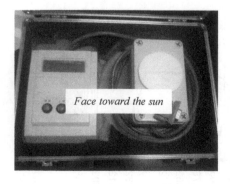

Face toward the sun

Face toward the canopy of rice

Fig. 3. RERI sensor meter

Fig. 4. RERI sensor used in field experiment. (In the 4th field experiment, handheld RERI sensor was used to measure rice canopy RERI values. The handheld RERI sensor was held 100 cm above the canopy under cloudless or partly cloudy conditions.)

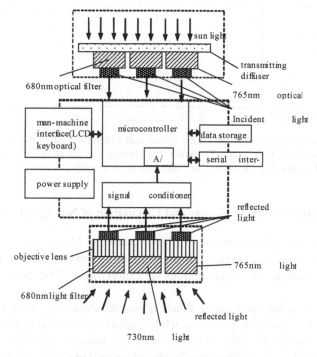

Fig. 5. Working principle diagram

This meter uses sunshine as light source and optical filters as optical components to measure the reflectance of crops at 680 nm, 730 nm, and 765 nm. Then, the RERI values are calculated. Low power consumption TI single-chip with six filtering systems is used as core component. Three filtering systems are installed under the transmitting diffuser which is on the top of the instrument (toward sun). Sun light reaches the sensors after going through transmitting diffuser and optical filter. Then, the sun optical signals at 680 nm, 730 nm, and 765 nm are obtained. The next set of three filtering systems is installed on the bottom of the instrument (toward crop canopy). The filtering systems installed on the bottom of the instrument collect canopy reflected light and send them to the sensors after going through optical filter and objective lens. Subsequently, the crop canopy reflected light signals are obtained. Every channel signal is transformed into digital signals through Analog-to-Digital Converter. RERI values are calculated with digital signals. Meanwhile the results are shown on the LCD. All data files are stored in the memory and they can be downloaded on to a computer by RS 232 or USB serial port (figure 5). Nitrogen content of rice canopy is automatically calculated and displayed by the onboard software (figure 6).

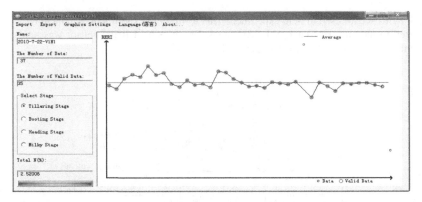

Fig. 6. Software for elimination of coarse errors and calculation of nitrogen content. (Rice genotype is Zhendao88. Tiller stage. The line is the average line. Small circles are the measured data using RERI sensor. Big circles are the valid data after removing coarse errors.)

2.3   Elimination of Coarse Errors and Calculation of Nitrogen Content

In order to ensure the accuracy of RERI Nitrogen Meter, when using RERI Nitrogen Meter, we should select as many repetition points as possible (at least 30). Because of the milliseconds response time, very short time will be spent on measuring process.

A software with data processing function was developed to select and eliminate errors caused by operation processes while predicting the nitrogen content (N%) (see figure 6). When the number of data points is less than or equal to 30, Romanvschi rule (T distribution) is used, otherwise Grubbs rule is used to remove coarse errors from the measured data. In this software, measured data files can be imported by selecting the menu "import". Then, the file name and the amount of data are shown automatically. After selecting rice growth stages, object models will be called by the software to calculate the nitrogen content automatically. The results are saved as log files.

2.4   Verification of the Precision of Diagnosis

The precision of diagnosis of RERI Nitrogen Meter was verified by using the data from the 4th experiment. In addition, the meter's feasibility and practicability were also confirmed.

Comparing the RERI values calculated from canopy spectral reflectance with those measured by the RERI Nitrogen Meter showed that calculated values were significantly correlated to the measured values (correlation coefficients more than 0.8). Significant correlation coefficients were more than 0.7 between the RERI Nitrogen Meter readings and the level of nitrogen fertilizer. Both measured RERI using RERI Nitrogen Meter and calculated RERI using spectral reflectance increased with increasing nitrogen fertilizer levels (figure 7). As expected, when the growth stages changed from tiller to heading stage, RERI Nitrogen Meter readings increased (figure 8).

After importing RERI Nitrogen Meter readings from the 4th experiment into the onboard software (figure 6), the regression models (table 1) were called and the nitrogen contents of rice canopy leaves were shown automatically. Correlation analysis between the N content predicted by the RERI Nitrogen Meter and the N content measured using the common laboratory Dumas method showed that the precision of total N content diagnosis was more than 80% at tiller stage and 90% at booting stage at the 0.01 probability level (table3).

Therefore, this study indicated that the RERI Nitrogen Meter can not only qualitatively classify the level of nitrogen, but can also be used for quantitative diagnosis of rice nitrogen content of canopy leaves. The precision of diagnosis reaches 80-90% and even higher.

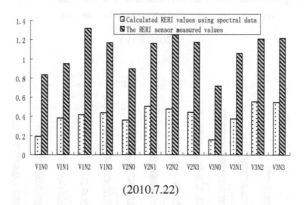

(2010.7.22)

Fig. 7. RERI values among genotypes and fertilizer levels. (V1:Zhendao88, V2:Shengdao16, V3:Shengdao15)

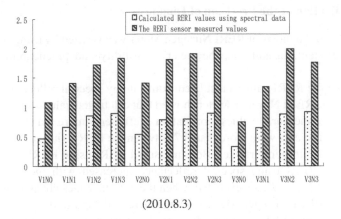

(2010.8.3)

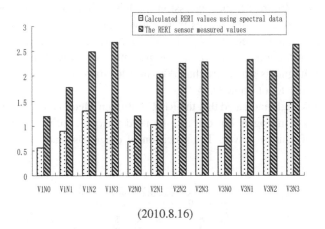

(2010.8.16)

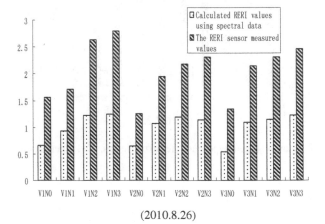

(2010.8.26)

Fig. 7. (*continued*)

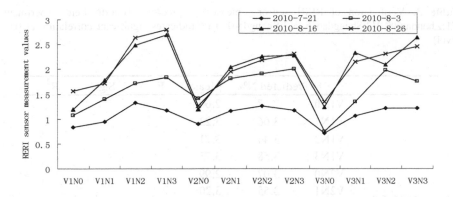

Fig. 8. RERI sensor measurement values among growth stages (V1:Zhendao88, V2:Shengdao16, V3:Shengdao15)

Table 1. Canopy leaf nitrogen content prediction models (n = 12) [14] (The third field experiment)

Stage	Model	R	R^2	F	P
Tiller	N% = 1.2007RERI+1.384	0.919	0.844**	43.389	0.000
Booting	N% = 0.7408RERI + 1.5727	0.888	0.788**	29.777	0.000
Heading	N% = 0.8618RERI + 1.5364	0.801	0.642**	17.911	0.002
Milky	N% = 0.7809RERI + 1.5889	0.663	0.439*	7.824	0.019

Table 2. Correlation between predicted and actual nitrogen contents in the first and second field experiments [14]

Experiment/Stage		R	R^2	F	Sig.
First Experiment (n = 32)	Tiller	0.931**	0.866	200.240	0.000
	Booting	0.966**	0.933	430.024	0.000
	Heading	0.973**	0.946	564.014	0.000
Second Experiment (n = 12)	Tiller	0.861**	0.742	28.689	0.000
	Jointing	0.946**	0.896	85.756	0.000
	Booting	0.964**	0.930	131.897	0.000
	Heading	0.984**	0.969	308.563	0.000

Table 3. Verification of RERI sensor's measuring precision (Fourth field experiment. V1:Zhendao88, V2:Shengdao16, V3:Shengdao15) (**indicates significant correlation at 0.01 level)

		Predicted N%	Measu	F	Sig.	R^2
	V1N0	2.67	2.60			
	V1N1	3.06	3.23			
	V1N2	3.44	3.71			
	V1N3	3.58	3.73			
	V2N0	3.07	2.99			
2010-8-3	V2N1	3.55	3.20			
Tiller stage	V2N2	3.67	3.78			
	V2N3	3.79	4.00			
	V3N0	2.28	2.63			
	V3N1	2.99	3.02			
	V3N2	3.77	3.56			
	V3N3	3.49	3.85			
				38.875	0.000**	0.7954
	V1N0	2.45	2.33			
	V1N1	2.89	2.73			
	V1N2	3.41	3.10			
	V1N3	3.56	3.08			
	V2N0	2.46	2.36			
2010-8-16	V2N1	3.08	2.64			
Booting stage	V2N2	3.24	2.87			
	V2N3	3.26	3.03			
	V3N0	2.49	2.46			
	V3N1	3.30	3.11			
	V3N2	3.12	2.77			
	V3N3	3.53	3.11			
				108.107	0.000**	0.9153

3   Conclusions

A RERI Nitrogen Meter developed based on red edge reflectance index (RERI) was investigated for practical application in agricultural production management. Based on the investigation, it can be concluded that because of the millisecond response time and the precision of diagnosis more than 80%, the meter can be used as a rapid nitrogen content diagnostic tool, and is suitable for not only handheld but also low altitude platforms such as helicopters and hot air balloons. Practical applications indicated that

RERI Nitrogen Meter is suitable for real time diagnosis of nitrogen content from canopy level, and should be an important part of the precision agriculture technology to improve variable fertilization technology.

Acknowledgments. Project supported by the Hi-Tech. Research and Development Program of China (863 Program) (2007AA10Z205) and the National Natural Science Foundation of China (40601062).

References

1. Curran, P.J.: Remote sensing of foliar chemistry. Remote Sensing of Environment 30, 271–278 (1989)
2. Goel, P.K., Prasher, S.O., Landry, J.A., Patel, R.M., Bonnellr, R.B., Viau, A.A., Miller, J.R.: Potential of airborne hyperspectral remote sensing to detect nitrogen deficiency and weed infestation in corn. Computers and Electronics in Agriculture 38, 99–124 (2003)
3. Serrano, L., Filella, I., Peñuelas, J.: Remote sensing of biomass and yield of winter wheat under different nitrogen supplies. Corp SCI 40(3), 723–730 (2000)
4. Lukina, E.V., Raun, W.R., Stone, M.L., Solie, J.B., Johnson, G.V., Lees, H.L., Ruffa, J.M., Phillips, S.B.: Effect of row spacing, growth stage, and nitrogen rate on spectral irradiance in winter wheat. Journal of Plant Nutrition 23(1), 103–122 (2000)
5. Card, D.H., Peterson, D.L., Matson, P.A., Aber, J.D.: Prediction of leaf chemistry by the use of visible and near in-frared reflectance spectroscopy. Remote Sensing of Environment 26, 123–147 (1988)
6. Curran, P.J., Dungan, J.L., Macler, B.A., Plummer, S.E., Peterson, D.L.: Reflectance spectroscopy of fresh whole leaves for the estimation of chemical content. Remote Sensing of Environment 39(2), 153–166 (1992)
7. Zhang, J.H.: Rice nitrogen nutrition diagnosis using continuum-removed reflectance. Journal of Plant Ecology 30(1), 78–82 (2006)
8. Zhang, J.H., Wang, K., Bailey, J.S., Wang, R.C.: Predicting nitrogen status of rice using multispectral data at can-opy scale. Pedsphere 16(1), 108–117 (2006)
9. Strachan, I.B., Pattey, E., Boisvert, J.B.: Impact of nitrogen and environmental conditions on corn as detected by hyperspectral reflectance. Remote Sensing of Environment 80, 213–224 (2002)
10. Blackmer, T.M., White, S.E.: Using precision farming technologies to improve management of soil and fertilizer nitrogen. Aust J. Agric. Res. 49(3), 555–564 (1998)
11. Ma, B.L., Morrison, M.J., Dwyer, L.M.: Canopy light reflectance and field greenness to assess nitrogen fertilization and yield of maize. Agron J. 88(6), 915–920 (1996)
12. Buschmann, C., Nagel, E.: In vivo spectroscopy and internal optics of leaves as basis for remote sensing of vegetation. Int. J. Remote Sens. 14(4), 711–722 (1993)
13. Gamon, J.A., Peñuelas, J., Field, C.B.: A narrowwaveband spectral index that tracks diurnal changes in photosynthetic efficiency. Remote Sensing of Environment 41, 35–44 (1992)
14. Zhang, J., Lv, Y., Han, C., Li, D., Yao, Z., Jiang, X.: New Reflectance Spectral Vegetation Indices for Estimating Rice Nitrogen Nutrition III: Development of a New Vegetation Index Based on Canopy Red-Edge Reflectance Spectra to Monitor Rice Canopy Leaf Nitrogen Concentration. Sensor Lett. 9, 1201–1206 (2011)

Applying Axiomatic Design Theory to the Multi-objective Optimization of Disk Brake[*]

Zhiqiang Wu, Xianfu Cheng, and Junping Yuan

School of Mechanical and Electronical Engineering, East China
Jiaotong University, Nanchang 330013, China
chxf_xn@sina.com

Abstract. The multi-objective optimization involves multiple, competing functionality requirements, which is mainly limited to downstream detailed design. Axiomatic design provides the theory to design a complex system top down and deals with multiple functional requirements (FR). It has demonstrated its strength in various types of design tasks. In fact, the objective function is a FR and those variables affecting the objective function are the design parameters (DPs). This paper presents an application of axiomatic design to multi-objective optimization. First, identify the relationship between FRs and DPs in terms of contribution of each DP to each FR by using orthogonal experiment and analysis of variance (ANOVA); then identify important design parameters to a FR and classify design variables into groups based on uncoupled design philosophy; and then establish the function dependence table, and sequentially optimize every objective function. An application in a disk brake design is used to demonstrate the use of the proposed method in dealing with real-world design problems. The results show that the proposed method provides a promising approach to optimize multiple, competing design objectives.

Keywords: Axiomatic design, Multi-objective optimization, ANOVA, Disk Brake.

1 Introduction

Multi-objective optimization is generally more difficult to achieve each objective optimum because of tradeoff between the various objectives, so the absolutely optimal solution may not exist. Axiomatic design approach has demonstrated its strength in various types of large-scale system design, including vehicles, aircrafts, manufacturing facilities, and so on [1]. Liu [2], Hwang [3] and Jeff [4] apply independent axiom of axiomatic design theory to improve and optimize multi-objective and large-scale engineering systems. In this paper, a systematic method is presented for applying independent axiom to multi-objective optimization problems. Firstly, identify the relationship between FRs and DPs in terms of contribution of

---

[*] Foundation: Project supported by the National Natural Science Foundation of China (51165007).

D. Li and Y. Chen (Eds.): CCTA 2011, Part III, IFIP AICT 370, pp. 62–73, 2012.

each DP to each FR by using orthogonal experiment and analysis of variance; secondly, important design parameters to a specific objective are identified and could be grouped into one set of parameters by means of the "uncoupled" philosophy of axiomatic design; then establish the function dependence table, and optimize every objective function in sequence.

2   Multi-objective Optimization Formulation

The mathematical model of multi-objective optimization is generally expressed as

$$\text{Min: } F(\mathbf{x}) = \left\{ f_1(\mathbf{x}), f_2(\mathbf{x}) ; \cdots , f_m(\mathbf{x}) \right\}^{\text{T}}$$

$$\text{s.t. } g_j(\mathbf{x}) \leq 0 \ \ j = 1, \cdots , q$$

$$h_k(\mathbf{x}) = 0 \ \ k = 1, \cdots , p$$

(1)

where, $\mathbf{x} = (x_1, x_2, \ldots , x_n)^{\text{T}}$ is n-dimensional design variables; $F(\mathbf{x})$ is the vector of objective functions; $f_i(\mathbf{x})$ is the ith sub-objective function and m is the number of sub-objective function; $g_i(\mathbf{x})$ is the jth inequality constraint and q is the number of inequality constraint functions, $h_k(\mathbf{x})$ is the kth equality constraints and k is the number of equality constraint functions.

In the above equation, achieving the optimum of each objective is generally difficult. Specially, when there are tradeoffs between the various objectives, namely, the optimization problem has conflicting goals, it is impossible to make each sub-objective simultaneously attain optimum. Thus, it should be required that the optimal solutions of all sub-objectives are balanced, so that the totally satisfactory solutions can be obtained. Compared to single objective optimization, the theory and computational methods on multi-objective optimization are not perfect. Therefore, it is necessary to introduce other relative design theories, such as axiomatic design, to further promote multi-objective optimization theory and methodology.

3   Optimization Design Based on "Uncoupled" Philosophy

In fact, the objective function is a FR and those variables affecting the objective function are the DPs already mentioned. But, in this case, the FR must be able to be expressed by the DPs in the form of a mathematical equation. It is obvious that optimization design is the method mapping between one FR and a set of DPs at a lower or the lowest level of FR and DP hierarchies in the process of axiomatic design [5]. For the design with only a FR, FR is clearly independent, and the optimal value of FR can be easily obtained by adjusting the corresponding DPs. Here, optimal design is very effective. For those with multiple objective functions, it is difficult to tune the corresponding DPs to simultaneously obtain the optimal solutions of FRs. For example, in order to obtain the optimum of FR1, the value of DPs should be tuned. In order to improve the FR2, the value of DPs should be further tuned, but the

FR1 will be changed. Therefore, it is needed to return to tune the DPs to optimize FR1; on the contrary, the FR2 will be changed. So again, this is a trade-off among multiple objectives.

In the axiomatic design, uncoupled or decoupled design is a good design [1]. The functional forms of the relations with two functional requirements are as follows:

For uncoupled design: $f_1 = f_1(x_1), f_2 = f_2(x_2)$

For decoupled design: $f_1 = f_1(x_1), f_2 = f_2(x_1, x_2)$

where f_1 and f_2 are functional requirements and x_1 and x_2 are corresponding design parameters. For uncoupled design, the design parameters can be determined separately. For decoupled design, x_1 and x_2 should be determined sequentially. In the first step of the decoupled design, the value of x_1 can be get by optimizing f_1, and x_1 is fixed in the next step as x_1^*. In the second step, the value of x_2 can be obtained by optimizing f_2. The solution obtained from the above process could not be the optimum when x_1 is not fixed in the second step. Therefore, the decoupled design may not be good one when the design solution is calculated by a mathematical optimization. It is necessary to make the design to be uncoupled design.

In the multi-objective optimization problems, there are usually two different solving methods. The one is that the most important FR is selected as an objective function and the other FRs are ignored. Thus multiple FRs are transformed into single FR, and optimization is effective to determine the optimal value of FR and the value of corresponding DPs, but the other FRs can't be optimized. The other is that every FR is weighted to form the aggregate objective function. Although it is also single FR optimization, it can't optimize FRs directly. Additionally, it is difficult to identify the weight. Therefore, in order to satisfy the independence axiom, FRs should be redefined or DPs should be reselected, and the different FRs is controlled by corresponding DPs independently. For uncoupled design, each sub-objective of multi-objective optimization is independent mutually, which is equivalent to single objective optimization.

For coupled design problem: $f_1 = f_1(x_1, x_2)$, $f_2 = f_2(x_1, x_2)$. If the influence of x_1 on f_1 is far greater than that of x_2 on f_1, and the influence of x_2 on f_2 is far greater than that of x_1 on f_2, the problem can be considered as a nearly uncoupled problem. Thus the axiomatic design process can be applied. When the influence of design parameters on the rest of design objectives can't be ignored, it is a strong coupling problem that can't be dealt with by axiomatic design.

Generally, there are more design variables than objective functions in optimization design. However, according to axiomatic design theory, the number of design variables (design parameters) must be the same as that of the objective functions (functional requirements in axiomatic design). Therefore, these designs are generally redundant, or may be coupled, and they violate the independence axiom and are not good designs. When the number of design variables is large, the variables can be grouped to have similar characteristics via the sensitivity information. That is, important variables to a specific objective function can be grouped into one set of parameters, and the number of the groups is the same as that of the objective functions. Thus the design is rearranged to be a nearly uncoupled design. The pertinence is backed up by the Theorem 8 in axiomatic design theory.

Theorem 8: Independence and Tolerance.

A design is an uncoupled design when the designer-specified tolerance is greater than

$$\Delta R_i > \left| \sum_{\substack{j=1 \\ j \neq i}}^{n} (\partial R_i / \partial P_j) \Delta P_j \right| \quad i = 1, 2, \cdots, n. \tag{2}$$

in which case the non-diagonal elements of the design matrix can be neglected from design consideration.

A multi-objective optimization problem will be transformed into single objective optimization problem in sequence by utilizing the method of large-scale optimization system or decomposition and coordination method of multi-disciplinary optimization. As the optimal solution of each sub-objective function may be not the optimum of multi-objective optimization, among of sub-objective function should be coordinated. According to optimization method on decomposition and coordination, the design variable of the previous objective function is fixed in the next objective function in the optimization process; the next objective function only optimize those design variables that is classified into this group, and the optimal variables will be returned to the previous objective function. By an iterative manner again and again, the optimization process continues until it satisfies the convergence condition. The key question of the "decomposition/coordination" optimization is how to identify the corresponding design variables and constraints of each objective function. In large-scale / multi-disciplinary optimization, the design variables are grouped according to the locations of parts in structural design or experts-based domain knowledge. In this research, the decomposition is based on the relationship between DPs and FRs, which is defined as "logical decomposition".

4   Optimization Design Method Using Independent Axiom

The steps of multi-objective optimization design using independent axiom in axiomatic design can be given as in the following:

Step 1. Select design variables and identify objective functions and constraints.

Consider an optimization design problem that consists of six design variables, three objective functions and three constraints functions which is given by the following design equation.

$$\text{Min} \quad F(\mathbf{X}) = \text{Min} \ \{f_1(\mathbf{x}), f_2(\mathbf{x}), f_3(\mathbf{x})\}^{\text{T}}$$
$$\text{s.t.} \quad g_1(x_1, x_2) \leq 0$$
$$g_2(x_1, x_4, x_5) \leq 0 \tag{3}$$
$$g_3(x_1, x_3, x_5, x_6) \leq 0$$

The vector of design variables is $\mathbf{x} = \{x_1, x_2, x_3, x_4, x_5, x_6\}^{\text{T}}$.

Step 2. Put the optimization objectives and design variables into a design matrix. The relationship between design variables and optimization objectives is expressed as

$$
\begin{bmatrix} FR1 \\ FR2 \\ FR3 \end{bmatrix} = \begin{bmatrix} 1 & 1 & 1 & 1 & 0 & 0 \\ 1 & 0 & 0 & 1 & 1 & 1 \\ 0 & 1 & 1 & 1 & 1 & 1 \end{bmatrix} \cdot \begin{bmatrix} x_1 \\ x_2 \\ x_3 \\ x_4 \\ x_5 \\ x_6 \end{bmatrix} \tag{4}
$$

where FRi is the ith functional requirement, namely design objective. The sign "1" means a relation exists and "0" means there is no relation between FR and design variable.

If the design matrix is rearranged into a new matrix by making it as diagonal matrix as possible, it shows the optimization objectives are independent, then turn to step 4.

Step 3. Use orthogonal experiment and ANOVA to identify the contribution of each design variables to objective functions, and determine the principal design variables and ignore those design variables with small influence. In design matrix, the sign "×" means design variable has significant effect on FR and "+" means design variable has little effect on FR. The equation (4) is rewritten as

$$
\begin{bmatrix} FR1 \\ FR2 \\ FR3 \end{bmatrix} = \begin{bmatrix} \times & \times & + & + & 0 & 0 \\ + & 0 & 0 & \times & \times & + \\ 0 & + & \times & + & + & \times \end{bmatrix} \cdot \begin{bmatrix} x_1 \\ x_2 \\ x_3 \\ x_4 \\ x_5 \\ x_6 \end{bmatrix} \tag{5}
$$

Rearrange the design matrix to make it as diagonal matrix as possible.

$$
\begin{bmatrix} FR1 \\ FR2 \\ FR3 \end{bmatrix} = \begin{bmatrix} \times & \times & 0 & + & + & 0 \\ + & 0 & \times & \times & 0 & + \\ 0 & + & + & + & \times & \times \end{bmatrix} \cdot \begin{bmatrix} x_1 \\ x_2 \\ x_4 \\ x_5 \\ x_3 \\ x_6 \end{bmatrix} \tag{6}
$$

The design variables are grouped and the number of the groups is the same as that of optimization objectives. Thus, the design will be nearly uncoupled design. According to equation (6), the design variables are classified into three groups. The design parameters DP1 include x1 and x2, DP2 include x4 and x5, and DP3 include x3 and x6. Then the formula can be rewritten as

$$\begin{bmatrix} FR1 \\ FR2 \\ FR3 \end{bmatrix} = \begin{bmatrix} \times & + & + \\ + & \times & + \\ + & + & \times \end{bmatrix} \begin{bmatrix} DP1(x_1, x_2) \\ DP2(x_4, x_5) \\ DP3(x_3, x_6) \end{bmatrix} \tag{7}$$

Step 4. Suppose x_p and x_q lie in the same group $f_i(\mathbf{x})$, if one constraint is only relative to x_p and x_q, this constraint will be classified into this group. All other constraints are classified into different groups by analogy, and then go to step 6. Otherwise, go to the next step.

Step 5. According to the relationship between the design functions (including the objective function and constraint functions) and design variables, establish the dependence matrix on the design functions and design variables, which is named as the function dependence table (FDT). If a constraint function relates to one design variable, the corresponding position in FDT is marked as "1", otherwise marked as "0". Here, the contribution values of design variables on the constraint function arc not considered. The relationship between the objective function and design variables is still marked as "×" or "+".

Table 1. Function Dependence Table

	x_1	x_2	x_4	x_5	x_3	x_6
f_1	×	×	+	+		
g_1	1	1				
g_2	1			1		
g_3	1			1	1	1
f_2	+		×	×		+
g_2	1		1	1		
g_3	1			1	1	1
f_3		+	+	+	×	×
g_3	1			1	1	1

In any case, the constraints must be met, so they can be classified into the different groups. Namely, if a constraint relates to design variables of multiple groups, it can be respectively classified into those groups. As shown in table 1, $g_1(\mathbf{x})$ only relate to $\{f_1(\mathbf{x}); x_1, x_2\}$, it will be classified into this group; $g_3(\mathbf{x})$ relate to design variables of three groups $\{x_1; x_5; x_3, x_6\}$, it will be respectively classified into these groups.

Step 6. If the design functions of each group are independent, the multi-objective optimization problem can be solved by single objective optimization manner. Then go to step 10. However, in many cases, even if the objective functions are independent, the constraint functions are often closely linked to each other. So, it can not be solved in single objective optimization manner and should be optimized in sequence.

Step 7. Determine the order of each group and optimize them in sequence. According to the order of optimization, if the optimization objective and constraints in one group not only relate to the design variables in this group, but also they relate to that in other group, the design variables in this group is only optimized and that in other group will be fixed. In the next group, the values of design variables obtained from the previous group are fixed. Each group is optimized in sequence, and set k = 1.

Step 8. Start from the first group continuously, the design variables in other groups are fixed. The other groups will be optimized in sequence and set k =k+1.

Step 9. Determine the optimization results whether meet the convergence criteria. If $\left|\left(\mathbf{x}^{k+1} - \mathbf{x}^k\right)/\mathbf{x}^{k+1}\right| < \varepsilon$, then return to step 10, where ε is the convergence precision and is usually set $\varepsilon = 10^{-3} \sim 10^{-4}$. Otherwise return to step 8 and continue for the next cycle.

Step 10. Output the optimal solution $\left(\mathbf{x}^*, F^*\right)$.

The algorithm flow of optimization design using "uncoupled" idea of axiomatic design is shown in figure 1.

5   Case Study

In the optimization design for caliper disc brake used in automobile, the short braking time and small nave parameter under controllable temperature are required. When the vehicle is full-loaded the load of a single wheel W is 3400N; the vehicle's running speed v is 160km/h; the radius of a wheel r is 350mm; the number of brakes (i.e. number of wheels) m is 4; the allowed maximum diameter for brake disk $[D_{max}]$ is 300mm; the allowed maximum temperature $[T_{max}]$ is 260°C; the material of brake disc is steel and the original temperature T_i is 35°C; the diameter of nave D_h is 75mm; the friction coefficient between pad and brake disc μ is 1 and the adhesion coefficient between tire and road surface φ is 1; the allowed maximum pressure of pad $[p_{max}]$ is 3MPa; the allowed maximum oil pressure of hydro-cylinder $[p_{0max}]$ is 7MPa; the thickness of hydro-cylinder wall t_c is 6.5mm.

The structural relationship between caliper and brake disc is shown in fig. 2. The circular friction surface of pad is discretized as an arc concentric with the disc, as shown in fig. 3. Considering that asymmetrical wear process lead to pv' (unit-pressure × Rotate-speed) become balance gradually on the whole fiction plane, so we suppose that $pv' = C = const$.

The force of pad acting on disc:

$$F = \int_{R-d/2}^{R+d/2} \frac{C}{r} l dr \tag{8}$$

where $l = r \cdot \beta = 2r \cdot \cos^{-1}\left(\dfrac{R^2 + r^2 - (d/2)^2}{2Rr}\right)$.

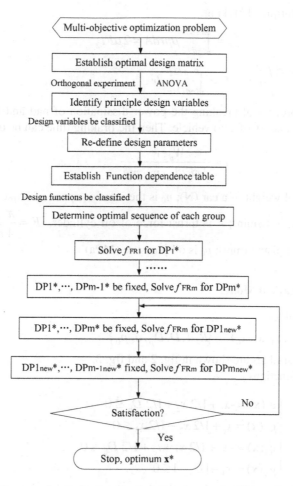

Fig. 1. The flow diagram of optimization design using "uncoupled" idea of axiomatic design

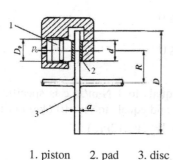

1. piston   2. pad   3. disc

Fig. 2. The structure diagram of disk brake

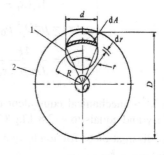

1. pad   2. pad disc

Fig. 3. Calculation diagram of brake

The friction torque of braking:

$$T_f = \int_{R-d/2}^{R+d/2} \mu p r dA = 2\mu F I_2$$

(9)

where $I_2 = \int_{R-d/2}^{R+d/2} \dfrac{l}{I_1} dr$, $I_1 = \int_{R-d/2}^{R+d/2} \dfrac{l}{r} dr$.

During the process of breaking the power dissipation of pad and brake disc is as much as kinetic energy of auto vehicle. Then the braking time can be derived:

$$t = \frac{W_a \cdot v^2}{4\pi F \mu I_2 \cdot n_0 \cdot mg}$$

(10)

where W_a is total weight of a car (N); n_0 is the rotation speed of brake discs or wheels when start braking (r/min); F is thrust force of oil cylinder, $F = \dfrac{\pi}{4} D_p^2 \cdot p_0$, where D_p is diameter of piston (mm); p_0 is oil pressure (MPa)

5.1   Mathematical Model

(1) Design variables

$$\mathbf{x} = \{x_1, x_2, x_3, x_4, x_5, x_6\}^T = \{R, d, D, D_p, a, p_0\}^T.$$

The design variables are shown in fig. 2 and fig. 3.
(2) Constraint functions

$$
\begin{cases}
g_1(\mathbf{x}) = -x_1 + 1/2\, x_2 + 1/2\, D_h \leq 0 \\
g_2(\mathbf{x}) = x_1 + 1/2\, x_2 - 1/2\, x_3 \leq 0 \\
g_3(\mathbf{x}) = -x_1 + 1/2\, x_4 + t_c + 1/2\, D_h \leq 0 \\
g_4(\mathbf{x}) = x_3 - [D_{max}] \leq 0 \\
g_5(\mathbf{x}) = x_6 - [p_{0max}] \leq 0 \\
g_6(\mathbf{x}) = \dfrac{\pi x_4^2 \cdot x_6}{4I_1(x_1 - x_2/2)} - [p_{max}] \leq 0 \\
g_7(\mathbf{x}) = \mu \pi D_p^2 p_0 I_2/2 - Wr\varphi \leq 0 \\
g_8(\mathbf{x}) = \dfrac{4E}{J\pi c\rho x_3^2 x_5} + T_i - T_{max} \leq 0
\end{cases}
$$

(11)

where J is mechanical equivalent of heat and equals to 1 N·m/J。 c is specific heat capacity and equals to 472.8 J/kg°C; ρ is density and equals to $7.8\times10^{-6} kg/mm^3$; E is power dissipation of friction torque and equals to $W_a \cdot v^2/(2mg)$.
(3) Objective functions

To assure the safety of vehicle, it is essential to improve the work efficiency of brakes and to shorten the braking time, so minimizing braking time should be considered as optimization objective. In addition, minimizing thickness and temperature of the brake disc can be also considered as other two objectives. i.e.:

$$\text{Min } F(\mathbf{x}) = \text{Min } \{f_1(\mathbf{x}), f_2(\mathbf{x}), f_3(\mathbf{x})\}^{\text{T}} \quad . \tag{12}$$

where $f_1(\mathbf{X}) = t$, $f_2(\mathbf{X}) = a$, $f_3(\mathbf{X}) = \dfrac{4E}{J\pi c\rho x_3^2 x_5}$.

5.2   Computing Process and Results

(1) Identify the relationship between optimization objectives and design variables in terms of design matrix, and then rearrange the design matrix to make it into a nearly diagonal matrix or triangular matrix.

$$\begin{bmatrix} \text{FR1} \\ \text{FR2} \\ \text{FR3} \end{bmatrix} = \begin{bmatrix} 1 & 1 & 1 & 1 & 0 & 0 \\ 0 & 0 & 0 & 0 & 1 & 0 \\ 0 & 0 & 0 & 0 & 1 & 1 \end{bmatrix} \cdot \begin{bmatrix} x_1 \\ x_2 \\ x_4 \\ x_6 \\ x_5 \\ x_3 \end{bmatrix} \quad . \tag{13}$$

As FR1 is independent of FR2 and FR3, and FR2 is only related to x_5, so we only need to determine the contribution of x_3 and x_5 to FR3. Since there are three sub-objectives in optimization design, the design variables can be grouped and the number of the groups is three.

Table 2. Level of factor (unit: mm)

Factor	Level		
	1	2	3
x_3	200	250	300
x_5	4	5	6

(2) Identify the contribution of x_3 and x_5 to FR3 using orthogonal experiment and ANOVA. Three levels are determined for both x_3 and x_5, as shown in table 2, and the orthogonal table $L_9(3^4)$ is selected.

The results of ANOVA show that x_3 has great influence on FR3 and x_5 has small influence on FR3. Then the equation (13) can be rewritten as

$$\begin{bmatrix} \text{FR1} \\ \text{FR2} \\ \text{FR3} \end{bmatrix} = \begin{bmatrix} 1 & 0 & 0 \\ 0 & 1 & 0 \\ 0 & + & \times \end{bmatrix} \begin{bmatrix} \text{DP1}(x_1, x_2, x_4, x_6) \\ \text{DP2}(x_5) \\ \text{DP3}(x_3) \end{bmatrix} \quad . \tag{14}$$

(3) Establish the function dependence table. The FDT of disc brake is shown in Table 3.

Table 3. FDT of disc brake

	x_1	x_2	x_4	x_6	x_5	x_3
f_1	1	1	1	1		
g_1	1	1				
g_2	1	1				1
g_3	1		1			
g_5				1		
g_6	1	1	1	1		
g_7	1	1	1	1		
f_2	+				1	
g_8					1	1
f_3					+	×
g_2	1	1				1
g_4						1
g_8					1	1

(4) According to table 3, $f_1(\mathbf{x})$ is independent of $f_2(\mathbf{x})$ and the relation between $f_3(\mathbf{x})$ and $f_2(\mathbf{x})$ is nearly uncoupled. Thus, $f_1(\mathbf{x})$ and $f_2(\mathbf{x})$ can be optimized simultaneously. But both the constraint g_2 in the group $\{f_1(\mathbf{x})\}$ and g_8 in the group $\{f_2(\mathbf{x})\}$ relate to x_3 in the group $\{f_3(\mathbf{x})\}$, x_3 should be fixed in the optimization process of $f_1(\mathbf{x})$ and $f_2(\mathbf{x})$. When $f_3(\mathbf{x})$ is optimized, x_1, x_2 and x_5 should be fixed.

Continue the next iteration until convergence criterion is satisfied. Then the optimal solutions are obtained.

The initial sizes of disc brake and the results of the weighted optimization method and the proposed method in this paper are summarized in table 4, here weighting factors w_1, w_2 and w_3 are 0.495, 0.495 and 0.01 respectively. According to the results and process of calculation, it shows that results obtained from the weighted optimization method will change with different weighting factors, so it is difficult to balance every objective. The optimal results based on the proposed method are more satisfactory, which consider the influence of design variables to design objectives and make the design to be nearly uncoupled design. The values of the first two objectives are smaller except the third objective, which is consistent with the importance of the first two objectives.

Table 4. The optimal results

	x_1(mm)	x_2(mm)	x_3(mm)	x_4(mm)	x_5(mm)	x_6(MPa)	$f_1(\mathbf{x})=t$ (s)	$f_2(\mathbf{x})=a$ (mm)	$f_3(\mathbf{x})=T$ (°C)
Initial value	100	60	280	40	5	3	7.241	5	378.938
Weighted optimization	100.016	60.036	280.145	40.077	7.272	3.516	6.153	7.272	207.484
Proposed method	100.052	60.121	300	40.258	5.848	4.727	4.535	5.848	224.997

6   Conclusions

In this paper, a new method of multi-objective optimization is presented. The concept of contribution of design variables to design objectives is used to identify the relation between them. Following the "uncoupled design" idea of axiomatic design, the design matrix is rearranged to be as diagonal matrix as possible. If the design is a nearly uncoupled design, an iterative method is suggested. The important design variables to a specific objective are identified and can be grouped into one set of parameters, and then establish the function dependence table and optimize every objective function in sequence. The optimization design of disc brake has been solved to show the validity of the proposed method.

References

1. Suh, N.P.: Axiomatic design: advances and applications. Oxford University Press, New York (2001)
2. Liu, X.P., Soderborg, N.: Improving an existing design based on axiomatic design principles. In: First International Conference on Axiomatic Design, Cambridge, U.S., June 21-23, pp. 199–202 (2000)
3. Hwang, K.H., Lee, K.W., Park, G.J., et al.: Robust design of the vibratory gyroscope with unbalanced inner torsion gimbal using axiomatic design. In: Second International Conference on Axiomatic Design, pp. 1–7. Massachusetts Institution of Technology, Boston (2002)
4. Jeff, T., Ge, P.: Applying axiomatic design theory to the evaluation and optimization of large-scale engineering systems. Journal of Engineering Design 17(1), 1–16 (2006)
5. Chen, K.Z.: Identifying the relationship among design methods-key to successful applications and developments of design methods. Journal of Engineering Design 10, 125–141 (1999)

Energetic and Exergetic Performances Simulating of GSHP Greenhouse Cooling System in Northern China[*]

Lilong Chai[1,**], Chengwei Ma[2,***], Gangyi Xu[1], Mingchi Liu[1], and Yong Xu[1]

[1] Vegetable Research Center,
Beijing Academy of Agriculture and Forestry Sciences, Beijing 100097, China
lchaipurdue@gmail.com
[2] College of Water Conservancy & Civil Engineering, China
Agricultural University, Beijing 100083, China
macwbs@cau.edu.cn

Abstract. The Energetic and Exergetic performances evaluating models were built for a agricultural greenhouse cooling with groundwater-style GSHP system (GSHPs) in Northern China. The Exergy destruction (Ex_{dest}), Exergy efficiency(ε) and coefficient of performance (COP) were estimated and presented based on summer cooling test monitored data and the simulation models. Analyzed results indicate that the evaporator has the highest Exergy efficiency compared with other sections of the system, which reached 92% during cooling test that means the evaporator has a brilliant performance of reversibility in cooling mode. The condenser and compressors have lower reversibility relatively. Generally, GSHPs has an Exergy efficiency of 36%. Besides, COP of GSHPs cooling in greenhouse reached 3.09, which is higher than 2.0 of conventional air source heat pump systems COP by 50%.

Keywords: greenhouse, Ground source heat pump, cooling, Exergy efficiency, COP.

1   Introduction

The utilizing of renewable and clean energy source, such as solar energy and shallow geothermal energy for building air-conditioning were conducted more frequent with the strengthen of global warming and environmental pollutant [1-4]. The shallow geothermal energy (the solar energy stored in shallow soil layer and groundwater) has been well developed and applied in cooling and heating industrial and civilian constructions by making use of ground source heat pump (GSHP) technology [5, 6], which has been proved with the characteristics of effective, environmental friendly and multi-functional of buildings heating, cooling and dehumidifying [7,8], which is indeed one of the most fast growing clean energy utilizing air-conditioning

---

[*]This study was supported by the earmarked fund for Modern Agro-industry Technology Research System (CARS-25-D-04).
[**] Research Assistant.
[***] Professor, Corresponding author.

D. Li and Y. Chen (Eds.): CCTA 2011, Part III, IFIP AICT 370, pp. 74–84, 2012.

technologies at present. By the end of 2005, the utilization scale of ground source heat pump air–conditioning in resident or office buildings had reached $3000{\times}10^4$ m^2 in mainland China [9], and some research on GSHP technology in agricultural facilities cooling or heating were conducted in recent years [10,11].

Although the energy saving performance of GSHPs in greenhouse cooling or heating has been estimated in past studies with many methods [12-14], most of analysis were limited in first law of thermodynamics, which describes the heat quantity transfer process in GSHPS, such as the COP was calculated based on this method. However, the quality of energy utilizing was taken into consideration in Carnot Cycle based heat transferring process such as heat pump system [15]. The quality analysis of the energy was defined as Exergy analysis that is based on second law of thermodynamics and is the combination of Enthalpy and Entropy. Exergy can be described as the maximum amount of work that a thermodynamic system can achieved when it is reach equilibrium with the reference environment [16, 17]. Exergy analysis method has been utilized in various fields [18]. Dincer [12] has come up with that the potential usefulness of Exergy in addressing and solving environmental problems as well as attaining sustainable development is crucial. Ozgener and Hepbasli [19] have assessed the relations between thermodynamic losses and capital costs for devices, and suggested possible generalizations in the relation. Generally, the Exergy analysis method was proved to be a more comprehensive method in assessing the energy transferring [20, 21]. Therefore, the combined method of energetic and exegetic performances study on agricultural greenhouse cooling need to be built for the utilizing of GSHPs.

The objects of this study is but not limited to (1) build the energetic and exergetic performance estimating method and simulation models for agricultural greenhouse cooling with GSHPs. (2) presents GSHPs greenhouse cooling performances based on the theories of first and second laws of thermodynamics.

2   Materials and Methods

2.1   GSHP Greenhouse Cooling System

The GSHPs and tested greenhouse (Fig. 1) were located in the in Haidian district (latitude 39°40' N) of Beijing of China. The GSHPs system had three principal circuits, as shown in Fig.2.

(i) Groundwater drawing and refilling part (there are five wells with the depth of about 100m, one water drawing well, four water refilling wells. The groundwater drawing and refilling circuit consisted of one water drawing well, four water refilling wells, a water drawing pump, and a water refilling pump. Each water pump had 11 kW rated input power and 33.2 m3 h-1 maximum water flow rate. The distances between the drawing well and refilling wells ranged from 100 to 300 m;

(ii) GSHP energy enhancing circuit, which consisted of four Danfoss Hermetic scroll compressors connected in series. GSHP unit contained about 58 kg R22 refrigerant and had total capacity of 380 kW for heating and 450 kW for cooling, the rated power of the electric motor for each compressor was 16.08 kW;

(iii) Heat transportation and fan coil heating units. This circuit contains many water circulating pipes and two water pumps.

Fig. 1. GSHPs and agricultural greenhouse in test

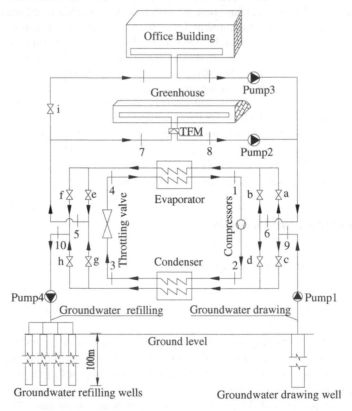

Fig. 2. Schematic diagram of GSHP cooling system in the study, a–i are valves installed on different water pipes; Pump1 represents the drawing water pumps; Pumps 2 and 3 represents circulating water pumps; Pump 4 represents backfilling water pumps; 1-10 represents each thermodynamic state position of refrigerant or water in each circle

During summer cooling test, the GSHPs operated cooling cycle, the water valves of b, c, e and h were turned on, and keep the valves of a, d, f and g shut off. In groundwater circle, the groundwater was drawn out from the well and pumped into heat exchanger connected with condenser via valve c, and then was recharged back via valve h to refilling wells after heat exchange in condenser. In greenhouse and building heating circle, the cold circulating water was sent to greenhouses and office buildings to cooling the house via valve e after released heat exchange in evaporator, and then was sent back via valve b to the heat exchanger connected with evaporator.

2.2   Energetic Performance Simulating Models

The coefficient of performance (COP) was often used as indicator to analyze the GSHP system under cooling operation, which is an important index for evaluating the energy efficiency in a thermodynamics system. Referred to previous research [12, 21], the energy transfer and performance analytical model of the system can be put forwarded as Eqs. (1) - (7). The cooling COP of the GSHP unit, total system and greenhouse subsystem are analyzed in the study.

Groundwater,

$$Q_{\text{well}} = m_{\text{well}} (h_{10} - h_9) \tag{1}$$

Where, Q_{well} is the groundwater heat transfer rate in condenser, in kW; m_{well} is the mass flow rate of underground water, in kg·s^{-1}; h_9 is the specific enthalpy of underground water entering condenser, in kJ·kg^{-1}; h_{10} is the specific enthalpy of groundwater leaving condenser, in kJ·kg^{-1}.

Condenser,

$$Q_{\text{cond}} = m_{\text{ref}} (h_{2e} - h_3) \tag{2}$$

Where, Q_{cond} is the heat rejection rate in the condenser, in kW; m_{ref} is the mass flow rate of refrigerant R22, in kg·s^{-1}; h_{2e} is the specific enthalpy of refrigerant leaving compressor/entering condenser in isentropic process, in kJ·kg^{-1}; h_3 is the specific enthalpy of refrigerant leaving condenser /entering throttling valve, in kJ·kg^{-1}.

Evaporator,

$$Q_{\text{evap}} = m_{\text{ref}} (h_1 - h_4) \tag{3}$$

Where, Q_{evap} is the heat transfer rate in the evaporator, in kW; h_1 is the specific enthalpy of refrigerant leaving evaporator /entering compressor, in kJ·kg^{-1}; h_4 is the specific enthalpy of refrigerant leaving throttling valve /entering evaporator, in kJ·kg^{-1}.

Compressor,

$$W_{\text{comp}} \eta_e \eta_c = m_{\text{ref}} (h_{2e} - h_1) \tag{4}$$

Where, W_{comp} is the power input to the compressors in kW; η_e is the compressor iso–entropy work efficiency; η_c is the compressor cubage work efficiency. In this study the product of η_e and η_c was considered as 75% as manufacturer rated.

Throttling valve,

$$Q_{\text{thro}} = m_{\text{ref}} (h_4 - h_3) \tag{5}$$

Where, Q_{thro} is the heat transfer rate in the throttling valve, in kW.

$$Q_{\text{cir}} = m_{\text{wa}} (h_6 - h_5) \tag{6}$$

Where, Q_{fc} is the total heat transfer rate of circulating water system, in kW; m_{wa} is the mass flow rate of circulating water, in kg·s^{-1}; h_5 is the specific enthalpy of circulating water leaving evaporator, in kJ·kg^{-1}; h_6 is the specific enthalpy of circular water entering evaporator, in kJ·kg^{-1}.

Circulating water system via greenhouse,

$$Q_{fc,g} = m_{wa,g}(h_8 - h_7) \tag{7}$$

Where, $Q_{fc,g}$ is the cooling capacity of fan–coil units in greenhouse, in kW; $m_{wa,g}$ is the mass flow rate of circulating water in greenhouse, in kg·s^{-1}; h_7 is the specific enthalpy of flowing in water in greenhouse, in kJ·kg^{-1}; h_8 is the specific enthalpy of flowing out water in greenhouse, in kJ·kg^{-1}.

The COP was usually applied as an indicator for assessing the performance of GSHPs in civilian and industry buildings heating and cooling research [17, 22]. The greenhouse heating COP of GSHPs was estimated with Eqs. (8) -(10).

$$COP_{GSHP} = \frac{Q_{evap}}{W_{comp}} \tag{8}$$

$$E_e = \sum_{i=1}^{n} \sum_{j=1}^{m} E_{i,j} \tag{9}$$

$$COP_{sys} = \frac{E_g}{3600E_e} \tag{10}$$

Where, $E_{i,j}$ is the electricity energy consumed by equipment j at time i, kWh, the electricity energy consuming equipment in greenhouse cooling including GSHP compressors, water pumps, and fan coil units; E_e is total electric energy consumed by GHSPs, kWh; E_g is cooling quantity in greenhouse provided by GHSPs, kJ; COP_{GSHP} is cooling COP of GSHP unit, dimensionless; COP_{sys} is greenhouse cooling COP of GSHPs, dimensionless.

2.3   Exergic Performance Simulating Models

Exergy analysis is based on the second law of thermodynamics, which takes the entropy portion into consideration by including irreversibilities, and is the combination between enthalpy and entropy. Exergy reflects both quantity and quality of thermodynamic process [12, 13]. The Exergy efficiency (Ex_{dest}) and Exergy destruction rate (ε) are core content of Exergy analysis, which was applied in this study to demonstrate the performance of GSHPs in greenhouse and buildings cooling. The estimation of Exergy transferring in each section of GSHPs was conducted with Eqs. (11)- (17).

Compressor,

$$ex_2 - ex_1 = (h_{2i} - h_1) - T_0(s_{2i} - s_1) \tag{11}$$

Condenser,

$$ex_2 - ex_3 = (h_{2i} - h_3) - T_0(s_{2i} - s_3) \tag{12}$$

Throttle valve,

$$ex_3 - ex_4 = (h_3 - h_4) - T_0(s_3 - s_4) \tag{13}$$

Evaporator,

$$ex_4 - ex_1 = (h_4 - h_1) - T_0(s_4 - s_1) \tag{14}$$

Heat exchanger of circulating water and evaporator,

$$ex_5 - ex_6 = (h_5 - h_6) - T_0(s_5 - s_6) \tag{15}$$

Heat exchanger of circulating water and greenhouse fan-coil units,

$$ex_7 - ex_8 = (h_7 - h_8) - T_0(s_7 - s_8) \tag{16}$$

Heat exchanger of groundwater and condenser,

$$ex_9 - ex_{10} = (h_9 - h_{10}) - T_0(s_9 - s_{10}) \tag{17}$$

Where, $ex_1 \sim _{10}$ represent the specific Exergy at each position of $1 \sim 10$ in Fig.2, in kJ·kg^{-1}; $h_1 \sim _{10}$ are the specific enthalpy at each position of $1 \sim 10$, respectively, in kJ·kg^{-1}; $s_1 \sim _{10}$ are the specific entropy at each position of $1 \sim 10$, respectively, in kJ·kg^{-1}·K^{-1}.

2.3.1   Exergy Destruction Rate

Exergy destruction rate embodies the quantity of devalued energy [13, 22], which was estimated with Eqs. (18) - (23) in each section of GSHPs.

Compressor,

$$Ex_{dest,comp} = W_{comp} - m_{ref}(ex_2 - ex_1) \tag{18}$$

Condenser,

$$Ex_{dest,cond} = m_{ref}(ex_9 - ex_{10}) - m_{ref}(ex_3 - ex_2) \tag{19}$$

Throttle valve,

$$Ex_{dest,thro} = m_{ref}(ex_3 - ex_4) \tag{20}$$

Evaporator,

$$Ex_{dest,evap} = m_{ref}(ex_4 - ex_1) - m_{ref}(ex_6 - ex_5) \tag{21}$$

Groundwater circle,

$$Ex_{dest,gw} = Q_{well}(1 - \frac{T_{10}}{T_0}) - m_{well}(ex_{10} - ex_9) \tag{22}$$

Heat transportation circle,

$$Ex_{dest,cir} = Q_{evap}(1 - \frac{T_5}{T_0}) - m_{cir,w}(ex_5 - ex_6) \tag{23}$$

Where, $Ex_{dest,comp}$, $Ex_{dest,evap}$, $Ex_{dest,cond}$, $Ex_{dest,thro}$, $Ex_{dest,cir}$ are exergy destruction rate in compressor, evaporator, condenser, throttling valve, circulating water system, respectively, dimensionless. T_5, T_6, T_9 are water temperatures at positions 5, 6 and 9, respectively, in K.

2.3.2   Exergy Efficiency

The Exergy efficiency of various sections and total system of GSHPs were estimated with the Eqs. (24)- (30).

Compressor,

$$\varepsilon_{comp} = \frac{Ex_2 - Ex_1}{W_{comp}} \tag{24}$$

Throttle,

$$\varepsilon_{\text{thro}} = \frac{Ex_3 - Ex_4}{W_{\text{comp}}} \tag{25}$$

Evaporator,

$$\varepsilon_{\text{evap}} = 1 - \frac{E_{\text{dest,evap}}}{W_{\text{comp}}} \tag{26}$$

Condenser,

$$\varepsilon_{\text{cond}} = 1 - \frac{E_{\text{dest,cond}}}{W_{\text{comp}}} \tag{27}$$

Circulating water system,

$$\varepsilon_{\text{cir}} = 1 - \frac{E_{\text{dest,cir}}}{W_{\text{fc}} + W_{\text{pump,cir}}} \tag{28}$$

GSHP unit,

$$\varepsilon_{\text{hp}} = 1 - \frac{Ex_{\text{dest,evap}} + Ex_{\text{dest,comp}} + Ex_{\text{dest,thro}} + Ex_{\text{dest,cond}}}{\dfrac{Ex_{\text{dest,evap}}}{1 - \varepsilon_{\text{evap}}} + \dfrac{Ex_{\text{dest,comp}}}{1 - \varepsilon_{\text{comp}}} + \dfrac{Ex_{\text{dest,thro}}}{1 - \varepsilon_{\text{thro}}} + \dfrac{Ex_{\text{dest,cond}}}{1 - \varepsilon_{\text{cond}}}} \tag{29}$$

GSHP system,

$$\varepsilon_{\text{sys}} = 1 - \frac{Ex_{\text{dest,evap}} + Ex_{\text{dest,comp}} + Ex_{\text{dest,thro}} + Ex_{\text{dest,cond}} + Ex_{\text{dest,cir}}}{\dfrac{Ex_{\text{dest,evap}}}{1 - \varepsilon_{\text{evap}}} + \dfrac{Ex_{\text{dest,comp}}}{1 - \varepsilon_{\text{comp}}} + \dfrac{Ex_{\text{dest,thro}}}{1 - \varepsilon_{\text{thro}}} + \dfrac{Ex_{\text{dest,cond}}}{1 - \varepsilon_{\text{cond}}} + \dfrac{Ex_{\text{dest,cir}}}{1 - \varepsilon_{\text{cir}}}} \tag{30}$$

Where, $\varepsilon_{\text{comp}}$, $\varepsilon_{\text{evap}}$, $\varepsilon_{\text{cond}}$, $\varepsilon_{\text{thro}}$, ε_{cir}, ε_{hp}, ε_{sys} are Exergy efficiencies of the compressor, evaporator, condenser, throttle, circulating water system, GSHP unit and GSHP system respectively, dimensionless.

2.4 Data Acquisition

The following data was collected in this test,

(1) Measuring mass flow rates of the water by using rotameters (Beijing jingyuan liquid apparatus company, China). Rotameters were installed at inlet of all water flow tubes;

(2) Measuring the temperature of the water inlet and outlet of the condenser, evaporator, and the greenhouse by using resistance thermometers PT1000 (Jingyuan liquid apparatus company, China, error limitation is ± (0.3+0.005Δt °C)), each couple of thermometers were installed at inlet and outlet of water flow respectively;

(3) Measuring the temperature and humidity of air inside and outside of greenhouse by using temperature–humidity sensors RS–11 (ESPEC, Japan), the error limitation is ±0.5 °C in temperature and ±5% in relative humidity;

(4) Recording input power of different electric motor driving equipments by using ammeters (Shanghai Huaxia ammeters manufactory).

All the simulation calculation was conducted in Micro-soft Excel file. The results was calculated by following assumptions (i) The temperature at 1, 2, 3 and 4 points in GSHP unit was gained from manufacturer (*Chongke High–Technology Development Co.,Ltd, Beijing,China*), and assumed that the running was kept on steadily, as well as the temperature at 1,2,3 and 4 points. (ii) In this study, the restricted dead state was taken to be the state of environment, the temperature and the atmospheric pressure are 0 °C and 101.325 kPa, and don't take the Exergy destruction of water pumps and pressure change into account for the limited condition.

3   Results and Discussion

3.1   The Energetic Performance of GSHPs

For a great deal of water was needed for staff living and farm irrigation at experiment station in summertime, the pumped underground water were not backfilled into well during the test, and the Pump3 was not used in fact, so neglecting the effect of Pump3 and backfilled well. The refrigeration capacity of evaporator Q_{evap} is 190kW, and the actual heat transfer rate between evaporator and circular water system was 164.15kW on average according to the calculation based on the measurements made during Aug.13–18th, 2007, the power input is 53.32kW. Besides, the refrigeration capacity rate to greenhouse during test is 40.18 kW on average. Detailed information about the energy input and COP calculated results as shown in Table 1. The greenhouses cooling COP with GSHPs is 3.09, which is higher than air source heat pumps of 2.0 by more than 50% [22].

Table 1. Cooling performance of the GSHPs in greenhouse（Aug.13-18, 2007）

Parameters	GSHPs-Greenhouse section	GSHPs-whole system
Fan-coil unit cooling rate, kW	40.2	157.2
Heat exchanging rate of Groundwater, kW	-	131.7
Compressors energy input rate, kW	8.1	32.2
Water pumps energy input rate, kW	4.6	18.5
Total energy input rate, kW	13.0	53.3
COP of Heat pump unit	-	5.90
COP of GSHPs	3.09	2.95

3.2   Exergetic Performances

Exergy analysis reflect the quality and quantity of a thermodynamic system, it is closely connected with each element of GSHP system, including compressor, evaporator, condenser and throttle valve. Exergy efficiencies and Exergy destruction are two of important indexes for evaluating energy utilizing system. The state of circulating water, groundwater and R-22 refrigerant was monitored or calculated according the test during Aug.13-18, 2007, as shown in Table 2.

Table 2. State parameters of Liquids in system（Aug.13–18th, 2007）

Positions	Liquids	Mass flow rate m, kg·s^{-1}	Temperature t, °C	Specific enthalpy h, kJ·kg^{-1}	Specific entropy s, kJ·kg^{-1}·K^{-1}
1	R22 refrigerant in vapor	1.145	10.0	409	1.738
2	R22 refrigerant in vapor	1.145	65.0	430	1.738
3	R22 refrigerant in Liquid	1.145	35.0	243	1.146
4	R22 refrigerant in mixture of vapor and liquid	1.145	3.0	243	1.158
5	Total circulating water	15.033	10.1±0.50	42	0.152
6	Total circulating water	15.033	12.7±0.55	53	0.190
7	Greenhouse inlet circulating water	0.923	10.2±0.48	43	0.154
8	Greenhouse outlet circulating water	0.923	20.8±0.83	88	0.305
9	Groundwater	9.220	14.1	59	0.211
10	Groundwater	9.220	17.6	74	0.261

Note, The state parameters value at different thermodynamic positions was calculated according to the recorded data during the test and published value [12, 22, 23] under rated compressor summer operating efficiency of 75%.

In Exergetic performance simulating, the reference temperature T_o was set as averaged outdoor air temperature 306.25. The Exergetic performances including of Exergy destruction rate and Exergy efficiency of GSHPs were listed in Table 3. In GSHPs, the section of evaporator shows highest Exergy efficiency of 92.5, which indicates that this section has higher energy utilizing quality. The condensers Exergy efficiency is about 65.8%. According to the Ozgener [22] reported result, the condenser has the Exergy efficiency of 80.5% when the GSHPs in heating mode, and 28.6% for evaporator. Therefore, the conclusion of higher Exergy efficiency for condenser and lower Exergy efficiency for evaporator in winter heating mode, and lower Exergy efficiency for condenser and higher Exergy efficiency for evaporator in summer cooling mode could be given.

Table 3. Exergetic performances （Aug.13-18th, 2007）

Elements	Exergy destruction rate, kW	Exergy destruction efficiency,%	Exergy efficiency,%
Compressor	8.14	25.3	74.7
Evaporator	1.83	7.5	92.5
Throttle valve	11.22	-	-
Condenser	5.84	34.2	65.8
Circulating water system	6.26	61.7	38.3
GSHP unit	27.03	42.0	58.0
GSHP system	33.29	64.0	36.0

Throttling valve consist of many capillaries, the Exergy destruction rate was high theoretically. As the R22 passing throttling valve was considered as adiabatic process, so the destruction of Exergy of R22 was caused by the increase of Entropy. Besides, as there no energy input in throttle valve, so the Exergy efficiency of throttling valve could be positive infinity or negative infinity, the study on it is insignificance. If the throttle valve was replaced with Expansion valve, the Entropy increase of R22 would be declined, but the cost of GSHPs would increase. The key object of energetic and exergetic performance analysis is to balance the relationship between economics and thermodynamics.

Generally, the total Exergy efficiency of GSHPs in greenhouse cooling is 36%, which is higher than published value of 15% [23] in residential buildings cooling. However, the Exergy efficiency of GSHPs in this study has the potential to be improved by reducing the Exergy destruction of water circulating and fan-coil units operating.

4   Conclusions

The following conclusions were drawn based on the results in this study,

1) The Enegetic and Exergetic simulation models and performance evaluating method were built in this study for greenhouse GSHPs performance analysis;

2) According to simulated results, total Exergy efficiency of GSHPs in greenhouse cooling is 36%, which is higher than published value of 15% in residential buildings cooling. The Exergy efficiency of GSHPs in this study has the potential to be improved by reducing the Exergy destruction of water circulating and fan-coil units operating.

3) The Energetic and Exergetic performances of GSHPs are associated with the economical performance closely, the optimizing of the Exergy reversibility and COP usually at the cost of economic performance degradation. The key object of energetic and exergetic performance analysis is to balance the relationship between economics and thermodynamics.

Acknowledgments. This study was supported by the earmarked fund for Modern Agro-industry Technology Research System （CARS-25-D-04）.

References

1. Zheng, D.: Modeling of standing column well in ground source heat pump system. Ph.D Thesis, Oklahoma State University, Stillwater (2004)
2. Mao, H., Wang, X., Wang, D.: The design and test of greenhouse solar energy heating system. Acta Energiae Solaris Sinica 25(3), 305–309 (2004)
3. Michopoulos, A.: Three–years operation experience of a ground source heat pump system in Northern Greece. Energy and Buildings 39, 328–334 (2007)
4. Ptasinski, J., Prins, M.J., Pierik, A.: Exergetic evaluation of biomass gasification. Energy 32, 568–574 (2007)
5. Zeng, H., Diao, N., Fang, Z.: A finite line–source model for boreholes in geothermal heat exchangers. Transfer—Asian Research 31(7), 558–567 (2002)
6. Hamada, Y., Nakamura, M., Saitoh, H., et al.: Improved underground heat exchanger by using no-dig method for space heating and cooling. Renewable Energy 32(3), 480–495 (2007)
7. Li, X., Chen, Z., Zhao, J.: Simulation and experiment on the thermal performance of U–vertical ground coupled heat exchanger. Applied Thermal Engineering 26, 1564–1571 (2006)
8. Karlsson, F., Fahlén, P.: Capacity–controlled ground source heat pumps in hydronic heating systems. International Journal of Refrigeration 30, 221–229 (2007)
9. Xu, W.: Investigation and analysis on utilization of ground source heat pump in China. Construction and Design for Project 12, 16–19 (2006)
10. Chai, L., Ma, C., Zhang, Y., et al.: Energy consumption and economic analysis of ground source heat pump used in greenhouse in Beijing. Transactions of the CSAE 26(3), 249–254 (2010)
11. Fang, H., Yang, Q., Sun, J.: Application of ground-source heat pump and floor heating system to greenhouse heating in winter. Transactions of the CSAE 24(12), 145–149 (2008)
12. Dincer, I.: The role of Exergy in energy policy making. Energy Policy 30, 137–149 (2002)
13. Sciubba, E., Ulgiati, S.: Emergy and Exergy analysis, Complementary methods or irreducible ideological options. Energy 30, 1953–1988 (2005)
14. Winter, C.-J.: Energy efficiency, no, It's Exergy efficiency. International Journal of Hydrogen Energy 32, 4109–4111 (2007)
15. Miu, D.: Refrigeration Compressor. China Machine Press, Beijing (2002) (in Chinese)
16. Zhang, J.: Brief Manual for Air Conditioning Worker. China Machine Press, Beijing (1999) (in Chinese)
17. Yan, J., Wang, Y.: Engineering Thermodynamics, 3rd edn. Higher Education Press, Beijing (2001)
18. Som, K., Datta, A.: Thermodynamic irreversibilities and Exergy balance in combustion. Progress Energy Combustion Science 34(3), 351–376 (2008)
19. Ozgener, O., Hepbasli, A.: Exergoeconomic analysis of a solar assisted ground-source heat pump greenhouse heating system. Applied Thermal Engineering 25, 1459–1471 (2005)
20. Bisio, G., Rubatto, G.: Work and entropy production aspects of irreversible processes in closed and steady-state open systems. Exergy, an International Journal 2, 192–205 (2002)
21. Ebru, K.A., Hepbasli, A.: A comparative study on exergetic assessment of two ground–source (geothermal) heat pump systems for residential applications. Building and Environment 42, 2004–2013 (2007)
22. Ozgener, O., Hepbasli, A.: A parametrical study on the energetic and exergetic assessment of a solar–assisted vertical ground–source heat pump system used for heating a greenhouse. Building and Environment 42, 11–24 (2007)
23. Zhao, H., Yang, Z.: The thermodynamic analysis of water source heat pump. Energy Conservation Technology 22(3), 29–32 (2004) (in Chinese)

Vague Weighted Decision-Making Method
and Its Application in Sugarcane Breeding

Hongxu Wang[1], FuJin Zhang[1], and Yunsheng Xu[2]

[1] College of Science and Engineering,
[2] College of Electronic Information Engineering, Qiongzhou University,
Sanya Hainan 572022, China
zfj56801@163.com, whx16233@yahoo.cn

Abstract. Similarity measure formula between Vague set A and B is put forward:

$$M_m(A,B) = \sum_{i=1}^{n} \left[1 - \frac{\left| u_{a_i}^{(m)} - u_{b_i}^{(m)} \right| + \left| v_{a_i}^{(m)} - v_{b_i}^{(m)} \right|}{2} \right] \cdot \left[1 - \frac{\left| t_{a_i}^{(m)} - t_{b_i}^{(m)} \right| + \left| f_{a_i}^{(m)} - f_{b_i}^{(m)} \right|}{2} \right]$$

Vague weighted decision-making method is the pattern recognition method of the Vague set. It is a weighted decision method applied to sugar cane. Vague strains preferred specific methods and steps are discussed, the preferred method is applied to sugar cane lines. The case shows that these formulas and methods are practical, and comparison with other methods, this one has greater advantages.

Keywords: Vague weighted decision-making method, data into formulas, similarity measure formula, sugar cane, Department of preferred varieties.

1 Introduction

In 2001, Hainan Sugarcane Breeding Farm bred identified as BC_1 hybrid strains of Erianthus real sugar cane for the first time. Fuzzy comprehensive evaluation method in Reference [1] studied and analyzed two strains of sugar cane major economic traits of Erianthus hybrids BC_1 17 to have determined it is the fine lines. Fuzzy comprehensive evaluation method, mainly relying on fuzzy matrix, has a great quantity of calculation. Vague set theory is an extension and development of fuzzy set theory, so in this paper we use vague set theory to study the same problem, with a view to agricultural research issues such as these, given the simplicity of the new research methods, and its application in the agricultural field is of a great potential area. And the formula (1), (2), (3), (4) and (5) put forward in this paper provide the technical support for it.

2 Basics

Definition 1 [2] Suppose C be a collection, $\forall c \in C$, G on C Vague set functions with a true membership function t_G and a false membership function f_G. $t_G(c)$ is from C

D. Li and Y. Chen (Eds.): CCTA 2011, Part III, IFIP AICT 370, pp. 85–91, 2012.
© IFIP International Federation for Information Processing 2012

evidence to support the recognition of the degree of membership derived lower bound, while the $f_G(c)$ is the evidence from the object C derived the lower bound of the negative membership. $t_G(c)$ and $f_G(c)$ in the range [0,1] a real number and C the point of linking that is mapped $t_G : C \rightarrow [0,1], f_G : C \rightarrow [0,1]$, and $t_G(c) + f_G(c) \leq 1$. Vague set G can be recorded at the element c is $G(c) = [t_G(c), 1 - f_G(c)]$. Vague can also be abbreviated as $c = [t_c, 1 - f_c]$.

It can be seen from the definition of $c = [t_c, 1 - f_c] \subseteq [0,1]$. $\pi_c = 1 - t_c - f_c$ represents the element of uncertainty on the Vague Set G function. If $C = \{c_1, c_2, \cdots, c_n\}$ is a discrete universe of discourse, the Vague on the set G can be written as $G = \sum_{i=1}^{n} [t_G(c_i), 1 - f_G(c_i)] / c_i$, which can also be abbreviated as

$$G = \sum_{i=1}^{n} [t_{c_i}, 1 - f_{c_i}] / c_i.$$

3   Vague of the Original Data

When we solve practical problems with Vague set theory, we must consider the practical problems of the original data to be blurred to create Vague environment, it will not be used to Vague set management Here is one the formula to turn the single-value data into Vague data, which will be discussed later on.

Definition 1. Suppose trait evaluation index set is $C = \{c_1, c_2, \cdots, c_n\}$, C is on the set of $G_i (i = 1, 2, \cdots, m)$; target ($c_j (j = 1, 2, \cdots, n)$) data for the $c_{ij} (\geq 0)$. If the single-value data $c_{ij} (\geq 0)$ into the data Vague $G_i(c_j) = c_{ij} = [t_{ij}, 1 - f_{ij}]$, and $G_i(c_j) = c_{ij} = [t_{ij}, 1 - f_{ij}]$ Vague can meet criteria and output criteria, then the single-value data into the conversion formula Vague data are called output-oriented transformation formula. If the single-value data $c_{ij} (\geq 0)$ into the data $G_i(c_j) = c_{ij} = [t_{ij}, 1 - f_{ij}]$ Vague can mee Vague standards and the investment criteria, then the single-value data into the conversion formula Vague data type conversion formula is known as input. Here:

a. Vague criteria $0 \leq t_{ij} \leq 1 - f_{ij} \leq 1$;

b. Output guidelines When $c_{xj} > c_{yj} \geq 0$, rather than negative data c_{xj} and c_{yj} single value, respectively, turning into the Vague data $G_x(c_j) = c_{xj} = [t_{xj}, 1 - f_{xj}]$ and $G_y(c_j) = c_{yj} = [t_{yj}, 1 - f_{yj}]$, and satisfies: $t_{xj} \geq t_{yj}, 1 - f_{xj} \geq 1 - f_{yj}$.

c. When $c_{xj} > c_{yj} \geq 0$, rather than negative data c_{xj} and c_{yj} single value, respectively, turning into the Vague data $G_x(c_j) = c_{xj} = [t_{xj}, 1 - f_{xj}]$ and $G_y(c_j) = c_{yj} = [t_{yj}, 1 - f_{yj}]$, and satisfies: $t_{xj} \geq t_{yj}, 1 - f_{xj} \leq 1 - f_{yj}$.

Theorem 1. If the mind $c_{j\max} = \max\{c_{1j}, c_{2j}, \cdots, c_{mj}\}$, $c_{j\min} = \min\{c_{1j}, c_{2j}, \cdots, c_{mj}\}$, $(i = 1, 2, \cdots, m; j = 1, 2, \cdots, n)$, then:

1)
$$G_i(c_j) = c_{ij} = \left[\frac{c_{ij}}{c_{j\max}}, \left(\frac{c_{ij}}{c_{j\max}} \right)^{\frac{1}{3}} \right] \tag{1}$$

$c_{ij} (\geq 0)$ expressed by the single-value data into the formula is the output Vague data type conversion formula.

2)
$$G_i(c_j) = c_{ij} = \left[1 - \left(\frac{c_{ij}}{c_{j\max}} \right)^{\frac{1}{3}}, 1 - \frac{c_{ij}}{c_{j\max}} \right] \tag{2}$$

$c_{ij} (\geq 0)$ expressed by the single-value data into the formula is the output Vague data type conversion formula.

4　Similarity Measure between Vague Values

In order to offer the similarity measure between the Vague values, we should recall the data mining Vague value method in Reference [4] first: Vague value $c = [t_c, 1 - f_c]$ for the definition of $t_c^{(0)} = t_c, f_c^{(0)} = f_c, \pi_c^{(0)} = \pi_c$:

$$t_c^{(m)} = t_c \cdot (1 + \pi_c + \pi_c^2 + \cdots + \pi_c^m),$$
$$f_c^{(m)} = f_c \cdot (1 + \pi_c + \pi_c^2 + \cdots \pi_c^m), \pi_c^{(m)} = \pi_c^{m+1};$$
$$u_c^{(m)} = t_c^{(m)} - f_c^{(m)}, v_c^{(m)} = t_c^{(m)} + f_c^{(m)}, (m = 0,1,2,\cdots).$$

The data mining of Vague value, we can construct a similarity measure between Vague value formula.

The so-called constructing Vague environment is turning the raw data into Vague data. This step is a prerequisite for the application of Vague sets. Reference [3] proposed the single-value data into the data definition Vague, here again we mention the assessment of new wheat varieties applying to single-value data into a formula Vague data.

Definition 2. There are two Vague values $a = [t_a, 1 - f_a]$ and $b = [t_b, 1 - f_b]$ called the similarity measure between Vague value A and Vague value B: $M(a, b)$, if $M(a, b)$ meets the following criteria:

　a. 0-1 criteria $0 \leq M(a, b) \leq 1$;
　b. Symmetric norms $M(a, b) = M(b, a)$;
　c. reflexive criteria $M(a, a) = 1$;
　d. the minimum criteria If when $a = [1,1], b = [0,0]$, or when $a = [0,0], b = [1,1]$, there is $M(a, b) = 0$.

Theorem 2. The following formula is Vague value similarity measures between $a = [t_a, 1 - f_a]$ and $b = [t_b, 1 - f_b]$ $(m = 0,1,2,\cdots)$:

$$M_m(a,b) = \left[1 - \frac{\left|u_a^{(m)} - u_b^{(m)}\right| + \left|v_a^{(m)} - v_b^{(m)}\right|}{2}\right] \cdot \left[1 - \frac{\left|t_a^{(m)} - t_b^{(m)}\right| + \left|f_a^{(m)} - f_b^{(m)}\right|}{2}\right]. \quad (3)$$

Theorem 3. Let the domain of $C = \{c_1, c_2, \cdots, c_n\}$, C on Vague set

$$A = \sum_{i=1}^{n} [t_A(c_i), 1 - f_A(c_i)] / c_i \quad \text{and} \quad B = \sum_{i=1}^{n} [t_B(c_i), 1 - f_B(c_i)] / c_i.$$

They were abbreviated as $A = \sum_{i=1}^{n} [t_{ai}, 1 - f_{ai}] / c_i$ and $B = \sum_{i=1}^{n} [t_{ai}, 1 - f_{ai}] / c_i$.

Vague set, the following formula is the similarity measure between a and b measure $(m = 0,1,2,\cdots)$.

$$M_m(A,B) = \sum_{i=1}^{n} \left[1 - \frac{\left|u_{a_i}^{(m)} - u_{b_i}^{(m)}\right| + \left|v_{a_i}^{(m)} - v_{b_i}^{(m)}\right|}{2}\right] \cdot \left[1 - \frac{\left|t_{a_i}^{(m)} - t_{b_i}^{(m)}\right| + \left|f_{a_i}^{(m)} - f_{b_i}^{(m)}\right|}{2}\right]. \quad (4)$$

Note. Vague sets A and B the similarity measure between the value of $M(A,B)$ is used to indicate the similarity between Vague sets A and B. The higher the value of $M(A,B)$ is, the more similar of Vague sets A and B are; in particular to obtain the maximum value 1 between $M(A,B)$, then A and B,of Vague sets are the most similar. The lower the value of $M(A,B)$, the more dissimilar between Vague sets A and B. In particular to obtain the minimum value 0, then A and B, of Vague sets are the least similar.

Theorem 4. If, in the condition of Theorem 3, and note the weighted number of elements in $\omega_i \in [0,1]$, and satisfying $\sum_{i=1}^{n} \omega_i = 1$, then the following formula is the weighted similarity measure between Vague set Q and P $(m = 0,1,2 , ...)$:

$$WM_m(A,B) = \sum_{i=1}^{n} \omega_i \left[1 - \frac{\left|u_{a_i}^{(m)} - u_{b_i}^{(m)}\right| + \left|v_{a_i}^{(m)} - v_{b_i}^{(m)}\right|}{2}\right] \cdot \left[1 - \frac{\left|t_{a_i}^{(m)} - t_{b_i}^{(m)}\right| + \left|f_{a_i}^{(m)} - f_{b_i}^{(m)}\right|}{2}\right]. \quad (5)$$

5   Vague Program Optimization Methods

The weighted decision-making method of Vague sets in Reference [6] is constructed into integrated decision-making rules, the general steps of its application are:1. Trait evaluation index selection set;2. Extracting to be sorted (or to be preferred) strains programs;3. Establishing the most reasonable set of lines program plan; 4. Vague of the original data to get the strains programs Vague sets;5. Determining the traits evaluation index weights; 6 Calculating the weighted similarity measure between lines to be sorted (or to be preferred) Vague sets and the best lines program;③. the conclusion based on the size of the weighted similarity measure available:

Conclusion 1 the one with greatest value-weighted similarity measure of the program is the best strains; or **conclusion 2** Being sorted in accordance with the size of similar sorting program strains. Vague weighted decision-making method is a pattern recognition method.

6   Case of Its Application

Re-examine the issue under discussion in Reference [1]with Vague weighted decision-making method.

6.1   Screening Trait Evaluation Index Set

Targets set for the judge to determine the characteristics $C = \{c_1, c_2, c_3, c_4, c_5\}$, in which c_1: Brix (%); c_2 height (cm); c_3: stem diameter (cm); c_4: effective number of stems (of / bundle);: c_5 empty heart of Po.

6.2   Extracting the Program to Be Sorted Strains of Sugarcane

Take care of (then called Guangdong Province, now Hainan Province) sugarcane germplasm nursery of Erianthus a1 strains and hybrids a217 a program composed of strains of sugarcane to be sorted.

Among them, the program A_1: strain called YCE01-33; A_2: YCE01-34; A_3: YCE01-35; A_4: YCE01-36; A_5: YCE01-37;A_6: YCE01-38; A_7: YCE01-39; A_8: YCE01-40; A_9: YCE01-41; A_{10}: YCE01-42; A_{11}: YCE01-43;A_{12}: YCE01-44; A_{13}: YCE01-45; A_{14}: YCE01-46; A_{15}: YCE01-47; A_{16}: YCE01-48; A_{17}: YCE01-49.

Table 1. Indicators of economic traits of the model of the original data

program	Indicators of economic traits of the model of the original data				
	c_1	c_2	c_3	c_4	c_5
A_1	19.1	273	2.0	11	1
A_2	19.1	276	2.3	1	2
A_3	23.4	249	2.4	4	1
A_4	18.6	159	1.8	6	2
A_5	18.6	242	2.1	10	1
A_6	16.4	127	2.6	3	1
A_7	21.6	175	1.6	10	3
A_8	19.5	169	2.5	2	1
A_9	13.7	165	2.0	4	1
A_{10}	18.2	174	1.9	2	1

Table 2. Indicators of economic traits of the model data Vague

program	Indicators of economic traits of the model data Vague				
	c_1	c_2	c_3	c_4	c_5
A_1	[0.816,0.934	[0.989,0.996]	[0.989,0.996]	[1.000,1.000]	[0.307,0.667]
A_2	[0.816,0.934]	[1.000,1.000]	[0.885,0.960]	[0.091,0.450]	[0.126,0.333]
...	...	...	...	...	...
A_{17}	[0.808,0.931]	[0.783,0.922]	[0.808,0.931]	[0.636,0.860]	[0.000,0.000]
B	[1.000,1.000]	[1.000,1.000]	[1.000,1.000]	[1.000,1.000]	[0.307,0.667]

6.3   Establishing the Most Ideal Strains of Sugar Cane Program

As in the strains of economic traits in the evaluation index, the Brix, plant height (stem diameter and the effective number to the value stems are much good); and empty heart of the small value of Po for the best, so the strain evaluation index, the best economic traits data can be composed of the best strains of sugar cane program, denoted by B. The strains of sugar cane, cane pattern data and the ideal scenario B strains of the original data are listed in Table 1 (from Reference [1]).

6.4   Vague of the Orginal Data

In the formula (1) and (2), turn the Table 1 into Table 2.Table 2 shows the various strains of sugarcane strains aaab and best mode B, Vague set of data.

6.5   Calculating the Similarity Measure between the Program of the Vague Set to Be Sorted and the Most Ideal Program of Vague Set

Reference [1] gives the index of the weighted factor traits: c_1 (Brix) of 0.30; c_2 (height) of 0.10; c_3 (stem diameter) of 0.15; c_4 (effective number of stems) is 0.30; c_5 (empty Po heart level) is 0.15; and take parameters $m=2$, application of the formula (8). Calculate the strain of sugarcane Vague set to be sorted and the best solution a1 ~ a17 strains of sugar cane similarity measure between scenario B, the results are as follows:

$$WM_2(A_1,B) = 0.899, \quad WM_2(A_2,B) = 0.567, \quad WM_2(A_3,B) = 0.775,$$
$$WM_2(A_4,B) = 0.677, \quad WM_2(A_5,B) = 0.899, \quad WM_2(A_6,B) = 0.619,$$
$$WM_2(A_7,B) = 0.761, \quad WM_2(A_8,B) = 0.645, \quad WM_2(A_9,B) = 0.602,$$
$$WM_2(A_{10},B) = 0.603, \quad WM_2(A_{11},B) = 0.824, \quad WM_2(A_{12},B) = 0.844,$$
$$WM_2(A_{13},B) = 0.511, \quad WM_2(A_{14},B) = 0.878, \quad WM_2(A_{15},B) = 0.547,$$
$$WM_2(A_{16},B) = 0.620, \quad WM_2(A_{17},B) = 0.700.$$

The purpose to calculate the similarity measure is: comparing each program to be sort of sugarcane strains $A_i (i = 1,2,\cdots,17)$ with the best sugar cane program model B, the first value is the first priority lines, the second number is the second priority strain, ..., the minimum value is ranked in the final lines, so according to the above results, the strains of sugar cane obtained to be sorted are as follows:
A1 and A5 tied 1, A4 No. 3, A12 No. 4, A11 No. 5, A3 No. 6, A7 No. 7,...,A15 No. 17.

The conclusion both in this paper and in Reference [1] are basically the same, but the fuzzy comprehensive evaluation method in Reference [1] requires a lot of matrix calculations with a large quantity of the calculation. This method in this paper is simple and replace fuzzy evaluation method.

7   Conclusion

The similarity measure formula between Vague sets discussed in this paper provides more choice of means for fuzzy information processing, but from the application data we can see the two similarity measure conversion formula turning a single value into Vague data sets is the referred method of the two basic options. Vague program for the study of the preferred method also provides a new method to solve the issues related to agriculture, which is an alternative method of fuzzy comprehensive evaluation method.

Acknowledgments. The Hainan Provincial Natural Science Fund Project No.610224;the Hainan Provincial Social development projects for science and technology development fund No.2010SF004 and Sanya City College, 2009 special fund project funding issues (YD09027).

References

1. Liu, S.-M., Fu, C., Huang, Z.-X.: Fuzzy comprehensive evaluation on the clones of Erianthus arundinaceou. Guangdong Agricultural Science (8), 16–18, 21 (2008)
2. Gau, W.-L., Buehrer, D.J.: Vague Sets. IEEE Transactions on Systems, Man and Cybernetics 23(2), 610–614 (1993)
3. Wang, H.-X.: Definition and transforming formulas from the single valued data to the vague valued data. Computer Engineering and Applications 46(24), 42–44 (2010)
4. Liu, H.-W., Wang, F.-Y.: Transformations and Similarity Measures of Vague Sets. Computer Engineering and Applications 40(32), 79–81, 84 (2004)
5. Wang, H.-X.: Similarity measure between vague sets and their application. Computer Engineering and Applications 46(26), 198–199 (2010)
6. Wang, H.-X.: Synthesis decision rule of vague sets and its application in scheme optimum seeking. Computer Engineering and Applications 46(27), 145–147 (2010)

Driver Safe Speed Model Based on BP Neural Network for Rural Curved Roads

Xiaolei Chen[1], Ruijuan Chi[1], Jianqiang Wang[2], Changle Pang[1,*], and Qing Xiao[1]

[1] College of Engineering, China Agricultural University,
Tsinghua East Road No.17, Beijing, 100083
pangcl@cau.edu.cn
[2] State Key Laboratory of Automotive Safety and Energy, Tsinghua University,
Shuangqing Road No.30, Beijing, 100084

Abstract. In order to improve the safety and comfort of the vehicles on rural curved roads, the paper proposed a safe curve speed model based on the BP Neural Network. A series of drivers' manual operation state data during cornering were gathered and observed according to the driver experiments under real traffic conditions. Three factors, referring to the speed calculated based on road trajectory parameters, the adhesion workload and the yaw rate computed from the processed data, were used as inputs of the model to obtain the target vehicle speed. Finally, tests verify the applicability of the modified model. It indicates that the developed speed model can adjust to the individual curve speed behavior of each driver.

Keywords: Rural curved road, driver behavior, adhesion workload, yaw rate, BP Neural Network.

1   Introduction

Curves of the rural roads are those places where the accidents take place more frequently than other parts of the road due to their intricate road condition. Recently in China, statistics on traffic accidents from the Chinese Ministry of Transportation in 2009 showed that 25,146 road accidents occurred on curved road, which is up to 10.56% of the total accidents [1]. Besides, the occurrence of these accidents is increasing. Mistakes during steering is one of the main factors, which fundamentally results from the driver's incorrect recognition or misjudgment of road condition, vehicle performance or surrounding environment, that normally let the driver enter a corner at a high speed [2].

In order to solve the aforementioned problems, many studies have been conducted to calculate the safe speed for cornering and several models have been developed during the last few decades [3-8]. According to [3], a predicting model of the 85th percentile speed was developed by Krammers in 1993, and Polus built four speed models based on numbers of speed data to estimate the operating speed for the two-lane rural roads. Another curve safe speed model which was used in accident

---

* Corresponding author.

D. Li and Y. Chen (Eds.): CCTA 2011, Part III, IFIP AICT 370, pp. 92–102, 2012.

reconstructions was developed in [5].Taking the acceptable lateral acceleration into account, a safe speed was presented by the Spanish Road Administration [7]. It was found in [8] that a differential speed model of the 85th percentile speed and the operating speed had been suggested for the two-lane rural roads according to the experiment data. In general, all the speed models above had determined the safe speed according to the road trajectory, yet considering the driver's individual characteristic. Sometimes it would make the drivers feel uncomfortable when cornering. As a result, the curve safe speed model should take into account of the individual characteristic of each driver.

Meanwhile, some researches had been undertaken focusing on the driver behavior on curved roads in recent years [9-13]. According to [9], the lateral force coefficient is a very important parameter to the safety and comfort of driving. It was indicated in [12] that drivers chose their comfortable speed mainly depending on curvature and driving conditions. Besides, the comfort of driving was bound up with the value of lateral acceleration. However, the common objective of existing researches regarding driver behavior on curved roads is to meet the requirement of geometric design of highways. Therefore existing models may be unsuitable to improve the safety and comfort on curved roads.

In this study, a driver safe speed model on curved roads is developed based on real experimental data gathered from a series of driver behavior experiments. With a view of adapting to driver's individual curve speed behavior, the Neural Network method is used in the driver safe speed model. Tests verify the applicability of the modified model.

2   Driver Behavior Experiments

2.1   Data Acquisition System

As shown in Table 1, three types of data, which could reflect driver behavior and vehicle states, were recorded with the data acquisition system.

Table 1. Data collected based on real traffic experiments

Type	Variables
Vehicle states	Vehicle speed
	Yaw rate
	Lateral acceleration
	Longitudinal acceleration
	Relative speed
Driver operation	Steering wheel angle
	Brake pedal depression
	Gas pedal depression
Road information	GPS coordinates
	Road conditions

The data were collected from CAN bus of the instrumented vehicle and some appendix sensors. Besides, the curvature and the friction coefficient of the road could be estimated in accordance with the GPS data and the vehicle states.

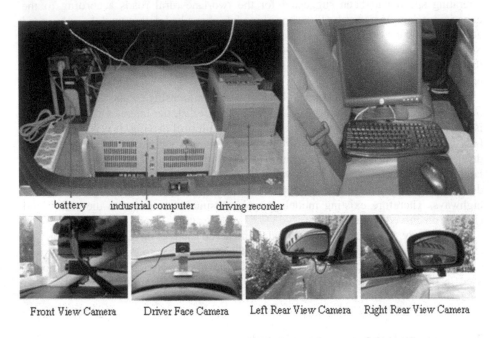

battery   industrial computer   driving recorder

Front View Camera   Driver Face Camera   Left Rear View Camera   Right Rear View Camera

Fig. 1. Data acquisition system

As indicated in Fig. 1, the data acquisition system consists of a battery, an industrial computer, and a driving recorder which were installed in the car boot. A monitor was fixed on the back of the co-pilot seat for the experiment recorder. In addition, four cameras were fixed in the system to record different images in real time. The data collection frequency of this system was 30 Hz.

2.2   Experiment Route and Design

Considering the requirement and purpose of the experiments, the sample route was required to be roads with regular curves. So we chose a section of a highway that started from the south entrance of the Beijing-Tibet highway to Badaling as the experiment area, as shown in Fig. 2.

A sample of 18 participants with full China driving license was enrolled to accomplish the experiments from Beijing. These drivers were acquainted with the road conditions and were required to drive with a safe and comfortable speed in free traffic flow. Data were collected and saved with the data collection system. It should be noted that only part of each experiment data from the curve entry to the curve exit were used for the analysis.

Fig. 2. Experiment route

3 Data Observation

Direct data could not satisfy the requirements of the model due to error and noise. The observation of the original data, such as longitudinal acceleration, lateral acceleration, and yaw rate, was taken place in the next section.

3.1 Kalman Filter of the Original Data

The Kalman Filter is a set of mathematical equations that provides an efficient computational (recursive) means to estimate the state of a process, in a way that minimizes the mean of the squared error [14]. It is widely used in many fields because of its powerful features.

Assume that the original data is x_k, and develop it by the formula of Tailor in time domain. The state equation is shown in Eq.1 taking x_k and x'_k as state variables.

$$X_k = \varphi X_{k-1} + Aw_k \tag{1}$$

Where, $X_k = \begin{bmatrix} x_k, & x'_k \end{bmatrix}^T$, $\varphi = \begin{bmatrix} 1 & \Delta T \\ 0 & 1 \end{bmatrix}$, A$=\begin{bmatrix} \dfrac{\Delta T^2}{2} \\ \Delta T \end{bmatrix}$, $w_k = x''_k$ is the random noise, ΔT is the sampling time, and ΔT =1/30 s.

The measurement equation is shown in Eq.2.

$$z_k = HX_{k-1} + n_k \tag{2}$$

Where, z_k is the measurement value of the data, $H = \begin{bmatrix} 1 & 0 \end{bmatrix}$, and n_k is the measurement noise.

The optimal estimation of the parameters based on Kalman Filter is shown in Eq.3.

$$\hat{X}_k = \hat{X}_k^- + K_k(z_k - H_k\hat{X}_k^-) \tag{3}$$

Where, $\hat{X}_k$ is the optimum estimate of X_k, $\hat{X}_k^-$ is the priori estimate of X_k, K_k is the Kalman gain, and z_k is the measurement vectors.

The recursive process of the system is as follows:

$$\hat{X}_k^- = \varphi\hat{X}_{k-1}^- \tag{4}$$

$$P_k^- = \varphi P_{k-1}\varphi^T + AQ_kA^T \tag{5}$$

$$K_k = P_k^-H_k^T(H_kP_k^-H_k^T + R_k)^{-1} \tag{6}$$

$$P_k = (1 - K_kH_k)P_k^- \tag{7}$$

Where, Q_k is the process noise covariance, R_k is the measurement noise covariance. P_k, P_k^- are the optimum estimate error covariance and the posteriori estimate error covariance, respectively. Their initial values are set to be zero matrixes.

The comparison result of data before and after filtering is shown in Fig. 3 taking longitudinal acceleration as example.

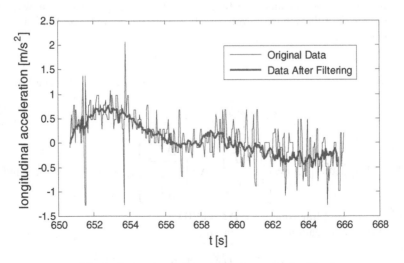

Fig. 3. Comparison of the data before and after filtering

3.2   Error Compensation of the Original Data

In order to reflect the real states of the vehicle, the deviation compensation between the measurement data and the real values caused by installation error, the roll and the pitch of the vehicle is extremely essential.

The influence of the roll and pitch of the vehicle to the parameters is shown in Fig. 4. The approximation of the roll angle can be estimated with the model [15].

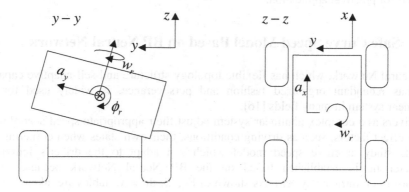

Fig. 4. Influence of the roll and pitch of vehicle to data

As shown in Eq.8, a steady -state moment equation is determined from Fig. 4 based on the static suspension model.

$$(K_{\phi,f} + K_{\phi,r})\phi_r = ma_{ys}h'\cos\phi_r - mgh'\sin\phi_r \qquad (8)$$

Where, $K_{\phi,f}$, $K_{\phi,r}$ are the roll angle rigidity of the suspension, ϕ_r is the roll angle of the vehicle, a_{ys} is the measurement lateral acceleration, and h' is the distance between mass center and roll center.

It can be considered that $\cos\phi_r \approx 1$ and $\sin\phi_r \approx 0$ when the value of the roll angle is small. Eq.8 can be converted to the form as Eq.9.

$$\phi_r = \frac{ma_{ys}h'}{K_{\phi,f} + K_{\phi,r} - mgh'} \qquad (9)$$

The actual values of the parameters can be calculated with Eq.10, Eq.11 and Eq.12.

$$a_y = \frac{a_{ys} + g\sin\phi_r}{\cos\phi_r} \qquad (10)$$

$$w_r = \frac{w_{rs}}{\cos\phi_r} \qquad (11)$$

$$a_x = a_{xs} - l_y w_r'$$ (12)

Where, w_r is the measurement yaw rate, and a_{xs} is the measurement longitudinal acceleration. l_y is the distance between mass center and installation position.

The data which had been compensated are more close to the actual values, and can be used for practical application.

4   Safe Curve Speed Model Based on BP Neural Network

BP Neural Network, which has flexible topology structure and self-adaptive capacity and has redundant organized fashion and perseverance, is widely used for the nonlinear system in many fields [16].

Drivers as a complex nonlinear system adjust their appropriate speed according to many effect factors, such as driving conditions, their own states when cornering etc. In this study, a curve speed model which can adapt to the driver's individual characteristic is established based on the BP Neural Network because of its superiority on intricate system. As shown in Fig. 5, three variables are taken as input data. A two layers feed–forward BP Neural Network is used to simulate the motion state of the vehicle on curved roads. The output data of the model is the target vehicle speed.

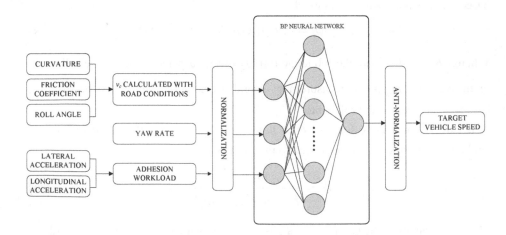

Fig. 5. Driver safe speed model based on BP Neural Network

There are three factors taken as inputs of the BP Neural Network. The first one is the speed calculated considering road trajectory. As shown in Eq.13, three parameters are chosen to describe the curved road conditions.

$$v_c = \sqrt{\frac{g}{c}(\frac{\phi + \mu}{1 - \phi\mu})} \tag{13}$$

Where, v_c is the safe speed on curved road, c is the curvature, ϕ is the road superelevation angle, and μ is the friction coefficient.

The second one is the yaw rate collected from the real road experiments. The last one is the adhesion workload which can reflect the ratio of the friction coefficient used by drivers. It is varied with different characteristics of the drivers, and the calculative method of it is shown in Eq.14.

$$\eta = \sqrt{\frac{a_x^2 + a_y^2}{\mu_{max} g}} \tag{14}$$

Where, η is the adhesion workload, a_x is the longitudinal acceleration, a_y is the lateral acceleration, and μ_{max} is the maximum friction coefficient.

Firstly, calculate the values of the speed, adhesion workload, and the yaw rate based on a fifty seconds length of data chosen from the abovementioned experiments. Then, normalize the input data and the output data into the range 0–1, and take them as the training set to train the networks. After that, set up the parameters of the networks. The number of the hidden layer nodes is set to 60 considering the complexity of the driver's characteristic. The transfer functions of the hidden layer and the output layer are "logsig" and "pureline", respectively. The root mean square error value used for the stopping signal was set to 0.001, and the number of epochs was set to 100. All the iterations realize the target mean square error in less then 7 epochs. The output data could be converted to the target speed based on anti-normalization.

5   Evaluation and Discussion

5.1   Evaluation

The evaluation was carried out based on the data gathered from real road experiments. Firstly, several parameters, such as speed (v_c), adhesion workload, yaw rate etc was calculated or processed according to the actual data of the drivers on curved roads. Secondly, train the Neural Networks with the information above to make it adapt to the driver's characteristic. Finally, when the vehicle driving into the curve, the model began to work and provided a safe and comfortable speed for the driver.

The comparison result of the real speed and the target speed known as the output of the model is shown in Fig. 6.

As shown in the figure, the model can reflect the curve speed behavior of the drivers, and provide a safe and comfortable speed when turning.

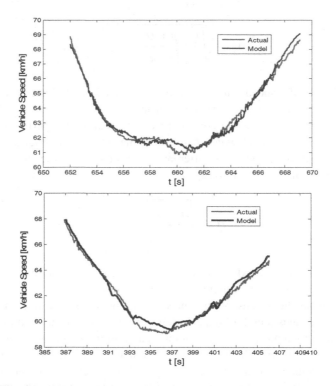

Fig. 6. Validation of driver safe speed model (No.11 and No.12 drivers)

5.2   Discussion

Two factors referring to the road trajectory (e.g. curvature, the road superelevation angle, and the friction coefficient) and the characteristic of driver (e.g. the adhesion workload and the yaw rate) were considered in the curve speed model in this paper. However, there are several parameters that had not been taken into account, including the visibility, the slope angle of the road and the initial velocity etc. Besides, the driver behavior experiments were carried out with no vehicles ahead, the driver's characteristic might change when following other cars. A further study with accordance into these factors will be done in the next reach.

In addition, some of the drivers participated in the experiments didn't obey the rules strictly we had made earlier, which might impact the data validity. Besides, the sample size of the experiments also has influence on the result. It is assumed that the result would be improved by increasing the amount of the experimental data.

6   Conclusion

This paper focused on a driver safe speed model on rural curved roads by considering the driver's curve speed characteristic. From what had been discussed above, the conclusions could be drawn as follows:

(1) The developed safe speed model is proposed on account of the actual driver behavior experimental data, and is able to provide a more suitable speed for drivers when cornering.

(2) The processed parameters taken as the inputs of the model can reflect the real conditions of the rural curved roads and the actual curve speed behavior of the drivers.

(3) The driver safe speed model based on BP Neural Network is adaptive to the individual curve speed characteristic of each driver. It can improve the safety and comfort of the vehicle on curved roads.

Acknowledgements. The research reported herein was supported by the Chinese National Programs for High Technology Research and Development, No. 2011AA110402. The authors would like to thank Dezhao, Zhang (Tsinghua University) for his kind support for the paper preparation.

References

1. Statistical Yearbook on Road Traffic Accidents of China (2008). Ministry of Transportation of China (2009)
2. Lee, Y.H., Deng, W.: Speed Control Method for Vehicle Approaching and Travelling on a Curve. US Paten, No.0150157 (2007)
3. Stamatiadis, N., Gong, H.: Analysis of Inconsistencies Related to Design Speed, Operating Speed and Speed Limits. University of Kentucky College of Engineering (2007)
4. Pomerleau, D., Jochem, T., Thorpe, C.: Run-off-road Collision Avoidance Using IVHS Countermeasures. National Highway Traffic Safety Administration (1999)
5. Sledge, N.H., Marshek, K.M.: Formulas for Estimating Vehicle Critical Speed from Yaw Marks. A Review, SAE (1997)
6. Zhong, X., Ren, F., Rong, J.: The Two-step Model of Operating Speed on Horizontal Curves Based on Driver's Information Collection and Processing. Transportation Engineering, 307–312 (2004)
7. Mopu.: Señalización Vertical. Instrucción Decarreteras. Norma 8.1-IC. Centro de Publicaciones Del Ministerio de Fomento (2000) (in Spanish)
8. Misaghi, P., Hassan, Y., Asce, M.: Modeling Operating Speed and Speed Differential on Two- Lane Rural Roads. Journal of Transportation Engineering, 408–417 (2005)
9. Zheng, K., Rong, J., Ren, F.: Analysis of Relation between Curve's Radius and Steering Speed on Expressway. Journal of Highway and Transportation Research and Development 20(2), 28–30 (2003)
10. Abdelwahab, W.M., Aboul-Ela, M.T., Morrall, J.F.: Geometric Design Consistency Based on Speed Change on Horizontal Curves. Road Transport Res. 127(1), 13–23 (1998)
11. Zhang, K., Jiang, L., Rong, J., Ren, F.: Study on Mental and Physiological Effects of Horizontal Radius of Expressway on Driving Reaction. Journal of Highway and Transportation Research and Development 21(5), 5–7 (2004)
12. Canadian Researchers Test Driver Response to Horizontal Curves. Journal of Road Management and Engineering (1998)
13. McFadden, J., Elefteriadou, L.: Evaluating Horizontal Alignment Design Consistency of Two-lane Rural Highways: Development of New Procedure. Transportation Research Record, 1737, 9–17. Transportation Research Board, Washington, D.C (2000)

14. Welch, G., Bishop, G.: An Introduction to the Kalman Filter. Department of Computer Science University of North Carolina at Chapel Hill (2006)
15. Li, L.: Cooperative Control of Vehicle Stability Based on AFS and DYC, Doctoral Thesis of Tsinghua University (2009)
16. Wei, L., Yumin, S.: Prediction of Energy Production and Energy Consumption Based on BP Neural Networks. In: Proceedings of the IEEE International Symposium, pp. 176–179. IEEE Press (2008)

Solving Motion Law by Numerical Simulation on Bowl Seeding Transplanting Robot

Chunhui Qi, Jianping Hu, Jun Ma, and Jianbing Zhang

Key Laboratory of Modern Agricultural Equipment and Technology,
Ministry of Education & Jiangsu Province, Jiangsu University,
High-tech Key Laboratory of Agricultural Equipment & Intelligentization
of Jiangsu Province, Zhenjiang 212013, China
hujp@ujs.edu.cn

Abstract. The paper using the inverse kinematics theory of the parallel mechanism, studied the movable needs of the transplanting robot,deduced the inverse kinematics formula of transplanting robot. Considered the demand of the "fetch and plant" operations, made an important research on the two trajectory planning methods of the moving platform: quintic and septic polynomial motion laws, acquired their variation rules of displacement, velocity, acceleration and saltus by using matlab software, and to make choice. After selected the law of motion equation, through numerical simulation of inverse kinematics by matlab, acquired kinematic parameters angular speed and acceleration of the two active motors, can be used as the priority basis for control the movement of the manipulator.

Keywords: Parallel mechanism, transplanting bowl seeding, trajectory planning, inverse position, numerical simulation.

1 Preface

Pot seeding technology has many advantages, such as reduce man-hour, raise working efficiency and protect the agricultural ecology environment, and it has been used in production of vegetable and flower widely, transplanting bowl seeding is an important link. Although transplanting bowl seeding is easy, it needs amount of hand labour, the average speed of artificially transplanting is 800—1000 trees per hour, and the workers work continuously will get tired easily, a low production efficiency, and hard to realize large-scale operations. So, to research high-speed automatic bowl seedling transplanting machine is particularly important, it has important significance in improve labor productivity, reduce the labor intensity, promote potted tray seeding technology development. Currently, transplanting machines with the industrial robot as body have many shortcomings, such as many freedoms, complicated structure and so forth, have many difficulties to fit for greenhouse automatic assembly line working facilities, so the type of automatic potted tray seedling transplanting machine fails to get promotion.

The paper will put forward a Two-DOF parallel transplanting robot of independent mechanical and electrical system, as shown in Figure 1, the mechanism consists of a five-bar parallel mechanism, two groups parallelogram chain and a moving platform,

D. Li and Y. Chen (Eds.): CCTA 2011, Part III, IFIP AICT 370, pp. 103–111, 2012.

driven by the active motors, pneuncatic manipulator could achieve two-dimensional translational. Due to the driving motors fixed on the frame, driven arms are made into light bars, so could make the moving platform achieve a high speed and acceleration, to meet bowl seedlings transplanting demand of high speed and short to medium distance.

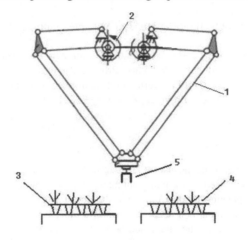

Fig. 1. Schematic diagram of transplanting robot 1. parallel mechanism 2. motor 3. seeding tray 4. plant seeding tray 5. manipulator

2   Select Bowl Seeding Transplanting Robot Motion Law

2.1   Motion Law Requirement of Two-DOF Parallel Transplanting Robot

Two-DOF parallel mechanism used to pick up and placed the object, its main job is pick up object in the initial position, then move to the target position placed the object, kinematic sketch is shown in Figure 2.

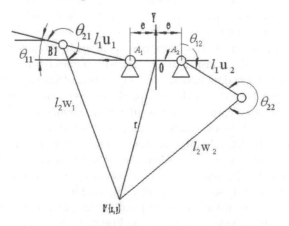

Fig. 2. Kinematic sketch

Working space of the mechanism is 600 * 150 mm, maximum speed of the manipulator is 4.5m/s, the maximum acceleration is 60m/s2. Maximum load weight is 0.3Kg, the average frequency of transplanting reach 100 times/minute.

To make the moving platform under the condition of the maximum acceleration allowed, the fastest way to fetch seedling from a certainl position of the seedling tray, then set the seeding to the corresponding position of the plant seedling tray, must be based on position, velocity and acceleration to plan trajectory.

2.2   Motion Trajectory Planning on Transplanting Manipulator

In the process of transplanting bowl seedings, manipulator required fetch seeding and plant seeding the two motion process for each seeding transplanting. While each process, the manipulator would pass through rising, translation, decline three stages. Transplanting motion requires the manipulator on the rise and decline section must keep a certain distance of straight-line movement, as AB and CD section shown in Figure 3:

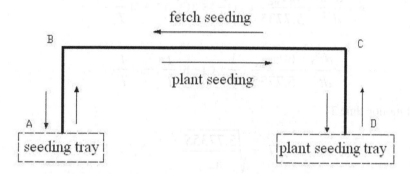

Fig. 3. Manipulator trajectory of transplanting process

For each straight line track, set motion law of the manipulator is cease-speed up- speed down-cease. So to achieve this rule, must meet the following points:

1) Moving platform velocity and acceleration at the start and end of the trajectory is zero;
2) First and second derivatives of displacement motion law must be continuous;
3) The third-order derivative of the displacement motion law f (the derivative of acceleration) is limited; otherwise it will cause shock; to ensure that the manipulator avoid to be impacted.

2.3   Mathematical Representation of the Two Motion Laws

In less than a given maximum acceleration condition, base on the movement theory, there are many motion laws to meet the above requirements, such as sine law, cycloidal law, trapezoidal law, quintic polynomial motion law, septic polynomial motion law and so on. Because quintic and septic polynomial are more likely to achieve above motion requirements accurately, therefor, only conduct analysis on them. They are under the condition of known the displacement S and the maximum acceleration amax , the calculation formula is as follows:

1) Quintic polynomial motion law

　　Displacement equation

$$s = \frac{a_{max}}{5.7735} T^2 \left(10 \left(\frac{t}{T}\right)^3 - 15\left(\frac{t}{T}\right)^4 + 6\left(\frac{t}{T}\right)^5 \right) \tag{1}$$

Derivative of (1), acquire velocity, acceleration and saltus equation

$$v = \frac{ds}{dt} = \frac{30a_{max}}{5.7735} T \left(\left(\frac{t}{T}\right)^2 - 2\left(\frac{t}{T}\right)^3 + \left(\frac{t}{T}\right)^4 \right) \tag{2}$$

$$a = \frac{d^2s}{dt^2} = \frac{60a_{max}}{5.7735} \left(\left(\frac{t}{T}\right) - 3\left(\frac{t}{T}\right)^2 + 2\left(\frac{t}{T}\right)^3 \right) \tag{3}$$

$$j = \frac{d^3s}{dt^3} = \frac{60a_{max}}{5.7735} \frac{1}{T} \left(\frac{t}{T}\right) \left(1 - 6\left(\frac{t}{T}\right) + 6\left(\frac{t}{T}\right)^2 \right) \tag{4}$$

Total motion time T

$$T = \sqrt{\frac{5.7735S}{a_{max}}} \tag{5}$$

2) Septic polynomial motion law

　　Displacement equation

$$s = \frac{a_{max}}{7.51} T^2 \left(35\left(\frac{t}{T}\right)^4 - 84\left(\frac{t}{T}\right)^5 + 70\left(\frac{t}{T}\right)^6 - 20\left(\frac{t}{T}\right)^7 \right) \tag{6}$$

Derivative of （6）, acquire velocity, acceleration and saltus equation

$$v = \frac{ds}{dt} = \frac{140a_{max}}{7.51} T \left(\left(\frac{t}{T}\right)^3 - 3\left(\frac{t}{T}\right)^4 + 3\left(\frac{t}{T}\right)^5 - \left(\frac{t}{T}\right)^6 \right) \tag{7}$$

$$a = \frac{d^2s}{dt^2} = \frac{420a_{max}}{7.51} \left(\left(\frac{t}{T}\right)^2 - 4\left(\frac{t}{T}\right)^3 + 5\left(\frac{t}{T}\right)^4 - 2\left(\frac{t}{T}\right)^5 \right) \tag{8}$$

$$j = \frac{d^3s}{dt^3} = \frac{840a_{max}}{7.51}\,(\frac{1}{T})\,(\ (\frac{t}{T})-6(\frac{t}{T})^2+10(\frac{t}{T})^3-5(\frac{t}{T})^4\ ) \qquad (9)$$

Total motion time T

$$T = \sqrt{\frac{7.51S}{a_{max}}} \qquad (10)$$

2.4 Simulation Analysis of the Two Motion Laws

Applied Mathematics software matlab, obtain the following motion law of Figure 4 to Figure 7.

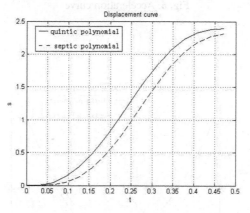

Fig. 4. Displacement curve

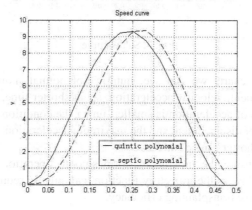

Fig. 5. Speed curve

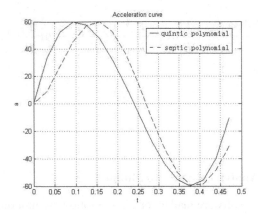

Fig. 6. Acceleration curve

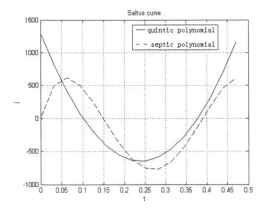

Fig. 7. Saltus curve

From the above charts we can see, quintic polynomial motion law arrive the maximum displacement, velocity, acceleration, spent shorter time, more stable saltus, indicating the saltus of acceleration is smaller; under the condition of the motion laws have the same size of displacement and the maximum acceleration, quintic polynomial motion law uses a shorter time of 0.07s.

In the case of ensure the moving platform smooth operation, select the quintic polynomial motion law as the trajectory function, can greatly reduce the time used in transplanting, improve transplanting efficiency.

3   Solving the Active Motor Motion Laws of the High-Speed Parallel Transplanting Robot

3.1   Position Inverse Model

Refer to Figure 2, in fixed reference coordinate system O-xy, establish equation:

$$r\text{-}sgn(i)ee_1\text{-}l_1u_i=l_2w_i \tag{11}$$

and, $u_i=(\ \cos\theta_{1i}\ \ \sin\theta_{1i})^T$, $w_i=(\ \cos\theta_{2i}\ \ \sin\theta_{2i})^T$,

$$e_1=(\ 1\ \ 0\ )^T\ , sgn(i)=\begin{cases}1 & i=1 \\ -1 & i=2\end{cases}$$

so: $A_i\sin\theta_{1i}+B_i\cos\theta_{1i}+C_i=0$

$$\theta_{1i}=2\arctan\frac{-A_i+sgn(i)\sqrt{A_i^{\,2}-C_i^{\,2}+B_i^{\,2}}}{C_i-B_i} \tag{12}$$

among that, $A_i=-2l_1y$

$B_i=-2l_1(x\text{-}sgn(i)e)$

$$C_i=x^2+y^2+e^2+l_1^{\,2}-l_2^{\,2}-2sgn(i)ex$$

3.2   Velocity, Acceleration Model

First and second order derivation of time for formula（11）, can get system speed and acceleration model:

$$\dot{\theta}_1=\frac{1}{l_1}Jv \tag{13}$$

$$Ja=l_1\ddot{\theta}_1-l_1f(\dot{\theta}_1) \tag{14}$$

In the formula, v and a are speed and acceleration of O, speed Jacobian matrix i:

$$J=\frac{1}{l_1}\begin{bmatrix} w_1 & w_2 \\ w^T_{\ 1}Qu_1 & w^T_{\ 2}Qu_2 \end{bmatrix}^T \tag{15}$$

$$Q = \begin{bmatrix} 0 & -1 \\ 1 & 0 \end{bmatrix}^{T} \tag{16}$$

3.3   Numerical Simulation Curve of the Two Active Motors

Set the manipulator horizontal moving distance 600mm, vertical moving distance 150mm, in the condition of a given mechanism parameter, inverse simulation by software matlab, acquire the following curves of the active motors:

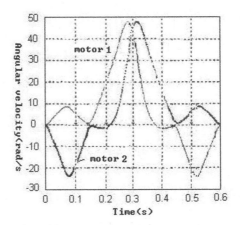

Fig. 8. Angular velocity curve

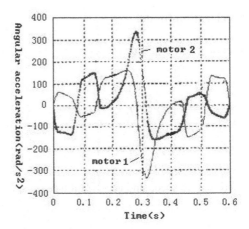

Fig. 9. Angle acceleration curve

Obtain the motors numerical parameters from above figures, provided theoretical basis for control the manipulator and optimal design the physical prototype.

4   Conclusion

1) Using the inverse kinematics theory of the parallel mechanism, studied the movable needs of the transplanting robot, deduced the inverse kinematics formula of transplanting robot.
2) Motion trajectory of transplanting robot was planned, conducted numerical analysis for quintic and septic polynomial by matlab software, selected the better motion polynomial.
3) Apply quintic polynomial motion law, under a certain condition of motor motion law, the operating cycle to be shorter, meet the requirement of high-speed robot for transplanting, can reduce the transplanting time of 0.07s, improve the transplanting efficiency.

Acknowledgements. This work was financially supported by Three Engineering of Agricultural Machinery, Jiangsu province(NJ2009-41), by Qing Lan Project of Jiangsu Province (Su teacher (2010)no.27) and the Priority Academic Program Development of Jiangsu Higher Education Institutions (Su financial teacher(2011)no.8).

References

1. Choi, W.C., Kim, D.C., Ryu, I.H., et al.: Development of a seeding pick-up device for vegetable transplanters. Transactions of the ASAE 45(1), 13–19 (2002)
2. Kutz, L., Miles, G.E.: Robotic transplanting of bedding plants. Transactions of the ASAE 30(3), 586–590 (1987)
3. Huang, T., Li, Z.X., Li, M., et al.: Conceptual design and dimensional synthesis of a novel 2-DOF translational parallel robot for pick-and-place operations. ASME Journal of Mechanical Design 126(5), 449–455 (2004)
4. Borubakis, N., Kydonas, G.: An Autonomous Hybrid Robot:Walking and Climbing. IEEE Robotics and Automation Magazine 11(6), 52–59 (1998)
5. Hiller, M., Fang, S.Q., Mielczarek, S.: Design Analysis and Realization of Parallel Tendon-based Manipulators. Mechanism and Machine Theory 40(4), 429–455 (2005)
6. Ryu, K.H., Kim, G., Han, J.S.: Development of a robotic transplanter for bedding plants. Journal of Agricultural Engineering Research 78(2), 141–146 (2001)
7. Guo, Z., Li, L., Sun, S.: Trajectory Planning and Simulation on 3-RPC Parallel Mechanism. The Chinese Mechanical Engineering 18(5), 1036–1038 (2007)
8. Ting, K.C.: Automate flexibly with robots. Greenhouse Grower 5(11), 24–28 (1987)
9. Youcef, T.K., Kuo, A.T.Y.: High-speed trajectory control of a direct-drive manipulator. IEEE Transactions on Robotics and Automation 2(1), 102–108 (1993)
10. Arai, T., Funabashi, H., Nakamura, Y., Takeda, Y., Koseki, Y.: High speed and high precision parallelmechanism. In: Proceedings of the 1997 IEEE/RSJ International Conference on Intelligent Robots and Systems, vol. 3(7-11), pp. 1624–1629 (1997)
11. Ji, Z.M.: Dynamics decomposition for Stewart platforms. J. of Mechanical Design 116, 67–69 (1994)
12. Lee, K.M., Shan, D.K.: Dynamic analysis of a Three-Degrees-Freedom In-Parallel actuated manipulator. IEEE Transactions On Robotics and Automation 4(3), 361–367 (1988)

Development of an Automatic Control System for Pot-Grown Rice Inspection Based on Programmable Logic Controller

Wanneng Yang[1,2], Chenglong Huang[1,2], and Qian Liu[1,2,*]

[1] Britton Chance Center for Biomedical Photonics, Wuhan National Laboratory for Optoelectronics-Huazhong University of Science and Technology, 1037 Luoyu Rd., Wuhan 430074, P.R. China
[2] Key Laboratory of Biomedical Photonics of Ministry of Education, College of Life Science and Technology, Huazhong University of Science and Technology, 1037 Luoyu Rd., Wuhan 430074, P.R. China
ywnhust@163.com

Abstract. Rice improvement breeding is one of the most important research fields in China. With the development of modern rice breeding technology, hundreds to thousands of new varieties are produced daily, creating the impetus for rapid plant phenotyping evaluation. However, traditional measurement is inefficiency, contact-interferential, and lack-objectivity. Thus a high-throughput and automatic extraction system for rice plant is imperative. In this article we developed a rice phenotyping automatic extraction system and designed the automatic control for the system based on programmable logic controller (PLC). Subsequently, the prototype was test under industrial conditions continuous 24 h workdays and the error probability was less than 0.01%. In sum, base on PLC, we provide an efficient and stable automatic control system for pot-grown rice phenotyping inspection.

Keywords: Rice breeding, phenotyping inspection, automatic control system, programmable logic controller, phenomics.

1 Introduction

Rice is the supreme production and consumption food in China, and thus rice improvement breeding is one of the most important research fields in China [1]. During every breeding stage, plenty of phenotyping parameters, such as plant height, green leaf area, tiller numbers, and leaf temperature et al., must be extracted and evaluated prior to next breeding stage. With the development of modern rice breeding technology, hundreds to thousands of new varieties are produced daily, creating the impetus for high-throughput phenotyping evaluation [2].

However, the conventional measurement, including counting and recording, is still manual, which is inefficiency, contact-interferential, lack-objectivity and

___

* Corresponding author.

D. Li and Y. Chen (Eds.): CCTA 2011, Part III, IFIP AICT 370, pp. 112–118, 2012.

lack-repeatability. The prevalent commercial instruments, such as seed counter and leaf area meter, are inefficiency and single function. The Plant Accelerator (University of Adelaide, Australia), is designed for plant phenotyping with the throughput of 2400 plants per day. With the facility, the plant mass, tissue water content, leaf temperature, photosynthetic machinery, and protein content et al., are extracted equipped with color image, near IR imaging, far IR imaging, fluorescence imaging, and hyperspectral imaging technology, respectively [3]. However, each imaging instrument is designed and fixed with one chamber, and thus five imaging chambers are necessary, which would lead unwanted time-consumption and unstable factors due to the interacting of each imaging chamber. What is more, the spatial and money cost would be incremental and unaccepted in some developing countries [4].

Programmable Logic Controller (PLC) is widely used in agriculture automatic control, such as efficient management of greenhouse [5], temperature-humidity control [6], and so on. Previously, we designed a novel facility to count tillers equipped with X-ray CT, termed the high-throughput system for measuring automatically rice tillers (H-SMART) [7]. In order to incorporation with color imaging technology and far IR imaging technology, we developed a rice phenotyping automatic extraction system and this article focus on the design for the system automatic control based on programmable logic controller (PLC), which provides higher efficiency, higher spatial utilization, and lower cost.

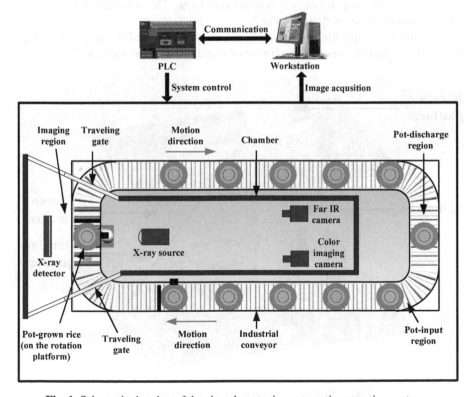

Fig. 1. Schematic drawing of the rice phenotyping automatic extraction system

2   System Description

The schematic drawing (top view) of the rice phenotyping automatic extraction system is shown in Fig.1. In order to describe the imaging device of the system more clearly, the top of the chamber is treated transparently. The system consists of four units: imaging unit, industrial conveyor, chamber, and control unit.

2.1   Imaging Unit and Industrial Conveyor

To acquire the different phenotyping parameters of the rice plant, three imaging devices, including color imaging camera, far IR camera, and X-ray system, are fixed into the imaging module. When the pot-grown rice plant (each pot with one pallet) is fed in the pot-input region, the pot is transported to the imaging region automatically.

In order to acquire image with different angles while the imaging devices remain stationary, a rotation platform is designed on the centre of the imaging region. The pot-grown rice plant is transported onto the rotation platform driven by the servo motor (MBDDT2210, Panasonic Corporation, Japan). What is more, before rotation, to jack the pot from the pallet, a jacking device, including jacking motor and ball screw, is designed and fixed under the rotation platform. Both the rotation platform and jacking device are driven via synchronous belts. The structure diagram of the jacking-rotation device is shown in Fig.2.

After imaging acquisition, the examined rice is transported to the pot-discharged region. The motion direction of the conveyor is indicated as the arrow in Fig.1.

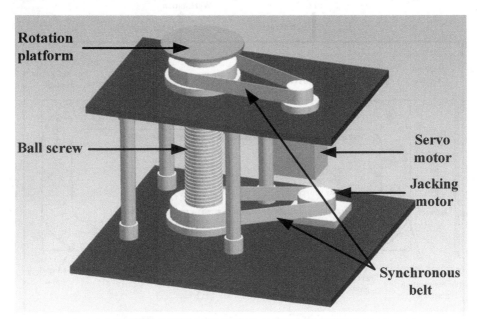

Fig. 2. Structure diagram of the jacking-rotation device

2.2   Chamber and Control Unit

For ensure the safety of the work area, a lead chamber is constructed for x-ray radiation shielding. And to avoid the interference of the external light, two traveling gates, which are open except the pot arrives at the rotation platform, are designed in the chamber. The whole system is controlled with PLC (CP1H-Y20DT-D, Omron Corporation, Japan) and computer workstation (HP xw6400, Hewlett-Packard Development Company, USA).

3   System Control

As mentioned above, the automatic control core of the system are programmable logic controller (PLC) and computer workstation, which control the conveyer unit, imaging unit, and traveling gates.

3.1   Workstation Communication

The system allows the user control the system via a friendly interface, provided in computer workstation. Once receiving the protocol "ON", transmitted by the workstation, PLC controls the system starts. Then the computer sends the instruction "R?" (every 2 seconds) and judges whether the pot arrives in the imaging region via the instruction returned by PLC. Once receiving the protocol "OF", representing the measurement task is finished, PLC controls the system stops. Additionally, the rotation angles and rotation speed could be predefined by the value sent by the workstation. The communication instructions are transmitted via the serial port (RS-232), and the communication protocol between workstation and PLC is illustrated in Table.1.

Table 1. Communication protocol between workstation and PLC

Instruction		Message
Workstation	PLC	
ON	-	System starts
	Y	New pot with rice plant arrives in imaging region
R?	P	New pot without rice plant arrives in imaging region
	N	No pot arrives in imaging region
S+	-	The rotation platform rotates with a predetermined angle
PU**	-	The predetermined value (**) of rotation angle
SP**	-	The predetermined value (**) of rotation speed
OF	-	System stops

3.2   PLC Control

Besides indirectly controlled by workstation, the system control is mainly designed and accomplished with PLC. As described in Fig. 3, photoswitch 1 and baffle 1 are used to block the path of next pot while the previous pot has arrived in imaging region. And the photoswitch 3 and baffle 2 are fixed to keep the awaiting-inspection pot in the centre of the rotation platform. The photoswitch 2 is used for detecting whether here is one pot in the coming pallet.

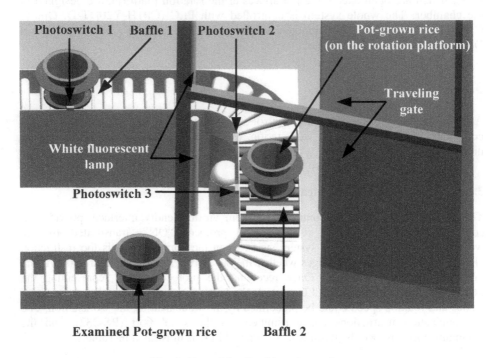

Fig. 3. Control details of imaging region

In order to avoid the interference of the external light, two traveling gates are closed when the awaiting-inspection pot has arrived in the imaging region. It is noticed that when the rice is jacked up for far IR imaging, the lamps must be turned off to eliminate the interference of the white fluorescent lights. After IR image acquisition, the lamps should be turn on for color imaging. The control flow chart based on PLC is shown in Fig. 4.

4   Results and Discussions

To evaluate the efficiency and stabilization of the system, 12 pot-grown rice plants were fed and test in the system continuous 24 hours workday. Without manual intervention, these pots were measured successively and cyclically. After 3 days continuous test, there was no error and approximate 12965 pot-data were inspected and stored in the system. Thus, with the error probability less than 0.01%, the facility has the throughput of 4320 pots per continuous 24 hours workday. What is

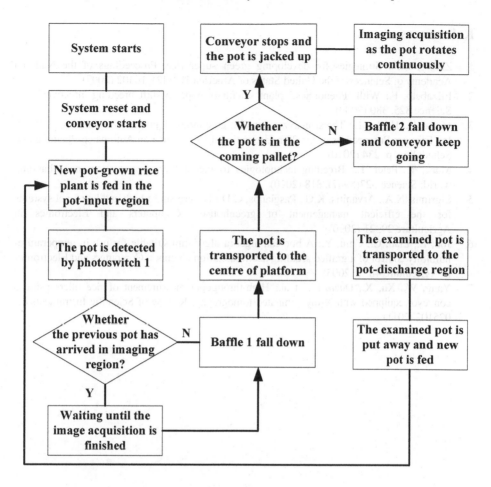

Fig. 4. Control flow chart based on PLC

more, merging the three imaging technologies in one chamber, the system is designed with high spatial utilization. Correspondingly, the cost is lower with this compact design.

5   Conclusion

In this article, we demonstrate a rice phenotyping automatic extraction system and design the system automatic control based on programmable logic controller (PLC). Under the condition of industrial test, the facility provides high efficiency and high stability. Additionally, more modern imaging technologies, such as near IR imaging and hyperspectral imaging, could be incorporated into the system. In sum, base on PLC, we provide an efficient and stable automatic control system for pot-grown rice phenotyping inspection.

References

1. Zhang, Q.F.: Strategies for developing green super rice. Proceedings of the National Academy of Sciences of the United States of America 104(42), 16402 (2007)
2. Elizabeth, F.: With 'Phenomics,' plant scientists hope to shift breeding into overdrive. Science 325, 380 (2009)
3. Malte, H., Hauke, L.: The scanalyzer domain: greenhouse logistics as a planning problem. In: Toronto: Proceedings of the 20th International Conference on Automated Planning and Scheduling, p. 234 (2010)
4. Mark, T., Peter, L.: Breeding technologies to increase crop production in a changing world. Science 327(5967), 818 (2010)
5. Sigrimis, N.A., Arvanitis, K.G., Pasgianos, G.D.: Synergism of high and low level systems for the efficient management of greenhouses. Computers and Electronics in Agriculture 29, 21 (2000)
6. Jou, L., Liao, C., Chiu, Y.: A boolean algebra algorithm suitable for use in temperature-humidity control of a grafted seedling acclimatization chamber. Computers and Electronics in Agriculture 48, 1 (2005)
7. Yang, W., Xu, X., Duan, L., et al.: High-throughput measurement of rice tillers using a conveyor equipped with X-ray computed tomography. Review of Scientific Instruments 82, 025102 (2011)

Bee Products Quality Control
and Emergency Management Mechanism
Research Based on Multi-Agent

E. Yue[1], Yongsheng Cao[2], and Yeping Zhu[1]

[1] Research Institute of Agriculture Information,
Chinese Academy of Agricultural Science,
Key Laboratory of Digital Agricultural Early Warning Technology
of Ministry of Agricultural, Beijing, China, 10008
eyue@mail.caas.net.cn
[2] Institute of Crop Science, Chinese Academy of Agricultural Science,
Beijing, China, 10008

Abstract. Based on the characteristics about distribution, intelligent, and coordination of Multi-Agent system, In this article, Agent theory and technology is applied to bee products quality control and emergency management system of information interaction and coordination, we constructed the bee products quality control and emergency management system of the frame structure, and put forward bee products quality control and emergency management system of the blackboard communication mechanism, and used the blackboard structure on the bee products quality control and emergency decision mechanism for research.

Keywords: Multi-Agent, Bee products, quality control, emergency management, communication mechanism, distributed blackboard structure, Maize, Purity identification, Density, Color, Core area.

1   Introduction

Bee products quality control and emergency management can to provide timely, quick, efficient, high quality emergency services for our country bee products quality control department when there are many quality problems, or natural disaster situation. To the question about Bee products quality problem, all kinds of emergencies independence and the correlation, need many departments and units of collaborative and cooperate in emergency decision and rescue that process. Bee products quality control and emergency management system must know accident of real-time information, and more effective interaction for rapid comprehensive decision-making system.

However, China's bees industry in the information, intelligence bee products quality control and emergency management has just starting, emergency response and transfer mode the lack of effective information release mechanism, use of not enough real-time information and feedback information, Department of the different response system, information platform and software platform lead to share data, response and scheduling model is not the same. All of these lead to the emergency rescue operation can't efficient conduct. With the rapid development of information technology,

D. Li and Y. Chen (Eds.): CCTA 2011, Part III, IFIP AICT 370, pp. 119–128, 2012.
© IFIP International Federation for Information Processing 2012

network has entered into the public's daily life and work, therefore, we can use of the distributed technology based on the network to construct distributed emergency response system, MAS because its have distribution, expansibility, parallelism, flexibility, intelligence and so on, the more suitable for bee products quality control and emergency management system construction.

MAS (Multi-Agent System) is a system concept on the basis of the Distributed Artificial Intelligence (Distributed Artificial Intelligence, DAI)[1]. Each Agent has the ability about independently solving problems or independently finished function, each Agent through information interaction, negotiated, coordinate complete complex task, Agent can be parallel to transmission and control information. However, in distributed open environment, each Agent is often heterogeneous, dynamic and unpredictable, it has the distribution and the internal correlation, how to through the communication mechanism to realize more effective interaction is a key issue. we must through the interaction between the Agent to realize resource sharing, the coordination of the conflict in order to achieve overall goal.

In this article, based on the characteristics about distribution, intelligent, and coordination of Multi-Agent system, Agent theory and technology is applied to bee products quality control and emergency management system of information interaction and coordination, we constructed the bee products quality control and emergency management system of the frame structure, and put forward bee products quality control and emergency management system of the blackboard communication mechanism, and used the blackboard structure on the bee products quality control and emergency decision mechanism for research. For bee products quality control and emergency management to provide an effective research ideas and methods.

2   Multi-Agent Communication Mechanism

The communication mechanism is Agent that in what ways does realize communication. Many of the Agent communication mechanism not only to realize the bottom of communication between the computer, but also to run in different network platform for communications connection, Agent in the environment of networks which position can be effective play its function and other collaborative interaction Agent. The communication mechanism design and choose plays an important role in between maintaining cooperation, to solve the conflict and to realize information exchange between agent, it will directly affect the overall efficiency of the system, robustness and expansibility.

At present, many of the main communication Agent system has there kinds: blackboard, federation, peer-to-peer [2,3,4].

2.1   The Blackboard

The blackboard is actually a shared knowledge structure, it for each Agent provides a share data area, used in between Agent of information and data exchange and sharing. Each Agent can write directly to the blackboard information, also can from the blackboard read other Agent of information. Allow many Agent through to the blackboard content directly to read and write to distribute and get news [5], it could achieve a send perform multiple tasks of communication. In the central control system, the blackboard way can share data structure and realizing efficient communication. The blackboard has advantages during the central control and high efficient, yet for complexity, interaction, and safety requirements high task, a blackboard way has some limitations.

2.2   Federation

All members of agent constitute different groups on the basis of federation, each Agent group set a Agent medium, Each Agent only communication with in the group media Agent, media Agent according to the request of the Agent, the news sent to the agent in group. This method greatly reduces the direct communication link between Agent, but if the number of Agent less, frequent communication between Agent, through the media Agent communication efficiency but is not high.

2.3   Peer-to-Peer

A peer-to-peer using TCP/IP protocol, establish the communication is the direct physical connection link. The packet to ensure the safe arrival, for TCP/IP protocol can realize the end-to-end confirmation. At present, most of the Agent platform established using direct communication mode. Using a peer-to-peer realize the physical connection between Agent for the sender Agent must know the receiving Agent physical location in the system.

3   Bee Products Quality Control and Emergency Management Communication Mechanism Based on the Agent

The core of Bee products quality control and emergency management is integration information resources and emergency management resources about our country different management and testing department, to achieve the emergency coordination effect between different departments, On the whole, enhance the system of the emergency response and decision making. Multi-Agent system has many good properties, it more suitable for the construction of bee products quality control and emergency management system. This section we will be structure bee products quality control and emergency management frame structure based on Agent, and use the Agent communication coordination technology research bee products quality control and emergency management system of communication mechanism.

3.1   Bee Products Quality Control and Emergency Management System Structure Based on Agent

Bee products quality control and emergency management system based on Agent, each Agent is real-time and autonomy basic modules, each Agent mutual cooperation and coordination, and compose a real-time function entity.

In the bee products quality control and emergency management system, Bee products quality control and emergency management organizations included ministry of agriculture, the national testing center, weather and environmental protection department and so on. They assume the bee products quality control and emergency management tasks. Every department is independent agent, and each main department Agent included many other auxiliary function agent, such as implementation agent and monitoring agent and so on. In the bee products quality control and emergency management organization, in order to better coordinate emergency management, optimize emergency management resources, to achieve the effective emergency decision knowledge together, we set up an emergency management center agent, the emergency management center agent include Central agent and Local agent, Every province is a Local agent, these agents jointly responsible for bee products quality control and emergency management in the system.

In figure 1 description of the typical distributed bee products quality control and emergency management structure based on Multi-Agent. Central management Agent in the global scheduling and decision-making position, then, according to China's bees products feature, The local   agent of the province mainly complete emergency management functions (such as: daily management, emergency command).   When need resources sharing and information collaboration between province, each of local Agent through communication network and information platform for exchange information. Central Agent plays a comprehensive coordination and decision-making role, integration and coordination each local Agent task.

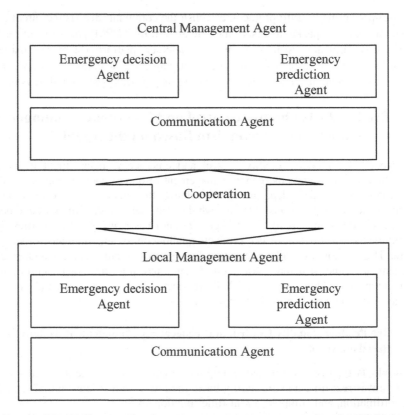

Fig. 1. Bee products quality control and emergency management structure based on Multi-Agent

3.2   Emergency Management Communication Mechanism Based on Agent

Different local Agent distribution in different environment, Heterogeneous platforms and information produced some obstacles to information of interaction and coordinate. In order to promote the cooperation between local Agent, to realize the integration of heterogeneous knowledge, in this paper, we use distributed blackboard structure to describe emergency management of communication coordination mechanism. Distributed blackboard structure can provide concurrency control, interactive, real-time control etc.

Among them, each Agent are adopted the blackboard to transfer information form the communication interface between Agent, enhance the efficiency about cooperation and communication between Agent. Every function agent has a blackboard, the blackboard is communication and information storage area, and is an information communication interface channel with other agent. At the same time, central agent and local agent have emergency blackboard, accept and response to each function agent of information, and send coordination and decision-making information to function agent.

In the process, there is two tasks collaborative request response mechanism.

3.2.1   Cooperative Mechanism between Regional

When department Agent can't alone finish emergency task, it through the blackboard structure to the local Agent sends a work request, if the local Agent think the request need other agent collaborative, the local agent release information on the blackboard, At the same time, the local agent analysis the task, send out task collaborative request to corresponding function agent, corresponding function agent received collaborative request, according to oneself circumstance to provide the service. Communication Agent is a control unit, to a certain extent, to realize department Agent communication request, equivalent to router, as shown in figure 2 shows.

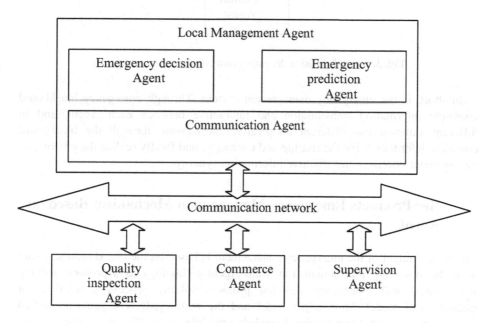

Fig. 2. Cooperative mechanism between regional

3.2.2   Overall Situation Decomposition Collaborative Mechanism

Central Agent establish an emergency task decomposition and task execution situation evaluation, first, overall emergency task decomposition, and assigned to each local agent, and then, appraise task execute condition, to more control effectively scheduling. The difference between overall situation decomposition collaborative mechanism and cooperative mechanism between regional, Central Agent monitoring the emergency blackboard information, if find local Agent is not able to accomplish task, must trans-regional information coordination, at this time, central agent control all emergency task, and then task decomposition, release the task decomposition to the local Agent, this is a cross-regional emergency "big synergy". Due to cooperative mechanism between regional, First, local agent accept department agent collaborative request, then build synergy between department Agent, and execute emergency task, as shown in figure 3.

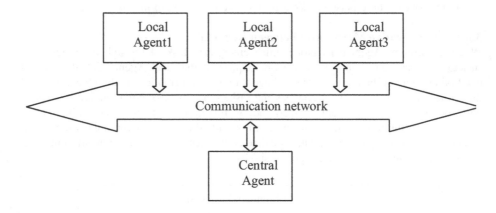

Fig. 3. Overall situation decomposition collaborative mechanism

In short, in the emergency management system, Through emergency blackboard complete information transmission and interactive between each Agent, and in different situation use different cooperative mechanism, through the blackboard complete information for the sharing and exchange, and finally realize the emergency management system of the effective information synergy.

4   Bee Products Emergency Management Mechanism Based on Agent

The basic thought of the emergency management is based on the blackboard structure as problem solving mechanism, the Multi-Agent technology as a problem solving way. Agent will emergency decision problem solving process simulation for mathematical model, knowledge model and the man's judgment package unified format, and form problem solving knowledge module, in intelligent solving process, their external behavior is consistent, behavior act on their own and environment, and can respond to the environment, through operation the blackboard, and cooperating problem solving.

Emergency decision simulation intelligent blackboard model consists of three parts: the Emergency blackboard, the Emergency decision Agent, Emergency prediction Agent, shown in figure 4.

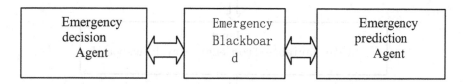

Fig. 4. Emergency decision simulation intelligent blackboard model

4.1 Emergency Blackboard

Emergency blackboard is a global database, it store the original data, problem solving solutions. In Emergency decision, Emergency decision information defined as a group of variables, according to the variable physical meaning divided into two categories: state variables, events variables.

(1)State variables: included production data, processing data, testing data, geography data, climate data, and so on. The variable is a function of time, the value with the advancement of crisis changes, it Can be a (0, 1) between the quantitative value digital.

Events variables: Defined as all events in the process of the crisis happened; the variable is a function of time, the value with the advancement of crisis changes, it Can be a (0, 1) between the quantitative value digital.

The emergency information of emergency simulation through state variables to reflect.

The emergency participants perceive the current crisis through emergency state variables, and decision making based on state variables. Decision making behavior of participants to display a series of events, the occurrence of events led to the change of state variables, and promote the development of the crisis. Otherwise, even if no decision action, the state variables will still be the advancement of change over time. So decision action and time is direct reason to promote action and situation change. The situation is interaction between variables, the mutual influence, part of the trend of the change will cause other variable situation of a series of variable chain reaction.

4.2 Emergency Decision Agent

Emergency decision Agent mainly complete crisis situations of the situation analysis, risk assessment, strength analysis, scheme generation, scheme evaluation and so on. the operation modes is when the state variables change up to a certain value, and the value(between 0-1) match crisis decision Agent executive premise, the Agent will be motivated to perform some action. For each one of the Emergency decision work, Emergency decision to realize the function of the Agent essence of a crisis situation analysis, decision making, evaluation model.

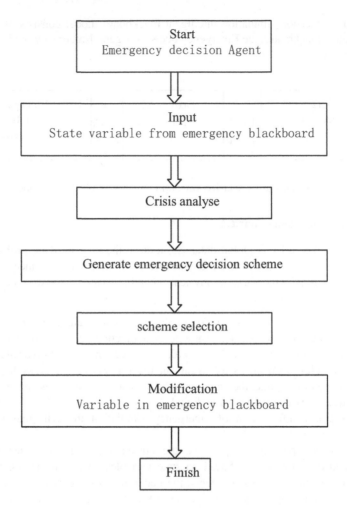

Fig. 5. Emergency decision Agent activity diagram

4.3   Emergency Prediction Agent

Emergency prediction Agent main complete crisis analysis of results, crisis situation variables revision and so on, the operation modes is when the situation variables change up to a certain value, and the value(between 0-1) match crisis decision Agent executive premise, the Agent will be motivated to perform some action. For each one of the Emergency decision work, Emergency prediction to realize the function of the Agent essence of Crisis result analysis, variable modification, to understand that a self-learning model.

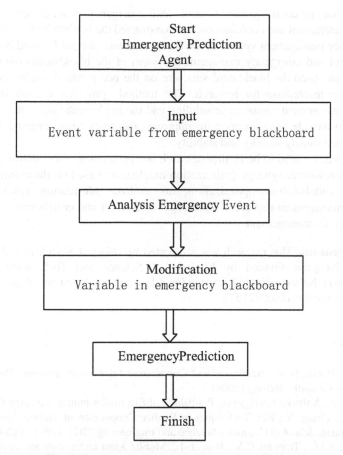

Fig. 6. Emergency prediction Agent activity diagram

Through the argument that, each Agent by conditions and action of two parts, the condition is the use of Agent premise, is a set of information about the blackboard changes of judgement, action description of the operation about the Agent usually process. They are the whole emergency decision core part, they can understand crisis in time of the current state changes, can to the change of state to make timely response ability, to have Reasoning and prediction capability through the reasoning mechanism based on the knowledge and experience, to can response crisis situation change and independent judgment in no manual intervention case.

5   Conclusion

With the fast development of the economy, bee products quality security is increasingly prominent, bee products related administrative departments for emergency management needs become very urgent. Considering the emergency management system of the distributed and autonomy characteristics, in this paper, Agent theory and technology is applied to bee products quality control and emergency management system of information interaction and coordination, we constructed the bee products quality control and emergency management system of the frame structure, we put forward bee products quality control and emergency management system of the blackboard communication mechanism, and used the blackboard structure on the bee products quality control and crisis decision mechanism for research. The method   provides a good strategy for emergency management resources scheduling and the implementation of the emergency measures,   to provide strong support, to improve emergency management level, ensure the bee products quality security and stability.

In the future, we need to be further research bee products quality control and urgent management resources synergy optimization mechanism based on the communication mechanism collaborative optimization, to realize information resources and emergency management resources of emergency interact and collaborative allocation in the emergency management.

Ackonwledgements. This research was supported by National Scientific and Technical Supporting Programs Funded by Ministry of Science and Technology of China (nyhyzx07-041). National Natural Science Foundation about Agent-based quality control of agricultural products (60972154).

References

1. Yao, L., Zhang, W.M.: Intelligent and Cooperative Information Systems. Publishing of Electronics Industry, Beijing (2008)
2. Luger, G.F.: Artificial intelligence. Publishing of Electronics Industry, Beijing (2008)
3. Wang, L., Zhang, Y.: Key Techniques to Realize Cooperation of Mobile Agent in MAS Environment. School of Computer Science and Engineering 32(2), 158–163 (2009)
4. Trappey, A.J.C., Trappey, C.V., Hou, J.-L.: Mobile agent technology and application for online global logistic services. Industrial Management & Data System 104(1/2), 169–183 (2008)
5. Zhao, J.M., Zhuang, X.P.: An agent-oriented requirement analysis and modeling method 4, 33–35 (November 2009)
6. Zhao, J.: Bee product quality and safety analysis of the key technology research and development. China Apiculture 57(12), 30–32 (2006)
7. DeLoach, S.A.: Engineering Organization-Based Multiagent Systems. In: Garcia, A., Choren, R., Lucena, C., Giorgini, P., Holvoet, T., Romanovsky, A. (eds.) SELMAS 2005. LNCS, vol. 3914, pp. 109–125. Springer, Heidelberg (2006)
8. Chang, M.-H., Harrington Jr., J.E.: Agent-based models of organizations. In: Handbook of Computational Economics II (2006)
9. Yi, S.C.: Computing based on Agent. Publishing of Tsinghua University (2007)
10. Zhi, S.Z.: Advanced Artificial Intelligence. Publishing of Science (2006)

Evaluating Simulation Model Based
on Generated Weather Data

Shijuan Li and Yeping Zhu

Laboratory of Digital Agricultural Early-warning Technology of Ministry
of Agriculture of China; Institute of Agricultural Information, CAAS,
100081 Beijing, China
{lishijuan,zhuyp}@mail.caas.net.cn

Abstract. The daily weather series simulated with observed weather data and
weather data generated with conventional WGEN model taking dry and wet day
as stochastic parameter and DWS model were statistically compared and
analyzed. These three weather data were respectively used to drive maize
growth simulation model. The corresponding yield results were compared. The
results showed there was no significant difference between observed weather
data and weather data generated with DWS model. The difference between
yield simulated with DWS model and yield simulated with WGEN model was
not significant.

Keywords: Weather generator, Dry and wet spell, Growth simulation.

1   Introduction

Crop growth simulation is to analyze the growth and development mechanism and the
quantitative relationship with environment with the help of computer [1-4]. The
dynamic processes of crop growth and development are expressed by mathematical
methods. Crop simulation model evolves with the development of computer
technique, systemic analysis theory and agricultural research achievements. It is the
core of precise agriculture and information agriculture, furthermore is the foundation
of agricultural production management and resources optimization.

Agriculture is a complicated huge system with many controllable objects. The
development and application successively of crop models promoted the change from
qualitative description to quantitative analysis for crop growth and development
discipline, established good foundation for development of crop growth decision system.
The mature models of developed countries had been applied in many fields such as yield
estimation, drought evaluation and variety breeding under deferent environments. As a
research tool, crop simulation model plays an important role in the domains of
environment, resource, continuous development and climate change impacts etc.

Besides solar radiation and temperature, crop simulation considers water and
fertilizer restrict too. Disease, insect pest, weeds and other biological factors will be
evolved in great simulation model. Many of the factors are linked with weather and
management measures. Lack of accurate and timely weather data restricts the regional
and large-scale application of crop simulation model.

D. Li and Y. Chen (Eds.): CCTA 2011, Part III, IFIP AICT 370, pp. 129–135, 2012.

Weather generator provides an effective measure and tool for weather data simulation. Weather simulation is to generate weather data in common use such as daily maximum temperature, daily minimum temperature, rainfall and solar radiation based on the observed historical weather materials. The common methods applied are stochastic process theory, probability theory and statistics. When there is no enough observed weather data in certain region, weather generator can provide daily meteorologic materials with parameter interpolation method.

International researches on weather generator began in the 1960s. For China it was in the 1980s [5-7]. The main works were to introduce the foreign weather models to test their simulation effects and improve the model parameters. Weather Generator of NCC/RCC-WG that can simulate four parameters of rainfall, maximum temperature, minimum temperature and sunshine duration was developed by National Climatic Data Center, China Meteorological Bureau. Now only the simulation effect about rainfall was reported, and there was no comparison with other weather generators [8]. Shen et al exploited their own weather generator to drive vegetable disease popularity model and construct insect dynamic diversification [9]. This weather generator is limited to laboratory, and has not been applied and test in a large scale.

2   Weather Generators Used in This Study

2.1   WGEN Model

The WGEN model is a common used weather generator based on the time series stochastic process constructed by Richardson et al [10]. The precipitation component of WGEN is a two-parameter Markov chain and gamma distribution model. The occurrence probability of wet or dry days is determined, and the precipitation is generated independently of the other variables for a given day. The residual of the three variables of daily values of maximum and minimum temperature and solar radiation are generated using a multivariate normal generation procedure. The WGEN model offers daily values for rainfall, maximum and minimum temperature, and solar radiation for an n-year period at a given location.

2.2   DWS Weather Generator

For WGEN model a given day is wet or dry depends on the Markov chain. So the bigger statistic error of dry and wet spell is gotten. DWS model adopts dry and wet spell but not dry and wet day as stochastic parameter. This is the essential difference with WGEN model. Researcher had studied the statistical discipline of dry and wet spell [11,12]. The modeling approach and test results were listed in reference [13].

3   Maize Growth Simulation Model

Making use of programming language Visual C++ and Visual Basic 6.0 on the operation system of Windows 2000 server, Digital Maize Planting and Management

System was designed in accordance with maize growth and development discipline using technologies of system engineering theory, software engineering theory, computer and animation and image processing [14]. The system consists of cooperative models, database and interface etc. The main cooperative models contain maize growth model, maize development, water balance model, nitrogen balance model, and 3D visualization model which lay out maize growth and yield formation process. Database was built in Access 2000, and forms and graphs output was carried out by Teechart control unit. In addition, databases, variety parameter test module and weather creation module programmed by Visual C++ are included. Basic parameter database consists of information about location, fertilizer type, fertilizer management, irrigation management, cultivation variety, phenology data, soil texture and soil parameter. Weather data day by day are kept in weather database. The simulation and predicting results of models were transported into result database. Interface functions implement the data transfer between models and databases.

The system simulates several kinds of production fashions, i. e. experiential irrigation, optimal irrigation, no fertilization, no irrigation, rainfall agriculture, potential crop production. This paper uses the production fashion of experiential irrigation to test the weather generation. We run the system according to the irrigation and fertilization amounts commonly applied by farmer, then compared the deference between simulation yield and observed yield.

4   Results Analysis

For this study, two sites were selected that have weather stations with long-term reliable historical daily data. They include Beijing and Zhengzhou. For each location, daily solar radiation, precipitation, and maximum and minimum temperature were available for 31 years (1973–2003). The day with daily precipitation greater than 0.1 mm is set as wet day, contrarily as dry day. At first, two 100-year daily weather data generated by WGEN and DWS models respectively was analyzed. Then Digital Maize Planting and Management System was run making use of the observed, generated weather data by above two models to compare the yield difference.

4.1   Weather Data Simulation Results Analysis

DWS model simulated weather series well. There was no significant difference between simulated monthly statistics and observed values at the level of 0.01. Table 1 showed that the absolute error for monthly maximum temperature generally was less than 0.2°C at two sites. The highest simulation error was in January, Zhengzhou, but didn't exceed 0.8°C. The absolute errors for monthly minimum temperature generally were less than 0.2°C at two sites. The simulation errors of January, July and August in Zhengzhou exceeded 0.4°C, but were less than 0.6°C. In general the absolute errors for monthly precipitation day were less than 1 day. For monthly total solar radiation, the simulation effect difference of DWS and WGEN models is minor. Overall, simulation results for Beijing site were better than Zhengzhou site.

Table 1. Significance test of difference between observed daily weather data (O) and simulated with DWS (D) and WGEN (W) ($t0.01/2 = 2.819$. $df = 22$)

Sites	Month	Maximum temperature(°C) O	D	W	Minimum temperature(°C) O	D	W	precipitation day (d) O	D	W	precipitation (mm) O	D	W	Solar radiation(KJ·m⁻²) O	D	W
Beijing	1	1.9	1.8	1.9	-8.2	-8.1	-8.1	1.8	2.1	1.7	2.9	3.5	3.0	8.2	8.3	8.4
	2	5.3	5.5	5.8	-5.3	-5.2	-4.8	2.4	2.4	2.4	4.6	5.2	4.9	11.1	10.	10.
	3	11.9	12.0	11.7	0.7	0.6	0.7	3.3	3.4	3.1	8.5	8.2	9.1	14.7	14.	13.
	4	20.3	20.7	20.4	8.1	8.3	8.3	4.8	4.6	4.3	22.5	23.	24.	17.9	17.	17.
	5	26.2	26.2	26.4	13.8	13.8	14.0	5.7	5.6	5.6	33.8	35.	34.	20.5	20.	20.
	6	30.1	30.2	30.2	18.9	19.0	19.0	9.8	9.9	9.5	77.3	76.	83.	19.7	20.	20.
	7	31.0	31.0	31.0	22.1	22.1	22.2	13.6	13.	12.	174.	182	173	17.2	19.	19.
	8	29.9	29.8	29.8	20.9	20.9	20.9	11.9	11.	11.	158.	153	147	16.3	17.	16.
	9	26.0	26.0	26.2	15.0	15.0	15.3	7.6	7.4	6.8	42.7	39.	44.	15.0	14.	14.
	10	19.0	19.4	19.0	8.0	8.3	7.9	5.4	5.4	5.0	25.7	25.	25.	11.6	11.	11.
	11	10.0	9.9	9.8	0.0	-0.2	-0.1	3.5	3.4	2.6	8.9	9.6	7.1	8.3	8.6	8.6
	12	3.7	3.8	3.9	-5.7	-5.5	-5.5	2.0	2.4	1.7	3.0	3.4	3.0	7.0	7.6	7.7
$t_{0.01}$	D-O	0.018			0.010			0.003			0.0			0.069		
	W-O	0.015			0.02			0.2			0.0					
Zhengzhou	1	6.9	6.1	6.4	-3.2	-3.8	-3.6	3.8	4.4	3.2	15.0	13.	12.	8.8	8.6	8.9
	2	10.2	10.0	10.1	-0.6	-0.7	-0.6	4.0	4.8	3.6	12.3	16.	14.	11.0	10.	10.
	3	15.4	15.6	15.2	4.2	4.4	4.1	6.6	6.3	6.1	37.8	32.	30.	13.3	13.	13.
	4	22.0	21.8	21.8	10.1	9.8	9.9	6.7	6.0	6.2	35.9	30.	35.	16.6	16.	16.
	5	27.2	27.0	26.8	14.9	15.0	14.8	6.7	6.8	6.9	61.4	54.	65.	18.6	18.	18.
	6	31.2	31.3	31.1	19.7	19.7	19.6	8.4	7.8	7.5	70.2	63.	71.	18.8	19.	19.
	7	31.0	31.4	31.1	22.1	22.5	22.2	11.6	12.	11.	140.	147	144	16.8	18.	18.
	8	29.4	29.8	29.7	20.7	21.2	21.1	10.4	11.	9.8	118.	120	122	15.7	16.	16.
	9	25.9	25.9	26.2	15.6	15.7	15.9	7.9	9.2	7.6	70.7	81.	72.	13.4	13.	13.
	10	21.1	20.7	21.1	9.6	9.4	9.6	6.6	7.2	6.4	42.9	53.	42.	11.4	10.	10.
	11	14.1	14.1	13.9	2.9	3.0	2.7	4.8	4.9	4.5	19.2	21.	19.	9.2	9.0	9.0
	12	7.7	8.0	8.3	-2.2	-1.9	-1.7	4.0	3.9	3.8	10.8	10.	9.6	7.4	8.0	8.2
$t_{0.01}$	D-O	0.005			0.011			0.2			0.0			0.0		
	W-O	0.009			0.00			0.3			0.1			0.1		

Table 1 also showed that DWS model got the similar effect with WGEN model. All the absolute errors for monthly maximum and minimum temperature between DWS model and WGEN model was less than 0.4°C. The absolute errors of monthly precipitation day were less than 1.5 d, and the errors of average monthly precipitation day were less than 0.5 d. The absolute errors of monthly precipitation were less than 3 mm at Beijing site except for July and August. For Zhengzhou site the value was 5 mm, but didn't exceed 10 mm. the average monthly precipitation difference between the two models was less than 3mm. the difference of solar radiations generated by DWS and WGEN was under $0.3KJ \cdot m^2$.

4.2   Analysis of Simulation for Maize Yield

We run the digital maize plant and management system with the observed and generated weather data by DWS and WGEN to test the influence of irrigation period on maize yield. Four irrigation periods were set, i. e. 1st July, 10th July, 20th July, 30th July. The irrigation amount was 100 mm. The simulation sites were Beijing and Zhengzhou. Maize variety of Nongda 108 was used. Table 2 is the t value (p=0.05) between yield simulated with observed weather data versus generated weather data based on DWS or WGEN. We can see that there was no significant difference between observed yield and simulated yield by DWS or WGEN.

Table 2. t values between yield simulated with observed weather data versus generated weather data based on DWS or WGEN ($t_{0.05}$=2.595, df=129)

Sites	Irrigation period	DWS-Observed	MG-Observed
	1st July	0.2	0.936
	10th July	0.154	0.843
Beijing	20th July	0.103	0.557
	30th July	0.944	0.341
	1st July	0.011	0.392
	10th July	0.011	0.318
Zhengzhou	20th July	0.022	0.301
	30th July	0.027	0.256

From figure 1 we got the yields simulated with generated weather data by DWS or WGEN were all higher than that with observed weather data. The yields simulated with generated weather data by WGEN were very similar with observed weather data. With the delay of irrigation period, all the maize yields simulated with three sources of weather data increased gradually. Jointing stage in July is the key stage for maize growth. Irrigation in this stage is advantageous to grain increase. But July belongs to rainy season, so rainfall may weaken the yield increase extend.

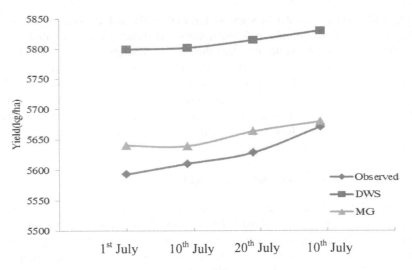

Fig. 1. Response of grain yield to irrigation period for maize simulated with observed weather data and weather data generated with DWS or WGEN

5   Conclusion

This paper introduced the DWS model taking dry and wet spell as stochastic parameter, compared statistically the weather data generated with DWS and WGEN. There was no significant difference between observed weather data and generated data. Three source of weather data were used to run the digital maize plant and management system to simulate maize yield. And different irrigation periods were set to test the influence on maize yield. The results showed there was no significant difference between observed yield and simulated yield by DWS or WGEN. The yields simulated with generated weather data by DWS or WGEN were all higher than that with observed weather data. The yields simulated with generated weather data by WGEN were very similar with observed weather data. With the delay of irrigation period, all the maize yields simulated with three sources of weather data increase gradually.

Acknowledgments. This research is kindly supported by Special Fund of Basic Scientific Research and Operation Foundation for Commonweal Scientific Research Institutes and Beijing Nova program.

References

1. Williams, J.R., Jones, C.A., Kiniry, J.R., et al.: The EPIC Crop Growth Model. Trans. ASAE 32(2), 497–511 (1989)
2. McCown, R.L., Hammer, G.L., Hargreaves, J.N.G., et al.: APSIM: a novel software system for model development, model testing and simulation in agricultural systems research. Agricultural Systems 50, 255–271 (1996)

3. Gao, L.Z., Jin, Z.Q., Huang, Y., et al.: Rice Cultivational Simulation-Optimization-Decision Making System (RCSODS). China Agricultural Scientech Press, Beijing (1992) (in Chinese)
4. Zhao, C.J., Zhu, D.H., Li, H.X., et al.: Study on intelligent expert system of wheat cultivation management and its application. Scientia Agricultura Sinica 30, 42–49 (1997) (in Chinese)
5. Chen, M.C., Zhang, Q., Yang, J.L.: Stochastic simulationmodeland its verification of precipitation, temperature and sunshining hours. Agricultural Research in the Arid Areas 12(2), 17–26 (1994) (in Chinese)
6. Wu, J.D., Wang, F.T.: Study on the creation of daily climatic variation scenarios with a stochastic weather generator and various interpolations. Quarterly Journal of Applied Meteorology 11(2), 129–136 (2000) (in Chinese)
7. Zhu, Y.P., Wang, S.Q.: Stochastic Modeling of Daily Weather and Its Implementation in Java. Acta Electronica Sinica 12, 2267–2271 (2007) (in Chinese)
8. Liao, Y.M., Zhang, Q., Chen, D.L.: Precipitation simulation in China with a weather generator. Acta Geographica Sinica 59(5), 689–698 (2004) (in Chinese)
9. Ma, X., Shen, Z.: Visual programming stochastic weather generator and its applications to ecological study in future. Scientia Agricultura Sinica 35(12), 1473–1478 (2002) (in Chinese)
10. Richardson, C.W., Wright, D.A.: WGEN: A model for generating daily weather variables. USDA, ARS-8 Washington, DC (1984)
11. Jorgenson, D.L.: Persistency of rain and no-rain periods during the winter at San Francisco. Mon. Weather. Rev. 77(9), 303 (1949)
12. Gabriel, K.R., Neumann, J.: On distribution of weather cycles by length. Quart. J. R. met. Soc. 83, 357–375 (1957)
13. Wang, S.Q., Zhu, Y.P., Li, S.J.: Stochastic simulation for dry and wet spell. Journal of Applied Meteorological Science 20(2), 179–185 (2009) (in Chinese)
14. Li, S.J., Zhu, Y.P., Yan, D.C.: Study on digital maize management system based on model. In: Progress of Information Technology in Agriculture: Proceeding on Intelligent Information Technology in Agriculture(ISSITA), pp. 240–243. China agricultural science and technology press, Beijing (2007)

On Integral Sum Numbers of Cycles

Ergen Liu, Qing Zhou, and Wei Yu

School of Basic Sciences, East China Jiaotong University
Nanchang, jiangxi China, 330013
liueg65@126.com, leg_eg@sina.com

Abstract. In this paper we determine that integral sum number of graph C_n, namely for any integer $n \geq 5$, then $\xi(C_n) = 0$, therefore we prove that the graph $C_n \, (n \geq 5)$ is an integral sum graph.

Keywords: Integral sum number, Integral sum graph, Graph C_n.

1   Introduction

The graph in this paper discussed are undirected, no multiple edges and simple graph, the unorganized state of definitions and terminology and the symbols in this paper referred to reference [1],[2].

F. Harary [3] introduce the concept of integral sum graphs. The integral sum graph $G^+(S)$ of a finite subset $S \subset Z$ is the graph (V, E), where $V = S$ and $uv \in E$ if and only if $u + v \in S$. A graph G is an integral sum graph if it is isomorphic to the integral sum graph number of $G^+(S)$ of some $S \subset Z$. The integral sum number of a given graph G, denoted by $\xi(G)$, is defined as the smallest nonnegative integer S such that $G \bigcup sk_1$ is an integral sum graph. For convincing, an integral sum graph is written as an integral sum graph in references [3, 4]. Obviously, graph G is an integral sum graph if $\xi(G) = 0$.

It is very difficult to determine $\xi(G)$ for a given graph G in general. All paths and matchings are verified to be integral sum graph in references [3], and we see from references [4] that $\xi(C_n) \leq 1$ for all $n \neq 4$. And further, an open conjecture was posed in references [4] as follows:

Conjecture [4]: Is it true that any old cycle is an integral sum graph?

Definition 1.1. If a graph is isomorphism graph $G^+(S)$, then we call graph G is Integral sum graph, denoted by $G \cong G^+(S)$.

D. Li and Y. Chen (Eds.): CCTA 2011, Part III, IFIP AICT 370, pp. 136–139, 2012.
© IFIP International Federation for Information Processing 2012

Definition 1.2. For graph G, if it exists nonnegative integer S such that $G \cup sk_1$ is an integral sum graph, then we call number s is integral sum number of G, denoted by $\xi(G) = s$.

2   Main Results and Certification

Theorem 2.1. For any integer $n \geq 3$, then

$$\xi(C_n) = \begin{cases} 3, & \text{when } n = 4; \\ 0, & \text{when } n \neq 4. \end{cases}$$

Proof. It is immediate from references [3, 4] that $\xi(C_3) = 0$ and $\xi(C_4) = 3$. And it is clear that $C_5 \cong G^+\{2, 1, -2, 3, -1\}$ and $C_7 \cong G^+\{1, 2, -5, 7, -3, 4, 3\}$.

Next we consider two cases: For all $C_{2j}(j \geq 3)$ and $C_{2j+1}(j \geq 4)$, we will show that the two classes of cycle are integral sum graph.

Let the vertices of $C_{2j}(j \geq 3)$ and $C_{2j+1}(j \geq 4)$ be marked as the methods in Fig.1 and Fig.2.

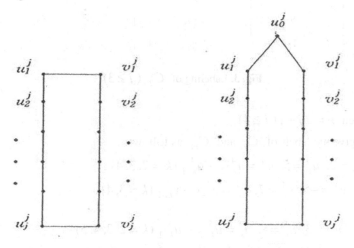

Fig. 1. Marking of C_{2j} **Fig. 2.** Marking of C_{2j+1}

Case 1. When $n = 2j \ (j \geq 3)$

We first give the labels of C_6 and C_8 as follows:

Let $u_1^3 = 4,\ u_2^3 = -1,\ u_3^3 = 5;\quad v_1^3 = 1,\ v_2^3 = 3,\ v_3^3 = -2$.

and

$$u_1^4 = 7,\ u_2^4 = -2,\ u_3^4 = 9,\ u_4^4 = -11;\quad v_1^4 = 2,\ v_2^4 = 5,\ v_3^4 = -3,\ v_4^4 = 8.$$

Then $C_6 \cong G^+\{4, -1, 5, -2, 3, 1\}$ and

$C_8 \cong G^+\{7, -2, 9, -11, 8, -3, 5, 2\}$, therefore $\xi(C_6) = 0$ and $\xi(C_8) = 0$.

When $j \geq 5$, we give the labels of C_{2j} as follows:

Let $\quad u_1^j = u_1^{j-1} + u_1^{j-2} \quad (j \geq 5); \quad u_2^j = u_2^{j-1} + u_2^{j-2} \quad (j \geq 5);$

$\quad\quad v_1^j = v_1^{j-1} + v_1^{j-2} \quad (j \geq 5); \quad v_2^j = v_2^{j-1} + v_2^{j-2} \quad (j \geq 5).$

and

$$u_k^j = u_{k-2}^j - u_{k-1}^j \quad (k = 3, 4, \cdots, j);$$

$$v_k^j = v_{k-2}^j - v_{k-1}^j \quad (k = 3, 4, \cdots, j).$$

By labeling of above, we know $\xi(C_{2j}) = 0 \, (j \geq 5)$.

The labeling of above is illustrated in Fig.3.

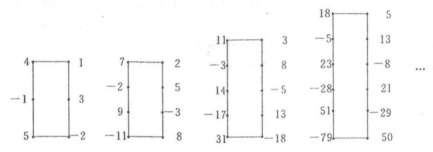

Fig. 3. Labeling of $C_{2j}(j \geq 3)$

Case 2. When $n = 2j + 1 \, (j \geq 4)$

We first give the labels of C_9 and C_{11} as follows:

Let $\quad u_0^4 = 2, \ u_1^4 = 5, \ u_k^4 = u_{k-2}^4 - u_{k-1}^4 \ (k = 2, 3, 4);$

$\quad\quad v_1^4 = -5, \ v_2^4 = 7, \ v_k^4 = v_{k-2}^4 - v_{k-1}^4 \ (k = 3, 4).$

and

$$u_0^5 = 3, \ u_1^5 = 8, \ u_k^5 = u_{k-2}^5 - u_{k-1}^5 \ (k = 2, 3, 4, 5);$$

$$v_1^5 = -8, \ v_2^5 = 11, \ v_k^5 = v_{k-2}^5 - v_{k-1}^5 \ (k = 3, 4, 5).$$

Then $C_9 \cong G^+\{2, 5, -3, 8, -11, 19, -12, 7, -5\}$ and

$C_{11} \cong G^+\{3, 8, -5, 13, -18, 31, -49, 30, -19, 11, -8\}$, therefore $\xi(C_9) = 0$ and $\xi(C_{11}) = 0$.

When $j \geq 6$, we give the labels of C_{2j+1} as follows:

Let $\quad u_0^j = u_0^{j-1} + u_0^{j-2} \quad (j \geq 6); \quad u_1^j = u_1^{j-1} + u_1^{j-2} \quad (j \geq 6);$

$\quad\quad v_1^j = v_1^{j-1} + v_1^{j-2} \quad (j \geq 6);$

and

$$u_k^j = u_{k-2}^j - u_{k-1}^j \quad (k = 2, 3, \cdots, j) ;$$
$$v_k^j = v_{k-2}^j - v_{k-1}^j \quad (k = 2, 3, \cdots, j) .$$

Where $v_0^j = u_0^j$ for $j \geq 6$.

By labeling of above, we know $\xi(C_{2j+1}) = 0 \, (j \geq 6)$.

The labeling of above is illustrated in Fig.4.

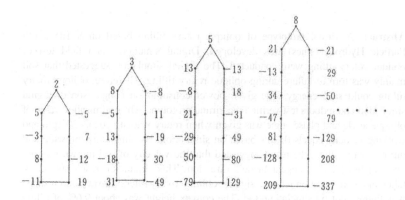

Fig. 4. Labeling of $C_{2j+1} (j \geq 6)$

Theorem 2.2. For any integer $n \geq 5$, the graph C_n is integral sum graph.

Proof. From theorem 2.1, we know $\xi(C_n) = 0 \, (n \geq 5)$, therefore for any integer $n \geq 5$, the graph C_n is integral sum graph.

References

1. Harary, F.: Graph Theory. Addison-Wesley, Reading (1969)
2. Bondy, J.A., Murty, U.S.R.: Graph Theory with Applications. Elsevier North-Holland (1976)
3. Harary, F.: Sum graphs over all the integers. Discrete Math. (124), 99–105 (1994)
4. Xu, B.: On integral sum graphs. Discrete Math. (194), 285–294 (1999)
5. Achaya, B.D., Hegde, S.M.: Arithmetic graphs. Journal of Graph Theory 18(3), 275–299 (1990)
6. Yu, H.: The Windmill W_n^* is the intergral sum Graph and Mod intergral sum Graph. Journal of Heze University 28(3), 18–19 (2006)
7. Gao, X.-L.: Several kinds Interal Sum Tree. Journal of Dezhou University 17(2), 18–22 (2011)

Soil-Cutting Simulation and Test of Oblique Rotary Tiller

Jianmin Gao and Yongchao Jin

Key Laboratory of Modern Agricultural Equipment and Technology,
Ministry of Education & Jiangsu Province, Jiangsu University, Zhenjiang 212013, China
jmgao@ujs.edu.cn

Abstract. A virtual prototype of oblique rotary tilling based on SPH(Smooth Particle Hydrodynamics) was developed. Digital simulation and field test of oblique rotary tilling were conducted. The digital simulation suggested that soil mainly was torn to failure during oblique rotary tilling. Therefore, oblique rotary tilling could save energy. The given power consumption comparison of digital simulation and indoors test verified the virtual prototype. The optimization value of oblique angle and phase angle was given when rotary velocity equals 200rpm and working velocity equals 0.4m/s based on simulation. By simulating throwing soil during rotary tilling, the result suggested that the velocity of soil thrown was not uniform but lean to tangent blade's direction. This simulation result should be taken into consideration while designing oblique rotary tiller. Furrow bottom shape was figured out by simulating, too. The convex height was about 9.6% of tilling depth. All of the research result suggested that oblique rotary tilling might be a very potential tilling method which could save tilling energy greatly.

Keywords: oblique rotary tilling, simulation, SPH, specified power consumption, throwing soil.

1 Preface

In the oblique rotary tillage, there was a sub-movement which made edge of the sub-exercise to apply force to the soil along the axis in the lateral when rotary blade was around the axis of rotation.

If the soil in the certain width direction along with the lateral force completely or partially lifted constraints (had been cultivated), then lateral edge of a lateral tear of the role of the soil causing more soil would be broken due to tension. From this perspective, oblique rotary tillage may reduce energy consumption, coupled with a better performance off the grass, it may be a promising new cultivation. The structure of cultivated soil was complex and very different in time and space and the movement of oblique rotary blade was more complex, so it was difficult to quantitative study of soil oblique rotary tilling mechanism by physical prototype testing of soil causing great difficulties in the development of the relevant equipment.

2 The Research of Oblique Rotary Virtual Prototyping System

The soil, nonlinear material, was damaged in high-speed collision was involved in this process of oblique rotary tilling. Soil high-speed cutting process has been an

D. Li and Y. Chen (Eds.): CCTA 2011, Part III, IFIP AICT 370, pp. 140–150, 2012.

important and difficult problem with the method computer simulation in the study of tillage mechanics. Because this involves cultivated soil which is multi-phase, loose and scattered in the working parts of soil failure under high speed and describes the state of soil movement after the destruction process. Theory of continuous physical and numerical solution (finite element method or boundary element method) are difficult to describe the process(such as finite element method for large deformation conditions mesh distortion occurs, leading to failure calculated).Therefore, traditional numerical simulation methods based on the continuous mechanics could not do high-speed cutting mechanism of the soil.

SPH (smoothed particle hydrodynamics) is without grid and no mesh distortion problems, so it could be dealt with under the Lagrange large deformation. Meanwhile, the method of SPH permits material interface, so you could simply and accurately get the complex constitutive behavior and the method of SPH also applies to materials at high loading rates of fracture and other issues.

SPH does not use discrete units, but use a fixed point of the movable mass particles or nodes. The quality is fixed on the particle's coordinate system, so that discretization is closer to the physical properties of cultivated soil. SPH do not use mesh and do not have mesh distortion problems, so it could be accurately described the object as well as destruction of nonlinear large deformation process. Hence, SPH is very suitable for the dynamic description of the process of farming.

By the basic equation of dynamic, we could get the acceleration of Lagrange particle volume of soil under stress.

$$\frac{d\dot{u}^{\alpha}}{dt} = -\frac{\partial}{\partial x^{\beta}}(\frac{\sigma^{\alpha\beta}}{\rho}) - \frac{\sigma^{\alpha\beta}}{\rho^2}\frac{\partial\rho}{\partial x^{\beta}}$$

(1)

In the formula: ρ is a relevant variable for the density, $\dot{u}^{\alpha}$ is velocity vector and $\sigma^{\alpha\beta}$ is stress tensor. The spatial coordinates x^{β} and time t were the independent variables. The acceleration of point x could be estimated by the formula (1) and the neighboring information. SPH's weight function w was multiplied on the right of the formula (1) and the result was integral in the domain of whole space.

$$\frac{d\dot{u}^{\alpha}}{dt} = -\frac{\partial}{\partial x^{\beta}}\int w\frac{\sigma^{\alpha\beta}(x')}{\rho(x')}dx' - \frac{\sigma^{\alpha\beta}(x)}{\rho(x)}\frac{\partial}{\partial x^{\beta}}\int w\rho(x')dx'$$

(2)

If the adjacent information was only valid in the discrete point j and the volume element was shown by $\frac{m_j}{\rho_j}$, then formula (2) could be got by formula (3).

$$\frac{d\dot{u}_i}{dt} = -\frac{\partial}{\partial x_i^{\beta}}\sum_j m_j\frac{\sigma_j^{\alpha\beta}}{\rho_j^2}w_{ij} - \frac{\sigma_j^{\alpha\beta}}{\rho_j}\frac{\partial}{\partial x_i^{\beta}}\sum m_j w_{ij}$$

(3)

A simple soil and crushable foam model was advanced by Krieg in 1972.If the yield stress was too low, this model feature was close to the fluid.

According to equation (3), combined with the pressure - volume deformation relationship, it's easy to calculate the force between soil particles.

Because this test was mainly carried out in indoor soil, SPH model of the soil was established according to indoor soil tank model.

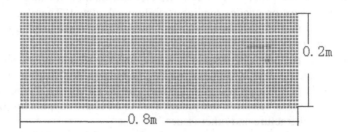

Fig. 1. Saltus curve the SPH model of soil

In this paper, soil and crushable foam model is as a soil model. The mechanical model about the tool contacting with soil was shown in Figure 2.Virtual prototyping system of oblique rotary was developed was shown in Figure 3. Rotary blade shaft was consists of three cutter head and each cutter head install two rotary cutter blade, so a total of six rotary blade was installed on the cutter shaft. Variables contains tillage depth, oblique angle, phase angle could be controlled in virtual prototyping system.

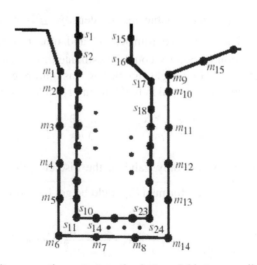

Fig. 2. Saltus curve the contact mechanical model between soil and cutter

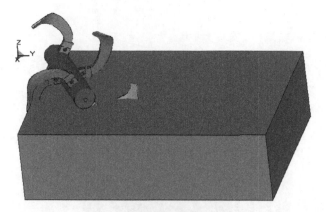

Fig. 3. Virtual Prototype of oblique rotary tilling

3   Numerical Simulation about the Process of Oblique Rotary Tilling Soil

Because the structure of soil which has time and space diversity is extremely complex, it is difficult to observe the process of cutting soil by Oblique rotary in the physical prototype test. The numerical simulation could accurately describe the damage process of cutting soil by Oblique rotary and the force of machine, and then the mechanism of Oblique rotary tilling soil could be revealed.

3.1   The Research on Lateral Tear of Soil

Tillage machinery approach to design was best "destroyed pull" and followed by "destroyed by cutting" and avoided "was destroyed by pressure" as far as possible to reduce energy consumption and improve the economy. In Oblique rotary, the soil was torn lateral that was possible main reason for oblique rotary saving energy. Through the physical prototype of lateral tear of the lateral edge effects on soil was more difficult, but the numerical simulation could be more clearly reveal the process. The particle of soil no.166,544 which was to be cutting by the rotary blade was selected (Figure 4). The coordinates of x, y, z were 0.045, 0.226, -0.05 and unit forward speed was 0.5m / s and rotate speed was 200 rpm,then the acceleration in X direction was shown in Figure 5.

Soil particle no.166,544 generated acceleration of 1370m/s^2 in the X positive, that was to say, the lateral movement of rotary blade torn soil along the positive of X when rotary blade was cutting soil in the soil near the particle no.166,544. Because the rotary cutter blade lateral torn the lateral effect to the soil, the soil was destroyed by "pull" was verified from the perspective of numerical simulation. From this perspective, oblique rotary tillage could greatly reduce energy consumption.

Fig. 4. The location of soil element no.166544

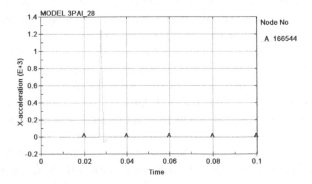

Fig. 5. The acceleration of soil element no.166544

Fig. 6. The location of soil element no.166562

Fig. 7. The location of soil element no.166482

The soil particles no.166562 (Figure 6) and no.166482 (Figure 7) which were near the two other lateral edge cutters were chosen. Soil particles no.166,562, and no.166,482 had the same coordinates of the no.166 544 in Y, Z directions and its acceleration in X direction was shown in Figure 8.

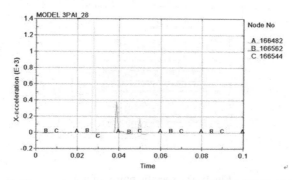

Fig. 8. The acceleration of soil element no.166544, 166562,166482

It could be seen from Figure 8:

Soil particles no.166544, no.166562, and no.166482 all had a instantaneous acceleration in the same direction which was along lateral edge of the direction of lateral movement indicating that the soil near the three cutter disc cutter were destroyed by the lateral movement of soil caused by tearing.

Soil particles no.166544, no.166562, and no.166482 of the coordinate of Y were consistent, but the failure time was not the same. This was because the tool axis was inclined to make that the soil produced ordered cut.

The tensile strength of soil particles no.166544, no.166562, no.166,482 reduced in correct order. This is because the tool axis was inclined, cutter head near soil particles no.166544, no.166562 and no.166482 cut soil in proper order to make the follow-up sword plate achieve all or part of the unconfined cut. From the literature, we could get that, unconfined soil strength is much smaller than confined soil strength. The cutter head near the soil particles no.166,544 first cut soil was confined soil cutting, so the tensile strength of it was more larger than the other two cutter heads. On the contrary point of view from the numerical simulation, the correctness of the theory of the side of the limit on soil strength which was introduced in the literature 4 was proved.

3.2   The Research of Specified Power Consumption

The specified power consumption was important parameter to measure the performance of a rotavator. To the oblique rotary tiller, the computing formula of specified power consumption is:

$$N_s = \frac{N}{(B\cos\alpha + 2R\sin\alpha)Av_m} \tag{4}$$

In the formula (4): N- output (N.m) B- width (cm) α- Oblique angle (°) R-Rolling radius of the blade. In the Figure 9,connection in specified power consumption, phase angle and oblique angle were obtained through laboratory test when the rotational speed was n = 200rpm and V = 0.4m / s.

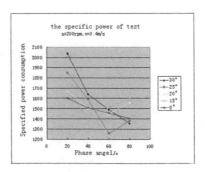

Fig. 9. The specific power of test

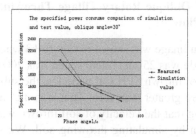

Fig. 10. The specified power consume comparison of simulation and test value, oblique angle=30°

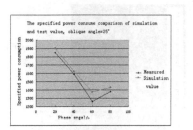

Fig. 11. The specified power consume comparison of simulation and test value, oblique angle=25°

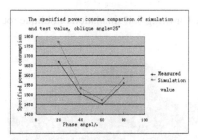

Fig. 12. The specified power consume comparison of simulation and test value, oblique angle=15°

Figure 10, Figure 11 and Figure 12 showed the contrast between measured value and simulated values at different oblique angle and phase angle when the rotational speed was n = 200rpm and V = 0.4m / s.

It could be seen from these figures:

Measured and simulated values were basically the same and the maximum relative prediction error is 6% indicating that the accuracy of the virtual prototype system could meet the analysis requirements.

Whether actual or simulated results showed that when the phase angle was 60° and oblique angle was 25°, the specified power consumption was minimum when speed was n = 200rpm and V = 0.4m / s. It could be used as design reference designing oblique rotary tiller.

3.3   The Analysis of Oblique Rotary Tillage Throwing Soil and the Shape of the Ditch after Plow

Throwing soil simulation image was shown in Figure 13 when unit forward speed was 0.5m / s and oblique angle was 25°and rotate speed was 200 rpm and deep tillage was 25 cm. By the statistics of thrown SPH soil particles, the sub-speed X of 93.4% of the thrown soil particles were greater than zero. That was the same as the lateral edge of the axial speed indicating that the velocity of soil thrown was not uniform but lean to tangent blade's direction by simulating throwing soil. We should fully consider the factors when design shell oblique rotary equipment. The shape of ditch after plowing was shown in Figure 14.

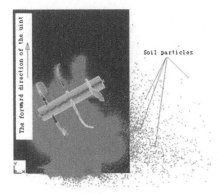

Fig. 13. Throwing Soil simulation of oblique rotary tilling

Fig. 14. Furrow bottom shape

As could be seen from Figure 14: when forward speed of the unit was 0.5m / s and oblique angle was 25°and rotate speed was 200 rpm and deep tillage was 25 cm, the maximum raised height was 2.4 cm which was 9.6% of the tillage depth and it was accounting for 7.1% of the whole ditch area indicating that after oblique rotary ditch was basic level could meet the farming requirements.

4   Conclusion

Through this study, we could obtain the following conclusions:

The result of digital simulation indicates that soil mainly was torn to be destroyed during oblique rotary tilling. The failure modes made more soil "destroyed pull" significant savings in energy work. This could also explain the phenomenon that oblique rotary tilling soil was easier in testing process.

The correctness of the simulation system was verified by the comparison of the test of oblique rotary tilling in specified power consumption between indoor and numerical simulation. At the same time, the best oblique angle and the optimum phase angle was given when the speed was n = 200rpm and V = 0.4m / s.

By simulating throwing soil, the velocity of soil thrown was not uniform but lean to tangent blade's direction. We should fully consider the factors when design shell oblique rotary equipment.

When forward speed of the unit was 0.5m / s and oblique angle was 25°and rotate speed was 200 rpm and deep tillage was 25 cm, the maximum raised height was 2.4 cm which was 9.6% of the tillage depth and it was accounting for 7.1% of the whole ditch area indicating that after oblique rotary ditch was basic level could meet the farming requirements.

Acknowledgements. This work was financially supported by Science and Technology research project of Jiangsu Province (BE2007355), by NSF grants of Jiangsu Province (SBK201123237), by Agricultural Science and Technology project of Zhenjiang City (NY2008003) and "Qinglan" Project of Jiangsu Province.

References

1. Gao, J., Sang, Z.: Study on Three-dimensional Simulation of an Oblique rotary Tiller. Transactions of the Chinese Society of Agricultural Machinery (5), 40–43 (2005)
2. Li, L., Huo, C.: The research and development of our country's rotary tiller. Modern Agriculture (10), 37–38 (2004)
3. Ding, W., Xu, Z., Wang, X.: Grass Sliding Cutting Angles and Their Equations of Oblique rotary Blades. Transactions of the Chinese Society of Agricultural Engineering (3), 49–52 (2002)
4. Jiao, P.: Research on Numerical Algorithm and Engineering Application of Fuild Simulation Based on Smoothed Particle Hydrodynamics.[Ph.D. Thesis],Ji Nan,Shandong University (2010)
5. Gao, J., Zhou, P., Zhang, B., Li, F.: Development and test of high speed soil-cutting simulation system based on smooth particle hydrodynamics. Transactions of the Chinese Society of Agricultural Engineering 23(8), 20–26 (2007)
6. Jia, J., Li, Z., Yang, J., Zhao, L., Yao, X.: A Study of Bird Impact on Aircraft Windshield Using SPH and Finite Element Method. Acta Aeronautica ET Astronautica Sinica 1000-6893 (2010) 01-0136-07
7. Hallquist, J.O.: LS-DYNA Theoretical Manual. Livermore Software Technology Corporation, pp. 1121–1130 (May 1998)

8. Anjami, N., Basti, A.: Investigation of rolls size effects on hot ring rolling process by coupled thermo-mechanical 3D-FEA. Journal of Materials Processing Technology 210, 1364–1377 (2010)
9. Jianmin, G.: Oblique rotary Mechanical CAD three-dimensional simulation and the realization of the key technology.[Ph.D. Thesis], Zhenjiang, Jiangsu Polytechnic University (2001)
10. Sun, Y., Gao, X., et al.: The mechanics of Agricultural soil. Agricultural Publishing House, Beijing (1985)

Image Recognition of Grape Downy Mildew and Grape Powdery Mildew Based on Support Vector Machine

Guanlin Li, Zhanhong Ma, and Haiguang Wang*

Department of Plant Pathology, China Agricultural University, Beijing 100193, China
wanghaiguang@cau.edu.cn

Abstract. In order to realize automatic disease diagnosis and provide related information for disease prediction and control timely and accurately, the identification and diagnosis of grape downy mildew and grape powdery mildew was conducted based on image recognition technologies. The method based on K_means clustering algorithm was used to implement unsupervised segmentation of the disease images. Fifty shape, color and texture features were extracted from the images of the diseases. Support vector machine (SVM) classifier for the diseases was designed based on thirty-one effective selected features. The training recognition rates of these two kinds of grape diseases were both 100%, and the testing recognition rates of grape downy mildew and grape powdery mildew were 90% and 93.33%, respectively. The recognition results using the SVMs with different kernels indicated that the SVM with linear kernel was the most suitable for image recognition of the diseases. This study provided an effective way for rapid and accurate identification and diagnosis of plant diseases, and also provided a basis and reference for further development of automatic diagnosis system for plant diseases.

Keywords: Grape downy mildew, grape powdery mildew, image recognition, support vector machine.

1   Introduction

Grape downy mildew caused by *Plasmopara uiticola* (Berk.dt Curtis) Berl. Et de Toni and grape powdery mildew caused by *Uncinula necator* (Schw.) Burr., are two kinds of common grape diseases in greenhouse [1]. They could cause serious damage via affecting grape quality and yield. The pathogens causing plant diseases are always difficult to be identified by using naked-eye observation method directly and disease symptoms are always influenced by various factors. So it is difficult to diagnose plant diseases accurately and effectively by using the traditional plant disease diagnosis method that is mainly dependent on naked-eye observation. Instead of using naked eyes, plant diease images could be processed using computer vision. This method could eliminate the image noise caused by environmental factors and image capture elements, and could diagnose the plant diseases by computer automatically. And then

---

* Corresponding author.

D. Li and Y. Chen (Eds.): CCTA 2011, Part III, IFIP AICT 370, pp. 151–162, 2012.

diagnosis results could be output directly. Thus the intuitive, practical, reliable and accurate information of plant disease diagnosis could be provided to the agricultural technicians and the farmers, and then could be used to guide plant disease control.

Real-time diagnosis of plant disease could be conducted quickly and accurately by using computer vision. Computer image recognition technologies have been widely used in plant disease studies. Image recognition of plant diseases is usually conducted based on shape features [2], [3], color features [4], [5], [6], [7], [8] or texture features [9] by using the methods, such as artificial neural network (ANN) [10], support vector machine (SVM) [6], [7], [11] and discriminant analysis [9], [12].

SVM is a new kind of pattern recognition algorithm based on VC dimension theory and structural risk minimization principle, which can solve the small sample, nonlinear problems, high dimension and local minimum points and other practical issues [13]. SVMs have been used for image recognition of plant diseases, such as corn leaf diseases [6], [14], cucumber leaf diseases [15] and cotton diseases [11]. However, the SVM based on multiple feature parameters has not yet been applied to image recognition of grape diseases.

In order to provide quick and reliable identification and diagnosis methods for grape downy mildew and grape powdery mildew in greenhouse, image recognition of these two kinds of grape diseases was conducted by using the method based on SVM and multiple feature parameters according to the properties of the disease images in this study.

2   Image Acquisition and Image Processing

2.1   Disease Image Acquisition and Image Preprocessing

Disease images were acquired from grape leaves that were naturally infected by downy mildew and powdery mildew. In order to obtain clear vertical projection images of diseased single leaves, the diseased grape leaves which surfaces were clean were selected, and then disease images were taken by using common digital camera that was perpendicular to the leaves. Fifty images of grape downy mildew were obtained and thirty-five images of grape powdery mildew were obtained. The size of the original images obtained was 2592×1944 with format of jpg, 24 bitmap. To improve the operation speed of computer programs, the images were compressed from 2592×1944 to 800×600 in the same proportion without changing the image resolution using the nearest neighbor interpolation method. And then the plant disease images were denoised with median filter algorithm.

2.2   Disease Color Image Segmentation

The obtained grape disease images were composed of diseased regions and normal leaf regions. In order to extract effective features, disease color image segmentation was conducted to segment diseased regions from the images. It included binary segmentation and color segmentation. The former was to extract shape features from the segmented images and the latter was to extract color features and texture features from the segmented images. Currently, the methods used for plant disease image segmentation are edge detection method [16], fuzzy C-means clustering method [17], segmentation method based on statistical pattern recognition [18], etc. In this study, K_means clustering algorithm was used to segment plant disease images. This algorithm is an unsupervised real-time clustering algorithm proposed by Mac Queen [19]. The basic idea of this algorithm is to identify the regions where the different colors belong to based on the different colors in the image color space, so as to achieve the purpose of image segmentation. The implementation process of this segmentation method has been used in [20]. Using the K_means clustering algorithm, binary segmentation and color segmentation of the images of grape downy mildew and grape powdery mildew were conducted, and the results were as shown in Fig. 1. The results indicated that this method could segment the diseased regions from the color images of the diseases with good accuracy and robustness, and that the binary segmentation images and the color segmentation images of the grape diseases could be used for subsequent image feature extraction.

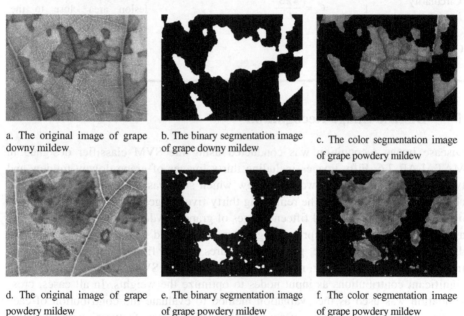

a. The original image of grape downy mildew

b. The binary segmentation image of grape downy mildew

c. The color segmentation image of grape powdery mildew

d. The original image of grape powdery mildew

e. The binary segmentation image of grape powdery mildew

f. The color segmentation image of grape powdery mildew

Fig. 1. Results of image segmentation of grape downy mildew and grape powdery mildew

3   Disease Image Feature Extraction

Fifty features including four shape features (Table 1), twenty-one color features (Table 2) and twenty-five texture features (Table 3), were extracted from the segmented images of the diseases. These features were regarded as candidate features for subsequent classification and recognition of grape diseases. Among these features, color features and texture features were based on RGB color model and HSV color model.

Table 1. Four candidate shape features and their corresponding calculation formulas

Features	Number of measurements	Calculation formulas	Comments
Area (S)	1	$$S = \sum_{x=0, y=0}^{N} f(x, y)$$ in which, N is lesion area and $f(x,y)$ is unit coordinate of lesion area.	S refers to the total number of pixels contained in the lesion areas in the segmented image.
Perimeter (L)	1	$$L = \sum_{i=1}^{N} \Delta l_i$$ in which, N is lesion area, and Δl_i is unit coordinate at the edge of the contour of the lesion area.	L refers to the total number of pixels at the edge of the contour of the lesion areas in the segmented image.
Circularity (C)	1	$$C = \frac{4\pi S}{L^2}$$	C describing the extent of lesion area close to the circle is between 0 and 1.
Complexity (E)	1	$$E = \frac{L^2}{S}$$	E describing the complexity and dispersion degree of lesion area is greater than 1.

4   Disease Image Recognition

Disease image recognition was conducted using the SVM classifier designed in MATALAB 7.6. Fifty images including thirty images of grape downy mildew and twenty images of grape powdery mildew which size was 800×600 were randomly chosen as the training set. The remaining thirty-five images including twenty images of grape downy mildew and fifteen images of grape powdery mildew were regarded as the testing set. After preprocessing, segmentation and feature extraction of each disease image, each feature, groups of features and all fifty features were used as inputs to the SVM classifier, respectively. And then the SVM used the features with significant contributions as input nodes to optimize the weights. In all cases, cross validation was used as the evaluation method to evaluate the contribution of each feature to the recognition effect of the SVM. The features with negative contributions to the recognition effect were removed. Finally, the optimal combination of the features was selected to achieve the image recognition of grape downy mildew and grape powdery mildew. Based on the optimal combination of the features, the SVMs with the four basic kernels, i.e. linear, polynomial, radial basis function (RBF) and sigmoid, were used to recognize the disease images with fifty images as the training set and thirty-five images as the testing set, in order to determine which kernel function was the best suitable for image recognition of grape diseases.

Table 2. Twenty-one candidate color features and their corresponding calculation formulas

Features	Number of measurements	Calculation formulas	Comments
Mean of gray values of R/G/B component	3	$$\mu = \frac{1}{G}\sum_{j=1}^{G} f_j p(f_j)$$ in which, G is the total number of pixels contained in the diseased region, f_j is an arbitrary coordinate in the diseased region, and $p(f_j)$ is color value of the point at f_j.	This feature is the mean of color values in the diseased region in color segmentation image.
Variance of gray values of R/G/B component	3	$$\sigma^2 = \frac{1}{G}\sum_{j=1}^{G} (f_j - \mu)^2 p(f_j)$$ in which, G, f_j and $p(f_j)$ are the same as above.	This feature is the square difference of color values in the diseased region in color segmentation image.
Skewness of gray values of R/G/B component	3	$$\varepsilon^3 = \frac{1}{G}\sum_{j=1}^{G} (f_j - \mu)^3 p(f_j)$$ in which, G, f_j and $p(f_j)$ are the same as above.	This feature is the cubic difference of color values in the diseased region in color segmentation image.
Color ratio in RGB color model: r, g, b	3	$$r = R/(R+G+B)$$ $$g = G/(R+G+B)$$ $$b = B/(R+G+B)$$	
Mean of gray values of H/S/V component	3	$$\mu = \frac{1}{G}\sum_{j=1}^{G} f_j p(f_j)$$ in which, G, f_j and $p(f_j)$ are the same as above.	
Variance of gray values of H/S/V component	3	$$\sigma^2 = \frac{1}{G}\sum_{j=1}^{G} (f_j - \mu)^2 p(f_j)$$ in which, G, f_j and $p(f_j)$ are the same as above.	
Skewness of gray values of H/S/V component	3	$$\varepsilon^3 = \frac{1}{G}\sum_{j=1}^{G} (f_j - \mu)^3 p(f_j)$$ in which, G, f_j and $p(f_j)$ are the same as above.	

Table 3. Twenty-five candidate texture features and their corresponding calculation formulas

Features	Number of measurements	Calculation formulas	Comments
Contrast in RGB color model	3	$f_1 = \sum_{n=0}^{P-1} n^2 \left\{ \sum_{i=0}^{P-1} \sum_{j=0}^{P-1} p(i,j) \right\}$, $n = \|i-j\|$ in which, P is the total number of pixels contained in the diseased region, (i,j) is an arbitrary coordinate in the diseased region, and $p(i,j)$ is color value of the point at (i,j).	Contrast is used to measure the clarity of texture.
Correlation in RGB color model	3	$f_2 = \sum_{i=0}^{P-1} \sum_{j=0}^{P-1} (i,j)^2 \, p(i,j)$ in which, P, (i,j) and $p(i,j)$ are the same as above.	Correlation is used to measure the degree of similarity of the elements of gray-level co-occurrence matrix (GLCM) at the row direction or the column direction.
Energy in RGB color model	3	$f_3 = \sum_{i=0}^{P-1} \sum_{j=0}^{P-1} p^2(i,j)$ in which, P, (i,j) and $p(i,j)$ are the same as above.	Energy is used to measure the distribution uniformity of image gray.
Homogeneity in RGB color model	3	$f_4 = \dfrac{\sum_{i=0}^{P-1} \sum_{j=0}^{P-1} p(i,j)}{1+(i-j)^2}$ in which, P, (i,j) and $p(i,j)$ are the same as above.	Homogeneity is used to measure the texture consistency between each pixel in the lesion area.
Contrast in HSV color model	3	$f_1 = \sum_{n=0}^{P-1} n^2 \left\{ \sum_{i=0}^{P-1} \sum_{j=0}^{P-1} p(i,j) \right\}$, $n = \|i-j\|$	
Correlation in HSV color model	3	$f_2 = \sum_{i=0}^{P-1} \sum_{j=0}^{P-1} (i,j)^2 \, p(i,j)$	
Energy in HSV color model	3	$f_3 = \sum_{i=0}^{P-1} \sum_{j=0}^{P-1} p^2(i,j)$	
Homogeneity in HSV color model	3	$f_4 = \dfrac{\sum_{i=0}^{P-1} \sum_{j=0}^{P-1} p(i,j)}{1+(i-j)^2}$	
4×4 binary fractal dimension (D)	1	$D = \lim_{r=0} \dfrac{\ln N_r(I)}{\ln r}$ in which, I is the total number of pixels contained in the diseased region, r is an arbitrary pixel in the diseased region, and N_r is box's size.	D is used to measure the fractal characteristics. Box's size is 4×4.

5   Results and Analysis

5.1   Optimization Results of the Features and Analysis

Based on the SVM classifier with the default RBF as kernel function in MATALAB 7.6, optimization of the features and image recognition of grape downy mildew and grape powdery mildew were conducted using the method described above. The results were as shown in Table 4. While each feature was used as input to SVM classifier, the obtained recognition rate was regarded as individual recognition rate. While group of features was used as inputs to SVM classifier, the obtained recognition rate was regarded as group recognition rate. While all fifty features were used as inputs to SVM classifier, the obtained recognition rate was regarded as total recognition rate. And while the optimal combination of the features was used as inputs to SVM classifier, the obtained recognition rate was regarded as best recognition rate.

The results indicated that every individual recognition rate was not exactly the same and that group recognition rate was different with each other. In the groups of color features, recognition effect of the SVM with the first-order moments of color or the second-order moments of color as inputs was better than that with the third-order moments of color as inputs. In the groups of texture features, recognition effect of the SVM with parameters of gray-level co-occurrence matrix (GLCM) in HSV color model as inputs was better than that with parameters of GLCM in RGB color model as inputs.

The results showed that there were eight features with no contributions to the recognition effect, eleven features with negative contributions to the recognition effect and thirty-one features with positive contributions to the recognition effect. Using these thirty-one features as inputs to SVM classifier, the best recognition effect was obtained. Based on these thirty-one features, optimal parameters were obtained after training using SVM classifier, i.e. $c=128$ and $g=0.0625$. The best recognition rate for the fifty images in the training set was 100%, and the best recognition rate for the thirty-five images in the testing set was 91.43%.

5.2   Results of Image Recognition Based on the SVMs with Different Kernel and Analysis

Based on the SVMs with different kernel functions, the images of grape downy mildew and grape powdery mildew were recognized using the selected thirty-one features as inputs and the comparison of corresponding recognition effects was conducted. The results were as shown in Table 5. The results showed that, for grape downy mildew and grape powdery mildew, the SVM with linear kernel had the best recognition effect and the average recognition rate of the training set and the testing set was 95.83%. The average recognition rate using the SVM with RBF kernel was 95.42% and that using the SVM with sigmoid kernel was 94.17%. The average recognition rate using the SVM with polynomial kernel was only 54.17%. Therefore, the SVM with linear kernel was the most suitable method for image recognition of grape downy mildew and grape powdery mildew based on multiple feature parameters. Using the SVM with linear kernel, the recognition rates of these two kinds of grape diseases were both 100% for the training sets, and for the testing sets, the recognition rates of grape downy mildew and grape powdery mildew were 90% and 93.33%, respectively.

Table 4. Optimization results of candidate features for image recognition of grape downy mildew and grape powdery mildew

Group	Feature	Individual recognition rate/%	Group recognition rate/%	Total recognition rate/%	Cross validation
Shape	Area	60.00/57.14	80.00/82.86	100/85.71	+
	Perimeter	92.00/88.57			+
	Circularity	82.00/88.57			+
	Complexity	82.00/88.57			−
The first-order moments of color	Mean of gray values of R component	76.00/74.29	94.00/88.57		−
	Mean of gray values of G component	78.00/71.43			+
	Mean of gray values of B component	60.00/57.14			+
	Color ratio of R component	90.00/57.14			+
	Color ratio of G component	74.00/57.14			+
	Color ratio of B component	60.00/57.14			+
	Mean of gray values of H component	68.00/51.43			o
	Mean of gray values of S component	88.00/60.00			+
	Mean of gray values of V component	74.00/82.86			−
The second-order moments of color	Variance of gray values of R component	98.00/60.00	100/82.86		o
	Variance of gray values of G component	74.00/85.71			+
	Variance of gray values of B component	84.00/48.57			o
	Variance of gray values of H component	68.00/54.29			+
	Variance of gray values of S component	80.00/40.00			o
	Variance of gray values of V component	84.00/48.57			+
The third-order moments of color	Skewness of gray values of R component	74.00/77.14	88.00/80.00		−
	Skewness of gray values of G component	76.00/80.00			+
	Skewness of gray values of B component	76.00/82.86			+
	Skewness of gray values of H	66.00/51.43			+

Table 4. (*continued*)

Group	Feature	Individual recognition rate/%	Group recognition rate/%	Total recognition rate/%	Cross validation
	component				
	Skewness of gray values of S component	60.00/57.14			+
	Skewness of gray values of V component	88.00/40.00			+
Texture in RGB color model	Contrast of R component	68.00/80.00	78.00/74.29		o
	Correlation of R component	76.00/80.00			—
	Energy of R component	80.00/54.29			o
	Homogeneity of R component	74.00/77.14			o
	Contrast of G component	74.00/71.43			+
	Correlation of G component	74.00/80.00			—
	Energy of G component	72.00/51.43			+
	Homogeneity of G component	74.00/82.86			+
	Contrast of B component	70.00/60.00			—
	Correlation of B component	72.00/77.14			+
	Energy of B component	72.00/48.47			+
	Homogeneity of B component	60.00/57.14			+
Texture in HSV color model	Contrast of H component	78.00/82.86	92.00/85.71		+
	Correlation of H component	74.00/62.86			+
	Energy of H component	62.00/77.14			+
	Homogeneity of H component	74.00/85.71			—
	Contrast of S component	74.00/77.14			—
	Correlation of S component	72.00/28.57			+
	Energy of S component	68.00/80.00			—
	Homogeneity of S component	72.00/85.71			o
	Contrast of V component	68.00/80.00			+
	Correlation of V component	76.00/80.00			—
	Energy of V component	80.00/54.29			+
	Homogeneity of V component	74.00/77.14			+
Fractal dimension	Fractal dimension	60.00/57.14	60.00/57.14		+

Note: The feature with positive contribution to the recognition effect was recorded as "+". The feature with no contribution to the recognition effect was recorded as "o". And the feature with negative contribution to the recognition effect was recorded as "—".

6   Conclusions

In this study, the binary segmentation and the color segmentation of diseased regions from the color images of grape downy mildew and grape powdery mildew were implemented using K_means clustering algorithm. This method could segment the diseased regions from the color images of the diseases with good accuracy and robustness. Using the SVM classifier with linear kernel based on the thirty-one features selected from the fifty shape, color and texture features extracted from the images of grape downy mildew and grape powdery mildew, the best recognition rate for the training set including fifty disease images was 100% and the best recognition rate for the testing set including thirty-five disease images was 91.43%. The average recognition rate of the training set and the testing set was 95.83%. For these two kinds of grape diseases, the SVM classifier with linear kernel had the best and stable classification performance. This study provides an approach for rapid and accurate identification and diagnosis of grape downy mildew and grape powdery mildew under the greenhouse environment.

Table 5. Results of image recognition using the SVMs with different kernel functions

Kernel function	Disease	Sample size		Number of correct recognition		Recognition rate/%	
		Training set	Testing set	Training set	Testing set	Training set	Testing set
Linear	Grape downy mildew	30	20	30	18	100	90
function	Grape powdery mildew	20	15	20	14	100	93.33
Polynomial	Grape downy mildew	30	20	30	20	100	100
function	Grape powdery mildew	20	15	2	1	10	6.67
Radial basis	Grape downy mildew	30	20	30	19	100	95
function	Grape powdery mildew	20	15	20	13	100	86.67
Sigmoid	Grape downy mildew	30	20	30	19	100	95
function	Grape powdery mildew	20	15	19	13	95	86.67

7   Discussion

The symptoms are always different during the development of plant disease. And the symptoms on the upper and lower surfaces of a diseased leaf are not always the same. For example, the grape leaves infected with downy mildew shows chlorotic at the early stages, and the color changes of the lesions are not obvious, so it is difficult to carry out image processing. Without taking into account the symptoms at the early stages, this study only dealt with the images with typical symptoms on the upper surfaces of the diseased leaves.

Image acquisition is often influenced by many kinds of factors including ambient lighting conditions, the differences between samples collected, the differences between acquisition devices, etc. In recent years, the common low-resolution digital cameras and even cell phones are used to capture images of plant diseases during the research on image recognition of plant diseases [21]. The common digital cameras or cell phones that are more portable and widely used, are very important to promote practical application of image recognition technologies to the plant diseases.

The methods of plant disease image segmentation in many studies are based on gray differences. The method bases on K_means clustering algorithm used in this study had good accuracy and robustness, and it could be an effective method to segment plant disease images. However, this method demands high image quality and needs computer to run a long time. Therefore, it is important to control the impact of complex environmental factors in the process of collecting disease images, and it is better to compress the images in the same proportion without changing the image resolution in order to improve the running of computer programs.

The features of the lesions of different plant diseases are not the same. However, only one feature or no enough features were used in many studies on image recognition of plant diseases, and it is difficult to meet the needs of identification and diagnosis of different targets. It is necessary to utilize shape, color and texture features to image recognition of plant diseases. Fifty shape, color and texture features extracted from the images of grape downy mildew and grape powdery mildew were regarded as candidate features for image recognition in this study. Guan et al [22] extracted sixty-three parameters of shape, color and texture features from disease images for image recognition of rice diseases.

With the development of agricultural informatization, more and more agricultural technicians and farmers could get access to the internet and solve the problems in agricultural production using web-based expert systems. With the popularity of digital photography products, the acquisition of plant disease images is easier. Web-based systems for image recognition of plant diseases should be developed to meet the needs of the agricultural technicians and the farmers. When the users upload digital images of plant diseases to the systems, the names of plant diseases and related information could be provided for plant disease control.

Acknowledgments. The work was supported by National Key Technology R&D Program (2007BAD57B02).

References

1. Li, H.Y., Chen, Z.Y., Zhou, J.C., Zhang, J.X.: Occurrence and Damage of the Main Diseases of Grape in Greenhouse During Growth Period and Shelf Life (in Chinese). Modern Agricultural Sciences and Technology 20, 187–189, 191 (2010)
2. Sasaki, Y., Okamoto, T., Imou, K., Torii, T.: Automatic Diagnosis of Plant Disease-recognition Between Healthy and Diseased Leaf. Journal of the Japanese Society of Agricultural Machinery 61, 119–126 (1999)
3. Zhao, Y.X., Wang, K.R., Bai, Z.Y., Li, S.K., Xie, R.Z., Gao, S.J.: Research of Maize Leaf Disease Identifying System Based Image Recognition (in Chinese). Scientia Agricultura Sinica 40, 698–703 (2007)
4. Sanyala, P., Patel, S.C.: Pattern Recognition Method to Detect Two Diseases in Rice Plants. Imaging Science Journal 56, 319–325 (2008)
5. Cui, Y.L., Cheng, P.F., Dong, X.Z., Liu, Z.H., Wang, S.X.: Image Processing and Extracting Color Features of Greenhouse Diseased Leaf (in Chinese). Transactions of the CSAE 21(supp.), 32–35 (2005)
6. Tian, Y.W., Zhang, C.H., Li, C.H.: Study on Plant Disease Recognition Using Support Vector Machine and Chromaticity Moments (in Chinese). Transactions of the Chinese Society of Agricultural Machinery 35, 95–98 (2004)
7. Tian, Y.W., Niu, Y.: Applied Research of Support Vector Machine on Recognition of Cucumber Disease (in Chinese). Journal of Agricultural Mechanization Research 31, 36–39 (2009)

8. Cen, Z.X., Li, B.J., Shi, Y.X., Huang, H.Y., Liu, J., Liao, N.F., Feng, J.: Discrimination of Cucumber Anthracnose and Cucumber Brown Speck Based on Color Image Statistical Characteristics (in Chinese). Acta Horticulturae Sinica 34, 1425–1430 (2007)
9. Pydipati, R., Burks, T.F., Lee, W.S.: Identification of Citrus Disease Using Color Texture Features and Discriminant Analysis. Computers and Electronics in Agriculture 52, 49–59 (2006)
10. Pydipati, R., Burks, T.F., Lee, W.S.: Statistical and Neural Network Classifiers for Citrus Disease Detection Using Machine Vision. Transactions of the ASAE 48, 2007–2014 (2005)
11. Camargo, A., Smith, J.S.: Image Pattern Classification for the Identification of Disease Causing Agents in Plants. Computers and Electronics in Agriculture 66, 121–125 (2009)
12. Wang, N., Wang, K.R., Xie, R.Z., Lai, J.C., Ming, B., Li, S.K.: Maize Leaf Disease Identification Based on Fisher Discrimination Analysis. Scientia Agricultura Sinica 42, 3836–3842 (2009)
13. Vapnik, V.N.: The Nature of Statistical Learning Theory. Springer, New York (1995)
14. Song, K., Sun, X.Y., Ji, J.W.: Corn Leaf Disease Recognition Based on Support Vector Machine Method (in Chinese). Transactions of the CSAE 23, 155–157 (2007)
15. Ren, D., Yu, H.Y., Wang, J.H.: Research on Plant Disease Recognition Based on Linear Combination of the Kernel Function Support Vector Machine (in Chinese). Journal of Agricultural Mechanization Research 29, 41–43 (2007)
16. Zhang, J., Wang, S.X.: A Study on the Segmentation Method in Image Processing for Plant Disease of Greenhouse (in Chinese). Journal of Inner Mongolia Agricultural University 28, 19–22 (2007)
17. Mao, H.P., Zhang, Y.C., Hu, B.: Segmentation of Crop Disease Leaf Images Using Fuzzy C-means Clustering Algorithm (in Chinese). Transactions of the CSAE 24, 136–140 (2008)
18. Tian, Y.W., Li, C.H.: Color Image Segmentation Method Based on Statistical Pattern Recognition for Plant Disease Diagnose (in Chinese). Journal of Jilin University (Engineering and Technology Edition) 34, 291–293 (2003)
19. Selim, S.Z., Ismail, M.A.: K-means-type Algorithm: a Generalized Convergence Theorem and Characterization of Local Optimality. IEEE Transactions on Pattern Analysis and Machine Intelligence 6, 81–87 (1984)
20. Li, G.L., Ma, Z.H., Huang, C., Chi, Y.W., Wang, H.G.: Segmentation of Color Images of Grape Diseases Using K_means Clustering Algorithm. Transactions of the CSAE 26(supp.2), 32–37 (2010)
21. Li, Z.R., He, D.J.: Research on Identify Technologies of Apple's Disease Based on Mobile Photograph Image Analysis (in Chinese). Computer Engineering and Design 31, 3051–3053, 3095 (2010)
22. Guan, Z.X., Tang, J., Yang, B.J., Zhou, Y.F., Fan, D.Y., Yao, Q.: Study on Recognition Method of Rice Disease Based on Image (in Chinese). Chin. J. Rice Sci. 24, 497–502 (2010)

Monitoring Wheat Stripe Rust
Using Remote Sensing Technologies in China

Haiguang Wang[*], Jiebin Guo, and Zhanhong Ma[*]

Department of Plant Pathology, China Agricultural University, Beijing 100193, China
{wanghaiguang,mazh}@cau.edu.cn

Abstract. Many studies on remote sensing monitoring of plant diseases have been conducted. Remote sensing (RS) has played an important role in monitoring some kinds of plant diseases and making decisions for the management of the diseases. Progress on remote sensing monitoring of wheat stripe rust in China was summarized from four aspects including remote sensing monitoring stripe rust of single wheat leaves and monitoring this disease using ground, aerial and space remote sensing technologies. The phenomena of same object with different spectra and different objects with same spectrum, the lowest threshold of disease prevalence for remote sensing monitoring, the spectral information distilling technologies, and the methods to develop inversion models based on spectral information were also discussed. Moreover, the development trends of multi-pest remote sensing, space remote sensing and integrated utilization of RS, geographical information system (GIS) and global positioning system (GPS) in monitoring wheat stripe rust were prospected.

Keywords: Wheat stripe rust, remote sensing, monitoring.

1 Introduction

Remote sensing (RS) is to acquire spectral information or images of an object in a far distance by receiving electromagnetic waves that the object reflects or radiates using either recording or real-time sensing devices. Since the 1960s, remote sensing technologies have being developed quickly. In the 1980s, with the rise of hyperspectral remote sensing, more and narrower wavebands of electromagnetic waves could be used to acquire related information from certain object, and then the application areas of remote sensing technologies were broadened further [1]. Now remote sensing technologies have been widely applied in many disciplinary fields, such as geography, geology, meteorology, ecology, oceanography and agronomy.

When plant disease occurs, biochemical components and organization structure inside plant leaves would be induced to change. Accordingly, the changes of the spectral characteristics of the plants and remote sensing images would be caused, and would show some specificity, which provides a basis for remote sensing monitoring of plant diseases [2], [3]. Generally, either crop plant pests, fruit tree pests, forest

---

[*] Corresponding authors.

D. Li and Y. Chen (Eds.): CCTA 2011, Part III, IFIP AICT 370, pp. 163–175, 2012.

pests or grassland pests that could cause discoloration or deformation of the leaves, or produce residues on the leaf surfaces, could be monitored using remote sensing technologies [4]. There have been many reports about remote sensing monitoring of plant diseases in the world [5], [6], [7], [8], [9], [10], [11], [12], [13], [14]. The reports about remote sensing monitoring of wheat stripe rust caused by *Puccinia striiformis* f. sp. *tritici*, were almost published by Chinese researchers.

In China, stripe rust is the most important disease of wheat [15]. The four most destructive epidemics of this disease occurred in 1950, 1964, 1990 and 2002, which caused yield losses up to 6.0, 3.2, 1.8 and 1.3 million metric tons, respectively [15], [16]. Prevention and control of the disease is very important for wheat production and even for food security in China. In order to control wheat stripe rust effectively, it is necessary to carry out disease monitoring to obtain the information on the incidence of the disease timely and accurately. Traditionally, monitoring of this disease in China mainly relies on field surveys by human power, which is time-consuming and energy-consuming. The subjectivity of the monitoring results and a certain hysteretic nature of the acquired information seriously affect the accuracy of disease forecast. The development of remote sensing technologies could make quickly, conveniently, economically and accurately real-time monitoring wheat stripe rust come true. In recent years, a lot of funds have been invested in the studies on remote sensing technologies for monitoring wheat stripe rust in China and a lot of results have been obtained. In this paper, the progress on remote sensing monitoring of wheat stripe rust in China was reviewed from four aspects, namely, remote sensing monitoring stripe rust of single wheat leaves and ground, aerial and space remote sensing monitoring of wheat stripe rust. Furthermore, some problems in the studies were discussed and the development trends of remote sensing monitoring wheat stripe rust were prospected.

2   Monitoring Single Wheat Leaves Infected by Stripe Rust Using Remote Sensing Technologies

The studies on monitoring single wheat leaves infected by stripe rust using remote sensing technologies could provide theoretical basis for remote sensing monitoring the prevalence of this disease. The results obtained by Huang et al [17] indicated that the wavebands in 446-725 nm as well as 1380-1600 nm were sensitive to the severity level of wheat stripe rust. In their study, using the established mathematical models (shown in Table 1) with designed spectral angle index (*SAI*), designed absorption area index (*AAI*), absorption depth and absorption area as independent variable, respectively, the disease severity level of winter wheat leaf could be inversed with high accuracy. It has been found that spectral reflectance of diseased areas of wheat leaves was positively correlated with disease severity when the wavelength was in 350-1600 nm [18]. On the wave band from 670 nm to 690 nm where reflectance rate was correlated with disease severity significantly, regression model (*P*<0.0001) (shown in Table 1) elucidating the relationship between wavelength and disease severity was established [18]. Wang et al [19] applied support vector machine (SVM) to process hyperspectral data obtained from 88 leaves including healthy leaves and infected leaves over a range of disease severity levels. The identification model was built based on 44 proof-read samples to estimate 44 proof-test samples and the identification accuracy was totally 97%. The results indicated that SVM could be used in the classification and identification of severity of wheat stripe rust based on obtained spectral data.

Table 1. Remote sensing inversion models of disease severity (S) of wheat leaves infected by *Puccinia striiformis* f. sp. *Tritici*

Selected wave band	Inversion model	Independent variable
666 nm, 758 nm	$S=1/tg\theta \times SAI$	$SAI = 7.289 \times R_{666nm} - R_{758nm}$, in which R_{666nm} and R_{758nm} mean the reflectance rates on 666 nm and 758 nm, respectively.
540-740 nm	$S= -3.494\ Depth + 2.827$	$Depth$ means absorption depth in 540-740 nm.
540-740 nm	$S= -0.014\ Area + 1.532$	$Area$ means absorption area in 540-740 nm.
540-740 nm	$S= 2.459 AAI - 0.019$	AAI means absorption area index.
685 nm, 690 nm	$S= -0.5768 + 0.7953 R_{685nm} - 0.6036 R_{690nm}$	R_{685nm} and R_{690nm} mean the reflectance rates on 685 nm and 690 nm, respectively.

Note: The first four models were established by Huang et al [17] and the last one was established by An et al [18].

3   Monitoring Wheat Stripe Rust Using Ground Remote Sensing Technologies

There have been many studies on monitoring wheat stripe rust using ground remote sensing technologies. They mainly focused on canopy spectral properties, inversion of disease index (*DI*), changes and inversion of biochemical parameters of wheat infected by stripe rust. Some spectral indexes (shown in Table 2) were used to analyze spectral properties, and some inversion models of wheat stripe rust were built based on spectral information (shown in Table 3). The inversion effects of the models were relatively insensitive to wheat varieties [21], [22]. Therefore, these models could be applied to monitor stripe rust on different wheat varieties. The studies clarified the mechanism of remote sensing monitoring of wheat stripe rust and provided the theoretical basis for monitoring this disease by using aerial and space remote sensing technologies.

The relationship between canopy reflectance and *DI* of wheat infected by stripe rust has been analyzed. Different results were obtained in different studies. Huang et al [20] found that 630-687 nm, 740-890 nm and 976-1350 nm were sensitive bands to *DI* of winter wheat stripe rust and the red edge position of diseased wheat shifted to the blue. The study conducted by Cai et al [26] showed that 769-938 nm was the sensitive band to *DI*. It has been found that *DI* of wheat stripe rust was highly correlated with the first derivative data of the canopy reflectance of winter wheat in the regions of 432-582 nm, 637-701 nm and 715-765 nm [22], [23]. The results obtained by Li et al [24] and Jiang et al [25] showed that the first derivative values of winter wheat infected by stripe rust increased at the green edge (500-560 nm), while decreased at the red edge (680-760 nm) with *DI* increasing. The ratio of the sum of derivative within the red region (*SDr*) and that within the green region (*SDg*) and the ratio of *SDr'* and *SDg'* were both highly correlated with *DI* of wheat stripe rust, and could be used to identify the disease effectively twelve days before symptoms appearing [24], [25]. The study conducted by Guo et al [21] indicated that *DI* has positive correlation with canopy reflectance in visible region and that it has significant negative correlation in the near infrared region and has stable negative correlation with the first derivative in the region of 700-760 nm. Zhang et al [27] found that with *DI* increasing, canopy reflectance in 600-703 nm decreased distinctively and that in 770-930 nm increased distinctively. Wang et al [30] used partial least square (PLS) to build a regression model for disease severity inversion based on canopy reflectance, and analysis results of regression coefficients of PLS showed that the first derivatives on the two sides of the chlorophyll absorption valley (505-550 nm, 640-670 nm, 680-700 nm) were very important for the assessment of disease severity.

Table 2. Some spectral indexes used in the studies on monitoring wheat stripe rust using ground remote sensing technologies

Spectral index	Definition	References
NDVI	Normalized differential vegetation index	[20], [21]
RVI	Ratio vegetation index	[20], [21]
TVI	Transformed vegetation index	[20]
SDb	Sum of first derivative within blue region	[21], [22], [23]
SDg	Sum of first derivative within green region	[21], [22], [23], [24]
SDr	Sum of first derivative within red region	[22], [21], [23], [24]
SDr'	Sum of first derivative within red peak region	[22], [25]
Dx	First derivative value of reflectance in x nm	[22], [23]
Dr	The maximum of first derivative in red region	[22, 23]
Dg	The maximum of first derivative in green region	[22]
SDg'	Sum of first derivative within green peak region	[22, 25]
Rx	Reflectance in x nm	[21], [26], 27]
DSr	Thinness of the first derivative of red edge spectra	[28]
Ar	Asymmetry of the first derivative of red edge spectra	[28]
REP	Red edge position	[29]
YEP	Yellow edge position	[29]

Wang et al [28] put forward two new red-edge indexes (*DSr* and *Ar*) to predict wheat stripe rust. *DSr*, an index describing thinness of the first derivative of red edge spectra (Dred) of winter wheat infected by stripe rust, was defined as the ratio of maximum value of Dred and sum of Dred. Ar, an index describing asymmetry of Dred, was defined as $(S_2-S_1)/(S_2+S_1)$, where S_1 and S_2 were the sums of Dred in 680-700 nm and 701-775 nm, respectively. Jiang et al [29] analyzed the relationship between *DI* and two spectral features, namely, the red edge position (*REP*) and yellow edge position (*YEP*) of the first derivative values. The results showed that with disease severity increasing, *REP* gradually shifted to the short-wave band, and the *YEP* gradually shifted to the long-wave band, however, the variable (*REP-YEP*) quickly became smaller. The model built using *REP-YEP* as independent variable has the best estimation precision for *DI* than that built using *REP* or *YEP*.

Table 3. Some inversion models of wheat stripe rust for monitoring wheat stripe rust using ground remote sensing technologies

Inversion model	References	Inversion model	References
$DI=-143.11NDVI+165.41$	[20]	$DI=752.477R_{690}-167.356R_{850}+66.966$	[21]
$DI=-7.288RVI+111.74$	[20]	$DI=696.934R_{690}-233.908R_{850}+108.023$	[21]
$DI=-304.16TVI+398.17$	[20]	$DI=148.657R_{690}-60.547R_{850}+26.385$	[21]
$DI=-4.6208RVI+55.496$	[21]	$DI=530.009R_{690}-131.489R_{850}+55.063$	[21]
$DI=-3.4151RVI+32.161$	[21]	$DI=-42.341R_{690}-234.475R_{850}+111.813$	[21]
$DI=-2.2092RVI+29.582$	[21]	$DI=46.637R_{690}-85.05R_{850}+46.745$	[21]
$DI=113.142-143.01Dr$	[23]	$DI=116.739-11.924\times(D_{731}/D_{525})$	[22]
$DI=126.16-3.648SDr$	[23]	$DI=118.523-12.234\times(Dr/Dg)$	[22]
$DI=-10.035+86.602SDb$	[23]	$DI=117.507-11.012\times(SDr'/SDg')$	[22]
$DI=-229.03SDr+106.11$	[21]	$DI=115.557-7.576\times(SDr/SDg)$	[22], [23]
$DI=-275.87SDr+127.4$	[21]	$DI=153.787\times\exp[-0.034\times(SDr/SDb)]$	[22], [23]
$DI=-79.056SDr+33.574$	[21]	$DI=549.302\times\exp[-0.627\times(SDg/SDb)]$	[22], [23]
$DI=-149.09SDr+76.168$	[21]	$DI=-489.43+1806.08\times[(SDr-SDg)/(SDr+SDg)]-1421.3\times[(SDr-SDg)/(SDr+SDg)]^2$	[22], [23]
$DI=-236.63SDr+80.265$	[21]	$DI=-533.34+2801.06\times[(SDr-SDb)/(SDr+SDb)]^2-2276.0\times[(SDr-SDb)/(SDr+SDb)]^3$	[22], [23]
$DI=-92.751SDr+41.246$	[21]	$DI=152.456-173.95\times[(SDg-SDb)/(SDg+SDb)]$	[22], [23]
$DI=-273.71NDVI+251.1$	[21]	$DI=137.682-26.602\times(D_{725}/D_{702})$	[23]
$DI=-454.68NDVI+403.7$	[21]	$DI=-11.805\times(SDr'/SDg')+117.8$	[25]
$DI=-113.99NDVI+96.975$	[21]	$DI=-2.5173R_{930nm}+1.2217$	[26]
$DI=-253.68NDVI+216.35$	[21]	$DI=13.03R_{650nm}-0.67R_{850nm}+10.22$	[27]
$DI=-118.24NDVI+96.078$	[21]	$DI=48.63R_{650nm}-2.41R_{850nm}-41.51$	[27]
$DI=-97.558NDVI+85.853$	[21]	$DI=24.42R_{650nm}-5.10R_{850nm}+67.77$	[27]
$DI=-6.697RVI+93.292$	[21]	$DI=-111.3DSr^2+314.1DSr-134.1$	[28]
$DI=-6.937RVI+101.96$	[21]	$DI=-567.1Ar^2+504.9Ar-36.5$	[28]
$DI=-2.9087RVI+32.279$	[21]	$DI=-2419.2+37.216\times(REP-YEP)-0.1383\times(REP-YEP)^2$	[29]

The studies on monitoring the changes of biochemical components of wheat infected by stripe rust were also conducted by using ground remote sensing technologies. The canopy reflectance spectral data of winter wheat at the wavelength of 550-1160 nm had good correlation with DI of stripe rust and some physiological parameters such as chlorophyll content and water content, and chlorophyll content and water content can be used as two important indicators in remote sensing monitoring of the disease [31]. Chlorophyll fluorescence sensing based on Fraunhofer lines could be used to detect wheat stripe rust [32]. The model established by Jiang et al [33] could be used to estimate the contents of chlorophyll a, chlorophyll b and carotenoid in the diseased wheat with good accuracy. The regression model with satisfactory accuracy was established between the content of wheat chlorophyll and the hyperspectral data of wheat infected by stripe rust [34]. The inversion model with the first derivative index $(D_{750}-D_{550})/(D_{750}+D_{550})$ as independent variable could be used to estimate canopy chlorophyll densities (CCDs) [35]. Jiang et al [36] found that the leaf total nitrogen (LTN) of the wheat infected by stripe rust gradually decreased with disease aggravating, and there was high correlation between LTN and first derivative data of canopy reflectance in 430-518 nm, 534-608 nm, 660-762 nm and 783-893 nm, and that the model established with the ratio of sum of the first derivative within red edge and sum of the first derivative within blue edge (*SDr/SDb*) had satisfactory accuracy. The canopy spectral reflectance of winter wheat under stripe rust stress gradually decreased in the near-infrared region (900-1300 nm) with the reduction of relative water contents, while that gradually increased in the short-wave-infrared region (1300-2500 nm) [37].

4   Monitoring Wheat Stripe Rust Using Aerial Remote Sensing Technologies

The studies focusing on aerial remote sensing monitoring of wheat stripe rust have been done in recent years. A study was done to obtain the reflectance data of the wheat infected by stripe rust in field at a fire-balloon flight and near ground, respectively [38]. The results showed that the reflectance data from the fire-balloon were dramatically higher than that from near ground in the visible region, while the sum of first derivatives of the reflectance data from the fire-balloon was lower than that from near ground in 537-582 nm and 700-1000 nm. This study provided some certain basis for further studies on monitoring wheat stripe rust by using aerial remote sensing technologies. Liu et al [39] analyzed the multi-temporal hyperspectral airborne image data acquired from winter booting stage to milking stage using pushbroom hyperspectral imager (PHI) on Yun-5 plane. The results showed that compared with normal wheat, the image spectral reflectance of diseased wheat was higher in 560-670 nm bands, lower in near infrared bands and the absorption depth of chlorophyll well in red band and the height of chlorophyll peak in green band were relatively reduced. The model built to inverse *DI* was fitted well to the practical disease index and occurrence ranges. Yang and Guo [40] analyzed the multi-temporal PHI airborne wheat image data, and the information of wheat stripe rust was recognized in PHI images in terms of wheat spectral features and spectral angle mapping (SAM) technique. The analyses of the PHI images conducted by Luo et al [41] showed that red bands (620-718 nm) and near infrared bands (770-805 nm) were the sensitive bands to wheat stripe rust. With the inversion model established using the mean reflectance of red bands and near infrared bands as independent variables and the observed disease indexes as dependent variable, wheat stripe rust was monitored successfully based on PHI images.

5   Monitoring Wheat Stripe Rust Using Space Remote Sensing Technologies

Fruitful results have been obtained in monitoring forest pests and crop insect pests by using space remote sensing technologies in the world [42], [43]. However, the studies on monitoring crop diseases using space remote sensing technologies are less, especially for wheat stripe rust. Huang [44] reported that the sensitive spectral bands to *DI* were similar for three wheat varieties with different susceptibility including Jing 411, 98-100 and Jingdong 8, and that the bands included TM2 (520-600 nm), TM3 (630-690 nm) and TM4 (760-900 nm) of Landsat/TM. Thus, it is possible to monitor wheat stripe rust using the Landsat/TM remote sensed data, and meanwhile the wheat variety parameter could be neglected. Preliminary studies on remote sensing monitoring of wheat stripe rust based on SPOT5 image have been conducted by the researchers from China Agricultural University [45], [46]. They found that SPOT satellite remote sensing spectral information could be used to monitor wheat stripe rust, and the third band of SPOT image or normalized difference vegetation index (*NDVI*) and *RVI* calculated using the reflectance values extracted from SPOT image were useful for further studies. Zhang et al [47] used three PHI images that included different severity levels of stripe rust as a medium to establish the spectral knowledge base of relationships between *DI* and the simulated reflectance of TM bands by using the empirical inversion model of *DI* and the relative spectral response (RSR) function of TM-5 sensor. And then Mahalanobis distance or SAM was used to monitor and identify winter wheat stripe rust. The results showed that the infected pixels could be identified accurately from the simulated TM pixels in pustulation and milk stages of winter wheat. Liu et al [48] used multi-temporal remote sensed data to monitor and evaluate the diseases including stripe rust and powdery mildew and the yield of winter wheat. Four Landsat TM images used to analyze were acquired at erecting stage, booting stage, anthesis stage and grain filling stage. The results showed that both the spectral reflectance of diseased wheat at visible and short infrared regions and the red edge position decreased, and that the spectral reflectance at near-infrared region increased. An early yield prediction model developed using the Landsat TM images acquired at the erecting and booting stages was used to evaluate wheat yield loss.

6   Problems in the Studies on Remote Sensing Monitoring of Wheat Stripe Rust

6.1   The Phenomena of Same Object with Different Spectra and Different Objects with Same Spectrum

The acquisition of remote sensing spectral data of wheat stripe rust is affected by various conditions. The stability of the spectrum of the disease is often influenced by the device(s), wheat density in the field, soil types, meteorological conditions and other pests. Therefore, the phenomena of same object with different spectra and different objects with same spectrum are caused easily. That is a difficult problem for remote sensing monitoring. To solve this problem, it is important to obtain the specific spectrum or the diagnostic spectrum via basic studies on spectral properties of the wheat infected by stripe rust under different conditions.

6.2   The Lowest Threshold of Disease Prevalence for Remote Sensing Monitoring

It is an important objective of remote sensing monitoring of wheat stripe rust to realize early monitoring of the disease and even monitoring the disease under its economic injury level or in incubation period. Reflectance spectra of the diseased wheat in incubation period showed different with that of normal wheat and could be used to identify wheat stripe rust [24], [26]. However, could the disease be found out using remote sensing technologies when a small quantity of wheat leaves infected by stripe rust in the field? Is there the lowest threshold of disease prevalence for remote sensing monitoring of wheat stripe rust? If yes and it is determined, it would be very useful for guiding the early control of wheat stripe rust by using the remote sensing information.

6.3   The Spectral Information Distilling Technologies

The distilling of spectral property information is the premise of application of spectral data of wheat stripe rust and *DI* inversion. The common methods to distil spectral property information include the methods based on K-L transform, separability criterion, nonlinear criteria and spectral recomposition [49]. For information distilling from remote sensing images, the technologies such as image enhancement and image classification seem a bit rough and poor because of the affects of sun elevation angle, meteorological conditions and seasonal variation on the remote sensing images at different time. The image processing methods such as Gramm-Schmidt transformation, principal component analysis (PCA), tasseled cap transformation (TCT), spectral mixture analysis and change vector analysis (CVA), and remote sensing image classification methods such as maximum likelihood classification, artificial neural network (ANN) and SVM, could be used to improve information distilling from remote sensing images.

6.4   The Methods to Build Inversion Models Based on Spectral Information

The ultimate goal of remote sensing is the inversion and the use of inversion results for decision-making. For the inversion of wheat stripe rust using remote sensing technologies, it is the key to determine the relationship between disease prevalence and the changes of original spectra, vegetation indexes, derivative spectra and so on, and then to determine sensitive bands and sensitive period for monitoring the disease. In the studies on remote sensing monitoring, generally, spectral reflectance in sensitive bands or the model parameters obtained from its differential transformation are used to build the inversion models of wheat stripe rust by using the methods such as linear regression and nonlinear regression. These methods always have the shortcomings such as the deficiency of sample size and the instability of the errors in application and extension. In order to overcome these shortcomings, it is better to use the methods such as nearest neighbor algorithm, ANN and SVM, to establish the inversion models with minor error, wide application scope and high stability.

7   Future Prospects of Remote Sensing Monitoring of Wheat Stripe Rust

7.1   The Studies on Remote Sensing Monitoring of Multiple Pests of Wheat

There are many kinds of wheat pests, and there are more than eighty wheat diseases in China, of which there are more than twenty diseases causing severe losses [50]. Some different wheat pests cause similar symptoms that make it difficult to distinguish between the pests. Moreover, there are always obvious differences between the symptoms caused by the same wheat pest in different wheat growth stages. So it is very important to carry out the studies on remote sensing identification of multiple pests and the pests in multiple growth stages of wheat. There is still much work to be done in this area. The damages caused by wheat powdery mildew, wheat stripe rust and aphid have been successfully identified by using stepwise discriminate analysis and hierarchical clustering based on the canopy reflectance data [51].

7.2   Further Studies on Monitoring Wheat Stripe Rust by Using Space Remote Sensing Technologies

Now space remote sensing has been widely used in various fields. High resolution remote sensing satellites such as IKNOS, QuickBird, SPOT-5 and ORBVIEW-3, promoted the development of space remote sensing. In China, remote sensing monitoring of many kinds of great natural disasters such as flood disasters, drought disasters, fire disasters of forests and grasslands, sandstorms and red tides, is used to keep abreast of emergency disaster information and make timely decisions. The space remote sensing technologies used in other areas are worth making use for reference in development and exploration of space remote sensing of wheat stripe rust. If the studies on multi-platform, large-scale, multi temporal and multi-band remote sensing are conducted successfully and relationship models between different platforms are built, remote sensing monitoring of wheat stripe rust will come true finally.

7.3   The Integrated Application of 3S Technology in Remote Sensing Monitoring of Wheat Stripe Rust

The term, 3S technology, refers to RS, geographical information system (GIS) and global positioning system (GPS). GIS is a computer decision support system to display, manage and analyze geographic spatial data and to show the processing results in the means of maps, graphics or data. GIS has been widely used in military, agriculture, environmental protection, traffic and transportation, urban planning, and so on. GIS has been well applied in the analysis of spatial dynamics of plant pathogen population, monitoring, forecasting and risk analysis of plant diseases [52]. GPS could be used to realize the localization in the investigations of plant diseases. Thus, the investigations of some plant disease in fixed locations in many consecutive years could be realized. It is very useful for the studies on epidemic dynamics of plant disease during many years and more precise management of plant disease. The integration of RS, GIS and GPS could be implemented in real-time monitoring of plant disease [53], [54], [55], [56]. The localization using GPS is absolutely necessary for the realization of aerial and space remote sensing monitoring of wheat stripe rust. The essential information could be distilled from the remote sensing images more precisely via the localization of target objects. A monitoring and warning information system for remote sensing of wheat stripe rust could be established via the integrated application of 3S technology in future.

Acknowledgments. This work was supported by National Natural Science Foundation of China (Grant No.: 30671341, 31071642).

References

1. Pu, R.L., Gong, P.: Hyperspectral Remote Sensing and Its Applications (in Chinese). Higher Education Press, Beijing (2000)
2. Liu, S.B., Liu, Y.: Preliminary Feasibility Exploration of Prediction of Crop Pests Using Remote Sensing Technologies (in Chinese). Heilongjiang Agricultural Science 6, 31–32 (1996)
3. Chen, P.C., Zhang, J.H., Lei, Y.H., Li, M.M.: Research Progress on Hyperspectral Remote Sensing in Monitoring Crop Diseases and Insect Pests (in Chinese). Chinese Agricultural Science Bulletin 22, 388–391 (2006)
4. Li, D.K.: Application of Remote Sensing Technologies in Investigation of Plant Pests (in Chinese). Journal of Shaanxi Meteorology 3, 27–30 (1998)
5. Greaves, D.A., Hooper, A.J., Walpole, B.J.: Identification of Barley Yellow Dwarf Virus and Cereal Aphid Infestation in Winter Wheat by Aerial Photography. Plant Pathology 32, 159–172 (1983)
6. Malthus, T.J., Maderia, A.C.: High Resolution Spectroradiometry: Spectral Reflectance of Field Bean Leaves Infected by *Botrytis fabae*. Remote Sensing of Environment 45, 107–116 (1993)
7. Adams, M.L., Philpot, W.D., Norvell, W.A.: Yellowness Index: an Application of Spectral Second Derivatives to Estimate Chlorosis of Leaves in Stressed Vegetation. International Journal of Remote Sensing 20, 3663–3675 (1999)
8. Steddom, K., Heidel, G., Jones, D., Rush, C.M.: Remote Detection of Rhizomania in Sugar Beets. Phytopathology 93, 720–726 (2003)
9. Nutter Jr., F.W., Guan, J., Gotlieb, A.R., Rhodes, L.H., Grau, C.R., Sulc, R.M.: Quantifying Alfalfa Yield Losses Caused by Foliar Diseases in Iowa, Ohio, Wisconsin, and Vermont. Plant Disease 86, 269–277 (2002)
10. Guan, J., Nutter Jr., F.W.: Quantifying the Intrarater Repeatability and Interrater Reliability of Visual and Remote-sensing Disease-assessment Methods in the Alfalfa Foliar Pathosystem. Canadian Journal of Plant Pathology 25, 143–149 (2003)
11. Nakane, K., Kimura, Y.: Assessment of Pine Forest Damage by Blight Based on Landsat TM Data and Correlation with Environmental Factors. Ecological Research 7, 9–18 (1992)
12. Wu, S.W., Wang, R.C., Chen, X.B., Shen, Z.Q., Shi, Z.: Effects of Rice Leaf Blast on Spectrum Reflectance of Rice (in Chinese). Journal of Shanghai Jiaotong University (Agricultural Science) 20, 73–76, 84 (2002)
13. Liu, Q.W., Wu, H.G., Shi, J., Jiang, L.Y., Ye, Q.W.: A Remote Sensing Monitoring System for the Damage Caused by Forest Insects and Diseases Using TM Images (in Chinese). Remote Sensing Information 2, 46–49, 97 (2007)
14. Qiao, H.B., Jian, G.L., Zou, Y.F., Cheng, D.F.: Influence of *Fusarium* Wilt to Different Resistance Cultivars on Spectrum of Cotton (in Chinese). Cotton Science 19, 155–158 (2007)
15. Li, Z.Q., Zeng, S.M.: Wheat Rust in China (in Chinese). China Agriculture Press, Beijing (2002)
16. Wan, A., Zhao, Z., Chen, X., He, Z., Jin, S., Jia, Q., Yao, G., Yang, J., Wang, B., Li, G., Bi, Y., Yuan, Z.: Wheat Stripe Rust Epidemic and Virulence of *Puccinia striiformis* f. sp.*tritici* in China in 2002. Plant Disease 88, 896–904 (2004)

17. Huang, M.Y., Huang, W.J., Liu, L.Y., Huang, Y.D., Wang, J.H., Zhao, C.J., Wan, A.M.: Spectral Reflectance Feature of Winter Wheat Single Leaf Infected with Stripe Rust and Severity Level Inversion (in Chinese). Transactions of the CSAE 20, 176–180 (2004)
18. An, H., Wang, H.G., Liu, R.Y., Cai, C.J., Ma, Z.H.: Preliminary Study on Spectral Characteristics of Single Leaf Infected by *Puccinia striiformis* (in Chinese). China Plant Protection 25, 8–11 (2005)
19. Wang, H.G., Ma, Z.H., Wang, T., Cai, C.J., An, H., Zhang, L.D.: Application of Hyperspectral Data to the Classification and Identification of Severity of Wheat Stripe Rust (in Chinese). Spectroscopy and Spectral Analysis 27, 1811–1814 (2007)
20. Huang, M.Y., Wang, J.H., Huang, W.J., Huang, Y.D., Zhao, C.J., Wan, A.M.: Hyperspectral Character of Stripe Rust on Winter Wheat and Monitoring by Remote Sensing (in Chinese). Transactions of the CSAE 19, 154–158 (2003)
21. Guo, J.B., Huang, C., Wang, H.G., Sun, Z.Y., Ma, Z.H.: Disease Index Inversion of Wheat Stripe Rust on Different Wheat Varieties with Hyperspectral Remote Sensing (in Chinese). Spectroscopy and Spectral Analysis 29, 3353–3357 (2009)
22. Jiang, J.B., Chen, Y.H., Huang, W.J., Li, J.: Study on Hyperspectral Remote Sensing Retriveral Models about Winter Wheat Stripe Rust Severity (in Chinese). Journal Nanjing Agricultural University 30, 63–67 (2007)
23. Jiang, J.B., Chen, Y.H., Huang, W.J.: Using Hyperspectral Derivative Indices to Diagnose Severity of Winter Wheat Stripe Rust (in Chinese). Optical Technique 33, 620–623 (2007)
24. Li, J., Chen, Y.H., Jiang, J.B., Cai, H.C.: Using Hyperspectral Derivative Index to Identify Winter Wheat Stripe Rust Disease (in Chinese). Science&Technology Review 25, 23–26 (2007)
25. Jiang, J.B., Chen, Y.H., Huang, W.J.: Using Hyperspectral Derivative Index to Monitor Winter Wheat Disease (in Chinese). Spectroscopy and Spectral Analysis 27, 2475–2479 (2007)
26. Cai, C.J., Wang, H.G., An, H., Shi, Y.C., Huang, W.J., Ma, Z.H.: Remote Sensing Research on Monitoring Technology of Wheat Stripe Rust (in Chinese). Jour. of Northwest Sci-Tech Univ. of Agri. and For (Nat. Sci. Ed.) 33(supp.), 31–36 (2005)
27. Zhang, Y.P., Guo, J.B., Ma, Z.H.: Correlation Analysis of Multi-temporal Canopy Reflectance and Disease Index of Wheat Stripe Rust (in Chinese). Acta Phytophylacica Sinica 34, 507–510 (2007)
28. Wang, Y.Y., Chen, Y.H., Li, J., Huang, W.J.: Two New Red Edge Indices as Indicators for Stripe Rust Disease Severity of Winter Wheat (in Chinese). Journal of Remote Sensing 11, 875–881 (2007)
29. Jiang, J.B., Chen, Y.H., Huang, W.J.: Using the Distance Between Hyperspectral Red Edge Position and Yellow Edge Position to Identify Wheat Yellow Rust Disease (in Chinese). Spectroscopy and Spectral Analysis 30, 1614–1618 (2010)
30. Wang, Y.Y., Chen, Y.H., Li, J., Jiang, J.B.: The Application of Partial Least Square to the Inversion of Severity of Winter Wheat Stripe Rust Disease (in Chinese). Remote Sensing for Land & Resources 1, 57–60 (2007)
31. Huang, M.Y., Huang, Y.D., Huang, W.J., Liu, L.Y., Wang, J.H., Wan, A.M.: The Physiological Changes of Winter Wheat Infected with Stripe Rust and the Remote Sensing Mechanism of Disease Incidence (in Chinese). Journal of Anhui Agricultural Sciences 32, 132–134 (2004)
32. Zhang, Y.J., Huang, W.J., Wang, J.H., Liu, L.Y., Ma, Z.H., Li, F.L.: Chlorophyll Fluorescence Sensing to Detect Stripe Rust in Wheat (*Triticum aestivum* L.) Fields Based on Fraunhofer Lines (in Chinese). Scientia Agricultura Sinica 40, 78–83 (2007)

33. Jiang, J.B., Chen, Y.H., Huang, W.J.: Study on Hyperspectra Estimation of Pigment Contents in Canopy Leaves of Winter Wheat Under Disease Stress (in Chinese). Spectroscopy and Spectral Analysis 27, 1363–1367 (2007)
34. Jiang, D.H., Li, Z.C., Zhou, Q.B., Li, S., Liu, J.: Estimation of the Content of Winter Wheat Chlorophyll Influenced by Yellow Rust with Hyper Spectrum (in Chinese). Chinese Agricultural Science Bulletin 23, 376–380 (2007)
35. Jiang, J.B., Chen, Y.H., Huang, W.J.: Using Hyperspectral Remote Sensing to Estimate Canopy Chlorophyll Density of Wheat Under Yellow Rust Stress (in Chinese). Spectroscopy and Spectral Analysis 30, 2243–2247 (2010)
36. Jiang, J.B., Chen, Y.H., Huang, W.J., Li, J.: Hyperspectral Estimation Models for LTN Content of Winter Wheat Canopy Under Stripe Rust Stress (in Chinese). Transactions of the CSAE 24, 35–39 (2008)
37. Jiang, J.B., Huang, W.J., Chen, Y.H.: Using Canopy Hyperspectral Ratio Index to Retrieve Relative Water Content of Wheat Under Yellow Rust Stress (in Chinese). Spectroscopy and Spectral Analysis 30, 1939–1943 (2010)
38. Cai, C.J., Ma, Z.H., Wang, H.G., Zhang, Y.P., Huang, W.J.: Comparison Research of Hyperspectral Properties Between Near-ground and High Altitude of Wheat Stripe Rust (in Chinese). Acta Phytopathologica Sinica 37, 77–82 (2007)
39. Liu, L.Y., Huang, M.Y., Huang, W.J., Wang, J.H., Zhao, C.J., Zheng, L.F., Tong, Q.X.: Monitoring Stripe Rust Disease of Winter Wheat Using Multi-temporal Hyperspectral Airborne Data (in Chinese). Journal of Remote Sensing 8, 275–281 (2004)
40. Yang, K.M., Guo, D.Z.: Analysis of Hyperspectral Features and Extraction of Disease for Vegetation (in Chinese). Geography and Geo-Information Science 22, 31–34 (2006)
41. Luo, J.H., Huang, W.J., Gu, X.H., Ji, N., Ma, L., Song, X.Y., Li, W.G., Wei, Z.L.: Monitoring Stripe Rust of Winter Wheat Using PHI Based on Sensitive Bands (in Chinese). Spectroscopy and Spectral Analysis 30, 184–187 (2010)
42. Guo, Z.H., Xiao, W.F., Zhang, Z., Chen, C.J., Zhao, X.W.: Utilization of Remote Sensing for Detecting Forest Damage Caused by Insect Infestations or Diseases (in Chinese). Journal of Natural Disasters 12, 73–81 (2003)
43. Ni, S.X., Jiang, J.J., Wang, J.C.: Progress in Application of Remote Sensing and GIS to the Study of Locust Prevention and Control (in Chinese). Advance in Earth Sciences 15, 97–100 (2000)
44. Huang, M.Y.: Monitoring of Winter Wheat Stripe Rust Using Hyperspectral Remote Sensing Data (in Chinese). Anhui Agricultural University, Hefei (2004)
45. Zhang, Y.P., Guo, J.B., Wang, S., Wang, H.G., Ma, Z.H.: Relativity Research on Near-ground and Satellite Remote Sensing Reflectance of Wheat Stripe Rust (in Chinese). Acta Phytophylacica Sinica 36, 119–122 (2009)
46. Guo, J.B., Huang, C., Wang, H.G., Ma, Z.H.: Preliminary Study on Remote Sensing Monitoring Wheat Stripe Rust Based on SPOT5 Image (in Chinese). Acta Phytophylacica Sinica 36, 473–474 (2009)
47. Zhang, J.C., Li, J.Y., Yang, G.J., Huang, W.J., Luo, J.H., Wang, J.H.: Monitoring of Winter Wheat Stripe Rust Based on the Spectral Knowledge Base for TM Images (in Chinese). Spectroscopy and Spectral Analysis 30, 1579–1585 (2010)
48. Liu, L.Y., Song, X.Y., Li, C.J., Qi, L., Huang, W.J., Wang, J.H.: Monitoring and Evaluation of the Diseases and Yield Winter Wheat from Multi-temporal Remotely-sensed Data (in Chinese). Transactions of the CSAE 25, 137–143 (2009)
49. Tong, Q.X., Zhang, B., Zheng, L.F.: Hyperspectral Remote Sensing and It's Multidisciplinary Applications (in Chinese). Publishing House of Electronics Industry, Beijing (2006)

50. Liu, D.Q., Dong, J.G.: Introduction to Plant Pathology (in Chinese). Science Press, Beijing (2007)
51. Qiao, H.B., Xia, B., Ma, X.M., Cheng, D.F., Zhou, Y.L.: Identification of Damage by Diseases and Insect Pests in Winter Wheat (in Chinese). Journal of Triticease Crops 30, 770–774 (2010)
52. Shi, S.D., Ma, Z.H., Wang, H.G., Zhang, W.M.: The Application of Geographical Information System in Plant Protection (in Chinese). Agriculture Network Information 3, 7–10 (2004)
53. Everitt, J.H., Escobar, D.E., Appel, D.N., Riggs, W.G., Davis, M.R.: Using Airborne Digital Imagery for Detecting Oak Wilt Disease. Plant Disease 83, 502–505 (1999)
54. Yang, C.D., Chen, D.Q., Wei, Y.M.: Application of Remote Sensing in Monitoring and Management of Forest Disease and Insect Damage (in Chinese). Journal of Catastrophology 14, 6–10 (1999)
55. Orum, T.V., Bigelow, D.M., Cotty, P.J., Nelson, M.R.: Using Predictions Based on Geostatistics to Monitor Trends in *Aspergillus flavus* Strain Composition. Phytopathology 89, 761–769 (1999)
56. Verreet, J.A., Klink, H., Hoffmann, G.M.: Regional Monitoring for Disease Prediction and Optimization of Plant Protection Measures: the IPM Wheat Model. Plant Disease 84, 816–826 (2000)

Research on Automatic Inspection Methods of Flight Quality of Digital Aerial Photography Results

Yanwei Zeng[1], Yong Liang[2,*], Wencong Jiang[2], and Xiaojun Wang[2]

[1] Quality Supervision and Testing Center of National Surveying and Mapping Products,
Chengdu, Si Chuan Province 610081, China
[2] School of Information Science & Engineering, Shandong Agricultural University, Tai'an,
Shandong 271018, P.R. China
yongl@sdau.edu.cn

Abstract. Aerial photogrammetry is one of the main methods obtaining geospatial information. After entering the 21st century, aerial photogrammetry technology has fully entered the digital age, and the quality of digital aerial photography results will directly affect the quality and accuracy of results of surveying and mapping .Therefore, it is necessary to inspect the quality of digital aerial photography results. In the process of digital aerial photography, flight quality directly affects the quality of the results. It is of great importance to make its flight quality inspection. Based on the analysis of flight quality index of the results of digital aerial photography and domestic and international current situation of quality inspection technology of aerial photography results, the author has researched and has posed inspection index and automatic inspection methods of flight quality of the results of digital aerial photography; they can be applied to check index, such as longitudinal overlapping degree, lateral overlapping degree, rotation angle, and *the curvature of airline* of images, to realize automatic quality inspection of flight quality of the results of digital aerial photography.

Keywords: Digital aerial photography, Flight quality index, Flight quality, Quality inspection, Automatic inspection.

1   Introduction

Digital aerial photography results are the important data sources of basic surveying and mapping, which quality will directly affect the quality of results of follow-up surveying and mapping. Therefore, it is necessary steps to make the comprehensive quality inspection to guarantee the quality of data, and it's of important application value and meaning [1]. In the process of digital aerial photography, flight quality directly affects the quality of the results, and it's important to check flight quality. It's high efficient and practical to make automatic quality inspection of flight quality based on digital image.

---

* Corresponding author.

D. Li and Y. Chen (Eds.): CCTA 2011, Part III, IFIP AICT 370, pp. 176–187, 2012.
© IFIP International Federation for Information Processing 2012

2   Index of Flight Quality

In this paper, based on the national standards and regulations(in table 1), the author studied and put forward quality inspection index system of flight quality of the box type digital aerial photography results(in table 2).

The index of flight quality includes longitudinal overlapping degree, lateral overlapping degree, inclination angle of picture, rotation angle of picture, the curvature of airline, measurement area coverage guarantee, division area coverage guarantee, the difference between the biggest navigation height and the smallest navigation height and the difference between the actual navigation height and the design navigation height and so on [2] [3].

Table 1. National standards and regulations

National standards and regulations	GB/T 6962－2005 《Aerial Photographic specification for 1: 500、1:1000、1:2000 Scale Topographic maps》
	GB/T 15661－1955 《Aerial Photographic specification for 1: 5000、1:10000、1:25000、1:50000、1:100000 Scale Topographic maps》
	GB/T 19294－2003 《Design specification of Aerial Photography Technology》
	MH/T 1006－1996 《Inspection specification of Aerial Photography Instruments》
	《Provisions of GPS Supplemental Aerial Photography Technology》（Trying）
	GB/T 24356—2009 《Quality Inspection and Acceptance of Surveying and Mapping Results》
	《Topographic Map Based on The Scale of 1:10000、1: 50000 IMU/DGPS Supplemental Aerial Photography Technology Provisions 》（Trying）
	《Implementation Detailed Rules of Inspection and Acceptance and Quality Evaluation of The National Basic Aerial Photography Results》（Trial Draft）
	《Supplement Technology Regulations of The National Basic Aerial Photography 》
	《Implementation Detailed Rules of Inspection and Acceptance and Quality Evaluation of The National Basic Aerial Photography Results》（Submissions）
	《The Format and Note of Material of The National Basic Aerial Photography Results》
	《Data Arrangement and Explains of Digital Aerial Photography Results》 （Trying）

Table 2. Flight quality index system of digital aerial photography results [4] [5]

Index of the second class	Description of function	Accuracy
longitudinal overlapping degree	Calculate the overlapping degree on the direction of airline between two photos according to the image matching method	General is for 60%-65%, and individuals are not more than 75% and not less than 56%
lateral overlapping degree	Calculate lateral overlapping degree on the direction of airline between two adjacent airline photos according to the image matching method	30%-35%
inclination angle of photos	The angle between the main beam axis of aerial photography machine and the plumb line	Not more than 3 degrees
rotation angle of photos	Get maximum according to calculating the angle of the attachment line between the photo lord point and box standards of two photos	Not more than 12 degrees
the curvature of airline	Calculate the line length of the photo lord point at ends of airline, then Calculate the distance from the photo lord point that deviates farthest from the line to the line, finally get the ratio between the distance and the line length	Not more than 3 degrees
measurement area coverage guarantee	Check the aerial photography results containing the range of design measurement area or not, and judge whether to exist airline gap or not	lateral coverage beyond the measurement area border is not less than 50% of photos and at least 30%
division area coverage guarantee	Check the aerial photography results containing the range of design division area or not, and judge whether to exist gap or not	lateral coverage beyond the division area border is not less than 30% of photos and at least 15%

Table 2. (*continued*)

the difference between the biggest navigation height and the smallest navigation height	Calculate the difference between the biggest navigation height and the smallest navigation height in the scope of navigation tape and calculate the difference between the biggest navigation height and the smallest navigation height in division area	Not more than 50m
the difference between the actual navigation height and the design navigation height	Calculate the difference between the actual navigation height and the design navigation height on airline and calculate the difference between the actual navigation height and the design navigation height of all photos in division area	Not more than 5% of the design navigation height

3   Pretreatment

Make pretreatment for the purpose of Building the image pyramids and the image matching. Before the flight quality inspection, we should make the matching of adjacent photos on airline and lateral overlapping photos among airlines to make sure relative position and judge overlapping degree and the rotation angle [6].

Because the original image is bigger, this paper uses the method of pyramid matching from level to level. Firstly, establish multistage thumbnail images for all images according to a certain proportion. Make feature point extracting and matching operation in the smallest level images to make sure the relative position of photos.

3.1   Steps of Image Matching

3.1.1   Search for Homologous Image Points

Use SIFT operator to search for homologous image points in thumbnail images. SIFT algorithm firstly put forward by D. G. Lowe in 1999, and is Summarized and perfected in 2004. Now SIFT feature matching algorithm is hot and difficult in feature point matching research field at home and abroad. The algorithm use feature point to extract feature descriptor, and looking for matching optimum point among descriptors and its matching ability is strong.

In quality inspection data of digital aerial photography results, there may be some aviation images which pitch, inclination and rotation angle is big and navigation height is not stable. SIFT feature keeps invariant for rotation, scale zoom and brightness variations and keeps certain stability for perspective variations, affine transformation and noise, and is suitable for image matching for quality inspection of aviation images. Figure 1 is the results scheme using SIFT operator to search for homologous image points. The top half of the picture is the left image, the bottom half is the right image and Purple lines links homologous image points.

Fig. 1. Search for homologous image points in adjacent images using SIFT operator

3.1.2 Make Sure of Relative Position between Photos

After Searching for enough homologous image points using SIFT operator, we should use quadratic polynomial model and least square method to make relative position relationship of two images, and put the coefficient of quadratic polynomial into database as initial value to use bigger accuracy matching. In this process, it can get the right result using Constraint of deformation and rotation to eliminate the mismatching homologous points.

$$X_l = \sum_{i=1}^{2} \sum_{j=1}^{2} A_{ij} X_r^{\,i} Y_r^{\,j}$$

$$Y_l = \sum_{i=1}^{2} \sum_{j=1}^{2} B_{ij} X_r^{\,i} Y_r^{\,j} \qquad \text{(Formula 1)}$$

This research combined with the relative position relationship between photos uses least square method to automatically set the threshold of feature points matching and its Result is better.

Through the experiment, when overlapping degree of the left and the right photos is right, the number of the effective homologous points is more than 50. When there is no overlap, it also gives error. Figure 2 is the relative position scheme of a pair of photos in experimental results.

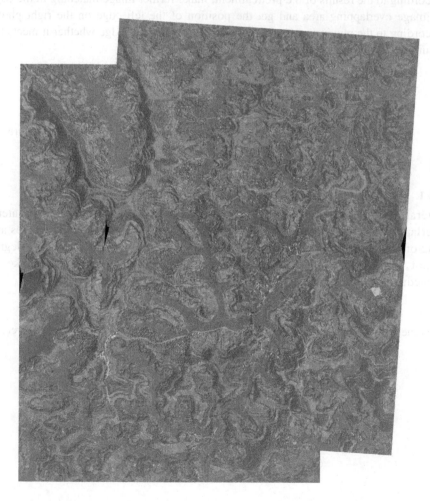

Fig. 2. Montage charts of adjacent images according to the calculation

4   Automatic Inspection Method of Flight Quality

4.1   Longitudinal Overlapping Degree

4.1.1   Longitudinal Overlapping Degree

Longitudinal overlap is overlapping photography of adjacent photos on the same airline. Longitudinal overlapping degree is a ratio between side length of overlap images and long and wide of picture format and expresses as a percentage. If overlapping degree is not enough, there will be aerial photography gap and it needs to make up immediately.

4.1.2   Calculation Method of Longitudinal Overlapping Degree

According to the results of the pretreatment, make further image matching in the edge of image overlapping area and get the position of the left edge on the right photo. According to the requirements of the specifications we can judge whether it meets the requirements of longitudinal overlapping degree.

$$\text{Longitudinal overlapping degree} = \frac{l_1}{L_1} \quad (\%)$$

l_1—Longitudinal minimum overlap width; L_1—The length of the picture

4.2   Lateral Overlapping Degree

4.2.1   Lateral Overlapping Degree

Lateral overlap is overlapping photography between adjacent airlines, and lateral overlapping degree is a ratio between side length of lateral overlapping images and long or wide of picture format and expresses as a percentage. If overlapping degree is not enough, there will be aerial photography gap and it needs to make up immediately [7].

4.2.2   Calculation Method of Lateral Overlapping Degree

This method is similar to the inspection method of longitudinal overlapping degree.

$$\text{Lateral overlapping degree} = \frac{l_2}{L_2} \quad (\%)$$

l_2—Lateral minimum overlap width; L_2—The width of the picture

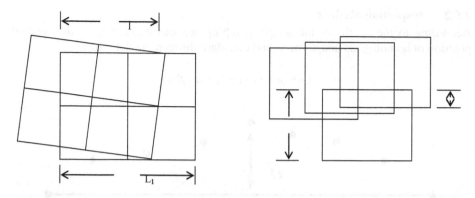

Fig. 3. Calculation schemes of longitudinal overlapping degree and lateral overlapping degree

4.3   Angle of Inclination of the Picture

4.3.1   Angle of Inclination of the Picture
Angle of inclination of the picture is the angle of main axis of the aerial camera and the plumb line.

4.3.2   Calculation Methods of Angle of Inclination of the Picture
View aerial apparatus records or use photogrammetry methods to check.

4.4   Angle of Rotation of the Picture

4.4.1   Angle of Rotation of the Picture
Angle of the attachment line between the photo lord point and box standards of two photos.

4.4.2   Calculation Methods of Angle of Rotation of the Picture
Calculate the angle according to image matching of adjacent pictures. The specific method: The existence of the rotation angle will make the whole route serrated and it affects overlapping degree. According to relative position of adjacent photos after pretreatment, we need to make further matching nearby homologous image points and get the precise location of homologous image point in the left photo relative to the right photo and homologous image point in the right photo relative to the left photo. Then we can calculate the angle according to the definition.

4.5   Curvature of Airline

4.5.1   Curvature of Airline
The maximum deviation degree from homologous image points of all photos to the line connecting homologous image point of the first photo with that of the last one[8].

4.5.2   Inspection Methods

According to the results of the image matching we can make sure of the relative position of homologous image points and calculate through the definition.

$$\text{Curvature of airline} = \delta / L$$

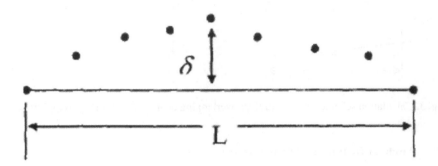

Fig. 4. Calculation scheme of curvature of airline

4.6   Navigation Height Keeping

4.6.1   Navigation Height

Navigation height is the vertical distance from remote sensing platform to datum of Photography division. We can calculate the difference of navigation height between adjacent images through the length of corresponding features in topographic map and images.

If there is GPS data, it will be easy to calculate the difference of navigation height. We only need to get all navigation height on one airline and obtain the difference between the maximum value and the minimum value. If no, we can get the difference between all photography stations and the first photo according to foreign elements got by calculating topological relationship and obtain the difference between the maximum value and the minimum value of foreign elements in each photo.

4.6.2   Inspection Methods

You can get parameters Z_i (i=1, …, n) of foreign elements of homologous image points in each photo and that is navigation height. Then, you can calculate variance of all navigation height to keep navigation height.

$$S^2 = \frac{\sum_{i=1}^{n} (S_i - \bar{S})^2}{n}$$

4.7   Difference between the Biggest Navigation Height and the Smallest Navigation Height

Inspection methods: Get the maximum value Z_{max} and the minimum value Z_{min} through parameters Z_i of foreign elements and the difference is as follows:

$$\Delta Z = Z_{max} - Z_{min}$$

4.8   Difference between the Actual Navigation Height and the Design Navigation Height

Inspection methods: Get the difference between parameters Z_i of foreign elements in images of all measurement areas and Design Navigation Height Z.

$$\Delta Z = Z_i - Z$$

4.9   Coverage Guarantee of Measurement Area

4.9.1   Coverage Guarantee of Measurement Area

Airlines completely cover the whole measurement area and control design on aerial photography images is checked with homologous features nearby control line marked on topographic map [9].

4.9.2   Inspection Methods

Get coordinates of image center on peripheral airlines to calculate the range of coverage S^A, and compare with the range of design measurement area and specific steps are as follows:

　①Draw closed polygon S according to boundary peripheral series coordinates (x^i, y^i), i=1, ···n, given by the map of design measurement area;

　② Draw closed polygon S^A by getting coordinates of image center on peripheral airlines (x^i_1, y^i_1), i=1, ···n;

　③Automatically judge S^A whether contains S or not, or judge through the human-computer interaction drawing polygon S^A and S in different color lines.

4.9.3   Input Data Requirements

Coordinate system of design measurement area map is the same to that of aerial photography photos. And input data includes design map of measurement area, aerial photography photos and foreign elements.

4.9.4   Realization Methods

In data preparation, we should provide the dialog box that needs to be input boundary dots and coordinates, and set the type of input data. According to the input data point coordinates, it can generate closed polygon and it's the range of design measurement area. Generate closed polygon through coordinates of image center on peripheral airlines.

4.9.5   Airline Boundary

If aviation coverage is one baseline beyond measurement area boundary, coordinates of image center need to be one baseline beyond boundary.

4.9.6   Realization Methods

It's shown by designing map polygon in measurement area and polygon connecting images center on peripheral airlines.

4.10   Coverage Guarantee of Division Area

Control design on aerial photography images is checked with homologous features nearby partition line marked on topographic map, and the specific method is the same to inspection of measurement area coverage guarantee [10].

5   Conclusions

In this paper, based on research and analysis of technology situations of quality inspection for aerial photography results, the author studies and puts forward results inspection index and method of flight quality of box type digital aerial photography and Applies to check the index such as longitudinal overlapping degree, lateral overlapping degree, inclination angle of picture, rotation angle of picture, the curvature of airline and so on.

References

[1] Yu, C., Zeng, Y.: Design on Automatic Quality Inspection System of Digital Aerial Photography Results. Information and Engineering of Surveying and Mappin 36(1), 8–10 (2011)

[2] GB/T 6962−2005:Aerial Photographic specification for 1: 500、 1:1000、 1:2000 Scale Topographic maps

[3] GB/T 15661−1955:Aerial Photographic specification for 1: 5000、 1:10000、 1:25000、 1:50000、 1:100000 Scale Topographic maps

[4] Implementation Detailed Rules of Inspection and Acceptance and Quality Evaluation of the National Basic Aerial Photography Results. Bureau of National Surveying and Mapping (2001)

[5] Data Arrangement and Explains of Digital Aerial Photography Results. Bureau of National Surveying and Mapping (2007)

[6] Yuan, J.: Information Management System of Aerial Photography. Information Engineering University of Zhengzhou (2002)

[7] Wu, S.: Design and Implementation on Digital Acceptance System of Aerial Photography Flight Quality. Information Engineering University of Zhengzhou (2005)

[8] Yuan, J., Xu, B.: Inspection Technology of Flight Quality Based on Digital images and GPS data. Journal of the PLA Surveying and Mapping Institute 22(1), 22–26 (2011)

[9] Zhang, Z., Zhang, J.: Digital Photogrammetry Science. Technology of Surveying and Mapping of Wuhan University (1996)

[10] Yuan, G., Huang, J.: Quality Control and Inspection of Digital Aerial images. Surveying and Mapping society of Jiangsu Province (2003)

Application of Machine Vision Technology in the Diagnosis of Maize Disease

Liying Cao, Xiaohui San, Yueling Zhao, and Guifen Chen[*]

College of Information and Technology Science, Jilin Agricultural University,
Changchun 130118
{caoliying99,umbrella,zyueling,guifchen}@163.com

Abstract. In order to identify the rapid diagnosis of diseases of corn, to take timely preventive measures to improve the diagnosis of diseases of corn. Machine vision technology will be introduced to the diagnosis and identification of maize diseases, laboratory tests show that the uses of machine vision technology, disease recognition model for the disease sample collection process to identify, analyze findings and to get the real practical applications, consistent with the conclusions, to meet the agricultural production practical application. The technology for the diagnosis of diseases of corn provides a quick, inexpensive, non-destructive testing of possible means.

Keywords: corn diseases, machine vision technology, mathematical morphology, neural network algorithm.

1 Introduction

With the computer image processing technology, machine vision technology in agriculture more and more attractive. As in the agricultural production process, there are a lot of man-made and natural factors, if applied only to the traditional manual way, not only time consuming, laborious and supplies, and production efficiency is very low, to a large extent affect the production of precision. Machine vision technology is the human eye and brain function extension, instead of using machine vision systems or auxiliary manual operation is a trend in modern agriculture [1].

Huge collection of agricultural information work, the reality of the information, timeliness and accuracy of agricultural production and scientific research issues of common concern, maize growth and development process, often subject to various factors, leading to occurrence of disease[2]. Common corn disease diagnosis is mainly by virtue of experience in human judgments. How timely to quickly determine the exact disease to corn has been the field of computer technology for agricultural research is an important content. Corn disease control methods in order to achieve the automation and modernization of the urgent need for a way to simulate the human visual function and can exceed the performance of machine vision systems [3-4].

---

[*] Corresponding author.

D. Li and Y. Chen (Eds.): CCTA 2011, Part III, IFIP AICT 370, pp. 188–194, 2012.

2   The Experimental Data

2.1   Experimental Method of Image Data Acquisition

The experimental design of a high 1 m, the length and width are 30 cm, black box, the box laying opaque, non-reflective black cloth, fixed a steady flow connected to the power of the ring light source, the light source stability, uniform to meet the needs of image acquisition, decrease the natural light conditions, brightness, color differences produced by the uncertainty and shadow noise, the acquisition results more clear, precise, easier to analyze. Devices and photographic equipment, according to meters, computer work together to build the image acquisition hardware platform. Foliar disease first collection of white flat on the cardboard, then use HP camera to shoot. Then use the scanner with a resolution set at 4800 dpi, scan and generate 256 gray values of digital images, sample images were normalized to 148 × 256 pixel size. Here the use of gray value image processing to meet the needs of both can also reduce the amount of information operations, to bring up a great deal of convenience.

Fig. 1. Experimental images

2.2   The Characteristic Analysis of the Common Corn Plant Diseases and Insect Pests

(1) Corn big spot disease

Main symptom: There is the shuttle type disease spot, generally the disease spot length is 5-10 cm, the breadth is 1-2 cm, sometimes the length can be 20 cm above, and breadth is over 3 cm.

(2) Corn small spot disease

Main symptom: There is the oval, circular type disease spot, size is 5-10(mm)×3-4(mm), the disease spot often connects with each other to a slice when disease spot crowded, becoming a bigger and withered spot.

(3) Corn gray spot disease

Main symptom: There is the rectangle disease spot, the disease spot size is: 2-4 (mm)×1-6 (mm).

(4) Corn Curvularia lunata (Wakker) Boed spot disease

Main symptom: The typical symptom is that it have circular or oval type disease spot with green and transparent, and center withered white, the edge is dark and brown, having a thin and yellow and dizzy turn around, the disease spot all of the general0.5-4 (mm) ×0.5-2 (mm), big of them can reach to 7 (mm) × 3(mm).

(5) The corn circle spot disease

Main symptom: There is the circular going to egg circular spot round a vein. size is 5～15(mm)×3～5(mm)。

(6) Corn brown spot disease

Main symptom: There is the Circular, oval spot, swell up the pimple type, the diameter is 1 mm or so, can greatly reach to 3-5 mm more on the main vein.

To sum up, this kind of disease usually concentrated on corn's leaf, and there is apparently different between the disease leaf and normal leaf, normal leaf present green or deeply green, but the ill leaf appear tan or dark brown spot, which their shape is circular, oval, rectangle and the shuttle type so on. So we withdraw the characteristic from both the color and the shape.

3   Experimental Methods and Experiment

3.1   Experimental Methods

The main experimental methods and processes shown in Fig, 2

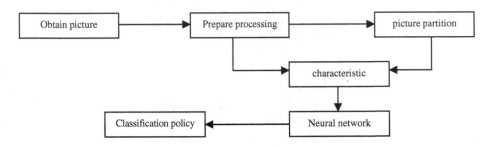

Fig. 2. Experimental procedures

3.2   Image Denoising

First, the background noise in the image analysis of information characteristics, type in VC + + development platform, smoothing filter-based image denoising method of beans. Smoothing filter mask is used to determine the neighborhood of pixel values instead of the average gray value of each pixel image, this method can significantly reduce the gray-scale image of the "sharp" change that "noise" [6]. Bean disease in this study applied the linear image smoothing method, select the 3 × 3 neighborhood template smoothing filter, it can effectively filter out noise and to maximize the retention of soybean clear image of the target image.

3.3   Objectives and Background Segmentation

In order to extract the characteristics of disease, disease need to target and background segmentation. Background separation method is based on the classic gray threshold segmentation method. It does this by setting the threshold, the pixel grayscale divided into several categories, in order to achieve image segmentation. To a gray image into binary image thresholding is the most simple form [7]. Set a grayscale image of f (x, y), first to certain criteria in f (x, y) to find a gray value of t as the threshold, the image is divided into two parts, that is greater than or equal to the threshold pixel value is set to 1, less than the threshold pixel value is set to 0 [8].

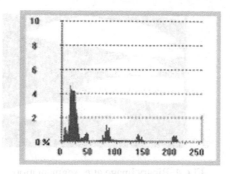

Fig. 3. Histogram

3.4   Image Segmentation

This study uses the iterative type threshold selection method. First choose a threshold value as the initial estimate, and then according to certain rules, continuously improve the estimated value until meet given standards [9] so far. In the iterative process, to select the right threshold value improvement measure. In general to meet two conditions: one is enough, the second is the rapid convergence in each iteration threshold value better than the last time new produce threshold. This paper will be divided into several images, areas in each area for the first for the biggest image segmentation grey value and minimum gray value, and then ask Zk Z1 and maximum and minimum gray value of the mean value T0 [10];

$$T^0 = \frac{Z_1 + Z_2}{2} \tag{1}$$

According to mean the image into two parts A and B. Then A, B, respectively for the two parts of the Z0 average gray and the ZB,

$$Z_0 = \frac{\sum_{z(i,j)<T^0} z(i,j) * N(i,j)}{\sum_{z(i,j)<T^0} N(i,j)} \tag{2}$$

$$Z_B = \frac{\sum_{z(i,j)<T^B} z(i,j) * N(i,j)}{\sum_{z(i,j)<T^B} N(i,j)} \tag{3}$$

Type (3) z (I, j) is the image (I, j) point gray value, N (I, j) is (I, j) point, take the weight coefficient of general 1.0. According to the two parts average gray new threshold value calculation, j N (I) = 1.0.

$$T^{k+1} = \frac{Z_0 + Z_B}{2} \tag{4}$$

Will the new threshold toshimi koitabashi + 1 and former a threshold, meet some comparison, toshimi koitabashi requirements then stop the iteration, or access to the circulation. Using vc + +, program set a cyclic number 60 times, so that when the history of not termination conditions met, could force terminated. Using this method adhesion effect is good after grain segmentation, as shown in Fig. 4 shows.

Fig. 4. Binary image after segmentation

3.5 Feature Extraction

In fact we consider classification problem is in the feature space, always identify some characteristics of the object, whether physical or form, to the digital, and according to the principle of certain chosen, thus forming characteristics of a vector space, and used to represent a consider recognition object, such, can in the feature space to these vector classified discrimination. Feature extraction involve is very wide, identification of the object the parameters can be used as a measure of the way, table 1 below.

3.6 BP Neural Network Based Detection of Lesions

This study needs to be fine-spot disease identification, which is the output vector to be determined with a link with the input vector process. Therefore, we as a development platform based on Matlab using the function to build a three-newff BP neural network. One hidden layer neurons using tan-sigmoid transfer function type function taming, the last layer of the network is prelim linear neurons, so that the entire output of the network can take any real number. When building a neural network input into the number of neurons is 23, the output layer node number is 1.

Table 1. Each disease of the characteristic parameters

No.	Area(pixel)	Perimeter(pixel)	Circular degree	The position of gravity (pixel)
0	21718	928.82	0.1410	（215.320）
1	2308	274039	0.2149	（324.107）
2	9460	352.85	0.3256	（401.196）
3	4152	894.63	0.2658	（490.098）
4	8570	367.98	0.0948	（584.469）

Experimental procedure, we set the number of iterations to 150, learning rate 0.2,momentum factor of 0.9, the maximum number of 1000 training, the training accuracy of $1 \times 10\text{-}6$. We selected 640 samples for training, 160 samples for testing. After 720 times training, Figure 7 can be introduced by the mean square error of approximation error fitting convergence objective, to achieve the intended accuracy.

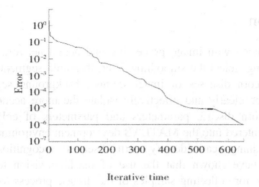

Fig. 5. Training result

Collected by a group of diseases of the data analysis of the sample picture identification, the system identified by the diseased sample and the actual disease situation, and so the comparison sample and found that not all diseases can be identified correctly identified the system, there are some error, the applicability of our results given by table 2 and comparative analysis of the actual situation.

Table 2. Results comparison table

The category of Corn plant diseases and insect pests	Identified to discovered the number of Plant diseases and insect pests I1	In the sample actual the number of plant diseases and insect pests I2	Recognition accuracy
Big spot disease	29	34	85.3%
Small spot disease	35	32	92.3%
Gray spot disease	13	18	72.3%
The corn Curvularia lunata (Wakker) Boed spot disease	14	16	87.5%
Circle spot disease	23	24	95.8%
Brown spot disease	23	22	95.7%

At the different disease conditions discussed, the system identified the disease as the number of I1, the actual sample data with the disease represented by I2.

Identified by the experimental data of disease data and real data for comparison of disease, identify disease found in corn can be used in agricultural production, that we plant diseases in agriculture in the actual application is valid.

4   Conclusion

In this study, combined with image processing and neural network technology, using VC + + programming, select the smoothing filter, threshold segmentation algorithm on the acquisition of corn diseases of image demise, background segmentation, image segmentation, can be clearly and effectively isolate the more accurate morphological characteristics of corn disease parameters and parameters of color features. These parameters will be entered into the MATLAB development environment to construct the neural network training; can identify corn diseases, recognition rate of 88.2%. Experimental tests have shown that the use of machine vision technology, disease identification system for collecting samples of the disease process to identify, meet the practical application of agricultural production. Illustrates the system's effectiveness in the field of agricultural production.

Acknowledgments. This work was funded by the Youth Foundation of Jilin Agricultural University under Grant No.2010041, 201136; the National High-Tech Research and Development Plan of China under Grants Nos.2006AA10A309 and 2006AA10Z245; the National Spark Program Nos. 2008GA661003. Changchun Technology Correspondent Project (2009245).

References

1. Chen, B., Sun, M.: The Visual C++ Practical Image Processing. Tsinghua University Press, Peking (2004)
2. Yuan, Q.: The Digital Image Processing. Alectronics Industrial Press, Peking (2001)
3. Zhang, H., Liu, S.: The Corn Pest Image Identifies A Medium Mathematics To Statistics A Characteristic To Withdraw. The Computer Application And Software 22(3), 126–127 (2005)
4. Mingwu, R., Jingyu, Y., Han, S.: Tracing Boundary Contours in A Binary Image. Image and Vision Computing 20(2), 125–131 (2002)
5. Sankur, B., Sezgin, M.: Image Thresholding Techniques: A Survey over Categories. Pattern Recognition (2001)
6. Zhou, C.: Mastering In The Visual C++ Image programing. Electronics Industrial Press, Peking (2000)
7. Sonka, M., Hlavac, V., Boyle, R.: The Image Processing, Analysis, The And Machine Vision. People The Post And Tele Press, Peking (2002)
8. Wang, Y.N., Li, S., Mao, J.: The Calculator Image Processsing And Identification Technique. The Higher Education Press (2000)
9. Li, M., Zhang, C.L., Wang, X.N.: Based on image processing technology of wheat form detection method. Journal of Northeast China Agricultural University 40(3), 111–115 (2009)
10. Cui, Y.: The Image Processing And Analysis Mathematics Appearance Learn The Method And Application. Science Press, Peking (2000)

Analysis of the Rigidity of Arc Flexible Hinge with Different Geometrical Parameters

Hongjiang Chen

School of Mechanical and Electrical Engineer, Jiangxi Science & Technology
Normal University, Nanchang, Jiangxi 330013, P.R. China
hongjiangc@163.com

Abstract. Flexible hinges are widely used in micro robotic. Its rigidity directly influences an organization's terminal localization. Its actual structure geometry size cannot satisfy the theoretical analysis completely in a theoretical supposition condition. In this paper, we analyzed the rotation rigidity of arc flexible hinges in different parameters using finite element software ANSYS. The errors are discovered and compared with theoretical result. An analysis of changes of parameters on the performance of arc flexible hinge was carried out, though the graph of the flexible hinge's parameters and its performance. The key manufacture parameters that affect the performance of arc flexible hinge the most and rules of design are given, which can provide directions of design precision for the flexible hinge.

Keywords: arc flexure hinge, finite element analysis, rigidity.

1 Introduction

Flexible hinge have some characteristics, such as small volume, without rubs, ceaseless, good rigidity and high sensitivity. With microcomputer electrical system series (MEMS) technical rapidly expanding, flexible hinge are widely applied in the displacement which requests small angular and high-precision rotation, such as gyroscopes, accelerometers, precision instruments and so on. It has broad application prospects in the micron level domain.

The common flexible hinge is in two kinds: beam-shape flexible hinge and arc-shaped flexible hinge. The beam-shaped flexible hinge has a big slewing area, but the movement precision is bad. The arc-shaped flexible hinge's movement precision is high, but the slewing range is relatively small [1]. In order to take into account the movement precision and scope, the following several rotation flexible hinges have been generated: parabolic flexure hinge, an arc flexure hinge and a hyperbola-shaped flexure hinge, etc [2].The properties of flexible hinges are rigidity, precision and stress characteristic, etc. The rigidity performance reflects the stress ability and also manifests movement to a vice-flexible degree. In 1965, Paros et al [3] announced his design development of the circular flexible hinge for the first time, and gave the rigidity formula. Smith et al used the similar method to obtain an elliptic flexible hinge mechanics expression [4]. Nicolae Lodonitu inferred the parabola and the hyperbolic flexible hinge's rigidity formula [5].

D. Li and Y. Chen (Eds.): CCTA 2011, Part III, IFIP AICT 370, pp. 195–200, 2012.

Wei Xu and Tim King analyzed the rectangular and ellipse flexible hinge's rigidity and rotation precision using the finite element method [6].

In this paper the arc flexible hinge stiffness to different geometrical parameters is analyzed with software ANSYS10.0. Compared with results of theoretical analysis and finite element analysis (FEA), the errors are analyzed. Through the graph of the flexible hinge parameters and its performance, an analysis of changes of parameters on the performance of the arc flexible hinge was carried out. The key manufacture parameters that affect the performances of an arc flexible hinge the most and rules of design are given, which can give directions of design precision for the flexible hinge.

2   Rigidity Formula of the Arc Flexible Hinge

An arc flexible hinge, as shown in Figure 1, is a particular type of flexure that consists of a necked down section. Parameters t, h, b are flexible hinge's smallest thickness, height and width, respectively, parameter R is the radius of arc, and θ_m is the centre angle of arc.

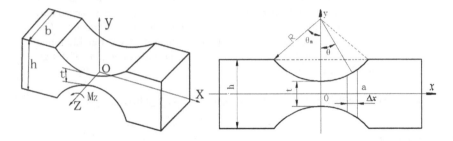

Fig. 1. Model of arc flexible hinge

As shown in Figure 1, the infinitesimal is intercepted in the abscissa axis that is $\Delta x = \Delta(\rho \sin \theta)$. To begin, the infinitesimal section is vertical to the abscissa axis. The flexible hinge's angular deformation a_z is generated under torque M_Z as given in Eq.1 [1].

$$\alpha_z = \int_{-R\sin\theta_m}^{R\sin\theta_m} \frac{M_z(x)}{EI_z(x)}dx = \frac{12M_z}{EbR^2}\int_{-\theta_m}^{\theta_m} \frac{\cos\theta}{(\frac{t}{R}+2-2\cos\theta)^3}d\theta \tag{1}$$

$$f_1 = \int_{-\theta_m}^{\theta_m} \frac{\cos\theta}{(\frac{t}{R}+2-2\cos\theta)^3}d\theta = \frac{8\gamma^4(2\gamma+1)\tan\frac{\theta_m}{2}}{(4\gamma+1)^2[1+(4\gamma+1)\tan^2\frac{\theta_m}{2}]^2} + $$

$$\frac{4\gamma^3(6\gamma^3+3\gamma+1)\tan\frac{\theta_m}{2}}{(4\gamma+1)^2[1+(4\gamma+1)\tan^2\frac{\theta_m}{2}]} + \frac{12\gamma^4(2\gamma+1)}{(4\gamma+1)^{5/2}}\arctan(\sqrt{4\gamma+1}\tan\frac{\theta_m}{2}) \tag{2}$$

Where the parameters r can be expressed by Eq.3.

$$\gamma = \frac{R}{t} \tag{3}$$

The rotation rigidity formula of arc flexible hinge is given by Eq.4.

$$K_1 = \frac{M_Z}{\alpha_Z} = \frac{EbR^2}{12f_1} \tag{4}$$

3　FEA Model of Arc Flexible Hinge

ANSYS has some characteristics that the general finite element analysis technology, powerful computing, and reliable result. The arc flexible hinge's basic structure size is b=10mm, t=1mm, R=2.5mm, θ_m.=90° The material is Spring steel, E=200GPa, $v = 0.3$.

Fig. 2. FEA model of arc flexure hinge

The arc flexible hinge FEA model is shown in Figure 2.The model left end surface is restrained completely; the right end surface exerts bending moment $M = 0.1N.m$. The special node 1 of the grid model right end surface represents the output displacement. The unit type chooses 3-D the entity SOLID92 unit model, the entire model uses smart size to free mesh. The FEA model and the output displacement have been obtained with changing arc flexible hinge's parameters E, b, t and R as well as θ_m.

4　Performance Analysis of Stiffness

The theoretical calculation and FEA rotational stiffness are obtained through changing arc flexure hinge parameters E、b、t and R as well as θ_m, as shown in Figure 3 to7. The theoretical value of arc flexible hinge stiffness is simplified theory. FEA is FEA value of arc flexible hinge stiffness.

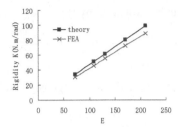

Fig. 3. Comparison of FEA value and the theoretical value of flexure hinge with changing E

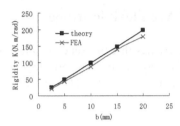

Fig. 4. Comparison of FEA value and the theoretical value of flexure hinge with changing width b

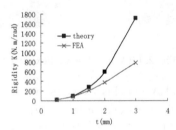

Fig. 5. Comparison of FEA value and the theoretical value of flexure hinge with changing thickness t

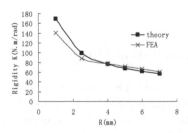

Fig. 6. Comparison of FEA value and the theoretical value of flexure hinge with changing radius R

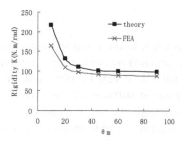

Fig. 7. Comparison of FEA value and the theoretical value of flexure hinge with changing centre angle θ_m

From Eq.1, Eq.2and Figures 3 to 7 the following conclusions can be observed.

(1)From Figures 3 and 4 it can be observed that the rotation stiffness is a linearly increasing relation with material young's modulus E and width b. The theoretical value is bigger than the FEA value. When E and b are smaller, the FEA value and the theoretical value are closer.

(2) From Figure 5 it can observed that the rotation of the stiffness FEA value and the theoretical value is a curve increasing with thickness t, end the speed-up is getting quicker and quicker. When t is bigger, the difference of the theoretical value and the FEA value is bigger. When t<2mm, the FEA value and the theoretical value are close.

(3) From Figure 6 it can be observed that the relation of rotation rigidity and radius R is a decreasing curve, and the rate of reduced scope is gradually decreased. When R>2mm, the FEA value and the theoretical value are closer.

(4) From Figure7 it can be observed that the relation of rotation rigidity and centre angle θ_m is a decreasing curve, but the decreasing scope is small. The theoretical value is bigger than the FEA value. When θ_m>20° the FEA value and the theoretical value are closer.

From Figures 3 to 7 it can be observed that the influence of flexure hinge's parameter to its rotation stiffness is: the influence of thickness t is biggest, followed by radius R, centre angle θ_m, width b and E.

The theoretical value and the FEA value of an arc flexible hinge rotation rigidity is not equal, even if has a big differential value. The reasons are:

(1) The flexible hinge theoretical model that is established using materials mechanics' bending strain theory is built on the basis of certain assumptions.

(2) From Figure 2 it can be observed that the FEA model not only has the displacement in the y axis direction, but also has the displacement change on the z axis direction, when the torque M_z exerted on the z axis for the model. In other words, the flexible hinge not only has the bending strain, but also will have the shearing force to cause upward deformation. Under certain design parameters, the flexible hinge's theory and FEA solution achieve a good match.

5   Conclusions

The different design parameters to the flexible hinge rotation rigidity influence and the linear relationship are obtained by comparing the rotation rigidity theory solution and the finite element analysis. It can be observed that the influence of flexible hinge's parameter to its rotation stiffness is: the influence of thickness t is biggest, followed by radius R, centre angle θ_m, width b and E. The reasons that the theoretical value and the FEA value of an arc flexible hinge's rotation rigidity is not equal is that the flexible hinge not only has the bending strain, but also will have the shearing force to cause upward deformation. It is helpful to further analyze the movement of the mechanical deformation mechanism, using the finite element technology to simulate the flexible hinge performance.

Acknowledgments. This research is financially supported by the Hangzhou Binteng Technology Co., LTD, Hangzhou Province, China.

References

1. Zuo, X.Y., Liu, X.M.: Calculation and analysis of rotational stiffness for three types of flexure hinges. Chinese Journal of Scientific Instrument 27, 1725–1728 (2006)
2. Lobontiu, N., Garcia, E.: Analytical model of displacement amplification and stiffness optimization for a class of flexure-based compliant mechanisms. Computer & Stuctures 81, 2797–2801 (2003)
3. Paros, J.M., Weisibord, L.: How to design flexure hinge. Machine Design 37, 151–157 (1965)
4. Smith, T.S., Badami, V.G.: Arc flexure hinges. Review Scientific Instruments 68, 1474–1483 (1997)
5. Lobontiu, N., Paine, J.S.N.: Corner-filleted flexure hinges. Journal of Mechanical Design 123, 346–352 (2001)
6. Xu, W., King, T.G.: Flexure hinges for piezo-actuator displacement amplifiers: flexibility, accuracy and stress considerations. Precision Engineering 19, 4–10 (2002)
7. Abdellatif, H., Benimeli, F., Heimann, B., Grotjahn, M.: Direct identification of dynamic parameters for parallel manipulators. Presented at International Conference on Mechatronics and Robotics, MechRob 2004, Aachen, Germany (2004)

A Study of Image Processing
on Identifying Cucumber Disease

Yong Wei[1], Ruokui Chang[1], Yuanhong Wang[2,*], Hua Liu[1], Yanhong Du[1],
Jianfeng Xu[1], and Ling Yang[3]

[1] Department of Electromechanical Engineering
[2] Department of Horticulture, Tianjin Agricultural University,
Tianjin, P.R. China 300384
[3] The Center for Agri-Food Quality and Safety, MOA, Beijing P.R. China 100210
weiytj@sohu.com

Abstract. Plant disease has been a major constraining factor in the production of cucumber, the traditional diagnostic methods usually take a long time, and the control period is often missed. We take computer image processing as a method, preprocessing the images of more than 100 sheets of collected samples of cucumber leaves, using the region growing method to extract scab area of leaves to get three feature parameters of shape, color and texture. And then, through the establishment of BP neural network pattern, the model identification accuracy of cucumber leaf disease can reach 80%. The experiment shows that by using this method, the diseases of cucumber leaves can be identified more quickly and accurately. And the feature extraction and automatic diagnosis of cucumber leaf disease can be achieved.

Keywords: cucumber disease, texture feature, feature extraction.

1 Introduction

As an important component of plant pathology, leaf disease is increasingly valued by botanists and pathologists. Computer vision technology provides new research ideas and methods for rapid automatic identification and diagnosis of plant disease. As early as 1999, Yuataka Sasaki studied the automatic diagnostics of cucumber anthracnose from the perspective of spectral reflectance properties and shape characteristics[1].Wang Shuangxi of Shanxi Agricultural University has taken the cucumber disease leaf in greenhouses as an example to carry out in-depth research on image segmentation, image enhancement and feature extraction. In this study, we regard the common cucumber angular leaf spot, powdery mildew and downy mildew as the main research objects, exploring the way of achieving rapid and accurate diagnosis of diseases of cucumber through extracting three characteristic values of shape, texture and color. It will provide technical support for the safe production of cucumber.

---

* Corresponding author.

D. Li and Y. Chen (Eds.): CCTA 2011, Part III, IFIP AICT 370, pp. 201–209, 2012.

2   Materials and Methods

The experimental images are collected from cucumber greenhouses of Dangcheng village, Xinkou town, Xiqing District of Tianjin. To ensure leaf image are of comparability, after making the leaves which are infected by different diseases clean and dry, we take some photos from the same angle and height under the same environmental conditions. Digital camera of Olympus FE5030 is used in the experiment, with the pixel of 14 million. The processor is Intel Core i3, 2GB memory, and the captured image is 1820 * 960 pixels.

It took about two hours to deal with image processing of one picture because of the high pixel. So we use screenshot tool to reduce it to 750 * 650 pixels. This can greatly save the time of single image processing, increase availability and meet the requirements of the pixels in the follow-up experiments.

In the experiment, we use the matlab image processing tool; comprehensively use the knowledge of image processing, plant pathology, color science and pattern recognition to diagnosis cucumber angular leaf spot, powdery mildew and downy mildew.

We can get scabs on the leaves and extract three eigenvalues of shape, texture and color by processing the known disease of cucumber leaf image. It will be sent into the neural network. Finally, by using the trained neural network we can identify unknown disease in cucumber leaves.

3   Image Processing of Cucumber Leaves

3.1   Image Processing of Cucumber Leaves

This section includes image preprocessing, image binarization, morphological image enhancement, the extraction of image background with region growing method, the binary image of Scab by using image subtract operation to obtain color images of the scab. As is shown in Fig.1.

3.2   Image Preprocessing

As a pre-processing of Image pre-processing feature extraction and image recognition, It is an important part of the process of disease identification. The purpose of preprocessing is to improve the image of intelligibility, It includes three links of image denoising, image background segmentation and binary image. Experiments show that median filtering is the best denoising, matlab implement median filter by calling function of medfilt . Deal with the effects is shown in Fig.2.

We find that the applicability of using region growing method to extract background is the strongest by comparing region growing, quadtree segmentation and robert / prewitt operator in the experiment. By using this method, we can extract a clearer pre-treated gray background.

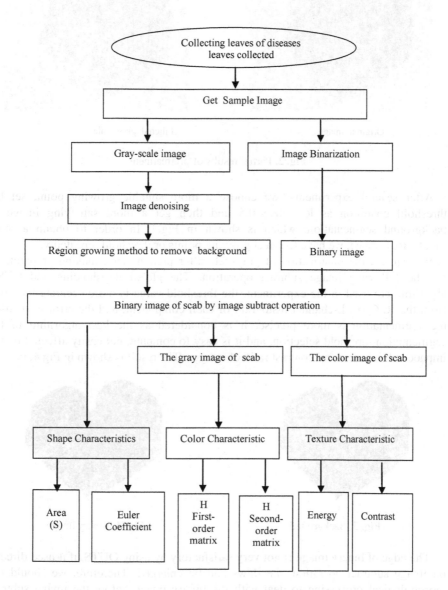

Fig. 1. Flow chart of image feature extraction

Original image   Filtered gray scale

Fig. 2. Partial results of pretreatment

After several experiments, we choose a more suitable growing point, set the threshold condition as less than 0.5 and then get a more satisfying image of background segmentation, which is shown in Fig.3. In order to obtain a more satisfactory image, we have to select growing points or threshold repeatedly.

We can get the binarization of grayscale after pretreatment, making preparations for the following image subtract operation. The global thresholding and OTSU algorithm are used in the experiment, the threshold value is more accurate than that from the R, G, B, L-channel histogram of each component, and the error is smaller, the segmentation is more precise. It is considered as the best algorithm of the segmentation threshold selection, and it is easy to compute, not easily affected by the impact of brightness and contrast ratio of images. The result is shown in Fig.4.

Fig. 3. Background   **Fig. 4.** Binary image

The edge of binary image is not very satisfactory by using OUTS, if it used directly on image subtract operation, the flaws can be enlarged. Therefore, we should use morphological processing to deal with the binary image before the image subtract operation. There are four methods available: expansion, erosion, opening operation (erosion after the first expansion) and closing operation (after the first expansion of corrosion). If we compare the results of treatment (Fig.5), we can see that the result of closing operation is more in line with the original image. Therefore, we can use closing operation to enhance the binary figure in experiments.

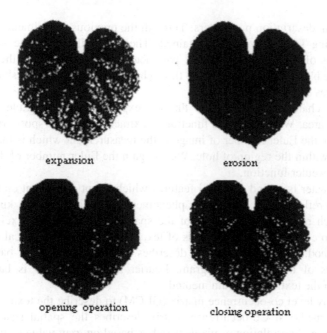

Fig. 5. Results of morphological processing

We will get the binary image of scab with scab only if we make subtraction between the background image obtained in the experiment (Fig.3) and binary image. It is shown in Fig.6. According to the Binary image of scab, we can determine the pixel position of scab area, extract three-channel value of R, G, B from the original rgb map, then use cat function to gain color picture of scab with scab only, it is shown in Fig.7.

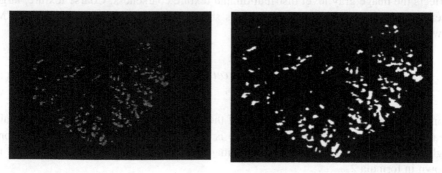

Fig. 6. Binary image of scab   Fig. 7. RGB image of scab

3.3   The Extraction of Feature Parameters

In order to create a system to identify different types of diseases of cucumber leaves, we must determine what characteristics of the objects to be diagnosed have, and then it will result in description parameters. Through the previous experiments, the images only containing scabs have been obtained. Then we will begin the study of the characteristics of scabs to find out the parameters that can describe these features. Typically, the blade can be divided into three characteristic values: the shape features, texture features and color features.

The shape characteristics selected through experiments is the Euler number of disease spots area. We use bwarea function to extract the disease spots area of binary image (Fig.6); the Euler number of image is the measurement which is the number of empty holes within the region of hole. We can gain the Euler number of disease spots through by Bweuler function.

Grain character is a kind of visual features which is not dependent on the color or brightness to reflect the homogeneous phenomenon in images; it is a kind of image features which reflect the properties of the spatial distribution of pixel gray level. There are two commonly used methods of texture description: statistical method and spectral method. Statistical method describes the texture that is based on the characteristics of the image histogram. Fourier spectral method is based on the description of the texture spectrum method.

We use gray level co-occurrence matrix (GLCM) to describe the texture, it belongs to statistical methods. Co-occurrence matrix describes the spatial structure of the characteristics and correlation of pixels which is based on gray value of image. In the experiment, we construct the GLCM of image which is based on joint probability density function of the location of two pixels. GLCM is the second-order statistical measure of gray-scale image. The structural parameters of Co-occurrence matrix is determined that d take 1, θ take 0 degrees. In matlab, use out = cooccurrence (I, 0, 1, 1) to be GLCM of grayscale images; Co-occurrence is the sub-function of extracted GLCM Functions. We can obtain texture characteristic parameters by extracting energy and contrast ratio of GLCM (**Fig.2**). Energy is a measure of image texture; it reflects the image gray level distribution and texture coarseness. Coarse texture, large energy; texture thin, energy is small. It is shown in formula 1.M, N for the GLCM rows and columns.

$$\text{Energy} = \sum_{i=1, j=1}^{M,N} out_{i,j}^{2} \tag{1}$$

Contrast (moment of inertia) is average of the image difference of all pixel gray-scale treatment of | i-j |. Gray level difference is the contrast of gray pixels of the more higher the value. It is the clarity of the image, the texture of the deep grooves. It is shown in formula 2.

$$\text{Contrast} = \sum_{i=1, j=1}^{M,N} (i - j)^{2} out_{i,j} \tag{2}$$

Colors are the main features for people to pay attention to and memorize images. Experiments show that the leaves in the H channel of HSV color space are the color feature parameter under the first moment and second moment. We can extract color feature parameters of disease spots, namely, the first moment and second moment of H color.

Among them, the tone of the first-order matrix and second-order matrix equation is shown as follows(3),(4).

$$\text{M1}= \frac{1}{N} \sum_{i=1,j=1}^{M,N} H_{i,j} \tag{3}$$

$$\text{M2}= \left[\frac{1}{N} \sum_{i=1,j=1}^{M,N} (H_{i,j} - M1)^2 \right]^{\frac{1}{2}} \tag{4}$$

4   Cucumber Leaf Disease Identification System

BP neural network is mainly used in function approximation, pattern recognition, classification and data compression. It is a one-way transmission of multi-layer feedforward network. It consists of input layer, hidden layer (may have multi-layer) and output layer, each layer is formed by different nodes. For the cucumber disease diagnosis problem, the symptoms can be seen as input to the output of disease name (type number) of the nonlinear mapping problem. We chose input parameters of the network from the extracted six characteristic parameters of cucumber leaves image, which are, scab size S, EULER of scab area, first moment M1 of H color channel, second moment M2 of H color channel, gray degree of co-occurrence matrix of energy and contrast. The output vector of neural network is the type of cucumber disease. From the foregoing, the neural network input nodes n = 6, the output nodes for the m = 1. The structure of neural network model is shown in Fig.8.

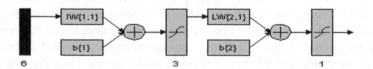

Fig. 8. Neural network structure

The experiment verifies that if we choose three layers from the middle layers, the training error is 0.01, the training step is 10000, the input layer and hidden layer transfer function is tansig, the hidden layer and output layer transfer function is purline, network training function is trainlm, and when Network output error range is 0.01, we find a good trained neural network model to recognize successfully, the error is shown in Fig. 9.

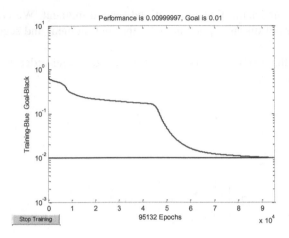

Fig. 9. Neural network training error

Using the test samples to detect trained network, we discover that the correct rate of identification can reach 80%. It shows that the trained BP neural network can complete the basic disease recognition task. Due to fewer samples, recognition error rate was higher; Secondly, experimental results are vulnerable to the interference from other factors such as leaf images. For example, some of the leaves have been infected more than one virus. To improve the recognition rate caused by neural network requires the sample to be comparable experimental and statistical.

5   Conclusions

The experiments proved that the use of Matlab toolbox can be realized on cucumber leaf disease identification, Through the preprocessing operation of images, the experiment shows us that median filtering was an effective way to de-noising, the application of "Image Subtraction method" and "region growing" is an effective way to separate effective areas and extract image feature parameters of the region in a complex background. Experiment using the region growing method to extract leaf scab area, we established BP neural network model by obtaining the shape, color, texture characteristic parameters, the model identification accuracy of cucumber leaf disease can reach 80%.

According to the conclusions of this paper, there are some design limitations; it is proposed the following visions for the future:

(1) To achieve the degree of cucumber disease classification, at present, we can only identify the disease and we can not give the classification data of the extent of disease, and also, we should give the appropriate classification of treatment options to growers.

(2) The optimization algorithm and the processing speed should be improved. The current algorithm contains nested, loops and subroutine calls and so on, And with high pixels of leaves photo, the processing time takes about 40 minutes. This will be improved in the future.

(3) Simplify the structure, expert systems should be made to achieve product-oriented.

Acknowledgements. We acknowledge the funding of this work by National Spark program of China (No:2011GA610014) and Spark Project of Tianjin in China(No:10ZHXHNC08300).

References

1. Sasaki, Y., Okamoto, T., Imou, K., Torii, T.: Automatic Diagnosis of Plant Disease. Journal of JSAM 61(2), 119–126 (1999)
2. Muhammed, H.H.: Hyperspectralcrop reflectance data for characterizing and estimating fungal disease severity in wheat. Biosystems Engineering 91(1), 9–20 (2005)
3. Jing, Z., Shuangxi, W., Xiaozhi, D.: A study on method of extract of texture characteristic value in image processing for plant disease of greenhouse. Journal of Shenyang Agricultural University 37(3), 282–285 (2006)
4. Changxing, G., Junxion, Z.: Recognition and Features Extraction of Cucumber Downy Mildew Based on Color and Texture. Transactions of the Chinese Society for Agricultural Machienry 42(3), 170–174 (2011)
5. Bingqi, C., Xuemei, G., Xiaohua, L.: Image diagnosis algorithm of diseased wheat. Transactions of the Chinese Society for Agricultural Machienry 40(12), 190–195 (2009)
6. Hanping, M., Guili, X., Pingping, L.: Diagnosis of nutrientdeficiency of tomato based on computervision. Transactions of the Chinese Society for Agricultural Machienry 34(2), 73–75 (2003)

Dynamic Compensation for Impact-Based Grain Flow Sensor

Junwan Hu[1,*], Changlai Gong[1], and Zhigang Zhang[2]

[1] Electronic Information Engineering College, JiaYing University, Meizhou 514015, China
hujunwan@jyu.edu.cn
[2] Key Laboratory of Key Technology on Agricultural Machine and Equipment
of Ministry of Education, South China Agricultural University,
Guangz hou 510642, China

Abstract. The impact-based grain flow sensor is widely used in the combine harvester yield monitor systems to measure the crop yield .but its accuracy wrecked by false signal of excessive natural vibration. A step response experiment was carried to identify the math function of the sensor. Experiment found that the math function of the sensor was a second-order vibration system, its Damping Ratio was 0.037, and its natural frequency was 125Hz, the overshoot reached 20%.To reduce the effect of the overshoot and natural vibration signal on the measurement accuracy, a dynamic compensation algorithm was designed with the series correction method. Step response experiment showed that the overshoot of the compensated sensor was reduced from 20% to 2%.

Keywords: impact-based grain flow sensor, system identification, transfer function, dynamic compensation.

1   Introduction

As an important element of the combine yield monitor system The impact-based grain flow sensor measure the grain flow of the harvester by detecting the impact of grain. With the characteristics of simple structure, and low cost, the impact-based grain flow sensor is widely used in the combine harvester yield monitor systems to measure the crop yield [1-11], But its accuracy was influent by vibration and tilt [12-15].

With a high velocity, the grain jet out of the crop outlet of the combine harvester, and impact the detect plate of the sensor and reflect quickly. The yield monitor system acquires the impact force and calculates the grain flow rapidly. But, after impacting, a false signal last a while by overshoot and nature vibration.

A Damping material was adopted to enhance Damping Ratio of sensor, and then eliminate the affection of overshoot and nature vibration [16-18], but reduce the sensitivity.

To investigate the dynamic characteristic, a step response experiment was carried to identify the math function of the sensor. And a dynamic compensation algorithm was designed with the series correction method in this paper.

---

* Lecturer, Research on agricultural automation.

D. Li and Y. Chen (Eds.): CCTA 2011, Part III, IFIP AICT 370, pp. 210–216, 2012.

2   The Impact-Based Grain Flow Sensor

As show in Fig. 1, the single plate impact-based grain flow include bracket. elastic body, impact plate.

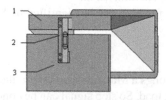

Fig. 1. Structure of impact-based grain flow sensor

The impact plate is made of a Plexiglas board with the dimensions 260mm ×120mm×4mm. It fixed at the end of elastic body which bean made of a hard aluminum-Alloy with the dimensions of 80mm ×12mm×12mm, and 2 parallel through-holes in its center.

As show in the Fig.2, a Wheatstone bridge with 4 electrical-resistance strain gages with 320 Ω bean pasted at the most sensitive surface of the elastic body.

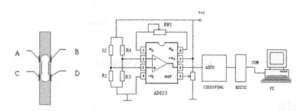

Fig. 2. Data acquiring circuit for sensor

The grain impact the plate of the sensor when the combine harvester working, and then, the output signal of the sensor have a liner relationship with the impact force. The signal is amplified from 0~5mV into 0~5V by a AD623 instrumentation amplify circuit. In this way, we can calculate the grain flow by the output voltage of the sensor.

The output voltage of the sensor can be acquired by a embed ADC of C8051F040 MCU, and send to a computer by RS232 Bus.

3   System Identifications

The impact-based grain sensor belong A Mass-elastic-Damper system. According to the basic theory of automatic, the impact-based grain flow sensor is a typical attenuate vibration system of second order, its transfer function should be:

$$G(s) = \frac{\omega_n^2}{S^2 + 2\xi\omega_n S + \omega_n^2}$$ (1)

Where: ω --Free Vibration Frequency, rad/s;
         ξ --Damping Ratio, No dimension.

The parameter of transfer function can be identified by Step Response test.

3.1   Step Response Test

As the grain flow sensor belongs a Mass elastic system, the nature frequency could be changed by put a mass-block load. So step signal can be conducted by unload a pre-load suddenly.

As show in Fig.3, fix the sensor in level, and hang a 2kg mass-block as pre-load with a slender thread. Adjust the zero point; make sure the output of the sensor is 0V.

The step signal happened by unload the preload with a pair of shears suddenly.

Fig. 3. Step load method

3.2   Test Results

The output voltage under step signal excitation was acquired by C8051F040, and recorded by PC. As show in Fig.4, the step response curve indicates that the grain flow sensor is a typical Second Order System.

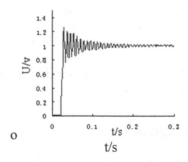

Fig. 4. Step response of the sensor

According to the basic theory of automatic, there is:

$$\omega_d = \omega_n \sqrt{1-\xi^2} \tag{2}$$

$$\xi\omega_n = \frac{1}{T}\ln(\frac{A_1}{A_2}) \tag{3}$$

Where ω_d -- angular frequency under damped vibration, rad/s;
     T--period of damped vibration, s;
     A_1 --the first peak voltages, V;
     A_2 -- the second peak voltages, V.
From the curve, T=0.008s, $A_1 = 0.265v$,
$A_2 = 0.210v$, $\cdot$ $\omega_d = 2\pi\frac{1}{T} = 785 rad/s$ Then $\omega_n \approx 785\ rad/s$, $\xi \approx 0.037$, the
transfer function of the grain flow sensor is:

$$G(s) = \frac{616225}{S^2 + 58S + 616225} \tag{4}$$

The overshoot reached 20%, the accuracy of the sensor could be damage by overshoot and free vibration.

4   Dynamic Compensation

4.1   Basic Theory of Compensation

For a second order system with small Damping Ratio, it's necessary to compensate the Damping Ratio up to 0.6~0.7 for the stability. Take an additional Damping material can improve the Damping Ratio in some degree, but it is not enough. Series/parallel correction methods are widely used in sensor dynamic compensation [15-16].

If the original transfer function is $G(s)$, the series correction system is $G_c(s)$, the after correction system should be:

$$G'(s) = G(s)G_C(s) \tag{5}$$

According to the formula (1), If the appropriate Damping ratio is 0.6 and keep the nature frequency, then the ideal corrected system should be:

$$G'(s) = \frac{616225}{S^2 + 942S + 616225} \tag{6}$$

By Matlab simulate, we got the step response curve of the original system and the corrected system. As show in Fig.5, the simulation result showed that the overshoot of the corrected system can be limited significantly. The corrected system should keep more stability.

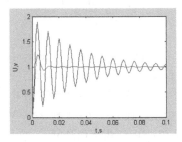

Fig. 5. Step response by simulation

According to the formula (5)and (6), the series correction system should be:

$$G_c(s) = \frac{S^2 + 58S + 616225}{S^2 + 942S + 616225} \tag{7}$$

4.2   Compensation Algorithm

It is difficult to reality the formula (7) by create a suitable hardware circuit. But it is easy for software. For that, the correction system must describe in discrete transfer function.

Make a Z Transform by Matlab function named C2D with a 0.001s sampling period, the formula (7) transform into discrete transfer function:

$$G_c(z) = \frac{0.6849z^2 - 0.9246z + 0.619}{z^2 - 1.01z + 0.03898} \tag{8}$$

According to formula (8), If the input of the correction system is x, the output is y, the second order difference equations of the correction system is:

$$y^*(t+2T) - 1.01y^*(t+T) + 0.03898y^*(t)$$
$$= 0.6849x^*(t+2T) - 0.9246x^*(t+T) + 0.619x^*(t) \tag{9}$$

Where y* -- discrete value of output variable y;

x* -- discrete value of input variable x;
T –sampling period, 0.001s.
According to formula (9), get the iterative equation:

$$y^*(k+2) = 0.6849x^*(k+2) - 0.9246x^*(k+1)$$
$$+ 0.619x^*(k) + 1.01y^*(k+1) - 0.03898y^*(k) \tag{10}$$

Where k—positive integer;
initial condition of the iterative equation:

$$
\begin{array}{ll}
x^*(0) = 1 & y^*(0) = 0 \\
x^*(1) = 1 & y^*(1) = 0
\end{array} \tag{11}
$$

Finally, program the compensation formula (10) and (11) into fire ware of C8051F040.

4.3 Compensation Result

Step response test carried again after compensation. Show as at Fig.6.

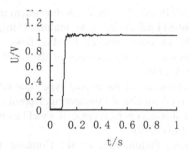

Fig. 6. Step response after compensation

The response curve of the compensated showed that the overshoot been limited from 20% to 2%, the dynamic characteristics improved significantly.

5   Conclusion

The impact-based grain flow sensor system was identified by a step response test. The step response curve indicated that the transfer function of the grain flow sensor is a under Damping second-order system with 125Hz free frequency and 0.037 damped Ratio.

A compensation algorithm was introduced to improve the dynamic characteristics without change the real damped Ratio. After compensation, the overshoot limited from 20% to 2%.The dynamic charactcristics have been improved significantly.

References

1. Luo, X., Zhang, Y., Zhou, Z.: Research progress in farming information acquisition technique for precision agriculture. Transactions of Agricultural Engineering 22(1), 167–173 (2006) (in Chinese)

2. Li, M.: The Technique of Crop Yield Monitor and Key Equipment. Agriculture Network Information (S1), 34–38 (2004) (in Chinese)
3. Reyns, P., Missotten, B., Ramon, H., et al.: A Review of Combine Sensors for Precision Farming. Precision Agriculture (3), 169–182 (2002) (in Chinese)
4. Sun, Y., Wang, M., Ma, D., Huang, J.: Experimental Research on Grain flow measurement System Using an Impact sensor. Transactions of Agricultural Machinery (04), 48–50 (2001) (in Chinese)
5. Chen, S., Zhang, W., Li, X., Li, M., Huang, J.: Experiment Research of Grain Mass Flow Sensor Based on Impact. Transactions of Agricultural Machinery (02), 82–84 (2005) (in Chinese)
6. Lee, C.K., Iida, M., Kaho, T., et al.: Development of impact type sensor for heading feeding combine. Journal of the JSAM 62(4), 81–88 (2000) (in Japanese)
7. Shoji, K., Kawamura, T., Horio, H.: Impact-based grain yield sensor with compensation for vibration and drift. Journal of the JSAM 64(5), 108–115 (2002) (in Japanese)
8. Chaplin, J., Hemming, N., Hetchler, B.: Comparison of impact plate and torque-based grain mass flow sensors. Transactions of the American Society of Agricultural Engineers 47(4), 1337–1345 (2004)
9. Schrock, M.D., Oard, D.L., Eisele, E.L., et al.: A diaphragm impact sensor for measuring combines grain flow. Applied Engineering in Agriculture 15(6), 639–642 (1999)
10. Strubbe, G., Missotten, B., De Baerdemaeker, J.: Mass flow measurements with a curved plate at the exit of an elevator. In: Proceedings of the 3rd International Conference on Precision Agriculture, USA, (1996)
11. Vansichen, R., De Baerdemaeker, J.: An impact type flow rate sensor for combines. In: International Conference on Agricultural Engineering, Uppsala, Sweden, pp. 15–16 (1992)
12. Arslan, S., Colvin, T.S.: Laboratory performance of a yield monitor. Applied Enginering in Agriculture 15(03), 189–195 (1999)
13. Burks, T.F., Shearer, S.A., Fulton, J.P., et al.: Combine yield monitor test facility development and initial monitoring test. Applied Engineering in Agriculture 19(01), 5–12 (2003)
14. Fulton, J.P., Sobolik, C.J., Shearer, S.A., et al.: Grain yield monitor flow sensor accuracy for simulated varying field slopes. Applied Engineering in Agriculture 25(1), 15–21 (2009)
15. Grisso, R.D., Jasa, P.J., Schroeder, M.A., et al.: Yield monitor accuracy successful farming magazine case study. Applied Engineering in Agriculture 18(02), 147–151 (2002)
16. Zhou, J., Zhou, G., Miao, Y., Liu, C.: Damping Design of Impact-based Grain Yield Sensor. Transactions of the Chinese Society for Agricultural Machinery 36(11), 121–123 (2005) (in Chinese)
17. Tu, J., Miao, Y., Zhao, S., et al.: Damping desige and signal proscession of the yield sensor on grain combine. In: Progress of Information Technology in Agriculture, Proceedings of the 4th International Symposium on Intelligent Information Technology in Agriculture(ISIITA), Beijing (2007)
18. Zhou, J., Liu, C.: Signal processing method for impact-based grain mass flow sensor with parallel beam load cell. Transactions of the Chinese Society of Agricultural Engineering 24(1), 183–187 (2008) (in Chinese)
19. Chen, S., Yang, H., Li, Y., Hu, J., Zhang, L.: Experiment of Dual-plates Differential Impact-based Grain Flow Sensor. Transactions of the Chinese Society for Agricultural Machinery 41(08), 172–173 (2010) (in Chinese)

Research on the Simulation Model of Above-Ground Organs Morphogenesis of Flue-Cured Tobacco

Shuping Xiong[1], Lei Xi[2], Jucai Wang[2], Guanghui Xu[1,3], and Xinming Ma[1,2,*]

[1] Agronomy College of Henan Agricultural University, zhengzhou 450002, China
[2] College of Information and Management Science,
Henan Agricultural University, zhengzhou 450002, China
[3] Yexian Branch of Pingdingshan Tobacco Company, Yexian 467200, China
xinmingma@126.com, shupxiong@163.com

Abstract. In order to create the simulation model of Above-ground Organs Morphogenesis of Flue-cured Tobacco, the dynamic model of organ morphology in different growing step of tobacco was built with potting experimental methods with which the biomass of tobacco organ in different growth period can be systematically determined. As simulation of organ morphology of tobacco measured in 2007 shows that the correlation coefficient between the simulated value and the measured value of above-ground organ of tobacco in different growth cycle is 0.735 to 0.9997 at significant level which proved that the dynamic of above-ground organ morphogenesis of tobacco can be predicted well by the model. The regulation of growth of tobacco morphology can be reflected well by the model of above-ground organ morphogenesis; furthermore, the model can also be a theoretical basis for virtual growth of tobacco.

Keywords: Flue-cured Tobacco, above-ground organ, morphogenesis, model of simulation.

With the dynamic development of information technology on agriculture, more and more researches on virtual plant have been taking. The morphogenesis model, a key technology in virtual plants, has aroused our attention. Ulam [1] and Cohen [2] were the pioneers on research to models of plant branches. These were followed by Lindermayer and his L-system [3], basing on the analysis to the plant organ growth, Hunt [4] produced a plant organ-growing model. Besides, de Reffye, a France man, and his assistants developed a plant-growth system, named AMAP [5, 6]. Combining the L-system and computer graphics, A.R. Smith and Prusinkiewicz made the visualization of plant morphology come true [7-10]. Considering the environment model (e.g. Light and disease and pest injury) and measured data from tri-dimension plant on the L-system, virtual plant model was built in the research center CPAI, Australia [11]. The virtual plant system GROGRA2.4 (Growth grammar Interceptor), which was basing on the L-system, was created by Kurth [12].

As a function-structure model, GREENLAB played an important role in the plant structure area [13-15]; it is brief and honest to mechanization. By building Recurrence

---

* Corresponding author.

D. Li and Y. Chen (Eds.): CCTA 2011, Part III, IFIP AICT 370, pp. 217–229, 2012.
© IFIP International Federation for Information Processing 2012

relations among several Mathematical formulas, the feedback relationship was parallel simulated. It only needed a few certain parameters to simulate the growth of plants like trees. Virtual structure model of plant, like cotton, maize, wheat etc, was produced by de Reffye [16], Zhan Zhigang etc [17], and GREENLAB. Technology frame on shape simulation and tri-demission visualization of corn, basing on growth model, was produced by Zhao Chunjiang etc [19], and it created a new idea and method. After researching the static model on maize canopy structure, Ivanov [20] and Fournier [21] rebuilt the tri-dimension canopy and analyzed the way how the light is used by canopy with the help of oriented-object program, Jin Mingxian [22] built the tri-dimension model for root -growth of maize. Besides, maize- visualization model, produced by Guo Yan and Li Baoguo [23-24], can be used to analyze tri-dimension structure character of maize canopy and the maize canopy space distribution under the effect of morphology. These researches above show that plant simulation has been developing fast in all the areas which it refers.

Tobacco is one of the very important cash crops. Researches about its under-ground organ such as root have been done. Ma Xinming [25-26] once described the dynamic relation between growth of root system and surrounding environment and built a mathematic model on morphological development of tobacco roots. However, researches on above-ground organs of tobacco are rare. Taking the existed researches [27-29] as references, basing on the measured data for building tobacco morphology, researching the dynamic relationship between tobacco morphogenesis regulation and the environment, visualization model about tobacco morphogenesis was built, with the help of morphology module produced by Song Youhong etc [18]. A purpose of this paper is to offer a theory for improving the quality of tobacco and increasing of production.

1   Material and Methods

1.1   Designing of Experiment and Materials in Use

This experiment was made in the scientific and educational experimental area of Henan Agricultural University during 2006-2007. All the tobacco seeds, seeds K326 in this experiment, were cultivated in the pots, diameter 40cm, depth 45cm, filled with sandy and tidal soil. Content of nutrient in the soil were listed as Table1:

Table 1. Content of Nutrient in the Sandy and Tidal Soil

Index of Soil	Organic Matter(g.kg^{-1})	Available N(mg.kg^{-1})	Available P(mg.kg^{-1})	Available K(mg.kg^{-1})	pH
Content	7.8	35	9.86	80	7.6

The weight of soil which should be air-dried and sifted before being used in each pot was 25kg. Chemical fertilizers used in this soil were AR $(NH4)_2SO_4$, KNO_3 and KH_2PO_4 and all of these chemical fertilizers should be scattered off as base fertilizer at the first time. The content of fertilizer N in every kilogram soil was 0.2 gram, and N:

P_2O_5: K_2O=1:1.5:3. Seeding growing with the float system was cultivated in artificial climatic box in the lab. Sixty days later, they were transplanted into the pot, laid in the soil under the shelter. In this way, the environment where they grow in can be similar with that of farmland. The amount of necessary water in different period of growing for tobacco is varied. The supply of water can be controlled with the help of time-domain reflector (TDR) whose type model is TRIME-FM and shelter should also be open in the raining day to prevent the rainwater in. The management of tobacco, planted in row spacing 1.1m, plant spacing 0.6m in this experiment, has noting different with that of farmland except entering rosette stage in their 30th day and pinching in 57th day after being transplanted.

1.2   Measured Items and Measuring Methods

1.2.1   Measured Items for Internodes: Fresh Weight, Length and Diameter

Three typical plants from the experimental area should be taken every 10 days after seeding restitution stage. Then, cut them apart by internodes. Fresh weight of internodes can be measured on milli electronic balance. Length of internodes can be measured by ruler which is correct to 0.1cm. Diameter can be measured by vernier caliper within the accuracy of 0.001cm.

1.2.2   The Length, Width and Area of Leaf

The maximal width on the middle of leaf (Abb. W) and leaf length (Abb. L) can be measured with ruler, and the fresh weight of leaf can be measured with electronic balance. Then, the leaf area (Abb. LA) can be figured out with this formula:

$$LA=L \times W \times 0.6345 \qquad (1)$$

Besides, meteorological data can be achieved from meteorological bureau.

1.3   Model Testing

The dynamic model for above-ground organs of tobacco while growing can be built with data measured in 2006 and be tested with the data measured in 2007. The conformity between analog value and observed value can be made a statistical analysis with root mean square error (Abb. RMSE) and 1:1 graphing method. The RMSE can be counted in this equation:

$$RMSE = \sqrt{\frac{\sum_{i=1}^{n}(OBS_i - SIM_i)^2}{n}} \qquad (2)$$

OBS_i: *Observed value;*
SIM_i: *Analog value;*
n: Sample size

1.4   Description on Tobacco Models

1.4.1   Model on Growth Cycle of Tobacco

Growth cycle (Abb. GC) was defined as a time span caused by two adjacent me tamers which including internodes, node and leaf growing from the node. It has been proved that the topological structure of plant is obviously affected by cumulative effect which is caused by temperature change of environment [17]. For that growing period of tobacco in field last for 120~130 days which is a pretty long time, the GC was defined as a time unit while modeling. Growing process can be predicted with the following formula (3) which reflect the relationship between tobacco growth and accumulated temperature.

$$NGC = DR \cdot SumT + 7 \qquad (3)$$

NGC: Number of Growth Cycle

DR ($°C^{-1}$) : Developing ratio

SumT ($°C$): Accumulated temperature which equals to the sum of temperature after being transplanted

The number 7 in formula (3) represented the number of unrolled leaf when the tobacco plant being transplanted, in other words, 7 Growth Cycles has been finished when being transplanted.

1.4.2   Internodes Morphology of Tobacco

Growing of tobacco stem can be described in two aspects including prolonging and thickening. Internodes morphology in different position should be built in different way. Leaf 1 to leaf 8, counted from the bottom of stem, are too short to measure when being transplanted. So, they were ignored in this experiment. Only internodes whose position was higher than that of the 8th internode were considered while building morphology.

As the shape of tobacco internode is like a cylinder, volume (V_e) of the internode can be figured out with formula (4):

$$Ve(j,i) = \frac{q_e(j,i)}{\rho_e(j,i)} = l_e(j,i) \cdot s_e(j,i) \qquad (4)$$

i: Growth cycle (Abb. GC)

j: Position of internodes

$q_e(j,i)$: *Accumulated biomass of the jth internode in its GC (g).*

$\rho_e(j,i)$: *The internode density (g/cm^{-3})*

$l_e(j,i)$: *The internode length (cm)*

$s_e(j,i)$: *Cross-sectional area (cm^2)*

The length and cross-sectional area of the tobacco internode change with the intercalary growth and primary thickening growth of the internode. Analyzing the experimental data, changing relationship can be built as following:

$$l_e(j,i) = k_e \cdot s_e(j,i)^\alpha \tag{5}$$

k_e, α: Fitting index which is possible to change with the change of the internode position

If defining the morphology index of the internode β and b_e as following:

$$s_b(j,i) = \frac{q_b(j,i)}{\xi_b} \tag{6}$$

Computational formula on length and cross-sectional area of tobacco internodes can be figured out with formulas (4), (5) and (6). It turns out to be formula (7):

$$\begin{cases} \beta = \dfrac{\alpha - 1}{\alpha + 1} \\ b_e = K_e^{1-\beta} \end{cases} \tag{7}$$

Value of the length and the cross-sectional area could be figured out in formula (7), only if knowing the biomass of internodes in a certain growing stage when morphology parameters of the internode β, b_e and density ρ_e were given. Then, simulation of internodes morphology can be carried out with biomass.

1.4.3   Morphology of Tobacco Leaf

What we need from tobacco is leaf. The leaf is not only a place for photosynthesis but also a place to store all kinds of chemical substances which directly decide the quality of tobacco. The area of leaf j, S_b, in i^{th} can be figured out in formula (8) with its biomass q_b.

$$\begin{cases} l_e(j,i) = \sqrt{b_e} \left[\dfrac{q_e(j,i)}{\rho_e(j,i)} \right]^{\frac{1+\beta}{2}} \\ s_e(j,i) = \sqrt{\dfrac{1}{b_e}} \left[\dfrac{q_e(j,i)}{\rho_e(j,i)} \right]^{\frac{1-\beta}{2}} \end{cases} \tag{8}$$

ξ_b : Specific leaf weight, in other words, value of dividing leaf area into leaf fresh weight (g/cm^2).

Showing from experimental data, the relationship between leaf length l_b (cm) and its fresh weight q_b (g) can be expressed with formula (9):

$$l_b(j,i) = k_i \cdot q_b(j,i)^r \qquad (9)$$

k_i and r in formula (9) are fitting indexes. For that leaf area is always figured out through multiplying a certain parameter λ with the product of leaf length and the maximum width of leaf in agronomy, the maximum width of leaf, w_b (cm), can be figured out after the leaf area and leaf length being simulated with the following formula:

$$w_b(j,i) = \frac{s_b(j,i)}{\lambda \cdot l_b(j,i)} \qquad (10)$$

So, the leaf area (Abb. LA), length and the maximum width of this plant can be figured out after the accumulated biomass of leaf in a certain time being simulated if parameters ξ_b, k_i, r and λ were given.

1.4.4   Ascertaining Parameters

Parameter in models can be divided into three kinds: parameters being used to describe the growing process of plant, parameters being used to build the internode model and parameters being used in morphology model. Value of Parameters like growing speed, accumulated biomass, cross-sectional area of the internode, the internode length, leaf area, fresh weight of leaf, leaf width, and specific leaf weight can get from experimental data. However, coefficients like fitting index k_e and α of the internode morphology, morphology index β and b_e of the internode, fitting index k_i and r of leaf are implicit parameters. Parameters of model are listed as following table 2.

Table 2. List of model parameters

	Parameter categories	Unit
Development parameters of tobacco	**DR:** *Developing ratio*	℃⁻¹
	SumT: *Accumulated temperature*	℃
Morphology parameter of the internode	**j :** *Position of the internode*	---
	i: *Growth cycle*	---
	$q_e(j,i)$: *Accumulated biomass of the jth internode in i^{th} GC(g)*	g
	$\rho_e(j,i)$: *The internode density*	g/cm³
	$l_e(j,i)$: *The internode length*	cm
	$S_e(j,i)$: *Cross-sectional area*	cm²
	k_e , α : *Fitting index of internode*	---
	β , b_e : *Morphology index*	---
Leaf morphology parameter	$S_b(j,i)$: *Leaf area*	cm²
	$q_b(j,i)$: *Fresh weight of leaf*	g
	ε_b : *Specific leaf weight*	g/cm²
	$l_b(j,i)$, $w_b(j,i)$: *Leaf length and leaf width*	cm
	k_i , r : *Fitting index of leaf*	---
	λ : *Leaf area index*	---

The following Figure 1 is a relation graph between the measured number of tobacco metamer which was defined to be 7 when being transplanted and the accumulated temperature starting from seeding restitution stage.

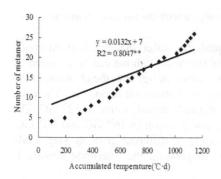

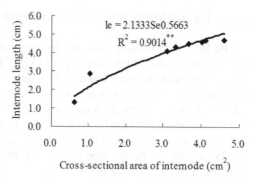

Fig. 1. The relationship between number of tobacco and sum of temperature

Fig. 2. Relationship between length and cross-sectional area during its elongation (9th internode)

As shown in Fig 1, the simulated number of metamer matches the measured number well. The number of GC equals that of metamer, in other words, one metamer could be produced in one GC. Slope in this model is the developing speed of tobacco, represented with DR($^{\circ}C^{-1}$). Meanwhile, a necessary accumulated temperature which is 75.76($^{\circ}C^{-1}$) in this model in a GC is represented with the reciprocal of slope. Real length of time in each GC is 2 or 3 days, changing with daily temperature.

Using experimental data, Fitting coefficients k_e, α can be figured out with formula (4) and the internode morphology coefficients β and b_e can also be figured out with formula (5), showed in Fig 3. As shown in fig 3, two peak values of b_e appeared in the 5th internode and the 14th internode with the rising of the internode position. The value of β grows with the growing of the internode position. For that morphology coefficient in different position of internodes differ, so, the value of β and b_e in different position should be considered while building the internode morphology model.

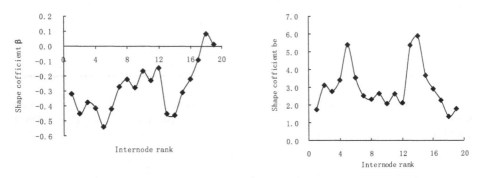

Fig. 3. Internode shape coefficient be and β varying with the internode position

The Internode density, showing in fig 4, equals the value that dividing internode volume into measured internode fresh heavy. The internode volume can be acquired by making internode diameter multiply its length. As shown in figure 4, the changing trend of the internode density is different with the position of internode in one GC. The peak value of the third internode density and the 8th internode density come in 12th GC. The internode density grows with rising of the internode position in 16th GC and 20th GC. The internode density should be selected according to different growing step while simulating the internode morphology for that, in general, the internode density is reducing with the growing of GC.

Through fitting analysis on the leaf fresh weight and its leaf area in different leaf position in different growth period measured in 2006, it appears that specific leaf weight ε_b :

$$\varepsilon_b = 0.045(r=0.869^{**}, \quad n=134)$$ as shown in figure 5. Leaf length in different position in different GC and its fresh weight can be fitted in formula (9) (Fig. 6). Leaf area of tobacco used to be figured out through multiplying among leaf length, leaf width and leaf area index. Leaf area index λ in formula (10) is settled as 0.6345.

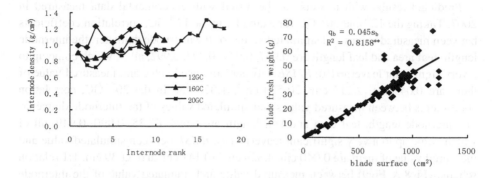

Fig. 4. The density of tobacco internodes

Fig. 5. The relationship between blade fresh weight and surface

2   Results and Analysis

In purpose of testing the simulation precision of model on metamer number of tobacco, the predicted results of model was tested with experimental data measured in 2007. The number of metamer was predicted with the help of formula (2) and the accumulated temperature which was measured after being transplanted in 2007. As shown in figure 7, correlation coefficient between the simulated value and actual value reached to 0.992(n=23) which comes up to a significant leave. Meanwhile, *RMSE* between simulated value and actual value is 1.857 which proves them a good uniformity. All tests above prove that it is feasible to simulate the metamer number of tobacco with model.

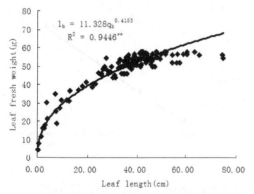

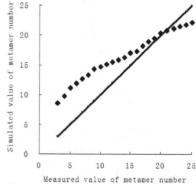

Fig. 6. Relationship between leaf length and its fresh weight

Fig. 7. Comparison between simulated value and mesaured value of metamer number

Predicted results with models can be tested with experimental data measured in 2007. Taking the 12th and 20th GC for example, in the 12th GC, correlation coefficients between measured values and simulated values of the internode diameter, the internode length, leaf area and leaf length are 0.997, 0.931, 0.997, 0.992, all of which come up to a very significant leave(n=10). *RMSE* between simulated value and measured value of them are 0.045 cm, 2.213 cm, 20.570 cm^2, 1.828 cm. In the 20th GC, correlation coefficients between measured values and simulated values of the internode diameter, the internode length, leaf area and leaf length are 0.994, 0.735, 0.990, 0.949, all of which come up to a very significant leave(n=19). *RMSE* between simulated value and measured value of them are 0.040 cm, 4.828 cm, 40.141 cm^2 and 4.039 cm. 1:1 relation schema (Fig8 & Fig9) between measured value and simulated value of the internode diameter, the internode length, leaf area, leaf length in 12th and 20th GC show that simulated value from the dynamic model of tobacco growth matches the measured value well.

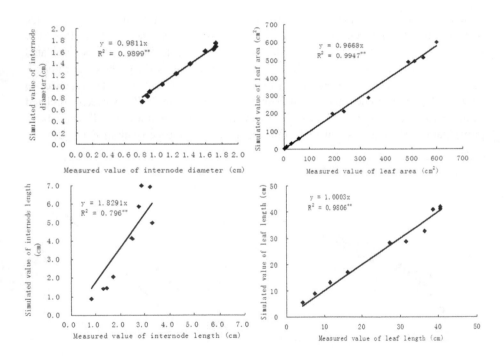

Fig. 8. Comparison between simulated value and measured value in the 12th GC

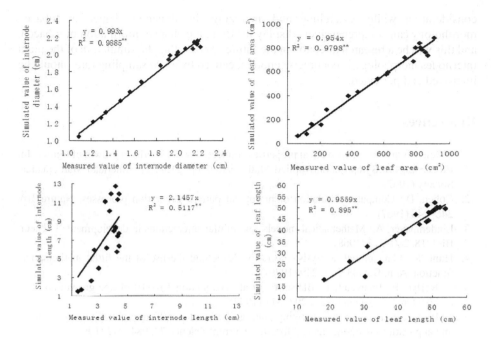

Fig. 9. Comparison between simulated value and measured value in the 20th GC

3   Conclusions and Discussion

The essential basis while building digital plant will be plant growing, structure simulation of plant morphology and union of the both. Interrelation between changing of above-ground organ morphology and GC during the growing process of tobacco was generally researched in this paper. Besides, basing on biomass-morphology relationship of tobacco organ, dynamic model on organ morphology was also built in this paper. It turns out that the model can express biological method well and that there is a high degree of uniformity between simulated results and measured values. They have made the model usable.

Growth period model of tobacco is a factorial index model which is using Rice Clock Model for reference and basing on mechanism of tobacco growing and to express growth process of tobacco [30]. Virtual growth system of tobacco, coupled with dynamic organ model and growth period model, will be a new research direction in the next step. The system is necessary while digitizing the tobacco growth. Information on tobacco growth in different stage can be obtained from the system only if the agriculture technician input few certain parameters of growing environment. With that information, cultivating and control technology, fertilizer rate in necessary and so on will be guided well.

Preparing for building the morphology model of above-ground organ of tobacco, the simulation model which based on the model of physiological and ecological process of tobacco, under the control of outside environment, like temperature, was created in this paper. Taking the spatial angle change during the period of tobacco growth into consideration while researching and analyzing the dynamic change of tobacco morphology can comprehensively display the dynamic change information of tobacco, and this will be a research direction in the future. At last, that the simulation of the plant internodes morphology is not precise enough, caused by a low sampling rate, should be improved and perfected.

References

1. Ulam, S.: On some mathematical properties connected with patterns of growth of figures. In: Proceedings of Symposia on Applied Mathematics, pp. 215–224. American Mathematical Society (1962)
2. Cohen, D.: Computer simulation of biological pattern generation processes. Nature 216, 246–248 (1967)
3. Lindenmayer, A.: Mathematical models for cellular interactions in development. J. Theor. Biol. 18, 280–315 (1968)
4. Hunt, R.: Plant growth analysis: the rationale behind the use of the fitted mathematical function. Ann. Bot. 43, 245–249 (1979)
5. de Reffye, P., Fourcaud, T., Blaise, F., et al.: A functional model of tree growth and tree architecture. Silva Fennica 31, 297–311 (1997)
6. de Reffye, P., Houllier, F.: Modeling plant growth and architecture: Some recent advances and applications to agronomy and forestry. Current Science 73, 984–992 (1997)
7. Prusinkiewicz, P., Lindenmayer, A., Hanan, J.: Developmental models of herbaceous plants for computer imagery purpose. Computer Graphics 22(4), 141–150 (1988)
8. Mech, R., Prusinkiewicz, P.: Visual models of plants interacting with their environment. Computer Graphics 30(3), 397–410 (1996)
9. Prusinkiewicz, P.: A look at the visual modeling of plant using L-systems. Agronomie 19, 211–224 (1990)
10. Prusinkiewicz, P., Hammel, M., Mjolsness, E.: Animation of plant development. Computer Graphics 27(3), 351–360 (1993)
11. Room, P.M., Hanan, J.S., Prusinkiewicz, P.: Virtual plants: New perspectives for ecologists, pathologists and agricultural scientists. Trends in Plant Science (1), 33–38 (1996)
12. Kurth, W.: Growth Grammar Interpreter GROGEA2.4: A Software tool for the 3-dimensional interpretations of stochastic, sensitive growth grammars in the context of plant modeling. In: Introduction and Reference Manual. Universitat gottingen, Gottingen (1994)
13. de Reffye, P., Hu, B.-G.: Relevant qualitative and quantitative choices for building an efficient dynamic plant growth model: GreenLab case. In: Hu, B.-G., Jaeger, M. (eds.) Plant Growth Modeling and Applications, pp. 87–107. Tsinghua University Press, Beijing (2003)
14. Guo, Y., de Reffye, P., Song, Y.H., et al.: Modeling of biomass acquisition and partitioning in the architecture of sunflower. In: Hu, B.-G., Jaeger, M. (eds.) Plant Growth Modeling and Applications, pp. 271–284. Tsinghua University Press, Beijing (2003)
15. Yan, H.P., Kang, M.Z., de Reffye, P., Dingkuhn, M.: A dynamic, architectural plant model simulating resource-dependent growth. Ann. Bot. 93, 591–602 (2004)
16. de Beffye, P., Yan, H.P., Leroux, J., et al.: Study on plant growth behaviors simulated by the function-structural plant model-Greenlab. In: Plant Growth Modeling and Applications Proceedings, pp. 118–128 (2003)
17. Zhan, Z., Wang, Y., de Reffye, P., et al.: Morphological Architecture-Based Growth Model of Winter Wheat. Transaction of the CSAE 17(5), 6–10 (2001)

18. Song, Y.-H., Guo, Y., Li, B.-G., et al.: Virtual maize model II. Plant morphological constructing based on organ biomass accumulation. Acta Ecologica Sinica 23(12), 2579–2586 (2003)
19. Guo, X., Zhao, C., Liu, Y., et al.: Three-dimensional visualization of maize based on growth models. Transaction of the CSAE 23(3), 121–125 (2007)
20. Ivanov, N., Boissard, P., Chapron, M., et al.: Estimation of the height and angles of orientation of the upper leaves in the maize canopy using sterovision. Agronomie 2, 183–194 (1994)
21. Fournier, C., Andrieu, B.: A 3D architectural and process-based model of maize development. Annals of Botany 81(2), 233–250 (1998)
22. Jin, M.-X., Wang, T.-D.: Simulation of Growth and Hydrotropism of Maize Roots. Acta Botanica Sinica 38(5), 384–390 (1996)
23. Ma, Y.-T., Guo, Y., Zhan, Z.-G., Li, B.-G., et al.: Evaluation of the Plant Growth Model GREENLAB-Maize. Acta Agronomica Sinica 32, 956–963 (2006)
24. Guo, Y., Ma, Y.T., Zhan, Z.G., et al.: Parameter optimization and field validation of the functional-structural model GREENLAB for maize. Annals of Botany 97, 217–230 (2006)
25. Ma, X.-M., Yang, J., Xiong, S.-P., et al.: A Model for Simulating Root Morphological Development of Tobacco. Scientia Agricultura Sinica 38(12), 2421–2427 (2005)
26. Ma, X.-M., Xi, L., Xiong, S.-P., et al.: Dynamic changes of morphological parameters of tobacco root in field. Chinese Journal of Applied Ecology 17(3), 356–357 (2006)
27. Qiao, Y., Yu, Z., Driessen, P.M.: Quantification of dry matter accumulation and distribution among different organs of winter wheat. Chinese Journal of Applied Ecology 13(5), 543–546 (2002)
28. Liu, X., Kang, S., Xia, W.: A mathematical model of water stress and light condition effects on cotton dry matter and yield formation. Chinese Journal of Applied Ecology 13(9), 1085–1090 (2002)
29. Yang, J., Wang, Z.: Crop growth simulation model and its application. Chinese Journal of Applied Ecology 10(4), 501–505 (1999)
30. Xiong, S., Ma, X., Shi, Y.-Y., et al.: Study on Dynamic Simulation Model for the Relationship between Growth and Environmental Factors at Different Tobacco Growth and Development Stage. Journal of Henan Agricultural University 39(3), 321–325 (2005)

Simulation on Magnetic Field Characteristics of Permanent-Magnet Seed-Metering Device

Jing Wang, Jianping Hu, Qirui Wang, and Xun Wang

Key Laboratory of Modern Agricultural Equipment and Technology,
Ministry of Education & Jiangsu Province, Jiangsu University,
High-tech Key Laboratory of Agricultural Equipment & Intelligentization
of Jiangsu Province, Zhenjiang 212013, China
hujp@ujs.edu.cn

Abstract. The cylindrical permanent magnet is the core part of the permanent-magnet seed-metering device, it can absorb single magnetic powder coated seed. The first, the magnetic induction intensity model of any point in the cylindrical permanent magnet external was established based on the equivalent current model of permanent magnet. The second, the mathematical formula was derived using the Biot-Savart law and the superposition principle of magnetic field. Then its magnetic induction intensity was calculated by multiple numerical integration function of MATLAB, and the characteristics and distribution were obtained. On this basis, the simulation and analysis of the permanent magnet with height 7mm and diameter 2mm was finished. The results showed that the closer the field point was to the permanent magnet end face, the stronger the magnetic induction intensity was, and the magnetic induction intensity at the edge of end face was stronger than at the center. So the diameter of the cylindrical permanent magnet should be less than magnetic powder coated seed, meanwhile, the air gap between the permanent magnet end face and the magnetic powder coated seed should be smaller as much as possible or the magnetic powder coated seed directly contacted with the permanent magnet end face.

Keywords: Magnetic seed-metering device, Permanent magnet, Magnetic field analysis, Numerical integration, Magnetic induction intensity, Equivalent current model of permanent magnet.

1   Introduction

In recent years, concerning the problem of accurate sowing for the small seed, the literature [1-3] carried out the research about Magnetic Precision Metering Technology which used electromagnet as the seed-metering component of the metering device. In the literature [4], a permanent-magnet seed-metering device was proposed and the simulation and experiment of sowing performance was studied. The structure diagram of the permanent- magnet seed-metering device was showed in Figure 1. The seed-metering component was a cylindrical permanent magnet. The permanent magnet was installed in the device which can make the permanent magnet to throw out and draw back. This device was installed in the drum. With the drum rotating, the magnetic powder coated seeds were absorbed by seed-metering components when it threw out, and were metered when it drew back. In order to analyze the characteristics and

D. Li and Y. Chen (Eds.): CCTA 2011, Part III, IFIP AICT 370, pp. 230–238, 2012.

distribution of magnetic field about the cylindrical permanent magnet, the paper adopted the equivalent current model of permanent magnet to derive and establish the mathematical model which can be used for calculating the magnetic induction intensity of any point in the permanent magnet external. The mathematical model of magnetic induction intensity about the permanent magnet can be calculated by the multiple numerical integration function of MATLAB, and the distribution can be expressed by the visualization function.

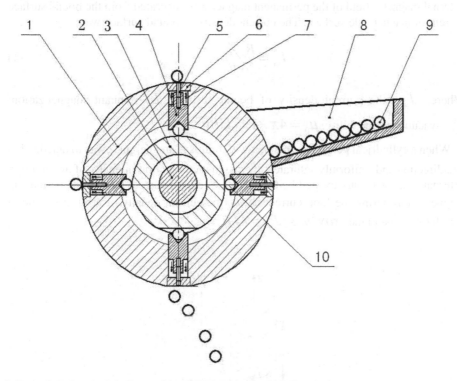

1. Drum 2. Drive shaft 3. Cam guides 4. Magnet jacket 5. Cylindrical permanent magnet 6. Cover plate 7. Spring 8.Seed box 9.Magnetic powder coated seed 10. Steel ball

Fig. 1. Structural diagram of roller-type metering device

2   Mathematical Model of the Magnetic Induction Intensity of any Point in the Cylindrical Permanent Magnet External

2.1   Analytic Derivation of the Magnetic Induction Intensity of the Cylindrical Permanent Magnet

At present, the methods of studying the distribution of magnetic field of the cylindrical permanent magnet are magnetic dipole and empirical formula. The magnetic dipole method requires the radius of field point much larger than the cylindrical magnet's, so its error is large when the radius of the cylinder cannot be ignored. The empirical formula can only estimate the magnetic induction intensity on the cylinder axis, and the experience factor in the empirical formula can only be got by a large number of experiments, so the method is less accurate. In order to seek an easy and accurate algorithm for magnetic field of the cylindrical permanent magnet, based on the equivalent current model of permanent magnet, the mathematical model was derived to calculate magnetic induction intensity of any point in the cylindrical permanent magnet external. The equivalent current model of permanent magnet can be considered that the external magnetic field of the permanent magnet was generated from the bound surface current of magnet side surface. The current density of bound surface was:

$$J_m = \frac{B_r}{\mu_0}. \tag{1}$$

Where: J_m - the current density of bound surface; B_r -remnant magnetization; μ_0 -vacuum permeability, $\mu_0 = 4\pi \times 10^{-7}\,\text{H/m}$.

When a cylindrical permanent magnet with radius r_0 and height h was magnetized in one direction and uniformly saturated, the magnetic induction intensity of any point in external space was only excited by the surface of closed current loop of the permanent magnet. Considering the loop current as I, the current density of arbitrary plane in parallel with the plane xoy was $J_m = I/h$.

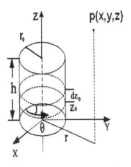

Fig. 2. Parameters of cylinder permanent magnet

The cylindrical coordinate was taken, a point inside the magnet was represented with (r_0, θ, z_0), and the coordinate system was established, as shown in Figure 2. Considering the thin layer consisted of plane z and $z + dz$, the magnetic induction intensity of any point $p(x, y, z)$ in its external space was generated by current loop $J_m dz$ to $d\vec{B}$. According to Bio-Savart law and the superposition principle of magnetic field, the magnetic induction intensity of any point $p(x, y, z)$ outside the cylinder was:

$$\vec{B} = \frac{\mu_0}{4\pi} \oint_l \frac{Id\,\vec{l} \times (\vec{r} - \vec{r}')}{\left|\vec{r} - \vec{r}'\right|^3}. \tag{2}$$

Where: $\vec{r}$ - the radius vector of source point (x_0, y_0, z_0); $\vec{r}'$ - the radius vector of field point $p(x, y, z)$.

In cylindrical coordinate, a point $M(x_0, y_0, z_0)$ on the surface of the cylinder can be expressed as $M(r_0, \theta, z_0)$, that is,
$$\begin{cases} x_0 = r_0 \cos\theta \\ y_0 = r_0 \sin\theta \\ z_0 = z_0 \end{cases}.$$

$$d\,\vec{l} \times r_0 = \begin{vmatrix} i & j & k \\ -r_0 \sin\theta d\theta & r_0 \cos\theta d\theta & 0 \\ x - r_0 \cos\theta & y - r_0 \sin\theta & z - z_0 \end{vmatrix}. \tag{3}$$

Order: $K = \left[(x - r_0 \cos\theta)^2 + (y - r_0 \sin\theta)^2 + (z - z_0)^2\right]^{3/2}$. $\tag{4}$

Generated from current loop, the magnetic induction intensity $\vec{B}$ in x, y, z directions were:

$$\begin{cases} dB_x = \frac{\mu_0 J_m dz_0}{4\pi} \int_0^{2\pi} \frac{(z - z_0) r_0 \cos\theta}{K} d\theta \\ dB_y = \frac{\mu_0 J_m dz_0}{4\pi} \int_0^{2\pi} \frac{(z - z_0) r_0 \sin\theta}{K} d\theta \\ dB_z = \frac{\mu_0 J_m dz_0}{4\pi} \left\{ \int_0^{2\pi} \frac{-r_0(x - r_0 \cos\theta)\cos\theta}{K} d\theta - \int_0^{2\pi} \frac{r_0(y - r_0 \sin\theta)\sin\theta}{K} d\theta \right\} \end{cases}. \tag{5}$$

The space magnetic induction intensity of the cylindrical permanent magnet was:

$$\left\{ \begin{array}{l} B_x = \dfrac{\mu_0 J_m dz_0}{4\pi} \int_0^h \int_0^{2\pi} \dfrac{r_0(z-z_0)\cos\theta}{K} d\theta \\[3mm] B_y = \dfrac{\mu_0 J_m dz_0}{4\pi} \int_0^h \int_0^{2\pi} \dfrac{r_0(z-z_0)\sin\theta}{K} d\theta \\[3mm] B_z = \dfrac{\mu_0 J_m dz_0}{4\pi} \left\{ \begin{array}{l} \int_0^h \int_0^{2\pi} \dfrac{-r_0(x-r_0\cos\theta)\cos\theta}{K} d\theta \\[3mm] -\int_0^h \int_0^{2\pi} \dfrac{r_0(y-r_0\sin\theta)\sin\theta}{K} d\theta \end{array} \right\} \end{array} \right. \qquad (6)$$

substituted (1) into (6)

$$\left\{ \begin{array}{l} B_x = \dfrac{Brdz_0}{4\pi} \int_0^h \int_0^{2\pi} \dfrac{r_0(z-z_0)\cos\theta}{K} d\theta \\[3mm] B_y = \dfrac{Brdz_0}{4\pi} \int_0^h \int_0^{2\pi} \dfrac{r_0(z-z_0)\sin\theta}{K} d\theta \\[3mm] B_z = \dfrac{Brdz_0}{4\pi} \left\{ \begin{array}{l} \int_0^h \int_0^{2\pi} \dfrac{-r_0(x-r_0\cos\theta)\cos\theta}{K} d\theta \\[3mm] -\int_0^h \int_0^{2\pi} \dfrac{r_0(y-r_0\sin\theta)\sin\theta}{K} d\theta \end{array} \right\} \end{array} \right. \qquad (7)$$

2.2   Calculation of the Magnetic Induction Intensity Using MATLAB

When the integral expression of function was known, it can be solved with Newton Leibniz formula in theory, but it was not practical in the calculation of the magnetic field, for integral functions of most functions can not be found. A lot of command functions of the numerical integration can be provided by MATLAB, and they can be called based on the actual situation, not only convenient but also accurate. The integral command used in this paper was dblquad. Actually, the dblquad was achieved by calling quad repeatedly. The principle of quad was adaptive Simpson quadrature method. If using the quadratic interpolation polynomial--the area of the curved trapezoidal surrounded by the parabola $y=g(x)$ approximate instead of the area of the curved trapezoidal surrounded by $y=f(x)$, the integral formula was called Simpson Formula:

$$I = \int_a^b f(x)dx \approx \frac{b-a}{6}[f(a) + 4f(\frac{a+b}{2}) + f(b)]$$

$$(8)$$

The interval $[a,b]$ was divided to K equally and $n = 2^k$ subinterval was obtained, then the composite Simpson formula further improved was:

$$I = \sum_{i=0}^{n-1} \int_{x_i}^{x_{i+1}} f(x)dx \approx s_n = \frac{h}{6} \sum_{i=0}^{n-1} [f(x_i) + 4f(\frac{x_i + x_{i+1}}{2}) + f(x_{i+1})]$$

$$(9)$$

When the variable step Simpson integration method was used to calculate the double integral, the numerical integration approach was to divide the double integral

$$I = \int_b^a dx \int_{y_1(x)}^{y_2(x)} f(x,y)dy$$

$$(10)$$

Into

$$g(x) = \int_{y_1(x)}^{y_2(x)} f(x,y)dy$$

$$(11)$$

And

$$I = \int_b^a g(x)dx .$$

$$(12)$$

In MATLAB, the model in (7) was written into M-file of $fun(\theta, z_0)$, and the integral of the model was realized by B=dblquad(fun, a, b, c, d, tol). Where a, b was the upper and lower limit of θ; c, d for was the upper and lower limit of z_0 separately; tol was integration accuracy (default accuracy was 10e-6).

3   Simulation and Analysis the Magnetic Induction Intensity of the Cylindrical Permanent Magnet

The magnetic coated and pelletized seeds, about 3mm in diameter, were used in the permanent-magnet seed-metering device. In order to further simulate, a cylindrical magnet with diameter 2mm and length 7mm was selected.

Figure 3(a) showed the gradient changes in the x direction of the magnetic induction intensity with the cylindrical permanent magnet in the plane with y=0,-5mm <x<5mm, 7mm <z<10mm; Figure 3(b) showed the gradient changes in the x direction of the magnetic induction intensity with the cylindrical permanent magnet in the plane with z=7mm,-5mm<x<5mm, -5mm<y<5mm; Figure 3(c) showed the gradient changes in the z direction of the magnetic induction intensity with the cylindrical permanent magnet in the plane with y = 0,-5mm <x<5mm, 7mm <z<10mm ; Figure 3(d) showed the gradient changes in the z direction of the magnetic induction intensity with the cylindrical permanent magnet in the plane with z=7mm,-5mm<x<5mm, -5mm<y<5mm.

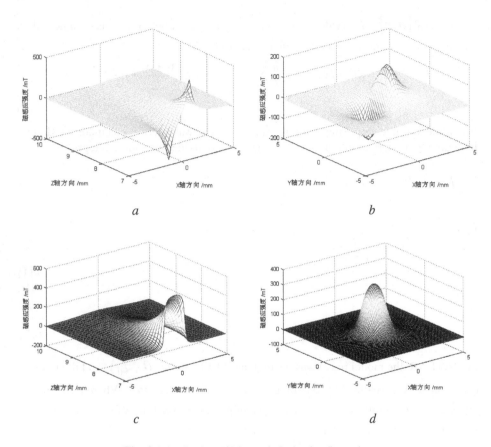

Fig. 3. Distribution of Magnetic Induction Intensity

The distributions of B_x, B_z in xoz plane were showed in figure 3(a) and figure 3(c). The B_x reached a maximum value at the x=1mm or x=-1mm, zero at the x=0, and had a rapidly decay then tended to zero within the radius; B_z reached a maximum value on the axis of a cylinder, and the magnetic induction intensity in the diameter range was relatively larger, decaying rapidly outside; the value of B_x and B_z had rapidly decay in the Z-axis direction and tended to zero. The distributions of B_x and B_z on the end face of the permanent magnet were showed in figure 3(b) and figure 3(d). The magnetic induction intensity was concentrated within a radius of the cylinder; and it was about zero at the place larger than the radius.

4   Conclusions

1)   The paper adopted the equivalent current model of permanent magnet and the Bio-Savart law to derive and establish the mathematical model which can be used for calculating the magnetic induction intensity of any point in the permanent magnet external. The calculated value would not produce errors for the method itself, because the magnetic induction intensity of field point only depended on all source points and the magnetic parameter of permanent magnet was constant. Compared to the magnetic dipole and the empirical formula, this method was more accurate.

2)   Using adaptive Simpson quadrature method and the numerical integration function of MATLAB, the precise calculation about the magnetic induction intensity of any point in the permanent magnet external was realized. Meanwhile, the complex derivation process of the discrete integral formula was eliminated and the problems of stability, accuracy and overflow were avoided in the integration formula of recursive process.

3)   The simulating calculation results showed that the space magnetic induction intensity of the cylindrical permanent magnet was concentrated on the end face of the permanent magnet. The magnetic induction intensity in z direction achieved maximum value on the end face of the permanent magnet, decreasing rapidly with the distance increased; the magnetic induction intensity in x, y directions achieved maximum value at the edge of the permanent magnet end face, and zero at the center. So, considering the effects of seeds filling, the diameter of the cylindrical permanent magnet should be less than magnetic powder coated seed, meanwhile, the air gap between the permanent magnet end face and the magnetic powder coated seed should be smaller as much as possible.

Acknowledgements. This work was financially supported by Three Engineering of Agricultural Machinery, Jiangsu province (NJ2009-41), sponsored by Qing Lan Project of Jiangsu Province (Su teacher(2010)no.27) and A Project Funded by Priority Academic Program Development of Jiangsu Higher Education Institutions (Su financial teacher(2011)no.8).

References

1. Hu, J., Zheng, S., Liu, W.: Design and experiment of precision magnetic cylinder seeder. Transactions of the Chinese Society for Agricultural Machinery 40(3), 60–63 (2009)
2. Hu, J., Wang, X., Yan, J., Zheng, S.: Analysis for Magnetic Field Characteristics of Magnetic Seed-metering Elements and Structure Optimization. Transactions of the Chinese Society for Agricultural Machinery 42(2), 67–70 (2011)
3. Hu, J., Li, X., Mao, H.: Magnetic field characteristic analysis for the magnetic seed-metering space of the precision seeder. Transactions of the Chinese Society of Agricultural Engineering 21(12), 39–43 (2005)
4. Hu, J., Wang, Q., Shao, X.: Simulation on Magnetic Precision Seed-metering Device. Transactions of the Chinese Society for Agricultural Machinery 41(12), 35–38 (2010)

5. Magrab, E.B., Azarm, S., Balachandran, B., et al.: An Engineer's Guide to MATLAB with Application from Mechanical, Aerospace, Electrical and Civil Engineering. Publishing House of Electronics Industry, Beijing (2006)
6. Zhang, X., Fang, L., Li, G.-L., Deng, F.-L., Li, J.-P.: Modeling and Simulation for Permanent Column in Wireless Endoscope. Journal of System Simulation 19(3), 494–497 (2007)
7. Hui, C.: Experimental Study on Magnetic Field Characteristic of Magnetic Marker. Wuhan Ligongdaxue, Wuhan (2007)
8. Kong, F., Chen, G., Cao, W.: Numerical calculation of magnetic field in magnetic couplings of magnetic pump. Chinese Journal of Mechanical Engineering 42(11), 213–217 (2006)
9. Liu, H.: Research of the Three-Dimensional Magnetic Field Distribution Around a Rectangular Permanent Magnet. Beijing Industrial University, Beijing (2006)

Maximum Entropy Niche-Based Modeling (Maxent) of Potential Geographical Distributions of *Lobesia Botrana* (Lepidoptera: Tortricidae) in China

Wencheng Lv[1], Zhihong Li[1,*], Xingxia Wu[2], Wenlong Ni[1], and Weiwei Qv[1]

[1] College of Agronomy and Biotechnology, China Agricultural University, Beijing, P.R. China
lizh@cau.edu.cn
[2] Administration of Quality Supervision, Inspection and Quarantine, Beijing, P.R. China

Abstract. *Lobesia botrana* (Denis & Schiffermüller, 1775) (Lepidoptera: Tortricidae) is one of the most destructive pests of grape in the Palearctic region. The potential geographical distribution of this pest is important to agriculture security. In this study, Maxent and ArcGIS were used to project the potential geographical distribution of *L. botrana* in China under the current climate. The result indicated that *L. botrana* was suitable in most parts of middle and southern China and the Maxent model was highly accurate for the AUC value of 0.970. Jackknife analysis revealed that low temperature influence the potential distribution of *L. botrana*. This study would be a decision-support of surveillance and quarantine measures.

Keywords: *Lobesia botrana*, potential geographical distribution, Maxent, ArcGIS.

Introduction

The grape berry moth, *Lobesia botrana* (Lepidoptera: Tortricidae) is an important pest of vineyards in many countries of the world [1,2]. It was first described in 1775 in Vienna, from samples collected in Italy. At present, it has spread to several European countries, North and West Africa and the Middle East. It was introduced into Japan before 1974 and recently into Chile [2]. In September 2009, it was reported for the first time from Napa County, CA in North America [3]. It is considered an economic pest of grape because the damage to the grape yield is twofold, direct damage by larvae feeding on all parts of the flower cluster in early spring, on green berries in mid summer, and on ripening fruit in late summer continuing through harvest, and indirect damage by fungi and bacterial growth [4]. In response to differences of climate, the number of generations completed by *L. botrana* within a year differs geographically. In general, two generations occur annually in northern areas of Europe, such as Austria,

---

* Corresponding author.

D. Li and Y. Chen (Eds.): CCTA 2011, Part III, IFIP AICT 370, pp. 239–246, 2012.
© IFIP International Federation for Information Processing 2012

Germany, Switzerland and northern France, whereas three generations occur in southern Europe, including Mediterranean countries [5,6]. High temperature and low humidity provide optimal conditions for *L. botrana*, while rainy in conjunction with low temperature conditions seem to reduce the frequency of mating and, subsequently, egg production [7]. Optimal conditions for its activity occur at temperatures over 20°C and at 40%-70% relative humidity [8]. The Chinese government classified *L. brotrana* as one of the quarantine pests [9,10]. Although to date there is no distribution of *L. brotrana* is unknown in China, the potential risk of it spreading from its original introduction [2] or being repeatedly introduced into China is increasing as the international grape trade increases. It is important to predict the potential geographical distribution of *L. brotrana* in China, which will present a decision-support of surveillance and quarantine measures.

There are several methods to predict the potential geographical distribution of organisms. The most commonly used methods are secological niche model such as CLIMEX, GARP and Maxent[11]. Maxent is a machine learning method, which estimates the distribution of a species by finding the probability dispersal of maximum entropy, subject to constraints representing incomplete information about the distribution. The constraints are the expected value of each environmental variable that should match its average over sampling locations derived from environmental layers. The algorithm evaluates the suitability of each grid cell as a function of environmental variables of that cell [12]. Maxent has been extensively used though it was just recently released [13-19]. In this study, Maxent software is used to predict the potential geographical distribution of *L. botrana* in China.

1   Material and Method

1.1   Material

1.1.1   Occurrence Data of *L. Botrana*

The species distributional data are gathered from literature published, the specimen records in the museum or herbarium, and authoritative electronic resources. In addition, the data are also obtained through on-the-spot investigation [20]. In this study, the data came from the distribution of papers published abroad [21-30]. Localities were geo-referenced based either on coordinates provided directly in papers or on the official gazetteers (GeoNet, http://gnswww.nga.mil/geonames/GNS/index.jsp). The 95 unique records in Fig. 1 were obtained after checking the location. According to Maxent software requirements, the reference points were saved in csv format by species name, longitude, and latitude in order.

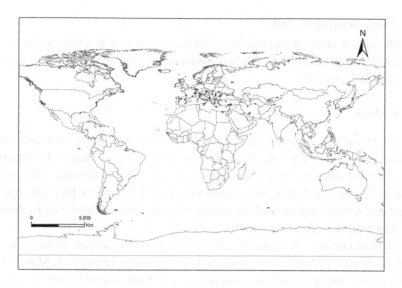

Fig. 1. The known distributions of *Lobesia botrana* in the world

1.1.2   Software Tools

Maxent: Downloaded from http://www.cs.princeton.edu/~schapire/maxent/, ver. 3.3.3e. ArcGIS: Purchased by the Plant Quarantine and Invasion Biology Laboratory of China Agricultural University (CAUPQL), ver. 9.3.

1.1.3   Environmental Variables

Nine biological climate variables (Table 1) were used as the main environmental data forprediction. The climate data with a resolution of 5arc-minutes in 1950-2000 were downloaded from http://www.diva-gis.org/climate.htm, and converted to asc format according to Maxent software requirements.

Table 1. Environmental variables used in potential distribution prediction of *L. botrana*

Environmental variables	
BIO6	Min temperature of coldest month
BIO19	Precipitation of coldest quarter
BIO11	Mean temperature of coldest quarter
BIO18	Precipitation of warmest quarter
BIO8	Mean temperature of warmest quarter
BIO2	Mean diurnal range
BIO4	Temperature seasonality
BIO3	Isotherm
BIO1	Annual mean temperature

1.1.4   Basic Geographic Data

The 1:400 million maps of national boundaries and province boundaries used in this paper were downloaded from the national fundamental geographic information system (http:// nfgis.nsdi.gov.cn/).

1.2   Methods

The distributional and environmental data were imported into the Maxent, and 75% of the distribution points were selected at random as the training dataset, the remaining points as the test dataset. Other parameters were the software defaults. The analysis resulted in the logistic format were outputted by ASCII type of file. The file was imported into ArcGIS and showed the results map. ArcGIS was also used to show the known distributions of *L. botrana* in the world.

The predicted results were usually classified based on the suitable values. The area under the curve (AUC) were directly calculated by Maxent. In addition, Maxent has a jackknife option through which the importance of individual environmental variables can be estimated (Fig. 4).

2   Results and Analysis

We graphed the potential geographical distribution of *L. botrana* in China under current climate conditions (Fig. 2). In the predicted results, the appropriate values of known regions of occurrence were more than 0.006; the values of Hokkaido in Japan were 0.107, It was reported that this pest had occurred in this region [31]; the values of the regions all had severe occurrences were more than 0.17. Therefore, the suitable area was divided into 4 grades.

Optimal regions: middle and southern Jiangsu, Zhejiang and Anhui; eastern and western Hubei; Jiangxi except northern region; northern Guangdong and Guangxi; eastern and southern Guizhou; western Hunan; southeastern Chongqing and Tibet; southern Henan and Taiwan.

Suitable regions: Southeastern and western Jiangsu; Northern Zhejiang and Guizhou; Mid south parts of Anhui and Hubei; Eastern and middle Hunan; Middle Taiwan, Guangdong and Guangxi; Eastern and western Yunnan; a small portion of Sichuan; Shanghai.

Marginal regions: Northern Jiangsu, Anhui and Hubei; Southern Shaanxi, Shanxi, Fujian, Guangdong and Guangxi; Eastern Gansu; Middle Hunan and Henan; eastern and western Yunnan and Sichuan; Northwestern Chongqing; Southeastern Tibet; Shandong except northern regions; most parts of Taiwan.

Maxent is a new software, which predicts the geographical distribution of species, AUC values are regularly used to evaluate the ability of the models to predict independent test points accurately. AUC values of 0.5–0.7 are usually taken to indicate low accuracy. Values of 0.7–0.9 indicate useful applications, and values > 0.9 indicate high accuracy [32].The AUC value reached 0.970 in this study (Fig. 3), indicating that the Maxent model performed well and that its predictions of the potential distribution of *L. botrana* were highly accurate.

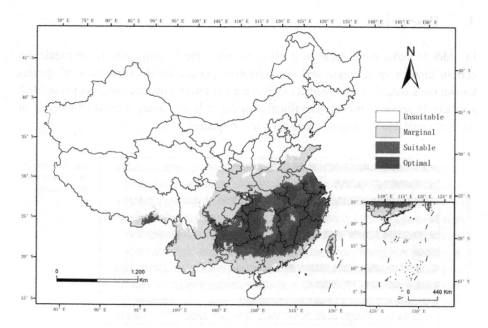

Fig. 2. The potential geographical distribution of *Lobesia botrana* in China under current climate conditions, as modeled using Maxent. White = unsuitable (Appropriate value≤0.006); yellow = marginal (0.006<Appropriate value≤0.1); brown = suitable (0.1<Appropriate value≤0.17) and red = optimal (0.17<Appropriate value≤1).

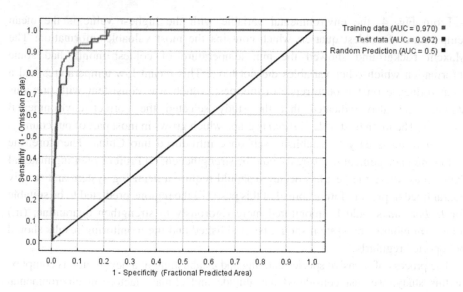

Fig. 3. Sensitivity vs. 1-Specificity for *Lobesia botrana*

3   Discussion

In order to make more accurate predictions using the Maxent model, we required a certain amount of accurate and representative geographical distribution of species known point data, but also needed to select the key environmental variables to establish a relatively accurate model. The foundation depends on having a good knowledge of the biological and ecological characteristics of species [33].

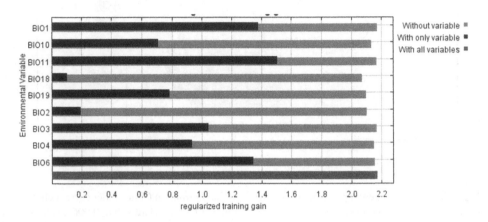

Fig. 4. Jackknife test for environmental variable significance performed by Maxent

From Fig. 4, the environmental variable with the highest value is the mean temperature of coldest quarter, which contains the most valuable information. The Maxent background showed the min temperature of coldest month had some information which other variables did not have. This meant low temperatures had a great influence on the occurrence of this pest, which was consistent with previous studies, and also indicated that the study selected the correct environmental variables.The main host of *L. botrana* is grape which grows in most part of our country, so *L. botrana* is easy to establish itself once introduced into China. Therefore, the following management measures should be strengthened: (i) Fruit or planting material from areas where the pest has occurred should require a licensing system and strictly quarantined to prevent future spread of this pest; (ii) the regions predicted to be suitable for *L. botrana* should be monitored more rigorously to strengthen quarantine; (iii) long-term monitoring system should be established and the monitoring results should be reported regularly.

The process of invasive species entering and establishing in a new region is complex. In this study, we just considered the altitude and climate factors in environmental variables. Soil type, vegetation and climate warming on the distribution of this pest have not been considered for lack of corresponding digital base map. More research on the influence of environmental variables on survival of *L. botrana* are needed.

Acknowledgments. The authors thank Prof. Stauffer at Pennsylvania State University for his valuable suggestions and modifying the draft. We thank all members of the Plant Quarantine and Invasion Biology Laboratory of China Agricultural University (CAUPQL). This study received financial support from the 973 project (2009CB119200).

References

1. Avidov, Z., Harpaz, I.: Family Tortricidae: Leaf roller moths. In: Plant Pests of Israel, pp. 380–384. Israel Universities Press, Jerusalem (1969)
2. CIE. *Lobesia botrana* (Schiff.). Distribution Maps of Pests, Series A, Map No. 70(revised). Commonwealth Institute of Entomology/Commonwealth Agricultural Bureau, Wallingford, UK (1974)
3. Monica, L., Lucia, G., Rhonda, J.: European Grapevine Moth:a New Pest of Grapes in California Farm advisors, pp. 20–28 (2010)
4. Louis, F., Schirra, K.: Mating disruption of *Lobesia botrana* (Lepidoptera: Tortricidae) in vineyards with very high population densities. IOBC/WPRS Bull. 24, 75–79 (2001)
5. Badenhausser, I., Lecharpentier, P., Delbac, L.: Contributions of Monte-Carlo test procedures for the study of the spatial distribution of the European vine moth, *Lobesia botrana* (Lepidoptera, Tortricidae) in European vineyards. Eur. J. Entomol 96, 375–380 (1999)
6. Venette, R.C., Davis, E.E., Dacosta, M., Heisler, H.: Mini Risk Assessment, Grape Berry Moth *Lobesia botrana* (Denis & Schiffermuller) [Lepidoptera: Tortricidae].USDA-APHIS, Center for Plant Health Science and Technology (Internal Report), Raleigh, NC, 38 pp (2003)
7. Deseo, K.V., Marani, F., Brunelli, A., Bertaccini, A.: Observations on the biology and diseases of *Lobesia botrana* Den. and Schiff (Lepidoptera: Tortricidae) in central-north Italy. Acta Phytopathologica Academiae Scientiarum Hungaricae 16, 405–431 (1981)
8. Roditakis, N., Karandinos, M.: Effects of photoperiod and temperature on pupal diapause induction of grape berry moth *Lobesia botrana*. Physiological Entomology 26, 329–340 (2001)
9. AQSIQ. Plant inspection and quarantine. In: AQSIQ ed. Manual of Inspection and Quarantine, 80 – 81. AQSIQ, Beijing (2005)
10. CABI. Crop Protection Compendium. CAB International Walling ford (2005)
11. Wang, Y.S., Xie, B.Y., Wan, F.H.: Application of ROC curve analysis in evaluating the performance of alien species' potential distribution models. Biodiversity Science 15(4), 365–372 (2007)
12. Phillips, S.J., Anderson, R.P., Schapire, R.E.: Maximum entropy modeling of species geographic distributions. Ecological Modeling 190, 231–259 (2006)
13. Elith, J., Graham, C.H., Anderson, P.R.: Novel methods improve prediction of species' distributions from occurrence data. Ecography 29(2), 129–151 (2006)
14. Perkins, S.L., Rothschild, A., Waltari, E.: Infections of the malaria parasite, Plasmodium floridense, in the invasive lizard, Anolis sagrei, in Florida. Journal of Herpetology 41(4), 750–754 (2007)
15. Wang, Y.S., Xie, B.Y., Wan, F.H.: Potential Geographic Distribution of *Radopholus similis* in China. Chinese Agriculture Science 40(11), 2502–2506 (2007)

16. Bigg, G.R., Cunningham, C.W., Ottersen, G.: Ice-age survival of Atlantic cod: agreement between palaeoecology models and genetics. Biological Sciences 275, 163–172 (2008)
17. Loiselle, B.A., Jorgensen, P.M., Consiglio, T.: Predicting species distributions from herbarium collections: does climate bias in collection sampling influence model outcomes. Journal of Biogeography 35(1), 105–116 (2008)
18. Zhao, W.J., Chen, L., Ding, K.J.: Prediction of potential geographic distribution areas of the maize downy mildew in China using MAXENT. Plant Protection 35(2), 32–38 (2009)
19. Feng, Y.M., Liang, J., Lv, Q.: Potential Suitability Analysis of *Hemiberlesia pitysophila* Takagi in China. Forest Research 22(4), 563–567 (2009)
20. Zeng, H., Huang, G.S., Lin, W.: Prediction of potential geographic distribution of *Microcyclus ulei* in the world using MaxEnt. Plant Protection 34(3), 88–92 (2008)
21. Sharon, R., Zahavi, T., Soroker, V.: The effect of grape vine cultivars on *Lobesia botrana* (Lepidoptera: Tortricidae) population levels. J. Pest. Sci. 82, 187–193 (2009)
22. Eghtedar, E.: Biology of *Lobesia botrana* in Fars province. Applied Entomology and Phytopathology 63(1/2), 5–6 (1996)
23. Casta±eda-Samayoa, O., Holst, H., Ohnesorge, B.: Evaluation of some Trichogramma species with respect to biological control of Eupoecilia ambiguella Hb. and *Lobesia botrana* Schiff. Zeitschrift fur Pflanzenkrankheiten und Pflanzenschutz 100(6), 599–610 (1993)
24. Burov, V.N., Sazonov, A.P.: A new preparation for orchards and vineyards. Zashchita Rastenii (Moskva) 10, 50–51 (1992)
25. Baumgartner, J., Baronio, P.: Phenological model of the flight of *Lobesia botrana* Den. & Schiff (Lep. Tortricidae) in relation to the environmental conditions of Emilia-Romagna. Bollettino dell'Istituto di Entomologia "Guido Grandi" della Universita degli Studi di Bologna 43, 157–170 (1989)
26. Fischer-Colbrie, P.: Present pests in viticulture and modern methods of control. Pflanzenarzt 33(4), 35–37 (1980)
27. Pavan, F., Sbrissa, F.: Damage of the grape berry moths, *Lobesia botrana* (Den. e Schiff.) and Eupoecilia ambiguella (Hb.), on late-harvested cultivars in north-eastern Italy. Frustula Entomologica 17, 43–53 (1994)
28. Pongracz, A.: Swarming dynamics of *Lobesia botrana* Schiff. in the Sopron wine-growing region. Novenyvedelem 18(1), 27–28 (1982)
29. Russo, A., Gurrieri, C., Bonfanti, S., Fici, P.: Flight dynamics of the grape berry moth in the vineyards of eastern Sicily. Rivista di Viticoltura e di Enologia 38(4), 219–222 (1985)
30. Schieder, F.: Investigations on the swarming dynamics of grape berry moths in Fejer County, Eastern Transdanubia. Novenyvedelem 20(7), 320–332 (1984)
31. Crop Protection Compendium, http://www.cabi.org/cpc/
32. Swets, J.A.: Measuring the accuracy of diagnostic systems. Science 240, 1285–1293 (1988)
33. Chang, Z.L., Zhou, Y.L., Zhao, Z.T.: Suitability analysis of *Karnal bunt* in China based on MaxEnt model. Plant Protection 36(3), 110–112 (2010)

A Design of Greenhouse Remote Monitoring System Based on WSN and WEB

Jun Wang[1,2] and Gang Liu[1]

[1] Key Laboratory for Modern Precision Agriculture System Integration Research,
Ministry of Education, China Agricultural University, Beijing 100083, China
[2] College of Vehicle & Motive Power Engineering, Henan University of Science and
Technology, Luoyang 471003, China

Abstract. Wireless sensor networks (WSN) are increasingly popular in the field of greenhouse environment monitoring. In this paper, a new design of greenhouse remote monitoring system based on WSN and WEB is presented. The system has a three-tier structure of node layer, distributed management layer and WEB service layer. Experiments showed that the node layer has excellent self-organization and communication ability. The maximum distance of one-hop is 856 m. The distributed management layer can acquire and manage the data of temperature, humidity, light and the level of the carbon dioxide, and simultaneously send the data to WEB server database through the Internet. The WEB service layer can complete format storage, statistical analysis and conditional query for database, also ordinary users can obtain the graphic display of the greenhouse environment data through web browser. Normal working time of system reaches 141 days in the experiment. Meanwhile, normal operation rate exceeds 92%. Packet transfer rate of each sensor node is higher than 89.6% and lower than 95.4%.The greenhouse remote monitoring system based on WSN and WEB can realize an organic combination between distributed management and remote data sharing throughout different regions.

Keywords: Greenhouse monitoring, Wireless sensor networks, WEB, Sensor, ARM7.

1   Introduction

Greenhouse has played a key role in the development of agriculture. Due to the increased demand of food, people are trying to put extra efforts and special techniques to multiply the food production. Use of different technologies towards greenhouse is one of such efforts. Apart from scientific technologies in greenhouse, information technology is now being heavily exercised to improve decision making capabilities in this area. Recently, wireless sensor networks (WSN) attract intensive research efforts due to easy deployment and a large variety of application scenarios. Wireless sensor networks provide the capability of self-organizing, self-configuring, self-diagnosing

D. Li and Y. Chen (Eds.): CCTA 2011, Part III, IFIP AICT 370, pp. 247–256, 2012.

and self-healing which enable un-interrupt, in-field sensing, measurement, and control [1,2]. Greenhouse production commonly features as remote, variable, harsh, and sometimes hard to access. Hence, continuous monitoring can be difficult to realize. With the advancement of wireless communication, micro-electronics, and computer technology, wireless sensor networks show advantages in these applications, and make it possible to acquire spatial and temporal knowledge about greenhouses [3,4].

The main purpose of wireless sensor networks in greenhouse is to keep the process of real-time monitoring and control the most suitable environment for growing crops in accordance with expert knowledge [5]. A large number of nodes can collect and transmit data cooperatively in different regions. However, the essence of wireless sensor networks is a distance-limited distributed system. Data management is the key problem of application. Different regional greenhouses need a remote background system to support the task. In recent years, greenhouse remote monitoring technology based on WEB has received more and more attention with the rapid development of the Internet [6]. The combination of WSN and WEB is a very positive direction in greenhouse practices. In this paper, we describe the features and architecture of the greenhouse remote monitoring system, and the approach of distributed data processing by Web application services.

2   System Architecture

Fig. 1 shows the system architecture, which comprises three basic tiers as below.

The sensor application tier: This tier contains the wireless sensor nodes and the sink node. For environment monitoring, sensor nodes are usually distributed to certain greenhouses determined by geographical constraints or user requirements. These nodes can self-organize themselves into a WSN, which continuously generates and delivers environment data to the sink node. The information may include temperature, humidity, light and carbon dioxide. Issues about the manner of sensing, reporting and communication protocol are critical in designing this tier.

The distributed management tier: The distributed management tier obtains each greenhouse group data from the sink node through the serial cable. The environment data is forwarded to local processing program for analysis, calculation and visualization. For more comprehensive data processing, some professional platform could be introduced, which is powerful in handling large amount of data.

The WEB service tier: The distributed management tier uploads environment data to the WEB server tier via the Internet. As an important feature of the system, remote users can access the data via Web interfaces. Following this way, users are able to gather, visualize the data from the server. In consideration of the WSN security, users are only provided with data surveillance but assumed having no authority to change parameters of the fundamental tier.

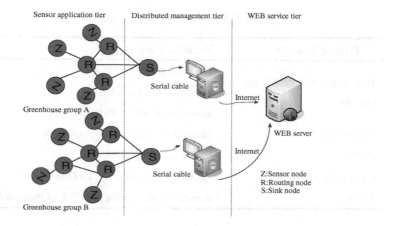

Fig. 1. System architecture

3   Design and Implementation

3.1   Sensor Application Tier

Sensor nodes should have abundant functions, such as data acquisition, data transmission and friendly interface [7]. In order to realize the above functions, sensor node mainly includes four units. First, sensor unit completes information collection and data transformation. Second, microprocessor unit is responsible for nodes control, data processing and the collected data transmission. LPC2131 is selected as processor. 12-Bit serial A/D converter MAX186 is used as the external A/D chip for conversion precision. Third, wireless communication unit adopts SZ05 wireless data communication module produced by shanghai shuncom network technology Co., LTD. The unit can effectively organize wireless network, send the collected data and receive instructions from distributed management tier. Liquid crystal display unit chooses graphic dot matrix unit LCM12864ZK, which undertakes the task of displaying greenhouse environment information.

The typical greenhouse environment is comprised of temperature, humidity, light, gas and soil, etc. Considering the impact on crop growth, the collection information includes temperature, humidity, light and carbon dioxide. Obviously, sensor is the basis of data gathering, the accuracy of sensor has an important effect on the whole system. The sensor selection should follow the principle of actual demand. The technical parameters of each sensor show in Table.1.

Table 1. The sensor technical parameters

Types and models	Technical parameters
Temperature& humidity sensor DHT85	Temperature:-40～123.8°C
	Humidity: 0～100%RH
	Sensor accuracy: 2.0%RH, 0.3°C@25°C
Light sensor SC-GZ	Measurement range: 0～200KLUX
	Sensor accuracy: ±5%
Carbon dioxide sensor T6004	Measurement range: 0～2000ppm
	Sensor accuracy: ±40ppm + 3% of measured value

SZ05 wireless data communication module is developed according to the standard ZigBee protocol. The topology structure of sensor application tier is designed as mesh network by considering transmission distance. Mesh network is a type of network where each node must not only capture and disseminate its own data, but also serve as a relay for other sensor nodes. All the nodes must collaborate to propagate the data in the network. The self-healing capability of mesh network enables a routing based network to operate when one node breaks down or a connection goes bad. As a result, the network is typically quite reliable, as there is often more than one path between a source and a destination in the network. In the sensor network, all the nodes have been set in advance. There is only one sink node in a greenhouse group, which controls the data transmission. Relay routing nodes can forward other nodes' data to sink node through the way of multi-hop, and work as ordinary nodes. In order to avoid network congestion, sink node uses tour collection pattern [8]. The detailed steps of communication process are: 1) sink node sends data transmission command to relay routing nodes one by one; 2) relay routing node transmits environment data after receiving the command; 3) sink node uploads data packet to the distributed management tier, if data obtained within a period of single node collection; 4) if not, then sink node skips over the node and sends instruction to the next node. As shown in Fig.2, one period of single node collection can be approximately described as the following equation:

$$T_{task} = T_b + T_{reg} + T_{trans} + T_{route} + T_{sleep} \qquad (1)$$

The communication testing of sensor nodes is carried out as follows: 1) first, sink node respectively sends 50 control frames to every node according to the interval of 5 s; 2) compute the time T, which is from sending control frame to receiving data packet, $215\text{ms} \leq T \leq 1453\text{ms}$. In addition to ensure the stableness of wireless communication modules, the sensor application tier still should have a reliable communication protocol. The data packet structure of monitoring system is designed, which is shown in Fig.3. The application message is consisted of network segment ID, node ID, type and information of sensor node, battery capacity. By using this packet structure, the sensor node periodically gathers sensing data and transmits through RF channel.

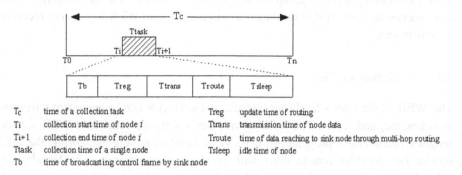

T_c	time of a collection task	T_{reg}	update time of routing
T_i	collection start time of node i	T_{trans}	transmission time of node data
T_{i+1}	collection end time of node i	T_{route}	time of data reaching to sink node through multi-hop routing
T_{task}	collection time of a single node	T_{sleep}	idle time of node
T_b	time of broadcasting control frame by sink node		

Fig. 2. Period of single node collection

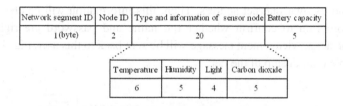

Network segment ID	Node ID	Type and information of sensor node	Battery capacity
1 (byte)	2	20	5

Temperature	Humidity	Light	Carbon dioxide
6	5	4	5

Fig. 3. Data packet structure

3.2   Distributed Management Tier

The core of greenhouse remote monitoring system is distributed management tier, which is responsible for searching sensor nodes, sending instructions, receiving data, information management, processing alarm information and uploading data to WEB server, etc. The software of distributed management tier adopts C # language as the tool in Visual Studio 2008, and uses SQL Server 2008 to build database. In this tier, dynamic data analysis and other possible algorithms could be easily proposed and directly applied, reinforcing the software's extensibility. The software consists of three modules:

(1)   Wireless communication control module: The module mainly operates RS232 interface to realize serial communication via the System.IO.Ports.SerialPort class. This module controls sink node to send instructions to sensor nodes in point-to-point pattern. All the nodes respectively respond in master-slave pattern.

(2)   Information management module: In the application process, the module completes a number of process functions, such as choosing greenhouses, setting

working frequency, connecting the database, inquiring data information, visualization, statistics and so on.

(3)   Data transmission module: The module sends the collected data to WEB server through the Internet. The steps for upload process are: 1) the distributed management tier establishes a Socket; 2) set up the WEB server IP address and service port; 3) issue a connection request; 4) start the data communication with WEB server after receiving a confirmation.

3.3   WEB Service Tier

The WEB service tier's hardware includes network connection equipments (routers, switches, etc) and server. The WEB service tier's software consists of WEB services program and database program [9]. In order to facilitate remote monitoring, the WEB service tier provides remote users with real-time data accessing, by broadcasting refined data packets over the Internet. In the opinion of data security, any user should first get permission from the server before browsing any information. In the system design, a user should first send a request to the server conveying its user name, password and its own Internet address. Then, this information will be checked by an embedded program to confirm whether the name and password are right. If it is permitted, an acknowledgement message will be sent back to this user. Fig. 4 shows the database table relationship of the tier.

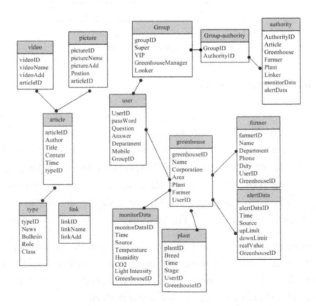

Fig. 4. Database table relationship

As an end-user interface, the WEB service tier generally accomplishes four functions:

(1) Basic information maintenance: Maintain the basic greenhouse data (crop species, planting history, unit yield, etc.), and manage user registration.

(2) Data collection and storage: Use TCP Socket to receive data from the distributed management tier, and then compare with standard data format to judge the legitimacy of data, finally storage the correct data.

(3) Data process and inquire: Manage the upload data, then output statistical analysis of the real-time monitoring data, and provide the service of data inquire.

(4) Dynamic data browse: Authorized users can access WEB server via browser, and obtain the dynamic information of greenhouses through clicking hot-points on the electronic map.

4   System Implementation and Test

4.1   System Deployment

In the experiment, 20×sensor nodes and 5×sink nodes are involved. All the nodes are assigned to five greenhouse groups respectively. Each greenhouse group only equips with a sink node. 6×PCs with one for the server and the other five for five greenhouse groups are used to test the ability of system. This experiment lasted for four months (August 2010-December 2010) and all the equipments ran to monitor in the greenhouse groups. Normal working time of system reaches 141 d. Meanwhile, normal operation rate is higher than 92%. The collection frequency of each node was set to 30 s. Sensor nodes were fixed on the wall in greenhouses. In order to prevent the influence of wall, the antennas of wireless communication modules extended 5 meters to the top of greenhouses.

Calculate the theoretical propagation distance of wireless communication in free space according the following equation:

$$[L_{fs}] = 32.44 + 20\lg d + 20\lg f \tag{2}$$

Where $[L_{fs}]$ is transmission loss. d is transmission distance and f is working frequency. The parameters of wireless communication module are: 1) working frequency is 2.425 GHz; 2) transmission power is 25 dBm; 3) antenna loss is 3 dBm per meter; 4) receive sensitivity is -94 dBm. The equation (2) can be expressed as the following equations:

$$[L_{fs}] = 10 - (-94) = 104 \tag{3}$$

$$104 = 32.44 + 20\lg d + 20\lg 2405 \tag{4}$$

The transmission distance d is 1.57 km through equation (4). Due to different kinds of interference, the actual propagation distance is less than the distance of theoretical calculation in practical application. The maximum distance of one-hop is 856 m.

4.2   Test Performances

Fig.5 shows the dynamic curve of humidity, which is displayed in distributed management tier by Dundas Chart. As shown in Fig.5, the humidity range is 47.8% to 49.4% in a short time. Considering the sensor precision, the changes of data accord with greenhouse characteristics. These results demonstrate that sensor application tier has the excellent capability of self-organizing in the greenhouse, and effectively obtains the greenhouse environment data.

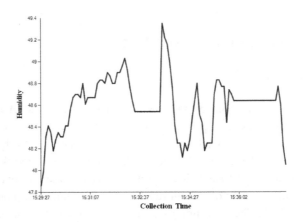

Fig. 5. Dynamic curve of humidity

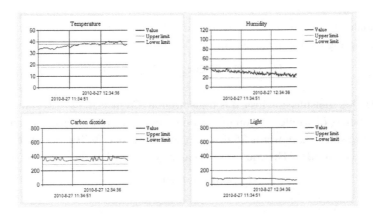

Fig. 6. Data monitoring curves

Fig.6 shows the data monitoring curves of a greenhouse on August 27, 2010 through WEB browser. As shown in Fig.6, Temperature is more than the maximum 38 □ at almost 12:00 pm. Due to ventilation and thermal transpiration, humidity in the greenhouse shows a slow decline trend. Carbon dioxide maintains a good level. Meanwhile, light does not appear remarkable changes in the whole time. Through the above analysis, it can be found that the remote monitoring technology can help users to make rapid response and reasonable management methods by collecting real-time data.

During the experiment period, the packets which are sent from each node to WEB service layer should be up to 2880 each day, according to packets received by the server, the packet transfer rate can be calculated through the following equation:

$$N = N_r / N_t \times 100\% \qquad (5)$$

Where N is packet transfer rate. N_r is actual number of received packets and N_t is ideal number of received packets. Each sensor node should send 2880 packets every day and the experiment lasted for 141 d. N_t can be expressed as 2880×141 = 406080. N_r is the received packets of each node in the server during the time. According to the equation (5), packet transfer rate of each sensor node can be calculated. The maximum rate is 95.4%, the minimum rate is 89.6%, and the average rate is 93.5%.

5   Conclusion

In this paper, a system based on WSN and WEB is presented, which has the capability of environment monitoring and data processing. Experiments are then demonstrated, which shows the system's well performance and the convenience to obtain data analysis. The system has made several achievements in: (1) The system is a practical environment monitoring application that sensor nodes periodically sense their ambience and the information can be eventually uploaded to the server. (2) Sensor information is extracted and visualized accounting for its authenticity. (3) The data from the server can be forwarded to all the users over the Internet which makes remote monitoring system feasible.

Future work will employ more nodes and powerful sink nodes to provide long-term monitoring of five greenhouse groups. Besides, this system can be reinforced by introducing more efficient hardware working styles to make it less aware of environment disturbances.

Acknowledgements. This research is funded by National High Technology Research and Development Program of China (No.2011AA100704) and Major National Science and Technology Programs of China (No.2009ZX03001-019-02).

References

1. Xu, N.: A survey of sensor network applications. IEEE Communications Magazine 40(8), 102–114 (2002)
2. Messer, H., Zinevich, A., Alpert, P.: Environmental monitoring by wireless communication networks. Science 312, 713–714 (2006)
3. Serodio, C., Cunha, J.B., Morais, R., et al.: A networked platform for agricultural management systems. Computers and Electronics in Agricultural 31, 75–90 (2001)
4. Li, L., Li, H.-X., Liu, H.: Greenhouse environment monitoring system based on wireless sensor network. Transactions of the Chinese Society for Agricultural Machinery 40, 228–231 (2009) (in Chinese)
5. Wang, N., Zhang, N., Wang, M., et al.: Wireless sensors in agriculture and food industry-Recent development and future perspective. Computers and Electronics in Agricultural 50(1), 1–14 (2006)
6. Yang, W., Lu, K., Zhang, D.: Development of wireless intelligent control terminal of greenhouse based on ZigBee. Transactions of the Chinese Society of Agricultural Engineering 26(3), 198–202 (2010) (in Chinese)
7. McKinion, J.M., Willers, J.L., Jenkins, J.N.: Wireless local area networking for farm operations and farm management. St. Joseph. ASAE Annual Meeting Papers, pp. 1–6. The American Society of Agriculture Engineers, Michigan (2004)
8. Zhang, R., Feng, Y., Shen, Z.: Communication method of star wireless sensor network for greenhouse dynamic measurement. Transactions of the Chinese Society of Agricultural Engineering 24(12), 107–110 (2008) (in Chinese)
9. Sun, Z., Cao, T., Li, H.: GPRS and WEB based data acquisition system for greenhouse environment. Transactions of the Chinese Society of Agricultural Engineering 22(6), 131–134 (2006) (in Chinese)

Research on the Monitor and Control System of Granary Temperature and Humidity Based on ARM

Liu Yang[1], Xinrong Cheng[2], Zhijie Jiang[3], and Zhijun Ren[1]

[1] Engineering College, China Agricultural University, 100083, Beijing China
[2] College of Information and Electrical Engineering,
China Agricultural University, 100083, Beijing China
[3] The Department of Automobile,
Beijing Jiaotong Vocational Technical University, 102200, Beijing China
yangliu@cau.edu.cn, hh0188@sina.com,
jiangzhijie@163.com, zhijunr@gmail.com

Abstract. The temperature, humidity, air composition and pH value are very important parameters in the granary that keep the grain safely store and good quality. Nowadays only temperature and moisture are used in most granary monitor and control system. Air composition, pH and insect pest are not monitored because classic industrial personal computer or microcomputer are not able to handle these real-time multiply tasks at the same time. So it is necessary to design a monitor and alarm system to monitor these parameters in the granary to minimize or curtail damage or loss. Applying the advanced embedded technology and sensor technology, a set of granary temperature and humidity monitor and alarm system is designed based on the ARM. Temperature sensor, humidity sensor, air composition sensor and pH value sensor are selected to monitor the parameters in the granary. Based on the ARM microprocessor LPC2290, the hardware system consists of serial communication module, LCD display module and alarm module. Based on the embedded operation system, the software completes the allocation design and testing of the tasks and realizes the functions such as pulse frequency signal acquisition, analog signal A/D convert, serial digital signal communication, alarm in different grades and LCD display. All the parameters can be real-time displaying on the LCD screen. The system meets the requirement of the monitor and alarm functions in the granary.

Keywords: Monitor, Alarm, Sensor, ARM.

1   Introduction

Grain storage safety is the important strategy relating to peoples' livelihood and has its social meaning and economic value. The temperature and humidity in the granary

D. Li and Y. Chen (Eds.): CCTA 2011, Part III, IFIP AICT 370, pp. 257–264, 2012.

varies when the environments and ventilation situation changes during the storage that leads to the grain becoming worse and insect damage. At the same time, the quality of the grain influenced by the air in the grain and microorganism. According to the specific of the grain storage, the temperature and humidity are the main parameters which should be monitored in the granary and the air composition and pH value are the auxiliary parameters [1].

In the old days the temperature and humidity in the granary are controlled by the workers. The granary workers check the temperature and humidity in the granary periodically in order to make decision how long and how strong the wind is supported to ventilate the granary. It is hard to control the temperature and humidity accurately in the granary just by the workers. With the developments in the electric and electronic technology, the sensors are used to monitor the temperature and humidity in the granary. At the beginning granary measure and control system consisted of only some electronic temperature measurement and several controlled fans [2]. Later on industrial personal computer and semiconductor PN temperature components are used in big and middle granary to control the limited parameters [3]. And then the digital sensors and industrial personal computer with windows operation were used in the control system [4]. Nowadays wireless technology is used in the monitor and control system [5].

Although in the 20 years monitor and control system have developed and applied greatly and achieved economic benefits, many problems still exist. In wireless system, it it hard to improve the system accuracy and reduce the repeated error because of the useful detected signal being added by surrounding wireless signals. In the wireless system communication data temporary disappearing with the environment temperature varied leads to unreliability [6]. On the other hard, nowadays only temperature and moisture are used in most granary monitor and control system. Air composition, pH and insect pest are not monitored because classic industrial personal computer or microcomputer are not able to handle these real-time multiply tasks at the same time [7]. However the ARM monitor system in this article solved the problems above. It can process multiple signals at the same time using the multiple tasks and real-time functions.

2   Scheme of the Hardware System

The monitor system mainly consists of controller, signal acquisition module, LCD display module, alarm module, testing module and power module. The controller makes the data acquisition and compares the values to the boundary condition values. The alarm beeps and at the same time lights flash if the real value is greater than the boundary ones. Every parameter can be real-time displaying on the LCD screen. This project is based on the LPC2290 belonging to ARM microcomputer of Zhi Yuan company. According to the functions, hardware part bases on the LPC2290 microprocessor and connects to inputs and outputs through the bus and interface circuit. The diagram of hardware system is shown in Fig.1.

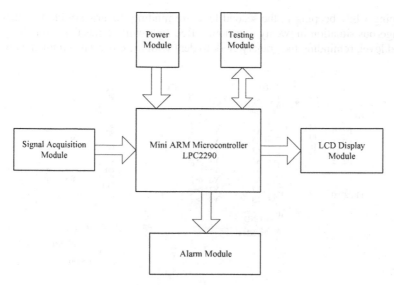

Fig. 1. The diagram of hardware

2.1   Sensor Signal Acquisition

There is four-channel & ten-digital converter in LPC2290 microcontroller which can successively convert analog signals to digital signals. The outputs of temperature sensor and humidity sensor signal are plus frequency signals which input into the AIN0 and AIN1 of LPC2290 after go through optical coupler. Air composition sensor and pH value sensor output the signals that directly go through the multiple serials converter and communicate with LPC2290 [8][9]. The interface diagram of sensor signal data acquisition is shown in Fig.2.

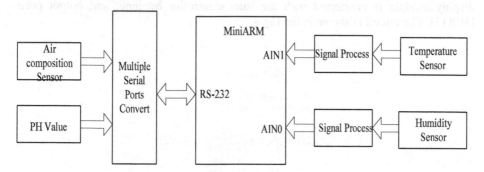

Fig. 2. Interface circuit of sensor data acquisition

2.2   Alarm Module Design

The alarm system is divided into three levels. When the acquisition data reach to the critical value, the system judge the type of the alarm level and output the related results. Also the alarm result is divided into three levels. Green light will be flashing in the first level, reminding the granary clerk to monitor the parameters carefully. Yellow light will be flashing while beeping in the second level, reminding the granary clerk to deal with the dangerous situation in twenty four hours. Red light will be flashing while beeping in the third level, reminding the granary clerk to deal with the emergency immediately.

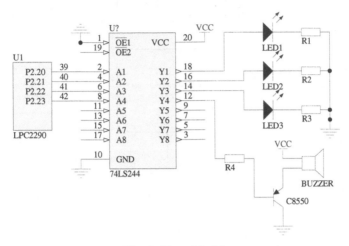

Fig. 3. Alarm Module

2.3   LCD (Liquid Crystal Display) Module

The LCD module is designed base on M240128-1A1 made by Xin Li company to display the temperature, humility, air composition and pH values. The LCD matrix dot is 240×128. The LCD display module consists of controller, line driver, row driver, display memory and LCD display screen assembled in one low-cost PCB board. The module can be real-time displaying the data monitored by the temperature sensor, humidity sensor, air composition sensor and pH value sensor. The LCD display module is connected with the microcontroller by input and output ports [10][11]. The circuit is shown in the Fig.4.

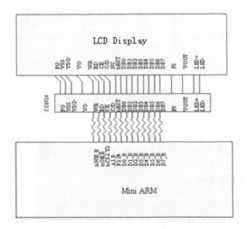

Fig. 4. LCD Display Interface Circuit

3   Software Scheme Based on μC/OS-II

The more powerful functions and system calling, the more effective and simple supports can be provided by the applying program and the less amount of maintain. TheμC/OS-II only provides a task scheduling kernel. In order to realize a complete and reality online multiple task operating system, the basic common task is built such as serial ports, LCD and A/D according to the function acquirement of the monitor and alarm system.

The bottom layer consists of the alarm hardware system whose kernel is LPC2290 (RM7 serial chip) and some surrounding devices such as LCD and alarm module. The middle layer consists of signal supported by operating system, mailbox and information line etc. communication mechanism, driving program library and API functions. The top layer is the customer applied program which is established in the main task and operated through calling API function by the customers to satisfy their requirements. Customers can establish their own tasks in their own applied programs. Multiple tasks complete the cooperative communication depending on the system information line.

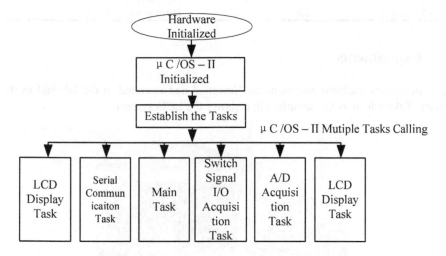

Fig. 5. Main Program Diagram

3.1   System Task Modules and Priority Level Division

The tasks division is the important step of the real-time software system development. The whole system will be low effective, poor real-time and less capacity if the division is unreasonable. According to the design requirement, the program establishes six tasks: the main task, A/D acquisition task, the switch signal I/O acquisition task, serial communication task, alarm task and LCD display task. The allocation of the tasks is shown in the table 1. Every task has its own stack space depending on the variety numbers and interruption numbers in the task after the priority is decided.

In the μ C/OS- II system, the static and active ways are used to allocate the stack space. The static stack allocation is completed when compiling while the active stack allocation is completed when operating. The static allocation is used in the design that keep the priority in the process of system operation is the same as before.

Table 1. Tasks Allocation

Task Name	Priority	Task Stack	Function Description
Main Task	17	256	Initialized Display Interface, Established Other Tasks
A/D Acquisition Task	18	128	Measure Temperature, Humidity
Switch Signal I/O Acquisition Task	19	128	Acquire I/O Signals
Serial Communication Task	20	256	Send Air composition Signals, pH Value Signals To Serial Ports
Alarm Task	21	128	Beep and Light Alarm
LCD Display Task	22	512	Display Measurement

4   Experiments

The experiments methods and steps are designed and operated in the lab and in the granary. Take wheat as the sample. Fig.6 shows the LCD system.

Fig. 6. LCD Module in the Monitor and Control System

Table 2. Compared Measured Value with Actual Value of the Granary Parameters

Parameters Name	Moisture(%)	Temperature(°C)	Air Composition (%)	pH Value
Measured Number 1	51.45	22.56	3.78	6.89
Actual Value	51.81	23.00	3.28	6.77
Measured Number 2	52.32	22.89	3.02	6.71
Actual Value	52.67	23.13	3.35	6.67
Measured Number 3	51.87	23.09	3.15	6.80
Actual Value	51.31	22.79	3.77	6.74
Measured Number 4	52.04	22.11	3.20	6.69
Actual Value	52.56	23.43	3.82	6.79
Measured Number 5	51.78	22.67	3.32	6.81
Actual Value	51.99	23.99	3.57	6.90
Measured Number 6	51.37	23.00	3.90	6.83
Actual Value	51.09	22.89	3.11	6.47
Measured Number 7	52.67	22.62	3.65	6.29
Actual Value	52.01	23.00	3.22	6.47
Measured Number 8	51.81	22.47	3.92	6.59
Actual Value	51.57	23.13	3.06	6.70
Measured Number 9	52.83	23.28	3.46	6.39
Actual Value	52.32	22.90	3.94	6.37
Measured Number 10	51.34	23.06	3.26	6.44
Actual Value	51.67	22.97	3.80	6.61

5   Conclusion

Applying the advanced embedded technology and sensor technology, a set of granary temperature and humility monitor and alarm system is designed based on the ARM he ARM microprocessor LPC2290. Temperature sensor, humidity sensor, air composition sensor and pH value sensor are selected to monitor the parameters in the granary. The hardware system consists of serial communication, LCD display and alarm module. The software is based on the embedded operation system that completes the allocation design and testing of the tasks. The system realizes the functions such as pulse frequency signal acquisition, analog signal A/D convert, serial digital signal communication, alarm in different grades and LCD display. The system meets the requirement of the monitor and alarm functions in the granary.

References

1. Liu, T.: The Design of Intelligent Granary Monitoring System Based on Wireless Sensor Network. Journal of Jinling Institute of Technology 26(4), 6–11 (2010)
2. Simulation of Temperature Measurement System forGrain Storage Based on ZigBee Technology, http://www.computer.org/portal/web/csdl/doi/10.1109

3. Zheng, S.: The Development and Application of the Granary Temperature Measure System. Wuhan Polytechnic University (2009)
4. Wang, Z., Wang, P., Li, C.: Wireless Oxygen Content Monitor Design in Metallurgy Gas Processing. Control & Automation 23(1), 109–110 (2007)
5. Cai, X.: Research and Design of Smart Online pH Detector and Recorder.D. Zhejiang Polytechnic University (2009)
6. Chi, T., Huang, D.: pH Detection's Realizer and Control Based on Transcendental Knowledge of Neuron Model. Journal of Zhengzhou University (Science Edition) 40(3), 32–34 (2008)
7. Li, T., Zhao, W., Huang, Z.: The pH Detecting System Based on nRF9E5 Wireless Transmission. Instrument Technique and Sensor (4), 62–63 (2009)
8. Zhou, L.: RM Embedded System Tutorial. Tsinghua University Press, Beijing (2004)
9. Shen, L., Song, T., Ye, Z.: Development and Application of Embedded System. Electronics Industry Press, Beijing (2005)
10. Zhou, L.: Basis and Practice of ARM Microcontrollers. Beijing Aerospace University Press, Beijing (2004)
11. Zhou, L.: ARM Embedded System Experimental Materials. Beijing Aerospace University Press, Beijing (2005)
12. Jean, L.J.: Embeded Real-time Operating System μC/OS- II. Beijing Aerospace University Press, Beijing (2003)

The Research of Support Vector Machine in Agricultural Data Classification

Lei Shi[1], Qiguo Duan[2], Xinming Ma[1], and Mei Weng[1]

[1] College of Information and Management Science, HeNan Agricultural University,
Zhengzhou 450002 China
[2] Zhengzhou Commodity Exchange, Zhengzhou 450008 China
{sleicn,dqgcn,xinmingma}@126.com, wengm@163.com

Abstract. The agricultural data classification is a hot topic in the field of precision agriculture. Support vector machine (SVM) is a kind of structural risk minimization based learning algorithms. As a popular machine learning algorithm, SVM has been widely used in many fields such as information retrieval and text classification in the last decade. In this paper, SVM is introduced to classify the agricultural data. An experimental evaluation of different methods is carried out on the public agricultural dataset. Experimental results show that the SVM algorithm outperforms two popular algorithms, i.e., naive bayes and artificial neural network in terms of the F_1 measure.

Keywords: Support Vector Machine, Agricultural Data, Classification.

1 Introduction

As a very promising field with a huge growth potential, agricultural data classification is a hot topic in the agriculture and computer science communities. In recent years, many popular algorithms in the machine learning field have been applied in the agricultural data classification, such as decision tree [1], kNN [2], artificial neural network [3, 4], etc. Support vector machine (SVM) [5, 6], introduced by Vapnik and Chervonenkis in 1971, is a machine learning algorithm based on statistical learning theory. By using nonlinear kernel functions, SVM can map original input data into a high dimensional feature space to seek a separate hyperplane, and then it can perform classification by using the constructed N-dimensional hyperplane that optimally separates the data into two categories. For the past few years, SVM has been widely used in different fields and it can obtain high performance in many real world classification applications such as image retrieval [7], cancer recognition [8], text classification [9, 10] and credit scoring [11-13].

In this paper, SVM is introduced to classify the agricultural data. Experiments on real agricultural dataset have been conducted and the experimental results indicate that the SVM algorithm outperforms two popular algorithms, i.e., naive bayes and artificial neural network in terms of the F_1 measure. Thus, SVM is an effective method for agricultural data classification.

D. Li and Y. Chen (Eds.): CCTA 2011, Part III, IFIP AICT 370, pp. 265–269, 2012.

The remainder of the paper is organized as follows: Section 2 gives an introduction of SVM in detail. Section 3 reports and discusses the experimental results and finally Section 4 states the conclusions of our work.

2   SVM

As a popular machine learning algorithm, SVM is a new generation learning system based on recent advances in statistical learning theory. It realizes the theory of VC dimension and principle of structural risk minimum to constitute an objective function and then find a partition hyperplane that can satisfy the class requirement. The basic idea of SVM can be described as follows. Firstly, search an optimal hyperplane satisfies the request of classification. Secondly, use a certain algorithm to make the margin of the separation beside the optimal hyperplane maximum while ensuring the accuracy of correct classification. Then, the separable data can be classified into classes effectively [6]. As a kind of structural risk minimization based learning algorithms, SVM have better generalization abilities comparing to other traditional empirical risk minimization based learning algorithms. An illustration of the SVM is shown in Fig. 1.

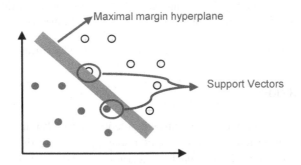

Fig. 1. An illustration of SVM

In a SVM classifier, let the training set be $\{(x_1, y_1), (x_2, y_2), \ldots, (x_n, y_n)\}$, where x_i is an input vector and y_i its label. The partition hyperplane can be defined as [6]

$$\omega \cdot x + b = 0 . \tag{1}$$

where b is the offset of hyperplane; ω is the normal vector of the partition hyperplane. A partition hyperplane to make the bilateral blank area, i.e., $2/\|\omega\|$, maximum must be found to make the partition hyperplane as far from the point in training dataset as possible, which can be defined as follows.

$$\text{Minimize} \phi(\omega) = \frac{1}{2} \|\omega\|^2 . \tag{2}$$

A constraint condition must be met, which is defined as follows.

$$y_i(\omega \cdot x_i + b) \geq 1.$$ (3)

The lagrange function can be defined as:

$$L(\omega, b, \alpha) = \frac{1}{2}(\omega \cdot \omega) - \sum_{i=1}^{n} \alpha_i (y_i(\omega \cdot x_i + b) - 1).$$ (4)

Subject to the following two conditions, i.e., $\sum_{i=1}^{n} y_i \alpha_i = 0$ and $\alpha_i \geq 0$, then the following formula can be defined for seeking the minimum of lagrange function.

$$\max Q(\alpha) = \sum_{i=1}^{n} \alpha_i - \frac{1}{2} \sum_{i,j=1}^{n} \alpha_i \alpha_j y_i y_j (x_i \cdot x_j).$$ (5)

The optimal class function can be defined as follows.

$$f(x) = \text{sgn}((\omega^* \cdot x) + b^*) = \text{sgn}(\sum_{i=1}^{n} \alpha_i^* y_i (x_i \cdot x) + b^*).$$ (6)

An important advantage of SVM is that it can be analyzed theoretically using concepts from computational learning theory, and obtain state-of-the-art performance. Recently, it has also been applied to a number of real-world problems such as handwritten characters recognition, information retrieval and the classification of biomedical data. In this paper, SVM is introduced to classify the agricultural data for improving the classification performance of agricultural data.

3   Experimental Results

To study the effectiveness of the SVM method for agricultural classification, we test it on agricultural data in this section. One agricultural dataset obtained from agricultural researchers in New Zealand, i.e., the white-clover dataset [14], is used in experiment. The objective of the white-clover dataset is to determine the mechanisms which influence the persistence of white clover populations in summer dry hill land.

We used the F_1 measure to evaluate the performance of algorithm. A confusion matrix contains information about actual and predicted classifications done by a classification system. The table 1 shows confusion matrix for two class classifier [15].

Table 1. Cases of the classification for one class

Class C		Result of classifier	
		Belong	Not belong
Real classification	Belong	TP	FN
	Not belong	FP	TN

Several standard terms can be defined for the two class matrix. The recall is the proportion of positive patterns that were correctly identified, as calculated using the equation:

$$recall = \frac{TP}{TP + FN}.$$ (7)

Precision is the proportion of the predicted positive patterns that were correct, as calculated using the equation:

$$precision = \frac{TP}{TP + FP}.$$ (8)

Then, the performance of the classification can be evaluated in terms of F_1 measure.

$$F_1 = 2 \times \frac{precision \times recall}{precision + recall}$$ (9)

For SVM, we used the LIBSVM [16] for SVM implementation and set linear function as default kernel function of SVM. To evaluate the effectiveness of SVM in agricultural data classification, two popular algorithms, i.e., naive bayes [17] and artificial neural network [18], are implemented and used as benchmarks for comparison. Performance is evaluated by 10-fold cross validation.

Fig. 2 shows the classification results of SVM, naive bayes and artificial neural network in terms of F_1 measure on the dataset. The F_1 value of SVM is 67.3%, which is approximately 6.9% higher than that of naive bayes algorithm and 4.8% higher than that of artificial neural network algorithm.

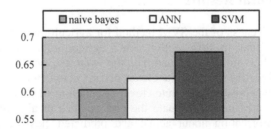

Fig. 2. Comparison of the F_1 of classification on dataset

4   Conclusion

The classification of agricultural data is an important application of information technology in agriculture. SVM is a powerful state-of-the-art classifier and has been applied in many fields. In this paper, SVM is introduced to classify the agricultural data for improving the classification performance. The experimental results show that the SVM is an effective method for classification of agricultural data.

References

1. Kirchner, K., Tolle, K.-H., Krieter, J.: The analysis of simulated sow herd datasets using decision tree technique. Comput. Electron. Agric. 42, 111–127 (2004)
2. Rajagopalan, B., Lall, U.: A k Nearest Neighbor Simulator for Daily Precipitation and Other Weather Variables. Water Resources Research 35(10), 3089–3101 (1999)
3. Chedad, A., Moshou, D., Aerts, J.M., et al.: Recognition System for Pig Cough based on Probabilistic Neural Networks. Journal of Agricultural Engineering Research 79(4), 449–457 (2001)
4. Schatzki, T.F., Haff, R.P., Young, R., et al.: Defect Detection in Apples by Means of X-ray Imaging. Transactions of the American Society of Agricultural Engineers 40(5), 1407–1415 (1997)
5. Vapnik, W.N., Chervonenkis, A.Y.: On the uniform convergence of relative frequencies of events to their probabilities. Theory of Probability and its Applications 16(2), 264–280 (1971)
6. Vapnik, V.: Statistical Learning Theory. John Wiley and Sons, New York (1998)
7. Tao, D.C., Tang, X.O., Li, X.L., Wu, X.D.: Asymmetric bagging and random subspace for support vector machines-based relevance feedback in image retrieval. IEEE Transactions on Pattern Analysis and Machine Intelligence 28(7), 1088–1099 (2006)
8. Giorgio, V., Marco, M., Francesca, R.: Cancer recognition with bagged ensembles of support vector machines. Neurocomputing 56, 461–466 (2004)
9. Hyunsoo, K., Peg, H., Haesun, P.: Dimension Reduction in Text Classification with Support Vector Machines. Journal of Machine Learning Research 6, 37–53 (2005)
10. Simon, T., Daphne, K.: Support Vector Machine Active Learning with Applications to Text Classification. Journal of Machine Learning Research, 45–66 (2001)
11. Bellotti, T., Crook, J.: Support vector machines for credit scoring and discovery of significant features. Expert Systems with Applications 36, 3302–3308 (2009)
12. Lee, Y.C.: Application of support vector machines to corporate credit rating prediction. Expert Systems with Applications 33(1), 67–74 (2007)
13. Huang, C.L., Chen, M.C., Wang, C.J.: Credit scoring with a data mining approach based on support vector machines. Expert Systems with Applications 33(4), 847–7856 (2007)
14. http://www.cs.waikato.ac.nz/~ml/weka/index_datasets.html
15. Yang, Y.: An evaluation of statistical approaches to text categorization. Journal of Information Retrieval 1, 67–88 (1999)
16. http://www.csie.ntu.edu.tw/~cjlin/libsvm/
17. Lewis, D.D.: Naive (Bayes) at Forty: The Independence Assumption in Information Retrieval. In: Nédellec, C., Rouveirol, C. (eds.) ECML 1998. LNCS, vol. 1398, pp. 4–15. Springer, Heidelberg (1998)
18. Bishop, C.M.: Neural networks for pattern recognition. Oxford University Press, Oxford (1995)

Study of Micro-vision Calibration Technique Based on SIFT Feature Matching

Tao Hu[1], Hui-lan Wu[2], and Guodong Liu[1]

[1] Harbin Institute of Technology, Department of Automatic Measurement and Control,
Harbin, China
{hutao,lgd}@hit.edu.cn
[2] Research Institute of Shanghai Academy of Spaceflight Technology,
No. 803, Shanghai, China
whl3003@163.com

Abstract. In the micro-vision system, precise calibration of the pixel equivalent is a prerequisite for accurate visual inspection. Traditional calibration process not only needs to take standard parts as the base, but also has strict requirements on their shape, manufacturing precision, placement and so on. Because of such shortcomings of traditional method, this paper gives an improved SIFT calibration algorithm for the pixel equivalent. Firstly, get the image's characteristic points before and after its' moving, using SIFT algorithm. Then filter the mismatched points through the second filtering algorithm so that the matching accuracy can be greatly improved. Compare moving distances of the characteristic point pixels to the reference distance of optical grating. Then accurate pixel equivalents can be obtained. Experiments show that the calibration algorithm is more accurate than traditional methods. So this algorithm can completely replace the standard-parts method in micro-vision system.

Keywords: Vision measurement, Calibration, Feature Matching.

1   Introduction

Measuring object size using CCD pixels as the scale is the core of vision measuring technology. So we need to acquire the actual size of CCD pixel. And because of the existence of optics system, the pixels' actual application size should be the one which is calculated through the optics system. During the application process of the vision system, an accurate enlargement of the optics system is hard to obtain because of many factors, just like the camera's relative position with CCD, and the camera's assembly quality differences. So, calibration of CCD pixel equivalent is the precondition and foundation of the measurement based on image [1-2].

Currently, standard-parts method is commonest among the calibration of CCD pixel equivalent. E.g.: figure 1(a) Standard mask. Test the standard part's geometrical shape, and then transmit its precise size to digital image. The precision of this method is subject to the standard part's accuracy of manufacture and the picture border's

D. Li and Y. Chen (Eds.): CCTA 2011, Part III, IFIP AICT 370, pp. 270–277, 2012.

inspection quality. Moreover, it has strict requirements on the shape of standard part. In addition, the standard part's border must be parallel to the direction of CCD pixel. Or the distance between parallel lines will correspond to slant image's pixel number. And there will be angular misalignment in the demarcated pixel equivalent, as the picture 1 (b) shows. To optimize the calibration method, this paper presents an improved SIFT-based method to demarcate the pixel equivalent of Microscopic inspection system, according to its calibration characteristics. SIFT-Feature point matching method is based on image's local gradient features. It has better adaptability to image's lighting change, fuzziness and distortion. It doesn't need to detect the object's border. And it's not sensitive to object's shape.

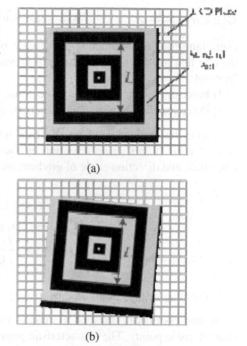

(a)

(b)

Fig. 1. Traditional method of calibration

2   Calibration Technique

Micro-vision system, which is based on SIFT- algorithm, can accomplish the calibration process with only the measured object. It doesn't have to draw support from standard part, which changes the traditional method that acquires the number of pixels of the reference distance. Detail calibration steps as follows: 1) Lay the object upon the one-dimensional translation stage; 2) Move the object. And collect the images of it separately before and after the moving; 3) Read the object's displacement L through the numerical reading device (optical grating or other displacement output unit); 4) Extract SIFT characteristic points of the collected images; 5) Match SIFT characteristic points; 6) calculate the number of pixel's corresponding distance the characteristic points moved; 7) L/N is the pixel equivalent of the vision system.

What is key in the calibration method base on SIFT algorithm is the extraction and matching of SIFT characteristic points.

2.1   Method of Abstracting SIFT Characteristic Points

The SIFT algorithm extracts extreme points of Difference of Gaussian scale-space(DoG) as characteristic points, which mainly contains the following 4 steps [3-8]:

1) Build a DOG and extracts its extreme points;

$$D(x, y, \sigma) = (G(x, y, k\sigma) - G(x, y, \sigma)) * I(x, y)$$
$$= L(x, y, k\sigma) - L(x, y, \sigma)$$

(1)

$G(x,y,\sigma)=\dfrac{1}{2\pi\sigma^2}e^{-(x^2+y^2)/2\sigma^2}$ is a scale variable Gaussian function. $L(x,y,\sigma)$ is an Gaussian image. k is a scale scaling factor. σ is a Gaussian scale. The extreme point is the one that has the biggest change in grayscale value compared with its surrounding 26 pixels.

2) Precisely position extreme value points through fitting 3-d quadratic function.

3) Direction distribution of characteristic points

Calculate the images' gradient of characteristic points in the DoG. Determine the characteristic points' main direction by the way of accumulating their gradient. The amplitude and direction angle of gradient are calculated as follows:

$$\begin{cases} m(x,y)=\left[\begin{matrix}(L(x+1,y)-L(x-1,y))^2\\+(L(x,y+1)-L(x,y-1))^2\end{matrix}\right]^{1/2} \\ \theta(x,y)=\tan^{-1}\dfrac{L(x,y+1)-L(x,y-1)}{L(x+1,y)-L(x-1,y)} \end{cases} \qquad (2)$$

4) Build descriptor of the characteristic point

Turn the coordinate axis of Gaussian image $L(x,y,\sigma)$ to the main direction of characteristic points. The characteristic points being the center, divide its surrounding 16×16 pixel window into 4×4 windows. In each small window, accumulate the Gaussian image's gradient projection in 8 directions. Then a characteristic vector F of 4×4×8=128 dimensions can be obtained.

2.2   Characteristic Points Matching and Mismatch Filtering

After detecting the SIFT characteristic points of the object's image, the points obtained after moving need to be matched with those before moving, thus confirm their one-to-one correspondence. The SIFT characteristic point matching methods that are in common used mainly include: NN(Nearest Neighbor), Exhaustive method, K-D(K-Discriminator Tree), BBF(Best-Bin-First) and so on. Above methods are all based on traditional SIFT characteristic point descriptor, all getting too much error matching.

In the calibration process of micro-vision system, even a few mismatches can bring great deviation to the result. In order to overcome the influence of the mismatches, this paper does a second filtering to the mismatches, using the space coordinate information of characteristic points, which is based on NN(Nearest Neighbor) method.

Suppose $K(I_{test})=\{k_1^{test},k_2^{test},...k_M^{test}\}$ is the set of characteristic points of the image before object's moving. And $K(I_{temp})=\{k_1^{temp},k_2^{temp},...k_M^{temp}\}$ is the set of characteristic points of the image after object's moving.

Calculate the nearest and the second nearest distance (MD_i and SMD_i) between each couple of characteristic points' descriptor (before and after the image's moving). And then calculate the value: SMD_i/MD_i as follows: .

$$MD_i = \min_{j=1}^{M}(dis(F(k_i^{test}), F(k_j^{temp}))) \tag{3}$$

$$SMD_i = \operatorname{second}\min_{j=1}^{M}(dis(F(k_i^{test}), F(k_j^{temp}))) \tag{4}$$

$$prop_i = \frac{SMD_i}{MD_i} \tag{5}$$

If $prop_i > th_1$, then point k_i^{test} and point k_j^{temp} are matching with each other. th_1 is an appointed threshold value. With this step, usually 80% mismatches can be filtered. The larger th1 is, the less the number of matching couples is, and the better the stability is. But when th_1 is too large, the number of matching point couples decreases so sharply that correct positioning is impossible, and not all mismatches can be eliminated. In practice, in most cases the value of th1 is around 1.5.

After initial characteristic point matching, point pairs can be obtained: $\{(s_1^{test}, s_1^{temp}), (s_2^{test}, s_2^{temp}), \ldots (s_L^{test}, s_L^{temp})\}$, which still contains many mismatches. Because the relative position of characteristic points doesn't change after object's moving, a second matching can filter mismatches with the space coordinates information. Calculate the nearest distance md_i^{test}, md_i^{temp} and the second nearest distance smd_i^{test}, smd_i^{temp} separately within each characteristic point space.

$$md_i^{test} = \min_{j=1, j\neq i}^{L}(dis(s_i^{test}, s_j^{test})) \tag{6}$$

$$smd_i^{test} = \operatorname{second}\min_{j=1, j\neq i}^{L}(dis(s_i^{test}, s_j^{test})) \tag{7}$$

$$md_i^{temp} = \min_{j=1, j\neq i}^{L}(dis(s_i^{temp}, s_j^{temp})) \tag{8}$$

$$smd_i^{temp} = \operatorname{second}\min_{j=1, j\neq i}^{L}(dis(s_i^{temp}, s_j^{temp})) \tag{9}$$

If both $md_i^{test} / md_i^{temp}$ and $smd_i^{test} / smd_i^{temp}$ are smaller than the appointed threshold value th_2, with $md_i > 10$pixel, then this couple of matching points be kept. If not, delete it. The value of th_2 is about 0.9 in common case. As is in picture 2, k_1 and k_3, k_2 and k_4 are all considered correct match before the second filtering. But

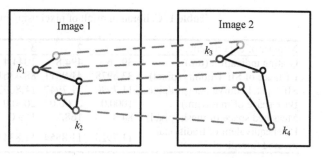

Fig. 2. Filter out the mismatches using space coordinates

actually, only k_1 and k_3 are the correct couple. k_2 and k_4 are the mismatches. After the second filtering, only the couple of k_1 and k_3 will be retained.

Lots of experiments show that after the second time filtering, correct correspondence (before and after the object's moving) of object's SIFT characteristic points can be gained. And through affine transformation between images, the number of pixels corresponding to the SIFT characteristic points' moving distance can be calculated. With the reference displacement given, the pixel equivalent of micro-vision system can be demarcated.

3   Experiments and Analysis

In order to examine above ideology, this paper designed two experiments.

3.1   Experiments of Standard Parts' Calibration and Comparison

Firstly, lay a standard part (masking layer) upon the one-dimensional electric transition stage which has a grating readout device. Resolution of the optical grating is 0.2μm, using backlit lighting. CCD's type is Japan's Watec 902H, with a nominal pixel size value of 8.6*8.3μm. To make a contrast, pixel equivalent calibration of the standard parts is done separately with the traditional method (including border detection, subpixel subdivision, parallel fitting) and this paper's method. Figure 3 shows the result of SIFT characteristic point matching. And table 1 shows the result of calculation.

Fig. 3. SIFT matching point of the mask

Table 1. Calibration result of pixel using mask

Number of experiments	1	2	3	4	5
Grating indication (μm)	397.6	494.8	1044.4	1545.4	2192.2
Distance of SIFT points (pixel)	33.6978	41.9511	88.4361	130.7644	185.8332
SIFT pixel equivalent (μm/pixel)	11.7990	11.7947	11.8097	11.8182	11.7966
Base space of mask(μm)	1000.0	2000.0	2000.0	3000.0	3000.0
Measured space of mask (pixel)	84.8	168.7	169.0	254.6	254.5
Pixel equivalent of traditional method (μm/pixel)	11.7925	11.8554	11.8343	11.7832	11.7878

From table 1, the mean value of pixel equivalent is 11.8036 μm/pixel with this paper's method. While with traditional method, the mean value is 11.8106 μm/pixel. Being influenced by border detection's degree of precision, the result of traditional methods has less stability.

In order to check the accuracy of this paper's method further, move the standard part to a certain distance. The displacement can be read out by Renishaw ML10 two-frequency laser; Calculate the displacement's number of pixels with this paper's SIFT algorithm. And then calculate the actual displacement separately with above two calibration results. Table 2 shows the result.

As can be seen in table 2, the measuring result of this method is better than traditional method in application.

Table 2. Moving test error of mask image

Number of experiments	1	2	3	4	5
Displacement by Dual-frequency laser (μm)	494.6	504.2	507.4	498.7	495.1
Movement distance of characteristic points (pixel)	41.9270	42.7070	43.0163	42.2561	41.96
Error of pixel equivalent by mine(μm)	0.2895	-0.1037	0.3472	- 0.0741	0.1791
Error of pixel equivalent by traditional method(μm)	0.5830	0.1953	0.6483	0.3699	0.4728

3.2   Experiment of Workpiece's Self-movement

One obvious advantage of this calibration method is that the calibration algorithm is independent   from object's shape. So the calibration   can   be done without standard parts,   only   making use of   workpiece's self-moving. Keeping the   same   optical magnification   as previous experiment, table   3   gives   the

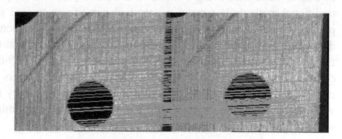

Fig. 4. SIFT matching point of the workpiece

Table 3. Calibration result 1 of work with a hole

Number of experiments	1	2	3	4	5	mean error
Pixel equivalent(μm/pixel)	11.7893	11.8225	11.8105	11.7934	11.8086	
Error 1 of pixel equivalent (μm)	-0.0213	0.0119	-0.0001	-0.0172	-0.002	-0.0057
Error 2 of pixel equivalent (μm)	-0.0143	0.0189	0.0069	-0.0102	0.0050	0.0013

results of vision system's calibration by workpiece with hole. Two images' matching result of SIFT characteristic points is given in figure 4. In table 3, pixel equivalent error 1 is the deviation of the two calibration results (the one that makes use of workpiece based on this paper's algorithm and the other by traditional method). Pixel equivalent error 2 is the deviation of the two results (the one that makes use of workpiece and the other that makes use of standard part, which all take this paper's algorithm).

Under different magnification, table 4 gives the calibration result of micro-vision system by workpiece with circular hole. In table 4, pixel equivalent error is the deviation of the two calibration results----the one that makes use of workpiece and the one with traditional method.

Table 4. Calibration result 2 of work with a hole

Number of experiments	1	2	3	4	5	mean error
Pixel equivalent (μm/pixel)	8.7949	8.7997	8.7959	8.8017	8.7892	
Error 1 of pixel equivalent (μm)	0.0052	0.0100	0.0062	0.0120	-.0005	0.0066

From table 3 and table 4, we can see that the calibration result by workpiece itself can maintain better repeatability with the method that uses mask. This further again proved this paper's method.

4   Conclusion

In micro-vision measuring system, calibration's precision of pixel equivalent applying traditional methods is subject to standard part. To overcome these shortcomings, this paper proposed a method based on improved SIFT local characteristic point matching to demarcate pixel equivalent. The experimental results show that the method presented in this paper has better stability than the traditional method. While reaching more stable calibration precision, the vision system's positioning accuracy is improved too. With this paper's calibration method, standard part is no more necessary in the process of micro-vision-detecting system's pixel equivalent calibration, overcoming the shortcoming that standard parts need to be positioned precisely.

References

1. Wu, J.-G., Bin, H.-Z.: Dimensional inspecting system of thin sheet parts based on machine vision. Optics and Precision Engineering 15, 124 (2007)
2. Wang, J., Pu, Z., Zhao, H., Lu, Z.: A new method for calibrating 2-D image measuring systems. Journal of Harbin Institute of Technology 32, 37 (2000)
3. Pan, X., Lyu, S.: Detecting image region duplication using sift features. In: Processing of IEEE International Conference on Acoustics, Speech and Signal, vol. 1706 (2010)
4. Bastanlar, Y., Temizel, A., Yardimci, Y.: Improved SIFT matching for image pairs with scale difference. Electronics Letters 46, 346 (2010)

5. Li, J., Allinson, N.M.: A comprehensive review of current local features for computer vision. Neurocomputing 71, 1771 (2008)
6. Lowe, D.G.: Distinctive image features from scale-invariant keypoints. Int. Journal of Computer Vision 60, 91 (2004)
7. Mikolajczyk, K., Schmid, C.: A performance Evaluation of Local Descriptors. IEEE Transactions on Pattern Analysis and Machine Intelligence 27, 1615 (2005)
8. Wu, H.-L., Liu, G.-D., Liu, B.-G., Pu, Z.-B.: Study on the circle center fast accurate-locating technique based on the SIFT. Journal of Optoelectronics.Laser 19, 1512 (2008)

Design of Fuzzy Control Algorithm
for Precious Irrigation System in Greenhouse

Ronghua Ji, Lijun Qi[*], and Zicheng Huo

College of Information & Electrical Engineering,
China Agricultural University,
Qinghua East Road. 17, 100083 Beijing, China

Abstract. The precious irrigation is of great significance for arid and semiarid area. According to the special environment of greenhouse, a fuzzy control algorithm was proposed to make an optimal irrigation strategy based on the actual measured soil humidity during the whole plant growth process. The fuzzy control system had two inputs (soil humidity error and its rate) and one output (water level difference). In this paper, the fuzzy control algorithm was introduced in detail which included the setting of input and output, the selection of membership function and the setting of fuzzy rules. The fuzzy control system was meaningful to the smart water-saving irrigation in greenhouse.

Keywords: soil humidity, fuzzy control algorithm, irrigation, greenhouse.

1 Introduction

Water is one of our precious natural resources. Water-saving irrigation is of great significance because there are many arid and semiarid areas in the word. The key in water-saving irrigation is striking to get balance for optimal plant grown with optimal usage of water. Many water-saving technologies were proposed by the researchers [1], such as drip irrigation [2] ,subsurface drip irrigation [3] and subsurface negative irrigation[4]. There were many research works which focused on the affection of different irrigation methods to crop. In order to find better irrigation scheduling with the compromise between high yield and great quality of greenhouse-grown tomato under limit water supply, two experiments of different irrigation treatments were conducted in the arid region of northwest China during spring to summer in 2008 (2008 season)and winter in 2008 to summer in 2009 [4]. Because the irrigation water use efficiency was very importance, the technical efficiency of unheated greenhouse farms in Tunisia was measured, and proposed a measure for irrigation water use efficiency (WUE) using an alternative form of the data envelopment analysis [5]. Application of the temporal and spatial deficit irrigation in field-grown crops had greater potential in saving water, maintaining economic yield and improving WUE [6].

Many conventional methods for controlling greenhouse irrigation were not effective since they were either based on on-off control methods or proportional

---

[*] Corresponding author.

D. Li and Y. Chen (Eds.): CCTA 2011, Part III, IFIP AICT 370, pp. 278–283, 2012.
© IFIP International Federation for Information Processing 2012

control methods which resulted in a loss of energy and productivity. A solution for an irrigation controller based on the fuzzy-logic methodology was presented [7]. The developed fuzzy logic controller could effectively estimate the amount of water uptake of plants in distinct depth using the reliable irrigation model, evaporation functions, environmentally conditions of the greenhouse, soil type, plant type and other factors affecting the irrigation of greenhouse. A fuzzy irrigation decision-making system was established by using virtual instrumentation platform [8]. The experiment results showed that the system had friendly interface and was easy to use; it could give comprehensive judgment and decision-making, and provide scientific basis for water saving irrigation. In our case, the irrigation system was very different.

The optimal water volume for plants was affected by many physical parameters such as air temperature, soil humidity, wind and stage of plant grown. Soil humidity was an important irrigation indicator to ensure the crop growing well. Because environment was controllable in greenhouse, some outside parameters were constant such as air temperature and wind. As for the irrigation system which was applied in greenhouse, the change of soil humidity was the most importance and direct parameter for irrigation strategy which included irrigation time and the irrigation volume. The fuzzy control algorithm was proposed for greenhouse precision irrigation system in this paper.

2   Materials and Methods

The soil water movement and distribution in soil was seriously affected by the irrigation strategy. In this paper, a precision irrigation system was used. The precision irrigation system consisted of five parts: a plant container, a built-in reservoir, a level control tank, a reservoir and a height adjuster. The scheme of precision irrigation system was shown in Fig. 1.

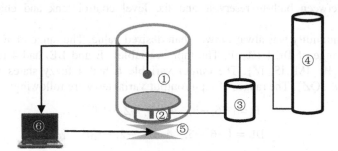

Fig. 1. The scheme of precision irrigation system

①the plant container; ②the built-in reservoir; ③ the level control tank; ④ the reservoir; ⑤ the height adjuster; ⑥ the fuzzy controller in computer.

The soil humidity of plant container was affected by the water level difference between built-in reservoir and the level control tank. The water level difference was adjusted by the height adjuster which was controlled by the fuzzy controller in PC. Fuzzy controller had been widely applied as a powerful methodology for complicated nonlinear delay systems which were difficult to set up accurate mathematic models. The control strategy in controller was selected as fuzzy control because soil humidity was large delay, great inertial, time-varying and non-linearity.

The fuzzy controller was determined by the height of height adjuster based on the soil humidity error and its rate. The principle diagram of fuzzy control in this system was shown as in Fig.2.

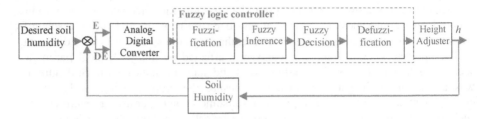

Fig. 2. The principle diagram of fuzzy controller

E was the soil humidity error which was defined as desired soil humidity minus actual soil humidity. DE was the rate of soil humidity error which was defined in equation (2).

$$E = H_d - H_a \tag{1}$$

$$DE = \frac{H_d - H_a}{H_d} \tag{2}$$

Where H_d was desired soil humidity, H_a was actual soil humidity. The best range of soil humidity in every crop growing stage was ascertained according to the previously experimental data. The medium value of the best range of soil humidity was taken as the desired soil humidity.

The output of fuzzy control system was h which was used adjusting the water level difference between built-in reservoir and the level control tank and changing soil humidity.

The soil humidity was always lower than desired value. The range of E was [-6%, 0] and the range of DE [-1%, 0]. The input variables (E and DE) had 4 fuzzy states which was {IL, IM, IS, IZ}. The output variable h had 4 fuzzy states which was {OL, OM, OS, OZ}. The ranges of input/output variables were following:

$$E = \{-6, -5, -4, -3, -2, -1, 0\}$$
$$DE = \{-6, -5, -4, -3, -2, -1, 0\}$$
$$h = \{0, 1, 2, 3\}$$

Because the input variables of fuzzy controller (E and DE) were measured as accurate, they should be fuzzed firstly according to the equation (3).

$$y = \frac{6(x - \frac{a+b}{2})}{b-a} \tag{3}$$

Where x was the accurate input variable and y was the fuzzed value. The accurate input variables changed from a to b. y should be taken as integer.

The membership function of variables was importance to the fuzzy controller. Every fuzzy variable's membership functions should be defined respectively. There were many kinds of membership functions to meet the requirement of various variables. The general rule to select membership function was following: the higher sensitivity membership for little error and the fine stability membership for larger error. According to the changing regularity of soil humidity error and the membership selection rule, the membership functions of variables (IL and IM) were taken as triangle function, the membership functions of variables (IS and IZ) were taken as Gaussian function and the membership functions of (DE and h) were triangle function. The membership function assignment table was shown in Table 1 to 3.

Table 1. The soil humidity error's membership function assignment table

Fuzzy variable	The soil humidity error (E)						
	-6	-5	-4	-3	-2	-1	0
IL	1.0	0.6	0.2	0	0	0	0
IM	0.2	0.6	1	0.6	0.2	0	0
IS	0	0	0	0.5	1	0.5	0
IZ	0	0	0	0	0	0.5	1

Table 2. The soil humidity error rate of membership function assignment table

Fuzzy variable	The error rate of soil humidity (DE)						
	-6	-5	-4	-3	-2	-1	0
IL	1.0	0.5	0	0	0	0	0
IM	0	0.5	1	0.5	0	0	0
IS	0	0	0	0.5	1	0.5	0
IZ	0	0	0	0	0	0.5	1

Table 3. The output membership function assignment table

Fuzzy variable	The error rate of soil humidity (h)			
	0	1	2	3
OL	0	0	0.5	1
OM	0	0.5	1	0.5
OS	0.5	1	0.5	0
OZ	1	0.5	0	0

According to the experimental data and irrigation experience, the fuzzy control rules were shown in Table 4.

Table 4. Fuzzy control rules table

Input		DE			
		IL	IM	IS	IZ
	IL	OL	OL	OM	OZ
E	IM	OM	OM	OS	OZ
	IS	OS	OS	OZ	OZ
	IZ	OZ	OZ	OZ	OZ

There were 16 fuzzy control rules in this system.
That was

If $E=A_i$ and $DE=B_j$ Then $h=C_{ij}$ (i, j=3, 2, 1, 0)

Where the value of A_i was set according to Table 1 and the value of B_j was set according to Table 2.

$$C_{ij} =A_i \times B_j$$

In this paper, the fuzzy control algorithm was simulated by the fuzzy control toolbox of Matlab. The fuzzy reasoning system surface was shown in Fig 3.

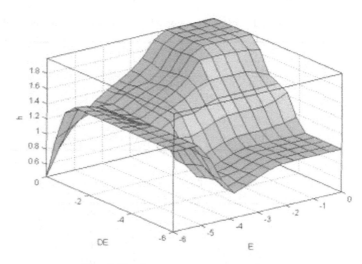

Fig. 3. The fuzzy reason system surface

3   Conclusion

In the greenhouse, the plant growth environment parameters were controllable, such as air temperature, wind and air humidity. The precious irrigation should be made the suitable irrigation strategy according to the requirements of plant growth. The irrigation strategy based on soil humidity and plant growth was an optimal irrigation to meet the actual need of plant growth.

The fuzzy control algorithm was effective for the dynamic characteristics of soil humidity which was large delay, great inertial, time-varying and non-linearity. The fuzzy control system was meaningful with the water-saving irrigation in greenhouse.

Acknowledgments. The research is supported by the National Natural Science Funds (Project No. 31101609) and Chinese Universities Scientific Fund (Project No. 2011JS144).

References

1. Tal, A.: Seeking Sustainability: Israel's Evolving Water Management Strategy. Science 313, 1081–1084 (2006)
2. Caldwell, D.S., Spurgeon, W.E., Manges, H.L.: Frequency of irrigation for subsurface drip irrigation corn. Transactions of the ASAE 37, 1099–1103 (1994)
3. Ayars, J.E., Phene, C.J., Hutmacher, R.B., Davis, K.R., Schoneman, R.A., Vail, S.S., Mead, R.M.: Subsurface drip irrigation of row crops: a review of 15 years of research at the Water Management Research Laboratory. Agricultural Water Management 42, 1–27 (1999)
4. Wang, F., Kang, S., Du, T., Li, F., Qiu, R.: Determination of comprehensive quality index for tomato and its response to different irrigation treatments. Agricultural Water Management 98, 1228–1238 (2011)
5. Frija, A., Chebil, A., Speelman, S., Buysse, J., Van Huylenbroeck, G.: Water use and technical efficiencies in horticultural greenhouses in Tunisia. Agricultural Water Management 96, 1509–1516 (2009)
6. Du, T., Kang, S., Sun, J., Zhang, X., Zhang, J.: An improved water use efficiency of cereals under temporal and spatial deficit irrigation in north China. Agricultural Water Management 97, 66–74 (2010)
7. Javadi Kia, P., Tabatabaee Far, A., Omid, M., Alimardani, R., Naderloo, L.: Intelligent Control Based Fuzzy Logic for Automation of Greenhouse Irrigation Systemand Evaluation in Relation to Conventional Systems. World Applied Sciences Journal 6, 16–23 (2009)
8. Zhengjun, Q., Xiaoxing, T., Jiehui, S., Yidan, B.: Irrigation decision-making system based on the fuuzy-control theory and virtual instrument. Transactions of the CSAE 23, 165–169 (2007)

Winter Wheat Yield Estimation Coupling Weight Optimization Combination Method with Remote Sensing Data from Landsat5 TM

Xingang Xu[1,2,3,*], Jihua Wang[1,2,3], Wenjiang Huang[1,2,3], Cunjun Li[1,2,3], Xiaoyu Song[1,2,3], Xiaodong Yang[1,2,3], and Hao Yang[1,2,3]

[1] National Engineering Research Center for Information Technology in Agriculture, Beijing 100097, China
[2] Department of Precision Farming Applications, National Remote Sensing Center of China Beijing 100097, China
[3] Beijing Research Center for Information Technology in Agriculture, Beijing 100097, China
xxg2007@yahoo.com.cn

Abstract. Crop yield models using different VIs (vegetation index) from remote sensing data show the various precision, but each of them can provide useful information related with yield. So it is very significant how to integrate the useful information of these models. In this study, a few of typical VIs, such as *NDVI* (Normalized Difference Vegetation Index), *SR* (Simple Ratio index), *TCARI/OSAVI* (Trans-formed Chlorophyll Absorption Ratio Index (*TCARI*), and Optimized Soil-Adjusted Vegetation Index (*OSAVI*)), *NDWI* (Normalized Difference Water Index) extracted from Landsat5 TM image covering Beijing region, are used to build yield modes of winter wheat, respectively. And then the Weight Optimization Combination (WOC) method is utilized to integrate the models by calculating optimized weights to form the combining model. It is proved that the combining model with WOC exhibits better performance with the slightly higher determination coefficient R^2 in comparison with each single yield models with four different VIs, respectively. The analysis of comparing the weights in the combining model with WOC indicates that the two VIs, *SR* and *NDWI* are more sensitive to winter wheat yield than the other two during the winter wheat jointing stage. The preliminary results of coupling the WOC method with remote sensing imply that WOC can be used to improve the accuracy of yield estimation based on remote sensing.

Keywords: Weight optimization combination, remote sensing, yield estimation, winter wheat, Landsat5 TM.

* Corresponding author.
Funding for this research is supported by 863 National High Technology R&D Program (No.2008AA10Z214), National Natural Science Foundation of China (No.40701120), and Beijing Natural Science Foundation (No.4092016 & 4092017) (P.R. China).

1   Introduction

Crop yield are impacted by a wide range of factors, not only natural environment conditions such as light, temperature, water, soil quality, terrain and so on, but also social factors, for instance, field management, agricultural machine, fertilizer, etc (Rieger et al., 2008; Xu et al., 2008). So it is difficult, and even impossible to establish the yield estimating models which can include all impact factors of crop yield. Although the factors influencing crop yield are many and complex, these factors are not independent and affect each other. In different stage, there are different dominant factors impacting crop growth, the estimating models of crop yield can be set up by using the dominating factors according to some principals and methods, Therefore, all kinds of models can all provide various useful-information more or less to some extent. If the scattered models are synthetically utilized to form the combining model and estimate crop yield, the precision of crop yield estimation will improve, Weight Optimization Combination (WOC) is just an algorithm for solving the type of problem. WOC aims at making best use of useful information from each of single models by giving the optimal weights to the single models to form the combining model with LSSE (Least sum of square error), and is often used in economic prediction and decision analysis fields (Tang, 1991, 1992; Tang et al., 1994), and seldom applied for yield estimation with remote sensing.

Remote sensing plays a unique role in estimating crop yield by its nondestructive, fast, and large-area-measurement characteristic. The typical vegetation indices (VIs) with different bands combination from remote sensing, such as *NDVI* (Rouse et al., 1974; Gitelson et al., 1994), *SR* (Jordan, 1969), *TCARI/OSAVI* (Daughtry et al., 2000; Rondeaux et al., 1996; Haboudane et al, 2002), *NDWI* (Gao, 1996) can monitor crop growth status in different stages, indirectly provide useful information on crop yield, and be used to estimate crop yield in this study. Since different VI can detect crop growth status from different views, crop yield models with different VIs can also provide some useful information from different ways, so if we integrate the scattered models together, and form the combining model in order to make full use of the useful information from each of the single scattered models, the precision of crop yield estimation can improve more or less.

The objective of the study is to compare the performance of the above VIs for estimating yield of winter wheat, and then the WOC principle is applied to integrate the single yield estimating models with the VIs to form the combining models, finally assess the performance of the WOC method with remote sensing for estimating yield of winter wheat.

2   Material and Method

2.1   Study Area and Data Acquisition

The study area covers Shunyi & Tongzhou District in Beijing, China. The plant area of winter wheat in the two districts accounts for about 50% of the whole Beijing. Fgure 1 showed the location of the study area (116.45~117.01°E, 40.0~40.3°N), the triangles in Fig. 1 represent the 30 measured yield plots in winter wheat field. Among the plots, there are 15 plots in Shunyi, and the other 15 in Tongzhou District.

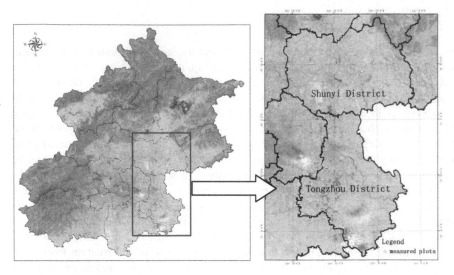

Fig. 1. Study area covering Shunyi & Tongzhou District(right), in Beijing(left), China

2.2   Remote Sensing Data and Preprocessing

In the study, a satellite image from Landsat5 TM which passed over the study area on April 15, 2009 is acquired to estimate yield of winter wheat for assessing the performance of WOC. Winter wheat is during the jointing stage. In order to eliminate some noises and improve data precision, the image is preprocessed by radiant calibration, atmospheric and geometrical corrections with ENVI software.

2.3   Vegetation Indices Used in the Study

In this analysis, the four vegetation indices, *NDVI, SR, TCARI/OSAVI* (the ratio of *TCARI* and *OSAVI* as a VI), and *NDWI* are utilized to estimate yield of .winter wheat in the study area in 2009. Table 1 showed the summary of the four vegetation indices, R is the land surface reflectance, and the subscripts *green, red, nir, and swir* were respectively band2, band3, band4 and band5 from the Landsat5 TM image.

NDVI (Normalized Difference Vegetation Index) should be the most extensively used VI which couples the reflection in the infrared with that in the red, and responds to changes in amount of biomass, chlorophyll and LAI. *SR* (Simple Ratio index) is directly formulated with the reflection in the infrared and that of the absorption in the red, and can enhance the contrast between soil and vegetation while minimizing the effect of the illumination conditions (Barnet and Guyot, 1991).

TCARI (Transformed Chlorophyll Absorption Ratio Index) is proposed to eliminate reflectance effect of background matters (soil and non-photosynthetic components) and to increase the sensitivity at chlorophyll content, and it is often formulated with 550,670, and 700nm in hyperspectral applications, the detailed description of the *TCARI* can be found in Daughtry et al. (2000). In the study, in order to use the multispectral wide-band image, the calculation of *TCARI* is modified with bands from Landsat5 TM as the formula in Table 1. *OSAVI* (Optimized Soil-Adjusted

Vegetation Index) belongs to *SAVI* family (Huete, 1988), and is developed to further reduce background soils. The ratio of *TCARI* and *OSAVI* as a new index is proposed by Haboudane et al. (2002), which integrate advantages of indices minimizing soil background effects and indices that are sensitive to chlorophyll concentration. So the index of *TCARI/OSAVI* can monitor crop nutritional status, and further assess crop yield.

NDWI (Normalized Difference Water Index) is based on liquid water absorption band near 1240nm, and a relative non-absorption reference band near 860nm (Gao, 1996), so it can detect crop water stress. In the analysis, *NDWI* is modified by the combination of the reflectance in the Nir with that in the Swir (short infrared) from Landsat5 TM image bands.

In the present study, the four indices are relatively related with crop growth, nutrition and water, all of which interact with crop yield, so it is possible that integrating the single models with these indices establishes the combining model to estimates crop yield with higher precision.

Table 1. Summary of the four vegetation indices for this analysis

VI	Full name	Definition	Described by
NDVI	Normalized Difference Vegetation Index	$(R_{nir} - R_{red})/(R_{nir} + R_{red})$	Rouse et al., 1974; Gitelson et al., 1994
SR	Simple Ratio Index	R_{nir}/R_{red}	Jordan, 1969
TCARI/ OSAVI	Transformed Chlorophyll Absorption Ratio Index / Optimized Soil-Adjusted Vegetation Index	$\dfrac{3*((R_{nir}-R_{red})-0.2*(R_{nir}-R_{green})*(R_{nir}/R_{red}))}{(1+0.16)*(R_{nir}-R_{red})/(R_{nir}+R_{red}+0.16)}$	Daughtry et al., 2000; Rondeaux et al., 1996; Haboudane et al, 2002
NDWI	Normalized Difference Water Index	$(R_{nir} - R_{swir})/(R_{nir} + R_{swir})$	Gao, 1996

2.4   Weight Optimization Combination Method

Weight optimization combination (WOC) is a method which computationally gives optimal weights of different models solving the same problem to form the combination model with the aim of the least errors (Xu et al., 2009). The principle of WOC is as the following:

There are different N models constructed with n samples for settling the same problem, where both N and n are the same as the following mentioned, respectively.

y_j: the measured value for j sample ($j = 1, 2, 3, \cdots, n$);

f_{ij}: the estimated result for j sample with i model($i = 1, 2, 3, \cdots, N$);

$e_{ij} = y_j - f_{ij}$: the error for j sample with i model;

The estimated value of the combination model formed by N models for j sample is defined as the following:

$$f_j = \sum_{i=1}^{N} k_i f_{ij} \tag{1}$$

Here, k_i are weights of N single models, and k is constrained by the following conditions:

$$\begin{cases} k_i \geq 0 \\ \sum k_i = 1 \end{cases} \tag{2}$$

The error of the combination model for j sample is formulated with the following:

$$e_j = y_j - f_j = \sum_{i=1}^{N} e_{ij} k_i \tag{3}$$

For determining k_i, e_j is usually looked on as independent variable of the objective function, and the mathematic framework of WOC is commonly expressed as the following:

$$\begin{cases} E = \min E(k_1, k_2, \ldots, k_i) \\ \sum k_i = 1 \\ k_i \geq 0 \end{cases} \tag{4}$$

Where, $\min E$ is the objective function that can be the minimum error square sum, or minimum absolute error sum, or the other cost function.

The process solving the formula (4) for the acquisition of k_i is a little complicated, and there are various solving algorithms for the formula (4) with different effectiveness. In the study, the iterative optimization algorithm based on dual optimal combination is selected to calculate the optimal weights, whose detailed description can be found in Tang et al. (1994)

3   Result and Discussion

3.1   Yield Estimation with Single Vegetation Index

To set up the combining model of winter wheat yield estimation base on WOC, the above four VIs is firstly used to establish the yield models with the field measured yield data and the preprocessed remote image from Landsat5 TM, respectively. The LLST(Linear Least Squares Fit) is the main modeling method in the study; and the equations of the models with different index are as the following (5) – (8):

$$f_{NDVI} = 6879 * NDVI + 1970 \tag{5}$$

$$f_{SR} = 483.6 * SR + 3868 \qquad (6)$$

$$f_{TCARI/OSAVI} = -1462 * TCARI / OSAVI + 6143 \qquad (7)$$

$$f_{NDWI} = 6801 * NDWI + 4764 \qquad (8)$$

In the equation (5) ~ (8), f is yield calculated by the individual model from different vegetation index, and the unit is kg/hm.

Figure 2 shows the correlation coefficients between the measured and estimated yield with four VIs models of winter wheat yield. From the figure, it is proved that the four models with different Vis have the approximate precisions, but the precisions of the models with three VIs, SR, TCAI/OSAVI and NDWI are more proximal, and the determinant coefficients R^2 are 0.368, 0.365 and 0.364, respectively.

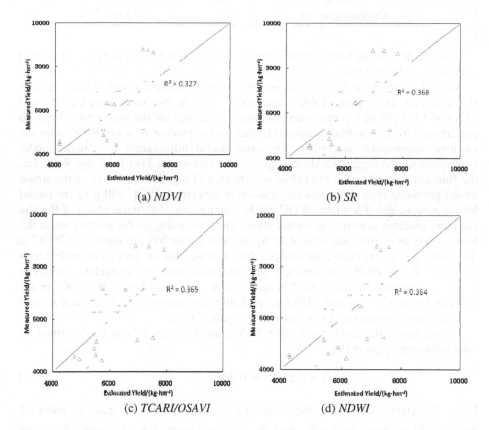

(a) NDVI   (b) SR

(c) TCARI/OSAVI   (d) NDWI

Fig. 2. Coefficients of correlation between the measured and estimated yield with different VI models of winter wheat

3.2   Estimating Yield with the Combining Model

In order to use WOC to build the combining model for estimating yield of winter wheat, the above four models from the equations (5) ~ (8) are input into WOC, and then the iterative optimization algorithm above mentioned is applied to calculate the weights. The result is as Table 2 shows.

Table 2. Optimum weights of the estimating models with different VIs based on WOC

Model with different VIs	Weights	R^2 of yield estimation
SR	0.54	0.368
NDVI	0.00	0.327
TCARI/OSAVI	0.00	0.365
NDWI	0.46	0.364
Combining model	--	0.379

From Table 2, it can been seen that the combining model has better performance in comparison with the four individual models with different VIs, and its determinant coefficient R^2 arrives at 0.379 (also see Fig. 3) and are slightly higher than the four single models. In addition, Table 2 also shows that the two models with *NDVI* and *TCARI/OSAVI* obtain the zero weights, which indicates that the two models have no contribution to the combining model. In fact, in the process of using WOC with the iterative optimization algorithm, the more useful information the single model contributes to, the bigger weight it is given, and vice versa. That is to say, WOC has the function of judging the redundant information (Tang, 1992). As far as the single model providing little or useless information is concerned, WOC will give the model less or zero weight. Therefore, WOC can be employed to determine which of the VIs are more probably sensitive to winter wheat yield according to the weights when the four models as constructed separately by the above four VIs are input into WOC at the same time. In this study, the analysis demonstrates that the two yield models with the VIs *SR* and *NDWI* are enough, and the other two are redundant, which is significant for how to select the VIs sensitive to crop yield based on WOC. In the analysis, the two VIs SR and *NDWI* are probably more sensitive to winter wheat yield than the others two during the winter wheat jointing stage.

According to the result from table 2, the combining model can be described by the following equation (9):

$$Y = 0.54 f_{SR} + 0.46 f_{NDWI} \qquad (9)$$

Here, Y is yield calculated by the combining model coupling the vegetation index *SR* with *NDWI* in terms of WOC, and the unit is kg/hm. both f_{SR} and f_{NDWI} are corresponding to dependent variables in the equations (6) and (8), respectively. Figure 3 displays the correlation between the measured and estimated yield with the combining model based on WOC by plotting scatter diagram.

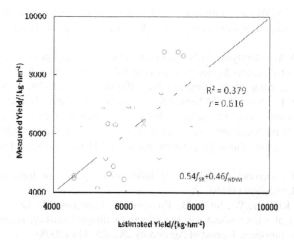

Fig. 3. Correlation between the measured and estimated yield with the combining model

4   Conclusion

In this study, the weight optimization combination method is introduced to the yield estimation of winter wheat with remote sensing data from Landsat5 TM. Firstly, the four typical vegetation indices, *NDVI, SR, TCARI/OSAVI* and *NDWI* are adopted to establish the yield estimating models, respectively, and then the four models with different VIs are input into WOC to calculate the optimum weights and form the combining model, and there are conclusions as the followings:

(1) In comparison with the single yield models of winter wheat with different vegetation indices from remote sensing data, the combining model based on WOC has slightly higher precision for estimating winter wheat yield.
(2) In the combining model using WOC with the four VIs yield models, the two models with *SR* and *NDWI* are given the non-zero weights, which indicate that the two VIs are probably more sensitive to winter wheat yield than the other two during the winter wheat jointing stage.

The study only discusses the ability of the WOC method for estimating winter wheat yield in one wheat growth period, and the following research work would focus on multi-periods with multi-temporal remote sensing data.

References

1. Baret, F., Guyot, G.: Potentials and limits of vegetation indices for LAI and APAR assessment. Remote Sens. Environ. 35, 161–173 (1991)
2. Daughtry, C.S.T., Walthall, C.L., Kim, M.S., Brown de Colstoun, E., McMurtrey III, J.E.: Estimating corn leaf chlorophyll concentration from leaf and canopy reflectance. Remote Sens. Environ. 74, 229–239 (2000)

3. Gao, B.C.: NDWI-A Normalized Difference Water Index for Remote Sensing of Vegetation Liquid Water from Space. Remote Sensing of Environment 58, 257–266 (1996)
4. Gitelson, A.A., Merzlyak, M.N.: Spectral reflectance changes associated with autumn senescence of Aesculus hippocastanum L and Acer platanoides L leaves-spectral features and relation to chlorophyll estimation. Plant Physiol. 143, 286–292 (1994)
5. Haboudane, D., John, R., Millera, J.R., Tremblay, N., Zarco-Tejada, P.J., Dextraze, L.: Integrated narrow-band vegetation indices for prediction of crop chlorophyll content for application to precision agriculture. Remote Sens. Environ. 81, 416–426 (2002)
6. Huete, A.R.: A soil-adjusted vegetation index (SAVI). Remote Sens. Environ. 25, 295–309 (1988)
7. Jordan, C.F.: Derivation of leaf area index form quality of light on the forest floor. Ecology 50, 663–666 (1969)
8. Rieger, S., Richner, W., Streit, B., Frossard, E., Liedgens, M.: Growth, yield, and yield components of winter wheat and the effects of tillage intensity, preceding crops, and N fertilisation. European Journal of Agronomy 28, 405–411 (2008)
9. Rondeaux, G., Steven, M., Baret, F.: Optimization of soil-adjusted vegetation indices. Remote Sens. Environ. 55, 95–107 (1996)
10. Rouse, J.W., Haas, R.H., Schell, J.A., Deering, D.W., Harlan, J.C.: Monitoring the vernal advancements and retrogradation of natural vegetation. In: NASA/GSFC, Final Report, Greenbelt, MD, USA, pp, 1–137 (1974)
11. Tang, X.: Study of computing method of combination forecasting. Forecasting 10(4), 35–39 (1991) (in Chinese with English abstract)
12. Tang, X.: Study of combination forecasting error information matrix. Journal of UEST of China 21(4), 448–454 (1992) (in Chinese with English abstract)
13. Tang, X., Zeng, Y., Cao, C.: An iterative algorithm for optimal combination forecasting of non-negative weights. Systems Engineering Theory Methodology Application 3(4), 48–52 (1994) (in Chinese with English abstract)
14. Xu, X., Wang, J., Huang, W., Li, C., Yang, X., Gu, X.: Estimation of crop yield based on weight optimization combination and multi-temporal remote sensing data. Transactions of the CSAE 25(9), 137–142 (2009) (in Chinese with English abstract)
15. Xu, X., Wu, B., Meng, J., Li, Q., Huang, W., Liu, L., Wang, J.: Research advances in crop yield estimation models based on remote sensing. Transactions of the CSAE 24(2), 290–298 (2008) (in Chinese with English abstract)

Application of Data Fusion Technology in Greenhouse Environment Monitoring and Control System

Xiangfei Meng[1,2] and Changming Wang[1]

[1] School of Mechanical Engineering, NUST, Nanjing 210094, China
[2] Changshu Institute of Technology, Changshu, 215500, China

Abstract. Multisensor data fusion technology is a new frontier technology. According to the demand of greenhouse environment monitoring, the paper puts forward a new kind of data fusion method based on Dempster-Shafer (D-S) evidence theory and agricultural expert system. The experimental results show that the method can improve the veracity of decision of measuring and controlling greenhouse environment parameters, and can significantly improve the control effect of greenhouse environment.

Keywords: greenhouse environment, multisensor data fusion, D-S evidence theory, agricultural expert system.

1 Introduction

The environmental conditions in the greenhouse play an important role in crop growth and development. It is a key point of the development of greenhouse technology that how to make the most suitable greenhouse environment for crop growth. Now a single sensor is mainly used to monitor the greenhouse environment, such as temperature monitoring, humidity monitoring, CO_2 monitoring, soil moisture monitoring, illumination monitoring, etc, since the lack of collaboration processing and comprehensive utilizing the multi-source and multidimensional information, there are varied defects in accuracy, reliability, practicability, etc. By better utilizing the information resources, data fusion technology is applied to the greenhouse environment monitoring and control system to incorporate and corresponding process multidimensional information from various sensors [1]. So more accurately reflection about the greenhouse environment condition can be got and more accurately and reliably greenhouse environment monitor can be carried out.

2 Data Fusion Technology

2.1 Data Fusion Process

Data fusion is the technology which makes full use of multisensor resources. It can combine the information, which is redundant and complementary in time and space, according to certain standards, by using the multisensor and observation information properly to get the consistent explanation or description of the tested object. The

D. Li and Y. Chen (Eds.): CCTA 2011, Part III, IFIP AICT 370, pp. 293–299, 2012.

processes of Data fusion mainly includes multisensor (signal acquisition), data preprocessing, data fusion center (feature extraction, data fusion Calculation) and result output [2].

2.2   Fusion Algorithm

As a data processing technology, data fusion is in fact the integration and application of traditional science and new technologies. Traditional multiple sensor fusion mainly includes simple filtering method, the weighted averages method, production rules, the Bayesian estimation, D-S evidence reasoning method, etc. In recent years, many new fusion methods have also been put forward, including expert system, neural network and fuzzy theory, etc. This paper put forward a kind of fusion method based on the evidence theory and the expert system to monitor the greenhouse environment [3].

The biggest characteristic of D-S evidence theory structure is introducing the uncertainty into evidence and establishing the axioms. For example, basic probability assignment function (BPAF), believe function (BEL), plausibility function (PL), etc. The most basic concept of D-S evidence theory is the recognition framework, recorded as Θ. Θ represents the set of all possible proposition in a domain, Every proposition is represented as a subset of Θ. 2^{Θ} is Θ Power set and makes up a set of proposition $\Omega(\Theta)$. If the elements meet the condition that incompatible with each other in a discernment frame , the m (A), values A assigns to function m, is a mapping form power set to $[0,1]$. If the function m meets the following conditions:

$$m(\Phi) = 0 \tag{1}$$

$$\forall A \in 2^{\Theta}, m(A) \geq 0, \ and \ \sum_{A \in 2^{\Theta}} m(A) = 1 \tag{2}$$

m (A) can be called as a basic probability assignment function of A. Among them Φ represents empty set, m (A) represents the precise degree of believe in proposition A and the directly support of A.

For a given basic probability assignment function m and $\forall A \in 2^{\Omega}$, the corresponding belief function is defined as:

$$Bel(A) = \sum_{B \subseteq A} m(B) \tag{3}$$

Plausibility function is defined as:

$$Pl(A) = 1 - Bel(\overline{A}) = \sum_{B \cap A \neq \Phi} m(B) \tag{4}$$

Bel function is called as lower limit function, expressed the degree of believe in proposition A, including Bel $(\Phi) = 0$, Bel $(\Omega) = 1$. Pl function also known as the upper limit function or not negative function, it is a sum of all the set of basic probability assignment functions that meet A. As the evidence refused to A, Pl $(A) = 0$, when there is no evidence against A, Pl $(A) = 1$, it is easy to prove Pl $(A) \geq Bel$ (A).

[Bel (A), Pl (A)] represents the belief range of *A*. If *A* is a subset in discernment frame and *m (A)*>0, *A* is called as a focal of belief function *Bel*. In this way, trust degree and plausibility have summarized the relations evidence of proposition *A*, the relations between them as shown in figure 1; this constitutes a complete range of evidence.

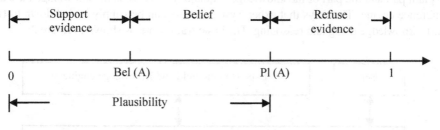

Fig. 1. Evidence range schemes

Basic rules of D-S evidence combination: Hypothesizing that there are two reasoning system, their basic probability assignment and belief function is m_1 m_2 and Bel_1, Bel_2 respectively, for subset *A*, the D-S rules composed of probability assignment of the two reasoning system:

$$m(A) = \frac{\sum_{A_1 \cap A_2 = A} m_1(A_1)m_2(A_2)}{\sum_{A_1 \cap A_2 \neq \Phi} m_1(A_1)m_2(A_2)} = m_1(A_1) \oplus m_2(A_2) \tag{5}$$

The corresponding *Bel* of *m* called synthesis or sum value of Bel_1 and Bel_2, recorded as $Bel=Bel_1 \oplus Bel_2$.

$$\sum_{A_1 \cap A_2 \neq \Phi} m_1(A_1)m_2(A_2) = 1 - \sum_{A_1 \cap A_2 = \Phi} m_1(A_1)m_2(A_2) = 1 - k \tag{6}$$

$1-k$ is a correction factor. In fact, the introduction of $1-k$ is in order to avoid assigning nonzero probabilities to empty sets when combining the evidences, so that the abandoned belief assignment of empty sets can be added to nonvoid set proportionally. The *k* objectively reflects the degree of conflict among evidences during the date fusion process. The range of *k* is $0 \leq k \leq 1$, the bigger *k* is the greater conflict will be. If *k* close to 1, it will probably produces unreasonable results and leads to the fusion decisions against intuition; If *k*=1, D-S theory cannot be use to fuse.

2.3   Expert System

Expert system is a branch of artificial intelligence. Its main purpose is to make the computers play the role of human experts in each field. It is a kind of intelligence program subsystems, which has a large number of domain knowledge and experiences on expert level. The expert system can solve the problems in the field by using the knowledge and methods that human experts will adopted. It is a computer program, which can finish general or humanoid simulation problem-solving strategies on expert level and combine the problem with operational knowledge and experience knowledge [4].

Expert system generally consists of knowledge base, database, inference engine, explain part and the part of the knowledge acquisition. Its core is the knowledge base and Inference engine. The ways that expert system works can be simply boiled down to two parts: knowledge using and reasoning. The basic framework as shown in figure 2:

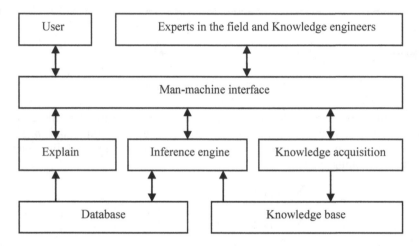

Fig. 2. The basic framework of expert system

3   The Greenhouse Environment Monitoring System Based on Multisensor Data Fusion

Environmental monitoring technology is the core of greenhouse technology. In a modern large greenhouse, all the environmental factors such as indoor temperature, light, wet and heat detecting, sensing and adjusting are managed by the computer comprehensively and controlled automatically [5]. The purpose of greenhouse environment controlling is overcome some or entire climate environment in outside world and the objective restrictions, according to the physiological property of different crop, to build a best environment for different crop to growth. At present, the greenhouse environment controlling mostly uses industrial control system. On the one hand, the industrial control system costs more, can't meet the low-cost requirement of establishment agriculture; on the other hand, it focuses on the computer technology during the development process, without the participation of agricultural expert system. It also lacks the expert system that includes physiological information of crops. Because of these reasons, the greenhouse environment controlling has some limitations in the management application [6] [7].

This paper adopts a method, which combined the D-S evidence theory with expert system, to do the fusion processing on the three main environment parameter, temperature, humidity and light intensity in greenhouse. According to what may happen in the greenhouse environment, a definition of the rational recognition framework can be worked out form expert knowledge, and the assignment on basic probability assignment can be down on the date which is fused locally. And then initial conditions of D-S theory can be acquired. After D-S evidence theory combination rules fusion, all the fusion results will be sent into the knowledge base of expert system to combine with the experiences of domain experts as the basis of inference in the expert system so that a accurate judgment will be worked out, and appropriate measures will be applied to adjust environmental parameters. Finally, the best environment conditions for crop to growth will be acquired. System structure fusion as shown in figure 3:

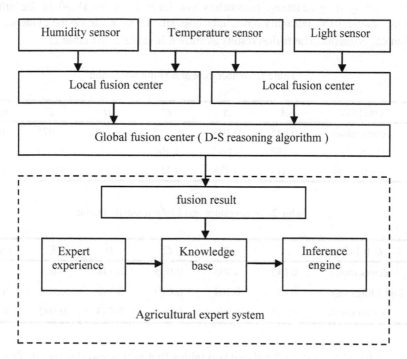

Fig. 3. Structure diagram of system fusion

4 The Experiment and Application Study for Greenhouse Cultivation

The simulation experiment of fusion algorithm has been down on specific environmental conditions of strawberry cultivation in a greenhouse trellis. Strawberry belongs to the thermophilic plants. A group of environmental data of greenhouse strawberry cultivation in March is collected for experiment. There is only one or two of the environmental factors play a leading role under certain conditions in the greenhouse. We call them the leading factor. During fruiting period of strawberry, temperature is the leading factor, which affects the yield and quality of strawberry, in sunlight greenhouse. So recognition framework can be built with the knowledge and experiences of domain expert. The recognition framework is as follows:

$\Theta = \{A, B, C, D, E\}$;

$A = \{$ appropriate, temperature 20°C~25°C, humidity 60%~70%, light intensity 2500 ~ 3000 $lx\}$;

$B = \{$ low temperature $\}$;

$C = \{$ low temperature, humidity is on the high side $\}$;

$D = \{$ low temperature, light intensity is insufficient $\}$;

$E = \{$ low temperature, humidity is on the high side, light intensity is insufficient $\}$;

Take a group of greenhouse parameters got form 16:30 to 18:30 in the afternoon $\{$ temperature 18°C, humidity 65%, light intensity 1500 $lx\}$ to do the evidence theory fusion experiments. The fusion results as shown in table 1 and table 2:

Table 1. Temperature and Humidity fusion

k=0.1812	A	B	C	D	E	$m(\Theta)$
Temperature	0.645	0.103	0.025	0.148	0.075	0.018
Humidity	0.382	0.067	0.460	0.042	0.115	0.027
Fusion result	0.844	0.018	0.116	0.016	0.015	0.009

Table 2. Temperature and Light intensity fusion

k=0.1125	A	B	C	D	E	$m(\Theta)$
Temperature	0.645	0.103	0.025	0.148	0.075	0.018
Light intensity	0.053	0.104	0.019	0.702	0.058	0.001
Fusion result	0.126	0.056	0.002	0.743	0.002	0.006

It can be inferred from the above two tables that m (Θ) was decreased. That means data fusion reduce the uncertainty of the system. At the same time, the fusion of the basic possibility is better separability than before fusion. Table 1 shows that after merging the temperature and humidity, basic probability function value of A is the largest one, and is more than before fusion temperature and humidity their basic possibility function value is bigger. Table 2 shows that after merging the light intensity and temperature, basic possibility function value of D is the largest one. Comprehensively considering the fusion results of the two tables, it can be judged that temperature, humidity is appropriate in the greenhouse now, but light intensity is insufficient. So it is necessary to do light supplement by using dysprosium lamp. Compared to high voltage sodium lamp and halide lamp, dysprosium lamp can make the light increased from 1000 lx to 4000 lx. Because of this, dysprosium lamp can be used in raining days, fog days and evening.

5   Conclusions

At present, Multisensor data fusion technology has been successfully applied to the automatic control, the military and aviation navigation. It is not a single technology, but an interdisciplinary comprehensive theory and method. We should actively learn the research results home and abroad. The research in the agricultural engineering area should be vigorously promoted. This paper through two-step data fusion, the fusion results will be sent into the knowledge base of expert system as the basis of inference in the expert system and then adds the experiences of agricultural expert, more accurate decision results can be got.

The combination of data fusion technology and agriculture expert system is the development direction of precision agriculture. With the continuous improvement and development of the data fusion technology, it is believed that technical support will be offered to informationization and better educated the agricultural production in the near future. The agricultural production will become more and more automated and precision. The pace of development of modern agricultural production in China will be speedup.

References

[1] Xu, F.: The Study of the Development of Establishment Agriculture in China, Shandong Agriculture University, pp. 1–5. (2008)
[2] (US) Hall (D.L.). Multisensor Data Fusion Manual, pp. 256–260. Publishing House of Electronics Industry, Pekin (2008)
[3] Kang, Y.: Data Fusion Theory and Application, pp. 165–168. Publishing house of Xi-Dian University, Sian (2006)
[4] Zhao, Z.: The Countermeasures of Developing Intellective Agriculture Expert System. China Science and Technology Review, 16–18 (2009)
[5] Liang, J.: The Research and Design of Intelligent Greenhouse Environment Temperature and Humidity Measurement and Control System, pp. 25–30. Taiyuan University of Technology (2005)
[6] Ding, W.: The Analysis of Greenhouse Environment Control and Situation of Greenhouse Simulation Modeled To The Current. Chinese Society of Agricultural Machinery. Journal of Agricultural Machinery 40(5), 44–48 (2009)
[7] Cheng, M., Yuan, H., et al.: The Research Based on Multisensor Data Fusion and Greenhouse Environment Control. Agricultural Mechanization Research 31(7), 213–217 (2009)

Improvement of the Capacitive Grain Moisture Sensor

Liu Yang[1], Yongjun Zheng[1], Zhijie Jiang[2], and Zhijun Ren[1]

[1] Engineering College, China Agricultural University, 100083, Beijing China
[2] The Department of Automobile, Beijing Jiaotong Vocational Technical University,
102200, Beijing China
{yangliu,zyj}@cau.edu.cn,
jiangzhijie@163.com, zhijunr@gmail.com

Abstract. Moisture is one of the most important factors affecting grain quality in storage. The grain must be dried as soon as possible after harvesting to lower moisture to a standard level. It is difficult to obtain satisfactory measurement effect on precision in capacitive grain's moisture measurement due to many influencing factors, such as temperature, species and weight. The data confusion method of Radial Basis Function nerve network is adopted with improved hardware of the measurement system. Tests show that the precision in moisture measurement of wheat has been improved.

Keywords: Moisture Measurement, Precision, Factors, Radial Basis Function Never Network.

1   Introduction

Safe storage of food is one of the most important strategic issues for a nation's economy and the people's livelihood. Moisture is a key factor to food storage. High grain moisture levels at harvest can result in heat, fermentation, deterioration and low burgeoning rate. To ensure safe storage, the grain must be dried as soon as possible after harvesting and is maintained at lower moisture levels.. It is, therefore, important to use an advanced sensor system to accurately monitor grain moisture levels. This paper examines the ways to improve accuracy and reliability of moisture sensors and to develop an advanced moisture monitoring system.

China urgently needs matching equipment with simple construction, low cost, high accuracy, reliable and good repetition of results. The capacitance sensor has advantages such as low cost, high sensitivity and good dynamic performance and it is suitable for online measurement. So the capacitance sensor is selected to measure the moisture.

1.1   The Current Situation of Online Moisture Sensors

The principle of the capacitance sensor is that it measures the capacitance value to obtain moisture levels of the grain which chang with the relative dielectric constant. There are two types of capacitance sensors: double electrodes and cylindrical [1].

D. Li and Y. Chen (Eds.): CCTA 2011, Part III, IFIP AICT 370, pp. 300–307, 2012.

(1) Change the hidden area

The capacitance value is proportional to the angle movement. The hidden area can be changed by using the line movement[2]. At the beginning the hidden area is the biggest and it changes when the relative electrodes changes. It is hard to measure moisture levels of the grain.

(2) Change the distance of the electrodes

This kind of sensor consists of two electrodes. One is grounded and the other is active with the measured object. The capacitance varies when the distance of the two electrodes changes. Accuracy of measurement is low when moisture levels of the grain are high.

(3) Change the dielectric constant[3]

One kind is cylindrical sensor probe. It has stable performance and high accuracy. But it is difficult to install this type of sensor on the dry machine and to achieve online measurement.

2   Research on Affecting Factors of the Capacitive Grain Sensor

The capacitance value can be expressed by the following equations.

$$C_x = K_0 e\varepsilon_3 + K_0(1-e)\varepsilon_1 + \frac{K_0 \gamma_d (1-e)(\varepsilon_2 - \varepsilon_1)}{1 + M(\gamma_d - 1)} M \tag{1}$$

$K0 = \dfrac{\varepsilon_0 LH}{D}$, LH is the front area and D is the distance between the two electrodes; ε_0 is the vacuum dielectric constant; M is the grain moisture; ε_1 is the object dielectric constant; ε_2 is the dielectric constant of water in grain; ε_3 is the dielectric constant of the air between grain holes; γ_d is the object volume of grain; e is the rate of hole gaps.

From the equation we can derive the following affecting factors:

1   The temperature is an important factor and should be eliminated.
2   Different grains have different dielectric constants which will affect the capacitance.
3   The rate of grain gaps is the main factor that affects precision and should be eliminated.

3   Hardware Circuit

3.1   Moisture Measurement

Fig.1 is the basic circuit of capacitance moisture senor. The driving electrode is connected with the oscillation circuit and sensor electrode and protecting electrode are connected to the ground. The frequency f is decided by induction L and measured capacitance C_x

$$f \propto \frac{1}{\sqrt{LC_x}} \quad . \tag{2}$$

Different grain moisture leads to changes in C_x, and the frequency changes. Thus we can obtain the moisture from the frequency.

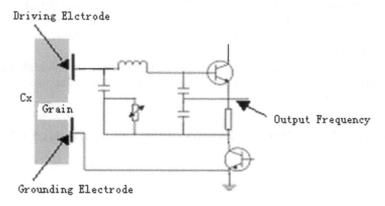

Fig. 1. Moisture Measurement Circuit

3.2 Temperature Measurement

Fig. 2 is the temperature to frequency transfer circuit. LM35 is the accurate temperature sensor. The output voltage is proportional to the Celsius temperature. The accuracy is ±0.5°C. Output voltage is -1.0~+6V. The output signals transfer into frequency signals.

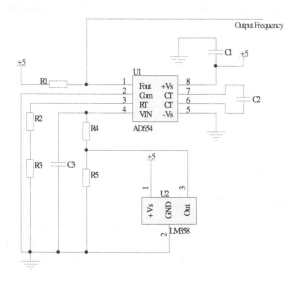

Fig. 2. Temperature Measurement Circuit

3.3   Weight Measurement

Fig.3 shows the weight measurement circuit. The resistance strain sensors are used in the measurement circuit. The difference amplifier is applied in the preamplifier to improve the input resistance and block the common noise. Two channels of low-pass filter the signals of the two arms. The signals send to slave computer.

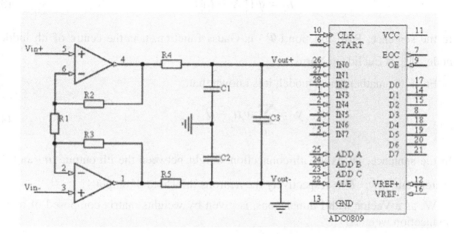

Fig. 3. Weight Measurement Circuit

4   Hardware Circuit

There are a few major factors affecting the measuring accuracy of grain moisture: the ambient temperature, the testing frequency and the wieght of the grain[4][5]. This model composes by input layer, hidden layer and output layer. The input layer has 3 neurons, the hidden layer has I neurons, the output layer has one neuron. The neural network topology is show in Figure 4.

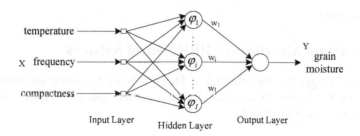

Fig. 4. RBF network structure of moisture measurement system

4.1   Mathematics Model

The input vector is $X = [x_1, x_2, x_3]$; x_1, x_2, x_3 are temperature, frequency and compactness. The output vector is Y = y, y is grain moisture.

RBF network hidden layer output (the ith node)[6].

$$u_i = \varphi(\|X - t_i\|) \tag{3}$$

In the sentence, RBF function (φ) is Gauss function, ti is the centre of ith hidden node, $\|\cdot\|$ is Euclidean Norm.

From the mathematical model, it is known that.

$$y = \sum_i w_i u_i - \theta . \tag{4}$$

In the sentence, w_i is the ith connection weight between the ith output u_i and the system output y, θ is respectively the neurons threshold of output.

W, as a Vector with I dimensions, is given by weights matrix composed of output connection weights.

$$W = [w_1, w_2, \cdots w_i \cdots w_I]. \tag{5}$$

To obtain RBF network[7] for a measuring system, which has N groups of inputs and outputs, can be described in mathematical model as: to get the optimum weights matrix W so as to achieve minimum error between output of RBF network and the expected output of the samples. The target function is.

$$\min \quad B = \frac{1}{2}\sum \|d_k - Y_k\|^2 = \frac{1}{2}\sum_{k=1}^{N}(d_k - y_k)^2. \tag{6}$$

Y_k is kth output vector of RBF network, d_k is kth expected output vector of training samples.

5   Training Algorithm of RBF Neural Network

There are 2 stages for this algorithm. Stage 1 is to determine the radial primary function for the hidden layer; stage 2 is the get the optimum weights matrix from nonlinear programming model.

5.1   Improved RBF Network OLS Algorithm

Three parameters are needed to be computed and learned: center vector in basis function, variance vector and weight value matrix. Structural optimization in network is a difficult. The general structure has large numbers of hidden nodes and leads to over-learn. The general orthogonal method is the traditional Gram-Schmidt which has rounding error[8][9]. The hidden network structure is optimized with the improved method in the article.

The I eigenvectors are obtained by K-mean clustering [10]. Suppose the output testing samples column vector is.

$$d = [d_1, d_2, \cdots, d_I] \cdot \qquad (7)$$

The hidden layer output vector is.

$$U = \left[u_1, u_2, \cdots, u_I \right]^T . \qquad (8)$$

The expected output vector can be expressed by hidden layer function output vector.

$$d = UW + E . \qquad (9)$$

In the sentence, E is error vector.

Make U as orthogonal triangular factorization with Gram-Schmidt orthogonal algorithm [11].

$$U = QR . \qquad (10)$$

The elements in upper triangular matrix R are computed in row but not in line in improved Gram-Schmidt method which lead to lower rounding error. For details, viewing q_1 as the result of u_1, at the same time $u_2, \cdots, u_I$ minus the parallel component of u_1 in advanced.

$$\begin{cases} R_{11} = u_{11}, q_1 = u_1 / \|R_{11}\| \\ R_{1j} = q_1^T u_j, u_j^{(1)} = u_j - q_1 R_{1j} \qquad 2 \le j \le I. \end{cases} \qquad (11)$$

After the computation, $u_2^{(1)}, u_3^{(1)}, \cdots, u_I^{(1)}$ are orthogonal with q_1.

Then, Ortho-normalized $u_2^{(1)}$: $u_3^{(1)}, \cdots, u_I^{(1)}$ minus the parallel component of $u_2^{(1)}$.

$$\begin{cases} R_{22} = u_{22}^{(1)}, q_2 = u_2^{(1)} / \|R_{22}\| \\ R_{2j} = q_2^T u_j^{(1)}, u_j^{(2)} = u_j^{(1)} - q_2 R_{2j} \quad 3 \le j \le I. \end{cases} \qquad (12)$$

Thus, $u_3^{(2)}, \cdots, u_I^{(2)}$ are orthogonal with q_1, q_2. Repeating the steps, the orthogonal matrix Q and upper triangular matrix R are obtained.

The structure network is optimized with improved Gram-Schmidt method and detail solving process is designed in the article. The improved optimized network structure is obtained by sentence (7).

$$d^T d \approx \sum_{i=1}^{I} g_i^2 + E^T E . \qquad (13)$$

In the sentence, $\sum_{i=1}^{I} g_i^2 = G^T G$

$$G = (g_1, g_2 \cdots, g_i, \cdots, g_I) = RW \approx Q^T d$$

Suppose the compression ratio is.

$$[err]_i = g_i^2 / d^T d \qquad 1 \le i \le I . \qquad (14)$$

The above results show that as the rounding error is lower in the improved Gram-Schmidt, the numbers of the hidden layer nodes can be computed precisely. The computation amount is decreased and over learned problem is avoided.

5.2   Data Analysis and Processing

Comparing experiments have been done to verify the function of the improved RBF algorithm in this article, which is supposed to achieve higher moisture detecting accuracy.

BP network, traditional RBF network and improved RBF methods are used to compare for data fusion process.

300 groups of wheat samples are prepared for the experiments. Among which, 250 samples are used for learning algorithm, and 50 groups are used for measuring.

Testing values and standard values of the two methods are listed in Fig.5.

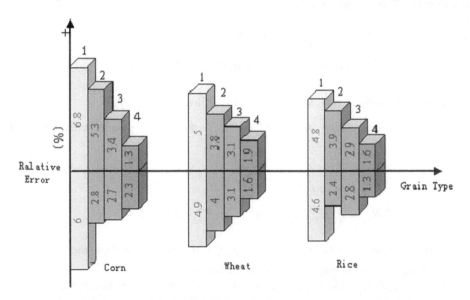

Fig. 5. Comparing Error of Three Kind of Grain With Four Methods
1 No RBF Algorithm   2 BP Algorithm   3 Regular Algorithm   4 Improved Algorithm

6   Conclusion

Factors such as temperature, species and weight affect measurement precision in capacitive grain moisture sensors are analyzed in this paper. The data confusion method of Radial Basis Function nerve network is adopted with improved hardware of the measurement system. Laboratory tests have been conducted on grains of wheat, rice and corns. The results demonstrate that the precision in wheat's moisture measurement has been improved, which shows that the proposed method is better than conventional methods.

References

1. Zhang, C., Zhang, J.: Introduction on the Capacitor Sensors Method for a Moisture Measuring Instrument on Line in Grains. Journal of ChangChun University of Science and Techenology 27(1), 19–21 (2004)
2. Meng, W., Yang, Y., Liu, Y.: Principle and Application of Capacity Sensor. Modern Electronic Technique 7(150), 78–79 (2003)
3. Baxter, L.K.: Capacitive Sensors. IEEE Press (1997)
4. Zhai, B., Chen, Q.: Data Processing of Moisture Content Measurement Based on Data Fusion. Journal of Liaoning Insitute of Technology 26(3), 158–160 (2006)
5. Hardy, R.: Multiquadric Equations of Topography and Other Irregualr Sufaces. Journal of Geophysics Research, 1905–1915 (1987)
6. Harder, R., Desmarais, R.: Interpolation using surface splines. Aircraft (9), 189–191 (1972)
7. Moody, J., Darken, C.: Fast learning in networks of locally-turned processing units. Neural Computation 1(2), 281–294 (1989)
8. Yan, P., Zhang, C.: Artificial Neural Networks and Evolutionary Computing. Tsinghua University Press, Beijing (2002)
9. Billings, S., Zheng, G.L.: Radial basis function network configuration using genetic algorithms. Neural Networks 8(6), 877–890 (1995)
10. Liu, J.: Study on RBF Neural Network Improvement and its Application. Lanzhou University, Lanzhou (2008)
11. Huan, Y., Di, C., Zhu, S.: Matrix Theory and its Application. University of Science and Technology of China Press, HeFei (2005)

Study on the Automatic Composition of Document Service Based on Semantic and Multi-agent Method

Haiyan Hu[1], Xianxue Meng[1], and Xiaolu Su[2,*]

[1] Agricultural Information Institute of Chinese Academy of Agriculture Science,
100081 Beijing, P.R. China
{huhaiyan,meng}@mail.caas.net.cn
[2] Key Laboratory of Digital Agricultural Early-warning
Technology Ministry of Agriculture, Beijing 100081, P.R. China
suxiaolu@mail.caas.net.cn

Abstract. This paper proposes a method which composes document services over the Internet automatically based on multi-agent and semantic technology, and discusses the implementation of three document service functions (catalog browsing, document information browsing and document full version downloading) with that method. We use service delegate agent to encapsulate services on the internet; use service purchase agent to decide which service delegate agents should be used and then to generate a composition script describing how these services being purchased should be used; use service provider agent to call these services according to the composition script and merge the results, translate the merged result into the system predefined format, finally return it to the requesting user. By doing so, service provider can simply composite existed services on the internet and provide full functional service.

Keywords: Document service, Automatic composition, Semantic Web, Multi-agent.

1   Introduction

Information services are becoming more and more specialized. There are many standalone indexing, searching, and online storage services on the Internet, provided by many providers respectively.

Traditional online library is a multi-function system, provides catalog, indexing, and electronic document downloading services. This type of system appears obsolete today. Regarding that there are better search services like Google, better storage services like Amazon S3[1], etc, why not simply use them but do everything self? Develop an all in one service is quite a big challenge, even can be done, it must not be as cost effective as those specialized services from above providers, and can not achieve the high quality standard of them. Composing the existing specialized services are the best way to build online library on today's Internet.

---

* Corresponding author.

D. Li and Y. Chen (Eds.): CCTA 2011, Part III, IFIP AICT 370, pp. 308–314, 2012.
© IFIP International Federation for Information Processing 2012

The core business of online library service provider is to give users the documents they want. To achieve this purpose, four fundamental functions are necessary, they are, document catalog and indexing, document searching, document metadata offering, and document full-text download. As the owner of the documents, providing document's full-text version is the only job must be done by provider himself. If everything is ideal, the online library provider can use online storage service stores his documents, and create a database stores the download links and basic metadata of these documents, and need do nothing else but compose 3rd party services on the web. The basic metadata should include a unique identity for each document, and some candidate identity fields such as title, publish date, author, etc. These fields may be used by some service agents to identify documents, preventing duplication of document metadata from multiple sources.

Semantic and multi-agent based Web Services automatic composing have became new hot spot for Web Services [2-6]. This article discusses the research based on multi-agent and semantic technology which automatically composes directories, document information and document texts in document services.

2   Technical Considerations

The best way to implement service composition system is multi-agent architecture. Using one single agent represents a service. Let these delegate agents promotes his service to the purchasers in a marketplace. After a process of competition, reasonable service consumption relations are established, from which the service cooperation framework can be derived out.

BDI model [7] is a multi-agent architecture that is widely used. A BDI model has three basic parts:

(1) The Belief. Belief is a set of theories about the world, which include the knowledge about the environment, the knowledge about other agents the agent may contact with, and the knowledge about the agent himself. It is the objective basis of the decision-making of the agent.
(2) The Desire. Desire is the motivation of agent, which represents the state the agent willing to achieve and to hold.
(3) The Intention. Intention is the current target of the agent. It is the most urgent desire among all the desires of that agent. It represents the direction of the agent's mind, and guides the actions the agent currently taking.

The system takes JADEX as the basic framework of agent's interaction [8]. Regarding that JADEX do not support ontology inference, it must be extended to meet our requirements. We created a new interface named "IMOWLBelief", two new classes named "MOWLBelief" and "MTypedOWLElement". The class "MTypedOWLElement" defines the attributes of the Ontology and their getters and setters, encapsulates OWL operations. The class "MOWLBelief" is extended from the class "MBelief". To make these newly defined classes accepted by JADEX framework, the JIBX binding file (binding.xml) must be changed. After doing that change, believes can be presented using OWL.

3   Architecture of Service Composition

Each kind of service is composited by a service provider agent, a service purchase agent, and a number of service delegate agents. Each service delegate agent delegates a single service source on the web. Service delegate agent 'knows' every detail of the service it delegated, in another word, that service delegate agent encapsulates its service. The desire of service delegate agents is to sell its service to service purchase agent as much as possible. A service delegate agent can trade with more than one service purchase agents, sells different functions to each of them. For example, a service delegate agent delegates a service source which provides catalogs as well as document metadata, it can sell catalog function to catalog service purchase agent as well as sell metadata function to metadata service purchase agent. Each service purchase agent serves for a single function, so in our system there should be four service purchase agents, work for document catalog, document search, document metadata, and document download respectively. Like service purchase agents, service provider agents are also dedicated to those four functions respectively.

Service purchase agents decide which service the service delegate agents delegated should be used in service composition. While done, the chosen services can be composited to serve users. Service purchase agents will generate a composition script to describe how these services it purchased should be used. A service provider agent is responsible to calling these services according to the script generated by the service purchase agent who work for the same function as it does, and then merges the results, and translates the merged result into the system predefined format; finally return it to the requesting user. The script generation will consume a large amount of computation resources, so it shouldn't be done frequently.

4   Functions of Service Composition

A typical document service provider provides catalog browsing; document searching; document information browsing; and document full version downloading. Regarding that the search service may returns a huge amount of data, and it is not fit for compositing, so we will only discuss composition of the other three functions.

4.1   Catalog Browsing

Catalog browsing service needs a catalog. In traditional way, catalog is created manually with some kind of classification method. Regarding that there may be different users expecting different classification methods, and the best practice is to provide each user what he needs. Creating catalogs manually is an exhausted task, and is apparently not cost effective. If we can reuse the catalogs currently exist on the web, it will become practicable to provide multiple catalogs with different classification method. The catalogs currently on the web are not created for your needs, so those catalogs must be customized.

In catalog service, the catalog itself is the belief of service delegate agent, and the desire of service delegate agent is to sell the service it delegated as much as possible. The service purchase agent will assess each delegate agent and calculate how much its catalog can complement the catalogs already purchased. The service purchase agent will purchase the services which can contribute the most content to current catalogs.

At the initial state, the service purchase agent does not purchase any service. The service delegate agents are added into system every time a new service is discovered. After created, each service delegate agent updates service information periodically to handles the possible changes of that service.

The periodical update of service information may introduce changes to existing service, and those changes may affects the purchase contract already signed. When changes occurred, the service delegate agent must notify the service purchase agent. While notified, the service purchase agent will expire the currently purchase contract, assess the changed service again, together with all other services not yet assessed, and decide how to purchase from all available services. Then the service purchase agent must regenerate service composition script.

The service purchase agent sorts the service delegate agents by the entry numbers in the catalogs their services provides, in descendent order, assesses them one by one. The catalog provides the more useful entries will be scored higher. After all services are assessed, the service purchase agent starts purchase from the service with highest score, until the service scored lower than threshold. The services with zero score will be excluded, until they got some changes and then triggered reassessment processes. The services scored above zero but lower than the threshold will not be purchased in the first round, and will be reassessed in the second round.

The second round purchase based on the result of first round purchase and composition. All the services scored above zero in the first round but not been purchased will be rescored in this round. There is no threshold of score in the second round, if a service is rescored more than zero against the new basis, it will be purchased. The initial score in the first round will be recorded for future use, but not the second round score.

The composition operation uses some simple rules. For example, there is a rule looks like this: "if equalsIgnoreCase (X.entryName, Y.entryName) and notEmpty(intersect (X.parents, Y.parents)) then X sameAs Y "; or "if equalsIgnoreCase (X.entryName, Y.entryName) and isEmpty(X.parents) and isEmpty(Y.parents) then X sameAs Y ". The catalogs the services provided may have multiple language versions. The same catalog entry or the same article title in different languages can be linked up automatically. The service purchase agent handles the merging of catalog entries, generates a script to tell the service provider agent how to composite these catalogs. When user requests, the service provider agent retrieves and composites catalogs according to the script generated by service purchase agent, then extracts out the part which meets the user's requirement, converts them to standard format, and return to the user. Let the service purchase agent handle catalog composition and the service provider agent do the real composition job is based on such considerations: the service purchase agent can present each catalog entry as an OWLClass, and each document as OWL Individual, in its belief, to convenient inference of catalog entry relations; the service provider agent can treat all catalog entries and documents as individuals at the same time, to convenient inference of merge operation. These two believes can not be mixed up, because there is some thing in one is represented as class and in another is represented as individual; if put them together, the merged belief will violate the OWL DL constraint, and can not be used in any inference. The service provider agent reads the script generated by service purchase agent, and revises its own belief according to that script. Considering mapping multiple languages to each other, the link between them needs a new predicate, to express that they can be translated to each other. Two language versions of one document are handled as two linked documents; two language versions of one catalog entry are also handled as two linked ones.

4.2   Document Information (Metadata) Browsing

Metadata of one document can be acquired from multiple sources, and they may not consist with each other. Data from multiple sources may have multiple structures, and these structures must be identified correctly and mapped to a standard structure. Some of the data is acquired from online libraries, this part appears well arranged, there is some other data come from none academic sources such as online book stores, may be organized according to their business needs, and not comply with their logical meanings.

There is still some fragmental data distributed in online forums, bokees, and other online information sources. This part of data often published personally, and just organized by the intendancy of these people, but may have some in-depth opinions. Because this part of data often appears in html pages, and can not be acquired from some kind of services, it can only be collected from search engine service. But search engine services are never designed to provide such data, and they may return many irrelevant data as well as some useful data, some the results the search engine returned must be filtered first.

Document metadata service composition is not the same as catalog service composition. The service purchase agent must organize the service delegate agents by each document, and then judge which source should be used for each document. There is no standard schema which all service delegate agent comply with. Fusion on attributes can only be done dynamically using inference.

There are 3 steps in the fusion process of each attribute:

(1) To judge whether current attribute can be merged with some attributes of another object.

(2) If two attributes from two objects can be merged, whether their value equal or compatible to each other.

(3) If both values not compatible to each other, determine which value should be kept.

There are two occasions that two different attributes can be merged. One is that they have the same meaning: attributes with the same meaning may have different names, for example, 'title', 'topic', and 'caption' may be the same, and can be merged, another is that one attribute can be deduced from another, for example the attribute 'age' can be calculated from the attribute 'birth date' but not vice versa, so the attribute 'age' can be removed. In the first occasion, a synonym table can handles the mapping well; in the second occasion, there must be a conversion function fit for that calculation, if such a function can be found by the service purchase agent, the merge will be allowed.

While mapped, compatibility between the values of attributes to be merged must be assessed. Because values are often digits, and mathematical calculation often needed, the assessment can not be completed by inference, but can only by dedicatedly designed functions. These functions are owned privately by the service purchase agent. The values to be assessed must have the data type which is acceptable to the assessment function. If some of the values are not in proper data type, data type conversion must be taken first, fail in conversion means not compatible. If compatible, the one with more accuracy will be kept, if not, there should be a method to choose the applicable one among them. If a value of attribute has more than one source, the value with the support of most of sources has the highest reliability; the less frequently changed values have higher reliability. For example, the 'age' attribute must be changed every year, but the 'birth date' attribute needn't do that change, so 'birth date' is more reliable than 'age'.

To get document metadata from search engine, the system need calling the search service with the title of that document as keyword. The result returned from search service includes the URL of target web page and a brief abstract of it. The search engine often break the title into words before search, so the result returned contains many irrelevant pages which just have some of the words we want to search. These entries are useless and should be eliminated first. While filtered, the remaining entries will be examined one by one, the target web page will be washed out peripheral contents and html tags, only core text content will be kept. The core text will be added to the description of that document.

4.3   Document Full Version Downloading

Document download service provides the binary versions of documents to users. There are many online store services on the web, they are often more reliable and accessible to common users than the server maintained by document provider itself. Most of the online storage services need user login first. Using multiple online storage providers to balance data flow and secure availability is also a good idea. So there is also motivation on composition of document storage services.

In document online storage service composition, the return of the composited service is the binary file of document, it needn't further processing, and can return to user directly. So in this part service provider agent is not necessary. Service purchase is also simpler than the other two parts. The service purchase agent will give higher privilege to the services which can provide storage of larger number of documents, and which has the higher download speed. The privilege is dynamic, if a service already has a number of live calling, its privilege will be lowered to make it less possible to be called again. This dynamic privilege system will balance the load.

5   Conclusion

Traditional way of "all in one" document service system has its downside: waste resources on developing already exist functions on the internet; make the providers lost focus from their core business; and create obstacles to integrating them together.

This paper proposes a method a of automatically compositing existed document services based on multi-agent architecture and semantic technology, and discusses the composition of three common document service functions, and provides a solution to solve the problems traditional document services have.

Acknowledgement. The research was supported by the 12th five-year national key technology support program, super-class scientific and technical thesaurus and ontology construction faced the Foreign Scientific and technical literature (2011BAH10B01) and special fund of basic commonweal research institute project of information institute of CAAS.

References

1. http://aws.amazon.com/s3/
2. Lian, W., Liang, Y., Zeng, Q.: Integrating semantics and agent technology to automatic Web service composition. In: IEEE Symposium on Web Society, 2nd Symposium on Web Society, pp. 201–206 (2010)
3. Kumar, S., Mastorakis, N.E.: Multi-Agent Negotiation based Semantic Web Service Composition Models. In: WSEAS International Conference on Software Engineering, Parallel and Distributed Systems (SEPADS 2010). Recent Advances in Software Engineering, Parallel and Distributed Systems, pp. 214–223 (2010)
4. Hao, T.: Agent-based semantic web service composition model. In: Second Pacific-Asia Conference on Circuits, Communications and System, vol. 2, pp. 67–70 (2010)
5. Falou, M.E., Bouzid, M., Mouaddib, A.-I., Vidal, T.: Automated Web Service Composition: A Decentralised Multi-agent Approach. In: 2009 IEEE/WIC/ACM International Joint Conference on Web Intelligence and Intelligent Agent Technology, Wi-iat, vol. 1, pp. 387–394 (2009)
6. Nouredine, G., Hassina, S.: Composition of web service based multi-agent. In: International Conference on Multimedia Computing and Systems (ICMCS 2009), pp. 51–55 (2009)
7. http://baike.baidu.com/view/1258913.htm
8. Braubach, L., Pokahr, A., Lamersdorf, W.: Jadex: A BDI Agent System Combining Middleware and Reasoning. In: Software Agent-Based Applications, Platforms and Development Kits, pp. 143–168 (2005)

Utilizing Model to Optimize Crop Plant Density: A Case Study on Tomato

LiLi Yang, QiaoXue Dong, and Daoliang Li[*]

College of Information and Electrical Engineering,
China Agricultural University, Beijing, 100083, China
li.daoliang@163.com

Abstract. Based on the functional-structural plant model GreenLab, a common plant category tomato was selected as a test case in order to analyze the impact of plant density on the yield. A yield optimization model was set up based on minimum ripe fruit weight constraints, fruit weight serve as the objective function for the bound-constrained optimization problem. Particle Swarm Optimization (PSO) algorithm was applied for maximizing the crop production, which will provide a theoretical reference for agronomy measures based on plant spacing.

Keywords: Tomato, Plant density, GreenLab model, Yield optimization, PSO.

1 Introduction

Tomato's economic benefit is related to fruit yield and quality, and these two factors are considerably affected by light condition [1][2]. Manipulation of plant spacing is a possible means to change light interception for peasant. Traditionally, plant density is based on empirical knowledge from filed experiments, and this is quite time consuming and expensive. While plant growth models provide a very important tool for realizing optimal yields of crops with an efficient means [3]. Functional-structure model GreenLab can simulate plant growth based on organ size, so it provides possibility for plant density optimization [4]. Combining plant mathematical model with optimization method can provide guiding for the optimization of planting density and horticultural practice such as pruning and environmental control in special constrained environment.

2 The Description of Optimization Problem

2.1 Greenlab Model

In GreenLab model, time scale, called a growth cycle, is often the phyllochron between appearances of two successive leaves in main stem [5]. Plant total product biomass at growth cycle n is $Q(n)$.

---

[*] Corresponding author.

D. Li and Y. Chen (Eds.): CCTA 2011, Part III, IFIP AICT 370, pp. 315–319, 2012.

$$Q(n) = AB \left(1 - \ell^{-\frac{S(n)}{A}} \right) \qquad (1)$$

A is the projection surface of single plant (m^2/m^2), which is in response to plant density. B is plant growth potential multiplied by an empirical resistance, which can be computed by environment data. $S(n)$ is total   leaves surface at n^{th} growth cycle.

D(n) is all organ demands at the nth growth cycle

$$D(n) = \sum_o P_o \sum_{t=1}^{n} f_o(t) N_o(n-t+1) \qquad (2)$$

Where P_o(unitless) is the sink of organ o (o=internode (i), blade (b), petiole (p), fruit (f)), which is defined as the ability of organs to compete for biomass. $N_o(n-t+1)$ is the number of organ o in t growth cycle. $f_o(t)$ is sink variation of organ o at t^{th} growth cycle, which is described by an empirical Beta function. α_o and β_o are the coefficients of the Beta function, and α_o is set constant.

A, P_o(unitless) and β_o (unitless) are hidden parameter. These parameters were identified by fitting the periodical destructively-measured data and environment data with the corresponding model output.

2.2   Fruit Weight Calculation

At the end of nth growth cycle, biomass for one chronological aged j (growth cycle) fruit can be calculated as below:

$$q_f(n,j) = \sum_{k=1}^{j} P_f(k) \frac{Q(n-j+k)}{D(n-j+k)} \qquad (3)$$

k is fruit growth cycle, all organs including fruit compete for biomass in a common pool. The formula for calculating the total fruit weight of an aged n (growth cycle) plant as follows:

$$Y = \sum_{k=1}^{t_{x\_f}} P_f(k) \frac{Q_{n-(t_{x\_f}-k)}}{D_{n-(t_{x\_f}-k)}} \qquad (4)$$

t_{x_f} is fruit extension time, which is an observation value.

2.3   Model Parameter Estimation of Greenlab for Tomato

For establishing the relationships between GreenLab model parameters and plant density, four gradient density tomatoes named by D1,D2,D3,D4 from low density to high density were planted in solar greenhouse at the Chinese Academy of Agricultural Science in Beijing (39.55°N, 116.25°E)[6]. The generalized least square method was used for fitting [6]. Four plant density model parameters are shown in table 1:

Table 1. Estimated parameter values of model

Parameters	Values			
	D1	D2	D3	D4
P_i	0.47	0.46	0.58	0.56
P_p	0.65	0.57	0.83	0.72
P_f	23.4	16	15	8
β_i	2.41	2.24	2.76	1.67
β_p	1.91	1.86	2	1.35
β_b	1.48	1.28	1.83	1.46
β_f	1.58	1.03	1.48	1.44
A	2228	2186	1783	1592

An equation is used to describe model parameter variation trend with plant density. The supreme fitting degree function is shown as below:

$$\Omega = a + b\exp(-cx) \tag{5}$$

x is plant density, a, b, c are constants which can be got by fitting, Ω is GreenLab parameters as table1 listed.

3   Tomato Optimal Plant Density Solution

3.1   Tomato Growth Simulation at Different Plant Density

Different density plants growth and development can be simulated using GreenLab model with parameters listed in table 1.

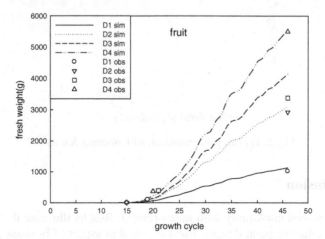

Fig. 1. Fitting results on fruit fresh weight evolution for a ground area plant of four densities symbols- measurement, lines- model

Model outputs show that increasing plant density results in a reduction of single plant fruit fresh weight (Figure is not shown) but in an increase of fruit fresh weight on a ground area (Fig.1), which is consistent with measured data.

3.2   Mathematical Solution for the Tomato Plant Density Optimization Problem

Considering market economic benefit, we define a minimum harvestable fruit weight as constraint. A single object non-linear optimization function is built as follow,

$$\begin{cases} \max_{d \in R} Y = S(d, \Omega) \\ G \ge g_{min} \end{cases}$$

Optimal object is maximum yield Y. Plant density d is an optimizing object variable and it varies in real field. All the GreenLab parameters Ω are control variables. g_{min} is a threshold value of tomato fruit referred to practice(100g). G is single fruit weight. The PSO(Particle Swarm Optimization) algorithm was implied to optimize.

The fruit weight output with respect to different plant density is shown as Fig 2. Fruit yield variation with plant density can be divided into three phases. During the first phase (1 to 8.2 plants per square meter) fruit yield grow bigger with density increasing. During the second phase (8.2 to 10.5 plants per square meter) fruit yield grow less with density increasing. In the following, fruit yield drop to zero. Because fruits get smaller and smaller with later density increasing, even it can't up to harvestable standard. Optimal plant density is 8.2 plants per square meter, and the fruit weight is close to 5kg per square meter.

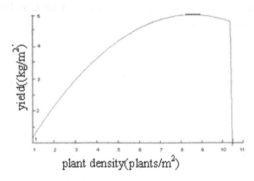

Fig. 2. Tomato yield evolution with planting density

4   Conclusion

Model output is well conformity with measurement. Results illustrate that model has the ability of reflecting plant density effect on yield in aspect of biomass production, distribution and organ number changing. We can infer model parameter, plant growth and development process in any environment from model calibration and parameter interpolation. Combining with optimization algorithm, we can get optimum plant conditions (in this paper plant density as an example). It provides a reference for decision-makers using limited experiment, and it can be used in plant growth prediction, manufacture management and so on.

Acknowledgments. This research was financially supported by Hi-Tech Research and Development (863) Program of China (#2008AA10Z218), NSFC(21020123) and the Start Fund for Scientific Research, CAU (2011JS156).

References

[1] Bertin, N.: Competition for Assimilates and Fruit Position Affect Fruit Set in Indeterminate Greenhouse Tomato. Annals of Botany 75, 55–65 (1995)
[2] Papadopoulos, A.P., Pararajasingham, S.: The influence of plant spacing on light interception and use in greenhouse tomato (Lycopersicon esculentum Mill.): A review. Scientia Hortticulturae 69, 1–9 (2003)
[3] Vos, J., Marcelis, L.F.M., de Visser, P.H.B., et al.: Functional-Structural Plant Modeling in Crop Production. In: Evers, J.B. (ed.). Springer, Netherlands (2007)
[4] Qi, R., Letort, V., Kang, M., et al.: Application of the GreenLab Model to Simulate and Optimize Wood Production and Tree Stability: A Theoretical Study. Silva Fennica 43(3), 465–487 (2009)
[5] Guo, Y., Ma, Y.T., Zhan, Z.G., Li, B.G., Dingkuhn, M., Luquet, D., De Reffye, P.: Parameter optimization and field validation of the functional–structural model GREENLAB for maize. Annals of Botany 97, 217–230 (2006)
[6] Yang, L.L., Wang, Y.M., Kang, M.Z., et al.: Relation between Tomato Fruit Set and Trophic Competition-a Modelling Approach. Plant Growth Modeling and Application Procedding. In: Third International Symposium on Plant Growth Modeling, Simulation, Visualization and Applications, PMA 2009, pp. 198–205. IEEE CPS, Beijing (2009)

Research on Automatic Inspection Methods of Image Quality of Digital Aerial Photography Results

Yong Liang[1], Yanwei Zeng[2,*], Wencong Jiang[1], and Xiaojun Wang[1]

[1] School of Information Science & Engineering, Shandong Agricultural University, Tai'an,
Shandong 271018, P.R. China
[2] Quality Supervision and Testing Center of National Surveying and Mapping Products,
Chengdu, Si Chuan Province 610081, China
zengyw@sbsm.gov.cn

Abstract. Aerial photogrammetry is one of the main methods obtaining geospatial information. After entering the 21st century, aerial photogrammetry technology has fully entered the digital age, and the quality of digital aerial photography results will directly affect the quality and accuracy of results of surveying and mapping .Therefore, it is necessary to inspect the quality of digital aerial photography results. In the process of digital aerial photography, image quality directly affects the quality of the results. It is of great importance to make its image quality inspection. Based on the analysis of image quality index of the results of digital aerial photography and domestic and international current situation of quality inspection technology of aerial photography results, the author has put forward the index system which consists of subjective evaluation index and objective evaluation index. Based on objective evaluation index which includes the maximal displacement of image points, image definition, uniform degree of image contrast and brightness and image integral color performance, the author has researched automatic inspection methods of image quality of the results of digital aerial photography, and has realized automatic quality inspection of image quality of the results of digital aerial photography.

Keywords: Digital aerial photography, Image quality index, Image quality, Quality inspection, Automatic inspection.

1   Introduction

Digital aerial photography results are the important data sources of basic surveying and mapping, which quality will directly affect the quality of results of follow-up surveying and mapping. Therefore, it is necessary steps to make the comprehensive quality inspection to guarantee the quality of data, and it's of important application value and meaning [1]. In the process of digital aerial photography, image quality directly affects the quality of the results, and it's important to check image quality. Digital aerial photography provides digital aviation image and makes it possible to take comprehensive and rigorous automatic inspection using computers.

---

* Corresponding author.

D. Li and Y. Chen (Eds.): CCTA 2011, Part III, IFIP AICT 370, pp. 320–331, 2012.
© IFIP International Federation for Information Processing 2012

2   Index of Image Quality

In this paper, based on the national standards and regulations(in table 1), the author studied and put forward quality inspection index system of image quality of the box type digital aerial photography results(in table 2).

The index of image quality includes the maximal displacement of image points, image definition, image color, image contrast, cloud and cloud shadow, splash and bad point and image noise and so on [2] [3].

Table 1. National standards and regulations

National standards and regulations	GB/T 6962－2005 《Aerial Photographic specification for 1: 500、1:1000、1:2000 Scale Topographic maps》
	GB/T 15661－1955 《Aerial Photographic specification for 1: 5000、1:10000、1:25000、1:50000、1:100000 Scale Topographic maps》
	GB/T 19294－2003 《Design specification of Aerial Photography Technology》
	MH/T 1006－1996 《Inspection specification of Aerial Photography Instruments》
	《Provisions of GPS Supplemental Aerial Photography Technology》（Trying）
	GB/T 24356－2009 《Quality Inspection and Acceptance of Surveying and Mapping Results》
	《Topographic Map Based on The Scale of 1:10000、1: 50000 IMU/DGPS Supplemental Aerial Photography Technology Provisions 》（Trying）
	《Implementation Detailed Rules of Inspection and Acceptance and Quality Evaluation of The National Basic Aerial Photography Results》（Trial Draft）
	《Supplement Technology Regulations of The National Basic Aerial Photography 》
	《Implementation Detailed Rules of Inspection and Acceptance and Quality Evaluation of The National Basic Aerial Photography Results》（Submissions）
	《The Format and Note of Material of The National Basic Aerial Photography Results》
	《Data Arrangement and Explains of Digital Aerial Photography Results》（Trying）

Table 2. Image quality index system of digital aerial photography results [4] [5]

Index of the second class	Description of function
the maximal displacement of image points	Check the deformation of features in images to judge whether to be beyond the range or not
image definition	Check image definition to judge whether to be read or not
image color	Check the partial color of images
image contrast	Check image contrast to judge whether to be moderate or not
cloud and cloud shadow	Check the coverage of cloud and cloud shadow and the percentage of the area of cloud and cloud shadow on images
image noise	Check the range of image noise
splash and bad point	Check whether there are splashes in images

3   Inspection Methods of Image Quality

It's a complicated process to make image quality assessment of digital images. The reasons of complication are that the images are two dimensional representations of three dimensional real worlds and not comprehensively reflect the properties of features. It's a perception process to make image quality evaluation and it's a comprehensive judgment using the brain and other organs. In addition, the evaluation results also depend on people's knowledge ability and image quality requirements of the evaluation. The complexity shows that the evaluation doesn't only depend on the quantitative index and it will appear a better result to use the method of the combination between subjective evaluation and objective evaluation.

3.1   Subjective Evaluation Index

It's difficult to distinguish characteristics texture, imaging injury and image quality degradation in the process and artificial qualitative evaluation results are given. The human eyes judge images whether there are cloud and cloud shadow, bad points and noise, according to the subjective feelings to give the evaluation.

3.1.1   Cloud and Cloud Shadow
View the data of images, select problem areas through the user circle, and calculate the area size of cloud and cloud shadow.

3.1.2   Splash and Bad Point
View the data of images and users judge splashes and bad points of images.

3.1.3   Image Noise
View the data of images and users judge noise of images.

3.2   Objective Evaluation Index

3.2.1   The Maximal Displacement of Image Points
Calculate by reading the data of images.

Space frequency can be used to make quantitative evaluation of the maximal displacement of image points. If the calculation value is smaller, the displacement is bigger, and if the calculation value is bigger, the displacement is smaller [6].

Space frequency: It reflects the overall activity degree of image space. And it includes space line frequency RF and space column frequency CF which can be expressed as:

$$RF = \sqrt{\frac{1}{m \times n} \sum_{i=1}^{m} \sum_{j=2}^{n} (f_{i,j} - f_{i,j-1})^2} \tag{1}$$

$$CF = \sqrt{\frac{1}{m \times n} \sum_{i=2}^{m} \sum_{j=1}^{n} (f_{i,j} - f_{i-1,j})^2}$$

(2)

Get the whole space frequency value:

$$SF = \sqrt{RF^2 + CF^2}$$

(3)

Among them, **m** and **n** stand for the width and height of images, and $f(i, j)$ is the gray value of image pixels (i, j).

Take a few pictures below as an example according to the above algorithms and calculate their maximal displacement of image points. From the results we can see that the **SF** value of three pictures above from left to right becomes smaller and smaller, and the results of three pictures below are the same. This conclusion is consistent with subjective evaluation.

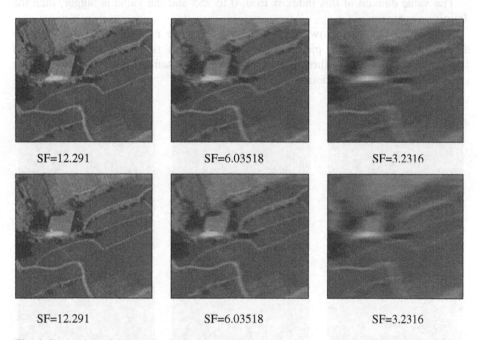

SF=12.291   SF=6.03518   SF=3.2316

SF=12.291   SF=6.03518   SF=3.2316

Fig. 1. Inspection of the maximal displacement of image points according to Space frequency

3.2.2   Image Definition

It depicts the clarity degree of image features, and it's the contrast degree of features and its background region.

It's more index of quantitative evaluation about definition. Definition is used to reflect diffusion degree of some characteristics of the edge of images, and if the diffusion degree is bigger, the definition is smaller, and if the diffusion degree is smaller, the definition is bigger. At present, the most mature evaluation method of definition is MTF which full name is modulation transfer function, but the determination of MTF is relatively complex [7]. In order to make it simple, we can take global point sharpness algorithm as the approximate evaluation. It can accurately and fast reflect tendency of definition of digital images. It's calculated by:

$$P = \frac{\sum_{i=1}^{m \times n} \sum_{a=1}^{8} |df / dx|}{m \times n} \tag{4}$$

Among them, m and n is the size of images, df is the grayscale amplitude and dx is the distance increment between the pixels. This formula can be described: Get the difference of each point and its eight neighborhood points and calculate the eight differences according to the average of the weighted distance and finally obtain the average results of the whole image and regard it as the relative evaluation index of image definition.

The value domain of this index is from 0 to 255 and the value is bigger, then the definition is bigger.

Take a few pictures below as an example. From the results we can see that the definition degree of three pictures above from left to right becomes smaller and smaller, and the results of three pictures below are the same. The results are also the same to the subjective evaluation.

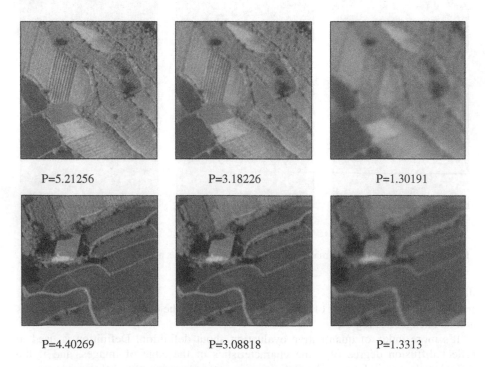

P=5.21256   P=3.18226   P=1.30191

P=4.40269   P=3.08818   P=1.3313

Fig. 2. Detection of image definition

3.2.3   Uniform Degree of Image Contrast and Brightness

The common data detection about remote sensing images and aviation images is image brightness uniformity and according to the absolute evaluation, we put forward a kind of quantitative index. Firstly according to image brightness distribution fitting quadric surface we judge whether it is level, that is, whether its variances is close to zero, and the variance is more closer to zero, then the brightness distribution is uniform. On the contrary it's not uniform [8]. And its calculation process is as follows:

Input sampling of image brightness component and obtain the size $（M \times N）$ of images.

(1) Generate average template according to window size ($w_w \times h_w$, such as 11×11) and get its three-dimensional coordinate (x, y, l). Among them, x, y is coordinates of each point $x \in \left[0, \lceil N / w_w \rceil\right]$, $y \in \left[0, \lceil M / w_h \rceil\right]$ and $\lceil \bullet \rceil$ stands for getting integer up and l is the brightness of each point.

(2) According to the explicit two-dimensional surface equation:

$$z = A + Bx + Cy + Dxy + Ex^2 + Fy^2 \tag{5}$$

Generate vertex equations based on least square principle:

$$
\begin{bmatrix}
m & \sum_{i=1}^{m} x & \sum_{i=1}^{m} y & \sum_{i=1}^{m} xy & \sum_{i=1}^{m} x^2 & \sum_{i=1}^{m} y^2 \\
\sum_{i=1}^{m} x & \sum_{i=1}^{m} x^2 & \sum_{i=1}^{m} xy & \sum_{i=1}^{m} x^2 y & \sum_{i=1}^{m} x^3 & \sum_{i=1}^{m} xy^2 \\
\sum_{i=1}^{m} y & \sum_{i=1}^{m} xy & \sum_{i=1}^{m} y^2 & \sum_{i=1}^{m} xy^2 & \sum_{i=1}^{m} x^2 y & \sum_{i=1}^{m} y^3 \\
\sum_{i=1}^{m} xy & \sum_{i=1}^{m} x^2 y & \sum_{i=1}^{m} xy^2 & \sum_{i=1}^{m} x^2 y^2 & \sum_{i=1}^{m} x^3 y & \sum_{i=1}^{m} xy^3 \\
\sum_{i=1}^{m} x^2 & \sum_{i=1}^{m} x^3 & \sum_{i=1}^{m} x^2 y & \sum_{i=1}^{m} x^3 y & \sum_{i=1}^{m} x^4 & \sum_{i=1}^{m} x^2 y^2 \\
\sum_{i=1}^{m} y^2 & \sum_{i=1}^{m} xy^2 & \sum_{i=1}^{m} y^3 & \sum_{i=1}^{m} xy^3 & \sum_{i=1}^{m} x^2 y^2 & \sum_{i=1}^{m} y^4
\end{bmatrix}
\begin{bmatrix} A \\ B \\ C \\ D \\ E \\ F \end{bmatrix}
=
\begin{bmatrix}
\sum_{i=1}^{m} l \\
\sum_{i=1}^{m} xl \\
\sum_{i=1}^{m} yl \\
\sum_{i=1}^{m} xyl \\
\sum_{i=1}^{m} x^2 l \\
\sum_{i=1}^{m} y^2 l
\end{bmatrix}
\tag{6}
$$

Among them m is the number of points in template, $m = \lceil N / w_w \rceil \times \lceil M / h_w \rceil$

(3) Use Gaussian elimination method of main elements selected to solve the above equation and get the coefficient of the explicit two-dimensional surface equation.

(4) Calculate square error according to the two-dimensional surface equation and it's shown as follows

$$\sigma_t^2 = \frac{1}{M' \cdot N'} \sum_{i=0}^{M'-1} \sum_{j=0}^{N'-1} \left[\hat{l} - \mu \right]^2 \tag{7}$$

Among them, M', N' is the size of template, $M' = \lceil M / w_w \rceil, N' = \lceil N / h_w \rceil$,

$\hat{l}$ is fitting brightness of each point in template according to the two-dimensional surface and μ is the average width of template.

If square error is smaller, the brightness distribution is uniform; On the contrary it's not uniform. From the calculation process we can found that the domain still is from 0 to 255. When square error is close to 0, the template is close to ideal level plane and it indicates that brightness distribution is uniform.

The pictures below give several square error values after processing. From the results we can see that the square error value of three pictures above from left to right becomes bigger and bigger, and the results of three pictures below are the same. This conclusion is consistent with subjective evaluation.

$\sigma_t^2 = 7.84994$ $\sigma_t^2 = 8.14565$ $\sigma_t^2 = 29.6955$

$\sigma_t^2 = 12.3018$ $\sigma_t^2 = 13.2876$ $\sigma_t^2 = 32.7956$

Fig. 3. Detection of uniform degree of image brightness

3.2.4   Image Integral Color Performance

It's used to depict integral tonal of images and evaluate the difference of adjacent images in image mosaic.

The method based on gray balance is to make statistics of the average brightness of three channels and judge whether the result is neutral grey according to assumption scene meeting the gray world. If it is neutral grey, there will be no partial color. Otherwise there will be partial color. The algorithm is shown below:

(1) Make statistics of the average brightness of three channels and they are $R_{mean}, G_{mean}, B_{mean}$.

(2) Suppose for the standard RGB color space coordinates and get the relatively uniform chromaticity coordinates through the color space transformation. The method of color space transformation is shown as follows:

The conversion of RGB and Lab chromaticity coordinates:

There are two kinds of methods to establish color space: One is the color reference system based on the psychological physical experiment (such as munsell table color system); the second is the color analytic expression system based on the psychological physics experiment (such as CIELAB, CIELUV color system). Color space used commonly can be divided into the base color space, CIE color space orthogonal color space and cognitive color space.

Base color space is the most basic and common RGB color space in image processing. Because the existing image acquisition and display equipment is mostly based on RGB value and intermediate storage is also mostly based on RGB value. Other color space used in image processing is the transformation from RGB color space and the processing results that need to display or storage out also need to convert back to RGB color space [9].

CIE chromaticity space based on colorimetric theories is launched by CIE (international lighting committee) and has been generally accepted as international measurement standards [10]. The common characteristics of all CIE chromaticity space have nothing to do with equipment.

The main principle of orthogonal color space is using color antagonist phenomenon of human visual perception to find out the orthogonal color component. According to different TV formats, color space which color component is approximating orthogonal has YUV color space (PAL TV), YIQ (NTSC TV) and so on. At present color space of the digital coding of standard television images which are recommended is YCbCr (ITU/ITU-R, 1994). In addition, there is the I1I2I3 color space put forward by Ohta, and three color components are completely irrelevant. Pratt made K-L transform for RGB and the results show that, Ohta component (I1 I2, I3) is a good approximation of K-L transforms for RGB.

In order to comply with people's subjective cognitive characteristics for the color, many researchers have studied various algorithms for get color attribute from RGB value, and they are collectively called cognitive color space which includes HIS, VHS, LHS HSB and GLHS and so on, and these color space in computer vision and digital image processing has a wide range of applications, so they also known as color models. Their common characteristics are based on the subjective psychological evaluation of human visual system for the color and mostly based on hue, saturation and brightness.

In comparison to other color space, RGB color space has the following characteristics:

It's not intuitive and it is difficult to directly recognize color from RGB value through the human visual system.

RGB color space is one of the least uniform color spaces. The perception difference of the two colors is nonlinear, and it can't be expressed as Euclidean distance between two color points.

There is a high correlation between RGB values (B-R: 0.78, R-G: 0.98, G-B: 0.94) (Palus, 1998). These high correlations make the challenge on the various treatments of the color information.

It is related to device. RGB value is actually the relative value of the device dynamic range quantity, and the same RGB values have different color performance on different display and output devices.

Just like cognition color space of HSV, HSL, and HSB, it is a subset of color space that the human can perceived.

In order to improve color space and imaging devices of the RGB and display devices relevance, the International Color Consortium introduced the sRGB color space to make image exchange in 1996, especially the standard format of network image exchange. sRGB color space provides handling the color methods from the operating system and device drivers, and uses a simple and robust device independent color to definite add the current ICC color management strategy. The definition of sRGB color space is based on the average effect of a typical CRT monitor under the conditions of reference and observation, but it is suitable for the flat panel display devices, television, scanners, digital cameras and printing systems. Due to these advantages, it has been adopted as an international standard by ICC. Because of the defined similarity of the display device of reference and real CRT monitors, when you use the sRGB color space, you usually do not need extra color space conversion to display images. However, you need to convert the data to sRGB, and then output to different dynamic range, color gamut and output device of the observe conditions. With regards to sRGB standard color space and ICC profile format, more details can be referred to the relevant references (Gasparin & Schettini, 2004).

The RGB color space is related to the device, but independent CIE color space has no relation with the device, therefore in the conversion process from RGB to CIE LAB, you need to describe the device properties.In the absence of profile and experimental conditions, you can usually assume image data based on the sRGB standard color space, and the light source referred is CIE D65, according to the following formula to achieve color coordinate transformation from the RGB to Lab.

$$R'_{sRGB} = R_{8bit} / 255.0 ; G'_{sRGB} = G_{8bit} / 255.0 ; B'_{sRGB} = B_{8bit} / 255.0 \quad (8)$$

$$I_{sRGB} = \begin{cases} I'_{sRGB} / 12.92, if\,(I'_{sRGB} \le 0.04045) \\ \left[(I'_{sRGB} + 0.055)/1.055 \right]^{2.4}, else \end{cases} \quad (9)$$

Among them,

$$I'_{sRGB} = \left\{ R'_{sRGB}, G'_{sRGB}, B'_{sRGB} \right\}, I_{sRGB} = \left\{ R_{sRGB}, G_{sRGB}, B_{sRGB} \right\} \qquad (10)$$

$$\begin{bmatrix} X \\ Y \\ Z \end{bmatrix} = \begin{bmatrix} 0.4124 & 0.3576 & 0.1805 \\ 0.2126 & 0.7152 & 0.0722 \\ 0.0193 & 0.1192 & 0.9505 \end{bmatrix} \begin{bmatrix} R_{sRGB} \\ G_{sRGB} \\ B_{sRGB} \end{bmatrix} \qquad (11)$$

$$S' = S / S_0, S' = \left\{ X', Y', Z' \right\}, S = \left\{ X, Y, Z \right\}, S_0 = \left\{ X_0, Y_0, Z_0 \right\} \qquad (12)$$

Among them, X_0, Y_0, Z_0 is the stimulation value of D65 light source:

$$X_0 = 0.9505, Y_0 = 1.00, Z_0 = 1.0891 \qquad (13)$$

$$S'' = \begin{cases} (S')^{1/3}, if\,(S' > 0.008856) \\ 7.787 \times S' + 16.0 / 116.0, else \end{cases}, S'' = \left\{ X'', Y'', Z'' \right\} \qquad (14)$$

$$\begin{cases} L^* = 903.3Y', a^* = 3893.5(X' - Y'), b^* = 1557.4(Y' - Z'), \\ if\,(X' \le 0.008856 \,\&\, Y' \le 0.008856 \,\&\, Z' \le 0.008856) \\ L^* = 116Y'' - 16, a^* = 500(X'' - Y''), b^* = 200(Y'' - Z''), \\ else \end{cases} \qquad (15)$$

(3) Calculate the distance of chromaticity of neutral grey

$$dis_{gray} = \sqrt{a^2 + b^2} \qquad (16)$$

(4) The value is bigger then the integral partial color is more serious.

Take three pictures below as an example. From the results we can see that the overall partial color of the left image is weak, that of the middle image turns to be blue and red and that of the right image becomes yellow and red. And the situation of partial color of the right image is the most serious and the left is the most light. This conclusion is consistent with subjective evaluation.

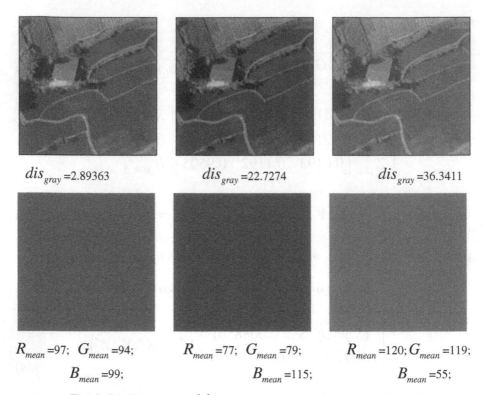

dis_{gray} =2.89363 dis_{gray} =22.7274 dis_{gray} =36.3411

R_{mean}=97; G_{mean} =94; R_{mean} =77; G_{mean} =79; R_{mean} =120; G_{mean} =119;

B_{mean} =99; B_{mean} =115; B_{mean} =55;

Fig. 4. Calculation of partial color based on the method of gray balance

4   Conclusions

In this paper, based on research and analysis of domestic and international situations of quality inspection technology of aerial photography results, the author studies and proposes inspection index and methods of image quality of box type digital aerial photography. Subjective evaluation index system which includes cloud and cloud shadow, splashes and bad points of images and image noise is difficult to recognize by computers and it needs to give the evaluation according to the subjective feelings. Based on objective evaluation index system which consists of the maximal displacement of image points, image definition, uniform degree of image contrast and brightness and image integral color performance, the author has put forward the quality inspection method of image appearance based on characteristics of the human visual system and image structure distortion, and has realized automatic quality inspection of image appearance quality of the results of digital aerial photography.

References

[1] Yu, C., Zeng, Y.: Design on Automatic Quality Inspection System of Digital Aerial Photography Results. Information and Engineering of Surveying and Mappin 36(1), 8–10 (2011)

[2] GB/T 6962−2005:Aerial Photographic Specification for 1: 500、1:1000、1:2000 Scale Topographic maps
[3] GB/T 15661−1955:Aerial Photographic Specification for 1: 5000、1:10000、1:25000、1:50000、1:100000 Scale Topographic Maps
[4] Implementation Detailed Rules of Inspection and Acceptance and Quality Evaluation of the National Basic Aerial Photography Results. Bureau of National Surveying and Mapping (2001)
[5] Data Arrangement and Explains of Digital Aerial Photography Results. Bureau of National Surveying and Mapping (2007)
[6] Wu, S.: Design and Implementation on Digital Acceptance System of Aerial Photography Flight Quality. Information Engineering University of Zhengzhou (2005)
[7] Wang, H.: MTF Measurement Research and Its Application of Satellite in Orbit. Nanjing University of Science and Technology (2004)
[8] Li, Q., Guo, B., Dong, L.: The Semi-automatic Extraction Algorithm Research of the road centerline on Aerial images. Information and Engineering of Surveying and Mapping 34(1), 23–25 (2009)
[9] Yuan, G., Huang, J.: Quality Control and Inspection of Digital Aerial images. Surveying and Mapping society of Jiangsu Province (2003)
[10] Yuan, J.: Information Management System of Aerial Photography. Information Engineering University of Zhengzhou (2002)

Simulated Analysis of a Wheeled Tractor on Soft Soil Based on RecurDyn[*]

Wenqian Huang[1,2,**], Feijun Xu[1,2], Jishuai Ge[1,2], and Chi Zhang[1,2]

[1] Beijing Research Center of Intelligent Equipment for Agriculture,
Beijing Academy of Agriculture and Forestry Sciences, Beijing, 100097, China
[2] National Research Center of Intelligent Equipment for Agriculture, Beijing, 100097, China
huangwq@nercita.org.cn

Abstract. A simulation model of a wheeled tractor was built using the multi-body dynamics software RecurDyn. The model consisted of four wheels, front and rear axles, and a body frame. An interaction model between tires and soft soil was established using the Soil-tire module of RecurDyn. The simulations of displacement and force of the tires were conducted on 20° up-slope, 44° ultimate up-slope, 20° down-slope and 34° ultimate down-slope roads respectively. The performance of a wheeled tractor over a cylindrical obstacle was analyzed under two different speeds. Results showed that forces of the front wheel were different on different slope roads. The maximum impact force of the front wheel increased by 68% as the up-slope increasing from 20° to 44°. The maximum impact force of the front wheel decreased by 8% when the down-slope changing from 20° to 34°. The maximum force of the front wheel decreased by 16% when the wheeled tractor over a cylindrical obstacle with the speeds decreasing from 1.356m/s to 0.678m/s.

Keywords: wheeled tractor, soft soil, RecurDyn, simulation.

1   Introduction

A modern wheeled tractor has the advantages such as reliability, mobility and applicability, especially its wheels has no destructive effect on the road surface and soil, which make it the main agricultural machinery widely applied in agriculture [1]. As the complexity of a tractor and its operation environment, the design of a tractor using the traditional method is a long period and high cost process. With the development of the theory of vehicle and terrain systems and multi-body dynamics, it is feasible for us to design a tractor or analyze its performance using the techniques of modeling and simulation.

The vibration of wheeled tractors traveled on the rough ground was studied while the mechanics mode and equation of vibration was set up [2]. Influences of the change of the amplitude and space frequency of road surface roughness on adhesion

---

[*] Beijing Municipal Science and technology Commission (Project No. D101105046310003).
[**] Corresponding author.

D. Li and Y. Chen (Eds.): CCTA 2011, Part III, IFIP AICT 370, pp. 332–342, 2012.

ability were simulated and analyzed by means of the nonlinear and time-varying tire mode [3]. The results showed that the adhesion ability of road to the tire reduced and the braking distance increased as the road surface roughness increased. The models of formative process of the effective spectrum of the soft terrain were developed and calculated [4]. A simplified, closed-form version of the basic mechanics of a driven rigid wheel on low-cohesion deformable terrain is studied [5].

In recent years, the development trend of a wheeled tractor is to design a compact structure, light, easy to operate and adaptable to different implements tractor. It is important to study the stability when a wheeled tractor was running on a slope land and over an obstacle. In this article, the interaction model of a tire and the soft land was developed using the Soil-tire module of the multi-body dynamics software-RecurDyn. The trafficability and terrainability of a wheeled tractor on a slope land and over an obstacle were studied.

2   Materials and Methods

2.1   Mechanical Relationship between Vehicles and Terrain

In order to measure the deformation of soil under different loads, penetration tests are necessary. In these tests, the interaction between of the tire and soil is simulated using a plate penetrating into the soil, and the pressure-sinkage relationship can be calculated. For the homogeneous soil, a pressure-sinkage relationship equation was proposed by M.G. Bekker as follow [6-7]:

$$p = \left(k_{\phi}/b + k_c\right)Z^n \tag{1}$$

Where:

b = plate width, m

p = vertical average contact pressure, kPa

k_{ϕ} = soil stiffness constant for sinkage, kPa/m^n

k_c = soil stiffness constant for sinkage, kPa/m^{n-1}

Z = depth of sinkage, m

n = soil constant related to the soil characteristics, non-dimensional

Equation (1) is suitable for the continuous loading process. For the unloading and loading cycle process, the calculation equation is showed as follow:

$$p = p_u - \left(k_0 + A_u Z_u\right)\left(Z_u - Z\right) \tag{2}$$

Where:

p_u = vertical average contact pressure at the start of unloading, kPa

Z_u = depth of sinkage at the start of unloading, m

k_0 and A_u = the characteristic parameters of the soil

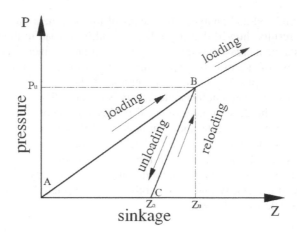

Fig. 1. The pressure-sinkage curve of the soil

The pressure-sinkage curve of the soil under the loading, unloading and reloading cycle process is shown in Fig.1. The line segment AB shows the continuous loading process. When reaching the maximum sinkage depth of Z_u, the unload process begins. The line segment BC shows the unloading process. When the pressure of soil reaches zero, a residual sinkage depth of Z_a still exists as the elastic deformation of soil. The line segment BC also shows the reloading process. When reaching the sinkage depth of Z_u, the new sinkage depth would be showed through the elongation line along the line segment AB.

2.2   Tire Mechanical Model

All ground forces are acting on the tractor through the tire when the tractor is moving. Mechanical properties of the tractor tire have a very significant impact on manipulation and stability of a tractor [8-12]. There are several tire models which are used in a dynamics simulation [13-14]. The Soil-tire toolkit enables the vehicle motion to be simulated on the flat and uneven soft ground. The soft ground is more complex than the solid ground, so the definition of the contact area is crucial for the effect of the simulation. The contact area is obtained from the equilibrium of forces while taking into account the tire deflection and the sinkage, considering the resistance of soil deformation and the wheel load. Therefore, the Soil-tire model was adopted in this study.

The wheel load of Rigid wheel with soil dynamics model in the Soil-tier model was adopted. The pressure-sinkage relationship which is the basis of the theory of BEKKER is measured quasi-statically with low velocities. However, when driving off-load, the soil stress is not quasi-static, but dynamic. In order to take account of these dynamic effects in the calculation, dynamics parameters characterizing the soil strength have to be used as the following equation. The dynamic pressure sinkage relationship formula is

$$p = \left(k_{stat} + k_{dyn} \cdot \dot{z}^m\right) \cdot z^n \tag{3}$$

Where: k_{stat} is the pressure-sinkage parameter. k_{dyn} is the pressure-sinkage parameter.

In the formula for the rigid wheel approach of BEKKER.

$$F_z = \frac{b * D}{2} \cdot \int_{\theta_{in}}^{\theta_{out}} \sin(\theta) \cdot p(\theta) d\theta \tag{4}$$

Where b is the tier width, m. F_z is the wheel load, N. D is the tier diameter, m. θ is the contact angle between tire and soil.

$p(\theta)$ is replaced by the dynamic equation, so that the connection between the wheel load F_z and sinkage z_0 is calculated as follows.

$$F_z = b \cdot \frac{D}{2} \int_{\theta_{in}}^{\theta_{out}} (k_{stat} + k_{dyn} \cdot \dot{z}^m) \cdot \left[\frac{D}{2} \cdot (\sin(\theta) - \sin(\theta_{in}))\right]^n \cdot \sin(\theta) d\theta \tag{5}$$

with

$$\theta_{in} = \arcsin\left(\frac{\frac{D}{2} - z_0}{\frac{D}{2}}\right) \; ; \; \theta_{out} = \frac{\pi}{2}.$$

2.3   Establishment of the Dynamic Model of a Wheeled Tractor

As the four tires of a wheeled tractor are running on the same soil condition, the hypothesis that the four tires have the same road spectrum was proposed in this study. A simplified model of a wheeled tractor was set up using the multi-body dynamics analysis software RecurDyn. The simplified model includes four tires, a front axle, a rear axles and a vehicle frame. A reasonable mass was imposed on the front and rear axles. The four tires were created using the Soil-tier model of RecurDyn.

The parameters of a wheeled tractor model were listed in Table 1. The fixed constraints were added between the vehicle frame and the front and rear axles. The revolution constraints were added between the tires and the front and rear axles. The model was driven using the motion imposed on the wheels. A step function was adopted in the creation of the motion shown as following.

$$\begin{cases} when \; x \le x_0 \, , \, step = h_0 \\ when \; x_0 \le x \le x_1 \, , \\ step = h_0 + (h_1 - h_0) \cdot \left(\frac{x - x_0}{x_1 - x_0}\right)^2 \cdot \left(3 - 2\left(\frac{x - x_0}{x_1 - x_0}\right)\right) \\ when \; x \ge x_1 \, , \, step = h_1 \end{cases} \tag{10}$$

The motion function imposed on the four tires was: $5 \times step(time, 0, 0, 0.1, 1)$. The formula means that the revolution speed of the tires will increase from 0 to 5 rad/s in 0.1 second. The contact parameters between the tires and the soil can be set in RecurDyn, which was shown as Fig.2.

Table 1. Simulated parameters of the tire model

Parameter name	Parameter values	Parameter name	Parameter values
Wheelbase(mm)	1400	Front Wheel track(mm)	900
Rear Wheel track(mm)	1000	Total Mass(kg)	2000

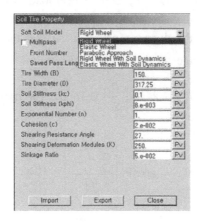

Fig. 2. Parameters of a tire model

2.4   Kinematic and Dynamic Simulations of the Wheeled Tractor

The wheeled tractor is a complex nonlinear multi-body system. The interaction process between the tire and the soil surface is a typical contact process [15-16]. RecurDyn is suitable to solve the multi-body dynamic problems with large-scale and complex contacts. The simulations of a wheeled tractor under three typical operation conditions were conducted respectively. The simulations of displacement and force of the tires were conducted on 20° up-slope, 44° ultimate up-slope, 20° down-slope and 34° ultimate down-slope roads respectively. The performance of a wheeled tractor over a cylindrical obstacle was analyzed under two different speeds. The road conditions of the simulation are the same as these in our another article [17].

3   Results and Discussion

3.1   The Simulation of a Wheeled Tractor on an Up-Slope Road

When the wheeled tractor is running on an up-slope rode, the front wheel contacts the road first. So the front wheel was chosen as the research object. As shown in Fig.3, 20°and 44°up-slope roads were created and a 500 sample times and 4 seconds simulation was conducted using RecurDyn.

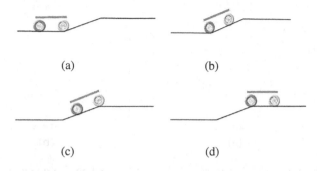

(a)   (b)

(c)   (d)

Fig. 3. The simulation process of a wheeled tractor on an up-slope road

As shown in Fig.4, the risk of a backwards rollover increased as the degree of the slope increased when the tractor was on an up-slope road, especially when the tractor was used to tow an implement or other heavy load. 44°up-slope road is an ultimate situation that a backwards rollover occurs. A counterweight for the wheeled tractor can afford optimum weight distribution and improve the stability of operation on a steep slope to decrease the risk of a backward rollover.

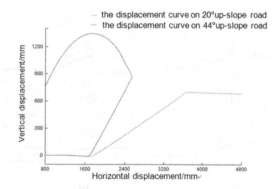

Fig. 4. The displacement curves of the front tire of a wheeled tractor on 20°and 44°up-slope roads

As shown in Fig.5(a), two peaks occurred in each normal force curve when the simulation time was 0.48 second and 1.4 second respectively, which were the transient normal impact forces generated in the contact-impact process between the front and rear tires and the steep slope road. The fluctuation reflected that there were a large amount of impacts when the complex non-linear tires were running over the road. As shown in Fig.5(b), when the simulation time was 1.7 second, the force on the front and rear tires was 0 when a backwards rollover happened. As shown in Fig.5(b), the force of the front tire when the wheeled tractor on a 44°ultimate up-slope road increased by 68% compared with that on a 20°up-slope road.

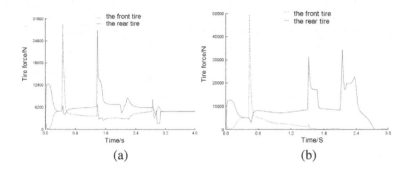

Fig. 5. The force curves of the front and rear tires on (a) 20°and (b)44°up-slope roads

3.2   The Simulation of a Wheeled Tractor on a Down-Slope Road

In the simulation of a wheeled tractor running on a down-slope road, the rear tire was chosen as the research objective. As shown in Fig.6, 20°and 34°down-slope roads were created and a 500 sample times and 4 seconds simulation was conducted using RecurDyn.

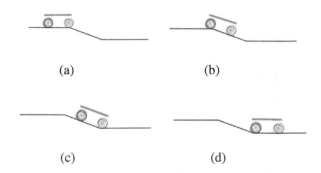

Fig. 6. The simulation process of a wheeled tractor on a down-slope road

As shown in Fig.7, the risk of a rollover still existed when the tractor was running on a down-slope road. 34°down-slope road is an ultimate situation that a rollover occurs. Because of the high speed and a large inertia when the tractor was running on a down-slope road, the risk of a rollover increased as the emergency brake or the collision with an obstacle occurred.

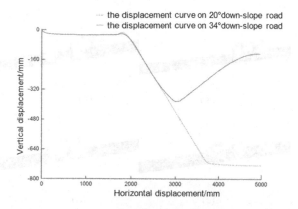

Fig. 7. The displacement curves of the rear tire of a wheeled tractor on 20° and 34° down-slope roads

The simulation result of a wheeled tractor on a 20°down-slope road was shown as Fig.8(a). When the simulation time was 0.46 second, the front tire began to contact with the road, and the force on the tire increased as the contact area between the tire and the road increased when the tractor was moving forward. When the simulation time was 1.22 second, the rear tire began to contact with the road, and the force between the rear tire and the road decreased dramatically as the front tire was moving forward steadily. The simulation result of a wheeled tractor on a 34°down-slope road was shown as Fig.8(b). As the force curves of the front tires shown in Fig.8(b), the maximum transient force of the front tire on the 34°down-slope road decreased by 8% compared with that on the 20°down-slope road. When the simulation time was 1.22 second, the force on the rear tires was 0 when a rollover happened.

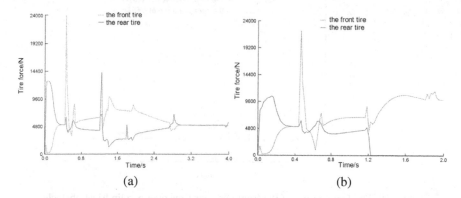

Fig. 8. The force curves of the front and rear tires on (a) 20°and (b) 34°down-slope roads

3.3   The Simulation of a Wheeled Tractor over an Obstacle

As shown in Fig.9, a cylindrical obstacle was created and a 500 sample times and 4 seconds simulation was conducted using RecurDyn. The diameter of the obstacle was 200mm and a half of it was embedded into the soil. The speeds that the wheeled tractor running over the obstacle were 1.356m/s and 0.678m/s in the simulation.

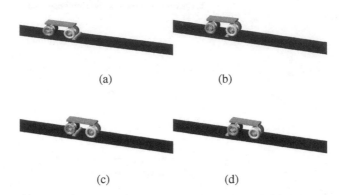

Fig. 9. The simulation process of a wheeled tractor over a cylindrical obstacle

The simulation result of the wheeled tractor over a cylindrical obstacle was shown as Fig.10. Two impact forces on the front and rear occurred respectively when the tractor was running over the cylindrical obstacle, and the force on the front tire was obviously larger than the one on the rear tire. The maximum force of the front tire when the wheeled tractor running over the obstacle at a speed of 0.678m/s decreases by 16% compared with that at 1.356m/s. It is necessary to increase the distance between the right tire and the left tire and decrease the speed for a stable operation on an uneven road and avoidance of a rollover in a sudden collision with an obstacle.

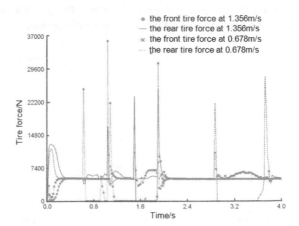

Fig. 10. The force curves of the front and rear tires over a cylindrical obstacle

4   Conclusion

The dynamic model of a wheeled tractor was established using Soil-tire module of RecurDyn. The simulations of displacement and force of the tires were conducted on

20°up-slope, 44°ultimate up-slope, 20°down-slope and 34°ultimate down-slope roads respectively. The tire force that the wheeled tractor runs over a cylindrical obstacle was analyzed at two different speeds. The conclusions are as following:

The forces of the front wheel were different on different slope roads. The maximum impact force of the front wheel increased by 68% as the up-slope increasing from 20°to 44°. The maximum impact force of the front wheel decreased by 8% when the down-slope changing from 20°to 34°.

The maximum force of the front wheel decreased by 16% when the wheeled tractor over a cylindrical obstacle with the speeds decreasing from 1.356m/s to 0.678m/s.

Acknowledgments. Our project is supported by Beijing Municipal Science and technology Commission (Project No. D101105046310003).

References

1. Wang, X.: Adaptability Comparison between Wheeled and Crawler Tractor. Tractor & Farm Transporter (2), 1–2 (2006)
2. Wang, X., Yu, Q., Hu, W., Xu, Y.: The Establishment of Traveling Vibration Mechanics Model and Equation of Vibration of Wheeled Tractors. Journal of Heilongjiang August First Land Reclamation University (3), 45–48 (1998)
3. Zuo, S., Cheng, Y.: Simulation Analysis of the Influence of Road Surface Roughness on Tyre Dynamic Performance in Vehicle Braking. Transactions of the Chinese Society of Agricultural Engineering 16(4), 42–45 (2000)
4. Zheng, L., Liu, M., Zhang, Y., Wang, D.: Formative Process Analysis of the Effective Spectrum of the Soft Terrain Surface. Transactions of the Chinese Society of Agricultural Engineering 10(2), 29–34 (1994)
5. Shibly, H., Iagnemma, K., Dubowsky, S.: An Equivalent Soil Mechanics Formulation for Rigid Wheels in Deformable Terrain. with Application to Planetary Exploration Rovers. Journal of Terramechanics 42, 1–13 (2005)
6. Bekker, M.G.: Theory of land locomotion-the mechanics of vehicle mobility. University of Michigan Press (1956)
7. Wong, J.Y.: Theory of Ground Vehicles. John Wiley & Sons, New York (1993)
8. Chen, Z., Yu, G.: Experimental Study on the Trafficability of Small-sized Desert Shrub Harvester and Its Effects on Sandy Land. Journal of Anhui Agricultural Science 36(31), 13521–13522, 13543 (2008)
9. Chen, W., Zhao, C., Liu, J.: Simulation Analysis on the Tractive Characteristics of Wheels in the Sands. Journal of Chongqing University (Natural Science Edition) 35(3), 15–18, 29 (2006)
10. Chen, W.: Analysis on Tractive Characteristics of a Wheel on Sands. Tractor & Farm Transporter 29(6), 22–23, 25 (2008)
11. Peng, Y.: Wheeled Tractor Pulling Characterize and Applied Research. Journal of Agricultural Mechanization Research (1), 173–175 (2007)
12. Bi, X., Wang, Y.: Factors Effect and Improving Measures on Traction Efficiency of Wheeled Tractor. Tractor & Farm Transporter 34(6), 11–12 (2007)
13. Hu, J., Li, T., Qin, D.: Modeling and Simulation of Electric Power Steering System Based on Vehicle Whole Dynamics. Journal of System Simulation 20(6), 1577–1581 (2008)
14. Leng, S., Gao, L., Wang, S., Zhu, Y.: Dynamics Model Analysis on Five-axle Vehicle with All-wheel Steering. Transactions of the Chinese Society of Agricultural Machinery 39(12), 39–44 (2008)

15. Schmid, I.C., Harnisch, C., Lach, B.: Terrain-Vehicle Interactions in Virtual Reality. In: Seoul 2000 FISITA World Automotive Congress, Seoul (2000)
16. Choi, H.D., Kang, H., Hyun, K.H., Kim, S., Kwak, Y.K.: Force Distribution Estimation of Wheeled Mobile Robot: Application to Friction Coefficients Estimation. In: 17th IFAC World Congress (IFAC 2008), Seoul (2008)
17. Xu, F., Huang, W., Chen, L.: Simulation analysis of tire force of wheeled tractor under typical road conditions. Transactions of the Chinese Society of Agricultural Machinery 25(S2), 61–65 (2009)

Identifying Apple Surface Defects Based on Gabor Features and SVM Using Machine Vision*

Wenqian Huang[1,2,**], Chi Zhang[2], and Baihai Zhang[1]

[1] School of Automation, Beijing Institute of Technology, Beijing 100081, China
[2] Beijing Research Center of Intelligent Equipment for Agriculture,
Beijing Academy of Agriculture and Forestry Sciences, Beijing, 100097, China
huangwq@nercita.org.cn

Abstract. In this paper, a novel method to recognize defect regions of apples based on Gabor wavelet transformation and SVM using machine vision is proposed. The method starts with background removal and object segmentation by threshold. Texture features are extracted from each segmented object by using Gabor wavelet transform, and these features are introduced to support vector machines (SVM) classifiers. Experimental results exhibit correctly recognized 85% of the defect regions of apples.

Keywords: defect identification, Gabor wavelet, SVM, apple quality grading.

1 Introduction

Tons of apples are produced, harvested and consumed throughout the world each year. Visual inspection of these apples is traditionally done by human experts. Even so, automation of this process is necessary to increase speed of inspection as well as to eliminate human inspection error and variation introduced. In recent years machine vision systems have been widely applied to evaluate external quality of apples [1-3]. However, these systems can't provide robust and accurate results yet, because high variability of defect types and skin color as well as presence of stem/calyx areas increases complexity of the problem. Computer vision systems are mostly confused in discriminating defect regions of apples from stem/calyx regions due to their similarity in appearance. In most machine vision based automated apple grading and sorting systems, it is important to distinguish apple stem/calyx from defect in apple images because stem/calyx region in apple images often exhibit patterns and intensity values that are similar to defect region in apple surface and result in false alarms during defect sorting. Hence, accuracy of apple sorting decreased by false identification of defect regions of apples.

* Young Scientists' Foundation of Beijing Academy of Agriculture and Forestry Sciences (Project No. QN201119) and National High-Tech Research and Development Program of China (863 Program) (Project No. 2011AA100703).
** Corresponding author.

D. Li and Y. Chen (Eds.): CCTA 2011, Part III, IFIP AICT 370, pp. 343–350, 2012.
© IFIP International Federation for Information Processing 2012

Several approaches have been introduced to recognize defects on apples using computer vision systems. T.G. Crowe et al. use structural illumination to detect apple defects, where concave dark spots are considered to be stem/calyx [4-5]. Zhiqing Wen et al. develop a rules-based NIR system and histogram densities are used to discriminate stem/calyx from defect areas [6]. Recognition rates of stems and calyxes are 81.4% and 87.9%, respectively. Their system is less reliable when stem/calyx regions are closer to the edge of fruit. Wen Z. et al. use an NIR and a middle-infrared (MIR) camera for apple detection, where image from the latter is used to segment ROI and about 99% of them are correctly recognized [7]. However, cost of cameras, which is not discussed by the authors, is an important problem for practical implementation of this method. Kleynen et al. utilize correlation-based pattern matching technique to detect stem/calyx on apples in a multispectral vision system [8]. Recognition rates for stems and calyxes are 91% and 92%, respectively. And 17% of defects are misclassified as stem/calyx. Pattern matching method has been widely applied for object recognition, but its main disadvantage is high dependency on the template used.

2-D Gabor wavelets have been successfully applied to face recognition. Its advantages are better time-frequency localization feature and better signal resolution in time and frequency domain which can be achieved by adjusting Gabor filter's direction and base-frequency width and central frequency. Tai Sing Lee extended 1-D compact wavelet to 2-D Gabor wavelet in 1996 [9]. Multi-channel filter technology, that is, a set of Gabor wavelets with different time-frequency characteristics are adopted in image transform, each channel can achieve some local feature from input image, so the input image can be analyzed on different-sized granularity. In all, Gabor wavelets optimally represent the texture structure with different locations and orientations. Because Gabor wavelets transform is better than others on texture feature extraction, it is adopted in this work for apple stem/calyx and defect characteristics extraction.

SVM is a strong classifier which can identify two classes [10], and defect identification is to tell the ROI image is defect or stem/calyx. Therefore SVM is suitable for this problem. In fact, SVM is also of some advantages. SVM is on the basis of Vapnik-Cheervonenkis (VC) dimension theory in SLT (Statistic Learning Theory) and structure risk minimization principle. In order to achieve the best generalization, SVM makes the compromise between model complexity and generalization. Compared to other classical learning methods, SVM can overcome traditional learning flaws, such as over-learning and less-learning and driven to local minimum as well. For the situation which input samples can't be separated in a linear space, SVM can carry on a non-linear transform and change this inseparable problem into a divisible question in a high-dimensioned space and figure out its optimal classification surface in this space. Classification can be realized through inner product computation with SVM core function in a high dimensioned space, but computation complexity is not increased.

2   Identifying Apple Surface Defects Using Gabor Transform

This section describes the method for the identification of the defect on apple surface using Gabor transform. First, Gabor wavelet representation of apple images derives desirable features characterized by spatial frequency, spatial locality, and orientation. Second, the Gabor wavelet features of apple images are used as the input space in SVM.

2.1 Gabor Transform

The Gabor wavelets can be defined as follows:

$$\psi_{\mu,v}(z) = \frac{\parallel k_{\mu,v} \parallel^2}{\sigma^2} e^{-\frac{\parallel k_{\mu,v} \parallel^2 \parallel z \parallel^2}{2\sigma^2}} [e^{ik_{\mu,v}z} - e^{-\frac{\sigma^2}{2}}] \tag{1}$$

Where $z = (x,y)$ are the spatial coordinates, the parameter μ and v define the orientation and scale of the Gabor kernels, $\parallel \cdot \parallel$ denotes the norm operator, and $k_{\mu,v}$ is defined as follows:

$$k_{\mu,v} = k_v e^{i\phi_\mu} \tag{2}$$

Where $k_v = k_{max}/f^v$ and $\phi_\mu = \pi\mu/8$. $k_{max} = \frac{\pi}{2}$, and $f = \sqrt{2}$.

In most cases one would use Gabor wavelets of eight orientations, $\mu \in \{0, \ldots, 7\}$, and five different scales, $v \in \{0, \ldots, 4\}$. Fig.1 shows the real part and magnitude of Gabor wavelets kernel under five scales and eight orientations. The Gabor wavelets exhibit desirable characteristics of spatial frequency, spatial locality, and orientation selectivity.

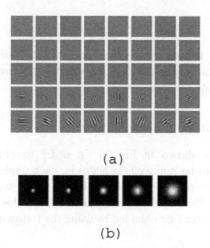

(a)

(b)

Fig. 1. Gabor Wavelets. (a) The real part of the Gabor wavelets at five scales and eight orientations. (b) The magnitude of the Gabor wavelets at five different scales.

The Gabor wavelet representation of an image is the convolution of the image with a family of Gabor wavelets as defined by Equation 1. Let $I(x,y)$ be the gray level distribution of an image, the convolution of image I and a Gabor wavelet is defined as follows:

$$O_{\mu,\upsilon} = I(z) * \psi_{\mu,\upsilon}(z) \tag{3}$$

Where $z = (x,y)$, and $*$ denotes the convolution operator, and $O_{\mu,\upsilon}(z)$ is the convolution result corresponding to the Gabor wavelets at orientation μ and scale υ. Therefore, the set $S = O_{\mu,\upsilon}(z) : \mu \in \{0, ,7\}, \upsilon \in \{0, ,4\}$ forms the Gabor wavelet representation of the image $I(z)$.

Applying the convolution theorem, we can derive each $O_{\mu,\upsilon}(z)$ from Equation 3 via the Fast Fourier Transform:

$$\mathcal{F}\{O_{\mu,\upsilon}(z)\} = \mathcal{F}\{I(z)\}\mathcal{F}\{\psi_{\mu,\upsilon}(z)\} \tag{4}$$

and

$$O_{\mu,\upsilon} = \mathcal{F}^{-1}\{\mathcal{F}\{I(z)\}\mathcal{F}\{\psi_{\mu,\upsilon}(z)\}\} \tag{5}$$

In order to obtain the input feature vector, we concatenate all these representation results and derive an augmented feature vector X. Before the concatenation, we first downsample each $O_{\mu,\upsilon}$ by a factor ρ to reduce the space dimension and normalize it to zero mean and unitvariance. We then construct a vector out of the $O_{\mu,\upsilon}(z)$ by concatenating its columns. Now, let $X_{\mu,\upsilon}$ denote the normalized vector constructed from $O_{\mu,\upsilon}$, the augmented Gabor feature vector X is then defined as follows:

$$X = (X_{0,0}X_{0,1} \ldots X_{4,7}) \tag{6}$$

The augmented Gabor feature vector thus encompasses all the elements (downsampled and normalized) of the Gabor wavelet representation as important discriminating information.

2.2   Defect Identification on Apple Surface

An image of apples is shown in Fig 2a. In order to obtain apple region, the background region has to be removed. In addition, each apple is a region of interest (ROI) and needs to be extracted individually. In this work, we use threshold method to extract apple image. That is, the R channel in RGB color channels is taken into account. The apple region can be obtained by using the following equation:

$$I(x, y) = \begin{cases} \text{background pixel} & R < 118 \\ \text{apple pixel} & \text{otherwise} \end{cases} \tag{7}$$

If $I(x,y)$ is identified as an background pixel, we let $I(x,y)$ be equal to 255. The segmented image is shown in Fig 2b. Each apple in a single image can be easily extracted from the segmented image individually.

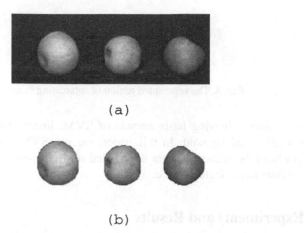

(a)

(b)

Fig. 2. (a) Original image of apples. (b) The segmented image.

In order to get the defect region in apple surface, we first convert the segmented color apple image into grayscale image by using the following equation:

$$I_{Gray} = 0.299I_{Red} + 0.584I_{Green} + 0.114I_{Blue} \tag{8}$$

Where I_{Red}, I_{Green}, and I_{Blue} are the 8-bit color value of a given pixel in the segmented image.

Then a threshold is used to extract dark areas within apples, such as defects, stem, and calyxes, as region of interesting. However, in our experiments, we find this method of extracting ROI in apple surface can't obtain all dark areas within apples.

In this study, a new method is proposed to extract dark areas within apples. We first use the following equation to get the grayscale of each apple.

$$I_{Gray} = \text{MAX}\{I_{Red}, I_{Green}, I_{Blue}\} \tag{9}$$

Then a threshold θ is used to get dark ROI in apple surface.

$$I_{Binary} = \begin{cases} 0 & I_{Gray} < \theta \\ 255 & \text{otherwise} \end{cases} \tag{10}$$

Finally, morphological operation is employed to refine the segmentation.

After segmentation operation is completed, we can utilize the central coordinate (x,y) of dark ROI to extract a 64× 64 region in original color apple image that centers on (x,y). The extracted color ROI in apple surface is show in Fig 3:

In this work, Gabor wavelet filter is used to extract Gabor wavelet features from ROI image. Two downsampling operations are employed to the features. So a 64×64 feature image becomes a 16×16 feature image. We then construct feature vector by concatenating its columns. The feature vector is used as input vector for SVM.

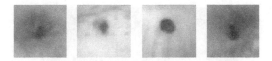

Fig. 3. The segmented region of interesting in an apple image

There are four following basis kernels of SVM: linear, polynomial, radial basis function (RBF), and sigmoid. In this paper, we use SVM with the linear function kernel as a black box classifier over the labeled set of feature vectors. Doing so yields support vectors in the feature space.

3   Experiments and Results

The machine vision system for apple quality inspection is shown in Fig.4. It consists of a computer-controlled frame grabber that is based on the PCI Express interface and an image sensing system, which is a digital progressive scan color CCD cameras (JAI CV-A70CL) with a C-mount lens of 8mm focal length. The color images are grabbed and analyzed by a host computer equipped with a Dalsa X64-CL Express frame grabber. A lighting chamber was designed to provide uniform illumination for the CCD sensor. The chamber size is 90(W)*100(L)*100(H) cm. In order to provide lighting, two warm-white lamps with color temperature 5400K are mounted above the conveyor. The CCD imaging sensor is mounted inside on the two sides of the chamber. A roller conveyor belt is built to hold and move apples in one lane. All apple samples are manually placed on the conveyer belt with a random orientation. The apples are rotating and moving when they pass through the view of the two CCD cameras. The whole surface of each apple can be covered by the CCD camera during the apple rotation. A drive controller and speed controller are connected with a photoelectric switch that provides precise timing signals for both on-line mechanical and electrical synchronization.

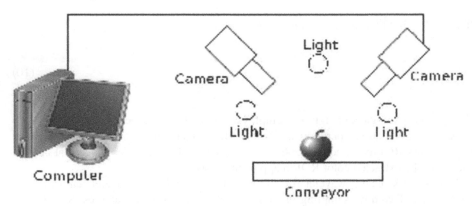

Fig. 4. The machine vision system

A total of 200 color apple images are acquired. From these apple images, we can obtain 90 stem regions, 90 calyx regions and 90 defect regions. The stem/calyx and defect images that are used in our experiments are show in Fig5: the first row is calyx image, the second row is stem image, and the last row is defect image.

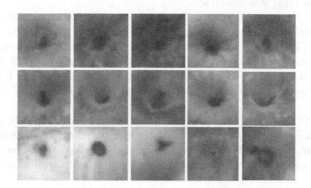

Fig. 5. The stem/calyx and defect images

We first segment the ROI in apple surface and convert the color ROI to grayscale image. For each gray image, Gabor wavelet filter is used to extract the texture features, and these features is employed to the input of SVM. Finally, the identification results are given by SVM. In our experiments, the training dataset includes 50 stem images, 50 calyx images and 50 defect images. The testing set includes 40 stem images, 40 calyx images and 40 defect images. The overall defect identification rate is 85%.

4 Conclusion

External quality grading of apple fruits by machine vision is still an open, tedious and challenging problem. Accuracy of this task depends on several subtasks, one of which is precise recognition of defect areas.

In this paper, a defect identification method based on Gabor wavelet features is introduced. Firstly, this method accurately obtains the ROI in apple surface. Then Gabor wavelet filter is used to extract the texture features of ROI, and these features are employed to the input of SVM. Finally, in the experiments were conducted and the overall defect identification rate is 85%.

Acknowledgments. Our project is supported by Young Scientists' Foundation of Beijing Academy of Agriculture and Forestry Sciences (Project No. QN201119) and National High-Tech Research and Development Program of China (863 Program) (Project No. 2011AA100703).

References

1. Heinemann, P.H., Varghese, Z.A., Morrow, C.T., Sommer III, H.J., Crasswelle, R.M.: Machine Vision Inspection of 'Golden Delicious' Apples. Applied Engineering in Agriculture 11(6), 901–906 (1995)
2. Paulus, I., Schrevens, E.: Shape Characterization of New Apple Cultivars by Fourier Expansion of Digitized Images. J. Agric. Engng Res. 72, 113–118 (1999)
3. Zou, X.-B., Zhao, J.-W., Li, Y.: Mel Holmes. In-line detection of apple defects using three color cameras system. Computers and Electronics in Agriculture 70, 129–134 (2010)
4. Crowe, T.G., Delwiche, M.J.: Real-time defect detection in fruit part I: Design concepts and development of prototype hardware. Transactions of the ASAE 39(6), 2299–2308 (1996)
5. Crowe, T.G., Delwiche, M.J.: Real-time defect detection in fruit-part II: an algorithm and performance of a prototype system. Transactions of the ASAE 39(6), 2309–2317 (1996)
6. Zhiqing, W., Yang, T.: Building a rule-based machine-vision system for defect inspection on apple sorting and packing lines. Expert Systems with Applications 16(3), 307–313 (1999)
7. Wen, Z., Tao, Y.: Dual-camera nir/mir imaging for stem-end/calyx identification in apple defect sorting. Transactions of the ASAE 43(2), 449–452 (2000)
8. Kleynen, O., Leemans, V., Destain, M.-F.: Development of a multi-spectral vision system for the detection of defects on apples. Journal of Food Engineering 69(1), 41–49 (2005)
9. Lee, T.S.: Image representation using 2d gabor wavelets. Pattern Analysis and Machine Intelligence. IEEE Transactions on Pattern Analysis and Machine Intelligence 18(10), 959–971 (1996)
10. Burges, C.J.C.: A Tutorial on Support Vector Machines for Pattern Recognition. Data Mining and Knowledge Discovery 2(2), 121–167 (1998)

Walking Goal Line Detection Based on DM6437 on Harvesting Robot

Gang Wu, Yu Tan[*], Yongjun Zheng, and Shumao Wang

College of Engineering, China Agricultural University, Beijing, China
wugang19771121@163.com, tanyu32@sina.com,
{zyj,wangshumao}@cau.edu.cn

Abstract. As to aided driving by harvesting robot, there is the large amount of image data processing, meanwhile, harvesting robot requires real-time image processing and to calculate the linear parameters in a straight line detection of the walking target process. This paper presents a hardware processing platform to TMS320DM6437 digital signal processor as the core processing chip, and an improved Hough transform algorithm which is based on a determined point is proposed to complete line detection. A camera is to be fitted on the left top of the combine harvester in order to capture images of farmland scenes in the process of harvesting. At first, according to different color characteristics of harvested areas and non-harvested areas, improved methods of Maximum entropy threshold segmentation and morphological approach are employed to determine candidate points of walking goal line. Then the candidate points are selected as the point set. Finally, the improved Hough transform based on a determined point is applied to complete line detection. The algorithm simplifies binary map to unitary map. Comparing with the traditional Hough transform, it saves computing time, and reduces the parameter space greatly. After multiple images processing, tests show that this detection method can detect real-time parameters of harvesting robot's walking goal line, and the algorithm is well proved with respect to its speed, anti-interference and accuracy.

Keywords: TMS320DM6437, Harvesting Robot, Line Detection, Hough Transform.

1 Introduction

Autonomous navigation research of Agricultural robot is the requirements of modern agricultural development, and it also has become a high-tech research direction such as intelligent control in the application of agricultural machinery and equipment. Currently, the ways of agricultural robot navigation are as follows: (1) Beacon navigation. Namely, beacons are set on the determined points of work environment; (2) Global Positioning

---

[*] Corresponding author.

D. Li and Y. Chen (Eds.): CCTA 2011, Part III, IFIP AICT 370, pp. 351–361, 2012.

System (GPS). The emergence of GPS is a major breakthrough of modern navigation technology, and it has high accuracy, unlimited users, all-weather work and other advantages. But it has a poor anti-interference ability. When it is obstructed by trees, houses and other blocks, the signal may be occasional lost; (3) Visual navigation. Visual navigation of agricultural autonomous walking robot, usually divides into two kinds: wireless guide and wired guide. Because of the complex operating environment of agriculture, we usually use wireless navigation, which robots accord a CCD camera's real-time detection of the surrounding environment to plan the required path, and it can follow the path without human intervention to move towards the target. Among them, due to its application is flexible and easy, visual navigation has become popular navigation way [1~3]. Agricultural robot's visual navigation requires not only an effective image processing algorithm, but also requires a stable platform of image processing with high executing speed and miniaturization. With the development of electronic technology, the signal processing hardware platform based on DSP [4~5] has been applied in image processing widely. This paper applies DSP hardware platform to complete image acquisition, image processing, external communications and other functions, at the same time, this hardware is very small, which applies improved Hough transform algorithm based on a determined point in the software.

2   System Hardware Components

System hardware consists of the signal processor TMS320DM6437, DSP program memory FLASH, and high-speed video A/D acquisition chip tvp5416. System hardware schematic diagram is shown in Fig.1. Firstly, TMS320DM6437 controls tvp5416 to do A/D conversion of the input analog video through the I2C bus and gets the digitized video signal. Then, image processing algorithms is used to detect linear parameters. Finally, the linear parameters by serial communication are sent to the steering control unit and the image is transmitted to the display unit.

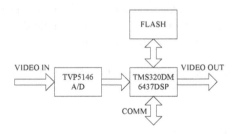

Fig. 1. System hardware schematic diagram

2.1   A/D Converter

Among the AD converter, there is a professional video A/D chip tvp5146 [6]. The chips do not need to use others to separate horizontal and vertical sync signals of video signal, because it can get vertical sync signals from the composite video signal. By horizontal and vertical sync signals, it can collect A/D converted digital images correctly. The chip programs the input original image via I2C bus and controls image brightness, contrasts and outputs effective range. In practice, the original composite video signal of camera outputting is selected to do pretreatment according to field in the A/D chip, and then the resulting digital video signal is put into the DSP.

2.2   High-Speed Image Processing Unit

TMS320DM6437 from TI company is introduced in 2006, specifically for high-performance, low-cost video application development, frequency of 600MHz and 32-bit fixed point DSP Leonardo (DaVinci (TM)) technology processor family, it can be applied to automotive vision, robotics and other fields [7]. TMS320DM6437 uses the TMS320C64x+DSP as its core which is TI's third-generation-long instruction set architecture (VelociTI.3), clocks at up to 600MHz, supporting eight 8-bit or four 16-bit parallel MAC operations, and the peak capacity up to 4800MIPS. It can also handle H.264 encoding algorithm of 8 channels CIF or 3 channels D1 format. DM6437 provides video-on-chip input/output interfaces which are called video subsystem VPSS. DM6437 video subsystem is composed by two parts, and one is video processing front end for digital video input data, which provides the input interface for a variety of standard digital video, at the same time, it also makes necessary pre-processing for the input digital video data. The other is the video processing back end, and it is used to output digital video data to drive the display video images.

Therefore, here we use DM6437, external 27M crystal, by frequency to 600MHz. The program is written into FLASH, and then the program is loaded into the DSP by the power.

3   Line Detection Algorithm

The imaging system is designed to detect the navigation path line when harvest wheat by combine-harvester. As the combine harvester unloading grain port is on the left, so we usually choose the left part to start harvesting, and it is easy to unload the grain, even the right direction of driving is non-harvested area, and the left is harvested area. The most common route methods of harvesting are dextrorotation method and four sides harvest method [8], and dextrorotation method is suitable for longer but not wider farmland. After cutting out of road, the long side direction of the harvest is followed, then the combine-harvester needn't to head back when the harvest has finished, finally the combine harvester turns right around to the other long side of partition to continue harvesting until the end of harvest; four sides harvest method is suitable for large fields, after cutting out of road, the combine harvester harvests along the left side of terraces until the end, then turns right to continue to harvest, and so forth, until the harvest ends. Based on the above practices, the detected straight line is put on the left side of combine harvester.

3.1   Image Processing Steps

Images are taken by JAI CV-M77 camera, shooting frame rate of 25s-1, 640×480 color images. Test image was shot in wheat field of suburb in Luoyang City, the weather was sunny. Before the test, the camera is mounted on top of the center-left position combines, apart from the ground about 3m, camera and horizontal's angle about 40°. Camera adopted isolation pads and protected cover with a dust wiper for dust treatment.

Image processing steps: (1) Grayscale processing. In such issues, as R(red) channel pixel values change more obviously, here R(red) channel is selected to do grayscale image processing; (2) Image noise reduction. In order to reduce noise interference, we use the level of five-point smoothing filter; (3) Thresholding. Because gray-scale distribution images of agricultural scene are complex, an improved maximum entropy thresholding method for image thresholding is chosen after the test; (4) Morphological processing. To further reduce interference, morphological processing is used with the binary image, processing methods are 3×3 structure element for corrosion and 3×3 structure element expansion; (5) Determination of the candidate point set. Figure 3 shows the average gray value distribution of each line (horizontal) pixels, we can see the gray value become smaller and smaller from top to down. In addition, because the camera is mounted on the top left of center combines harvester, and the straight line angle is generally between ±10°, so the line to be detected appears in the image between the 150 column-the 450 column, the collection point set D method is: scan the nearest point of left side of the 450 column from the 10 row to the 470 row, stop until the 140 column. If there is the point, it should be inserted point set D, if not, go to the next row; (6) At last, use improved HT based on a determined point to complete the line detection. The image processing steps are shown in Fig.2.

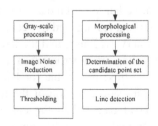

Fig. 2. Image processing flow chart

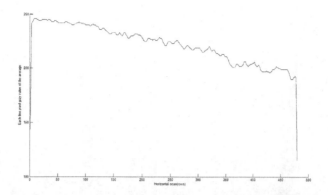

Fig. 3. Average gray value distribution of each line (horizontal) pixels

3.2   Improved Maximum Entropy Thresholding Method

Because Gray-scale distribution of agricultural scene images is complicated, it is difficult to use a fixed threshold segmentation method, so we choose the adaptive threshold segmentation, currently, adaptive thresholding methods are: Otsu thresholding method [9~10], iterative thresholding method [11] and maximum entropy thresholding method [12]. By using three methods of image segmentation, the segmentation results are shown in Fig.4. It is easy to see from four charts, Fig.4d is the best, so we choose the one-dimensional maximum entropy thresholding method as thresholding method of this study.

Maximum entropy thresholding method put the concept of Shannon entropy into image thresholding, whose basic idea is that image information entropy is defined by gray-scale image distribution density function and according to different assumptions or different perspectives, there is different entropy criteria, and finally get threshold through optimization of the threshold criteria. Maximum entropy thresholding method has two types: one-dimensional maximum entropy thresholding method and two-dimensional maximum entropy thresholding method.

(1) one-dimensional maximum entropy thresholding method

According to information theory, entropy is defined as

$$H = -\int_{-\infty}^{+\infty} p(x) \cdot \lg p(x) dx. \tag{1}$$

Where $p(x)$ is the probability density function of random variable x.

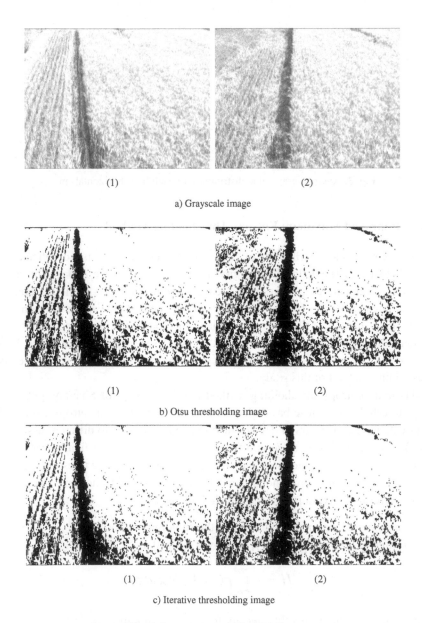

a) Grayscale image

b) Otsu thresholding image

c) Iterative thresholding image

Fig. 4. Image segmentation result

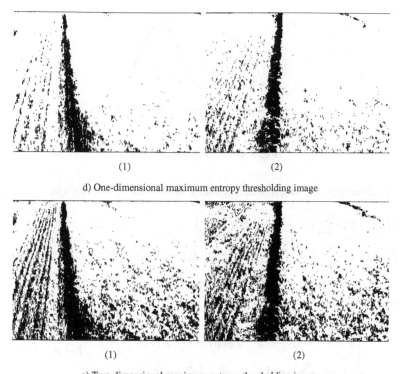

(1)   (2)

d) One-dimensional maximum entropy thresholding image

(1)   (2)

e) Two-dimensional maximum entropy thresholding image

Fig. 4. (*Continued*)

For digital images, random variable x can be gray value or regional gray, gradient and other characteristics. The words one-dimensional gray-scale maximum entropy mean that the threshold which is chosen can split image into two parts, and the two parts' first-order gray-scale statistics has maximum amount of information. The histogram is shown in Fig.5, we assume that the original grayscale image has L gray levels, pixel points that are lower than t gray level constitute the target area O, and pixel points that are higher than t gray level constitute the background area B, so the probability distribution in its region is as follows:

area O : p_i / p_t $i = 1, 2, \cdots, t$;

area B : $p_i / (1 - p_t)$ $i = t+1, t+2, \cdots, L$.

Thereinto,

$$p_t = \sum_{i=1}^{t} p_i \,.$$

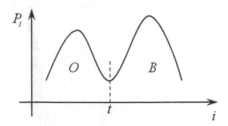

Fig. 5. One-dimensional histogram

For digital images, the target area and background area of entropy are:

$$\begin{cases} H_O(t) = -\sum_i (p_i / p_t) \cdot \lg(p_i / p_t) & i = 1, 2, \cdots, t \\ H_B(t) = -\sum_i [p_i /(1-p_t)] \cdot \lg[p_i /(1-p_t)] & t = t+1, t+2, \cdots, L \end{cases} \quad (2)$$

So the entropy function is defined as:

$$\begin{cases} \varphi(t) = H_O + H_B = \lg[p_t \cdot (1 = p_t)] + \dfrac{H_t}{p_t} + \dfrac{H_L - H_t}{1 - p_t} \\ H_t = -\sum_i p_i \cdot \lg p_i & i = 1, 2, \cdots, t \\ H_L = -\sum_i p_i \cdot \lg p_i & i = i+1, i+2, \cdots, L \end{cases} \quad (3)$$

When entropy function obtains the maximum, the corresponding gray value t^* is the desired optimal threshold, the calculation formula is as follows:

$$t^* = \arg \max \{\varphi(t)\}. \quad (4)$$

Because the process of finding t^* is global search, so the calculation time is too long, so we did some improvement with one-dimensional maximum entropy thresholding method as follows: Since gray level distribution of the medium shot is between the close shot and long shot, we select gray-scale image from the 200 row to the 249 row as a processing unit after numerous tests, then calculate the average gray value T of this unit, and $0.75T \le t^* \le 1.25T \le 255$, thus it greatly reduces the search space of t^* and saves computing time.

3.3   Improved Hough Transform

Linear equations in polar form as:

$$\rho = x \cdot \cos\theta + y \cdot \sin\theta. \tag{5}$$

Where (x, y) is the Cartesian coordinates of image; θ is the angle between the x-axis forward direction and normal line, the range of angle is $[-90°, 90°]$; ρ is the vertical distance from the line to the coordinates origin. According to geometry, we can see that any two points can determine the the line's parameters (ρ, θ). $a(x', y')$ which is supposed a determined point on a straight line, and $b(x_i, y_i)$ is a point from candidate set D, ρ and θ can use the formula (6) and formula (7) to calculate:

$$\theta_i = -\tan^{-1}(\frac{x_i - x'}{y_i - y'}). \tag{6}$$

$$\rho_i = x'\cos\theta_i + y'\sin\theta_i. \tag{7}$$

The value of θ is mapped to a set of accumulators, and each obtained θ_i makes the corresponding accumulator value plus 1. Because the points on a same line have the same value of θ, so when there is a straight line, its corresponding accumulator has partial maximum, θ_i which corresponded partial maximum become θ of the request line. According to θ and $a(x', y')$, the corresponding ρ value can be got from formula (7).

3.4 Walking Goal Line Parameter Calculation

In order to use the Hough transform based on a determined point[13~15], at first, we should confirm this point. As the long shot image has better effect, so we determine the method after many tests as follows: the first 40 points of the set of points $D(x_i, y_i)$ are taken, then we can determine a point $a(x', y')$ coordinates value as follows:

$$x' = \bar{x} = \frac{1}{40}\sum_{i=1}^{40} x_i; y' = \bar{y} = \frac{1}{40}\sum_{i=1}^{40} y_i. \tag{8}$$

First, the accumulator A is defined in $[-15°, 15°]$ range, and the range is divided into 100 equal parts A_i $(0<i<101)$, whose amplitude is $0.3°$. Then $a(x', y')$ and the candidate point set $D(x_i, y_i)$ as the basis, use formula (2) calculation θ_i, then map θ_i to 100 portions and make the cumulative device $A_i(0<i<101)$ value of the corresponding portions plus 1. When mapping has been completed, there must be an accumulator A_i maximum value, and use the midpoint of this accumulator corresponding parts as the request linear parameter θ, according to the formula (3) and $a(x', y')$, then calculate the other line A parameter ρ.

Test results of the image are shown in Figure 6, four images obtained a straight line parameters ρ and θ as follows: Fig.6a is 179.578, -6.45; Fig.6b is 312.155, 7.35; Fig.6c is 269.831, 1.95; Fig.6d is 250.817, -6.75.

(a)   (b)

(c)   (d)

Fig. 6. Image results of the experiment

4   Conclusion

In allusion to aided driving by harvesting robot, in order to make sure the entire image processing in real time and system can be working long-time stability, so this paper chooses TI's TMS320DM6437 as core processor for the system, meanwhile, the improved Hough transform based on a determined point is applied to complete line detection, the algorithm simplifies binary map to unitary map. Comparing with the traditional Hough transform, it saves computing time, reduces the parameter space greatly, and avoids invalid samples and cumulative problems. In addition, the algorithm is well proved with respect to its anti-interference and robustness etc. Tests show that the entire hardware system is capable of working stably, and the entire system operating time from the acquisition parameters to display is only 40ms or so, obviously, this design can meet the real-time processing requirements. Time is calculated by the time DSP debugging software CCS3.3.

Acknowledgements. The authors thank "Twelfth Five-Year" National Technology Key Project (Funding No.: 2011BAD20B00), for their financial support.

References

1. Zhou, J., Ji, C., Liu, C.: Visual navigation system of agricultural wheeled-mobile robot. Transactions of the Chinese Society for Agricultural Machinery 36(3), 90–94 (2005)
2. Shen, M., Ji, C.: Development and Prospect of Vision Guidance of Agricultural Robot. Transactions of the Chinese Society for Agricultural Machinery 32(1), 109–110 (2001)
3. Zhao, B., Wang, M., Mao, E., Zhang, X., Song, Z.: Recognition and classification for vision navigation application environment of agriculturalvehicle. Transactions of the Chinese Society for Agricultural Machinery 40(7), 166–170 (2009)
4. Ma, Z.-F., Zhao, B.-J., He, P.-K.: High-Speed Image Sampling And Dectection System Based on DSPC64X. Transactions of Beijing Institute of Technology 25(7), 628–631 (2005)
5. Cao, Q., Wang, K., Yang, Y., Shi, X.: Identifying the navigation route based on TMS320DM642 for agriculture visual robot. Transactions of the Chinese Society for Agricultural Machinery 40(7), 171–175 (2009)
6. Texas Instruments, TVP5146[S].8(SLES084C) (2007)
7. Texas Instruments, TMS320DM6437 Digital Media Processor[S], 6(SPRS345D) (2008)
8. Ni, C., Li, X., Wang, X.: Grain harvesting machinery Insider. Publishing house of electronics industry, Beijing (2008)
9. Navon, E., Miller, O., Averbuch, A.: Color image segmentation based on adaptive local thresholds. Image and Vision Computing 23(1), 69–85 (2005)
10. Otsu, N.: A Threshold Selection Method From Gray Level Histograms. IEEE Trans. on Syst. Man Cybernet SMC-9, 62–66 (1979)
11. Ridler, T.W., Calvard, S.: Picture thresholding using an iterative selection method. IEEE Transactions on Systems, Man and Cybernetics, 630–632 (1978)
12. Guo, H., Tian, T., Wang, L., Zhang, C.: Image Segmentation Using the Maximum Entropy of the Two-Dimensional Bound Histogram. Acta Optica Sinica 26(4), 506–509 (2006)
13. Zhang, F., Wang, K., Shi, X.: Vehicle flow detection system based on machine vision. Control & Automation 24, 138–140 (2008)
14. Cao, Q., Wang, K.: Vision Navigation Based on Agricultural Non-structural Characteristic. Transactions of the Chinese Society for Agricultural Machinery 40(1), 187–189 (2009)
15. Zhao, Y., Chen, B., Wang, S., Dai, F.: Fast detection of furrows based on machine vision on autonomous mobile robot. Transactions of the Chinese Society for Agricultural Machinery 37(4), 83–86 (2006)

Winter Wheat Seedtime Monitoring through Satellite Remote Sensing Data

Xiaoyu Song[1,*], Wenjiang Huang[1], Bei Cui, and Jihong Zhou[2]

[1] Beijing Agriculture Information Technology Research Center, Beijing, 100097, P.R. China
Songxy@nercita.org.cn
[2] Beijing Agro-Technical Extension Station, Beijing, P.R. China

Abstract. Winter wheat seedtime is important for wheat growth. It affects the wheat yield and quality. The objective of this study is monitoring the winter wheat seedtime through remote sensing imagery. Two HJ-1B images and one Landsat5 TM image were used in this study. Three Vegetation Indices, DVI, SAVI and RDVI were calculated. The correlation about the wheat seedtime and VIs were analyzed. The result indicated that wheat growth was negatively correlated with seedtime. Wheat VIs during 40-60 days after sowing is best for seedtime monitoring. The correlation coefficient for DVI of November 22th HJ-1B and seedtime reached -0.51. The seedtime for whole wheat plant field of Beijing area was inverted through the model. The results show that area for seeded before Sept 30th was about 12.7 thousands ha, 31. 8 thousands ha between Oct 1th and Oct 8th, and 16.2 thousands ha seeded after Oct 8th during 2009-2010 year.

Keywords: Winter wheat, Seedtime, Remote sensing, Landsat5 TM, HJ-1B.

1 Introduction

Recent years, warm winter appears in Beijing area frequently since the Global climate warming. High temperature in winter will affects the growth of overwinter crop. Seedtime is important for the management of the wheat [1]. Crop sowing date, sowing pattern, and nitrogen fertilization will affect on weed suppression and Yield [2-3]. Sowing prior to October generally provides enough time for wheat to establish canopy and develop sufficient roots to anchor the plant in the soil [4]. Proper late sowing can avoid wheat bloom before winter and help it safe live through winter Gao Q.L [5-6]. Winter wheat in the Beijing area is typically sown from late September through middle October. During 2009-2010, there are almost 61.3 thousands ha wheat fields in Beijing suburb and the seedtime for different fields is varied. So it is necessary for the farmer or manager to master the wheat area of different seedtime.

This study tries to monitor the winter wheat seedtime in Beijing suburb through satellite remote sensing imagery. Firstly, the wheat plant area was extracted using the threshold of NDVI of three satellite remote sensing images acquired before 2010

---

* Corresponding author.

D. Li and Y. Chen (Eds.): CCTA 2011, Part III, IFIP AICT 370, pp. 362–371, 2012.

spring. Then four Vegetation Indices (VIs) for 53 winter wheat fields were calculated and the relationship about the wheat seedtime and VI is analyzed. The study result indicated that the winter wheat growth was negatively correlated in wheat seedtime while it was positive correlated in wheat tiller number. The DVI of November 22th HJ-1B CCD2 image was highly related in the seeded time of wheat, and the correlation coefficient reached -0.51. Then winter wheat seedtime monitoring model was established based on the HJ-1B image DVI and the wheat sowing date. The seedtime for whole wheat plant field of Beijing area was inverted through the model. The results show that in 2009-2010 year, winter wheat area for seeded before Sept 30th was about 12.7 thousands ha, while area for seeded between Oct 1th and Oct 8th was 31. 8 thousands ha, and 16.2 thousands ha wheat was seeded after Oct 8th.

2   Materials and Methods

2.1   The Study Area

This study was carried on Beijing suburb which ranging from N 39°26′to 41°03′in latitude and from E 115°25′to 117°30′in longitude. During 2009-2010 the winter wheat growth season, 53 wheat fields distributed in Beijing suburb,including Shunyi, Tongzhou, Fangshan, Daxing, Changping, and Huairou were selected as the study samples area (Figure 1). One Landsat5 TM image and two Environment and Disaster Monitoring and Forecasting of small satellite Constellations 1B (HJ-1B satellite) CCD2 images were used in this study.

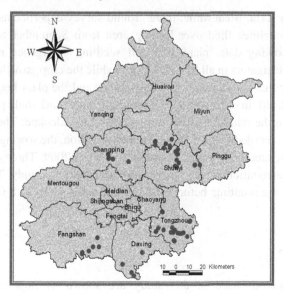

● Study wheat fields

Fig. 1. The location of the study area and the distribution of the study wheat fields

2.2   Data Collection

Remote sensing data. One Landsat5 TM image acquired on 24 October, 2009, two Environment and disaster monitoring and forecasting of small satellite constellations 1B (HJ-1B satellite) CCD2 images acquired on 22 November, 19 December, 2009 were used in this study. HJ-1B satellite is equipped with a Charge-Coupled Device camera (CCD) and Infrared Camera (IRS).HJ-1B satellite are designed nadir symmetrical placement, split field and parallel observations [7]. HJ-1B satellite is loaded CCD2 cameral of four spectrum push-broom imaging with the ground swath width of 360 km, the ground pixel resolution of 30 meters. The main parameters of CCD2 camera are shown in table 1 [8-9].

Table 1. Characteristics of HJ-1B CCD2

Satellite	Sensor	Bands	Wavelength range (μm)	Spatial resolution (m)	Swath width (km)	Sub-cycle (days)
HJ-1B	CCD2	1	0.43-0.52	30	360	4
		2	0.52-0.60	30	360	4
		3	0.63-0.69	30	360	4
		4	0.76-0.90	30	360	4

Ground survey data. Meanwhile, three ground survey experiments were carried out when the two satellites flied over Beijing area from September to December. The winter wheat sowing date, plant area and seedling emergence numbers data are collected by investigators in all 53 fields. Meanwhile the crop growth information such as wheat winter main stalk number, tiller number and the plant height for each field were also calculated. In order to get the exact data, three 1 m2 study plots for each filed where located in the middle of field were selected to calculate. Then the location of study plots was recorded by GPS. From the investigation, the sowing period for winter wheat of Beijing area lasts from 23 Sept to 15 Oct in 2009. Three classes of sowing calendar dates recognition namely: early, normal, late in this study. The date range for early is defined the seedtime before 30 Sept, normal is 1 Oct to 8 Oct and the late is after 9 Oct.

2.3   Methods

The overall methods used in this study are shown as flow chart in Figure.2. Conventional statistics were computed with Excel 2003. The remote sensing data processed and displayed with ENVI 4.1 (ITT 2003).

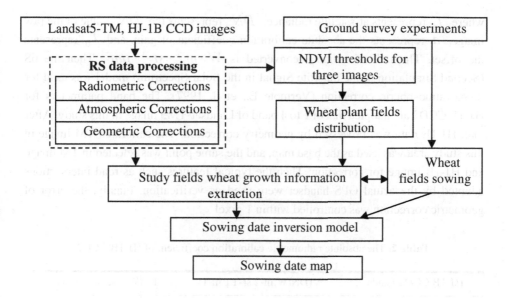

Fig. 2. The flow chart of the study methods

The sequence involves:

(1) TM and HJ-1 data processing, which includes radiometric, atmospheric and geometric corrections;

(2) Using three images NDVI thresholds to extract the winter planted area of 2009-2010 in Beijing suburb.

(3) Four Vegetation Indices (VIs) for 53 winter wheat fields were calculated and the correlation about the wheat seedtime, tiller number and VI were analyzed ,then winter wheat seedtime monitoring model was established.

(4) The seedtime for whole wheat plant field of Beijing area was inverted through the model.

3   Analysis and Conclusion

3.1   RS Data Processing

HJ-1B data was firstly processed by radiometric by convert the DN value of the raw image to the at-satellite radiance image using absolute calibration coefficients (table 2) [10].

$$L = DN / a + L_0 \qquad (1)$$

where L represents at-satellite radiance, DN represents the DN value of the raw image, a represents the absolute calibration coefficient of gain, and L_0 represents the offset. The unit of radiance converted is $W \cdot m^{-2} \cdot sr^{-1} \cdot \mu m^{-1}$ .Then the 6S (Second Simulation of the Satellite Signal in the Solar Spectrum) model was used for image atmospheric correction (Vermote E., et.al, 1997). The band parameters for HJ-1B CCD2 are adopted that of 1 to 4 band of Landsat-TM5 image in this study. After that, HJ-1B data was processed by geometry correction. The calibrated TM image in this study area was used as the base map, and the same point was selected in TM image and HJ-1B image for correction. Then the typical features such as road intersections adopted by the actual GPS handset were used as verification. Finally, the error of geometric correction was controlled within 1 pixel.

Table 2. The absolute radiometric calibration coefficient of HJ-1B CCD2

HJ-1B CCD2 bands	A (DN/W.m-2.sr-1.µm-1)	L_0 (W.m-2.sr-1.µm-1)
Band1	0.5759	3.4608
Band2	0.5488	5.8769
Band3	0.7537	8.0069
Band4	0.7753	8.8583

3.2   Winter Wheat Fields Extraction

The main plants in Beijing suburb are evergreen shrub and winter wheat in field from November to December.   During the winter, the plant can easily differentiate from the water body, city land and bare land for the plant NDVI threshold great than that of others features. Firstly, we use the NDVI to extract plant form other land types. In this paper, the threshold great than 0.05 in 24, Oct, 0.2 in 22, Nov, and 0.1 in 19, Dec is considered as the plant, which can easily differentiate the water body, city land and bare land. Then the winter wheat and the shrub were distinguished by the NDVI curve with the decision trees of ENVI. The evergreen shrub and the winter wheat have the different NDVI curve characters. The shrub NDVI curve shows obvious decrease from Oct to Dec while the winter wheat increases from Oct to Nov but decrease from Nov to Dec. Based on the difference of the NDVI curves, the winter wheat fields was extracted (figure 4).

■ Wheat fields   □ No-Wheat fields

Fig. 3. The winter wheat extraction map

3.3   Statistical Correlation

Spectral characteristics of crop fields are changed after sowing. Values of near infrared reflectance (band 2) increase during 40-60 days after sowing. Four vegetation indices (VI), NDVI, DVI, SAVI and RDVI are calculated from TM and HJ-1 image [11-14]. The definition for those four vegetation indices is listed in table 3.

Table 3. The vegetation index definition for Landsat5 TM and HJ-1B CCD2 image

Vegetation Index	Bands	Definition	Author
NDVI	B3,B4	$NDVI = (R_4 - R_3)/(R_4 + R_3)$	Rouse, et al., (1974)
DVI	B3,B4	$DVI = (R_4 - R_3)$	Jordan, et al., (1969)
SAVI	B3,B4	$SAVI = (1 + 0.5)*(R_4 - R_3)/(R_.$	Huete, et al., (1988)
RDVI	B3,B4	$RDVI = (R_4 - R_3)/\sqrt{(R_4 + R_3)}$	Rougean & Breon, (1995)

Then, analysis about the VI and the winter wheat growth investigation data are carried on. The sowing date has negative relationship with the winter wheat ground survey LAI. The correlation coefficient between sowing date and Oct LAI reached -0.23, increase to -0.54 in Dec then decrease to -0.12 in Nov. Meanwhile, the relationship between wheat VI and sowing date also analyzed (Table 4).

Table 4. The correlation coefficient between sowing date

Vegetation Index	sowing date	Vegetation Index	Sowing date	Vegetation Index	sowing date
10/24 TM-NDVI	-0.136	11/22 HJ-NDVI	-0.458**	12/19 HJ-NDVI	-0.142
10/24 TM-DVI	-0.111	11/22 HJ-DVI	-0.510**	12/19 HJ-DVI	-0.182
10/24 TM-RDVI	-0.124	11/22 HJ-RDVI	-0.487**	12/19 HJ-RDVI	-0.167
10/24 TM-SAVI	-0.136	11/22 HJ-SAVI	-0.458**	12/19 HJ-SAVI	-0.142

** : r(0.01, 53)=0.343

The table 4 indicated that wheat spectral characteristics during 40-60 days after sowing is best for seedtime monitored.the DVI of November 22th HJ-1B CCD2 image was highly related in the seeded time of wheat, and the correlation coefficient reached -0.510. Then winter wheat seedtime monitoring model was established based on the HJ-1B image DVI and the ground data (Figure 4). Three classes of sowing calendar dates recognition namely: early, normal, late in this study. The date range for early is before 30 Sept, for normal is 1 Oct to 8 Oct and the late is after 8 Oct.

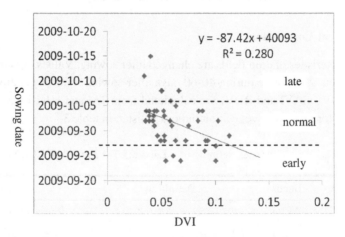

Fig. 4. The scatter-plot of sowing date and HJ-1 CCD2 DVI

3.4   Results

Figure 5 shows the result of winter wheat sowing date supervising through remote sensing data. The seedtime for whole wheat plant field of Beijing area was inverted through the model. The results show that in 2009-2010 year, winter wheat area for seeded before Sept 30th was about 12.7 thousands ha, while area for seeded between

Oct 1th and Oct 8th was 31. 8 thousands ha, and 16.2 thousands ha wheat was seeded after Oct 8th. Then the wheat planting area of different seedtime for five main crop counties, Daxing, Tongzhou, Shunyi, Fangshan and Changping was calculated through the seedtime map and the statistic results are list in table 5.

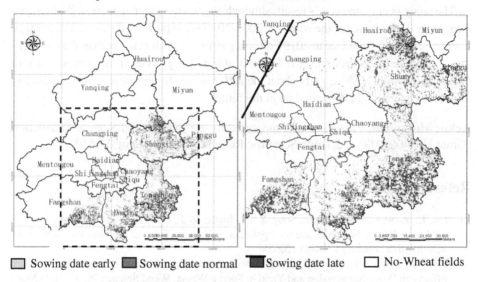

☐ Sowing date early ☐ Sowing date normal ☐ Sowing date late ☐ No-Wheat fields

a: Seedtime map for whole Beijing area

b: Seedtime map for main wheat planted counties of Beijing

Fig. 5. 2009-2010 Winter wheat Seedtime map of Beijing suburb

Table 5. Statistic results of wheat planting area of different sowing date for the main crop counties of Beijing suburb in 2009

Country name	Early sowing(ha)	Normal sowing	Late sowing
Daxing	2800.00	9666.67	1933.33
Tongzhou	3388.33	10727.20	1684.47
Shunyi	5066.67	8266.67	770.00
Fangshan	2010.67	9529.00	460.33
Changping	453.33	209.35	8.00

3.5   Conclusion and Discussion

In this paper, the winter wheat seedtime monitoring model was established based on the HJ-1B image DVI and the ground data. The seedtime for whole wheat plant field of Beijing area was inverted through the model. The result shows a good agreement with the statistic data from Beijing agriculture technique popularizing station. It indicated that the winter wheat growth was negatively correlated with wheat seedtime in winter and the wheat spectral characteristics during 40-60 days after sowing is best for seedtime monitoring. The results of this study suggest that seedtime monitoring using RS data was reliable and feasible.

The study is only one year's result, although the warm winter appears in Beijing area frequently in recent years, the winter of 2009-2010 is a typical cold winter. The average temperature from 2009 Dec to 2010 Feb is negative 3.5 °C, it is lower than the recent 10 year's average temperature by 1.6 °C. So it affects the growth of the winter wheat in different seedtime. More study about the different seedtime wheat growth characters in warm winter should be carried on in the future.

Acknowledgment. This work was supported by Beijing Natural Science Foundation (Grant No. 4092017) and Youth Scientific Research foundation of BAAFS.

References

1. Liu, L., Zhao, C.J., Wang, J.H., Song, X.Y., Huang, W.J., Li, C.J.: Satellite Remote Sensing of Winter Wheat Seedtime and its Application. Remote Sensing Information (in Chinese with English abstract) 1, 28–31 (2005)
2. Lars, K., Jannie, O., Jacob, W.: Crop Density, Sowing pattern, and Nitrogen Fertilization. Effects on Weed Suppression and Yield in Spring Wheat. Weed Science 56, 97–102 (2008)
3. Keyvan, S.: The effect of sowing date and row spacing on yield and yield components on Hashem chickpea variety under rainfed condition. African Journal of Biotechnology 9(1), 007–0014 (2010), http://www.academicjournals.org/AJB
4. Edwards, J.: Factors affecting wheat Germination and stand establishment in hot soils. Oklahoma Cooperative Extension Service. Division of Agricultural Sciences and Natural Resources, Pss-2256, August 18 (2008),
   http://pods.dasnr.okstate.edu/docushare/dsweb/Get/
   Document-5319/PSS-2256.pdf
5. Gao, Q.L., Xue, X., Liang, Y.J., Wu, Y.E., Ru, Z.G.: Studies on regulating sowing time of wheat under the warm winter conditions. Journal of Triticeae Crops (in Chinese with English abstract) 22(2), 46–50 (2002)
6. William, S., Donald, W., Harry, S., Steve, S., Robert, P.: Tillage Method and Sowing Rate Relations for Dryland Spring Wheat, Barley and Oat. Pacific Northwest Conservation Tillage Handbook Series No.30, Chapter 2- Conservation Tillage Systems and Equipment (2005)
7. Yi, L., Wang, X., Liu, B.: Researches on HJ-1 satellite image quality and land use classification precision. Remote Sensing for Land & Resources (in Chinese with English abstract) 81, 74–77 (2009)
8. Jia, F.J., Wu, Y.L., Huang, Y., Cao, D.J.: Design and On-orbit application of CCD Camera on HJ-1A/B Satellites. Spacecraft Engineering (in Chinese with English abstract) 18(6), 37–42 (2009)
9. Ren, P., Yang, C.J., Zhou, J.M.: The Evaluation and Application Study on CCD Multi-spectral Remote Data Characteristics of HJ-1A/B Satellites. Remote Sensing Technology and Application 25(1), 138–142 (2010)

10. Zhu, J., Wu, Y.L., Shen, Z., Li, T.: Analysis of System-level Radiometric Calibration Data for HJ-1A/B Wide Coverage CCD Camera. Spacecraft Engineering (in Chinese with English abstract) 18(5), 73–79 (2009)
11. Rouse, J.W., Hass, R.H., Schell, J.A., Deering, D.W.: Monitoring the vernal advancement of retrogradation of natural vegetation. NASA/GSFC, Type III, Final Report. Greenbelt, MD. 1974, 371 (1974)
12. Jordan, C.F.: Derivation of Leaf Area Index from Quality of Light on the Forest Floor. Ecology 50, 663–666 (1969)
13. Huete, A.R.: A Soil-Adjusted Vegetation Index (SAVI). Remote Sensing of Environment 25, 295–309 (1988)
14. Rougean, J.-L., Breon, F.M.: Estimating PAR absorbed by vegetation from bidirectional reflectance measurements. Remote Sens. Environ. 51, 375–384 (1995)

Guaranteed Cost Control for Uncertain Distributed Delay System with Neutral Type

Yuyan Zhang[*], Dan Zhao, Yan Zhao, and Na Zhang

Department of Automatic Control Engineering, Shenyang Institute of Engineering,
110136 Shenyang, China
{zhangyy,zhaodan,zhaoyan}@sie.edu.cn

Abstract. This paper investigates the problem of guaranteed cost control for a class of uncertain distributed delay systems with neutral type. A sufficient condition for the solvability of this problem is obtained. A novel Lyapunov-Krasovskii functional is constructed to reduce conservatism of the criterion in form of LMIs. Some mathematical techniques are utilized flexibly. Especially, the exchange of the order of repeated integral is required. Based the criterion, the control gain and the guaranteed cost are obtained. A numerical example is provided to illustrate the effectiveness of the proposed design methods.

Keywords: Distributed delay system with neutral type, Guaranteed cost control, Linear matrix inequality (LMI).

1 Introduction

Neutral delay systems are the general form of delay system and contain delays on the derivatives of some system variables. There are many physical examples for neutral delay system in practical systems (see, e.g., [1,2,8,11]). In recent years, the stability analysis and robust guaranteed cost control problems of neutral delay system have been considered extensively[1,2,5,8,11,12]. Different from some existing results, Lien[1] introduces a positive constant ω to obtain the corresponding LMIs using Lyapunov--Krasobskii theory and Leibniz--Newton formulae. An LMI optimization approach is proposed to find the robust non-fragile guaranteed cost control and used to minimize the guaranteed cost. Xu in [11] are concerned with the problem of non-fragile positive real control for uncertain neutral system with invariant delays in state. For both the cases with additive and multiplicative control uncertainties, sufficient conditions for the existence of the controllers are given in terms of LMIs.

On the other hand, with the increasing of the number of summands in a system equation and the decreasing of differences between neighboring argument values, systems with distributed delays will arise. Distributed delays can also be found in the

---

[*] This work is supported by the Natural Science Foundation of China under Grant No. 60972164, 60904101, 60904046 and the Science and Technology Program of Shenyang under Grant No. F11-264-1-70, F10-205-1-80.

D. Li and Y. Chen (Eds.): CCTA 2011, Part III, IFIP AICT 370, pp. 372–382, 2012.

modeling of feeding systems and combustion chambers in a liquid monopropellant rocket motor with pressure feeding [3,4]. Therefore, many efforts have been made for the distributed delays systems[5,6,7].

To the best of the authors' knowledge, there are a few notes on the problem of guaranteed cost control for distributed delay systems with neutral type, which motivates the present study. In view of the importance of the choice of an appropriate Lyapunov-Krasovskii functional for deriving good stability criteria for delay system, a class of special forms of Lyapunov-Krasovskii functionals are constructed to lead to simpler and less conservative sufficient conditions. Simultaneously, some mathematical techniques are applied flexibly. Finally, a numerical example is provided to illustrate the effectiveness of the proposed design methods.

2   Problem Statement and Preliminaries

Consider the following uncertain distributed delay systems with neutral type

$$\dot{x}(t) = \left[A + \Delta A(t)\right]x(t) + \left[A_\sigma + \Delta A_\sigma(t)\right]x(t-\sigma) + \left[A_\eta + \Delta A_\eta(t)\right]\dot{x}(t-\eta)$$

$$+ \left[A_\delta + \Delta A_\delta(t)\right]\int_{t-\delta}^{t} x(s)\,ds + \left[B + \Delta B(t)\right]u(t) \tag{1}$$

$$x(t) = \phi(t), t \in [-l, 0]$$

where $x(t) \in \mathfrak{R}^n$ and $u(t) \in \mathfrak{R}^m$ are the state and input of system, respectively. A, A_σ, A_η, A_δ, and B are known constant matrices of appropriate dimensions. $\phi(t)$ is the initial condition. σ, η, and δ are the time delays, $l = max\{\sigma, \eta, \delta\}$. Time-varying parametric uncertainties $\Delta A(t)$, $\Delta A_\sigma(t)$, $\Delta A_\eta(t)$, $\Delta A_\delta(t)$ and $\Delta B(t)$ are assumed to satisfy

$$\begin{bmatrix} \Delta A(t) & \Delta A_\sigma(t) & \Delta A_\eta(t) & \Delta A_\delta(t) & \Delta B(t) \end{bmatrix}$$

$$= DF(t)\begin{bmatrix} E_1 & E_\sigma & E_\eta & E_\delta & E_2 \end{bmatrix} \tag{2}$$

where matrices D, E_1, E_σ, E_η, E_δ, and E_2 are constant matrices of appropriate dimensions, and $F(t)$ is the unknown matrix function satisfying $F^T(t)F(t) \le I, \forall t \ge 0$.

Construct the following control law

$$u(t) = -Kx(t) \tag{3}$$

where $K \in \mathfrak{R}^{m \times n}$ is the control gain to be designed, the resulting closed-loop uncertain neutral system is obtained,

$$\dot{x}(t) = \left[A - BK + DF(t)(E_1 - E_2 K)\right]x(t) + \left[A_\sigma + DF(t)E_\sigma\right]x(t - \sigma)$$
$$+ \left[A_\eta + DF(t)E_\eta\right]\dot{x}(t - \eta) + \left[A_\delta + DF(t)E_\delta\right]\int_{t-\delta}^{t} x(s)\,ds \tag{4}$$

Define the following quadratic cost function

$$J = \int_0^\infty \left[x^T(t)S_1 x(t) + u^T(t)S_2 u(t)\right]dt \tag{5}$$

where $S_1 \in \Re^{n \times n}$ and $S_2 \in \Re^{m \times m}$ are two given symmetric positive definite matrices.

The objective of this note is to design a control (3) and determine a scalar J_u satisfying the following two conditions

    (a)   the closed-loop system (4) is asymptotically stable,

    (b) $J \le J_u$.

If the aforementioned control gain K and constant J_u exist, control (3) is the guaranteed cost control and J_u is the guaranteed cost for the considered system.

The following lemma is used for the proof of the main results.

Lemma 2.1 Let Z, X, S and Y be matrices of appropriate dimensions. Assume that Z is symmetric and $S^T S \le I$, then

$$Z + XSY + Y^T S^T X^T < 0$$

if and only if there exists a scalar $\varepsilon > 0$ satisfying

$$Z + \varepsilon XX^T + \varepsilon^{-1} Y^T Y = Z + \varepsilon^{-1}(\varepsilon X)(\varepsilon X)^T + \varepsilon^{-1} Y^T Y < 0 \cdot$$

3   Main Result

Theorem 3.1 Consider system (1) with (2) and (3). If there exist positive numbers ε, τ, some symmetric positive definite matrices Q, $\bar{H}_1$, $\bar{H}_2$, and matrix X such that the following LMIs hold

$$
\Xi = \begin{bmatrix}
\Xi_{11} & A_\sigma Q & A_\eta & A_\delta Q & QA^T - X^T B^T & Q & -X^T & \varepsilon D & \Xi_{19} \\
* & -\bar{H}_1 & 0 & 0 & QA_\sigma^T & 0 & 0 & 0 & QE_\sigma^T \\
* & * & -I_n & 0 & A_\eta^T & 0 & 0 & 0 & E_\eta^T \\
* & * & * & -\bar{H}_2 & QA_\delta^T & 0 & 0 & 0 & QE_\delta^T \\
* & * & * & * & -I_n & 0 & 0 & \varepsilon D & 0 \\
* & * & * & * & * & -S_1^{-1} & 0 & 0 & 0 \\
* & * & * & * & * & * & -S_2^{-1} & 0 & 0 \\
* & * & * & * & * & * & * & -\varepsilon I_n & 0 \\
* & * & * & * & * & * & * & * & -\varepsilon I_n
\end{bmatrix} < 0
$$

(6)

$$
\Gamma = \begin{bmatrix}
-I_n + \tau E_\eta^T E_\eta & A_\eta^T & 0 \\
* & -I_n & D \\
* & * & -\tau I_n
\end{bmatrix} < 0
$$

(7)

Then control (3) with $K = XQ^{-1}$ is the guaranteed cost control of system (1) with the following guaranteed cost

$$
J_u = \phi^T(0)Q^{-1}\phi(0) + \int_{-\sigma}^{0} \phi^T(s)Q^{-1}\bar{H}_1 Q^{-1}\phi(s)\, ds + \int_{-\eta}^{0} \dot{\phi}^T(s)\dot{\phi}(s)\, ds
$$

$$
+ \int_{-\delta}^{0} \left[\int_s^0 \phi^T(0)\, d0 \right] Q^{-1}\bar{H}_2 Q^{-1}\left[\int_s^0 \phi(\theta)\, d\theta \right] ds \qquad (8)
$$

$$
+ \int_0^\delta ds \int_{-s}^0 (\theta + s)\phi^T(\theta)Q^{-1}\bar{H}_2 Q^{-1}\phi(\theta)\, d\theta
$$

where $\Xi_{11} = AQ + QA^T - BX - X^T B^T + \bar{H}_1 + \delta^2 \bar{H}_2, \Xi_{19} = QE_1^T - X^T E_2^T$.

Proof: Choose $P = Q^{-1}, H_1 = Q^{-1}\bar{H}_1 Q^{-1}, H_2 = Q^{-1}\bar{H}_2 Q^{-1}$, and construct the following Lyapunov functional

$$
V(x(t),t) = V_1(x(t)) + V_2(x(t)) + V_3(x(t)) + V_4(x(t)) + V_5(x(t)) \qquad (9)
$$

where

$$
V_1(x(t)) = x^T(t)Px(t), V_2(x(t)) = \int_{t-\sigma}^t x^T(s)H_1 x(s)\, ds,
$$

$$
V_3(x(t)) = \int_{t-\eta}^t \dot{x}^T(s)\dot{x}(s)\, ds, V_4(x(t)) = \int_{t-\delta}^t \left[\int_s^t x^T(\theta)\, d\theta \right] H_2 \left[\int_s^t x(\theta)\, d\theta \right] ds,
$$

$$
V_5(x(t)) = \int_0^\delta ds \int_{t-s}^t (\theta - t + s)x^T(\theta)H_2 x(\theta)\, d\theta
$$

Obviously, $V(x(t),t) > 0$ for all $x(t) \neq 0$. The time derivative of $V(x(t),t)$ along the trajectories of system (1) with control (3) is given

$$\dot{V}(x(t),t) = \dot{V}_1(x(t)) + \dot{V}_2(x(t)) + \dot{V}_3(x(t)) + \dot{V}_4(x(t)) + \dot{V}_5(x(t)) \tag{10}$$

where

$$
\begin{aligned}
\dot{V}_1(x(t)) =\ & 2x^T(t)P\big[(A - BK + DF(t)(E_1 - E_2 K))x(t) \\
& + (A_\sigma + DF(t)E_\sigma)x(t-\sigma) + (A_\eta + DF(t)E_\eta)\dot{x}(t-\eta) \\
& + (A_\delta + DF(t)E_\delta)\int_{t-\delta}^{t} x(s)\,ds \\
\dot{V}_2(x(t)) =\ & x^T(t)H_1 x(t) - x^T(t-\sigma)H_1 x(t-\sigma), \\
\dot{V}_3(x(t)) =\ & \dot{x}^T(t)\dot{x}(t) - \dot{x}^T(t-\eta)\dot{x}(t-\eta) \\
=\ & \big[(A - BK + DF(t)(E_1 - E_2 K))x(t) + (A_\sigma + DF(t)E_\sigma)x(t-\sigma) \\
& + (A_\eta + DF(t)E_\eta)\dot{x}(t-\eta) + (A_\delta + DF(t)E_\delta)\int_{t-\delta}^{t} x(s)\,ds\big]^T \\
& \times \big[(A - BK + DF(t)(E_1 - E_2 K))x(t) + (A_\sigma + DF(t)E_\sigma)x(t-\sigma) \\
& + (A_\eta + DF(t)E_\eta)\dot{x}(t-\eta) + (A_\delta + DF(t)E_\delta)\int_{t-\delta}^{t} x(s)\,ds\big] \\
& - \dot{x}^T(t-\eta)\dot{x}(t-\eta), \\
\dot{V}_4(x(t)) =\ & 2\int_{t-\delta}^{t} (\theta - t + \delta)x^T(t)H_2 x(\theta)\,d\theta \\
& - \Big[\int_{t-\delta}^{t} x^T(\theta)\,d\theta\Big]H_2\Big[\int_{t-\delta}^{t} x(\theta)\,d\theta\Big] \\
\leq\ & \int_{t-\delta}^{t} (\theta - t + \delta)x^T(t)H_2 x(t)\,d(\theta - t + \delta) \\
& + \int_{t-\delta}^{t} (\theta - t + \delta)x^T(\theta)H_2 x(\theta)\,d\theta \\
& - \Big[\int_{t-\delta}^{t} x^T(\theta)\,d\theta\Big]H_2\Big[\int_{t-\delta}^{t} x(\theta)\,d\theta\Big] \\
=\ & \frac{1}{2}\delta^2 x^T(t)H_2 x(t) + \int_{t-\delta}^{t} (\theta - t + \delta)x^T(\theta)H_2 x(\theta)\,d\theta \\
& - \Big[\int_{t-\delta}^{t} x^T(\theta)\,d\theta\Big]H_2\Big[\int_{t-\delta}^{t} x(\theta)\,d\theta\Big], \\
\dot{V}_5(x(t)) =\ & \frac{1}{2}\delta^2 x^T(t)H_2 x(t) - \int_{t-\delta}^{t} (\theta - t + \delta)x^T(\theta)H_2 x(\theta)\,d\theta.
\end{aligned}
$$

Therefore, it follows from (10) that

$$\dot{V}(x(t),t) + x^T(t)S_1 x(t) + u^T(t)S_2 u(t) = \dot{V}(x(t),t) + x^T(t)S_1 x(t)$$

$$+ x^T(t)K^T S_2 K x(t) \qquad (11)$$

$$\leq \xi^T Y \xi$$

where

$$\xi^T = \begin{bmatrix} x^T(t) & x^T(t-\sigma) & \dot{x}^T(t-\eta) & \int_{t-\delta}^{} x^T(s)\,ds \end{bmatrix},$$

$$Y = \Omega + G_1 G_1^T + G_2 S_1 G_2^T + G_3 S_2 G_3^T,$$

$$\Omega = \begin{bmatrix} \Omega_{11} & P[A_\sigma + DF(t)E_\sigma] & P[A_\eta + DF(t)E_\eta] & P[A_\delta + DF(t)E_\delta] \\ * & -H_1 & 0 & 0 \\ * & * & -I_n & 0 \\ * & * & * & -H_2 \end{bmatrix},$$

$$\Omega_{11} = P[A - BK + DF(t)(E_1 - E_2 K)] + [A - BK + DF(t)(E_1 - E_2 K)]^T P$$

$$+ H_1 + \delta^2 H_2,$$

$$G_1 = \begin{bmatrix} (A-BK)^T + (E_1 - E_2 K)^T F^T(t)D^T \\ A_\sigma^T + E_\sigma^T F^T(t)D^T \\ A_\eta^T + E_\eta^T F^T(t)D^T \\ A_\delta^T + E_\delta^T F^T(t)D^T \end{bmatrix}, G_2 = \begin{bmatrix} I_n \\ 0 \\ 0 \\ 0 \end{bmatrix}, G_3 = \begin{bmatrix} -K^T \\ 0 \\ 0 \\ 0 \end{bmatrix}.$$

Define

$$\overline{Y} = \begin{bmatrix} \Omega & G_1 & G_2 & G_3 \\ * & -I_n & 0 & 0 \\ * & * & -S_1^{-1} & 0 \\ * & * & * & -S_2^{-1} \end{bmatrix} \qquad (12)$$

Pre- and post-multiplying the matrix $\overline{Y}$ in (12) by U^T and U, where

$$U = diag\left\{ P^{-1}, P^{-1}, I_n, P^{-1}, I_n, I_n, I_m \right\} = diag\left\{ Q, Q, I_n, Q, I_n, I_n, I_m \right\},$$

and substituting KQ, $QH_1 Q$, and $QH_2 Q$ with X, $\overline{H}_1$, and $\overline{H}_2$, respectively, the following matrix is obtained

$$\Theta = \begin{bmatrix} \bar{\Omega} & \bar{G}_1 & \bar{G}_2 & \bar{G}_3 \\ * & -I_n & 0 & 0 \\ * & * & -S_1^{-1} & 0 \\ * & * & * & -S_2^{-1} \end{bmatrix} \tag{13}$$

where

$$\bar{\Omega} = \begin{bmatrix} \bar{\Omega}_{11} & [A_\sigma + DF(t)E_\sigma]Q & A_\eta + DF(t)E_\eta & [A_\delta + DF(t)E_\delta]Q \\ * & -\bar{H}_1 & 0 & 0 \\ * & * & -I_n & 0 \\ * & * & * & -\bar{H}_2 \end{bmatrix},$$

$$\bar{\Omega}_{11} = AQ - BX + DF(E_1 Q - E_2 X) + QA^T - X^T B^T$$
$$+ (QE_1^T - X^T E_2^T)F^T(t)D^T + \bar{H}_1 + \delta^2 \bar{H}_2, \hspace{2cm} \text{I}$$

$$\bar{G}_1 = \begin{bmatrix} QA^T - X^T B^T + (QE_1^T - X^T E_2^T)F^T(t)D^T \\ QA_\sigma^T + QE_\sigma^T F^T(t)D^T \\ A_\eta^T + E_\eta^T F^T(t)D^T \\ QA_\delta^T + QE_\delta^T F^T(t)D^T \end{bmatrix}, \bar{G}_2 = \begin{bmatrix} Q \\ 0 \\ 0 \\ 0 \end{bmatrix}, \bar{G}_3 = \begin{bmatrix} -X^T \\ 0 \\ 0 \\ 0 \end{bmatrix}.$$

It is obvious that

$$\Theta = \begin{bmatrix} \Xi_{11} & A_\sigma Q & A_\eta & A_\delta Q & QA^T - X^T B^T & Q & -X^T \\ * & -\bar{H}_1 & 0 & 0 & QA_\sigma^T & 0 & 0 \\ * & * & -I_n & 0 & A_\eta^T & 0 & 0 \\ * & * & * & -\bar{H}_2 & QA_\delta^T & 0 & 0 \\ * & * & * & * & -I_n & 0 & 0 \\ * & * & * & * & * & -S_1^{-1} & 0 \\ * & * & * & * & * & * & -S_2^{-1} \end{bmatrix} \tag{14}$$

$$+ \Lambda^T F(t)\$ + \$^T F^T(t)\Lambda$$

where

$$\Lambda = \begin{bmatrix} D^T & 0 & 0 & 0 & D^T & 0 & 0 \end{bmatrix},$$
$$\$ = \begin{bmatrix} E_1 Q - E_2 X & E_\sigma Q & E_\eta & E_\delta Q & 0 & 0 & 0 \end{bmatrix}.$$

By **Lemma 2.1** and Schur complement formula, the condition $\Xi < 0$ in (6) is equivalent to $\Theta < 0$ in (14). According to (12), (13), and (14), $\Theta < 0$ is equivalent to $\overline{Y} < 0$. Applying Schur complement formula to $\overline{Y} < 0$, one can obtain $Y < 0$ in (11). From the condition $Y < 0$ in (11), there exists a constant $\rho > 0$, such that

$$\dot{V}(x(t),t) \le -\rho \| x(t) \|_2^2 \tag{15}$$

Another, by Schur complement formula, $\Gamma < 0$ in (7) is equivalent to the following one

$$\begin{bmatrix} -I_n + \tau E_\eta^T E_\eta & A_\eta^T \\ * & -I_n \end{bmatrix} + \tau^{-1} \begin{bmatrix} 0 \\ D \end{bmatrix} \begin{bmatrix} 0 & D^T \end{bmatrix} < 0 \tag{16}$$

that is

$$\begin{bmatrix} -I_n & A_\eta^T \\ * & -I_n \end{bmatrix} + \tau \begin{bmatrix} E_\eta^T \\ 0 \end{bmatrix} \begin{bmatrix} E_\eta & 0 \end{bmatrix} + \tau^{-1} \begin{bmatrix} 0 \\ D \end{bmatrix} \begin{bmatrix} 0 & D^T \end{bmatrix} < 0 \tag{17}$$

According to **Lemma 2.1**, inequality (17) is equivalent to the following one

$$\begin{bmatrix} -I_n & A_\eta^T \\ * & -I_n \end{bmatrix} + \begin{bmatrix} 0 \\ D \end{bmatrix} F(t) \begin{bmatrix} E_\eta & 0 \end{bmatrix} + \begin{bmatrix} E_\eta^T \\ 0 \end{bmatrix} F^T(t) \begin{bmatrix} 0 & D^T \end{bmatrix} < 0 \tag{18}$$

that is

$$\begin{bmatrix} -I_n & A_\eta^T + E_\eta^T F^T(t) D^T \\ * & -I_n \end{bmatrix} < 0 \tag{19}$$

By Schur complement formula, inequality (19) is equivalent to the following one

$$(A_\eta + DF(t)E_\eta)^T (A_\eta + DF(t)E_\eta) < I_n \tag{20}$$

that is

$$\| A_\eta + \Delta A_\eta \|_2 < 1 \tag{21}$$

This means that system (1) is Lipschitz in the term $\dot{x}(t - \eta(t))$ with Lipschitz constant less than 1.

Hence, by conditions (9) and (15), and (21), one can conclude that system (1) with (2) and (3) is asymptotically stable. From (11) with $Y < 0$, one can obtain

$$\int_0^\infty \dot{V}(x(t),t)\,dt = \lim_{t \to \infty} V(x(t),t) - V(x(0),0)$$

$$\le -\int_0^\infty [x^T(t)S_1 x(t) + u^T(t)S_2 u(t)]\,dt$$

Therefore,

$$\lim_{t\to\infty} V(x(t),t) = 0, \int_0^\infty [x^T(t)S_1 x(t) + u^T(t)S_2 u(t)]dt \le V(x(0),0) = J_u.$$

This completes the proof.

4   Illustrative Example

In this section, a numerical example is presented to show the validity of the control approach. A three-order system with two inputs is considered with the following parameters

$$A = \begin{bmatrix} -25.2 & 1.3 & 3.3 \\ 11.5 & -3.5 & 2.8 \\ 2.9 & -14.1 & -5.1 \end{bmatrix}, A_\sigma = \begin{bmatrix} -2.1 & -1.3 & 0.2 \\ 1.1 & 0.5 & 0.5 \\ 0.7 & -1.6 & 0.1 \end{bmatrix}, B = \begin{bmatrix} 1.5 & 2.2 \\ -2.3 & -0.1 \\ -3.5 & 1.5 \end{bmatrix},$$

$$A_\eta = \begin{bmatrix} 0.1 & -0.3 & -0.1 \\ 0.1 & 0.5 & -0.1 \\ 0.2 & 0.1 & -0.5 \end{bmatrix}, A_\delta = \begin{bmatrix} -2.1 & 0.2 & -0.4 \\ 0.1 & 0.2 & 0.2 \\ -0.8 & -0.4 & 1.4 \end{bmatrix}, \sigma = 0.1,$$

$$D = \begin{bmatrix} -0.5 & 0.2 & 0.1 \\ 0.1 & -0.7 & -0.2 \\ -0.1 & 0.3 & 0.1 \end{bmatrix}, E_1 = \begin{bmatrix} 0.3 & -0.1 & 0.1 \\ 0.4 & -0.5 & -0.1 \\ -0.1 & 0.2 & 0.1 \end{bmatrix}, \eta = 0.1,$$

$$E_\sigma = \begin{bmatrix} -0.1 & -0.1 & 0.1 \\ -0.1 & 0.2 & 0.1 \\ 0.1 & -0.1 & -0.2 \end{bmatrix}, E_\eta = \begin{bmatrix} 0.1 & 0.1 & -0.1 \\ -0.1 & 0.2 & -0.1 \\ -0.1 & -0.1 & 0.1 \end{bmatrix}, \delta = 0.2,$$

$$E_\delta = \begin{bmatrix} -0.2 & -0.2 & 0.3 \\ -0.3 & -0.2 & 0.1 \\ 0.1 & 0.4 & 0.4 \end{bmatrix}, E_2 = \begin{bmatrix} -0.6 & -0.3 \\ -0.1 & 0.1 \\ -0.4 & 0.2 \end{bmatrix}.$$

Let

$$S_1 = diag\{0.5, 0.5, 0.5\}, S_2 = diag\{2, 2\}$$

and the initial condition is given by

$$\phi(t) = [-0.1 + t \quad 0.15 \quad 0.2t + 0.05]^T$$

Applying Matlab toolbox [9,10] to solving the LMIs (6) and (7) with above parameters, one can obtain

$$Q = \begin{bmatrix} 0.0405 & -0.0193 & -0.0007 \\ -0.0193 & 0.0611 & -0.0810 \\ -0.0007 & -0.0810 & 0.1461 \end{bmatrix}, \varepsilon = 0.6067,$$

$$X = \begin{bmatrix} -0.1478 & 0.0268 & -0.2684 \\ -0.0149 & -0.0876 & 0.2976 \end{bmatrix}, \tau = 5.1734,$$

$$\bar{H}_1 = \begin{bmatrix} 0.3369 & -0.1033 & -0.0637 \\ -0.1033 & 0.1822 & -0.0344 \\ -0.0637 & -0.0344 & 0.2582 \end{bmatrix},$$

$$\bar{H}_2 = \begin{bmatrix} 7.8186 & -2.3760 & -1.4933 \\ -2.3760 & 4.0091 & -0.0089 \\ -1.4933 & -0.0089 & 5.0074 \end{bmatrix},$$

$$P = \begin{bmatrix} 60.5751 & 73.8035 & 41.2087 \\ 73.8035 & 151.7409 & 84.4717 \\ 41.2087 & 84.4717 & 53.8685 \end{bmatrix},$$

$$K = \begin{bmatrix} -18.0362 & -29.5139 & -18.2854 \\ 4.8911 & 10.7387 & 8.0133 \end{bmatrix},$$

$$H_1 = \begin{bmatrix} 1.2164 & 1.9843 & 1.1349 \\ 1.9843 & 3.8833 & 2.2436 \\ 1.1349 & 2.2436 & 1.3066 \end{bmatrix} * 10^3,$$

$$H_2 = \begin{bmatrix} 3.0276 & 5.0207 & 2.8767 \\ 5.0207 & 9.8562 & 5.7011 \\ 2.8767 & 5.7011 & 3.3162 \end{bmatrix} * 10^4,$$

$$J_u = 10.7543.$$

5   Conclusion

The guaranteed cost control for uncertain distributed delay system with neutral type is complex and challenging. In view of the importance of the choice of an appropriate Lyapunov-Krasovskii functional for deriving good stability criteria for delay system, a special form of Lyapunov-Krasovskii functional is constructed to lead to simpler and less conservative sufficient conditions. Simultaneously, some mathematical techniques are applied flexibly. Especially, the order of repeated integral is exchanged. Based the criterion, the control gain and the guaranteed cost are obtained.Finally, the numerical example has shown the validity of the present control approach.

References

1. Lien, C.H.: Non-fragile guaranteed cost control for uncertain neutral dynamic systems with time-varying delays in state and control input. Chaos, Solitons & Fractals 31(4), 889–899 (2007)
2. Ivanevescu, D., Niculescu, S.I., Dugard, L., Dion, J.M., Verriest, E.I.: On delay-dependent stability for linear neutral systems. Automatica 39(2), 255–261 (2003)
3. Xu, S., Chen, T.: An LMI approach to the H_∞ filter design for uncertain system with distributed delays. IEEE Trans. on Circuits and Systems-II 51(4), 195–201 (2004)
4. Zheng, F., Frank, P.M.: Robust control of uncertain distributed delay systems with application to the stabilization of combustion in rocket motor chambers. Automatica 38(3), 487–497 (2002)
5. Xu, S.Y., Lam, J., Chen, T.W., Zou, Y.: A delay-dependent approach to robust filtering for uncertain distributed delay systems. IEEE Transactions on Signal Processing 53(10), 3764–3772 (2005)
6. Cheng, Y.C., Hwang, C., Chen, C.T.: Evaluation of quadratic cost functionals for a class of distributed-delay systems. IET Control Theory Applications 1(1), 313–319 (2007)
7. Yuan, K., Li, H.X., Cao, J.D.: Robust stabilization of the distributed parameter system with time delay via fuzzy control. IEEE Transactions on Fuzzy Systems 16(3), 567–584 (2008)
8. Park, J.H.: Robust guaranteed cost control for uncertain linear differential systems of neutral type. Applied Mathematics and Computation 140(2-3), 523–535 (2003)
9. Gahinet, P., Nemirovski, A., Laub, A.J., Chilali, M.: LMI control toolbox user's guide. The Math Works Inc., Natick Mass (1995)
10. Boyd, S., Ghaoui, L.E., Feron, E., Balakrishnan, V.: Linear Matrix Inequalities in Systems and Control Theory. SIAM, Philadelphia (1994)
11. Xu, S.Y., Lam, J., Wang, J.L., Yang, G.H.: Non-fragile positive real control for uncertain linear neutral delay systems. System & Control Letters 52(1), 59–74 (2004)
12. Lien, C.H., Yu, K.W.: Non-fragile H_∞ control for uncertain neutral systems with time-varying delays via the LMI optimization approach. IEEE Transactions on Systems, Man, Cybernetics-Part B: Cybernetics 37(2), 493–499 (2007)

Sustainability Assessment of Regional Water Resources Use Based on PSO-PPE

Qiang Fu, Qiuxiang Jiang, and Zilong Wang

College of Water Conservancy & Architecture, Northeast Agricultural University,
Harbin, P.R. China 150030
fuqiang@neau.edu.cn, {jiangqiuxiang914,wzl1216}@163.com

Abstract. Aiming at poor valuing objectivity for indicator weight in sustainability assessment of water resources use (SAWRU), an indicator system and a projection pursuit evaluation model optimized by particle swarm optimization algorithm were structured for SAWRU, and then the method was applied to the SAWRU of Sanjiang Plain. The applied results indicated that the method not only avoided artificial disturbance when valuing indicator weight but also had the advantages of objective and precise assessment result, feasibility and availability. The assessment results showed that the sustainable grade of water resources use of Jiamusi, Shuangyashan and Jixi which located at Sanjiang Plain belonged to III, and the grade of the other regions of Sanjiang Plain belonged to IV. Thus, scientific water resource use scheme and reasonable socioeconomic development strategy need to be made based on the regional characteristics of water resources and socioeconomic development.

Keywords: Water resources sustainable utilization, Projection pursuit evaluation, Particle swarm optimization, Sanjiang Plain.

1   Introduction

Sustainability assessment of water resources use (SAWRU) is the key problem of water resources sustainability utilization research, the essential means for measuring water resources sustainable capacity and the main foundation of macro adjustment for regional water resources [1]. Presently, scholars, at home or abroad, usually use comprehensive grading method, fuzzy comprehensive evaluation method, grey clustering evaluation method, principal component analysis and factor analysis method to evaluate water resources sustainable utilization. However, human factors exist in the assignment of evaluation indicator weight of the above methods and cause poor objectivity of assessment results. For SAWRU with multiple indicators, the influence degree of each evaluation indicator on water resources sustainable utilization should be correctly analyzed under the least human factor effect, and then a comprehensive evaluation result reflecting the characteristic information of each indicator can be obtained. Projection pursuit evaluation (PPE) model is an exploratory data analysis method which drove by sample data [2]. The method firstly pursues the best projection direction on the basis of sample data characteristics, next judges the

D. Li and Y. Chen (Eds.): CCTA 2011, Part III, IFIP AICT 370, pp. 383–390, 2012.
© IFIP International Federation for Information Processing 2012

contribution degree of each evaluation indicator to comprehensive evaluation target based on the directions, and then obtains the projection values according to the best projection direction and the linear projection of evaluation indicators, comprehensively assesses water resources sustainable utilization with the projection values at last [3]. Thus, the paper used projection pursuit evaluation model based on particle swarm optimization (PSO-PPE) to assess regional water resources sustainable utilization and provided a new and effective evaluation method to the research of water resources utilization.

2   Methods

2.1   Projection Pursuit Evaluation Model

The modeling steps of projection pursuit evaluation (PPE) model based on assessment criterion of water resources sustainable utilization are as follows [4] and [5]:

Step 1: Normalizing the evaluation indicators of each sample

Set the classification criterion sample set of the SAWRU indicators as $\{x^*(i,j) \mid i = 1 \sim n, j = 1 \sim p\}$, where $x^*(i,j)$ is the indicator j value of sample i, n the number of samples and p the number of indicators. In order to eliminate the dimension influence and unify the variable scope of each indicator value, we can adopt the following formulas to normalize the extreme value:

$$x(i,j) = \begin{cases} \dfrac{x^*(i,j)}{x_{\max}(j)} & \text{in case the bigger the indicator the better} \\[3mm] \dfrac{x_{\min}(j)}{x^*(i,j)} & \text{in case the smaller the indicator the better} \end{cases} \tag{1}$$

where $x_{\max}(j)$ and $x_{\min}(j)$ stand for the maximum and the minimum value of indicator j, respectively, and $x(i,j)$ stands for the array of normalized indicator characteristic value in the classification criterion sample set.

Step 2: Constructing the projection indicator function $Q(a)$

Projection pursuit model is to integrate p-dimensional data, $\{x(i,j) \mid j = 1 \sim p\}$, into one-dimension projection value $z(i)$:

$$z(i) = \sum_{j=1}^{p} a(j)x(i,j) \quad (i = 1, 2, \cdots, n) \tag{2}$$

based on projection direction $a = \{a(1), a(2), a(3), \cdots, a(p)\}$, where a stands for unit length vector.

We then make a classification in accordance with one-dimension dispersion pattern of $\{z(i) \mid i = 1 \sim n\}$. A good classification for the method requires the local projection dots as close as possible and the integral projection dot groups as dispersive. Namely, the standard deviation and partial density values of multiple data interspersing among one-dimension space should be maximized at the same time. Thus, the projection indicator function can be expressed as follows:

$$Q(a) = S_z D_z \tag{3}$$

where S_z is the standard deviation of $z(i)$ and D_z the partial density of $z(i)$. Then we get

$$S_z = \sqrt{\frac{\sum_{i=1}^{n}(z(i) - E(z))^2}{n-1}} \tag{4}$$

$$D_z = \sum_{i=1}^{n}\sum_{j=1}^{n}(R - r(i,j)) \cdot u(R - r(i,j)) \tag{5}$$

where $E(z)$ is the average value of series $\{z(i) | i = 1 \sim n\}$, R is the window radius of partial density, which can be settled by test, but is assumed to equal $0.1S_z$ in normal practice, $r(i,j)$ is the distance between the samples, $r(i,j) = |z(i) - z(j)|$, and $u(R - r(i,j))$ is a unit step function. Let $t = R - r(i,j)$, then $u(t) = 1$ if $t \geq 0$ and $u(t) = 0$ if $t < 0$.

Step 3: Optimizing the projection indicator function

We can calculate the maximum value of $Q(a)$ to estimate the best project direction with restricted condition

$$\sum_{j=1}^{p}a^2(j) = 1 \tag{6}$$

It is a complex non-linearity optimization, in which $\{a(j) | j = 1 \sim p\}$ is taken as the optimized variable. Therefore, it is quite difficult to make calculations with the traditional method. We now may adopt particle swarm optimization (PSO) algorithm.

Step 4: Grade assessment of water resources sustainable utilization

We put the best projection direction $a*$ into Equation 2, and then we obtain the best projection value $z_s^*(i)$ of the separation dots of each grade in the classification criterion sample data. We normalize the indicator sample data of water resources sustainable utilization in the evaluated region and put the normalized data into Equation 2, and then we obtain the projection value $z^*(i)$ of the evaluated sample. Comparing $z^*(i)$ with $z_s^*(i)$, we obtain the grade that the regional water resources sustainable utilization belongs to.

2.2   Particle Swarm Optimization Algorithm

Particle swarm optimization (PSO) algorithm was proposed by Kennedy and Eberhart in 1995 [6] and [7], which is a kind of adaptive evolutionary computation technology and swarm intelligence algorithm. PSO algorithm considers each solution of optimization problem as a particle among the searching space and each particle have its own position, speed and adaptive value (*fitness*) decided by a certain optimization problem. The best position of each particle during the flight is the best solution found by the particle (the individual extremum, *pbest*), and then the best position experienced by the whole group is the best solution found by the whole group presently (the global extremum, *gbest*). Every particle constantly updates itself through *pbest* and *gbest*, and then a new population is created. At last, the whole population can comprehensively search the solution region [8].

Set the particle population size as N. The position of the i th particle ($i = 1, 2, \cdots, N$) can be expressed as x_i, speed as v_i and adaptive value as f_i. During each iteration after the initial position and speed generate randomly, a particle updates itself by following the individual extremum $pbest_i(t)$ and the global extremum $gbest(t)$. At the moment $t+1$, any particle i can update its own position and speed by the following equations:

$$v_i(t+1) = wv_i(t) + c_1r_1(t)(pbest_i(t) - x_i(t)) + c_2r_2(t)(gbest(t) - x_i(t)) \tag{7}$$

$$x_i(t+1) = x_i(t) + v_i(t+1) \tag{8}$$

where c_1 and c_2 are constants and called as learning factor, r_1 and r_2 are random numbers changing in the interval of $(0, 1)$ and w is inertia weight.

Then the individual extremum of each particle and global extremum of the whole particles can update by the equations as follows:

$$pbest_i(t+1) = \begin{cases} x_i(t+1) & f_i(t+1) \geq f(pbest_i(t)) \\ pbest_i(t) & f_i(t+1) < f(pbest_i(t)) \end{cases} \tag{9}$$

$$gbest(t+1) = x_{max}(t+1) \tag{10}$$

where $f_i(t+1)$ is the adaptive value of i particle at $t+1$ moment, $f(pbest_i(t))$ is the best adaptive value of i particle in its searching history, and $x_{max}(t+1)$ is the position of the particle among all the particles corresponded with the biggest $f(pbest_i(t))$ at $t+1$ moment. The adaptive value f_i of each particle is decided by an actual optimization.

3   Sustainable Assessment of Regional Water Resources Use

3.1   Study Area

Sanjiang Plain is located in the northeast of Heilongjiang Province (N45°01'~48°27'20", E130°13'~135°5'19") with the total area of 10.9×10^4 km^2, which boundary is the Heilongjiang River to the north, the Xingkai lake to the south, the east side of Xiao Hinggan Mountains to the west and the Wusuli River to the east. The cities and towns located in the region include Jixi, Hegang, Shuangyashan, Jiamusi, Qitaihe, Muling and Yilan. Sanjiang Plain has flat terrain, fertile soil, well climate and abundant water resources which natural conditions are suitable for agricultural development. After years of exploitation and construction, Sanjiang Plain has become the important commodity grain production base of China. Thus, a scientific assessment of sustainable utilization degree for water resources in Sanjiang Plain has the important realistic significance.

3.2   Establishing Indicator System for SAWRU

According to the comprehensive analysis of water resources influencing factors in Sanjiang Plain and the indicator system of supply and demand analysis of water resources in China [9], the indicator system for SAWRU of the region was established and shown in Table 1. The indicator system includes seven indicators (irrigation ration x_1, water resources use ration x_2, water resources development degree x_3, water supply modulus x_4, water demand modulus x_5, per capita water supply quantity x_6, environment water use ratio x_7). For the alternate use of average and interval of the classification criterion for SAWRU in reference [10] made the classification partition undefined, we gave five normalized values in the form of interval for the seven indicators of SAWRU in the study and the criterion was shown in Table 1.

Table 1. Classification criterion for sustainable assessment of water resources use

No.	Indicator	Type	Grade I	Grade II	Grade III	Grade IV	Grade V
1	x_1 (%)	positive	>60	45~60	35~45	20~35	<20
2	x_2 (%)	positive	>60	45~60	35~45	20~35	<20
3	x_3 (%)	positive	>70	55~70	45~55	30~45	<30
4	x_4 ($10^4 m^3/km^2$)	positive	>100	80~100	60~80	40~60	<40
5	x_5 ($10^4 m^3/km^2$)	positive	>100	80~100	60~80	40~60	<40
6	x_6 (m^3 per capita)	opposite	<1000	1000~1750	1750~2250	2250~3000	>3000
7	x_7 (%)	opposite	<2	2~3	3~4	4~5	>5

3.3   Evaluation Results and Analysis

The projection pursuit evaluation model based on particle swarm optimization algorithm (PSO-PPE) was programmed by MATLAB 7.0 software. In the program, we set the population size of PSO N as 400, the learning factors c_1 and c_2 as 2, the inertia weight w as 0.9965 and the maximum iteration time G_{max} as 50. Next we put the criterion and regional statistical data of SAWRU shown in Table 2 into the model and ran the PSO-PPE program under MATLAB environment. After that we obtained the best projection directions $a^* = (0.398, 0.398, 0.341, 0.366, 0.366, 0.404, 0.369)$, and then we put a^* into Equation 2 to calculate the best projection values of the classification criterion date set $z_s^* = (2.642, 1.927, 1.487, 0.986)$. Name, the sample for evaluation belongs to Grade I if $z^* > 2.642$, belongs to Grade II if $1.927 \leq z^* \leq 2.642$, belongs to Grade III if $1.487 \leq z^* \leq 1.927$, belongs to Grade IV if $0.986 \leq z^* \leq 1.487$ and belongs to Grade V if $z^* < 0.986$.

Considering Jixi, Hegang, Shuangyashan, Jiamusi, Qitaihe, Muling and Yilan located in Sanjiang Plain as the samples for evaluation of SAWRU and putting them into the above program, we obtained the best projection values z* of the seven regions for evaluation (shown in Table 2). Comparing it with the projection values of assessment criterion, we can judge which grade the water resources sustainable utilization of the regions for evaluation belong to.

Table 2. Indicator statistics value and the best projection value of SAWRU

Indicator	$x_1(\%)$	$x_2(\%)$	$x_3(\%)$	$x_4(10^4 m^3/km^2)$	$x_5(10^4 m^3/km^2)$	$x_6(m^3$ per capita)	$x_7(\%)$	z^*
Jixi	16.16	39	70.60	14.11	15.67	1663	0.52	1.874
Hegang	12.91	33	32.88	8.07	12.52	1082	0.36	1.465
Shuangyashan	12.86	40	53.00	8.89	12.47	1302	0.24	1.741
Jiamusi	18.82	38	82.17	13.16	18.25	1710	0.89	1.927
Qitaihe	3.07	35	15.69	2.11	2.98	145	0.35	1.215
Muling	1.44	43	5.53	1.10	1.40	219	0.23	1.144
Yilan	6.09	37	28.95	6.71	5.90	766	0.49	1.133

On the basis of the projection values of assessment criterion and the visual function of ArcGIS software, a spatial distribution map of evaluation grades for water resources sustainable utilization of Sanjiang Plain was drew and shown in Figure 1. In the region of Sanjiang Plain, the water resources sustainable utilization of Jiamusi, Shuangyashan and Jixi belonged to Grade III, which indicated that a balance existed between water resources sustainable utilization and socioeconomic development, but along with the rapid growth of economics and the increase of population size, water resources demand will increase day by day, thus making the best of the current water resources, strengthening management and exploiting water resources deeply were important to ensure a sustainable supply capacity of water resources for the socioeconomic development of these regions. However, the water resources sustainable utilization of Hegang, Yilan, Qitaihe and Muling belonged to Grade IV, which showed a low level of sustainable utilization, but the current exploitation degree and use ration of water resources of these regions were low, a good prospect for water resources sustainable utilization can be saw if increasing construction investment of water conservancy project and adopting strict water saving measures for industry and agriculture to enhance the water resources exploitation degree of these regions.

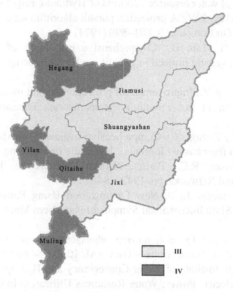

Fig. 1. Spatial distribution map of evaluation grades for regional water resources sustainable utilization

4   Conclusions

The PSO-PPE model for SAWRU cluster and evaluate the samples based on their own characteristics and do not need indicators' weight prior, which avoid human randomicity. At the same time, intuitiveness and good maneuverability are also the advantages of the model. The PSO-PPE model has been applied successfully in the SAWRU of Sanjiang Plain, and it was proved a feasible method and provided a new way for SAWRU with multiple influencing factors.

In the region of Sanjiang Plain, the SAWRU of Jiamusi, Shuangyashan and Jixi was Grade III showing a balance between water resources use and socioeconomic development. However, the SAWRU of Hegang, Yilan, Qitaihe and Muling was Grade IV showing a low level of water resources sustainable utilization capacity, thus a scientific exploitation and utilization plan for water resources combining the characteristics of the resources and socioeconomic development of these regions was required exigently.

Acknowledgements. The study was supported by the Program for New Century Excellent Talents In Heilongjiang Provincial University (1155-NCET-004).

References

1. Song, S., Cai, H.: Bossel indicator system and assessment method for sustainable utilization of regional water resources. Journal of Hydraulic Engineering 6, 68–74 (2004)
2. Friedman, J.H., Turkey, J.W.: A projection pursuit algorithm for exploratory data analysis. IEEE Transactions On Computer 9, 881–890 (1974)
3. Feng, Z., Zheng, H., Liu, B.: Comprehensive evaluation of agricultural water use efficiency based on genetic projection pursuit model. Transactions of the CSAE 3, 66–70 (2005)
4. Zhao, X., Fu, Q., Xing, Z.: Improvement of projection pursuit model and the application in integrated evaluation of eco-agricultural construction. Transactions of the CSAE 5, 222–225 (2006)
5. Wang, S., Hou, Y., Zhang, X.: Comprehensive evaluation method for water resources carrying capacity in river basins. Journal of Hydraulic Engineering 1, 88–92 (2003)
6. Kennedy, J., Eberhart, R.C.: Particle Swarm Optimization. In: IEEE International Conference on Neural Networks, pp. 1942–1948 (1995)
7. Eberhart, R.C., Kennedy, J.: A New Optimization Using Particle Swarm Theory. In: Proceedings of the Sixth International Symposium on Micro Machine and Human Science, pp. 39–43 (1995)
8. Wang, Z., Fu, Q., Jiang, Q.: Soil nutrient management zones based on particle swarm optimization algorithm. Transactions of the CSAE 10, 80–84 (2008)
9. Planning and Design Institute of Water Conservancy and Hydropower, Ministry of Water Conservancy and Electric Power: Water Resources Utilization in China. Water Resources and Electric Power Press, Beijing, 114–134 (1989)
10. Chen, S.: Theory model and a method for qualitative assessment of sustainable development of regional water resources. Engineering Science 2, 33–38 (2001)

Comprehensive Evaluation of Regional Agricultural Water and Land Resources Carrying Capacity Based on DPSIR Concept Framework and PP Model

Qiang Fu, Qiuxiang Jiang, and Zilong Wang

College of Water Conservancy & Architecture, Northeast Agricultural University,
Harbin, P.R. China 150030
fuqiang@neau.edu.cn, {jiangqiuxiang914,wzl1216}@163.com

Abstract. Aiming at the problems existing in the current use of agricultural water and land resources in China and in order to realize sustainable use of the two resources, we established an indicator system for comprehensive evaluation of agricultural water and land resources carrying capacity based on the Driving forces-Pressures-States-Impacts-Responses (DPSIR) concept framework. Then we took Sanjiang Plain as study area (including 6 cities and 1 county) and used projection pursuit (PP) model to evaluate regional agricultural water and land resources carrying capacity. The evaluation results indicated that seven indicators, including the arable wasteland rate, water resources utilization rate, urbanization rate, chemical fertilizer application in farmland per unit area, farmland irrigation rate, production GDP per unit water consumption and agricultural land output rate, were the key factors influencing agricultural water and land resources carrying capacity in Sanjiang Plain. Jiamusi, the main agricultural region of Sanjiang Plain, has the lowest carrying capacity of agricultural water and land resources. However, Muling has the highest carrying capacity. The evaluation results could provide scientific guidance for regional agricultural water and land resources sustainable use.

Keywords: DPSIR, Projection pursuit, Genetic algorithm, Agricultural water and land resources, Carrying capacity evaluation, Sanjiang Plain.

1 Introduction

Agricultural water and land resources are the basis of the people's livelihood and the development. China is a big agricultural country, and along with the speediness of the progress of industrialization and urbanization, the trend that the agricultural water and land resources are misappropriated can not be changed. Misappropriation and deficiency of agricultural water and land resources not only induce destruction of regional structure and attenuation of production, ecology and life function of the two resources, but also directly threaten the sustainable carrying capacity of agricultural water and land resources in China and the sustainable and security production of national food [1] and [2]. Sanjiang Plain has flat terrain, fertile soil, appropriate climate and abundant water resources, which is a good natural condition for

D. Li and Y. Chen (Eds.): CCTA 2011, Part III, IFIP AICT 370, pp. 391–398, 2012.
© IFIP International Federation for Information Processing 2012

agricultural development. After years of exploitation and construction, Sanjiang Plain has become an important grain production base of China and played an important role in guaranteeing national food security [3]. However, under the interference of high strength mankind's activity, the quantity, quality, spatial matching status and carrying capacity of water and land resources in Sanjiang Plain have obviously changed. In the study, we established the Driving forces-Pressures-States-Impacts-Responses (DPSIR) concept framework of agricultural of water and land resources system and used projection pursuit (PP) model to assessment their carrying capacity comprehensively. At last, we found the current status and influencing factors of water and land resources carrying capacity of Sanjiang Plain and expected the results and conclusions could provide scientific guidance for further exploitation and optimal allocation of regional agricultural water and land resources.

2   Methods

2.1   DPSIR Concept Framework

Establishing a concept framework for carrying capacity evaluation of agricultural water and land resources can provide specific research thoughts, principles, approaches and frameworks for researchers; can help them to choose corresponding elements and indicators and to organize data or information; can guarantee important elements and information not to be ignored; and can analyze and solve the problems to be researched [4]. After years of researches and practices, scholars proposed a lot of framework models for agricultural water and land resources carrying capacity evaluation, hereinto, the Driving Forces-Pressures-States-Impacts-Responses (DPSIR) concept framework is the most widely used one.

For the purpose of comprehensively analyzing and describing environmental problem and its relation with social development, the United Nations proposed and developed the DPSIR model by synthesizing the advantages of the PSR model and the DSR model in 1993. The DPSIR model, considering the interaction between human and environment system from the standpoint of system analysis, is a concept framework of evaluation indicator system. It was widely used in environment system and also in the researches of resource, population, environment and agriculture developments.

The components of DPSIR concept framework are Driving Forces, Pressures, States, Impacts and Responses. Each component stands for a type of indicator and each type of indicator includes a number of indicators. The five components of DPSIR concept framework establishing the agricultural water and land resources system can be described as follows [5]:

(1) Driving Forces describe the developments of society, economy and population and the corresponding changes of life-style, consumption and production form of human beings. In the evaluation of agricultural water and land resources carrying capacity, Driving Forces are the reasons causing the changes of agricultural water and land resources system.

(2) Pressure indicators are the pressures that directly exert on agricultural water and land resources system and make the system develop and change after Driving Forces effect. The similarity of Driving Forces and Pressures is that they are both the external force making the system changes, while the difference between the two components is that the action mode of Driving Forces on the system developments and changes is implicit and that of Pressures is explicit.

(3) States of agricultural water and land resources are the realistic performances of the system under various kinds of pressures and the results of joint action of Driving Force and Pressure.

(4) Impact indicators are the final effects describing the state changes of agricultural water and land resources system.

(5) Responses are the management measures used to exploit and utilize agricultural water and land resources system.

2.2   Projection Pursuit Model

Projection pursuit is a statistical method used to analyze and process nonlinear and nonnormal high dimensional data. For the purpose of analyzing high dimensional data, the method pursuits the projection that reflects the structure and characteristics of the data by projecting high dimensional data to low dimensional subspace [6]. The steps of modeling of projection pursuit (PP) model for agricultural water and land resources carrying capacity are as follows [7]:

Step 1: Normalizing the evaluation indicators of each sample

Set the classification criterion sample set of regional agricultural water and land resources carrying capacity as $\{x^*(i,j)\,|\,i=1\sim n, j=1\sim p\}$, where $x^*(i,j)$ is the indicator j value of sample i , n the number of samples and p the number of indicators. In order to eliminate the dimension influence and unify the variable scope of each indicator value, we can adopt the following formulas to normalize the extreme value:

$$x(i,j) = \begin{cases} \dfrac{x^*(i,j)}{x_{\max}(j)} & \text{in case the bigger the indicator the better} \\[3mm] \dfrac{x_{\min}(j)}{x^*(i,j)} & \text{in case the smaller the indicator the better} \end{cases} \tag{1}$$

where $x_{\max}(j)$ and $x_{\min}(j)$ stand for the maximum and the minimum value of indicator j , respectively, and $x(i,j)$ stands for the array of normalized indicator characteristic value in the classification criterion sample set. In the study, the number of samples for evaluation n is 8 and the number of evaluation indicator p is 17.

Step 2: Constructing the projection indicator function $Q(a)$

Projection pursuit model is to integrate p -dimensional data, $\{x(i,j)\,|\,j=1\sim p\}$, into one-dimension projection value $z(i)$:

$$z(i) = \sum_{j=1}^{p} a(j)x(i,j) \quad (i=1,2,\cdots,n) \tag{2}$$

based on projection direction $a = \{a(1), a(2), a(3), \cdots, a(p)\}$, where a stands for unit length vector.

We then make a classification in accordance with one-dimension dispersion pattern of $\{z(i) | i = 1 \sim n\}$. A good classification for the method requires the local projection dots as close as possible and the integral projection dot groups as dispersive. Namely, the standard deviation and partial density values of multiple data interspersing among one-dimension space should be maximized at the same time. Thus, the projection indicator function can be expressed as follows:

$$Q(a) = S_z D_z \tag{3}$$

where S_z is the standard deviation of $z(i)$ and D_z the partial density of $z(i)$. Then we get

$$S_z = \sqrt{\frac{\sum_{i=1}^{n}(z(i) - E(z))^2}{n-1}} \tag{4}$$

$$D_z = \sum_{i=1}^{n}\sum_{j=1}^{n}(R - r(i,j)) \cdot u(R - r(i,j)) \tag{5}$$

where $E(z)$ is the average value of series $\{z(i) | i = 1 \sim n\}$, R is the window radius of partial density, which can be settled by test, but is assumed to equal $0.1S_z$ in normal practice, $r(i,j)$ is the distance between the samples, $r(i,j) = |z(i) - z(j)|$, and $u(R - r(i,j))$ is a unit step function. Let $t = R - r(i,j)$, then $u(t) = 1$ if $t \geq 0$ and $u(t) = 0$ if $t < 0$.

Step 3: Optimizing the projection indicator function

We can calculate the maximum value of $Q(a)$ to estimate the best project direction with restricted condition

$$\sum_{j=1}^{p} a^2(j) = 1 \tag{6}$$

It is a complex non-linearity optimization, in which $\{a(j) | j = 1 \sim p\}$ is taken as the optimized variable. Therefore, it is quite difficult to make calculations with the traditional method. We now may adopt real coded accelerating genetic algorithm (RAGA). The modeling steps of RAGA can be found in reference [6].

Step 4: Comprehensive evaluation of agricultural water and land resources carrying capacity

We put the best projection direction $a*$ into Equation 2, and then we obtain the best projection value $z_s^*(i)$ of the samples for evaluation, namely, the comprehensive evaluation values of agricultural water and land resources carrying capacity.

3   Results and Analysis

3.1   Establishing DPSIR Concept Framework

On the basis of the choosing principles of indicators and the establishing theory of DPSIR concept framework and the characteristics of regional socioeconomic developments, a DPSIR concept framework for agricultural water and land resources carrying capacity evaluation in Sanjiang Plain was established and showed in Table 1. The framework was comprised of five influencing factors (Driving Forces, Pressures, States, Impacts and Responses) and each factor included a number of indicators. Then it formed a multilevel and closely associated evaluation indicator system. The specific indicators are as follows:

Table 1. DPSIR concept framework for agricultural water and land resources carrying capacity evaluation

Factor	Indicator	Jixi	Hegang	Shuang-yashan	Jiamusi	Qitaihe	Muling	Yilan	Sanjiang Plain	a^*
Driving Forces	x_1 (%)	12.3	12.3	15.2	15.9	26.1	13.4	17.6	16.11	0.158
	x_2 (‰)	3.67	0.67	0.38	4.66	7.71	2.99	8.32	3.58	0.017
	x_3 (%)	62.89	80.62	62.26	49.26	56.43	41.72	32.01	58.14	0.359
Pressures	x_4 (person/km^2)	85	75	68	77	145	50	88	79	0.142
	x_5 (%)	31.93	29.48	36.63	41.65	31.32	18.73	42.45	35.08	0.071
	x_6 (%)	93.4	96.4	96.3	98.8	72.9	78.6	98.5	96.1	0.075
States	x_7 (10^{4}RMB/hm^2)	1.56	1.26	1.42	1.38	0.99	1.69	0.7	1.36	0.221
	x_8 (%)	70.6	32.88	53	82.17	15.69	5.53	28.95	55.03	0.464
	x_9 (m^3 per capita)	2356	3292	2456	2081	927	3969	2647	2337	0.048
	x_{10} (%)	50.62	43.81	35.11	45.2	9.8	7.7	14.34	39.37	0.285
	x_{11} (kg/hm^2)	6643	6232	6249	6383	3779	2380	5270	6070	0.000
	x_{12} (kg/hm^2)	138.1	201.2	147	189.7	85.7	64.7	84.9	157.8	0.305
Impacts	x_{13} (hm^2 per capita)	0.38	0.4	0.54	0.54	0.22	0.37	0.48	0.44	0.155
	x_{14} (RMB/m^3)	9.95	15.6	13.28	9.26	142.69	89.17	16.82	13.13	0.260
	x_{15} (%)	16.45	11.4	11.75	20.2	8.34	2.41	5.14	14.17	0.531
Responses	x_{16} (%)	35.45	45.01	41.74	19.26	52.8	74.58	38.75	36.61	0.013
	x_{17} (kw/hm^2)	3.44	2.76	2.68	2.51	2.49	1.19	2.2	2.69	0.002

Note: The data in Table 1 comes from the reference [8].

(1) Driving Forces include GDP growth rate (x_1), population growth rate (x_2) and urbanization rate (x_3).

(2) Pressures include population density (x_4), reclaim rate (x_5) and agricultural water rate (x_6).

(3) States include agricultural land output rate (x_7), water resources utilization rate (x_8), water resource quantity per capita (x_9), farmland irrigation rate (x_{10}), grain yield per unit area (x_{11}) and chemical fertilizer application in farmland per unit area (x_{12}).

(4) Impacts include farmland area per capita (x_{13}), production GDP per unit water consumption (x_{14}) and arable wasteland rate (x_{15}).

(5) Responses include percentage of forest cover (x_{16}) and total motive power of farm mechanization per unit area farmland (x_{17}).

3.2   Evaluating Agricultural Water and Land Resources Carrying Capacity

On the basis of PP theory, we structured the projection indicator function and optimized the best projection direction a^* by using RAGA which simulated the mechanisms of creature survival of the fittest and chromosome information exchange in colony inside. The programs were realized in MATLAB 7.0 software. In the optimization process of RAGA, we set the initial population size of parent n as 400, the crossover probability p_c as 0.8, the variation probability as p_m 0.8, the amount of the excellent individuals as 20, the parameter α as 0.05 and the maximum accelerating time as 20. Then we put the best projection directions a^* (shown in Table 1) into Equation 2 and obtained the projection values $z^*(i)$ of the samples for evaluation, namely the comprehensive evaluation values of the agricultural water and land resources carrying capacity in the study area.

After projection transformation and the beat projection directions determination, the projection values $z^*(i)$ of the agricultural water and land resources carrying capacity evaluation in the study area are 0.847 (Jixi), 0.847 (Hegang), 0.876 (Shuangyashan), 0.836 (Jiamusi), 1.489 (Qitaihe), 2.349 (Muling), 1.490 (Yilan) and 0.853 (Sanjiang Plain). The results show that the agricultural water and land resources carrying capacity of the whole Sanjiang Plain region is relatively low (0.853); Muling is relatively high (2.349); Qitaihe and Yilan are moderate (1.489~1.490); and Jixi, Hegang, Shuangyashan and Jiamusi are relatively low (0.836~0.876).

3.3   Influencing Factor Analysis of Agricultural Water and Land Resources Carrying Capacity

The purpose of agricultural water and land resources carrying capacity evaluation is assessing the current states of resources utilization and their capacities supporting society-ecology-environment system, what more important is finding the influencing factors of agricultural water and land resources carrying capacity in order to adjust the current utilization policies for agricultural resources exploitation.

In the comprehensive evaluation of agricultural water and land resources carrying capacity based on PP model, the best projection direction $a^*(j)$ quantitatively shows the influence degree of the j indicator on regional agricultural water and land resources carrying capacity. Namely, the bigger $a^*(j)$ is the higher the influence degree of the j indicator on it. According to Table 1, the sequence of influence degree of the indicators on agricultural water and land resources carrying capacity is arable wasteland rate> water resources utilization rate> urbanization rate> chemical fertilizer application in farmland per unit area> farmland irrigation rate> production GDP per unit water consumption> agricultural land output rate>the other indicators. The influence degree summation of the former seven indicators on agricultural water and land resources carrying capacity is 0.917. Thus, they can be considered as the key influence factors of regional agricultural water and land resources carrying capacity.

In the process of socioeconomic developments and utilization policy adjustments of agricultural water and land resources in Sanjiang Plain, the measures, enhancing the exploitation and utilization degree of agricultural water and land resources, controlling the urban development speed, reducing chemical fertilizer application and increasing farmland irrigation rate, are the key points that can enhance the carrying capacity of agricultural water and land resources and ensure resources sustainable utilization.

4   Conclusions

On the basis of the choosing principles of indicators and establishing theory of DPSIR concept framework and the characteristics of regional socioeconomic developments, a DPSIR concept framework for agricultural water and land resources carrying capacity evaluation was established. And the framework includes 5 influence factors and 17 indicators.

A comprehensive evaluation model for agricultural water and land resources carrying capacity based on RAGA-PP was constructed and used for the 6 cities and 1 county in the Sanjiang Plain region. The evaluation results indicated that the agricultural water and land resources carrying capacity of the whole Sanjiang Plain region is relatively low. Thus, a reasonable plan for the exploitation and utilization of agricultural water and land resources should be made on the basis of the regional characteristics.

According to the sequence of the influence degree of the indicators on agricultural water and land resources carrying capacity, arable wasteland rate, water resources utilization rate, urbanization rate, chemical fertilizer application in farmland per unit area, farmland irrigation rate, production GDP per unit water consumption and agricultural land output rate are the key factors influencing the agricultural water and land resources carrying capacity in Sanjiang Plain. In the future adjustment of agricultural water and land resources exploitation and utilization, improving the key factors is the core that can enhance the carrying capacity of agricultural water and land resources and ensure resources sustainable utilization.

Acknowledgements. The study was supported by the Key Projects in the National Science & Technology Pillar Program during the Eleventh Five-Year Plan Period (2009BADB3B0205) and Research Fund for the Doctoral Program of Higher Education of Ministry of Education of China (20092325110014).

398   Q. Fu, Q. Jiang, and Z. Wang

References

1. Wu, Q., Chao, L., Zhao, G.: The fuzzy assessment of sustainable agriculture development potential of the soil and water resource in inner Mongolia. Research of Soil and Water Conservation 3, 141–145 (2008)
2. Xue, X., Yu, C., Huang, Q.: The model of water resources sustainable utilization and its application research. Journal of Xi'an University of Technology 3, 301–305 (2000)
3. Wang, Z., Guo, Z., Song, K.: Effects of land use/cover change on net primary productivity of Sanjiang plain, during 2000-2005. Journal of Natural Resources 1, 136–146 (2009)
4. Cao, F.: Research Manual for Indicator System of Urban Environment Sustainable Development in China. China Environmental Science Press, Beijing (1999)
5. Fu, Q., Jiang, Q., Jiao, L.: Researches on Sustainable Utilization of Water and Land Resources in Semi-arid Region of Heilongjiang Province. China WaterPower Press, Beijing (2010)
6. Fu, Q., Zhao, X.: Theory and Applications of Projection Pursuit Model. Science Press, Beijing (2006)
7. Zhao, X., Fu, Q., Xing, Z.: Improvement of projection pursuit model and the application in integrated evaluation of eco-agricultural construction. Transactions of the CSAE 5, 222–225 (2006)
8. Heilongjiang Provincial Bureau of Statistics: Heilongjiang Statistical Yearbook. China Statistics Press, Beijing (2009)

Investigating Image Enhancement in Pseudo-Foreign Fiber Detection

Xin Wang[1,3], Daoliang Li[1,*], and Wenzhu Yang[2]

[1] College of Information and Electrical Engineering, China Agricultural University,
Beijing 100083, PRC
[2] College of Mathematics and Computer, Hebei University, Baoding 071002, PRC
[3] Computer Network Center, China Agricultural University, Beijing 100083, PRC
dliangl@cau.edu.cn

Abstract. The detection of pseudo-foreign fibers in cotton based on AVI(Automatic Visual Inspection) is crucial to improve the accuracy of statistics and classification of foreign fibers. To meet the requirement of textile factories, a new platform is introduced in which cotton bulks are floating with relative high speed of six meters per second, and the throughput of detected lint could be above 20kg per hour. However, images captured by the new platform are blurred and not clear enough for post processes such as segmentation, feature extraction, target identification and statistics. Because thickness of the moving cotton bulks are not uniform, a part of or the whole object of pseudo-foreign fibers are blocked. Thus image enhancement algorithms should be investigated and implemented. In this paper the characteristics of the images acquired by the new platform are analyzed, and several image enhance algorithms are studied and compared on effectiveness and efficiency, which include Histogram Equalization, Wavelet Based Normalization, Homomorphic Filtering, Single Scale Retinex(SSR), Multiscale Retinex(MSR) and Variational Retinex. Result indicated that the Variational Retinex has a better performance and should be implemented in on-line pseudo-foreign fibers detection.

Keywords: Image enhancement, Histogram Equalization, Wavelet Based Normalization, Homomorphic Filtering, Single Scale Retinex, Multiscale Retinex, Variational Retinex.

1   Introduction

The foreign fibers in cotton refer to those non-cotton fibers and dyed fibers, such as hairs, binding ropes, plastic films, candy wrappers, polypropylene twines, etc., which are accidentally mixed into cotton during picking, storing, drying, transporting, purchasing and processing [1]. Similarly, the pseudo-foreign fibers in cotton are some trashes such as dried cotton leaves, cotton rod, cottonseed crumbs, straws, grass stems etc. which have the same color, size and shape as the foreign fibers. Because the quantity of pseudo-foreign fibers in cotton is much larger than that of the foreign

---

* Corresponding author.

D. Li and Y. Chen (Eds.): CCTA 2011, Part III, IFIP AICT 370, pp. 399–409, 2012.

fibers, in order to improve the accuracy of foreign fibers' detection and classification with AVI (Automatic Visual Inspection), pseudo-foreign fibers should be distinguished from the real foreign fibers clearly and efficiently.

Image enhancement is an important preprocessing stage in machine vision. The aim of image enhancement is to remove the noise while retaining significant features of the image [2]. In the past few decades, many image enhancement methods such as histogram manipulation techniques, wavelet based image enhancement and PDE(Partial Differential Equations) based image enhancement have been active and open to researches. And there is no single image enhancement method applicable to all kind of images [2]. Vicent Caselles et al. invented a novel approach for shape preserving contrast enhancement by means of a local histogram equalization algorithm which preserves the level-sets of the image [3]. Wang, X.; Liu, S.; Zhou, X. proposes a new algorithm called wavelet domain Inclusive-OR denoising algorithm (WDIDA), which distinguishes the wavelet coefficients belonging to image or noise by considering their phases and modulus maxima simultaneously and in order to enhance the edges of the image but not magnify noise, a contrast nonlinear enhancing algorithm is presented according to human visual properties [4]. Farrahi Moghaddam, R.; Cheriet, M. propose a novel PDE-based method for the restoration of the degradations in single-sided document images [5].

Previous image enhancement methods work well in the foreign fiber detection platform of low throughput where the cotton layers are thinner and the image of foreign fibers are clearer and more prominent. Yang, W.Z., et al. proposed a piecewise transform model that splits the distribution range of image pixels into two or more pieces, and performs transformation to each piece respectively to enhance the region of interesting [6]. But, in order to improve the detection efficiency, a new platform is constructed in which the speed of cotton flow is above 6 meters per second, and throughput of cotton is more than 20 kg per hour, so the images taken by this new platform will have a background like clouds in the sky and with pseudo-foreign fibers, uneven color spots and shadows mixed into them. Thus the tasks of identification are more complicated, and the probability of misclassification will be greater if we use the previous image enhancement algorithm.

The images acquired from the AVI system which contain pseudo-foreign fibers are usually not very clear because the clouds on of cotton layers. So the pseudo-foreign fiber objects are imaged under uneven lighting conditions and should be enhanced before other processes such as segmentation etc.. Many methods are developed for the enhancement of images which have cloud-like background, dim and non-uniform illumination, some of them are very successful in foreign matters detection in wool or cotton, power line detection in urban area, and face recognition under uneven lighting conditions. For example, LU Xiang-Ju, et al. posed a novel pseudo-color approach which can effectively mark all different particulars while it has the ability to divide foreign pieces with indiscernible brightness in fiber masses [7]. Jing Sun, et al. put forward a new method to detect and remove shadow from solo images of natural scenes [8]. Tang liang, et al. presented a fuzzy retinex to enhance the poor visibility of features in shadowed regions created by buildings in urban aerial images which prevents recognition of objects[9]. Although the above techniques present good results, several disadvantages of the reviewed methods still exist. For example, the contradiction between algorithm speed and precision degree exist almost in every method.

In order to find a better algorithm (relative) to use for the enhancement of images acquired by the new platform in pseudo-foreign fiber detection, several image enhancement methods are studied on principle and effectiveness, and experiment result are showed and analyzed.

In summary, the novelties of this paper are the following:

- A new pseudo-foreign fiber detection platform is introduced.
- Several illumination improve algorithms are investigated and applied to the images produced by the new platform.
- Experiment results are compared and analyzed, and best algorithm is chosen for further studies.

The rest of the paper is organized as follows. Section 2 briefly introduce the new platform, and images samples collected by it. In Section 3, the proposed method is described in details. Section 4 describes the result and presents experimental evidence, while concluding remarks are drawn in Section 5.

2   Image Acquisition and Samples

2.1   Image Acquisition

The images used in trial are taken from the foreign fiber detection platform constructed by the Agricultural Intelligence Research Laboratory of China Agricultural University and China Cotton Machinery & Equipment Co., Ltd. The schematic set-up of the computer vision system is presented in Fig.1.

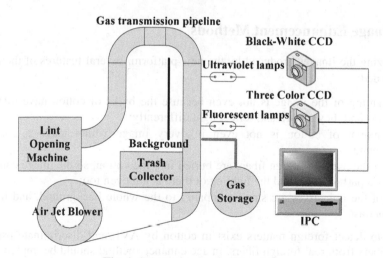

Fig. 1. Schematic set-up of the platform

The cotton processed by the Lint Opening Machine is passing through the Gas transmission pipeline then the computer triggers the flasher when an image is being grabbed by the Black-White CCD lighting by Ultraviolet lamps and the Three Color

CCD lighting by Fluorescent lamps respectively. The image then will be processed by the algorithms installed in the computer,   and both real foreign fibers and pseudo-foreign fibers would be detected. The algorithms should discern pseudo-foreign fibers from real foreign fibers, and the presence of real foreign fibers will trigger the subsequent cleaning processes.

Cotton, foreign fiber, and pseudo-foreign fiber samples are provided by the China Cotton Machinery & Equipment Co., Ltd. which are picked out by human workers, sorted and classified by engineers.

2.2   Image Samples

A typical image that contains pseudo-foreign fibers is presented in figure2 as an example. The size of the image is 4096*60. Because the width of the image, the presentation in Fig.2 is not very clear and we cannot discern the pseudo-foreign fiber in it, so a fraction of the image is cut out and presented as Fig.3. In this image a typical pseudo-foreign fiber maybe a grass leave is buried into the cotton layers and compared to the whole background tiny and dim.

Fig. 2. Image contains pseudo-foreign fibers

Fig. 3. A fraction of the above image

3   Image Enhancement Methods

By analyzing the images produced by the new platform, several features of them can be concluded:

- The lighting of the image is not even because the bulks of cotton have different thickness and they absorb and reflect light differently;
- The amount of cotton is not even in every image which make a complex background;
- Most of the pseudo-foreign fibers are buried into the cotton, so the image can only capture a part of them, and the lighting of them is not even too;
- Most of the objectives are small compared to the whole background, and have a low contrast.

In order to detect foreign matters exist in cotton by AVI, and discriminate pseudo-foreign fibers from real foreign fibers, image enhance method should be implemented before other processes such as segmentation and pattern recognition. Thus several algorithms used in face recognition under uneven lighting conditions and thin line detection in cloudy weathers are studied and compared, which include Histogram equalization, Wavelet based normalization, Homomorphic filtering, SSR(Single scale Retinex), MSR(Multi-scale Retinex) and Variational Retinex.

3.1   Histogram Equalization

Histograms are the basis for numerous spatial domain processing techniques. [10] Histogram equalization is a method that can usually increase the global contrast of many images, especially when the usable data of the image is represented by close contrast values. Through this adjustment, the intensities can be better distributed on the histogram. This allows for areas of lower local contrast to gain a higher contrast. HE is simple and effective in enhancing the low contrast image only if (a) it contains single object or (b) no apparent contrast change between object and background [11].

Suppose the gray probability density function) of image $f(x,y)$ is $p_f(f)$, if the gray scale on point (x,y) is f in original image $f(x,y)$, then we do some kind of transform to it as $g(x,y)$, $g(x,y) = T[f(x,y)] = \int_0^{f(x,y)} p_f(u)du$. So g is a probability distribution function and have attributes as follows:

- The transform from g to f is single-valued, monotonic, and increasing;
- $0 \leq g \leq 1$;
- g is a uniform random variable that distributed from 0 to 1.

As for digital image the histogram of it with intensity levels in the range [0,L-1] is a discrete function $h(r_k) = n_k$,where r_k is the k th intensity value and n_k is the number of pixels in the image with intensity r_k. A normalized histogram is given by $p(r_k) = n_k / MN$ $k = 0,1,...,L-1$ where $p(r_k)$ is an estimate of the probability of intensity level r_k in an image. So the gray scale on point(x,y) is $s_k = T[r_k] = \sum_{l=0}^{k} p(r_k) = s_{k-1} + p(r_k)$. Gray scales which have more pixels will be increased in differential with the previous scale after histogram equalization transform, and in general objective and background possess more pixels, hence the transform actually enhanced the contrast between the objective and the background. At the same time gray scales have little pixels will be decreased in differential with the previous scale after histogram transform, usually the number of pixels in the transition between border and background are small and they are incorporated either in border or in background, therefore the border will be more sharp after transform, so the contrast of image is enhanced.

Here we applied the transformation to all intensity levels, so the resulting intensities have a uniform PDF (probability density function). And all pixels in an image are ordered from the most negative to the most positive (from the one with the smallest intensity value to the one with the largest intensity value).There are other histogram equalization algorithms with different PDF and shape-preserving local histogram equalization, and we shall discuss them in other papers.

3.2   Wavelet Based Normalization

A wavelet is a wave-like oscillation with amplitude that starts out at zero, increases, and then decreases back to zero. It can typically be visualized as a "brief oscillation" like one might see recorded by a seismograph or heart monitor. Generally, wavelets are purposefully crafted to have specific properties that make them useful for signal processing. The main advantage of wavelet analysis is that it can provide abilities of local analysis and refinement in both spatial and frequency domain. And as for high frequency signals it adopt a gradually meticulous steps in frequency or spatial domain, so wavelet can focus on and be used to analyze any detail of objects in a signal or image. The formula of Continuous wavelet transforms is as follows.

$$c(s, p) = \int_{-\infty}^{\infty} f(t)\varphi(s, p)dt \qquad (1)$$

The results of Continuous wavelet transforms are many wavelet coefficients which are called scale factor s and translation function p respectively. If every possible scales or translation coefficients are calculated, the work will be too hard to accomplish, actually only scale factors and translation coefficients that are times of 2^j are chosen, thus the data for analysis would be decreased dramatically. And this kind of calculates are called Discrete wavelet transforms, in general Discrete wavelet transforms are also named dual-scale wavelet.

After the process of wavelet coefficients, the signal should be restored to its original form which is called wavelet restoration, wavelet synthesis or inverse wavelet transform.

The fundamental principle for wavelet transform used in image enhancement is that the coefficients matrix result from wavelet transform represent different frequency traits of image, by multiply them with different enhance factors different traits are enhanced, then through the inverse wavelet transform some part of the images can be enhanced.

Wavelet transfer has been used in many fields of image processing such as image enhancement, restoration, de-noising, compression and so on. All wavelet transforms may be considered forms of time-frequency representation for continuous-time (analog) signals and the method used in this tests equalizes the histogram of the approximation coefficients matrix and emphasizes (by scaling) the detailed wavelet coefficient in the three directions. As a final step it performs an inverse wavelet transform to recover the enhanced image.

In general wavelet can enhance the detail information in an image while give rise to a lot of noises, thus reduce the visual effect.

3.3   Homomorphic Filtering

Homomorphic filter is based on the theory which separate image into luminance component $L(x, y)$ and reflection component r(x, y) like the Retinex.

$$S(x, y) = R(x, y) \otimes L(x, y) \tag{2}$$

In an image luminance can be represented by a gradually changed space while reflection tend to be expressed by a rapid changed space. Thus we can relate the low frequency of log domain of an image to the luminance component and the high frequency of log domain to the reflection component. Because the luminance represent the dynamic range of pixels in an image while contrast of an image tend to be function of its reflection component, Homomorphic filter can achieve ideal control to both components of the image by decreasing the low frequency and increasing the high frequency at same time. As a result the process of homomorphic filter can both compress the dynamic range of pixels and enhance the contrast of an image. The flow chat of homomorphic filtering is presented as figure.

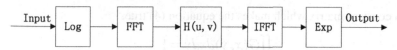

Fig. 4. Flow chart of Homomorphic filtering

The algorithm proposed first transform the image into the logarithm and then into the frequency domain. Here, the high frequency components are emphasized and the low-frequency components are reduced. As a final step the image is transformed back into the spatial domain by applying the inverse Fourier transform and taking the exponential of the result[12].

In practice ideal low pass and high pass filter used in homomorphic filtering which suitable for all kinds of image are hard to find, so the homomorphic filter build on the bases of Fourier transform sometime can't achieve good results .

3.4   Single Scale Retinex and Multi Scale Retinex

SSR and MSR are based on the theory of Retinex proposed by Land in the year 1963 which is an image enhancement and illumination compensation model of the lightness and color perception of human vision[4]. "Retinex" is a compound word came from Retina and Cortex. It is believed that our vision system is subjective when it comes to color perception. Our vision ensures that the perceived color of objects remains relatively constant under varying illumination conditions[13]. Because the principal of Retinex excludes the influences of variant lighting, a series of algorithm is developed based on this theory to detect objectives under uneven lighting or Remote Sensing images in cloudy day or other light lacking conditions.

The formula of Retinex is showed in equation (3).

$$S(x, y) = R(x, y) \otimes L(x, y) \tag{3}$$

The digital image S can be separated into two images: the reflectance R and the illumination L. Then the problem is that L should be estimated from S, and R is the enhanced image needed. There are many ways to calculate L from S, SSR and MSR are two of them and the detail of other algorithms would be discussed in other papers.

SSR and MSR are based on the principal of center/surround and the main idea of which is that the illumination component tends to change more smoothly than the surface reflectance, so this algorithm involves computing an average weighted by the distance from the point in question, and subtracting the logarithm of this average logarithm of the lightness [14].

$$\log[R(x, y)] = \log \frac{S(x, y)}{L(x, y)} = \log[S(x, y)] - \log[S(x, y) \otimes G(x, y)] \qquad (4)$$

$$G(x, y) = \lambda \bullet e^{\frac{-(x^2 + y^2)}{c^2}} \qquad (5)$$

λ is a constant matrix which makes the equation (4) true.

$$\iint G(x, y) dx dy = 1 \qquad (6)$$

The formula of MSR is showed as below:

$$r(x, y) = \sum_{i=1}^{N} w_i \{\log[S(x, y)] - \log[S(x, y) \otimes G_i(x, y)]\} \qquad (7)$$

N represents the number of scales, normally N is equal to 3, w_i is the weighting coefficient. Here w_i is 1/3. The parameter c in equation (3) is denoted as the scale of the algorithm, and experiments indicate that the best multi scales in MSR are 15, 80 and 200 respectively.

3.5   Variational Retinex

Variational Retinex is shown to be able to unify previous methods, leading to a new illumination estimation algorithm. Although it performs well, the computational complexity of this model is relatively high, [15] and quite a few algorithms are proposed to speed-up the method [16]. In this research calculus specifically Euler-Lagrange differential equation of variations are used, and the formulas is:

$$Minimize : F[l] = \int_{\Omega} ((|\nabla l|)^2 + \alpha(l - s)^2 + \beta |\nabla(l - s)|^2) dx dy \qquad (8)$$

$$Subject to : \quad l \geq s, and \left\langle \nabla l, \vec{n} \right\rangle = 0 \quad on \quad \partial \Omega$$

The illumination estimation problem can be formulated as a Quadratic Programming (QP) optimization problem. Here $\partial \Omega$ represents the image, l denotes the illumination component, s is the original image Ω, represents the edge of the image, β a and are non-negative coefficients.

$$\frac{\partial F[l]}{\partial l} = 0 = -\Delta l + \alpha (l - s) - \beta \Delta (l - s) \tag{9}$$

To solve equation (6), the partial derivative of F on l should be zero, and there are various numerical solutions to calculate l from formula (7). Here the idea of the steepest descent with an auxiliary variable is applied, and the initial value of l can be the image s. Through iterations of a given times we can get the estimation of the illumination image, and then the reflectance image or enhanced image can be calculated just as SSR .

4   Results and Discussion

The effect of six algorithms and their histogram are showed as follows.

Fig. 5. The Original image and its Histogram

Fig. 6. Image use Histogram Equalization and its Histogram

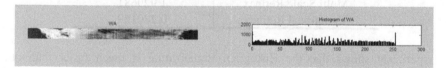

Fig. 7. Image after wavelet Normalization and its histogram

Fig. 8. Image by Homomorphic Filtering and its histogram

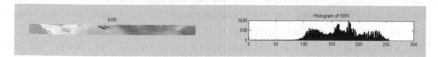

Fig. 9. Image with SSR and its histogram

Fig. 10. Image with MSR and its histogram

Fig. 11. Image with Variational Retinex and its histogram

By testing 40 images the average time cost of each algorithm is showed in Table1.The test images' size are 1000*60 pixels. The algorithms is implement in Matlab R2010a running on a PC with Intel(R) Core(TM) 2 Quad CPU Q6600 @ 2.4GHz 2.39G Hz , memory 3.25GB. If the algorithms is converted to C/C++ programs the speed of execution would be significantly increased, and if a DSP chip is designed and implemented the speed could be even faster than the C/C++ programs.

Table 1. Algorithms' Average speed

Algorithm name	Average speed(s)
Histogram Equalization	0.010004
Wavelet Normalization	0.049369
Homomorphic Filtering	0.036915
Single Scale Retinex	0.634774
Multi Scale Retinex	1.929681
Variational Retinex	0.280129

Experiment shows that the Histogram Equalization is much faster than other algorithms, but the enhanced image have more noises which came from the magnification of cotton shadows in the global enhance process.

The Wavelet Normalization is fast too, although the global frequency transform enhance the noises and shadows just as the Histogram Equalization.

The Homomorphic Filtering algorithm can smooth the edge between cotton bulk and the background, therefore make the foreign matters in the image more prominent. But verges of the foreign matter are blurred which are not conducive to object segmentation. And improvement of it should be investigated in the following works.

The SSR and MSR have the same enhancement effectiveness, but the speed of them are not suitable for online detection.

The Variational Retinex's comprehensive performance is better in object enhancement, shadow removal and process speed.

5   Conclusion

In this paper, a new foreign fiber detection platform is introduced. Images collected by the platform are studied and analyzed. Several methods are investigated for image enhancement in pseudo-foreign fiber detection, their enhance effect and algorithm speed are compared. Results indicate that the Variational Retinex is suitable for on-line pseudo-foreign fiber detection. Improvement on speed of it should be studied in further researches.

Acknowledgements. The authors thank National Natural Science Foundation of China (30971693) and Ministry of Education of People's Republic of China (NCET-09-0731), for their financial support, and China Cotton Machinery & Equipment Co., Ltd. for providing foreign fiber samples and technical support.

References

[1]   Yang, W., et al.: Fast recognition of foreign fibers in cotton lint using machine vision. Mathematical and Computer Modelling 54(3-4), 877–882 (2011)

[2]   Tasmaz, H., Ercelebi, E.: Image enhancement via space-adaptive lifting scheme exploiting subband dependency. Digital Signal Processing 20(6), 1645–1655 (2010)

[3]   Sengur, A., Guo, Y.: Color texture image segmentation based on neutrosophic set and wavelet transformation. Computer Vision and Image Understanding 115(8), 1134–1144 (2011)

[4]   Wang, X., Liu, S., Zhou, X.: New algorithm for infrared small target image enhancement based on wavelet transform and human visual properties. Journal of Systems Engineering and Electronics 17(2), 268–273 (2006)

[5]   Farrahi Moghaddam, R., Cheriet, M.: RSLDI: Restoration of single-sided low-quality document images. Pattern Recognition 42(12), 3355–3364 (2009)

[6]   Yang, W.Z., et al.: A new approach for image processing in foreign fiber detection 68(1), 68–77 (2009)

[7]   Lu, X., Ding, M., Wang, Y.: A New Pseudo-color Transform for Fibre Masses Inspection of Industrial Images. Acta Automatica Sinica 35(3), 233–238 (2009)

[8]   Sun, J., Du, Y., Tang, Y.: Shadow Detection and Removal from Solo Natural Image Based on Retinex Theory. In: Xiong, C.-H., Liu, H., Huang, Y., Xiong, Y.L. (eds.) ICIRA 2008. LNCS (LNAI), vol. 5314, pp. 660–668. Springer, Heidelberg (2008)

[9]   Tang, L., et al.: Removing Shadows from Urban Aerial Images Based on Fuzzy Retinex. Acta Electronica Sinica 33(3), 500–503 (2005)

[10]   Digital Image Processing Third Edition, p.142 (2010)

[11]   Cheng, H.D., Shi, X.J.: A simple and effective histogram equalization approach to image enhancement. Digital Signal Processing 14(2), 158–170 (2004)

[12]   An Investigation of Retinex Algorithms for Image Enhancement. Journal of Electronics (China) (05), 696–700 (2007)

[13]   Almoussa, N.: Variational Retinex and Shadow Removal. The Mathematics Department, UCLA (2008)

[14]   Inface: A Toolbox for Illumination Invariant Face Recognition Toolbox description (2009)

[15]   An Investigation of Retinex Algorithms for Image Enhancement. Journal of Electronics(China) (05), 696–700 (2007)

[16]   A fast algorithm for color image enhancement with total variation regularization. Science China (Information Sciences) (09), 1913–1916 (2010)

Assimilating MODIS-LAI into Crop Growth Model with EnKF to Predict Regional Crop Yield

Sijie Wu[1], Jianxi Huang[2,*], Xingquan Liu[1], Jinlong Fan[3],
Guannan Ma[2], and Jinqiu Zou[4]

[1] School of Geosciences and Info-Physics, Central South University,
410083, Changsha, China
[2] College of Information and Electrical Engineering,
China Agricultural University, 100083, Beijing, China
[3] National Satellite Meteorological Center, China Meteorological Administration,
100083, Beijing, China
[4] Institute of Agricultural Resources and Regional Planning,
Chinese Academy of Agricultural Sciences, 100081, Beijing, China

Abstract. Regional crop yield prediction is a vital component of national food security assessment. Data assimilation method which combines crop growth model and remotely sensed data has been proven the most potential method in regional crop production estimation. This paper takes Hengshui district as study area, WOFOST as crop model, MODIS-LAI as observation data to test and verify the efficiency of EnKF assimilation method. The results show that the precision of crop yield estimation are obviously improved with EnKF assimilation, in the WOFOST potential level the R^2 improved from 0.10 to 0.38 and RMSE was reduced from 2480 kg/ha to 880kg/ha. Our study indicates that EnKF assimilation method has great potential in regional crop production forecasting.

Keywords: Remote sensing, WOFOST, EnKF, Data Assimilation.

1 Introduction

Regional crop yield estimation plays an important role in the agriculture monitoring and food security. Traditional crop yield estimating methods such as investigation statistics, agro-meteorological model forecasting etc. These methods are hard to accurately predict the regional crop production due to costly and time-consuming. The satellite remote-sensing is characterized as fast, macroscopic, comprehensive, objective, dynamic, but restricted to spatio-temporal resolution, most of remotely sensed data only reflect the soil surface and crop canopy radiation information, cannot reveal the inherence mechanism of crop growth and yield formation. Crop growth models based on the crop photosynthesis, transpiration, respiration, nutrition are

---

* Corresponding author.

D. Li and Y. Chen (Eds.): CCTA 2011, Part III, IFIP AICT 370, pp. 410–418, 2012.

successfully applicable for yield forecasting in simple point scale. Because the model input parameters are high variable in the region scale, the simulated results are with high uncertainty. As a method that can integrate the crop growth model and remotely sensed data, data assimilation provides an approach to estimate the crop yield with high-accuracy and becomes the most promising method to predict the regional crop yield.

There are two category data assimilation algorithms: global assimilation such as variation algorithm and sequential assimilation like Kalman Filter. Evensen [2] firstly applied the EnKF data assimilation method in marine area. Vazifedoust [16] assimilated LAI and evapotranspiration (ET) retrieval from the remote sensing data into the SWAP model to explore whether data assimilation of LAI and ET can be used to forecast total wheat production as an indicator of agricultural drought, the results showed that predictions for in advance 1 month with assimilation at a regional scale were very promising with respect to the statistical data. However, longer-term predictions i.e. in advance 2 months, resulted in a higher bias between the simulated and statistical data. De Wit [1] used an EnKF to assimilate coarse resolution satellite microwave sensor derived soil moisture estimates (SWI) for correcting errors in the water balance of WOFOST model, the results showed that assimilation of SWI has clearly improved the relationship with crop statistical yield for winter wheat for the majority of regions where a relationship could be established.

In the study, EnKF was used to assimilate MODIS-LAI and WOFOST model to forecast winter wheat yield and assess the accuracy and applicability of the method. Since the MODIS - LAI data of study area contain some abnormal data, we corrected the MODIS-LAI with Savitzky-Golay Filter. Time-series LAI was assimilated through combined corrected MODIS-LAI and WOFOST simulated LAI. The assimilated optimal LAI was used to drive the WOFOST model in each pixel to obtain the regional yield.

2   Material and Experiments

2.1   Study Area

We chose Hengshui of Hebei province as the study area, since Hengshui is one of dominant winter wheat planting regions (Fig1). Hengshui is located in southeast Hebei and between 115° 10'–116° 34' E longitude and 37° 03'–38° 23' N latitude. Annual mean temperature in Hengshui is 9.0-15.3C and annual rainfall is 356.1-707.7mm. The winter wheat sow in the middle of October, seeding emerge 8-10 days later, grow into over-wintering stage in October, return green in late February, joint in late march, grow into anthesis stage in April, head out and fill in May every year. Winter wheat of Hengshui is usually harvested in early June. Because Hengshui is smaller, the growths of winter wheat of different areas are almost at the same time although growth stage in south is slightly earlier than in north.

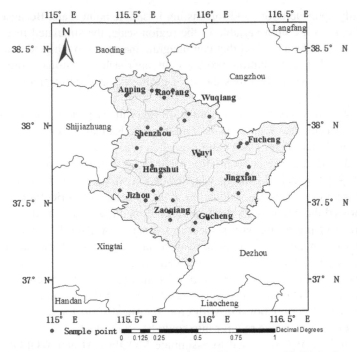

Fig. 1. Study Area(red points represent the filed measured LAI sites)

2.2   Crop Model

We used the world food studies (WOFOST) crop model of Wageningen University. WOFOST is a mechanistic crop growth model that describes plant growth with light interception, takes CO_2 assimilation as growth driving processes and takes crop phonological development as growth controlling [1].WOFOST model can be used in three different ways: a potential mode that crop growth is purely driven by temperature and solar radiation and no limiting factors are taken into count; a water-limited mode that is characterized by the aforementioned factors as well as water availability derived from root characteristics, soil physical properties, rainfall and evapotranspiration; a nutrient-limited mode that nutrient availability depends on the supply of nutrients to the plant roots and is estimated from soil characteristics. The potential mode was used in this study.

To drive the WOFOST model, we collected regional meteorological, soil, crop data. Meteorological data include daily maximum and minimum temperature, radiation, rainfall, wind speed, water pressure between January 2007 and December 2008 in the study area were collected. These meteorological data were interpolated by distance inverse weight method. Regional crop data (including Temperature sum from sowing to emergence, temperature sum from emergence to anthesis, temperature sum from anthesis to maturity, sowing date) and soil data(including field moisture capacity, wilting point, saturated water of soil) were also got with the same method. In the study 1:1000000 China Soil Database were also used.

2.3   Remotely Sensed Data

In this study, we chose MODIS 250m 8-day LAI data which were downloaded from the Earth Observation System data (EOS) gateway (http://eos.nasa.gov) as observation data. The original data were converted to Albers Equal-area projections at 1 km resolution and with a size of 136 * 162 pixels by MRT tool. The pixels without the planted winter wheat were excluded by overlaying the land use data extracted from the 30m TM data and MODIS-LAI data in winter wheat growth stage of from October 2007 to June 2008.

Due to the influence of clouds, vapor and aerosol, MODIS-LAI data are contaminated and needed to eliminate the abnormal data. In this study we used the Savitzky-Golay(S-G) filter method to smooth the time series of MODIS-LAI, restored the spatial-temporal continuum LAI data of fertility period of winter wheat. Fig shows LAI profile with S-G Filter.

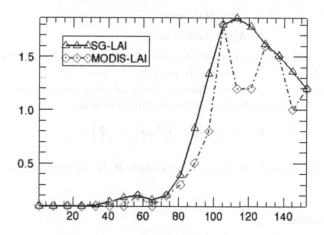

Fig. 2. (a) LAI profile with SG-Filter(Pixel[25,32])

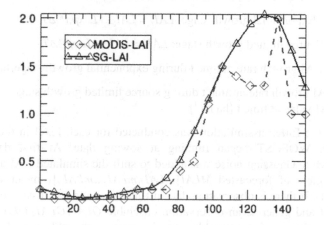

Fig. 2. (b) LAI profile with SG-Filter(Pixel[80,105])

2.4   Assimilating MODIS-LAI into WOFOST

Ensemble Kalman Filter

The Ensemble Kalman Filter is an optional recursive data assimilation method. The basic principle of EnKF is to construct a Monte Carlo ensemble such that the mean of the ensemble is the best estimate, and the ensemble error covariance is the estimate of the forecast covariance[3].At the current assimilation time t ,It assume that we have an ensemble of forecast $A^f_t=(a^f_{1,t}, a^f_{2,t},...,a^f_{N,t}) \in R(n \times N)$ (n: dimension, N:ensemble size) and an ensemble of observation $B_t=(b_{1,t}, b_{2,t}...b_{N,t}) \in R(n \times N)$. $A^a_t=(a^a_{1,t}, a^a_{2,t},...,a^a_{N,t}) \in R(n \times N)$ is the optional estimate Ensemble, the mean of A^a_t is the best estimate of time t. The relationship between A^f_t , B_t and A^a_t is shows in following equations:

$$B_t = HA_t + vt \tag{1}$$

$$A^f_t = MA^a_{t-1} + wt \tag{2}$$

$$A^a_t = A^f_t + Kt(B - HA^f_t) \tag{3}$$

where H is the observation operator that model states to the observations, M is the equation which transform state form time t to time $t+1$, vt is the noise of observation and wt the error which is produced when state transforms. Kt is the Kalman gain matrix; it is computed with following formulas:

$$K_t = P^f_t H^T (H P^f_t H^T + R_t)^{-1} \tag{4}$$

where P^f_t is the variance of forecast ensemble, R_t is the variance of observation ensemble.

EnKF Assimilation

In our study, LAI is the state variable of assimilation, observation data is corrected MODIS-LAI, $H=1(B_t=A_t+vt)$, M is defined as the LAI part of WOFOST model

$$\text{Exponential growth stage: } LAI_t = LAI_{t-1} + Lexp, t*\Delta T \tag{5}$$

$$\text{Source limited growth stage: } LAI_t = LAI_{t-1} + Lsc, t*\Delta T \tag{6}$$

where $Lexp, t$: LAI growth rate at time t during exponential growth stage[ha ha-1d-1]

Lsc, t : LAI growth rate at time t during source limited growth stage
LAI_t : LAI value at time t [ha ha^{-1}].

In this study, the EnKF assimilation was conducted for each pixel in the study area independently. WOFOST began running at sowing date. At first day of 2008 (DOY=1), a white Gaussian noise was added to shift the simulated LAI and generate the first ensemble of forecasted $MLAI\{mLAI_1, mLAI_2...mLAI_N\}$(mean value is the simulated LAI). If there is observation data at time t, we add a Gaussian perturbation-ensemble to it and generate an observation ensemble $OLAI\{OLAI_1, OLAI_2...OLAI_N\}$, then assimilate the forecast ensemble and observation ensemble with EnKF, obtain the optimal estimate ensemble ($MOLAI\{LAI_1, LAI_2...LAI_N\}$) which will be put into WOFOST model to get the forecast ensemble at time $t+1$. If there isn't observation LAI, the forecast ensemble is put into the model directly. Repeat the process until crop mature. The average of $MOLAI$ is the best estimate at time t.

Observation ensemble perturbation: after correction, the relations between MODIS-LAI data its size and actual values has been stable, in this research, the error of observation LAI is seted between 10% and 20%. EnKF Ensemble size: In EnKF assimilation, the ensemble size has great influence on the result and efficiency. In this study we test different size (10, 30, 50, 90) respectively and analyzed the relationship between the ensemble size and the assimilation results. EnKF Assimilation step: The ensemble size has great influence on the result. We set different size (1,4,8,16) to analyzed the impact and chose the best one to derive the finally result.

Finally, we put the optimal LAI into the WOFOST model and estimated the yield of each pixel. For getting convenient viewing of comparison results, we conducted spatial statistical analysis with the Geographic Information System (GIS) technology and calculated the forecast yield of each county and compared the estimated yield with statistical yield.

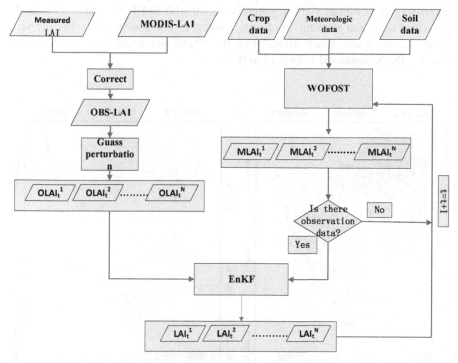

Fig. 3. The flowchart of LAI EnKF assimilation

3   Results and Discussion

Compared with the LAI simulated by WOFOST (WOFOST-LAI), LAI value with the assimilation (EnKF-LAI) are lower and indicates the trend that in over-wintering stage LAI decreased due to the death of leaves. Compared with the observation LAI, EnKF-LAI values are higher before 86th day and lower between 86th and 130th day. The EnKF adjust the time-series LAI trend and values effectively. In the research we found that at single point, when the EnKF ensemble size increases, the difference between the profiles of EnKF-LAI and observation LAI is become larger. For the whole study area, the bigger ensemble size, the better the result is obtained. The confidence coefficient(R^2) increased from 0.25 to 0.38 and the root mean square error (RMSE) decreased from 1020 kg/ha to 880 kg/ha as the size increased.

Figure 4(a) show the estimated yield of WOFOST potential mode. In potential mode, without assimilation most of pixels' estimated yield are higher than 7000 kg/ha, the spatial distribution of the yield has no obvious differences, the reason is probably that in potential level WOFOST assuming that crop growth conditions are the best, in the condition of model parameters are similar, estimated yield are similar and lead to the higher estimated yield.

Figure 4(b) indicate that the estimated yield of WOFOST potential level with EnKF assimilation(with ensemble size of 50 and assimilation step size of 1 day). Through data assimilation, estimated yield accuracy   improve greatly at the whole area, most of the estimate yield in potential mode with EnKF assimilation meets the requirement of spatial distribution of winter wheat production statistics. For the yield estimate accuracy with EnKF assimilation the RMSE decreased form 2480 kg/ha to 880 kg/ha, the R^2 improved from 0.13 to 0.38.

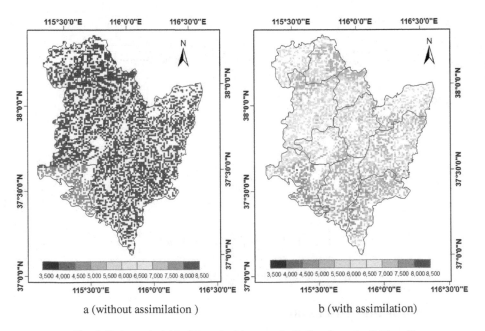

a (without assimilation)   b (with assimilation)

Fig. 4. Estimated yield with and without assimilation (in potential level)

4   Conclusion

In this study we use EnKF to assimilate corrected MODIS-LAI into WOFOST model to estimate winter wheat yield and assess the accuracy and applicability of the method. The EnKF assimilation results indicate that, in potential mode, production forecast precision by EnKF data assimilation is significantly higher than without assimilation. Future work will focus on how to integrate the light, temperature and water parameters information retrieval from the multi-source remote sensing data (visible-near infrared, thermal infrared, microwave radar) using EnKF multi-parameters algorithm to further improve the estimation accuracy.

Acknowledgements. This work is supported by the National Science Foundation of China (NSFC) project (NO.40901161), National High Technology Research and Development Program 863 of China (NO.2008AA10Z217) and Chinese Universities Scientific Fund (Project No. 2011JS142).

References

1. de Wit, A.J.W., van Diepen, C.A.: Crop model data assimilation with the Ensemble Kalman filter for improving regional crop yield forecasts. Agricultural and Forest Meteorology 146, 38–56 (2007)
2. Bach, H., Mauser, W., Schneider, K.: The use of radiative transfer models for remote sensing data assimilation in crop growth models. In: 4th European Conference on Precision Agriculture, Berlin, Germany (2003)
3. Lin, C., Wang, Z., Zhu, J.: An Ensemble Kalman Filter for severe dust storm data assimilation over China. Atmospheric Chemistry and Physics Atmos. ChemPhys 8, 2975–2983 (2008)
4. Doraiswamy, P.C., Hatfield, J.L., Jackson, T.J., Akhmedov, B., Prueger, J., Stern, A.: Crop condition and yield simulations using LANDSAT and MODIS. Remote Sensing of Environment 92, 548–559 (2004)
5. Evensen, G.: Sequential data assimilation with a nonlinear quasi-geostrophic model using Montre Carlo methods to forecast error statistics. Journal of Geophysical Research 99(CS), 10143–10162 (1994)
6. Evensen, G.: Data Assimilation The Ensemble Kalman, 2nd edn. Springer, Heidelberg (2009)
7. Evensen, G.: The Ensemble Kalman Filter:theoretical formulation and practical implemention. Ocean Dynamics 53, 343–367 (2003)
8. Guérif, M., Duke, C.L.: Adjustment procedures of a crop model to the site specific characteristics of soil and crop using remote sensing data assimilation. AgricEcosyst Environ. 81, 57–69 (2000)
9. Li, H.: Accounting for Model Error in Ensemble Data Assimilation. Mothly Weather Review 12, 3407–3419 (2009)
10. Komma, J., Bloschl, G., Reszler, C.: Soil moisture updating by Ensemble Kalman Filtering in real-time flood forecasting. Journal of Hydrology 357, 228–242 (2008)
11. Dente, L., Satalino, G., Mattia, F., Rinaldi, M.: Assimilation of leaf area index derived from ASRA and MERIS data into CERES-Wheat model to map wheat yield. Remote Sensing of Environment 112, 1395–1407 (2008)

12. Launay, M., Guerif, M.: Assimilating remote sensing data into a crop model to improve predictive performance for spatial applications. AgricEcosyst Environ. 111, 321–339 (2005)
13. Li, X., Huang, C., Tao, C., Rui, J., et al.: Progress and foresight of China land surface data assimilation system research. Progress in Natural Sciences (in Chinese) 217(2), 163–173 (2007)
14. Turner, M.R.J., Walker, J.P., Oke, P.R.: Ensemble member generation for sequential data assimilation. Remote Sensing of Environment 112, 1421–1433 (2008)
15. Nie, S.-P., Zhu, J., Luo, Y.: Comparison experiments of different model error schemes in ensemble Kalman filter soil moisture assimilation. Chinese Journal of Atmospheric Sciences (in Chinese) 34(3), 580–590 (2010)
16. Vazifedoust, M., van Dam, J.C., Bastiaanssen, W.G.M., Feddes, R.A.: Assimilation of satellite data into agrohydrological models to improve crop yield forecasts. International Journal of Remote Sensing 30(10), 2523–2545 (2011)

The Reputation Analysis Based on the Signal Game Theory Model of the Aquatic Products of Logistics Company

Jiansheng Zhang[1], Jinglai Zhang[2], Shangwu Liu, and Jianning Mu[3]

[1] College of Economics & Management, China Agricultural University,
Beijing, China 100083
[2] Beijing Commercial Information Consultation Center,
Beijing, China, 100029
[3] College of Water Conservancy and Civil Engineering,
China Agricultural University, Beijing, China 100083
bit@cau.edu.cn, zhangjinglai@263.net,
liu_shangwu@sina.com

Abstract. This article examines the reputation of the aquatic product logistics companies based on the signal model. We use the model to study these companies in separation equilibrium and pooling equilibrium situation and provide a static economic analysis. Suggestions are presented in the end to improve the reputation of these companies.

Keywords: Aquatic product logistics, Signal game theory, Reputation.

1   Introductions

In the operation process of logistics companies, the reputation problem is one of the critical factors that have an impact on their development in China. As with examples of reputation losses in our society, the reputation loss is also prevailing in logistics companies. One of the reasons is information asymmetry between logistics companies and their suppliers. The selection behaviors among those players actually become a strategy of game theory to pursue maximized benefits respectively. For example, logistics companies, who are aware of their own reputation status, tend to get larger benefits by frauds, while suppliers, without intelligence of logistics companies' reputation, are able to get the information to judge the situation only after products are delivered to destination. Thus the signal game method is a brilliant choice and will have a far-reaching influence on the information development.

Economists have long recognized the importance of trust in economic growth, judicial efficiency, government integrity, asymmetric information, and contractual enforcement. It is necessary to solve the asymmetry issue in the labor market in order to thoroughly use the labor market's information. Analyzing effects of information asymmetry on labor market, which is the study of the reputation problems, has started

D. Li and Y. Chen (Eds.): CCTA 2011, Part III, IFIP AICT 370, pp. 419–429, 2012.

from Spence since 1973 [1]. ZhangWeiYing conducted a profound discussion and gave a modeling argument to reputation theory in 1997 [2]. He also explained currently realistic reputation problems in China through reputation theory in 2001 [3]. WengJunYi [4] is an early researcher from this angle since 1996. In 1999, WangXiaoLong [5] explored reputation problems deeply from the view of business ethics. WangXinXin [6] introduced overseas reputation situation but failed to provide breakthroughs in 1998. Yet the reputation problem in his theory was merely a byproduct instead of a well-established systematic research. Other researchers, for instance, LiuBing, LuoYiMei(2000) [7], ZhangLiZi (1994) [8] and LiuGuangMing (2001) [8], LiBinYun(2005) [9] argued to enhance the power of the law in order to make a path for developing the reputation. Liu BinLian and LuYan(2007) [10] papered the aspects of the logistics companies' reputation loss , and its cause and negative effects. Wang HaiLan and WangLi (2008) [11], WangNing and LiuXiaoJin(2008) [12], LiuHongYu(2009) [13] and TaoGang(2010) [14] surveyed the present situation of logistics companies' reputation and reasons and provided resolutions in China. Data from the report of Chinese companies` repution in 2006 shows that the economic cost in the loss of companies' reputation is as high as 600 billion [15].

To sum up, domestic researches of logistics companies' reputation problem in China emphasize on unraveling the reasons and losses, leaving scopes for using practical model to solve the problem systematically and deeply. Nevertheless there are few articles discussing reputation problems in China from the perspective of information asymmetry.

2   Materials and Methods

The reputation problem is practical and puzzling in the transportation process for fish, where logistics companies and fish dealers can make an oral deal. However, due to the conflict of interest, fish dealers will design a considerable complicate contract to ensure their own interests, logistics companies will make a deviation to the fish dealers for their own interests. It is very difficult that   for fish dealers to select a high reputation logistics companies. The paper tries to deal with the problem using the theory of complete information dynamic game model.

2.1   Assumptions

The transaction time sequence between fish dealers and logistics companies is as follows:

(1) Assume the reputation level of logistics companies' isΘ,which may be high(H) or low(L). Let P be the probability of "$\Theta = H$" .

(2) Logistics companies realizes its reputation level and subsequently estimates a rough fresh fish rate as e (e$\geq$0,e$\in$E).

(3) Fish dealers propose a pay requirement according to e based on their observation of how logistics companies operate.

(4) The fish dealer offers the logistic company a payment rate according to the last shipment.

For the logistics company, the average income is positively correlated to the proportion of fresh fish in transportation, which is a widely accepted fact that makes e a preferred variable.

2.2   Model Contents

The model describes a signal game with two participants. One is fish dealers from the competitive market. The other one is a logistics company which sends the signal of the fresh fish rate level, $e(e \geq 0, e \in E)$. Assuming logistics companies are categorized into high (H) and low (L) according to their reputation level. The H company's prior probability is set for P.

Assume fish dealers pay ω to logistics companies. $c(\theta, e)$ is the cost of providing a fresh fish rate of e and $y(\theta, e)$ is the amount of fresh fish. When a logistics company is selected by a fish dealer, the logistics company's income is $\omega - c(\theta, e)$ and the fish dealer's income is $y(\theta, e) - \omega$. One basic assumption is that if a low reputation logistics company wants to get the same fresh fish rate, it has to cost more compared with a high reputation company. "e"s are $\dfrac{\partial c(L, e)}{\partial e} > \dfrac{\partial c(H, e)}{\partial e}$

When it is incomplete information, if the fish dealers observe the signals for e and then get a posteriori probability of H company for $\tilde{P}(H \mid e)$. Assuming the risk for fish dealers is neutral, then we can get a expectation output of the logistics company as follows:

$$\tilde{P}(H \mid e)y(H, e) + (1 - \tilde{P}(H \mid e))y(L, e). \tag{1}$$

Due to competition, fish dealers would take the [4] step.

$$W(e) = \tilde{P}(H \mid e)y(H, e) + [1 - \tilde{P}(H \mid e)y(L, e)]. \tag{2}$$

As a signal game, this model is discussed in two scenarios, namely separation equilibrium and pooling balanced equilibrium in certain conditions.

In separation equilibrium, low reputation companies can't imitate high reputation ones because the cost of high survival rate is not enough to compensate their own costs. Therefore we get:

$$W^*(L) - c(L, e^*(L)) > W^*(H) - c(L, e^*(H)). \tag{3}$$

See fig. 1

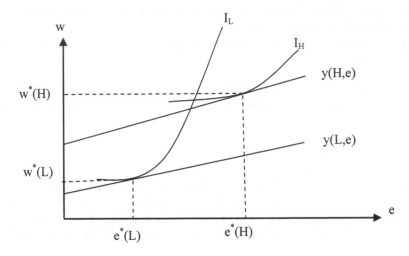

Fig. 1. Separation equilibrium condition

But in pooling equilibrium, low reputation companies can imitate high survival rate and therefore get larger benefits to compensate their own costs.

$$W^*(L) - C[L, e^*(L)] < W^*(H) - C[L, e^*(H)] . \tag{4}$$

See fig. 2

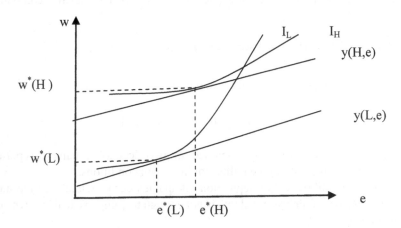

Fig. 2. Pooling equilibrium condition

2.2.1   Pooling Equilibrium

The assumption in pooling equilibrium is that both two types of logistics companies choose the same reputation level e_p , then fish dealers observe the e_p and get $\tilde{P}(H\,|\,e_p)=P$ (P is the prior probability of the H companies). According to the assumption, fish dealers' optimal wage rate is:

$$W_P = Py(H,e_p)+(1-P)y(L,e_p). \tag{5}$$

In the disequilibrium path, here we get:

$$\tilde{P}(H\,|\,e) = \begin{cases} P & e=e_p \\ 0 & e \neq e_p \end{cases}. \tag{6}$$

According to (2), the optimal choice for fish dealers is:

$$W(e) = \begin{cases} w_P & ,e=e_p \\ y(L,e) & , e\neq e_p \end{cases} \tag{7}$$

Given fish dealer's given reaction, logistics companies that have a reputation of θ will be forced to choose a e by the following condition:

$$\max_e [w(e)-c(\theta,e)]. \tag{8}$$

The equation (8) is really simple, logistics companies with reputation of θ choose a e_p or make $y(L,e)-c(\theta,e)$ get the optimal fresh fish rate and rightly equal to the low reputation logistics companies' $e^*(L)$. In fig. 3, the former choice is optimal for both types of companies that the low reputation companies' indifference curves through the point $[e^*(L),w^*(L)]$ are below the point (e_p,w_p)'s indifference curves and the high ones' indifference curves through the point (e_p,w_p) are above the payment function of $w = y(L,e)$. The outcome is that, according to the given indifference curves in fig. 3, the amount of products and the value in graph, the companies' strategy of $[e(L)=e_p,e(H)=e_p]$,the inference $\tilde{P}(H\,|\,e)$ in (6) and the dealers' strategy of $w(e)$ in (7)combined to the perfect bayesian pooling equilibrium of the game.

Even for the indifference curves and the amount of products in fig. 3, there are also many other perfect poolings, some of which are chosen the different fresh fish rate and of other which are in the different disequilibrium signals.

Obviously, in fig. 3, as long as the fresh fish rate is between e^* and e', it is easy to constitute more infinite pooling equilibriums.

It can be inferred that we can also get other pooling equilibriums by solely changing the path of information disequilibrium.

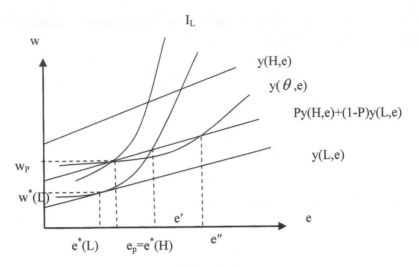

Fig. 3. Pooling equilibrium

Exchange the (6) to:

$$\tilde{P}(H|e)=\begin{cases} 0 & e\leq e'' \quad but \quad e\neq e_p \\ P & e=e_p \\ P & e>e'' \end{cases} \qquad (9)$$

The e_p is a random signal located in between $e^*(H)$ and e'. The fish dealers' strategy is :

$$W(e)=\begin{cases} y(L,e) & e\leq e'' \quad but \quad e\neq e_p \\ w_p & e=e_p \\ w_p & e>e'' \end{cases} \qquad (10)$$

For the H logistics companies, if they choose e_p, the benefits locate in the I_H through the (w_p,e_p). When they choose $e\leq e''$ but $e\neq e_p$, they locate in the indifference curve of $y(L,e)$. When they do $e>e''$, they make below the I_H. So e_p is the optimal choice. For the L logistics companies, if they choose e_p, the benefits locate in the I_L. when they choose $e\leq e''$ but $e\neq e_p$, they locate in the indifference curve of $y(L,e)$. When they do $e>e''$, they make below the I_L. So e_p is also the optimal choice.

2.2.2 Separation Equilibrium

Additionally, we investigate the separation equilibrium situation, see figure 1. Obviously, the most natural of separation of logistics company strategy equilibrium is for $[e(L)=e^*(L),e(H)=e^*(H)]$. After the signal, fish dealers get a posteriori probability for:

$$\tilde{P}(H \mid e^*(L)) = 0 \text{ and } \tilde{P}(H \mid e^*(H)) = 1.$$ (11)

According to (2) we get a result as follows :

$$W(e^*(L)) = W^*(L) \text{ and } W(e^*(H)) = W^*(H).$$ (12)

Under the disequilibrium condition, the provisions are as follows:

$$\tilde{P}(H \mid e) = \begin{cases} 0 & e < e^*(H) \\ 1 & e \ge e^*(H) \end{cases}.$$ (13)

The optimal choice for fish dealers are:

$$W(e) = \begin{cases} y(L,e) & e < e^*(H) \\ y(H,e) & e \ge e^*(H) \end{cases}.$$ (14)

For the H logistics companies, if they choose $e^*(H)$, the benefits locate in an indifference curve I_H and if they choose $e > e^*(H)$, it locates below it , so e is inferior to $e^*(H)$.When it comes to $e < e^*(H)$, they gets $y(L,e)$ .At this time , it locates below the I_H , and according to the fig.1 it is in the lower indifference curve . We have got the benefits for $y(H,e)$ when it is in the $e > e^*(H)$ and the income is inferior to $e^*(H)$. So the $e^*(H)$ is the optimal choice.

For the L logistics companies, if they choose $e < e^*(H)$, they get $y(L,e)$ that is necessarily less than the benefits when they choose $e^*(L)$ .Because $e^*(L)$ is the biggest fresh fish rate under the function of $w = y(L,e)$. When they do $e \ge e^*(H)$, they make $y(H,e)$ and their net income is paid for $y(H,e) - c(L,e)$. According to fig. 1, this negative net profit is obviously less than zero net profit when they choose $e^*(L)$. So $e^*(L)$ is the optimal choice.

If we assume geometric relations in figure 2 instead of in figure. 1, we study the separation equilibrium. At this point, due to the tendency of being imitated, high reputation logistics companies need to take actions to resist it and require higher costs to obtain a higher fresh rate, thus making it difficult for imitation to continue. At last it appears a separation equilibrium. Fish dealers, who observe the costs of the high fresh fish rate, also consider these companies as high reputation ones and then offer them a higher wage rate as a reward.

Thus, we know that the high reputation logistics companies need to choose $e_s > e^*(H)$ to constitute separation equilibrium. See fig.4.

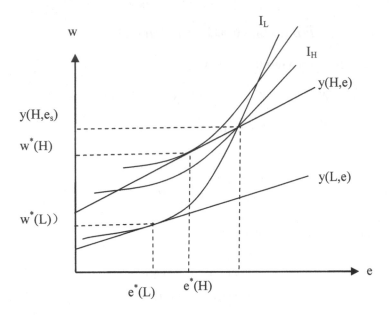

Fig. 4. Sending signals costs in separation equilibrium

Between $e^*(H)$ and e_s, if the imitation activities can confuse fish dealers in identifying reputation level, then low reputation logistics company has motivations to do so. When the high reputation logistics company sends a signal e_s, the low one replicates the choice . If it gets no difference with the imitation e_s to expose its own type of $e^*(L)$, it will choose $e^*(L)$.Then with logistics company's strategy the signals of the information set is given below and to prove that they make up a separate equilibrium.

Logistics company's strategy is

$$e(\theta) = \begin{cases} e^*(L) & \theta = L \\ e_s & \theta = H \end{cases} . \tag{15}$$

When fish dealers observe signals, there is a posteriori probability for

$$\tilde{P}(H \mid e) = \begin{cases} 0 & e < e_s \\ 1 & e \ge e_s \end{cases} . \tag{16}$$

The optimal choice of fish dealers is

$$W(e) = \begin{cases} y(L,e) & e < e_s \\ y(H,e) & e \geq e_s \end{cases}. \tag{17}$$

For the low reputation logistics company, selecting $e^*(L)$ and e_s gets a net earning of zero, but others gets a negative net earning , fore assumption results the optimal $e^*(L)$. For the high reputation logistics company, at that time, if they choose $e \geq e_s$, the benefits locate below an indifference curve I_H and if they choose $e < e_s$, it also locates below it, so e_s is the optimal choice.

The game also includes other separation equilibriums. In some separation equilibriums, high reputation logistics companies choose different fresh rates and low ones keep fixed $e^*(L)$. In other separation equilibriums, high reputation logistics companies stay put in e_s while the low ones keep $e^*(L)$, although signals in the disequilibrium path are different. As to the former one, setting $\hat{e}$ is higher than the fresh rate of e_s but high enough rather to be considered themselves as the low reputation logistics companies than to make the high ones want to choose $\hat{e}$, namely $\hat{e}$ in fig. 4. If we exchange the "e_s"s to "$\hat{e}$"s in $\tilde{P}(H|e)$ and $W(e)$ in fig. 4, the formed dealers' signals and strategies combined with logistics company strategies produce a separate equilibrium. As for the latter one, the fresh fish rate is between $e^*(H)$ and e_s, and strictly positive and small enough in order to get a strategy of $W(e)$ which is strictly below the indifference curve that the low reputation logistics companies go right through $[e^*(L), w^*(L)]$.

3   Conclusions and Discussion

Based on current achievements in economics and realistic information asymmetry problems, the article discusses the reputation theory between the fish dealers and the logistics companies in aquatic logistics supply chain, and analyzes the reputation relations between them using Spence's models from the perspective of game theory.

Several measures can be taken to establish more stable relations with fish dealers and enhance the development of modern logistics industry, for instance:

(1) Offer a price high enough to high reputation logistics companies in order to make them feel worthwhile to keep their reputation, and to ensure that long-term revenues are not less than short-term income.

(2) For low reputation logistics companies, effective regulations and punishment mechanism should be founded. Once frauds are found in such companies, fish dealers can fire them and discard them afterwards

(3) Use the "collectivism" punishment mechanism. If a logistics company's reputation is low, all dealers in one transaction region will participate in this mechanism and ensure that any company in blacklist will never be hired again.

(4) For the companies in the pooling equilibrium situation, namely low reputation ones that imitate high ones, government should on one hand establish stricter laws for prevention and punishment, and on the other hand launch favorable policies to promote the logistics industry. Try to turn the pooling equilibrium into the separation equilibrium, thus eliminating low reputation companies or helping them convert to high reputation companies.

Applications of strict measures to control dynamic information and to monitor the logistics companies' reputation can to some extent lead logistics industry to a better stage. However in face of many different equilibriums, it is crucial to understand why certain equilibrium is eventually chosen and its subsequent development. This article does not explore how to gradually squeeze out low reputation companies from the industry, or change into the high reputation companies, which, hopefully, I will be able to supplement in later researches.

Ackonwledgements. The authors would like to thank Project supported by the public welfare project of the agriculture industry of the Ministry of Agriculture, (200903009) & Chinese Universities Scientific Fund (2010JS027).

References

1. Spence, M.: Job Market Signaling. Quaterly Journal of Ecomomic, 355–374 (1973)
2. Zhang, W.Y.: The game theory and information economics. Shanghai Sanlian publishing (1997)
3. Zhang, W.Y.: The property rights, government and reputation, vol. (6). Shanghai Sanlian Publishing Company (2001)
4. Weng, J.Y: The enterprise reputation system dynamic game analysis.The Economist (January 1996)
5. Wang, X.X.: The management theory and development of reputation. The Economics of Dynamic (January 1998)
6. Liu, B., Luo, Y.M.: Dicussing a new stage reputation management on enterprise management. Chinese Soft Science (May 2000)
7. Zhang, L.Z.: Discussing the causes and management of the forged and fake commodity. The Economy Research (April 1994)
8. Liu, G.M.: The dissolve of the reputation and the economic reputation crisis. Journal of Economic Management (July 2001)
9. Li, B.Y.: The third logistics, the management of the supply line, reputation and law. The Science and Technology in China (November 2005)
10. Liu, B.L., Lu, Y.: The reputation in the third logistics and the exploring of its' regulation. The Logistic Science and Technology 26(1), 17–21 (2007)
11. Wang, H.L., Wang, L.: The reputation problems and the solution research in the process of the development of the logistics. ShanXi Finance and Economics University 30(2), 34–35 (2008)
12. Wang, N.: The discussing for the logistic companies' reputation in China. The Logistics' Science and Technology (9), 122–123 (2008)
13. Liu, X.J., Liu, H.Y.: The research of the logistic companies' reputation. The Running and Management 22, 111–112 (2009)

14. Tao, G.: The meditation for the system building of China's logistic reputation. Logistic Engineering and Management 32(6), 35–38 (2010)
15. Yu, Z.J.: The cost is highly 600 billions per year for the reputation of China's companies. The Times of the Construction 7(6) (2006)
16. Bai, C.Y.: Credit problems in the modern society. People's University of China, 4–14 (May 2006)
17. Hong, B.C., Hu, Z., Yan, X.Y.: The theory analysis of the companies' reputation loss in China. Economic Research Journal (9), 85–93 (2006)
18. Zhang, W.Y.: Reputational Foundation of the Legal System. Economic Research Journal (1), 3–13 (2002)
19. Long, Y.Y.: The reputation in game evolution. Southwestern University of Finance and Economics Research, 1–20 (April 2007)
20. Jin, J.: The game analysis of the companies' reputation behavior, pp. 20–22. Chongqing university (March 2003)
21. Xu, H.: The research of companies' reputation, pp. 12–16. Northwestern university (April 2002)
22. Cao, X.N.: The research of companies' reputation problems, pp. 3–8. Huazhong university of science and technology (May 2004)
23. Gibbons, R.: The game theory foundation, pp. 150–160. China social science press (March 1999)

Principal Component Analysis
of Anhui Agricultural Industrialization

Li Chen

Anhui Institute of Architectural and Industry, Hefei 230022, China
chinalichina@163.com

Abstract. This paper is discussed the Anhui agricultural industrialization using the method of principal component analysis. The indexes include per capita net income of farmers in Anhui province, non-agricultural employment rate, urbanization rate, the total power of agricultural mechanization, universal ratio of rural water, car villages, the proportion of industrial waste water by sewage treatment in total emission. Results show that Anhui agricultural industrialization is still at a relatively low level, thus accelerating the pace of agricultural industrialization has become the key of economic development in Anhui province. Finally, this article provides the specific policy recommendations to accelerate agricultural industrialization and reduces the gap of income.

Keywords: Agricultural Industrialization, Principal Component Analysis, Index System Introductions.

Introduction

The statistical data of Anhui from 2006 to 2010 shows that the gap of income between urban and rural residents in Anhui province is continued expanded. The gap between urban and rural residents is essential to the agriculture, and they correspond to three aspects, the industrialization of agriculture, rural urbanization and increasing the income of peasants. The important thing among them is the industrialization of agriculture. Industrialization of agriculture will realize the increase in farmers' income, and improve the rural economic development level, thus promote the development of the local economy.

What is the agricultural industrialization? Although definitions vary as to what industrialization of agriculture actually represents, one description provided by the council on food, agricultural and resource economics is as follows: Industrialization in agriculture refers to the increasing consolidation of farms and to vertical coordination among the stages of the food and fiber system. The internal structure of agriculture is optimized fundamentally. Integration and development in industrial and agricultural is realized.

Agricultural industrialization is the development of a region important to the performance of the agricultural economy.

This paper we propose the method of principal component analysis to discuss agricultural industrialization. The indexes include per capita net income of farmers in

D. Li and Y. Chen (Eds.): CCTA 2011, Part III, IFIP AICT 370, pp. 430–435, 2012.

Anhui province, non-agricultural employment rate, urbanization rate, the total power of agricultural mechanization, universal ratio of rural water, car villages, the proportion of industrial waste water by sewage treatment in total emission. As a multivariate statistical method, principal component analysis (PCA) is a powerful tool to empirical analysis.

1   The Empirical Model, Methods and Analysis

In order to analyze problems comprehensively and systematically, we must consider a number of factors. These factors referred to indicators which involved in the multivariate statistical analysis and they reflected the agricultural industrialization. The indexes of Anhui agricultural industrialization have correlation to each other, and they tend to get information from the statistical data which reflect to the extent overlap. Variables in the multivariate statistical method will increase the computational cost and increased complexity of the problem. The process of carrying out quantitative analysis will get more information, which involved fewer variables. Principal component analysis was generated to adapt to this requirement, and the idea is the tool to solve such problems.

PCA is known as matrix data analysis.It is a mathematical procedure that uses an orthogonal transformation to convert a set of observations of possibly correlated variables into a set of values of uncorrelated variables.

For example, We set up a number of indicators in the target system, and the number of such indicators are often large. There is a link between these indicators. Often, operation of PCA can be thought of as revealing the internal structure of the data in a way which best explains the variance in the data. In this case, the principal component analysis of the characteristics that can convert a large number of linear correlation index of indicators into the small number of linear independent. That is to say, this is done by using only the first few principal components so that the dimensionality of the transformed data is reduced. The number of principal components is less than or equal to the number of original variables.

2   Empirical Analysis of Anhui Agricultural Industrialization

2.1   Basic Ideas in Index System

The methods of industrial agriculture are technoscientific, economic, and political. They include innovation in agricultural machinery and farming methods, genetic technology, techniques for achieving economies of scale in production, the creation of new markets for consumption, the application of patent protection to genetic information, and global trade.

Only, single indicator can not fully show the level of agricultural industrialization in the region. It must establish a comprehensive assessment of the index system of agricultural industrialization, and scientific evaluation of agricultural industrialization approach is necessary.

Industrialization of agriculture is focused on the consumer. It implies that changes in agriculture are occurring so that the industry can better meet the demands of consumers. Anhui is a major agricultural province, and it is rich in agricultural resources. How to change the resource advantage into economic advantage of agricultural products is the key to revitalize the rural economy of Anhui. The development of agricultural product processing industry can improve the quality and agricultural products that value-added, and transfer rural labor. The focus of value-added agriculture is always on the final food product rather than the initial bulk commodity. Value-added agriculture is expected to provide higher profit margins, and it adds more value to the agricultural product. It can improve economic and social benefits, and promote rural economic development. Developing agricultural products can stimulate the development of related industries, and promote the process of industrialization in rural areas of Anhui. Appropriate understanding of the level of agricultural industrialization of Anhui and the existing problems and shortcomings, can speed up the process of agricultural industrialization. The promotion of prosperity and development of agricultural economy is the evaluation process of industrialization in agriculture to the highest standards. Often, the unity of the speed and efficiency can be thought of the important in agricultural industrialization, and we insist on the principle of comprehensive and coordinated development of the agricultural economy and rural society.

2.2   The Basic Framework of Indicator System

Per capita net income of rural is a reflection of the level of agricultural productivity, and it is development indicators. Structural indicators reflect the strength of a regional agricultural economy, agricultural technology advancement and improvement of the competitiveness. They speed up industrial restructuring and upgrading. The structure of agricultural labor force indicators reflected the process of industrialization, and can make labor from low productivity sectors to high productivity sectors of the transfer process. Representation is non-agricultural labor force indicators for the proportion of total agricultural labor force. Agricultural technology is a broad concept, which includes agricultural mechanization. Mechanization is the core of the new and the main features of agricultural industrialization. Agricultural mechanization level is a measure of essential new industrialization process of agriculture. Specific target is the total power of agricultural mechanization. It is science and technology indicator. Infrastructure indicators include number of villages benefited from water, car villages. Resources and environmental indicator is the proportion of industrial wastewater treatment by sewage treatment in total emission.

2.3   Empirical Analysis

PCA is one of the most widely used dimensionality reduction techniques for data analysis and compression. It is based on transforming a large number of variables into a smaller number of uncorrelated variables PCA is employed to reduce the high dimensional data vectors. The identification index of a network connection is represented as a single number.

We can obtain the variance of each principal component, which corresponds to the original principal components. In general, we only extract the first few principal components. The front four rate of cumulative eigenvalue contribution is 94.342 percent. It is more than 85 percent of the principle, so we select the first four eigenvalues. We decided to use four new variable to replace the original seven variables.

Integrated model values based on principal component can be calculated, the results can be seen from table 1.

According to the agricultural industrialization evaluation index system, we select the indicators of Anhui province during the year from 2005 to 2009. Average data of the five year is the raw data.We standardized the raw data, and then use SPSS software for data processing. We selected the comprehensive scores and total score in cities, such as Huaibei, Bozhou City, Huangshan City, Hefei, Chaohu City, Luan, Anqing City, Chuzhou, Wuhu City. The score of the cities are sorted to their average level of agricultural industrialization and the development of a comparative analysis.

Table 1. Principal component scores

City	principal component scores	rankings
Bozhou	1.47	1
Luan	1.16	2
Hefei	0.46	3
Anqing	0.21	4
Chaohu	0.05	5
Chuzhou	-0.30	6
Huaibei	-0.43	7
Chizhou	-0.47	8
Wuhu	-0.73	9
Huangshan	-1.41	10

2.4   The Results of Principal Component Analysis

Combined principal component analysis, we can get the following results:

Comprehensive value of Bozhou city and Luan is higher respectively, and they are the first and the second rows. Agricultural industrialization and urban development of the two cities is better. Although they are both the northern city of Anhui province, Bozhou and Huaibei have the different level of industrialization in agriculture. Mechanization of agriculture in its total power in Huaibei is much smaller than that of Bozhou City. The same for level of technology in the northern city of Huaibei ,it is far less than that of Bozhou.

Hefei, Anqing, Chaohu City are three to five rows in turn, and they are belong to middle level of agricultural industrialization in the urban area. Hefei and Chaohu are closer to the rows , and they are the third and fourth principal components. Urbanization rate of Chaohu is higher, which reach 90.73 percent, while it is only 58.58 percent of Hefei. The two principal component of the gap between the two cities is that the wastewater treatment rate of Hefei is 15.06 percent, while it is only 1.95 percent of Chaohu.

Chuzhou, Huaibei City, Chizhou City, Wuhu City, Huangshan City, they integrated values are negative, and they belong to the level of development in agricultural industrialization, which belong to poor category.

Rank of Chuzhou and Wuhu are relatively lower, one is six, and the other is nine. The scores are negative.The science and technology indicators of Wuhu City are too low, while ratio of non-agricultural employment and the urbanization rate in Chuzhou, is not high.

Luan, Anqing city both are relatively close to the top, and the composite score is relatively high. The western city of Anhui Agricultural industrialization is still quite early level of development. The indicators are not the leader, but they are in the middle front position, which makes the western city to balanced development of agricultural industrialization.

The southern city of Anhui Province is Chizhou, Huangshan. Chizhou and Huangshan are ranked last. Indicator of wastewater treatment is the proportion of resources, and the two city is zero. It is indicated that the two cities need to pay attention to the development of the protection of the environment, and it affects the sustainable development, so it also will affect the level of agricultural industrialization development assessment.

3   Conclusion

From the above analysis, the Anhui Agricultural industrialization is still in the lower level of development, thus accelerating the pace of industrialization of agriculture has become the focus of economic development in Anhui. Anhui Province will speed up the industrialization of agriculture from the following aspects:

In order to promote agricultural income ,we regard industrialization as the base. We will find a market for the agricultural products. In order to promote agricultural mechanization, we will promote the application of the entire agricultural sector comprehensively, thus promote the industrialization of agriculture and the industrialization process. Adjusting the agricultural structure is the main line, which include the adjustment of agricultural structure, the adjustment of the internal structure in agricultural and industry, and adjust the internal structure of urban and rural. Building a harmonious Anhui is the goal of the resource environment. We must put rural and agricultural ecological environment as a priority. Rural and agricultural development is based on natural resources and it is the time for us to strengthen agricultural sustainable development capacity, and promote the harmonious development between man and nature.

Acknowledgements. The authors would like to thank the Natural Science Project of Anhui   Education Department (Project No.: KJ2009A67). Scientific Research Project, Doctor- Master of aiai(2009) NO.94:

References

1. Chen, A.: Rural-urban Disparity and Sectoral Labour Allocation in china. Journal of Development Studies 35(3), 105–133 (2002)
2. Kargupta, H., Huang, W.Y., Sivakumar, K., Johnson, E.: Distributed Clustering Using Collective Principal Component Analysis. Knowl. Inf. Syst. 3(4), 422–448 (2001)
3. Greenwood, J., Jovanovic, B.: Financial Development. Growth. and the Distribotion of Income. Journal of Political Economy 98(5), 1076–1107 (1990)
4. Murate, Y.: Income and Inequality in China: Composition,Distribution and Growth of Household Income. Social Science Quarterly 75(4), 821–837 (2002)
5. Su, H., Hung, F.G., Jia, D.Y.: Principal Curve Component Analysis. Journal of Image and Graphics 10(4), 499–504 (2005)

Research on Change Monitoring Method of Cultivated Lands Level Based on Volatile Indicators

Yanqing Chen[1], Jianyu Yang[1,*], Chao Zhang[1], Zhouting Sun[1],
and Dongping Ming[2,**]

[1] College of Information & Electrical Engineering,
China Agricultural University, Beijing, 100083
[2] School of Information Engineering, China University of Geosciences,
Beijing, Xueyuan Road. 29, 100083 Beijing, China
mingdp@sohu.com, 1121704177@qq.com, ycjyyang@126.com

Abstract. With the second national land survey carried out, land grading method is nearly mature, but change monitoring of cultivated lands level has not yet been proposed an effective method. The paper makes the second national land survey as research basis for change monitoring. According to the differences of indicator monitoring periods, authors introduce the concept of volatile indicators. Change monitoring indicators are divided into volatile and non-volatile indicators. This way updates non-volatile indicators only when monitor can improve the efficiency of monitoring. For the region data is missing, this paper suggests filling the missing data through spatial correlation. In order to unify monitoring units, authors propose a new method- Be post-grading units as monitoring units, convert pre-grading values to post-grading units by area-weighted. Finally, we analyze the monitoring result by calculating the quantity, quality, layout, production levels and other aspects. The analysis will play a role in early warning for the quality of cultivated land.

Keywords: Cultivated Lands Level, Change Monitoring Method, volatile indicators, Grading Unit, Change analysis.

1 Introduction

Quality of cultivated land means the sum of natural factors and environmental conditions what constitute the land, which shows the level of production capacity and product quality and the merits of environmental conditions of arable land [1]. The level of cultivated lands is one of the critical factors which reflect its quality. Change monitoring of cultivated lands can accumulate the relevant information and improve

---

* Funded project: The development of the information management system for Farmland grading monitoring (201011006-5); Ministry of Land and Resources Industry research special funds for public welfare projects: Study on the fast recognition on Farmland grading monitoring information and data integration(201011006-4). This work was also supported by the National Natural Science Foundation of China (41001259).
** Corresponding author.

D. Li and Y. Chen (Eds.): CCTA 2011, Part III, IFIP AICT 370, pp. 436–445, 2012.

the content of the land resource management and also achieve the changes from the number of management to the quality and quantity management. Through long-term monitoring, with other relevant knowledge, analyze the monitoring results in all aspects and study the trends in land levels. The analysis can support land management science to decision-making.

In the second national land survey process, it has formed a set of relatively mature methods of Agricultural Land Classification system, but how to monitor the change of cultivated lands has not yet made a systematic approach. This paper combine he knowledge and previous research about grading for dynamic monitoring of Quality of cultivated land, and propose a new set of change monitoring method of cultivated lands level. Finally, we carry out a systematic analysis to achieve the quality of cultivated lands early warning role.

2   Current Situation of the Research

The methods of cultivated lands level's change monitor commonly use time-series model analysis combined with analysis of influencing factors. By comparing land grading indicators of different periods, reveal the variation of cultivated lands level and characteristics, combined with the variation of the factors and trends, forecasting the direction of the evolution of land level [2]. Chinese cultivated land soil survey started in 1985, but rapid progress. With development of computer and spatial technology, dynamic monitoring method of cultivated lands quality based on 3s technology has been used widely. This method completes land quality monitor using automatic discovery of computers and technology of overlay analysis with the RS, GIS, GPS and other software tools, and the data basis are remote sensing images, soil images and other data [3]. The second national land survey has done a lot of works in evaluation of land level, which provide a theoretical basis for monitor and data protection for future monitor in land levels. Peng Ru-yan and Zhang Xiao-pei [4] make the agricultural land classification rules as a basis, from the principle of the monitoring points' layout, monitoring index system, monitoring data collection, evaluation of monitoring results and spatial information technology, five-pronged approach, initially built national quality of cultivated land dynamic monitoring system which provide basis for China's cultivated land resources conservation and management decision for the future.

3   Research of Change Monitoring Method of Cultivated Lands Level

The assessment of cultivated lands level is premise of change monitor, "Agricultural Land Classification Regulations" [5] (Later referred to as "Regulations") clearly defines agricultural land classification process, as figure 1 shown, the whole process can be briefly summarized as: Target areas identified —>Grading unit identified—>Grading factors identified—>Index calculation—>Determine the level—>Summary acceptance.

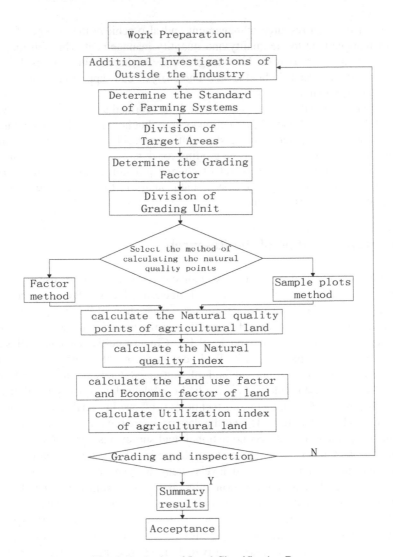

Fig. 1. Agricultural Land Classification Process

3.1   Volatile Index and Non-volatile Index

Level of agricultural land is affected by natural factors and socio-economic factors. Natural factors include climate, topography, soil, water, etc. Socio-economic factors include the socio-economic environment and geographic conditions, etc. In the "Regulations", all these factors are taken into account. All of the above factors will change with time. However, due to the intensity of driving force which makes them change is different, some factors change slowly and some are not. On this point, this paper introduces the concept of volatile index and non-volatile index. Volatile index is the indicators which are significant changes in agricultural land quality when driven forcefully in a short time, such as the status of land use. Non-volatile index refers to which can maintain a relatively stable index over an extended period in natural state [6], such as soil type. Different indicators have different change periods, and the same indicators at different index areas, the periods probably are different. Based on the differences of change monitoring scope and extent in land quality levels, monitoring cycle is divided into three categories: Regular monitoring: monitor and evaluate various indicators those cause cultivated land quality level changes, monitor once every three years. Real - time monitoring: monitor and evaluate various changed indicators caused by various types of engineering measures in the "increase, reduce, establish" process, monitor once every one year. Immediate monitoring: monitor and evaluate various changed indicators those caused by unpredictable natural and man-made destruction. It is measured only when the land level monitoring database changed .In practical application, it should set the change cycle based on the difference of driving forces which promote indexes changed in target area. Change monitoring gets the change information by comparing two cultivated grades. It also has a certain periodicity. If this cycle is less than the change cycle of the evaluation, these indicators can be seen as non-volatile. Others are volatile indexes which should be graded by the updated data. This rapid detection method can greatly reduce the workload of data collection and improve the efficiency of grading and monitoring. However, this method can not apply to mutated region, such as level evaluation and monitoring of land reclamation and development region. As figure 2 shown, this article will be divided into two kinds of areas-mutative and gradient regions-to monitor.

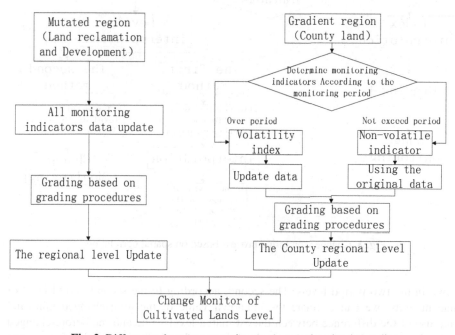

Fig. 2. Differences between mutations and gradual region in grading

3.2   The Changes Monitoring Process Based on Spatial Correlation

For the areas whose evaluations almost are known, it is desirable that combines with the concepts of volatile indicator and non-volatile indicator to grad. But if some areas are not able to acquire such these evaluation indexes or the data are missing, this method will be out of function.. For such problems, this paper proposes a level estimation method based on spatial correlation. We can use neighboring cells whose levels are known to estimate the levels value of the unknown elements through the spatial interpolation. In practice, on the basis of the characteristics of the data, we can select different interpolation methods for interpolating. It is worth to note that the level of mutations in the region can't be estimated by this method because the level does not have the continuity with the adjacent areas' level. For change monitoring, there are two different estimation methods: The first, according to the two period levels' difference of adjacent units, we can directly estimate the level of change in the value of the unit. This method does not involve any period level of the unit, so this method is applicable to this condition that two period levels of adjacent units are

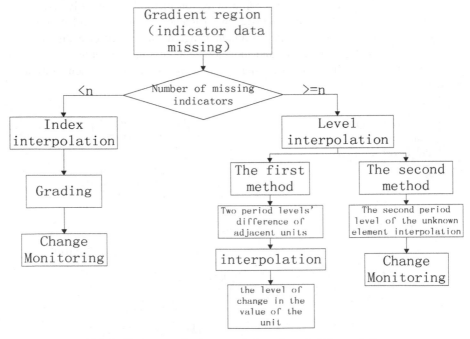

Fig. 3. Change monitoring process based on spatial correlation

known in the two period levels. The second, according to the second period level of adjacent units, we can estimate the unknown value of the after-changed unit, and make use of the difference between the estimated level value and the before-changed level value to acquire the value of grade changes. This method is suitable for the first period level of the estimated unit which is known. Due to the change monitoring is carried out on the basis of the second national land survey, the first period level of all units is known. In theory, the two methods are reasonable and practical. But in order to take full advantage of the known conditions to reduce the estimation error, this paper introduces the second method to estimate the unknown value of the second period level of the unit. When only a few indicators are missing, interpolation for index data is also feasible. We can specify a threshold value "n". When the number of missing data is greater than the index n, it is considered to directly operate on the level. On the contrary, it is considered to interpolate for these missing indicators. General process is shown as Figure 3.

3.3   The Method Research for the Unity of Change Monitoring Units

According to "Regulations", the division of agricultural land grading unit includes four ways: Overlay method: Land use map, topographic maps and soil maps in the same scale are superimposed, through this way it can be formed a new layer, the new layer can be seen as grading units layer; Land block method: Directly using polygons of the land use map as the grading units; Grid method: grids with certain sizes are used as grading units; Polygon method: All grading factor maps are superimposed. In these four methods, the second one-land block method-is common to use, but there is a problem for change monitoring: Assuming that we monitor the land level change between 2007 and 2010, grading units in 2007 are based on 2007 land use map, and grading units in 2010 are based on the 2010's, but the two land use maps can't be exactly the same, there is the case that the two period grading units do not correspond. So these units cannot be directly used in change monitoring. We have to make the two grading results correspond to each other in grading units. To facilitate the description, the grading result of an earlier phase is called pre-grading result. The later result of the grading is called post-grading result. No matter what technology is used to convert the arable land grading results, the law of natural grad ,using grad and economy grad after conversion must reflect the actual of regional resources and must match the distribution of regional characteristics about the light, temperature, soil and water [7-10]. The approach is as follows: post-grading units are seen as basic units of change monitoring. Making the area as converted weight, pre-grading result is transformed into post-grading unit. As figure 3 shown, shaded area is one of post-grading units which steps over the four pre-grading units. The numbers in the figure are the levels of pre-grading units. In addition to cultivated land, other land types' levels assign to "0".We calculate pre-grading level of the shaded unit by the ratio between area of intersection and the pre-grading level. This method can get two different time (Pre-grading and post-grading) levels at the same grading unit. The two values can be seen as two property value fields of change monitoring unit data. There are three levels in grading: natural grad, using grad and economy grad. In attribute table, we name them as "The value of pre-natural grad", "The value of post-natural grad", "The value of pre-using grad", "The value of post-using grad", "The value of pre-using grad" and "The value of post- economy grad", then post-grading value subtract pre-grading value, we can get the changed grading value. Add three fields to attribute table: "Changed natural level", "Changed using level" and "Changed economy level". When change in level is equal to 0, it means no change in grading unit level; when change in level is greater than 0, the land levels increased, indicating quality of arable land improved; when change in level is less than 0, the land levels decreased, indicating quality of arable land declined. About the judgment for new arable land, non-cultivated land's polygon of pre-data and cultivated land's polygon of post-data seek common ground by ARCGIS software. The common ground is the new arable land. About the judgment for disappeared arable land, non-cultivated land's polygon of post-data and cultivated land's polygon of pre-data seek common ground by ARCGIS software. By calculating the new land and the disappearance of arable land area, we monitor changes in the amount of cultivated land. By monitoring changes in levels, we can monitor changes in land quality, so as to achieve double control- the quantity and quality of arable land.

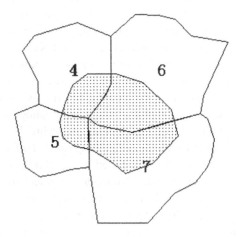

Fig. 4. Conversion figure of pre-grading result

4   The Analysis of Monitoring Results

Analysis for monitoring result is also very important. According to "Pilot monitoring land quality grade Technical Manual" [11], as shown in figure 5, the main change analysis can be divided into four parts: change analysis on arable land level, mutation analysis on arable land quantity, changes in the layout analysis and analysis of changes in the level of production capacity. The changes of number and grade have been analyzed in Section 3.3, this section will mainly analyze changes in the layout and production capacity.

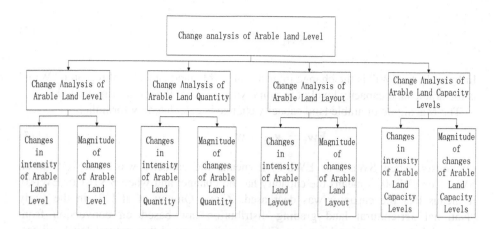

Fig. 5. Process of Change analysis of land level

Spatial layout can be measured by plaque fragmentation index of regional cultivated land "FN". "FN" can be calculated by "Np" and "Nc", "Np" is the total plaques of regional cultivated land and "Nc" is the ratio of cultivated land's total area and the smallest plaque area of the region. Specific calculation is as shown formula 1:

$$FN = \frac{N_p - 1}{N_c} \tag{1}$$

The change of spatial layout can be reflected in the intensity "SFN" and the margin "EFN" of regional cultivated land's plaque fragmentation. "SFN" can be calculated by plaque fragmentation index of regional cultivated area as formula 2 shown:

$$SFN = \frac{FN_n}{FN_{n-x}} \tag{2}$$

In formula 2, "FN_n" means regional cultivated land plaque fragmentation index of year n, "FN_{n-x}" is regional cultivated land plaque fragmentation index of year n-x. "x" is the discrepancy between two monitoring periods. "EFN" can be calculated by formula 3:

$$EFN = FNn - FNn - x \tag{3}$$

SFN> 1, which indicates the fragmentation degree of arable land is increased; SFN=1, which means there is no change in fragmentation; SFN<1, indicating the degree of fragmentation of arable land is decreased. The elevation of fragmentation, is not conducive to field management and mechanization, and indicates that the adjacent land probably has been destructed. From a regional point of view, the overall quality of arable land is decreased.

Like the spatial layout, change analysis of arable land capacity levels is also based on regions. The change intensity of the arable land capacity is calculated by formula 4:

$$SW_i = \frac{W_{i,n}}{W_{i,n-x}} \qquad (4)$$

In formula 4, "SWi" is the change intensity of arable land capacity of region i. "Wi,n" is the arable land capacity level of region i, year n. "x" is the monitoring period.

The Magnitude of arable land capacity change is calculated by formula 5:

$$Ew_i = W_{i,n} - W_{i,n-x} \qquad (5)$$

Obviously, when SWi>1 or EWi>0, it means the capacity was improved; when SWi=1 or EWi>0, it means the capacity has no change; and when SWi<1 or EWi<0, it means that the capacity was decreased. Zhang Qingpu et al [12] in the study "National agricultural land grading distribution law based on conversion from provincial level to national level in Chongqing" proposed that natural level indices, utilization index and economic index of Chongqing municipal agricultural land have linear correlation with the actual standard grain yield. That means, the capacity and quality of arable land has a direct relationship, so we can forecast trends in land quality through the change of capacity.

5   Conclusion

(1) Based on monitoring period, the concept of volatility index and Non-volatile index can be pointed out, which can greatly reduce the workload of data collection and improve the efficiency of grading and monitoring.

(2)This paper proposes to interpolate evaluation or rating value in order to obtain the unknown data by the spatial correlation of the data, and chooses different methods to operate on the basic of the characteristics of the data.

(3) It is the prerequisite for change monitoring that integrates the two periods' grading units. Pre-grading result is transformed into post-grading unit with the area for weight, and regards post-grading unit as basic unit of change monitoring. Through this method, the prerequisite can be achieved. Theoretically, both ensuring the uniform of two periods' grading units, and avoiding the situation that monitoring units and the latest land use map do not correspond.

(4) Analysis of monitoring results is very important for quality of cultivated land. Through analyze the quantity, quality, layout, production capacity and other changes, analysis of monitoring results can be used to forecast trends in cultivated land quality, which play a role of early warning for land quality.

References

1. Liu, Y.Z., Ma, X., Xu, M.: Preliminary Study on the Early Warning of Cultivated Land Quality. China Land Science 17(6), 10–12 (2003)
2. Yan, G., Yang, Y.: Research of Dynamic Monitor of Cultivated Lands Quality. National Land Resources Information (3), 29, 41, 43 (2005)

3. Tian, Y., Sun, T.-T., Ma, J.-C., Shen, R.: Research of Dynamic Monitor of Cultivated Lands Quality Based on 3S Technology. Animal Husbandry and Feed Science 30(6), 17–18 (2009)
4. Peng, R.-Y., Zhang, X.-P.: Designing Dynamic Monitoring System of National Plow Land Quality Based on Graduation. Resources & Industries 10(5), 96–98 (2008)
5. Agricultural Land Classification rules, People's Republic of land and resources industry standards: TD1004-2003
6. Chen, B., You, J., Pan, Y., et al.: Indices system and methods of monitoring gradation of agricultural land quality. Transactions of the CSAE 25(supp.2), 272–276 (2009)
7. Kong, X., Zhang, F., Jiang, G., et al.: Inspiration of foreign experience on arable land protection of Beijing. China Land Science 19(5), 50–56 (2005)
8. Zhang, Q., Wang, S., Zhang, F., et al.: Field quality limit to grain potential productivity based on farmland classification. Transactions of the CSAE 24(10), 85–88 (2008)
9. Su, Q., Zhang, L., Zhao, Y.: Verification of productive capacity of farmland graduation. Resources and Industries 10(5), 89–91 (2008)
10. Zhao, Y., Su, Q., Wu, K., et al.: Empirical analysis in the quality of the farmland in front and back land consolidation——the case of basic farmland demonstrate area land consolidation project in Tianhu town song county. Chinese Agricultural Science Bulletin 24(12), 514–518 (2008) (in Chinese with English abstract)
11. Level of Quality of cultivated land monitoring pilot technical manual, drafting by Ministry of National Land (February 2011)
12. Zhang, Q., Kong, X., et al.: National agricultural land grading distribution law based on conversion from provincial level to national level in Chongqing. Transactions of the CSAE 26(10), 297–303 (2010)

Feature Selection for Cotton Foreign Fiber Objects Based on PSO Algorithm

Hengbin Li[1], Jinxing Wang[1], Wenzhu Yang[2], Shuangxi Liu[1],
Zhenbo Li[2], and Daoliang Li[2,*]

[1] Mechanical and Electronic Engineering College,
Shandong Agricultural University, Taian 271018, China
[2] College of Information and Electrical Engineering,
China Agricultural University, Beijing 100083, China
{ytu-lhb,jingxingw,wzyservers,shuangxl,
zhboli,daoliangli}@163.com

Abstract. Due to large amount of calculation and slow speed of the feature selection for cotton fiber, a fast feature selection algorithm based on PSO was developed. It is searched by particle swarm optimization algorithm. Though search features by using PSO, it is reduced the number of classifier training and reduced the computational complexity. Experimental results indicate that, in the case of no loss of the classification performances, the method accelerates feature selection.

Keywords: Cotton, Foreign fiber, Feature selection, Particle swarm optimization.

Introduction

The foreign fibers in cotton is non-cotton fiber and non-nature color cotton fiber, such as chemical fiber, hair, hemp rope and so on, which are missing with the cotton and have serious influence on the quality of cotton and its product. Foreign fiber has serious impact on textile products even the quantity is very small. Once the fiber is mixed into cotton fiber, it will not only affect the textile spinning capacity, but also form color spots in dyed fabric which may seriously affect the appearance of the fabric and make a great damage to the cotton textile industry. In China, a number of cotton processing enterprises mainly rely on large numbers of workers employed to pick the foreign fiber. It takes a great deal of manpower and material resources. It's very necessary for improving efficiency and reducing costs to online monitoring technology in cotton foreign fiber based on machine vision.

Feature extraction of cotton foreign fiber can obtain the initial characteristics set, which can describe the feature. By the premise of he classification accuracy is not reducing, select the optimal feature subset with powerful ability of classification from the initial feature set. It can minimize complexity of the classifier design and increase classification speed, which is the premise and guarantee to real-time classification.

---

* Corresponding author.

D. Li and Y. Chen (Eds.): CCTA 2011, Part III, IFIP AICT 370, pp. 446–452, 2012.
© IFIP International Federation for Information Processing 2012

Particle swarm optimization (abbreviation: PSO) algorithm is a new global optimization algorithm. It searches optimal solution by the group of each particle kept moving and the motion of each particle is determined by current local optimal solution and global optimal solution. PSO as a heuristic search algorithm is concise, fast convergence, little parameters, etc., have been used in feature selection, classification and many other aspects. It can help the feature optimization and be able to extract optimal feature set of image by using the PSO in characteristics of cotton foreign fiber. The optimal feature subset can shorten the time of classification; even can be improve the classification accuracy in a certain extent.

1   Cotton Foreign Fiber Objects

It has many different foreign fibers in cotton. It is almost impossible to accurately classify in using certain features for the preprocessing foreign cotton fiber's target. Many different types of foreign fibers in cotton, the fiber pretreated to be the target of the opposite sex alone is almost impossible to use certain features on the accurate classification of foreign fibers of cotton, combined with the color, shape and texture features, you can improve the classification accuracy of the opposite sex fibers. So combing color, shape and texture features can improve the accuracy of foreign fibers' classification.

The characteristic of cotton foreign fibers can be expressed by 75-dimensional feature vectors, and the 75 characters include 24 color features, 43 texture features and 8 shape features.

It has 234 sample images, containing foreign fiber with 4000*500 24-bit true color images, in this sample image. These images were collected from real-time images of 4000election.

The sample image was processing segment and the small target was divided to six types, which are plastic, cloth, hemp rope, hair, polypropylene fiber silk and feather. Selected 135 small targets for each type. And obtained 810 samples of 75-dimensional feature data set according feature extracting to small target. The data set of sample characteristics randomly equal divided into 10 parts, each time taking one of them as a test set and the other 9 parts being merged into the training set.

2   Feature Selection Based on PSO Algorithm

2.1   Feature Selection

Feature selection can be described like that, selecting a feature subset which can make the categorizer have the best classification performance in the d-dimensional feature set. There are two problems which need to be solved, one is the criteria of selection, namely the evaluation criterion which is used to evaluate the properties of the different feature subsets; the other one is   the searching strategy, if d has been defined, there are C_D^d kinds of possible combinations. If all of the possible combinations are calculated in one pass, the amount of calculation is very large. Thus a effective searching method which can searched out a group of characteristics in the allowed time is needed.

The method of feature selection can be divided into two kinds: one is Filter method, the other is Wrapper method. Filter method is one kind of high efficient method which can eliminate the big kinds noise, it generally choose information entropy, correlation and class separation distance as the evaluation criterions. When the correlation between the categorizer and features is large, the method does not necessarily selectee a good feature subset. Although the sped of Wrapper method is slower than Filter method, the method is closely associated with the corresponding study arithmetic, then avoids the situation of selecting the wrong feature subsets. Nowadays,more and more   researchers choose Wrapper method to selecte features.

2.2   The Binary Basic Principle of Particle Swarm Optimization Algorithm

2.2.1   The Basic Principle of Particle Swarm Optimization Algorithm

PSO algorithm is the earliest be by Eberhart and Kennedy put forward 1995. Like other swarm algorithm, pso searches optimal solution by the continual moving of each individual. The motion direction of each particle is determined by local optimal solution Pbest and global optimal solution Gbest.

Each particle represents a D-dimensional solution space of a point, and its next position is determined by its current position and speed.

The location of i-th particle in the k-th iteration can be expreessed by

$$X_{id}(k) = (x_{i1}(1), x_{i2}(2),..., x_{iD}(k)).$$

And the speed $V_i(k) = (v_{i1}(1), v_{i2}(2),..., v_{iD}(k))$ is a vector in D-dimensional space.

Let $pBest_i(k) = (pBest_{i1}(1), pBest_{i2}(2),..., pBest_{iD}(k))$ be local optimal solution of X_i and $gBest_i(k) = (gBest_{i1}(1), gBest_{i2}(2),..., gBest_{iD}(k))$ be global optimal solution.   So in the iteration of K + 1 times, the entire particle positions and speeds is updated as following formula:

$$v_{id}(k+1) = wv_{id}(k) + c_1 r_1(k)[pBest_{id}(k) - x_{id}(k)] + c_2 r_2(k)[gBest_d(k) - x_{id}(k)] \tag{1}$$

$$x_{id}(k+1) = x_{id}(k) + \beta v_{id}(k+1) \tag{2}$$

In the formula, c_1, c_2 is learning factor, usually the value of its in the span 0 to 2. The r_1 and r_2 are random number , its value in the span 0 to 1. The w is weighted coefficients, and the β is constraint factor. d = 1, 2... D.

It can be used to deal with continuous space search problem by PSO, but can not be used to solve optimal combination problem. Therefore, Binary Particle Swarm Optimization (abbreviation: BPSO) is be by Eberhart and Kennedy put forward 1997 to solve discrete problem.

In BPSO, the value of X_{id} is 0 or 1, and V_{id} is the probability of X_{id} taking 1, limited by the transfer function to the range of 0 to 1. Usually Sigmond function is be used, which is

$$sig(v_{id}(k)) = 1/[1 + exp(-v_{id}(k))] \tag{3}$$

In BPSO, the formula of particle position update as follow:

$$x_{id}(k+1) = \begin{cases} 1, & r_{id} \le sig(v_{id}(k+1)) \\ 0, & otherwise \end{cases} \tag{4}$$

It is an important research direction to improve the speed of Wrapper by heuristic search method in order to overcome the shortcomings of slow speed of feature selection with Wrapper. As a heuristic search method, PSO has the characteristics of simple, few parameters, and fast convergence and so on. Therefore, BPSO was be used to be a search algorithm of feature selection in this article.

2.2.2   Fitness Function

Define particle's evaluation standard of evaluation standard performance as follows:

$$F(i) = p(i) / (1 + \lambda n(i)) \tag{5}$$

In the formula, $F(i)$ is fitness value of generating solution of particle i. And $p(i)$ is the mean rate of correct classification using this subset. $n(i)$ is the number of selected features,

$$n(i) = x_{i1} + x_{i2} + ... + x_{id} \tag{6}$$

λ is weight parameter of the number of feature, and λ generally is 0.01. The larger the value of F, the better indicate that the selected subset has better performance, obtaining a higher classification accuracy with fewer features.

2.3   Classification and Recognition Based on Support Vector Machine

A new optimum design criterion to linear classifier was put forward by Vapnik and others on the basis of year's research of statistical learning theory. The principle of support vector machine (abbreviation: SVM) is based on linearly separable, extended to linearly inseparable problem, even extended to using nonlinear function.

In this system, take optimal feature subset of cotton foreign fiber objects selected by BPSO algorithm as input vector of svm. And use radial basis function as kernel factions, which can obtain relatively superior classification effect. Classification learning of dataset, verify the quality of feature selection by the SVM classifier.

2.4   Algorithm Steps

The process of feature selection for cotton foreign fiber objects based on PSO algorithm:

1) Initializing the group of particle, obtain SVM classifier s according training samples set x, taking i=0;

2) For each particle $p_i = x_i$, calculate the characteristics of that subset of the new sample $x_j(k) Y$;

3) If the new moderate value is greater than moderate local optimal solution, the particle x_j local optimal solution update value: $pBest_i = x_i$;

4) If the new moderate value is greater than global optimal solution, the global optimal solution update value: $gBest_i = x_i$;

5) Calculating the particle's new speed:

$$v_{id}(k+1) = wv_{id}(k) + c_1 r_1(k)[pBest_{id}(k) - x_{id}(k)] + c_2 r_2(k)[gBest_d(k) - x_{id}(k)] \qquad (7)$$

6) Calculating the particle's new location:

$$x_{id}(k+1) = x_{id}(k) + \beta v_{id}(k+1) c_2 \qquad (8)$$

7) Self-increasing i, if I is less than the maximum the number of iterations, then turn step 2), otherwise the algorithm terminates.

3   Results of the Experiment and Discussion

The algorithm used java into programming, using K-fold cross-validation in this experiment, in which K is 10. The data set of sample characteristics randomly equal divided into 10 parts, each time taking one of them as a test set and the other 9 parts being merged into the training set. In this study, some parameters were set as: $c_1 = c_2 = 2$, PN (particle number) = 20, N (the maximum iteration number) = 1000.

In this experiment, performance of feature selection was compared between pso algorithm and ant colony algorithm [5] (abbreviation: IACA). Each algorithm run 10 times and takes the average. The iteration number of PSO is 718, and running time is 3120s; The iteration number of IATA is 1472, and running time is 5152s. The iteration number of PSO is less 52% than IACA and running time is less 40%, which can prove PSO has higher searching efficiency.

Table 1. Comparison of the number of original feature and selected feature set selection

Types	The original number of features	The number of features after feature select of IACA	The number of features after feature select of PSO
Color characters	24	10	11

Table 1. (*continued*)

Texture characters	43	11	9
Shape characters	8	1	0
All characters	75	22	20

To show the accuracy of PSO algorithm for improving the effectiveness of classification, compare the sets chose by two algorithms (show in Table 1) and its classification performance (show in Table 2). As can be seen from Table 1, optimal feature subset is smaller and more conducive to classifier design after feature selected by PSO. Table 2 shows that PSO can improve the classification accuracy of classifier after comparing. The above results indicate that PSO for feature selection methods to some extent improve the classification accuracy is valid.

Table 2. Comparison of classification performance of original feature set and selected future set

Types	Accuracy of original	Accuracy of selected by IACA	Accuracy of selected by PSO
Plastic	92	99	99
Cloth	82	94	95
Hemp rope	78	88	89
Hair	82	89	89
Polypropylene fiber	94	100	100
silk			
Feather	74	85	87

4   Conclusions

A fast feature selection for cotton foreign fiber objects based on PSO algorithm is be proposed in this paper. The time of feature selection is greatly reduced in the case of lossless of classification accuracy in this method. But the further research needs to improve the algorithm and its classification accuracy.

Acknowledgements. The authors would like to thank the Project supported by the National Natural Science Foundation of China (Grant No. 30971693) and supported by Program for New Century Excellent Talents in University (NCET-09-0731).

References

1. Zhao, N., Fu, C.X.: Real-time vision-based detecation of foreign fibers in cotton. Journal of Automation an Instrumentation 3, 24 (2008)
2. Liu, S., Zheng, W.X., Li, H.B., Wang, J.X.: Research of Dynamic Identification Techonlogy on Cotton Foreign Fibers. Computer and Computing Technologies in Angriculture IV, 389 (2010)
3. Zhu, Z.G., Ahi, D.J.: Digit limage processing. Publishing House of Elecronics Industry, Beijing (2003)
4. Wen, Z.Q., Cai, Z.X.: Conwergence analysis of Mean Shift algortithm. Journal of Software 2(18), 206–211 (2007)
5. Zhao, X.H., Li, D.L., Yang, W.Z.: Feature Selection for Cotton Foreign Fiber Objects Based on Improved Ant Colony Algorithm. Transactions of the Chinese Society for Agricultural Machinery 42(4), 168–173 (2011)
6. Yan, W.Z., Li, D.L., Wei, X.H., et al.: Feature selectiong for cotton foreign fiber objects based on improved genetic algorithm. Transactions of the Chinese Society for Agricultural Machinery 41(4), 173–178 (2010)
7. Lin, S.W., Ying, K.C., Chen, S.C., et al.: Particle swarm optimization for parametermianation and feature selection of support vector machines. Expert Systems with Applications 35(4), 1817–1824 (2008)
8. Shima, K., Todoriki, M., Suzuki, A.: SVM-based feature selection of latent semantic feature. Pattern Recognition Letters 25(9), 1051–1057 (2004)
9. Lin, J.Y., Ke, H.R., Chien, B.C., et al.: Classifier design with feature selection and feature extraction using layered genetic programming. Expert Systems with Applications 34(2), 1384–1393 (2008)
10. Uncu, Ö., Türkşen, I.B.: A novel feature selection approach: Combining feature wrappers and filters. Information Sciences 177(2), 449–466 (2007)
11. Horng, M.-H.: Multi-class support vector machine for classification of the ultrasonic images of supraspinatus. Expert Systems with Applications 36(4), 8124–8133 (2009)
12. Bermejo, S., Monegal, B., Cabestany, J.: Fish age categorization from otolith images using multi-class support vector machines. Fisheries Research 84(2), 247–253 (2007)

Optimization Model to Estimate Mount Tai Forest Biomass Based on Remote Sensing

Yanfang Diao[1], Chengming Zhang[2,3,*], Jiping Liu[2], Yong Liang[3], Xuelian Hou[4], and Xiaomin Gong[1]

[1] College of Water Conservancy and Civil Engineering,
Shandong Agricultural University, Taian, China
[2] Chinese Academy of Surveying and Mapping, Beijing, China
[3] School of Information Science and Engineering,
Shandong Agricultural University, Taian, China
[4] Information Center of Shandong Electric Power School, Taian, China
chming@sdau.edu.cn

Abstract. The development of low-carbon economy and the promotion of energy conservation are becoming a basic consensus of all countries. Therefore, global carbon cycle becomes a widespread concern research topic in scientific community. About 77% of the vegetation carbon stores in forest biomass in terrestrial ecosystems. So forest biomass is the most important parameter in terrestrial ecosystem carbon cycle. In this paper, for estimating the forest biomass of Mount Tai, a support vector machine (SVM) optimization model based on remote sensing is proposed. The meteorological data, terrain data, remote sensing data are taken into account in this model. In comparison the results of SVM with that of regressive analysis method, both the training accuracy and testing accuracy of regressive analysis method are lower than those of SVM, so SVM could obtain higher accuracy.

Keywords: forecast biomass, remote sensing, support vector machine (SVM).

1   Introduction

Because forest ecosystem is the most important part of terrestrial ecosystems, its research occupies a pivotal position in the global. Forest biomass is the energy-based of the entire forest ecosystem running and the sources of nutrients, which is the basis of studying biological productivity, net primary productivity (NPP), carbon cycle and global change research. Forest biomass includes tree layer biomass, living ground cover layer (shrub layer, herb layer and moss, lichen layer) biomass and animal and microbial biomass. There are three basic traditional research approaches to estimate biomass: by measuring photosynthesis; by measuring the carbon dioxide produced by respiration change; and by measuring the stock of organism. But above mentioned methods are difficult to estimate the biomass and NPP of large scale of forecast.

---

* Corresponding author.

D. Li and Y. Chen (Eds.): CCTA 2011, Part III, IFIP AICT 370, pp. 453–459, 2012.
© IFIP International Federation for Information Processing 2012

Spectral information of remote sensing images with good comprehensive and current trend has a correlation with forest biomass [1]. In our country, in spite of a large number of survey of biomass sample plots are carried out [2, 3], an abundant of data are accumulated, and the local site biomass data are gotten, but these data are difficult to estimate the biomass of large scale of forecast. How to combine these biomass plots survey data, topographical and meteorological data with remote sensing data, explore the establishment of remote sensing to study the biomass estimation model, is a worthy of study. In this paper, Mount Tai, for example, combining forest biomass with meteorological data, topographical data and remote sensing data, a support vector machine optimization model based on remote sensing information to estimate forest biomass in Mount tai is established.

2   The Source and Process of Data

2.1   Description of Mount Tai

Mount Tai is located in the central of Shandong province, 36°5'N~36°15'N, 117°5'E~117°24'E, and the highest peak is Yuhuangding, which altitude is 1545m. Mount Tai is a warm-humid and semi-humid monsoon climate and the vegetation type is the warm temperate zone deciduous broad-leaved forest. At present, the forest coverage rate reached 81.57%, and the vegetation coverage rate more than 90%. Vegetation types could be roughly classified into 19 types, including 11 types of forest, 2 types of shrub meadow, 3 types of meadow and 3 types of others. In the main forest types, Pinus tabulaeformis, Platycladus orientalis, Robinia pseudoacacia, Quercus variabilis account for about 92.9% [4].

2.2   The Source of Data

Air temperature, precipitation, humidity, sunshine, wind direction, wind speed and evaporation etc. are important ecological factors, which are also important factor that affect the forest ecosystem biomass. Meanwhile, the elevation and the types of vegetation are the very important factors. In order to determine above-mentioned factors' influence on the Mount Tai biomass, meteorological data, terrain data, remote sensing data are used to estimate forest biomass.

Meteorological data include temperature data and rainfall data. The temperature data includes annual mean temperature data (TA) and greater than 0 °C accumulated temperature data (T0), and the rainfall data is the annual mean rainfall data (PA).

Topographic data is primarily the 1:250 000 digital topographic map data. The contour lines could be obtained by topographic maps from digital data, and the digital elevation model (DEM) and slope data (ASP) could be obtained by ARC / INFO.

Remote sensing data uses Landsat-7 image data. Landsat-7 inherits technical parameters of the previous Landsat series, and the most important feature of it is to carry an Enhanced Thematic Mapper Plus ETM+. ETM+ is in developed on the basis of the Landsat-4, 5 satellite thematic mapper TM. Its band data cover larger scope from visible to infrared region, contain an abundant of information, and each band have different characteristics. At the same time, it is obvious that surface features in different spectral band are differences, so the band data of ETM+ have high practical value [5]. As the Landsat-7 ETM+ sensor has an advantage in spatial resolution, spectral resolution, and performance price ratio and other aspects. Therefore, ETM+ data has become one of the most commonly used remote sensing data at present, which is widely used in agriculture, forest and grassland resources survey, land use and mapping, geology, hydrology and other fields [6].

A series derived data of vegetation indexes are produced from Landsat-7 ETM+ data, for example normalized differential vegetation index (NDVI), ratio vegetation index (RVI), difference vegetation index (DVI), soil adjusted vegetation index (SAVI) and so on. The computational methods of above vegetation indexes are as follows.

Difference vegetation index: DVI=ETM4-A×ETM3

Normalized differential vegetation index: NDVI=(ETM4-ETM3)/(ETM4+ETM3)

Perpendicular vegetation index: PVI=(ETM4-A×ETM3-B)/SQR(1+A^2)

Ratio vegetation index: RVI=ETM4/ETM3

Soil adjusted ratio vegetation index: SARVI=ETM4/(ETM3+B/A)

Transformative Soil adjusted ratio vegetation index: TSAVI=A×(ETM4-A× ETM3- B)/(ETM3+A×ETM4-A×B)

Transformed vegetation index: TVI= (NDVI+0.5)$^{0.5}$

where TM3 and TM4 are red light and near infrared wave bands respectively. A and B equal 0.96916 and 0.084726 respectively.

2.3   From a Sample Survey Data of Forest Resources to Calculate Biomass Data

According to the types of forest of Mount Tai, the biomass estimation models of various organs are selected (such as Pinus tabulaeformis biomass estimation models [3,7], Quercus variabilis and other broad-leaved biomass estimation models [8]). Employing the breast-height diameter of per plant to calculate biomasses of every organs; the various biomasses of every organs are summed to be the biomasses of per plant; and the biomasses of every per plant are summed to be the biomasses of forest.

3   Optimization Model to Estimate Mount Tai Forest Biomass Based on Remote Sensing

3.1   Principle of Support Vector Machine (SVM)

The support vector machine (SVM) [9-11] proposed by Vapnik et al. is a novel approach for solving pattern recognition (binary) problems. SVM holds many advantages compared with other approaches. It is a quadratic programming (QP) problem, which assures that its solution is the global optimal solution. And its sparsity assures a better generalization. It implements the structural risk minimization principle, which minimizes the upper bound of the generalization error, instead of the empirical risk minimization principle. Moreover, it has a clear geometric intuition on the classification task. Due to the above merits, SVM has been successfully used in many fields and extended to regression problems [10-13].

SVM based on statistic learning theory is a novel learning machine, which balances learning ability and structural complexity of the model based on small samples, so this model can avoid effectively local optimization. And it has a small parameters set by people in advance which make it have better generalization and popularization ability [14,15]. The basic strategy of SVM is to seek decision rules with popularization ability. The analysis process of SVM is described as follows.

Firstly, suppose there is a sample aggregate named $\{x_i, y_i\}_{i=1}^N$, $x \in R^m$, $y_i \in \{\pm 1\}$, and then an SVM can be defined by possible mappings $\phi : R^m \to R^n$, where R^n are lower dimensional spaces aggregate and where R^n are higher dimensional spaces aggregate. The largest interval classification hyperplane can be shown as

$$A = \left[\omega \cdot \phi(x) \right] + b \tag{1}$$

where $\omega = \sum_{i=1}^N \alpha_i \phi(x_i)$ is obtained in the higher dimensional spaces, and where α_i and b are Lagrangian multipliers and constant, respectively.

According to the theory of Reproduce Kernel Hilbert Space (RKHS), the kernel function $K(x_i, x_j) = \left[\phi(x_i) \cdot \phi(x_j) \right]$ which satisfies the condition of Mercer can be obtained in lower dimensional spaces. Then the problem of seeking the optimal classification hyperplane using Lagrangian optimization method is conversed to the solution of its dual problem, which can be described as

$$\max Q(\alpha) = \sum_{i=1}^N a_i - \frac{1}{2} \sum_{i,j=1}^N \alpha_i \alpha_j y_i y_j K(x_i, x_j) \tag{2}$$

where α_i should subject to the constraint and where $K(x_i, x_j)$ is kernel function

$$\sum_{i=1}^N y_i \alpha_i = 0, \alpha_i \geq 0, i = 1, \cdots, N \tag{3}$$

Kernel functions usually adopt the follow three ones: Linear function, polynomial function, and the radial base function, which are shown as follows.

Linear Kernel function: $K(x_i, x_j) = x_i \cdot x_j$

Polynomial function: $K(x_i, x_j) = \left[s(x_i \cdot x_j) + c \right]^d$

Radial basis function:
$$K\left(x_i, x_j\right) = \exp\left(-\frac{\left\|x_i - x_j\right\|^2}{\sigma^2}\right)$$

Only a small number of nonzero solutions α_i are obtained from Eq.(2), these vectors corresponding to nonzero solution α_i are looked on as support vectors. Then the optimization decision function can be written as

$$f(x) = \text{sgn}\left\{\left[\omega \cdot \phi(x)\right] + b\right\} = \text{sgn}\left\{\sum_{i=1}^{N} \alpha_i y_i K\left(x_i, x_j\right) + b\right\} \tag{4}$$

If these data can not be classified with error-free in higher dimensional spaces, a relax quantum $\xi_i (\xi_i \geq 0)$ which is used to balance the maximum classification interval and the minimum misclassification samples is introduced to support vector machine. Then the optimum equation can be described as

$$\min \phi(\omega) = \frac{1}{2}\|\omega\|^2 + C\sum_{i=1}^{N} \xi_i y_i \left(\omega \phi(x_i) + \omega_0\right) \geq 1 - \xi_i, i = 1, \cdots, N \tag{5}$$

where C is penalty coefficient.

The optimum classification plane function can be written as

$$\max \omega(\alpha) = \sum_{i=1}^{N} \alpha_i - \frac{1}{2}\sum_{i=1}^{N}\sum_{j=1}^{N} \alpha_i \alpha_j y_i y_j K\left(x_i, x_j\right) \tag{6}$$

$$C \geq \alpha_i \geq 0 \quad \sum_{i=1}^{N} y_i \alpha_i = 0$$

Then the decision function $f(x)$ can be obtained using the Karush-Kutn-Tuker rules.

3.2   Estimate Mount Tai Forest Biomass

Fifty sample plots in the same size are selected in Mount Tai, in which forty sample plots are regarded as training samples and ten are testing samples. Ten independent variables TA, T0, PA, DEM, ASP, NDVI, PVI, RVI, SARVI, TSAVT are taken as input variables in the SVM and regressive analysis method. Then the SVM and regressive analysis method are applied to train the forty samples and test the ten samples. In this paper, the forest biomass calculated by the SVM and regressive analysis method are considered as predicted values, and those calculated by the method in the section 2.3 are considered as actual values. The accuracy function can be written as

$$Accuracy = \frac{1}{n}\sum_{i=1}^{n}\left(1 - abs\left(\frac{a_i - p_i}{a_i}\right)\times 100\%\right)$$

where i is the sequence number of samples, n is the amount of samples, a is actual value and p is predicted value.

The training and testing accuracy of the SVM and regressive analysis method are shown in Table 1.

Table 1. The accuracy of SVM and regressive analysis method

Accuracy Method	SVM	Regressive analysis
Training accuracy	86.09%	84.06%
Testing accuracy	84.62%	82.93%

4   Conclusion

(1) Because the training accuracy and testing accuracy of SVM and the regressive analysis method are high in Table 1, these are a close correlation between meteorological data, terrain data, remote sensing data and forest biomass. It is also shown that the independent variables selected in this paper could reflect the information of the Mount Tai forest biomass.

(2) From the Table 1, we could see that both the training accuracy and testing accuracy of regressive analysis method are lower than those of SVM, so SVM could obtain higher accuracy and it is a suitable method to estimate the forest biomass.

(3) In the current conditions, the proposed method to estimate Mount Tai forest biomass using remote sensing could replace the field survey methods. Its advantages are to reduce the amount of the field survey work, save the survey funds, reduce the labor intensity and have great social and economic benefits.

(4) The proposed method is relatively simple which is suitable to estimate biomass in larger area.

Acknowledgements. This study is funded by: (1) Basic Research Fund of Chinese Academy of Surveying and Mapping under Grant (Contract Number: 7771109); (2) Award Fund of Outstanding Young Scientist of Shandong Province (No. BS2011DX031).

References

1. Spencer, R., Green, M., Biggs, P.: Integrating eucalypt forest inventory and GIS in western Australia. Photogrammetric Engineering and Remote Sensing 63(12), 1345–1351 (1997)
2. Fang, J., Chen, A., Zhao, S., Ci, L.: Estimation biomass carbon of China's Forecast: Supplementary Notes on Report Published in Science (291: 2320-2322) by Fang etal. Acta Phytoecologica Sinica 26(2), 243–249 (2001) (in Chinese)
3. Fang, J., Liu, G., Xu, S.: Biomass and net production of forest vegetation in China. Acta Ecologica Sinica 16(5), 497–508 (1996) (in Chinese)

4. Guo, L., Yu, S.: Landscape Pattern of Taishan Mountain and Its Spatio Temporal Variation. Acta Scientiarum Naturalium Universitatis Sunyatseni 43(4), 61–65 (2004) (in Chinese)
5. Qian, L.: Remote sensing digital image processing and extracting geographic feature. Science Press, Beijing (2004) (in Chinese)
6. Xu, H.: Study on Data Fusion and Classification of Landsat 7 ETM + Imagery. Journal of Remote Sensing 9(2), 186–194 (2005) (in Chinese)
7. Wu, G., Feng, Z.: Study on the social characteristics and biomass of the pinus tabulaeformis forest systems in China. Acta Ecologica Sinica 14(4), 415–422 (1994) (in Chinese)
8. Wu, Z., Dang, C.: The biomass and net primary productivity of Pinus kesiya var langbianensis stands in Chang-Nin district, Yunnan. Journal of Yunnan University 14(2), 137–145 (1992) (in Chinese)
9. Christianini, V., Shawe-Taylor, J.: An Introduction to Support Vector Machines. Cambridge University Press, Cambridge (2002)
10. Vapnik, V.: The nature of statistical learning theory. Springer, New York (1995)
11. Vapnik, V.: Statistical learning theory. Springer, New York (1998)
12. Mukherjee, S., Osuna, E., Girosi, F.: Nonlinear prediction of chaotic time series using support vector machines. In: Proceedings of the 1997 IEEE Workshop, pp. 511–520. IEEE Press, Amelia Island (1997)
13. Jeng, J.T., Chuang, C.C., Su, S.F.: Support vector interval regression networks for interval regression analysis. Fuzzy Sets and Systems 138(2), 283–300 (2003)
14. Zhang, X.: Introduction to statistical learning theory and support vector machines. Acta Automatica Sinica 26(1), 32–42 (2000)
15. Burges, J.C.C.: A tutorial on support vector machines for pattern recognition. Data mining and Knowledge Discovery 2(2), 121–167 (1998)

Important Parameters Optimization
for Opening Cotton Device

Gaili Gao[1], Hefei Zhao[1], Jun Liu[1], and Daoliang Li[2,*]

[1] College of Engineering, China Agricultural University, Beijing 100083, China
ggl1965@126.com
[2] College of Information and Electrical Engineering, China Agricultural University,
Beijing 100083, China
dliangl@cau.edu.cn

Abstract. A new opening cotton device used in detecting and eliminating foreign fibers of cotton was presented in this paper. It is the first time to propose that the multi-variable nonlinear constrained optimization algorithm should be applied to obtain parameter values of the tooth profile of the opening roller and feed rollers as well as their diameter and rotating speed values. This approach was used to simultaneously consider the impact of all the performance parameters, and the important performance parameters may be weighted. As a matter of experience, the cotton fiber and foreign fibers were damaged small by the tooth profile of the opening roller and feed rollers. The foreign fibers could be easily detected and removed for they would not be torn.

Keywords: cotton, foreign fiber, opening roller, feed roller.

1 Introduction

Foreign fibers of cotton mainly include cloth strips, hemp ropes, the polypropylene fibers, plastic films, color yarns, feathers, hairs, and so on. In spinning process, the foreign fibers are not only eliminated difficultly, but also pulled, torn into shreds easily, and become tinier foreign fiber. They may have a strong impact on the strength of the yarn, and are not easy to be dyed [1-2]. In recent years, the domestic and foreign researchers have applied different techniques to identify various foreign fibers of raw cotton based on their characteristics of geometry, physics and spectroscopy. These techniques are machine vision at visible light and ultraviolet light wave, infrared spectroscopy, X-ray image, and so on [2-6]. Different kinds of sorter have been developed. However, some foreign fibers can only be detected and eliminated by the sorters. Two main factors may lead the foreign fibers in cotton not to be detected or eliminated. The first factor is that the polypropylene fiber which has the same color with cotton is hard to detect, and still exists in the yarn. The second factor is that the foreign fibers are increased dramatically after the cotton is opened, and it is hard to detect and eliminate the foreign fibers.

---

* Corresponding author.

D. Li and Y. Chen (Eds.): CCTA 2011, Part III, IFIP AICT 370, pp. 460–468, 2012.

At present, many researchers focus on the opening roller in rotor spinning. Duru and Babaarslan (2003) suggested the opening roller speed should be high [7]. Mwasiagi et al. (2005) also proposed that the opening roller speed be 6500 rpm [8]. However, Murugan et al. (2007) and Ulku et al. (1995) tested that fiber rupture had direct relationship with the opening roller speed and a high level of fiber damage caused by the opening roller occurred at high speed [9-10]. So the opening roller immediately influences the performance of the opened textile fiber, and then influences textile quality. The opening roller referred on rotor spinning is not suitable for the device of detecting and eliminating the cotton foreign fibers. Because the opening roller combs the cotton fiber too tiny, and cotton fiber is extremely injured. For this reason, a new opening cotton device used in detecting and eliminating the foreign fibers was proposed in this paper.

2 Model of Opening Cotton Device

A model of an opening cotton device for detecting and eliminating foreign fibers is shown in Fig. 1. The device mainly comprises a pressing roller, a conveying belt, two feed rollers, an opening roller and a cover plate. The pressing roller is set above the conveying belt. The two feed rollers are installed at one end of the conveyer belt. One of the two feed rollers is on the top of another. The opening roller is set under the cover plate, and near the two feed rollers.

When the opening cotton device is working cotton that is put on the conveying belt and compressed by the pressing roller is carried to the two feed rollers. The two feed rollers that rotate in opposite direction pick up the cotton and transfer it to the opening roller that rotates counterclockwise. The point and side of its saw teeth insert the cotton from the bottom to the middle and top gradually and cut up the cotton. When the cotton goes through separation zone between the opening roller and the cover plate cotton fiber is separated from the cotton. At the moment, the foreign fibers in the cotton are exposed in the surface of the cotton and can be detected effectively.

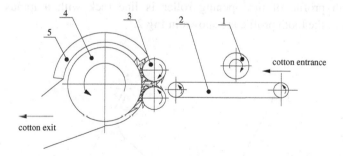

Fig. 1. Model of an opening cotton device.1-pressing roller; 2- conveying belt; 3- feed rollers; 4- opening roller; 5- cover plate.

3　Important Parameters Optimization for Opening Cotton Device

3.1　Building the Objective Function

There are two requests to be contented for conveying cotton in the opening cotton device: (1) The two feed rollers may provide enough cotton for the opening roller. (2) In order to prevent the cotton plug, the feed rollers cannot feed too much cotton to the opening roller. For these reasons, the absolute value of d-value of the cotton volume that is carried by the feed rollers and picked up by the opening roller in the unit time is as optimizing objective function. The objective function may be expressed as follows:

$$f = \left| C_1 f_1 - C_2 f_2 \right|. \tag{1}$$

Where f_1 is the cotton volume that is picked up by the opening roller in the unit time (mm^3 / s), f_2 is the cotton volume that is carried by the two feed rollers in the unit time (mm^3 / s), C_1 and C_2 are weight coefficient. For the influence on transferring and opening cotton, important degree of C1 and C2 is the same, so $C_1 = C_2 = 1$.

The cotton volume that is picked up by the opening roller in the unit time is the product of the total tooth number on the opening roller, rotational speed of the opening roller, the area of a single tooth profile and the width of base part of rack. The cotton volume may be described as follows:

$$f_1 = \frac{\pi}{25.4^2} d_1 l z_1 n_1 S_1 w_1. \tag{2}$$

Where d_1 is diameter of the opening roller (mm), l is length of the opening roller (mm), z_1 is tooth density of the opening roller teeth $/(25.4mm)^2$, n_1 is rotational speed of the opening roller (r / s), S_1 is area of a single tooth profile (mm^2), w_1 is width of base part of rack (mm).

The tooth profile of the opening roller is line rack with a minus angle δ. Parameters of the tooth profile are shown in Fig.2.

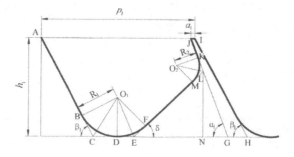

Fig. 2. Profile of the opening roller

Area of the tooth profile may be expressed as follows:

$$S_1 = S_{AJGC} - S_{BCD} - S_{DEF} - S_{MLK} - S_{ELG} .$$ (3)

Where

$$S_{AJGC} = h_1(p_1 - a_1) - \frac{h_1^2}{2}(\cot \beta_1 - \cot \alpha_1) .$$ (4)

$$S_{BCD} = R_1^2 \tan \frac{\beta_1}{2} - \frac{\beta_1 R_1^2}{2} .$$ (5)

$$S_{DEF} = R_1^2 \tan \frac{\delta}{2} - \frac{\delta R_1^2}{2} .$$ (6)

$$S_{MLK} = R_2^2 \cot \frac{\delta + \alpha_1}{2} - \frac{(\pi - \delta - \alpha_1)R_2^2}{2} .$$ (7)

$$S_{ELG} = \frac{\sin \alpha_1 \sin \delta}{2\sin(\delta + \alpha_1)} \left[p_1 - a_1 - h_1(\cot \beta_1 - \cot \alpha_1) - R_1 \left(\tan \frac{\beta_1}{2} + \tan \frac{\delta}{2} \right) \right]^2 .$$ (8)

Where h_1 is tooth height of the opening roller (mm), p_1 is tooth pitch of the opening roller (mm), a_1 is the tooth top width of the opening roller (mm), α_1 is working angle of the opening roller (rad), β_1 is tooth rack angle of the opening roller (rad), δ is minus angle (rad), R_1 is the radius of arc BF (mm), R_2 is the radius of arc MK (mm).

Substituting equations (4), (5), (6), (7) and (8) into equation (3) and rearranging terms gives:

$$S_1 = h_1(p_1 - a_1) - \frac{h_1}{2}(\cot \beta_1 - \cot \alpha_1) - R_1^2 \left(\tan \frac{\beta_1}{2} + \tan \frac{\delta}{2} \right)$$
$$+ \frac{R_1^2}{2}(\beta_1 + \delta) - R_2^2 \cot \frac{\delta + \alpha_1}{2} + \frac{(\pi - \delta - \alpha_1)R_2^2}{2}$$
$$- \frac{\sin \alpha_1 \sin \delta}{2\sin(\delta + \alpha_1)} \left[p_1 - a_1 - h_1(\cot \beta_1 - \cot \alpha_1) - R_1 \left(\tan \frac{\beta_1}{2} + \tan \frac{\delta}{2} \right) \right]^2 .$$ (9)

Substituting equation (9) into equation (2) yields:

$$f_1 = \frac{\pi d_1 l z_1 n_1 w_1}{25.4^2} \left\{ h_1 \left(p_1 - a_1 \right) - \frac{h_1}{2} \left(\cot \beta_1 - \cot \alpha_1 \right) - R_1^2 \left(\tan \frac{\beta_1}{2} + \tan \frac{\delta}{2} \right) \right.$$

$$+ \frac{R_1^2}{2} \left(\beta_1 + \delta \right) - R_2^2 \cot \frac{\delta + \alpha_1}{2} + \frac{\left(\pi - \delta - \alpha_1 \right) R_2^2}{2}$$

$$\left. - \frac{\sin \alpha_1 \sin \delta}{2 \sin \left(\delta + \alpha_1 \right)} \left[p_1 - a_1 - h_1 \left(\cot \beta_1 - \cot \alpha_1 \right) - R_1 \left(\tan \frac{\beta_1}{2} + \tan \frac{\delta}{2} \right) \right]^2 \right\}.$$

(10)

The cotton volume that is carried by feed rollers in the unit time is the product of the total tooth number on the two feed rollers, rotational speed of the two feed rollers, the area of a single tooth profile and the width of base part of rack. The cotton volume may be described as follows:

$$f_2 = \frac{2\pi}{25.4^2} d_2 l z_2 n_2 S_2 w_2. \tag{11}$$

Where d_2 is diameter of the feed rollers (mm), l is length of the feed rollers (mm), namely the length of the opening roller, z_2 is tooth density of the feed rollers, teeth $/(25.4mm)^2$, n_2 is rotational speed of the feed rollers (r / s), S_2 is area of a single tooth profile (mm^2), w_2 is width of base part of rack (mm).

The tooth profile of the feed rollers is line rack. Parameters of the tooth profile are shown in Fig.3.

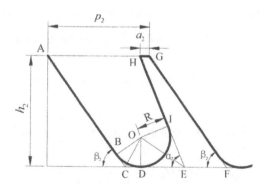

Fig. 3. Profile of the feed rollers

Area of the tooth profile may be expressed as follows:

$$S_2 = S_{AHEC} - S_{BCD} - S_{DEI}. \tag{12}$$

Where

$$S_{AHEC} = \frac{h_2}{2}\left(R\tan\frac{\beta_2}{2} + R\cot\frac{\alpha_2}{2} + p_2 - a_2 \right). \tag{13}$$

$$S_{BCD} = R^2 \tan\frac{\beta_2}{2} - \frac{\beta_2 R^2}{2}. \tag{14}$$

$$S_{DEI} = R^2 \cot\frac{\alpha_2}{2} - \frac{(\pi-\alpha_2)R^2}{2}. \tag{15}$$

Where h_2 is tooth height of the feed rollers (mm), p_2 is tooth pitch of the feed rollers (mm), a_2 is the tooth top width of the feed rollers (mm), α_2 is working angle of the feed rollers (rad), β_2 is tooth rack angle of the feed rollers (rad), R is the radius of arc BDI (mm).

Substituting equations (13), (14) and (15) into equation (12) and rearranging terms gives:

$$S_2 = R\left(\frac{h_2}{2} - R\right)\left(\tan\frac{\beta_2}{2} + \cot\frac{\alpha_2}{2}\right) + \frac{h_2}{2}(p_2 - a_2) + \frac{\pi - \alpha_2 + \beta_2}{2}R^2. \tag{16}$$

Substituting equation (16) into equation (11) yields:

$$f_2 = \frac{2\pi d_2 l z_2 n_2 w_2}{25.4^2}\left[R\left(\frac{h_2}{2} - R\right)\left(\tan\frac{\beta_2}{2} + \cot\frac{\alpha_2}{2}\right) \right.$$
$$\left. + \frac{h_2}{2}(p_2 - a_2) + \frac{\pi - \alpha_2 + \beta_2}{2}R^2 \right]. \tag{17}$$

Substituting equations (10) and (17) into equation (1), the objective function is:

$$f = \left| \frac{\pi d_1 l z_1 n_1 w_1}{25.4^2}\left\{ h_1(p_1 - a_1) - \frac{h_1}{2}(\cot\beta_1 - \cot\alpha_1) - R_1^2\left(\tan\frac{\beta_1}{2} + \tan\frac{\delta}{2} \right) \right.\right.$$
$$+ \frac{R_1^2}{2}(\beta_1 + \delta) - R_2^2 \cot\frac{\delta + \alpha_1}{2} + \frac{(\pi - \delta - \alpha_1)R_2^2}{2}$$
$$\left.- \frac{\sin\alpha_1 \sin\delta}{2\sin(\delta + \alpha_1)}\left[p_1 - a_1 - h_1(\cot\beta_1 - \cot\alpha_1) - R_1\left(\tan\frac{\beta_1}{2} + \tan\frac{\delta}{2} \right) \right]^2 \right\}$$
$$- \frac{2\pi d_2 l z_2 n_2 w_2}{25.4^2}\left[R\left(\frac{h_2}{2} - R\right)\left(\tan\frac{\beta_2}{2} + \cot\frac{\alpha_2}{2} \right) \right.$$
$$\left.\left. + \frac{h_2}{2}(p_2 - a_2) + \frac{\pi - \alpha_2 + \beta_2}{2}R^2 \right]\right|. \tag{18}$$

3.2   Choosing Optimized Parameters and Constraint Conditions

The magnitude of the cotton volume that is picked up by the opening roller or carried by the feed rollers in the unit time is mainly determined by the tooth profile, tooth density, length, diameter and rotational speed. The shape of the tooth profile is relevant to the tooth pitch, the tooth height, the tooth top width, the working angle, the tooth rack angle, the minus angle and the arc radius. By experience, the working angle α_1 and α_2 are 75 degree. The magnitude of the length l is proportional to the quantity of cotton that is carried by the device in the unit time, thus the magnitude of length l should be determined by the quantity of opening cotton. According to analysis above, the optimized parameters are d_1 , d_2 , n_1 , n_2 , z_1 , z_2 , $p_1, p_2, h_1, h_2, \beta_1, \beta_2, \delta, a_1, a_2, R_1, R_2$ and R . The parameters are converted to the form that may be used in the optimizing function. The corresponding relationship is:

$$
\begin{pmatrix} d_1 \\ d_2 \\ n_1 \\ n_2 \\ z_1 \\ z_2 \\ p_1 \\ p_2 \\ h_1 \\ h_2 \\ \beta_1 \\ \beta_2 \\ \delta \\ a_1 \\ a_2 \\ R_1 \\ R_2 \\ R \end{pmatrix} \Leftrightarrow \begin{pmatrix} x_1 \\ x_2 \\ x_3 \\ x_4 \\ x_5 \\ x_6 \\ x_7 \\ x_8 \\ x_9 \\ x_{10} \\ x_{11} \\ x_{12} \\ x_{13} \\ x_{14} \\ x_{15} \\ x_{16} \\ x_{17} \\ x_{18} \end{pmatrix}
$$

And the objective function may be written in the form

$$
f(x) = \left| f_1(x) - f_2(x) \right|. \tag{19}
$$

According to experimental data and experience formulas [11], the constraint conditions of the optimized parameters are given by:

$$320 \leq x_1 \leq 360 \quad , \quad 55 \leq x_2 \leq 65 \quad , \quad 15.8 \leq x_3 \leq 27.5 \quad , \quad 0.67 \leq x_4 \leq 1 \quad ,$$

$$30 \leq x_5 \leq 40 \quad , \quad 30 \leq x_6 \leq 50 \quad , \quad 5 \leq x_7 \leq 6 \quad , \quad 5 \leq x_8 \leq 6 \quad , \quad 3 \leq x_9 \leq 5.6 \quad ,$$

$$3 \leq x_{10} \leq 4 \quad , \quad \frac{5\pi}{18} \leq x_{11} \leq \frac{2\pi}{5} \quad , \quad \frac{5\pi}{18} \leq x_{12} \leq \frac{2\pi}{5} \quad , \quad \frac{\pi}{6} \leq x_{13} \leq \frac{2\pi}{9} \quad ,$$

$$0.25 \leq x_{14} \leq 0.4 , 0.25 \leq x_{15} \leq 0.4 , 3 \leq x_{16} \leq 4 , 1 \leq x_{17} \leq 2 , 2 \leq x_{18} \leq 4 .$$

3.3   Results and Discussions

Objective function $f(x)$ is nonlinear. Constraint conditions are linear. It is the more parameters and nonlinear constraint optimization. In this paper, we adopt "fmincon" optimization function from MATLAB software [12,13]. The optimal values of the parameters of the opening roller and feed rollers are given in the following table.

Optimal values of parameters of the opening roller and feed rollers

Names of parameters	Optimal values of parameters
Diameter of the opening roller d_1 (mm)	320
Diameter of the feed rollers d_2 (mm)	65
Rotational speed of the opening roller n_1 (r/s)	15.8
Rotational speed of the feed rollers n_2 (r/s)	1.0
Tooth density of the opening roller z_1 (teeth $/(25.4mm)^2$)	30
Tooth density of the feed rollers z_2 (teeth $/(25.4mm)^2$)	50
Tooth pitch of the opening roller p_1 (mm)	5.0
Tooth pitch of the feed rollers p_2 (mm)	6.0
Tooth height of the opening roller h_1 (mm)	3.0
Tooth height of the feed rollers h_2 (mm)	4.0
Tooth rack angle of the opening roller β_1 (degree)	72
Tooth rack angle of the feed rollers β_2 (degree)	72
Minus angle δ (degree)	30
The tooth top width of the opening roller a_1 (mm)	0.4
The tooth top width of the feed rollers a_2 (mm)	0.25
The radius of arc BF R_1 (mm)	3.0
The radius of arc MK R_2 (mm)	2.0
The radius of arc BDI R (mm)	4.0

4   Conclusions

(1)   In this paper, a new opening cotton device used in detecting and eliminating foreign fibers of cotton was presented. The cotton fiber and foreign fibers were damaged small by the new opening cotton device. The foreign fibers could be easily detected and removed for they would not be torn.

(2)   The multi-variable nonlinear constrained optimization algorithm was selected to obtain parameter values of the tooth profile of the opening roller and feed rollers as well as their diameter and rotating speed values.

(3)   It is the first time to propose that the multi-variable nonlinear constrained optimization algorithm should be applied to evaluate the design parameter values of the opening cotton device. This approach was used to simultaneously consider the impact of all performance parameters, and the important performance parameters may be weighted. This could get more reasonable parameter values.

References

1. Yang, W., Li, D., Zhu, L., Kang, Y., Li, F.: A new approach for image processing in foreign fiber detection. Comput. Electron. Agric. 68, 68–77 (2009)
2. Kang, Y., Li, W.: Development and application of lint foreign fiber cleaning equipment in cotton production line. China Cotton Processing (1), 12–14 (2010)
3. Li, B., Ding, T., Jia, D.: Design of a sophisticated foreign fiber separator. Nongye Jixie Xuebao 37, 107–110 (2006)
4. Guo, J., Ying, Y.: Progress on detecting technique and sorter of raw cotton foreign matters. Nongye Jixie Xuebao 39, 107–113, 106 (2008)
5. Zhang, X.B., Cao, B., Zhang, X.P., Shi, W.: Research on detecting heterogeneous fibre from cotton based on linear CCD camera. In: International Symposium on Photoelectronic Detection and Imaging 2009-Advances in Imaging Detectors and Applications, SPIE Digital Library, United States (2009)
6. Li, Y., Liang, K., Bai, H.Y.: Key technology in detecting and eliminating isomerism fibre in cotton. In: 2007 8th International Conference on Electronic Measurement and Instruments, ICEMI, pp. 4728–4732. Inst. of Elec. and Elec. Eng. Computer Society, United States (2007)
7. Duru, P.N., Babaarslan, O.: Determining an optimum opening roller speed for spinning polyester/waste blend rotor yarns. Text. Res. J. 73, 907–911 (2003)
8. Mwasiagi, J.I., Wang, X.H., Tuigong, D.R., Wang, J.: Study of rotor spun Basofil/cotton blended yarn quality characteristics during optimisation of processing parameters. J. Dong Hua Univ. 22, 1–5 (2005)
9. Murugan, R., Dasaradan, B.S., Karnan, P., Senthilkannan, M.S.: Fibre rupture phenomenon in rotor spinning. Fibers and Polymers 8, 665–668 (2007)
10. Ulku, S., Ozipek, B., Acar, M.: Effects of opening roller speed on the fiber and yarn properties in open-end friction spinning. Text. Res. J. 65, 557–563 (1995)
11. Fei, Q., Que, H., Chen, H., Wu, Q.: The technological characteristics, manufacture and use for carding. China Textile & Apparel Press, Beijing (2007) (in Chinese)
12. Edward, B.M., Shapour, A., Balahumar, B., James, H.D., Keith, E.H., Gregory, C.W.: Principle and application of MATLAB, 2nd edn. Electronics industry press, Beijing (2006) (in Chinese)
13. Su, J., Ruan, S., Wang, Y.: MATLAB engineering mathematics. Electronics industry press, Beijing (2005) (in Chinese)

Fast Segmentation of Foreign Fiber Image

Yutao Wu, Wenzhu Yang, Zhenbo Li, and Daoliang Li[*]

College of Information and Electrical Engineering,
China Agricultural University, Beijing 100083, P.R. China
dliangl@cau.edu.cn

Abstract. In the textile industry, different types of foreign fibers may be mixed in cotton, and the foreign fibers seriously affect the quality of cotton products. The step of image segmentation is of vital importance in the process of the foreign fibers identification, which is, in the same way, the foundation for cotton foreign fiber automated inspection. This paper presents a new approach for fast segmentation of foreign fiber images. This approach includes four main steps, i.e., image transformation, image block, image background extraction, image enhancement and segmentation. In the first step, we transform the captured color images into gray-scale images, and invert the color of the transformed images. In the second step, the proportion relationship between target image and background was analyzed, and then the whole foreign fibers image was divided into several blocks based on the analysis results. In the third step, the background of foreign fiber image was extracted by image corrosion and gray-level correction. In the final step, the histogram of the gray-scale image was analyzed, and a piecewise linear transform model was proposed to enhance the image blocks based on the analysis results, and then the image blocks were segmented by Otsu's method. The experiment results indicate that the proposed method can segment the foreign fiber image directly and precisely, and the speed of image processing is much faster than that of the conventional methods.

Keywords: Cotton, Foreign fibers, Fast segmentation, image processing, image block, background extraction, Ostu method.

1 Introduction

The foreign fibers in cotton refer to those non-cotton fibers and dyed fibers, such as hairs, binding ropes, plastic films, candy wrappers, and polypropylene twines, etc. Foreign fibers mixed with cotton during picking, storing, drying, transporting, purchasing and processing, are difficult to remove in spinning process, and can cause yarn breakage, even reducing the efficiency. Every low content of foreign fibers in cotton, especially in lint, will seriously affect the quality of the final cotton textile products, as they may debase the strength of the yarn, and are not easy to be dyed (Yang, et al., 2009). Since the price of the cotton for sale is affected by the content of

---

[*] Corresponding author.

D. Li and Y. Chen (Eds.): CCTA 2011, Part III, IFIP AICT 370, pp. 469–483, 2012.
© IFIP International Federation for Information Processing 2012

foreign fibers in it, the cotton farmers and traders are willing to keep the foreign fibers away to obtain a high price. This will lead to great economic loss for the cotton textile enterprises. Two main factors may lead to high level of foreign fiber content in cotton. One is the inappropriate picking technique. The foreign fibers are generally removed manually using human visual inspection, or mechanically using automated visual inspection (Lieberman et al., 1998; Su et al., 2006). When most western countries are using machines to pick up cotton automatically, Chinese cotton farmers in most regions are still picking cotton manually and putting them in polypropylene bags. Currently, foreign fibers are generally removed by hand picking methods using human visual inspection in most Chinese enterprises, which is time consuming and inefficient. So a machine vision system for online measurement of the content of foreign fibers in cotton is now being studied. High quality image acquisition, fast image processing, effective feature extraction, accurate object classification and precise content measurement are key factors in the implementation of the system (Li, et al., 2010).

The recognition of foreign fibers of targets is the key machine vision technology, in which image segmentation is an important step. Image segmentation is a process of partitioning an image into multiple regions and typically used to locate objects and boundaries (lines, curves, etc.). The aim of image segmentation is to partition the image into meaningful connected components to extract the features of the objects (Zhang et al., 2008).The segmentation results are the foundation of all subsequent image analysis and understanding, such as object representation and description, feature measurement, object classification, and scene interpretation, etc. Thus, throughout the image processing, image segmentation is an extremely important aspect. The popular approaches for image segmentation are: histogram-based methods, edge-based methods, region-based methods, model based methods and watershed methods (H. Zhang, J. E. Frittsb et al., 2008;Y. Jiang and Z.-H. Zhou et al., 2004).

Fast and precise segmentation has always been of great concern of people. Various image segmentation methods are reported in the literature (Bakker et al., 2008; Kim et al., 2003; Pichel et al., 2006) some of which are used in Automated Visual Inspection system in agriculture (Chen et al., 2002; Jiang et al., 2008). In recent years, researchers have developed more efficient, but also more complicated methods for segmentation. For example, Kainuller et al. (2007) used a statistical shape model combined with a constrained free-form model. Schmidt et al. (2007) presented a system that allows defining a set of rules, based on which abdominal organs are segmented (including the liver) using simple functions (like region-growing, or morphological operators). Liapis et al. (2004) proposed a wavelet-based algorithm for image segmentation based on color and texture properties. Furukawa et al. (2007) used a maximum posterior probability estimation for rough liver extraction subsequently refined with a level-set method. Seghers et al. (2007) presented an active shape model method, in which multiple local shape models are used. Susomboon et al. (2007) used intensity-based partition, texture-based classification, probability model, and thresholding to segment the liver.

The methods mentioned above may perform well in their specific circumstances, but it does not apply to segment images of cotton foreign fibers because of the low contrast. Due to the uneven thickness of the layers of cotton and foreign fibers of different colors and shapes, it is hard to attain a satisfying result by using the above conventional image segmentation methods. Therefore, we need to use the image pre-processing methods to eliminate the low image contrast and gray uniform of the background image. In the practice of image processing, image preprocessing refers to processing work in advance of the feature extraction, segmentation and matching of the image input. And the main aim of image preprocessing is to eliminate the irrelevant information in the origin image, regain the valuable and authentic information, and strengthen the detestability of relevant information, as well as to simplify date to the maximum, therefore to improve the reliability of feature extraction, segmentation, matching and recognition. In another words, image preprocessing provide better information base image for the image segmentation and makes it easy to image segmentation. In this article, a novel method based on image preprocessing and adaptive thresholding method is proposed to segment such low-contrast images.

In our research, the proportion relationship between target image and background was firstly analyzed, and then the whole foreign fibers image was divided into several blocks based on the analysis results. Thereafter improve the contrast ratio by means of the background subtraction of each image block. In the next step, a piecewise linear enhancement model was established based on the results of the histogram analysis, and applied to enhance the contrast of the image further. Finally, the best thresholding was determined by the Otsu's method.

2   Materials and Methods

2.1   Materials Preparation

The foreign fibers used in this research were collected from cotton mills including feathers, hair, hemp rope, plastic films, polypropylene twine, colored thread, cloth piece etc. as shown in Fig. 1. Adequate pure lint with no foreign fibers was also

Fig. 1. Foreign fiber samples

prepared for making the lint layer. The experiment selected a sufficient amount of lint cotton which does not include foreign fibers.

2.2   Image Acquisition

The Image Acquisition System has two cameras, two light sources, one shaft encoder, one synchronizing amplifier, two image acquisition boards and a computer, as shown in Figure 2. Colorful images are captured by a Canadian DALSA high-speed 3CCD color line scan camera under high-brightness LED lightning. The typical foreign fibers are concluded from the research on China's textile enterprises. To make the experiment easier, the foreign-fiber samples were dropping onto the surface of the pure lint one by one while the lint was feeding into the opening machine. After the lint with foreign fibers being opened, a continuous cotton layer is formed, 400mm wide and 2 mm thick, Totally 40 color images with 4000×500 in resolution were then obtained.

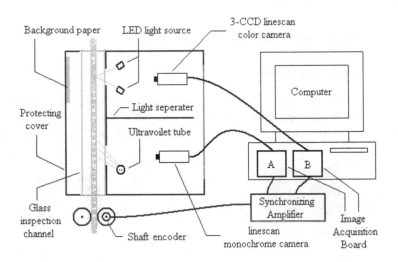

Fig. 2. The image acquisition system

By observing the images obtained, it was easy to find that the opened foreign fibers appeared in three typical forms, as shown in Fig. 3a–c, (1) sheet, such as plastic films, papers, etc., (2) wirelike, such as hair, color thread, etc., and (3) villiform, such as hemp rope, chemical fibers, etc.

As the original color image is too large but the target image is small, if the original image is directly inserted, it will result in an unclear target image, and affect the reader's vision. So same images in this paper are cut target images.

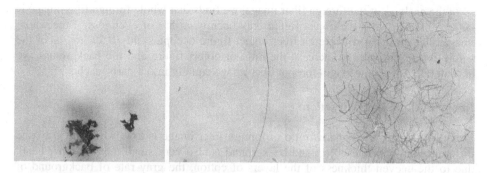

Fig. 3. Acquired color image examples: (a) opened plastic film, (b) opened hair, and (c) opened hemp rope

2.3   Image Segmentation

In the online detection of foreign fibers in lint using the machine-vision-based system, the speed and accuracy of algorithm are the key factors. Therefore, in order to ensure segmentation accuracy, the fastest segmentation algorithm should be chosen. Thresholding is a traditional method,which is widely used due to its computational simplicity, high speed and easy implementation. Ostu's Method, as an adaptive threshold method to confirm the threshold value, possesses the advantages of simple algorithm, high speed and so on. Moreover, it makes the biggest segmentation between-group variance implies getting the slightest chance to make errors, which means the Ostu's Method has the optimum segmentation threshold value so that the application of Ostu's method become widespread. However, due to the its problems existing in segmentation processing of images with heterogeneous background, small area proportion between object and background, or subtle difference of the gray rate between object and background, Otsu's Method has big variance in threshold value and therefore is unable to get segmented image with high quality. Nevertheless, cotton fiber image exactly belongs to the category small object image, which also has the characteristics such as small variance of gray rate and heterogeneous gray rate. Consequently, this paper employs preprocessing such as image block, image background extraction, gray-level correction, image enhancement, etc, to solve the problems.

Image Blocking

The segmentation result binarized by Otsu's method of an image is very satisfying for a good separation of figure and background. But, under the Otsu's method, only when object figure is larger than 25% of the whole image, the segmentation property is approximately optimum; when the area of moving object figure becomes smaller, the property of algorithm declines rapidly, which leads to smaller object figure and larger threshold value variance. Thus, to guarantee the segmentation accuracy and high-qualified segmentation result we divide the foreign fiber figure into several parts and combine them in sequence after image processing respectively, in order to resolve the problem of low ratio of the object figure and background area.

In the analysis of the foreign fiber image, we finds that whole foreign fiber image is 4000*500 large, with the object figure only occupying 5% or even less of the whole image. The most part of foreign fiber object figure occupies only 0.5% to 3% of the whole image. In order to increase the ratio of object figure and the background, we horizontally divide the origin foreign fiber image equally into 8 parts, each 500*500.

Image Background Extraction

Previously stated, the contrast ratio of foreign fiber image is low, while the gray rate difference between the object and background is also very small. On the other hand, due to the uneven thickness of the layers of cotton, the gray rate of background of foreign fiber image is heterogeneous. Meanwhile, the segmentation effects of Otsu's method on the low-ratio image or heterogeneous gray rate image is unsatisfying. Cotton foreign fiber image is just the case mentioned above. In order to get qualified segmentation effect, we need to enhance the image contrast ration by the use of the method of background subtraction and to eliminate the impact from the heterogeneous image background.

Background subtraction is to, by means of mathematical morphology or image gray-level correction and other methods, get the image background without the object, then subtracted from the origin image so as to reach the aim to highlight the object and reduce the influence of image background. This paper processes the foreign fiber image by image corrosion in mathematical morphology to obtain the image background.

$f(x, y)$ is the tight gradation function of $L^2(R)$, $g(i, j)$ is the gradation function for structural element.

The definition of corrosion for gradation function $f(x, y)$ is:

Corrosion definition:

$$f \Theta g(x, y) = \min_{(i,j)} \{ f(x+i, y+j) + g(i, j) \} \tag{1}$$

To make calculation convenient, the gray structure elements often take 0, that is

$g(i, j) = 0$. The structural element employed in the paper is round structural element

with the radius of 3. After the corrosion of foreign fiber image, we get a first-stage image background.

Image Gray-Level Correction

We can get background figure with comparative high quality by applying the above methods to the two kinds of foreign fiber image---wirelik and villiform, but we confront problems with the sheet foreign fiber image. The reason behind this is that the sheet foreign fiber image has larger object figure area, which incurs to the object figure remnants after the corrosion by radius 3 structural element. After the analyzing background figure of this type, we find that sheet foreign fiber image has greater gray-level and has more obvious difference with the cotton background. Therefore, we can improve the problems of this type via image gray-level correction to get highly-qualified background figure.

This paper utilized fixed threshold value 0.6 as a basic point to conduct image gray-level correction on image, that is, to replace the gray-level of all pixels that above 0.6 by certain needed gray-level value. The paper makes that certain value as 0 for convenience. Then we get a more satisfying background figure through image gray-level correction. Subsequently subtracting origin foreign fiber image with the obtained background figure, we get the foreign fiber image with the background extracted.

Image Enhancement Model

It is not difficulty to get the conclusion from the analysis result of the gray-level histogram of background-subtracted foreign fiber image that the gray-level of the background-subtracted foreign fiber image still exists in the low level part, as shown in Figure 4. This makes it difficult to perform the image segmentation to obtain the region of interesting. To solve this problem, we need to increase image contrast ration by image enhancement, so as to provide better image information basis for subsequent image segmentation. From Figure 6 we can see that the gray-level values of most pixels are below 0.08, which belongs to background figure, whereas pixels with gray-level value above 0.1 belongs to other parts of foreign figure image. And the pixels whose gray-level values are among 0.08-0.1 belong to the co-existing part of background and foreign fiber, that is, the gray edge of object and background, which exerts the most significant influences on subsequent image segmentation. Thus, a piecewise linear transform model was proposed, and the contrast of the image can be remarkably enhanced by this model, especially in the range from 0.08 to 0.1.

A piecewise transform model splits the distribution range of image pixels into two or more pieces, and performs transformation to each piece respectively to enhance the region of interesting. In our research, the main objective is to segment the foreign fiber objects out of the background, so a three-piece nonlinear model was proposed and described as follows.

Denote the original gray level in image position (i, j) to be GO (i, j), and the corresponding enhanced gray level to be GE (i, j). The gray-scale range need to focus on the image enhancement is [Ll, Lh]. The three-piece linear transform model for image enhancement is defined as

$$GE(i, j) = \begin{cases} GO(i, j) & GO(i, j) \leq L_l \\ 8*GO(i, j) & L_l < GO(i, j) < L_h \\ 0.5 & L_h \leq GO(i, j) \end{cases} \tag{2}$$

According to the histogram analysis, we set Ll=0.078 and Lh=0.1. The line of this three-piece enhancement model is shown in Fig.5.

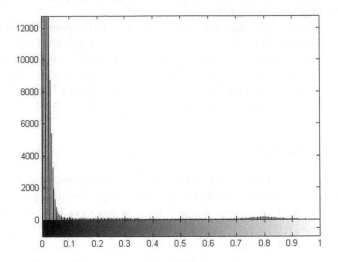

Fig. 4. Histograms of hair image

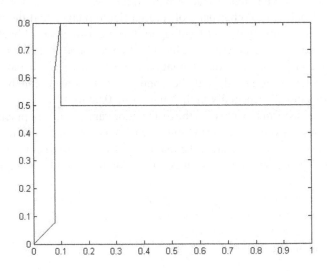

Fig. 5. Line of three-piece linear enhancement model

Image Segmentation

Speed and accuracy of an algorithm are key factors for the online visual inspection system (Golnabi and Asadpour, 2007). Hence, in addition to ensuring the segmentation accuracy, algorithms with faster speed are more attractive. The edge-based segmentation algorithm is effective when processing images with sharp edge and high contrast (Zhang, 2005). There are very little foreign fibers in lint, and the foreign fibers will be smashed by the opening machine before image acquisition. Therefore, the images of foreign fibers are of low contrast and are not suitable for using the edge-based segmentation algorithm. The special segmentation methods are also not fit for processing the foreign-fiber images due to their complexity and time consuming feature. Thresholding, a region-based segmentation technique, is then the preferred technique in segmenting the foreign-fiber images for its simplicity, speediness and stability.

The identification of cotton foreign fibers is carried out through real-time monitoring. However, different circumstances will have different light intensity. Therefore, the target segmentation for foreign fibers can not use a fixed thresholding value. The optimal threshold can be determined through a variety of ways, including histogram bimodal method (also known as the mode method), Otsu method and the iterative threshold method, etc. The Otsu's method (Otsu, 1979), which is also called maximum between-group variance method, is a kind of adaptive thresholding method which has the optimal threshold according to the statistics. The image is divided into two parts, namely, background and object, according to the gray character of the image. Computerizing between-group variance of background and object separated by every threshold value, we could find that when the between-group variance is the largest, the correspondent variance is optimum. The larger the variance is, the greater the difference of the two parts is. Therefore, the segmentation that has the largest between-group variance manifests the slightest chance of segmentation mistake, i.e., has the best threshold value in the sense of statistics. In this case, the dynamic thresholding was automatically selected by Ostu's method.

3   Results and Discussion

Seven typical foreign fibers, namely, plastic film, feather, polypropylene twine, hair, color thread, hemp rope and cloth piece, were used in the experiments. Ten samples were prepared for each type of foreign fibers. That is to say, there are totally 70 foreign-fiber samples. Adequate pure lint without foreign fibers was also prepared for making the lint layer. In our experiments, the pure lint with one type of foreign fiber dropped onto the surface at each time interval firstly was fed into the opening machine and then made into uniform thin layer, with 400mm in width and 2mm in thickness. The foreign fibers in the lint layer were presented in three forms, namely sheet, wirelike and villiform.

All the results of this paper were processed by the computer with the programming tools developed in Matlab7.0. Operating environment consists of: Inter Core2. PC-frequency: 2.60GHz, 2G Memory. and Windows XP was selected as the operation system.

3.1   Analysis of Image Background Subtraction

Foreign fiber image has low contrast ration and heterogeneous gray-level background, which brings a lot of troubles to the subsequent image processing. Therefore, we resort to the method background subtraction to solve to problem. Owing to the fact that foreign fiber image includes three types, i.e., sheet, wirelike, villiform, and the latter two are abundant in all foreign fibers, whereas the sheet fibers have a comparative low percentage. In addition, the connected area occupied by wirelike and villiform is so small that the foreign fiber image could be removed by erosion of smaller structural elements to get better background. On the other hand, because connected area occupied by the foreign fiber image of sheet type is comparatively large, so we need to use the large structural elements to corrode image. If we do so, the difference between the background figure subtracted and the original image will be too great to eliminate the influence of heterogeneity of background image. We can see from the gray-level analysis that the foreign fiber of sheet type mainly includes three subcategories as plastic film, feather and cloth piece, which all have deeper image gray-level and greater difference from the background figure. According to this, we could eliminate the remains of the object figure in the background by the Image gray-level correction, in order to get better background figure.

As mentioned above, the structural element employed In the process of image corrosion is round structural element with the radius of 3. After the corrosion of foreign fiber image, we get a first-stage image background as shown in Figure 6.

Fig. 6. Acquired background image examples: (a) background of plastic film, (b) background of hair, and (c) background of hemp rope

It is safe to say from Fig.6 we can get background figure with comparative high quality by applying the above methods to the two kinds of foreign fiber image---wirelik and villiform, but we confront problems with the sheet foreign fiber image. Thus, we could eliminate the remains of the object figure in the background by the Image gray-level correction, This paper utilized fixed threshold value 0.6 as a basic point to conduct image gray-level correction on image, that is, to replace the gray-level of all pixels that above 0.6 by 0. Then we get a more satisfying background figure through image gray-level correction. Subsequently, subtracting origin foreign fiber image with the obtained background figure, we get the foreign fiber image with the background extracted, as shown in Figure 7.

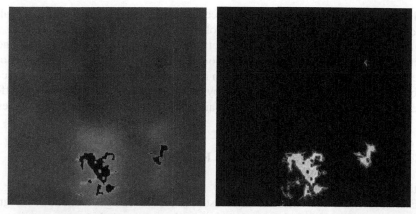

Fig. 7. (a) Acquired background image of plastic film after Image gray-level correction, (b) image of plastic film after background subtraction

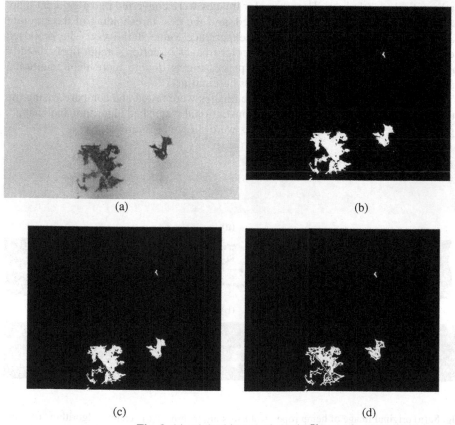

(a)   (b)

(c)   (d)

Fig. 8. (a) original image of plastic film
(b) Image of plastic film after background subtraction when the threshold is 0.5
(c) Image of plastic film after background subtraction when the threshold is 0.6
(d) Image of plastic film after background subtraction when the threshold is 0.7

In the course of image gray-level correction, the confirmation of threshold value is crucial step. Improper choice of threshold value---too high or too low, will exert negative influence on the details of object figure in the image whose background has been subtracted. Trough several comparison of experiment results, we determine on the threshold value 0.6. Figure 8 is the foreign fiber image got from plastic film image after its background subtracted and processed by the image gray-level correction by different threshold values. From the Figure 8 it is fair to say that threshold value 0.6 can reserve the details of origin image better.

3.2   Analysis of Image Segmentation Results

In the paper <
A Fast Segmentation Method for High-resolution Color Images of Cotton Foreign Fib ers> (Zhang et al., 2011), the author presents a fast approach for segmenting images of foreign fibers in cotton.。 Firstly, color images were captured, and the edge of color images were detected by edge detection method which is based on improved mathematical morphology. Then the color images were converted into a gradient map, the law of experience values was analyzed, and the best thresholding of the gradient map was chosen by selecting the best experience value iteratively. The proposed method can segment the high-resolution color images of cotton foreign fibers directly and precisely, and the speed of image processing is double more than traditional methods (referred to as zhang's algorithms hereinafter).

In our research, more than 2500 sample images were tested and compared using the Otsu's algorithm, Canny algorithm, the conventional watershed algorithm and zhang's algorithm. The image segmentation results were shown as figure 9.

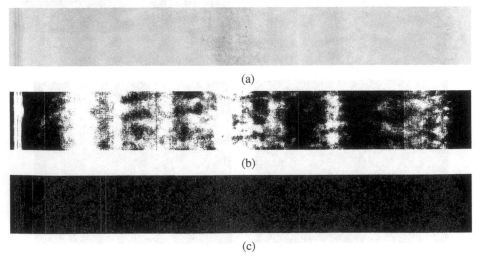

(a)

(b)

(c)

Fig. 8. (a) original image of hemp rope (b)Ostu's algorithm   (c) canny algorithm (d) the conventional watershed algorithms (e) zhang's algorithms (f)algorithm of this paper

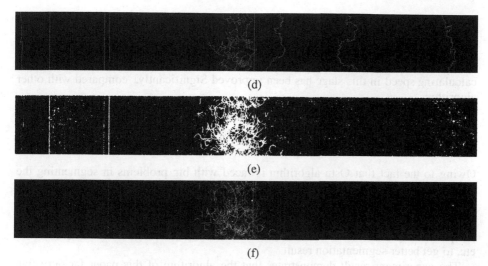

(d)

(e)

(f)

Fig. 9. (*continued*)

We can obviously see from the above figure the direct use of Ostu, Canny and the conventional watershed algorithms to segment image can not result in the clear segmentation of the object figure to meet our requirement. While Zhang's algorithms could get better segmentation result, the algorithm of this paper reserves more foreign fiber image details that make the segmentation result much clearer and higher segmentation accuracy.

3.3   Analysis of Image Calculating Speed

In our experiments of image segmentation, we have drew a comparison of the calculating speed of five methods, namely, Otsu's algorithms, Canny algorithms, the conventional watershed algorithms, zhang's algorithms and the algorithm of this paper.The results have shown that the average time for the five kinds of segmentation method of processing foreign fibers are: 0.26 s, 5.84 s, 9.23 s, 3.92s and 2.38s.Table 1 shows the average time of the five kinds of segmentation algorithm.

Table 1. Comparison of experiment results

time(s)	Segmentation method				
	Otsu	Canny	watershed	zhang's	this paper
average time of calculation	0.26	5.84	9.23	3.92	2.38

The results shown in Table 4 indicate that, the calculating speed of Canny algorithm, the conventional watershed algorithm and Zhang's algorithm for segmentation of images for foreign fibers are significantly slower than the one presented in this paper. Moreover, seen from the segmentation result, it is obvious that this algorithm has great advantages over other algorithm in segmentation accuracy. Exclusive use of Ostu algorithm without any other pre-processing to segment the image, though fast in speed, could not provide us with the result we expect.

Thus, the results of above analysis showed that we can acquire better segmentation results, whether in the case of wirelike, the villiform or the sheet foreign fibers. And the calculating speed in this stage has been improved Significantly⬜ compared with other algorithms.

4   Conclusion

Owing to the fact that Ostu algorithm is faced with big problems in segmenting the image that has low contrast ratio between object figure and background, small area of object figure or heterogeneous gray-level of background image---which type that foreign fiber image is unfortunately belongs to, we seek for solution by a series of pre-processing methods such as image block, background subtraction, gray balance, etc, to get better segmentation result.

The experiment result demonstrates that the algorithm of this paper far outweigh other algorithms in the past both in accuracy or speed.

The mandate of speed is a key factor for the online visual inspection system. Hence, in addition to ensuring the segmentation accuracy, algorithms of faster speed is now being studied.

References

1. Abouelela, A., Abbas, H.M., Eldeed, H., Wahdam, A.A., Nassar, S.M.: Automated vision system for localizing structural defects in textile fabrics. Pattern Recognition Letters 26(10), 1435–1443 (2005)
2. Bakker, T., Wouters, H., van Asselt, K., Bontsema, J., Tang, L., Muller, J., van Straten, G.: A vision based row detection system for sugar beet. Computers and Electronics in Agriculture 60(1), 87–95 (2008)
3. Chaira, T., Ray, A.K.: Threshold selection using fuzzy set theory. Pattern Recognition Letters 25(8), 865–874 (2004)
4. Chen, Y.R., Chao, K.L., Kim, M.S.: Machine vision technology for agricultural applications. Computers and Electronics in Agriculture 36(2–3), 173–191 (2002)
5. Funck, J.W., Zhong, Y., Butler, D.A., Brunner, C.C., Forrer, J.B.: Image segmentation algorithms applied to wood defect detection. Computers and Electronics in Agriculture 41(1–3), 157–179 (2003)
6. Zhang, H., Frittsb, J.E., Goldmana, S.A.: Image segmentation evaluation: A survey of unsupervised methods. Computer Vision and Image Understanding 110, 260–280 (2008)
7. Kim, B.G., Shim, J.I., Park, D.J.: Fast image segmentation based on multiresolution analysis and wavelets. Pattern Recognition Letters 24(6), 2995–3006 (2003)
8. Kwon, S.H.: Threshold selection based on cluster analysis. Pattern Recognition Letters 25(9), 1045–1050 (2004)
9. Lieberman, M.A., Bragg, C.K., Brennan, S.N.: Determining gravimetric bark content in cotton with machine vision. Textile Research Journal 68(2), 94–104 (1998)
10. Millman, M.P., Acar, M., Jackson, M.R.: Computer vision for textured yarn interlace (nip) measurements at high speeds. Mechatronics 11(8), 1025–1038 (2001)

11. Otsu, N.: A threshold selection method from gray-level histograms. IEEE Transactions on SMC 9(1), 62–66 (1979)
12. Pichel, J.C., Singh, D.E., Rivera, F.F.: Image segmentation based on merging of sub-optimal segmentations. Pattern Recognition Letters 27(10), 1105–1116 (2006)
13. Susomboon, R., Stan Raicu, D., Furst, J.: A hybrid approach for liver segmentation. In: MICCAI 2007 Workshop Proceedings of the 3D Segmentation in the Clinic: a Grand Challenge, pp. 151–160 (2007)
14. Su, Z.W., Tian, G.Y., Gao, C.H.: A machine vision system for on-line removal of contaminants in wool. Mechatronics 16(5), 243–247 (2006)
15. Yang, W., et al.: A new approach for image processing in foreign fiber detection. Comput. Electron. Agric. (2009), doi:10.1016/j.compag.2009.04.005
16. Zhang, H., Fritts, J.E., Goldman, S.A.: Image segmentation evaluation: a survey of unsupervised methods. Computer Vision and Image Understanding 110, 260–280 (2008)
17. Zhang, X., et al.: A Fast Segmentation Method for High-resolution Color Images of Cotton Foreign Fibers. Computers and Electronics in Agriculture (2011), doi:2011.06.005
18. Zhang, Y.J.: Image Engineering(II)Image Analysis. Tsinghua University Press, Beijing (2005)

A Portable Measurement Instrument for the Measurement of Water Body Chlorophyll-a in the Support of Fluorescence Detection

Cong Wang[1], Daoliang Li[1], Lingxian Zhang[1,*], Qisheng Ding[1,2], and Zetian Fu[1]

[1] College of Information and Electric Engineering,
China Agriculture University, Beijing, 100083, P.R. China
zlx131@163.com
[2] School of Electrical Engineering and Automation,
Xuzhou Normal University, Xuzhou, 2211116, P.R. China

Abstract. Chlorophyll-a was regarded as the important indicator to describe the marine primary production because the chlorophyll a content of phytoplankton in the ocean is related to its photosynthesis production. The concentration of chlorophyll a is also the major parameter to evaluate marine water quality, organic pollution and detect the fishing ground, and the temporal and spatial variation of chlorophyll a contains the basic information of sea areas. Based on the spectral characteristics of chlorophyll fluorescence, this document recommends a new dual optical detecting instrument for the measurement of chlorophyll-a concentration, the microcontroller MSP430F149 as the key control module, by controlling the ultra-high brightness LED which wavelength is 450nm to excite chlorophyll a to produce the fluorescent signal about 680nm, at the same time this LED is used as reference light, the dual-optical structure exclude the light fluctuations due to the impact of test results. At last, we get the relationship between relative fluorescence intensity and chlorophyll-a concentration with the spectrophotometer, we find the system has the good linear consistency when measures the low concentrations of chlorophyll-a.

Keywords: Chlorophyll-a, Relative fluorescence intensity, Dual-optical structure, Fluorescent signal.

1 Introduction

In recent years, China's Taihu, Wuhu lake, Songhua river and other water environment have emerged water crisis, due to the continued outbreak of blue-green algae classes in the water, making the phytoplankton in water sharply increase, the water oxygen exhaust, the water body is showing a large area of hypoxia and so large number of aquatic life is dying. As the rapid growth of algae, green algae accumulate on the

---

* Corresponding author.

D. Li and Y. Chen (Eds.): CCTA 2011, Part III, IFIP AICT 370, pp. 484–494, 2012.

surface of the water, causing water problems, water body cannot exchange air with the outside world, day by day become foul, to the people's production, life and health have brought great harm.

The evaluation of eutrophication can be achieved by tracking and monitoring the chlorophyll content in water, all of which chlorophyll a is highest concentrations of chlorophyll, chlorophyll a determination can thus trace the lake's eutrophication [1,2]. In the mid-1970s, Soviet oceanographers first use pulse xenon lamp as the light source, narrow band interference filter and pulse detection technology for the development of pulsed underwater fluorometer. From the late 1970s to the early 1980s, many developed countries had been studying multi-parameter, multi-purpose drag fluorometer /conductivity, temperature, depth (CTD) sensor system development [3]. In 1997, K.Wild-Allen simultaneously measured water color and chlorophyll concentration by using the sea buoy quipped with a color sensor and fluorometer [4]. R. Barbini established laboratory of the fluorescent sensors which supplied for large-scale walking route monitoring from different conditions of seawater, monitoring object included the concentration of phytoplankton, yellow substance, turbidity, biomass productivity and organic pollutants [5]. In the late 1990s, TriOS companies (German) used super-efficient blue LEDs (wavelength 470nm) and the internal reference diode control energy output, selected photodiode as a monitor, successfully developed a portable microFlu-chl-type sensors which can be directly related to the different instrument to read continuous data and collect data, measurement range of 0~100 μg/L, a resolution of 0.02 μg/L, the accuracy for the optical reading of 3% (http://www.trios.de/). Such as these foreign chlorophyll fluorometer, there are many, but they are expensive, and their operation is more cumbersome. Laboratory methods of measuring the concentration of chlorophyll-a include high-performance liquid chromatography (HPLC) and spectrophotometry they all need to extract chlorophyll from phytoplankton, not only the workload, and there is a lot of confounding factors in the whole process, the final result is likely to get the wrong data. Remote sensing methods need not extract, is an online measurement method, but only for a large area of water, and aerial work demanding, complex test results [6].

This paper presents a new site available for determination of chlorophyll fluorescence, high sensitivity, fast, real-time and good benefits, can be used for lakes, rivers, oceans and other water eutrophication on-site inspection [7,8,9,10].

2   Materials and Methods

2.1   Fluorescence Detection Principle

When chlorophyll a is excited by the wavelength of 450nm light around, it will send around a wavelength of 680nm fluorescence [11,12,13], the fluorescence emission intensity:

$$I_f = kQI_0 \left(1 - e^{-\varepsilon cb}\right) \tag{1}$$

Where: k is the instrument constant; Q is the fluorescence efficiency of material; I_0 is the light intensity of excitation source; c is the concentration of substance; b is the optical path difference of sample; ε is the molar absorption coefficient.

As long as the excitation light intensity is stable, the fluorescence intensity is only related with the concentration of chlorophyll a, chlorophyll-a concentration c and the relationship between the fluorescence intensity F:

$$c = A - B \lg (D - F)$$ (2)

Where: $A = 2.3 \lg(kQI_0)/\varepsilon b$; $B = 2.3/\varepsilon b$; $D = kQI_0$. Therefore, the chlorophyll-a concentration can be detected by the detection of the received fluorescence intensity.

When the solution is very dilute, the total excitation energy is absorbed less than 5%, or $\varepsilon cb \leq 0.05$, In Eq.(1), by power series expansion, since the second term is negligible, we get Eq.(3):

$$I_f = kQI_0\varepsilon cb$$ (3)

In Eq.(3), when a fluorescent substance concentration is very dilute and the related excitation source is stable, fluorescence intensity is proportional to the concentration of the solution. However, when the concentration $c > 0.05/\varepsilon b$, the fluorescence intensity and concentration is not proportional, but when the concentration increases to a certain extent, to further increase the fluorescence intensity of concentration no longer enhanced. Because at this time, $e^{-\varepsilon cb} \approx 0$, so Eq. (1) becomes $I_f = kQI_0$, At this point, no fluorescence intensity changes with concentration changes.

2.2   Dual Beam and Dual-Channel Measuring

By analyzing the Eq.(1), we can see, the changes in excitation light intensity has a great influence on the measurement results, so the system is designed with a dual optical path test structure(Fig.1). Two light paths are added interference filter and lens. By using the lens, the reference light and fluorescent light-gathering rate is enhanced, while the use of interference filter improves the conversion efficiency of photosensitive devices through filtering out most of the background light. In this System, photodiode converts the optical signal to light current, LEDs as the excitation light and reference light, its light intensity value is defined as I_0, and fluorescence signal intensity value is defined as I_f. Two signals processed through signal conditioning circuits are sent to the MSP430 microcontroller A/D side sampling (Fig.2), and finally by the microcontroller to calculate the ratio of two signals Eq.(4).

$$I_f/I_0 = kQ\left(1 - e^{-\varepsilon cb}\right)$$ (4)

For the dilute solution, we can get Eq.(5):

$$I_f/I_0 = kQ\varepsilon cb$$ (5)

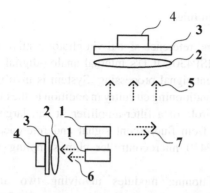

**1.Blue Leds 2.Convex Lens 3.Interference filter
4.Photodiode 5.Fluorometry 6. Reference light
7.Blue light**

Fig. 1. Fluorescence signal detection system

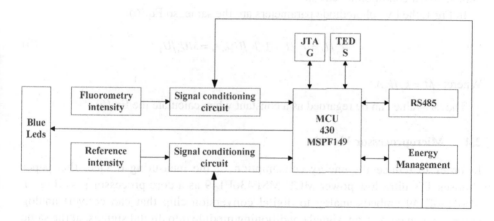

Fig. 2. Block diagram of the Chlorophyll a Intelligent instrument

Which can calculate the relative fluorescence intensity values to get the value of chlorophyll concentration. Therefore, the use of dual beam and dual-channel mode, by division and other operations to complete the normalization process, can effectively eliminate the excitation light intensity fluctuations on the measurement results, making the measurements more accurate.

2.3 Signal Conditioning Modules

In Fig.1, fluorescence signal and reference signal via photosensitive device, the light signals into current signals, MSP430 MCU's internal analog-digital conversion chip cannot be directly on the current signal processing. System is involved in the signal conditioning circuitry, signal conditioning circuitry in addition to the current signal into a voltage signal, but also the role of a filter-amplifier, it can largely filter out the background and circuit noise from fluorescent signal and reference signal, and its amplification meets the MSP430 microcontroller chip sampling within the A/D requirements.

Fluorescence signal conditioning modules involving two amplifier circuit, completes the first stage current-voltage conversion, the conversion factor is denoted as k_1, also completes the second level voltage amplification, magnification is recorded as A_1. The reference light signal conditioning module is relatively simple, according to the reference light intensity with the strong characteristics, using only one amplifier, the current voltage conversion circuit, the conversion factor is denoted as k_2. We can calculate $U_1 = I_A k_1 A_1$ and $U_2 = I_B k_2$, where: I_A is light current from the fluorescence signal ; I_B is light current from the reference optical signal; U_1 is output voltage from the fluorescence signal conditioning circuit; U_2 is output voltage from the reference optical signal conditioning circuit.

In Fig.1, the two photodiode parameters are the same, so Eq.(6).

$$I_A/I_B = I_f/I_0 = U_1 k_2/U_2 k_1 A_1 = M U_1/U_2 \tag{6}$$

Where: $M = k_2/k_1 A_1$.

The M value can be regarded as a constant when calculate the Eq.(6).

2.4 Microprocessor Module

In order to reduce the energy consumption of the measuring device, this paper chooses TI's ultra low power MCU MSP430F149 as a core processor [14] (Fig.2), MSP430F149 embeds analog to digital conversion chip that can convert analog signals which come from signal conditioning module into digital signals, at the same time with the external power management module , microprocessor module also can supply energy for signal conditioning module. By using MSP430F149 internal timer A, we can control the duty cycle and frequency of the blue LEDs flashes, the system LEDs blinking frequency is 10HZ, the ratio is 50% [15]. MSP430F149 single-chip system via the JTAG interface to debug and download program. Moreover, in order to make the measurement devices more intelligent, able to achieve record and store the channel parameters and calibration parameters table, we design the spreadsheets (TEDS) in the flash of MSP430F149. The system uses RS485 bus output(Fig.2).

2.5   Software Peak Detector Design

In laboratory experiments, we detect the chlorophyll-a fluorescence signal waveform (Fig. 3).

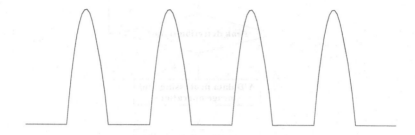

Fig. 3. Simulation of the Detection Waveform

This device which consists of interference filters ,largely reduces the external impact of background light and emit blue light when obtains the fluorescence signal, and part of the design of the signal conditioning module blocking circuit, band pass filter and 50HZ notch filter, as the implementation of these circuits make the extraction of the fluorescent signal more pure. After analyzing of chlorophyll-a fluorescence signal waveform (Fig.3), the paper designs a software peak detection method, by controlling the microcontroller A/D converter chip sampling delay, to achieve in a half-cycle-interval sampled 255 times, whichever maximum value is stored. We define the average of the 10 consecutive maximum as the original voltage U_1' of the fluorescence signal, software peak detection method is also applicable to the original value of the reference signal acquisition, the original definition of the reference signal voltage is U_2'. The final calculation of the relative fluorescence intensity can be expressed as $I_f/I_0 = MU_1/U_2 = MU_1'/U_2' = kQ(1-e^{-\varepsilon cb})$ or $U_1'/U_2' = kQ(1-e^{-\varepsilon cb})/M$, that is the results in theory which the system should get, so, we can see different concentrations of the measurement results should meet the negative exponential curve. Also we can get $U_1'/U_2' = kQ\varepsilon cb/M$ when the solution is very dilute, when, this should satisfy the linear time. Software flow chart shown as Fig.4.

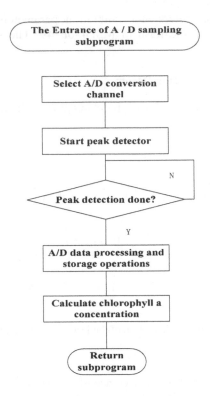

Fig. 4. A/D conversion module program

3   Result and Discussion

3.1   Preparation of Chlorophyll-a Standard Solution

In the preparation of chlorophyll a standard solution, we mainly extract chlorophyll-a by use of laboratory extraction method. First, select skeletonema costatum which was in the exponential phase of growth , weight class by its small to large is divided into A, B and C , respectively, filter through a diameter of 0.45 acetate membrane, the membrane is then placed in 100mL centrifuge tube, add 50 ml of 90% concentration of acetone, the tube extraction at 4°C refrigerator 2 hours, then to 4000 r/min centrifugation for 5 minutes, last, collect the supernatant with 50 ml brown flask in constant volume, and this solution as stock solution. When laboratory measurements, we can dilute the stock solution according to the needs of the required concentration. Through analysis of the nature of chlorophyll, we find the chemical properties of chlorophyll was unstable, so the prepared acetone solution of chlorophyll-a needs to be placed in dark place and the effective time for the solution is less 24 hours.

3.2   Evaluate of Instrument Performance and Standard Curve

The chlorophyll fluorescence measuring instrument measuring range is 0~25 µg/L, and the measuring minimum limit is 0.03 µg/L. Instrument in actual measurement, the value of the relative fluorescence intensity is very small, not easy to device calibration and instrument performance analysis, so we select U_1'/U_2' instead of I_f/I_0, the method has no effect on the calibration of instruments, and the rest of the photos or tables are processed in the same way. In the experiment of the instrument repeatability, we choose the prepared acetone solutions of the chlorophyll-a A and B as the experimental fluid, every 5 min, respectively, measure repeatedly the two solutions five times, the measurement results as shown in Table 1. According to the definition of repeatability, we could calculate the standard deviation 0.0024 and 0.0021 by Bessel's formula [16], that proves the instrument has good repeatability.

Table 1. The data of repeatability experiment

The number of measurements	The relative fluorescence intensity in acetone-A solution	The relative fluorescence intensity in acetone-B solution
1	1.422	2.114
2	1.425	2.114
3	1.421	2.111
4	1.427	2.112
5	1.425	2.109

In the linearity test for the measuring instruments, we must first divide the concentration levels of acetone solution of chlorophyll-a. Delineation of specific: non-chlorophyll acetone solution is defined as the 0 level; after a 1/8 fold dilution of the acetone solution of chlorophyll A is defined as 1/8 level; after 1/4 times the concentration of chlorophyll in acetone diluted solution A is defined as 1/4 level; after 1/2 times the concentration of chlorophyll in acetone diluted solution A is defined as 1/2 level; the original acetone solution of chlorophyll A is defined as 1 level; original chlorophyll acetone solution B is defined as Level 2 and the original chlorophyll acetone solution C is defined as the 3 level. The relationship between the average of relative fluorescence intensity from experimental measurement and chlorophyll concentration levels can be described as in Fig.5.

Fig.5 shows the measured relative fluorescence intensity close to the negative index, and theoretical analysis of the relative fluorescence intensity: $I_f/I_0 = kQ\left(1-e^{-\varepsilon cb}\right)$ is very close to this. It can be seen, if the concentration increased to a certain extent, the fluorescence intensity will not change significantly.

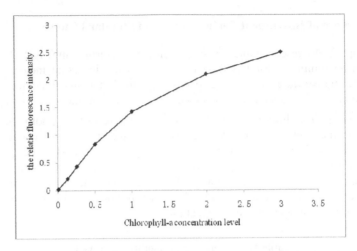

Fig. 5. Detecting results of the relative fluorescence intensity

In order to analyze the relationship between the relative fluorescence intensity and concentration, we has measured 0, 1/8, 1/4, 1/2 and 1grade acetone concentration of chlorophyll-a for getting the value of the relative fluorescence intensity. In theory, the relationship between the concentration of the diluted solution and the relative fluorescence intensity is $I_f / I_0 = kQ\varepsilon cb$. In Fig.6, the relative fluorescence intensity and concentration is in a linear relationship, which meets the theoretical results of the analysis, so the system design is feasible.

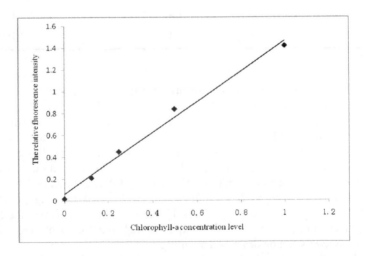

Fig. 6. Detecting results of the relative fluorescence intensity in weak acetone solution

According to national standard methods, we detect the concentration of the five levels of chlorophyll dilute solution with multi-wavelength spectrophotometer method [17], the measuring results is 0 μg/L, 3.05 μg/L, 6.32 μg/L, 12.53 μg/L and 19.82 μg/L from small to large order. As the Fig.7 shown, fluorescence intensity converted into concentration by the equation:

$$y = 14.2x - 0.01 \qquad (7)$$

Where: x is the relative fluorescence intensity; y is the chlorophyll-a concentration.

The linear regression coefficient is 0.997, that is, the measuring device in case of low value has a good linear consistency.

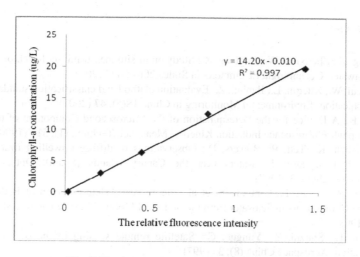

Fig. 7. Testing results using spectrophotometer

4   Conclusion

In this article, we carefully study the fluorescence detection method for measuring the chlorophyll-a content and chlorophyll-a fluorescence characteristics, combined with domestic and international issues related to research, design a low-power, low noise, high speed chlorophyll-a content measuring device.

(1) The system chooses MSP430F149 microcontroller as the core of the detection control unit, its rich pin function and the built-in functional unit simplify the system's design, while improve the system's stability and anti-jamming capability.

The system uses ultra-high brightness, a wavelength of about 460nm blue LEDs as (2) the excitation source, while the use of single-chip PWM output control, and other functional units select low-power devices for designing, effectively reduce the system power consumption, system overall average power consumption is only 0.03W.

(3) Due to the light fluctuations, test results may not be accurate, so, in order to exclude the impact, the system applies the structure of dual optical detection. When debugging is complete, we select different concentrations of chlorophyll acetone solution for measurement, analysis the relationship between the relative fluorescence intensity and concentrations of chlorophyll-a, and then complete the calibration

solution of chlorophyll with the spectrophotometer, the system repeatability tests and linearity tests. As can be seen from the experimental data, the system has the good linear consistency when measures the low concentrations of chlorophyll-a.

Acknowledgements. This work was supported by the programs "Development and Applications of sensor network applied to monitor bloom of blue-green algae in Taihu Lake" (2010ZX03006-006), and Beijing Natural Science Foundation "Integrations methods of digitalization technologies in intensive fish farming" (4092024).

References

1. Daying, X., Zhenxian, W., Jingfang, X.: Study on in-situ measuring set for chlorophyll-a in the seawater. Oceanologia Et Limnologia Sinica 20(4), 472 (2003)
2. Mingcui, W., Xueqin, L., Jianhui, Z.: Evaluation method and classification standard on lake eutrophication. Environmental Monitoring in China 18(5), 47 (2002)
3. Ruth, B.: A Device for the Determination of the Microsecond Component of the in vivo Chlorophyll Fluorescence Induction Kinetics. Meas. Sci. Technol. (1), 517 (1990)
4. Wild-Allen, K., Tett, P., Bowers, D.: Observations of diffuse upwelling irradiance and chlorophyll in case I waters near the Canary Islands (Spain). Optics & Laser Technology 29(1), 3 (1997)
5. Barbini, R., Colao, F., Fantoni, R., et al.: Fluorescence Determination of Pollutants and Natural Components in Seawater from the on Board Mobile Lidar Apparatus. SPIE (3534), 359 (1998)
6. Yunwu, L., Shuzhi, Z., Yunguo, G.: Satellite remote sensing in the ocean observing application. Aerospace China (8), 3 (1997)
7. Beutler, M.: A fluorometric method for the differentiation of algal populations in vivo and situ. Photosynthesis Research 72, 39 (2002)
8. Zhigang, W.: The phytoplankton classified measure based on excitation fluorescence spectra technique. China Environmental Science 28(3), 329 (2008)
9. Lianhua, C., Lei, L.: Application of the chlorophyll fluorescence in photosynthesis of alga. Jiangxi Science 25(6), 788 (2007)
10. Sharma, S., Schulman, S.G.: Introduction to fluorescence spectroscopy, pp. 22–23. John Wiley and Sons. Inc., New York (1999)
11. Ruth, B.: A Device for the Determination of the Microsecond Component of the in vivo Chlorophyll Fluorescence Induction Kinetics. Meas. Sci. Technol. (1), 517 (1990)
12. Guozhen, C.: Fluorescence analysis, p. 12. Science Press, Beijing (1975)
13. Brechet, E., Stay, D.M., Wakefield, R.D., et al.: A novel blue LED based scanning hand-held fluorometer for detection of terrestrial algae on solid surfaces. SPIE 3414, 184 (1998)
14. Lierda.MSP430F13X／F14X Chinese data sheet [EB／OL] (2005), http://www.lierda.com
15. Jian, Q., Guanling, Y., Zhenjiang, H., et al.: Atmospheric S02 concentration analyzer based on ultra-violet fluorescence. Chinese Journal of Scientific Instrument 29(1), 175 (2008)
16. Taylor, J.R.: An Introduction to Error Analysis, pp. 294–298. University Science Books (1981)
17. State Environmental Protection Administration 《Water and wastewater monitoring and analysis methods》 Editorial Board. Water and wastewater monitoring and analysis methods, 4th edn., pp. 670–671. China Environmental Science Press, Beijing (2002)

The Key Information Technology
of Soybean Disease Diagnosis

Baoshi Jin[1,2], Xiaodan Ma[3], Zhongwen Huang[4], and Yuhu Zuo[5,*]

[1] College of Agronomy Heilongjiang Bayi Agricultural University
DaQing China 163319
[2] General bureau of state farms of Heilongjiang Province Harbin China 150036
[3] College of Information Technology Heilongjiang Bayi Agricultural University
DaQing China 163319
[4] Academy of Sciences of Heilongjiang Land Reclamation Jia Musi China 154002
[5] College of Agronomy Heilongjiang Bayi Agricultural University
DaQing China 163319
zuoyhu@163.com

Abstract. Combining image processing and artificial neural network technology, a new diagnose method of soybean leaf diseases has been proposed, which identified the methods of division algorithm and eigenvalue computation, meanwhile, established a three-level neural network model to identify the diseased spot areas. According to the characteristics of soybean leaf disease, a new diagnose method has been formed, through extraction of geometric features, color and texture feature, which provided reference to Remote Intelligent diagnosis of soybean leaf disease.

Keywords: Soybean, Leaf Diseases, Image Processing, Neural network, Diagnose.

1   Introduction

At present, The image processing technology has become an important agricultural research content of digital agricultural information detection, the disease type, extent and damage control methods can be passed to agricultural producers synchronously after the disease images have been processed, segmented and recognized using image processing technology, through which, the diseases can be diagnosed automatically, comprising to traditional diagnose method, the method based on image processing technology has many advantages such as simple, rapid, real-time, objective, accuracy etc.

For the most of plants, the diseases can be reflected through its lamina at a great degree, so it is possible to get affected condition through researching laminas, and the identification of disease spots and its associated feature information become the basis

---

* Corresponding author.
The project supported by General bureau of state farms of Heilongjiang Province (HNK11A-06-02-02).

D. Li and Y. Chen (Eds.): CCTA 2011, Part III, IFIP AICT 370 , pp. 495–501, 2012.

for judging Diseases. As early as 1995, Tao[1] studied on color differences between apples and potatoes using machine vision, Zhou-Long[2] detected the image edge and Shen Zuo-rui[3] distinguished the geometrical characteristic among images using fuzzy enhancement and mathematics morphology separately.

Since the mid-20th century, 80, the image processing technology has been widely used in agricultural engineering studies. after retrieving a large number of crop diseases diagnosis technology[4-12], we found that, Ma Xiaodan[13] etc has achieved automatic recognition of soybean leaf diseased spots using neural network technology, CaoMin[14] has achieved determination of soybean nitrogen using image processing technology, Mari Oide[15] has recogonized 364 leaf shapes of 38 soybean varieties using Hopfield pattern recognition which did not require any shape feature extraction, the neural network determined right and wrong. in summary, soybean leaf disease diagnosis technology based on image processing and neural network have not been reported yet.

This article will focus on technology based on image processing and neural network to diagnose the soybean leaf diseases, in the field environment, through the machine vision to obtain image of leaf disease samples, to achieve automatic identification of disease, computer image processing and pattern recognition technology are proposed to diagnose the soybean leaf diseases, furthermore, has become the basement for remote intelligent diagnosis of soybean diseases.

2   Materials and Methods

2.1   Image Acquisition

The samples of soybean leaf diseases have been collected in open environment of field, which used non-destructive collection method, in natural light, soybean leaves have been loaded in home-made loading template, and used DSLR-α350 SONY digital cameras wih 14.2 million effective pixels to collect the images which would be stored into soybean leaf disease image database with JPEG format.

Fig. 1. The image of diseased leaf

2.2   Pre-processing of Plant Disease Image

Image of plant disease leaf could be affected by various noise sources in the generation and transmission which would lead to quality degradation. It is impossible to describe statistical model using random process, thus, this article used a local smoothing method to eliminate image noises, which named median filter approach.

A median filter window may be square (m×m), rectangular (m×n) or cross-shaped etc.

Firstly, Median filter will sort the gray value of template pixel, while n is odd number, the gray value of pixel Located in the middle is called the median number of these n numbers., while n is even number, the gray value of pixel Located in the middle of the average of the two values is called the median number, the expression is as follows:

$$g(i, j) = median[f_A(i, j)]$$

(1)

Where, the median represents the middle value of the window, $f_A(i, j)$ represents the gray value of pixel.

2.3   Recognition of Diseased Spots

BP network is one of the most widely used class of models, among of which the error is back propagation. From the topology point of view, BP network is a typical hierarchical network structure, is divided into input layer, hidden layer and output layer, between layers generally use the whole interconnect, the figure 1 is a three-layer BP neural network, i, j, k are input node, output node and hidden node separately.

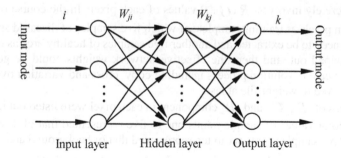

Fig. 2. Three-Layer BP network structure diagram

The input layer receives external input mode, and has been transmitted by the input node to the nodes of hidden layer. The hidden layer is a layer of internal processing units of BP network and pattern recognition has mainly achieved by the hidden layer nodes. Assume that there is a input mode $X_p = \{X_{pi}\}$, the each output of hidden layer nodes can be expressed as:

$$I_{pj} = \sum_i w_{ji} O_{pi}$$

(2)

Where, w_{ji} is the connection weights between input layer and hidden layer nodes, O_{pi} is the output value of input node, the output of hidden layer is expressed as follows:

$$O_{pj} = \frac{1}{1 + e^{-I_{pj}}}$$

(3)

Output layer produces the final classification result, that is the output mode, the output node of input layer is as follows:

$$I_{pk} = \sum_j w_{kj} O_{pj}$$

(4)

w_{kj} is connection weights between the node j of hidden layer and node k of output layer, O_{pj} is the output value of node j of hidden layer. The output of node k is as follows:

$$O_{pk} = \frac{1}{1 + e^{-I_{pk}}}$$

(5)

For the attraction of disease pathogen, the color of diseased spots area has often been influenced in a certain degree, which different with healthy area of lamina obviously, thus, the color characteristics of diseased area and healthy area would be used as input values, concretely involves R, G, B values of each pixel; In the course of the study, choosing ten pixels as training samples, of which five samples of diseased spots used as input value need to be extracted and another five samples of healthy area as input values should be wiped out, and then, the effective network weights could be got though a series complicated evolution process including copy, cross and variation over and over again, and saved to weight file at last.

The values of R, G and B component in each pixel were listed out in table 1 ,of which the color values of sample points one to five represented that of diseased spots, and anther five sample points six to ten represented that of background area.

Fig. 3. Soybean leaf diseased spot Image before and after recognized

2.4   Feature Calculation

1) Geometric Feature[16]

The characteristic parameters of the lesion is very important to determine the diseases, This region labeling and contour tracking has been used to calculate the geometric characteristics of lesion area.

Table 1. Values of Geometric Feature

No.	S	L	c	e	E	s
1	278	62	0.909	13.827	0.844	0.576
2	1311	139	0.853	14.738	0.950	0.638
......	......	......	......	......	......	......

2) Color Feature[17]

While diagnosis of crop diseases, the HSI model has great advantages, HSI model can reduce the light intensity to determine the impact of color, therefore, this study extract the color feature in   HSI color space, therefore, RGB space need to converted to HSI color space.

Table 2. Values of Color Feature

No.	H	S	I
1	64.71	32.53	78.21
2	69.72	33.00	66.52
......	......	......	......

3) Texture Feature[18]

The image of disease leaf includes not only geometric information, color information, but also contains the texture information, fiom which many valuable information can be abtained. Because different types of disease pathogens can produce different diseases, the lesion area showes different texture, thus, the texture features can provide an important basis for identification of disease.

Table 3. Values of Texture Feature

No.	m	R	μ_3	U
1	245.52	0.02	-3.61	0.70
2	226.81	0.06	-8.00	0.47
......	......	......	......	......

3   Result and Discussion

From figure 1, we see that the color of soybean brown spot is obviously different to that of healthy area, so it is feasible to use color characteristic as input value of the network, and the most of the diseased spots shown in figure 4 have been extracted, especially the bigger ones with distinct characteristic, so the algorithm accuracy can reach to more than 90%, furthermore, the main influenced factor lay in some aspects bellow:

1) The first factor is the number of samples, how many samples should be chosen depends on the complexity of the lamina itself, that is to say, the more complex types of diseased lamina, the more samples should be chosen.
2) The second factor is the resolution of the digital camera, which influenced the extraction accuracy of diseased spots.
3) The third factor is the light intensity which led to the loss of the image color, so reducing the interference of human factor and environmental factors should be taken into account when collecting the lamina images.

4   Conclusion

Based on the colorimetric mechanism, the soybean brown spots have been recognized successfully through training the artificial neural network, the method proposed in this paper overcomes the shortcomings of traditional threshold method. The experiments result shows that the precondition for accuracy reached to 100% is choosing enough samples seriously and combining with image processing technology.

In the paper, we have studied the key technology of Intelligent diagnosis of crop diseases. Firstly, proposed the image acquisition method, secondly, determined the preprocessing algorithms of diseased leaves image and the segmentation algorithm of soybean leaf lesion, at last, pre-research the Identification model of soybean leaf disease from the geometrical features, color and texture characteristic respectively, which provide the basement for intelligent diagnosis of diseased soybean leaf.

This study which can be applied not only in recognizing of soybean diseased spots, but also in that of other farm crop, such as rice, maize have been popularized in practical life and production, meanwhile, provides a practical scientific method for agriculture researchers and solid technology basement for species identification, characteristic recognition and diseased diagnosis.

References

[1] Tao, Y.: Machine vision for color inspection of potatoes and apples. Transactions of the ASAE 38, 555–1561 (1995)
[2] Zhou, L.: Research on Fuzzy Detection Method of Pest's Image in Stored Grain Based on Machine Vision. Computer Applications and Software (8), 24–25 (2005)
[3] Shen, Z.-R.: Use of math-morphological features in insect taxonomy
[4] Dong, J.: Agricultural Plant Pathology. China Agricultural Press (2001) (in Chinese)
[5] Lai, J., Li, S., Ming, B., Wang, N., Wang, K., Xie, R., Gao, S.: Advances in Research on Computer-Vision Diagnosis of Crop Diseases. Scientia Agricultura Sinica 42(4), 1215–1221 (2009)
[6] Georgieva, K., Georgieva, Y., Daskalov, D.: Theoretical substantiation of model of system for evaluation a state of vine plants and taking a decision for plant protection activities. Trakia Journal of Sciences (Series Social Sciences) 1, 30–32 (2003)
[7] Ying, Y., Zhang, W., Jiang, Y.: Machine vision technology in the agricultural harvest and process automation application. Agricultural Machinery 31(3), 112–115 (2000) (in Chinese)
[8] Shanwen, H.: Image processing technology in environmental applications. Electric Association Journal Featured, 455–458 (1985)
[9] Panigrahi, S.: Background Segmentation and Dimensional measurement of Corn Germplasm. Transactions of the ASAE 38(1), 291–297 (1995)
[10] Sasaki, Y., Okamoto, T., Imou, K., Tor, T.: Automatic Diagnosis of Plant Disease. Journal of JSAM 61(2), 119–126 (1999)
[11] Sasaki, Y., Suzuki, M.: Construction of the Automatic Diagnosis System of Plant Disease Using Genetic Programming Which Paid Its Attention to Variety. ASAE Meeting Presentation, paper No. 031049 (2003)
[12] Sanyala, P., Patel, S.C.: Pattern recognition method to detect two diseases in rice plants. The Imaging Science Journal 56(6), 319–325 (2008)
[13] Ma, X., Qi, G.: Investigation and recognition on diseased spots of soybean leaf based on neural network. Journal of Heilongjiang First Land Reclamation University 18(2), 84–87 (2006) (in Chinese)
[14] Cao, M.: Detecting Research of Soybean's Plant Nitrogen Based on image processing Technology. Jilin University, Changchun (2005) (in Chinese)
[15] Oide, M., Ninomiya, S.: Discrimination of soybean leaflet shape by neural networks with image input. Computers and Electronics in Agriculture, 59–72 (October 2000)
[16] Liu, S.: Based on fuzzy neural network diagnostic system of grape disease. Agricultural Engineering 9, 144–147 (2006) (in Chinese)
[17] Liu, S.: Based on fuzzy neural network diagnostic system of grape disease. Agricultural Engineering 9, 144–147 (2006) (in Chinese)
[18] Zhao, F., Zhao, R.: Texture segmentation and feature extraction Methods. Chinese Journal of Stereology and Image Analysis 3(4), 238–245 (1988) (in Chinese)

The Application of Wireless Sensor in Aquaculture Water Quality Monitoring

Wen Ding and Yinchi Ma[*]

Beijing Fisheries Research Institute, Beijing, 100068, China
{dingwen,mayinchi}@bjfishery.com

Abstract. The current means for aquaculture water quality monitoring have a weak infrastructure. We research to use wireless sensor technology, embedded computing technology, MEMS technology, distributing information processing technology and wireless communication technology to build the wireless network sensor network system. This system is a digital, networked, intelligent real-time dynamic for monitoring the aquaculture water quality. The system not only can deal the normal detection of the aquaculture environment indicators (temperature, PH, dissolved oxygen, turbidity, ammonia, etc.) in real-time monitoring, but also can detect indicators of data fusion and data mining to establish a history database of aquaculture environmental monitoring indicators. The system can gather the monitoring data by a local or remote way, and realize the real-time, dynamic display and analysis. So as to improve the process of aquaculture, water resources utilization, the quality of the culture environment and reduce emissions of pollutants. The system can provide an important technical means and scientific basis. The hardware architecture design is the core technology of this system. We will detail the part in this article.

Keywords: wireless sensor network, node, gateway, hardware platforms, aquaculture applications.

1   Introduction

Wireless sensor network is a kind of wireless network without infrastructure. It integrates the sensor technology, the embedded computing technology, the modern network technology, the wireless communication technology and the distributed intelligent information processing technology. The system can work under a state of long-term unattended [1]. It can detect, perceive and gather the information of the monitoring or environmental objects within the networks distribution region in real-time. It receives and sends messages through wireless and self-organization multi-hop routing [2]. Merging the logical information world and the real physical world together will change the interaction way between people and nature. The technology has good prospects in many areas, especially in agriculture area. Wireless sensor networks will be able to play a significant role in environmental monitoring, precision agriculture, section irrigation and livestock breeding [3-5].

---

[*] Corresponding author.

D. Li and Y. Chen (Eds.): CCTA 2011, Part III, IFIP AICT 370, pp. 502–507, 2012.
© IFIP International Federation for Information Processing 2012

This study is using the wireless sensor network technology to build an intelligent, network-based wireless monitoring system for aquaculture environment. The technology can be quickly applied to the field of aquaculture environmental monitoring, and promote the research and application of the wireless sensor networks technology. So as to improve the current traditional farming methods and aquaculture environmental monitoring instruments in the field of aquaculture in China. In this paper, we propose a set of practical hardware architecture design for the application of aquaculture.

2   System Design

The system mainly consists of the multi-parameter water quality sensors, the digital-analog transmission module, the wireless sensor network, the GPRS transmission unit, the data query and messaging real-time analysis of early warning system, and several other components. As shown in Figure 1, a set of wireless real-time water quality monitoring system includes the data acquisition node, the relay node and the gateway node.

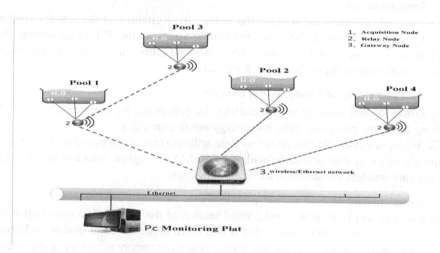

Fig. 1. Hardware architecture

3   Hardware Implementation

3.1   Acquisition Node

Monitoring can be arbitrarily placed in the desired area. Real-time collection includes water temperature, PH, dissolved oxygen, turbidity, ammonia, etc., and transmit the collected data to a wireless repeater or wireless gateway by wireless way.

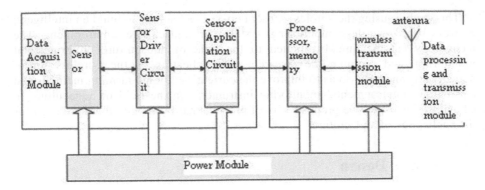

Fig. 2. Data Acquisition Node

As the figure 2 shows, the data acquisition node is an integrated structure. And it mainly contains the data acquisition module and the data transmission module, including the following several units divided by function:

● Sensor module

Sensor module contains the sensors, the sensor drive circuit and the sensors applied circuit. Sensors including the water temperature sensor, the PH value sensor, the oxygen sensor, the turbidity sensor, the ammonia nitrogen sensor for the water environment monitoring of the aquaculture water.

● Data processing and transmission module

I. Processor and memory unit: including the processor, the memory and the I/O. Among them, the processor is the low-energy micro controller.

II. Wireless transmitting/receiving module unit: the unit is composed of the wireless communication module according with IEEE802.15.4 / Zigbee. And this unit is used for the data wireless transmission and communication.

● Power module

Power supply unit is the power and control section of the system. The most important characteristic of the sensor node is that it will work under the condition of no lasting permanent power supply. This feature requires the work energy necessary of the sensor node is very low, and the sustainable power supply time of its own power must be long. According to the different application, appropriately adjusting the sleep time of sensor is the main task of the power control. Usually, the AA batteries and lithium battery can maintain a sensor node survival several months to 2 years. And adopting new technologies, such as solar energy, or using air micro vibration to produce electric power can make a sensor node survive longer. In the system, the scheme adopts the rechargeable efficient lithium battery.

3.2   Relay Node

The main function of relay nodes are forwarding sampling data from sensor node, and transmitting to gateway or other relay through wireless self-organization network. It can realize the transmission with a much longer distance. Relay node completely realized self-organizing network routing algorithms, within the wireless communication region, the relay nodes can immediately join in the network after powering, and establish the route of the data transmission.

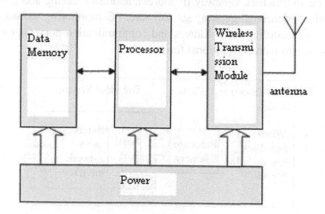

Fig. 3. Relay Node

As the figure 3 shows, the relay node mainly contains the data processing and wireless transmission modules with the same function as the data acquisition node. Among them according to their function, including the following several units divided by function:

● Data processing and transmission module

I. Processor and memory unit: including the processor, the memory and the I/O. Among them, the processor is the low-energy micro controller.

II. Wireless transmitting/receiving module unit: the unit is composed of the wireless communication module according with IEEE802.15.4 / Zigbee. And this unit is used for the data wireless transmission and communication.

● Data storage module

Data storage module is mainly composed of RAM or FLASH memory unit, and its main function is to store all kinds of sensor data and preserve the routing information of the whole network.

3.3   Gateway Node

The acquisition data by sensor node is transmitted to PC monitoring platform through Ethernet gateway.   The wireless network/Ethernet gateway has wireless sensor networks, IEEE802.3 Ethernet and GPRS communication function. It can transfer the wireless communication data to the Ethernet protocol and the GPRS data. It can put any wireless input data transparent transmission to a server with designated IP address, and the maximum data throughput can achieve 22.5 Kbytes/s. The RFIC adopt CC1100 of Chipcon Company. The processor adopts Mega128L of Atmel Company. The maximum visual transmission distance can be more than 800m. The transmission distance of a typical aquaculture site is more than 300m, and it supports IEEE802.3 Ethernet networks, GPRS wireless transmission, and TCP/IP, UDP protocol transparent data transmission.

Data communication can be set up through the Ethernet gateway, wireless networks and any other PC in Ethernet. Gateway IP address, address masking and communication port can be online set through gateway set software. PC monitoring software exchanges data with gateway according to IP address and communication port. Gateway will sent sensor network data to with conventional format.

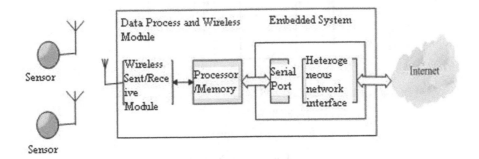

Fig. 4. Gateway Node

As the Figure 4 shows, the gateway node contains the data processing and wireless transmission module with the same function as the data acquisition node, and the embedded system connected with the heterogeneous network. As a IEEE802.15.4 and sensor network communication agent, the sensor node function modules must be equipped with a external I/O communication unit, used to communicate with the agency application server (Ethernet, RS232, USB, GPRS and satellite communication, etc.). The data from the sensor network accepted by the gateway node will be processed by the application server with stronger calculating function, but without power limit.

4   Conclusion

This study constructs an intelligent, networked aquaculture environment monitoring system using wireless sensor network technology. And the system is applied in the aquaculture environment monitoring field. It promotes the level of our wireless sensor network technology development and application. Ant it provides a new technical solution for improving the backward traditional breeding way and aquaculture environment monitoring method of the Chinese aquaculture field.

The low power consumption, low cost, and high reliability characteristics of the wireless sensor network make it have a broad application prospect in the wireless remote environment testing field [6 - 8]. We put forward the aquaculture water quality monitoring system construction program based on the study of Zigbee protocol of the wireless sensor network technology. And the water quality parameters collection and analysis was finished on this platform.

The results show that the development of the all-weather "wireless intelligent network real-time monitoring and warning system for aquaculture environment " can realize the real-time automatic monitoring, remote wireless transmission , automatic data processing and analysis, multi-platform control, intelligent warning, and SMS alarm for the water temperature, dissolved oxygen, PH, turbidity, ammonia and other indicator parameters of aquaculture environmental. So as to improve the utilization of aquaculture water maximum, provide the appropriate environmental condition for aquaculture objects, and control and ensure the quality security of aquatic products effectively. The system can realize automatic monitoring and scientific management for the aquaculture environment during the whole process. It will play a important role for protecting high-yield, efficient, safe, health of intensive aquaculture, improving aquatic product quality and safety in our city, and promoting the intensive, industrialization, refinement of aquaculture, and realizing the sustainable development of Beijing urban agriculture.

References

1. Wu, J.: Design of Wireless Sensor Network Node for Water Quality Monitorin. Computer Measurement & Control (12) (2009)
2. Du, Z.: Design of water quality monitoring wireless sensor network system based on wireless sensor. Computer Engineering and Design (17) (2008)
3. Liu, X.: Aquaculture security guarantee system based on water quality monitoring and its application. Transactions of the Chinese Society of Agricultural Engineering (6) (2009)
4. Ma, C., Ni, W.: The design of a factory aquiculture monitor system based on PLC. Industrial Instrumentation & Automation (02) (2005)
5. Zhu, W., Ran, G.: Research of aquaculture environment parameter automatic monitoring and controlling system. Freshwater Fisheries (01) (2001)
6. Guo, S., Ma, S., Wu, P.: The application research of remote monitoring system based on Zigbee technology of wireless sensor network in family. Application of Electronic Technique (6), 28–30 (2006)
7. Ren, X., Yu, H.: The wireless sensor network safety analysis based on ZigBee technology. Computer Science 6(10), 111–113 (2001)
8. Zhang, H., Li, W.: Study of a Wireless Sensor Network Based on ZigBee Technology. Journal of Wuhan University of Technology (Information & Management Engineering) (8), 12–15 (2006)

Prediction of Dissolved Oxygen Content in Aquaculture of *Hyriopsis Cumingii* Using Elman Neural Network

Shuangyin Liu[1,2], Mingxia Yan[1], Haijiang Tai[1], Longqin Xu[2], and Daoliang Li[1,*]

[1] College of Information and Electrical Engineering, China Agricultural University, Beijing 100083, P.R. China
[2] College of Information, Guangdong Ocean University, Zhanjiang Guangdong 524025, P.R. China
dliangl@cau.edu.cn

Abstract. Hyriopsis Cumingii is Chinese major fresh water pearl mussel, widely distributed in the southern provinces of China's large and medium-sized freshwater lakes. In the management of Hyriopsis Cumingii ponds, dissolved oxygen (DO) is the key point to measure, predict and control. In this study, we analyzes the important factors for predicting dissolved oxygen of Hyriopsis Cumingii ponds, and finally chooses solar radiation(SR), water temperature(WT), wind speed(WS), PH and oxygen(DO) as six input parameters. In this paper, Elman neural networks were used to predict and forecast quantitative characteristics of water. As the dissolved oxygen in the outdoor pond is low controllability and scalability, this paper proposes a predicting model for dissolved oxygen. The true power and advantage of this method lie in its ability to (1) represent both linear and non-linear relationships and (2) learn these relationships directly from the data being modeled. The study focuses on Singapore coastal waters. The Elman NN model is built for quick assessment and forecasting of selected water quality variables at any location in the domain of interest. Experimental results show that: Elman neural network predicting model with good fitting ability, generalization ability, and high prediction accuracy, can better predict the changes of dissolved oxygen.

Keywords: prediction, dissolved oxygen, Elman neural network, Hyriopsis Cumingii.

1 Introduction

Hyriopsis Cumingii is Chinese major fresh water pearl mussel, widely distributed in the southern provinces of China's large and medium-sized freshwater lakes. In recent years, aquaculture farmers to improve economic benefit in the production process, the use of livestock and poultry faeces or chemical fertilizer, lead to the water ecological unbalance, nitrogen and phosphorus excess water flooding, phytoplankton, nutrient runoffs, the serious influence of fresh-water cultured pearl's sustainable development.

---

* Corresponding author.

D. Li and Y. Chen (Eds.): CCTA 2011, Part III, IFIP AICT 370, pp. 508–518, 2012.
© IFIP International Federation for Information Processing 2012

Lacking of dissolved oxygen water quality exacerbate in the ponds in summer easily causes freshwater mussel disease (G.F.Zhang, 2005). Therefore, real-time monitoring and forecasting of Hyriopsis Cumingii ponds' water quality has becoming a priority issues, specifically dissolved oxygen prediction.

Aquaculture water quality is a complex system. It affected by many factors such as environment, drugs, climate and bait etc. In this field, to prevent breeding water quality deterioration, forecasting DO value accurately has been quite an imperative subject at present. Prediction of water quality at home and abroad focused mainly in rivers, lakes, reservoirs, estuaries and other large waters using the gray system theory, polynomial regression, mathematical statistics, time series models and the neural network, etc (Xiaoyi Wang,2011; Yan-ping GAO,2008; LEE JHW,2003, LiangPeng Wang,2010; Xiao-ping Wang,2007; Wei-ren Shi, 2009; Zhi-xia Sun, 2009). Yu first made a prediction model for water quality based on improved BP neural network (Ch.X. Yu, 2008); Palani et.al. developed a neural network mode to forecast dissolved oxygen in seawater (Palani, Liong, Tkalich, 2009); Li established the BP and AR of the short-term forecasting model (F.F. Li, 2010); Zhang had adopted Elnman neural network model to forecast the SO2 in the atmosphere pollution index (Qi Zhang, 2009); Wang Ruimei predicted dissolved oxygen using the fuzzy-BP neural network (Ruimei Wang, 2010).However, limited water quality data and the high cost of water quality monitoring often pose serious problems for process-based modeling approaches. ANN provide a particularly good option, because they are computationally very fast and require many fewer input parameters and input conditions than deterministic models. ANN does, however, require a large pool of representative data for training. The objective of this study is to investigate whether it is possible to predict the values of water quality variables measured by a water quality monitoring program; this task is quite important for enabling selective monitoring of water quality variables.

Elman regression network is a kind of typical dynamic neural network, it in feedforward neural network on the foundation of basic structure, through the internal storage condition caused it to have the function of dynamic features mapping, so that the system has the ability to adapt to the time-varying characteristic, is a current of the most widely used type feedback neural network. This paper, we adopting Elman dynamic neural network to establish 1 hour dissolved oxygen predicting model in the Hyriopsis Cumingii ponds. This paper aims to find an effective way for prediction of in the Hyriopsis Cumingii ponds.

The remaining parts of this paper are organized as follow. Section 2 covers some related work including data collection and reprocessing methods the Elman neural network model, Elman NN parameter selection and model performance evaluation. the experimental results are shown and evaluated in section 3. Finally, Section 4 presents our conclusions.

2   Relate Work

In this section, we survey some related research techniques in the area of data collection, Elman NN architecture, Elman NN parameter selection, data pre-processing, model performance evaluation.

2.1   Water Quality Data Collection

Ecological environment data of the Hyriopsis Cumingii aquaculture ponds are obtained by Digital Wireless Monitoring System of Aquaculture Water Quality (DWMS-AWQ) for real-time. It has been equipped at China Agricultural University-DuChang Aquaculture Digital System Research Center in DuChang city, Jiangxi province, China. The DWMS-AWQ consists of four parts: the data collection layer, the data transmission layer, the information processing layer and the application layer. The data collection layer directly connects to the intelligent sensor through RS485 connector and sends the data of intelligent sensor to routing node by wireless network. Then the routing node sends the data to the on-site monitoring center through a wireless network and to the remote monitoring center by GPRS.

In Hyriopsis Cumingii ponds, we installed two water quality data collection nodes101 and 102 collecting water level, water temperature, PH and DO at water level 1m and 2m, respectively, one meteorological data collection nodes 103 (collecting rainfall, temperature, humidity, wind speed, wind direction, solar radiation), routing node 1 and the GPRS module(Fig. 1).

Fig. 1. Hyriopsis Cumingii from breeding ecological environment data acquisition nodes

We refer to the knowledge of freshwater ecology to analyze the impact of dissolved oxygen factors, and choose water temperature(WT), solar radiation(SR), wind speed(WS), PH and dissolved oxygen(DO) five parameters of the ecological environment. The data used in this paper spanned 34 days, from July 2 to August 4, 2010. Data collection time interval is 1 hour. So we choose the dates every hour as the forecast value, which means 24 sets of data collected per day, the total samples is 816.

2.2   Structure of Neural Network Model

2.2.1   Elman NN Architecture

An artificial neural network (ANN) is a new generation of information processing system, which can model the ability of biological neural network by interconnecting many simple neurons. The neural network consists of layers of parallel processing elements called neurons; it is a simplified, simulation and abstract of human brain. They have the similarities in two main aspects: to acquire knowledge through learning from the external environment, and to store obtained knowledge use of the internal neurons. It is one of the well-known prediction models as it has excellent ability of mapping complex and highly nonlinear input-output patterns without the knowledge of the actual model structure. The feature of dealing with nonlinear problems makes ANN popular in many fields, such as financial signals prediction, language processing, biology, biochemical simulation and so on.

There are many types of artificial neural networks. The Elman network is one kind of globally feed-forward locally recurrent network model proposed by Elman (J. Elman, 1990). It has a set of context nodes to store the internal states. Elman neural network is a kind of internal feedback, can store and use the last moments of the input and output information, and has a strong computing power. Elman neural network consists of four layers: the input layer (signaling effect), the hidden layer, the context layer. As shown in Fig. 2. There are adjustable weights connecting each two neighboring layers. Generally, it is considered as a special kind of feed-forward neural network with additional memory neurons and local feedback (P. S. Sastry, G. Santharam and K.P. Unnikrishnan, 1994). The self-connections of the context nodes in the Elman network make it also sensitive to the history of input data which is very useful in dynamic system modeling (J. Elman, 1990).

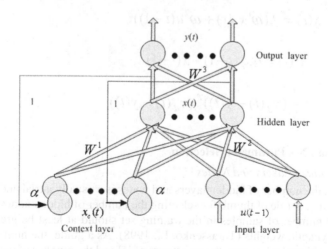

Fig. 2. Elman neural network architecture

The basic structure of a multilayer feed-forward network model can be determined as consist of an input layer, one or more hidden layer and an output layer. The input layer neurons receive input patterns from the external environment and propagate them on to the first hidden layer neurons. In this layer any data processing is not carried out. Input values distributed from each of the input layer neurons are multiplied by each of the adjustable connection weights linking the input layer neurons to hidden layer neurons. At each neuron in the hidden layer weighted input values are summed and a bias value is added. Then combined input value is passed through a nonlinear transfer function like sigmoid to obtain the output value of the neuron. This output value is an input for the neurons situated in the following layer. Finally, the output layer neurons produce the output value of the network model (Fatih Ozcan. Cengiz D. Atiş. Okan Karahan. Erdal Uncuoğlu, 2009).

Set x is the n-dimensional hidden layer node vectors, y is the m-dimensional output node vectors, u is the r-dimensional input vector, x_c is the n-dimensional feedback state vector; ω^1 is the weight matrix of the context layer to the hidden layer, ω^2 is the weight matrix of the input layer to the hidden layer, ω^3 is the weight matrix of the hidden layer to the output layer; $x(t)$, $x_c(t)$ and $y(t)$ are output of the hidden layer, context layer and output layer at time t, respectively. $\alpha(0 \leq \alpha < 1)$ is the self-connecting feedback gain factor, here set 0; $f(x)$ is the sigmoid function, such as the Formula 1. Elman neural network mathematical model shows in the following Eq.(2), (3), (4). Suppose the tth step of real output of system is $y_d(t)$, desired output is $y(t)$. The objective function of Elman neural network can be expressed as Eq. (5).

$$f(x) = 1/(1+e^{-x}) \tag{1}$$

$$y(t) = g(\omega^3 x(t)) \tag{2}$$

$$x(t) = f(\omega^1 x_c(t) + \omega^2 u(t-1)) \tag{3}$$

$$x_c(t) = \alpha x_c(t-1) + x(t-1) \tag{4}$$

$$E(t) = \frac{1}{2}(y_d(t) - y(t))^T (y_d(t) - y(t)) \tag{5}$$

2.2.2   Elman NN Parameter Selection

2.2.2.1   Hidden Layers and Nodes

Determining the number of hidden layers and nodes is a usually a trial and error task in ANN modeling. A rule of thumb for selecting the number of hidden nodes relies on the fact that the number of samples in the training set should at least be greater than the number of synaptic weights (Tarassenko, L., 1998). As a guide, the number of hidden nodes M should not be less than the maximum of I/3 and the number of output nodes O, where I is the number of input nodes. The optimum value of M is determined by trial and error.

For neural network training, the appropriate number of nodes in hidden layer is very important. In dealing with more complex problems, use of too few hidden units, the network can not remember all of the input-output model, the training of divergence; if too many neurons, the network will not only lengthen the training time dramatically, may be "overfitting "phenomenon, and will greatly reduce the generalization. Therefore, the model must be taken into account the training speed and generalization ability, choose the best number of hidden layer neurons.

Let q for the output layer nodes, n nodes for the input layer, p hidden nodes for the common choice of several nodes in one hidden layer of valuation as follows:

(1) Maximum number of nodes in hidden layer p= q (n+1)
(2) Maximum number of nodes in hidden layer p=q×3
(3) Input nodes is larger than the output layer node p=(q×n)1/2

(4) $p = \sqrt{n+q} + a$, Where a is constant between [1,10]

In this study, a trial and error procedure for hidden node selection was carried out by gradually varying the number of nodes in the hidden layer.

2.2.2.2.   Learning Rate (eta) and Momentum (alpha)

The models were calibrated using the back-propagation algorithm, as it has already been used successfully for the prediction of coagulant doses (van Leeuwen et al.,1999) and other water resources and environmental variables (Maier and Dandy, 2000) and, unlike second order optimisation algorithms, has the ability to escape local minima in the error surface (White, 1989). Optimal values of the parameters controlling the size of the steps taken in weight space as part of the back-propgagation algorithm (i.e. learning rate and momentum values) were found by trial and error. There is no specific rule for the selection of values for these parameters. However, the training process is started by adopting one set of values (i.e. $\eta = 0.2$, range 0 to 1, and $\alpha = 0.5$, range 0 to 0.9) and then adjusting these values as necessary (i.e. if the error reduction of the network is too slow or begins oscillating). The learning process in this study was controlled by the method of internal validation. Roughly 20% of calibration data was withheld and used to test the error at the end of each epoch. The weights were updated at the end of each epoch. The number of epochs with the smallest internal validation error indicates which weights to select. The ANN with the best performance when applied to the validation set was selected.

2.2.2.3.   Initial Weights

The weights of a network that is to be trained by BP must be initialized to some small, non-zero random values. If a network stops training before reaching an acceptable solution because a local minimum has been found, a change in the number of hidden nodes or learning parameters will often fix the problem; alternatively, we can simply start over with a different set of initial weights. When a network reaches an acceptable solution, there is no guarantee that it has reached the global minimum. The synaptic weights of the networks were initialized with normally-distributed random numbers in the range of -1to1.

2.2.3   Selection of Input Variables

According to the principles of ecological, there are three main sources of dissolved oxygen in the outdoor pond: production of phytoplankton photosynthesis, atmospheric oxygen dissolved in water, and increased by oxygen machine. Atmospheric oxygen dissolved in water is mainly affected by temperature, wind speed. But the gas in water diffusion is proceeding slowly, if not all kinds of mixed water masses (as well as horizontal flow fluctuations and vertical flow), this process limited to the surface. In the fertilizer ponds, the production of phytoplankton photosynthesis is the main source of oxygen; atmospheric dissolved oxygen played a secondary role.

Aquatic animals consume a large amount of oxygen when breathing. Aquatic plants in photosynthesis during the day also carry out respiration, but respiration rate much lower than the intensity of photosynthesis. At night, respiration of plants (especially algae) for water gas has a great influence. In addition, bacterial respiration is the oxygen consumption of the most important factor, both in the bottom water layers and bacterial decomposition of organic matter. When the dissolved oxygen super saturation in surface water, it may also occur oxygen escaping. Wind disturbance on the surface of the water can accelerate the process of escaping.

Therefore, the factors affecting pond dissolved oxygen is mainly reflected in the impact factors of photosynthesis. Solar radiation intensity, water temperature, air temperature are the most important factors affecting photosynthesis. Cooperation with the intensity of light with the intensity of solar radiation, water temperature, air temperature increases, reaching saturation values will decline.

Phytoplankton photosynthesis, biological respiration and decomposition of organic matter led to changes in pH value. In summer, when water phytoplankton blooms, they tend to happen: the night at the deep water layer, in the biological process of respiration, due to the accumulation of carbon dioxide, pH value will decrease. High fishing pond, high aquatic life, strong biological photosynthesis and respiration more strongly, the variation of pH value is large[1]. This shows that pH is an important sign of reflecting the dissolved oxygen content.So in this paper we choose solar radiation(SR), air temperature(AT), water temperature(WT), wind speed(WS), PH and oxygen(DO) six parameters as Elman neural network input parameters.

2.2.4   Data Pre-processing

In order to improve the training speed and accuracy, all data are normalized in this paper. Standardized function used in this paper is as follows Eq. (6).

$$x' = \frac{(y_{max} - y_{min})(x - x_{min})}{x_{max} - x_{min}} \tag{6}$$

Where x denote the original data point here, xmin and xmax are the minimum and maximum values in the data set, respectively. Here, we set ymax is 1, and ymin is -1. In this way, all the input signals are changed to the interval [-1, 1].

2.2.5   Model Performance Evaluation

A model trained on the training set can be evaluated by comparing its predictions to the measured values in the overfitting test set. These values are calibrated by systematically adjusting various model parameters. The performances of the models are evaluated using the root mean square error (RMSE) [Eq. (7)], the mean absolute error (MAE) [Eq. (8)], the Nash–Sutcliffe coefficient of efficiency (R2) [(Eq. (9)], and the correlation coefficient (r). Scatter plots and time series plots are used for visual comparison of the observed and predicted values. R2 values of zero, one, and negative indicate that the observed mean is as good a predictor as the model, a perfect fit, and a better predictor than the model, respectively. Depending on sensitivity of water quality parameters and the mismatch between the forecasted water quality variable and that measured; an expert can decide whether the predictability of the Elman NN model is accurate enough to make important decisions regarding data usage.

$$RMSE = \sqrt{\frac{1}{N} \sum (X_{observed} - X_{predicted})^2} \qquad (7)$$

$$MAE = \frac{1}{N} \sum | X_{predicted} - X_{observed} | \qquad (8)$$

$$R^2 = 1 - (\frac{F}{F_0}) \qquad (9)$$

$$F = \sum (X_{observed} - X_{predicted})^2 \qquad (10)$$

$$F_0 = \sum (X_{observed} - X_{mean-observed})^2 \qquad (11)$$

where N is the total number of observations in the data set.

3   Results and Discussion

The Elman NN model was developed to simulate every hour DO concentrations in the Hyriopsis Cumingii freshwater pond with training of variable learning rate momentum gradient descent algorithm. The quality of a neural network, is different with the traditional least square fitting evaluation (mainly based on residuals, goodness of fit, etc.), not reflect in the data fitting on the existing capacity, but a later predictive ability (the ability of generalization). Predictive ability of the network (also known as generalization ability) and training capacity (also called approximation ability, learning ability) is contradictory. In general, training is poor, the forecasting ability poor, and to some extent, with the ability to improve training, improve forecasting ability. However, this trend has a limit, when reached this limit, with the training capability, predictability declines and that the so-called "over-fit" phenomenon. At this point, samples of learning too many details, but the law does not reflect the sample contains. In this paper we use the methods of data classification and disrupting to improve Elman neural network generalization and avoid over-fitting phenomenon. We selected first 4 days of 96 sets of data as the Elman NN as training data, and the fifth day data sets data as the variable data, and 24 sets of data as test data. The variable data play a role in preventing over-fitting.

Typical Elman NN DO prediction model results are shown as Table 1. 24 group training in the use of data fitting Elman NN prediction model, select a different number of hidden layer neurons, the model has a different fitting precision

Table 1. The performance for different number of hidden layer neurons

	3	4	5	6	7	8	9	10	11
RSME	0.24	0.29	0.29	0.23	0.29	0.30	0.30	0.30	0.30
MSE	0.23	0.23	0.23	0.29	0.24	0.24	0.24	0.24	0.24
R	0.23	0.20	0.18	0.17	0.16	0.15	0.14	0.14	0.13

The Elman NN model of DO in freshwater pond was successful in simulating patterns in measured DO concentrations that result from seasonal temperature variations, periodic blooms of phytoplankton (production of DO), and point-source discharges of oxygen-consuming substances like ammonia and BOD. In tropical ponds where there are frequent phytoplankton blooms to increase DO levels, DO concentrations fluctuate and supersaturate during these blooms. The DO models simulate the dynamics of the measured concentration and are within the range of the measured values. Elman NN models were successful in predicting patterns in the hourly DO data, and they can be applied on daily, weekly, monthly, and seasonal time scales. The Elman NN model's performance was good, but the outdoor environment is complex and the measuring system has the larger error.

More data sampling is thus required, and future work should recalibrate and revalidate the models to generalize our conclusions. The DO predicting model for freshwater will be further fine-tuned for higher accuracy by more accurate data. The result of the Elman NN DO predicting model was shown in Fig. 3(hidden layer neurons:8).

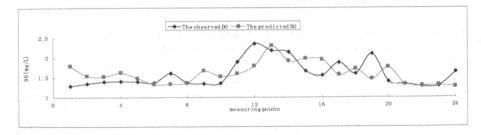

Fig. 3. The test curve of Elman prediction model

4   Summary and Conclusion

Elman NN model was developed to predict dissolved oxygen in Hyriopsis Cumingii pond waters both temporally and spatially using continuous measurements of water quality variables. In spite of largely unknown factors controlling pond freshwater quality variation and the limited data set size, a relatively good correlation was observed between the measured and predicted values. The Elman NN modeling technique's application for dynamic pond freshwater quality prediction was presented in this study. The Elman NN model has tremendous potential as a forecasting tool. An Elman NN prediction capability was tested and found to be faster than that from a process-based model with minimal input requirements.

In particular, we observed that the Elman NN methods were able to "learn" the mechanism of convective transport of water quality variables quite well. Based on the "best performance" in water quality parameter forecasting, we observed that Elman NN method with 7 or 8 hidden layer nodes is the better architecture for DO models, but the accuracy is not better for DO models. Also, the front part and last part of the forecast test data has a marked disturbance, which is Elman neural network inherent problem. The limitations of this study include its limited data set. The available data size is relatively small, reasonably good results were obtained for the water quality prediction of unseen validation dataset at locations separate from the training dataset stations. If more data become available, the proposed approach should provide better predictions3.

Acknowledgements. This research is financially supported by the National Key Technology R&D Program in the 12th Five year Plan of china (2011BAD21B01), Beijing Natural Science Foundation (4092024), National Major Science and Technology Project of China (2010ZX03006-006) and 948 Project of Ministry of Agriculture of the people's Republic of China (2010-Z13).

References

1. Zhang, G., Wang, D.: Advances of the studies on diseases of Hyriopsis cumingii and its control. Journal of Shanghai Fisheries University, 313–317 (September 2005)
2. Li, R.: Advance and trend analysis of theoretical methodology for water quality forecast. Journal of Hefei University of Technology 29(1), 26–30 (2006)
3. Wang, X., Zhao, X., Liu, Z.: Research on Lake Eutrophication Forecasting Methods Based on Grey Theory. Computer Simulation 28(1), 17–19 (2011)
4. Gao, Y.-P., Yu, H., Cui, X.: Prediction model and realization for water quality in an intensive aquaculture based on LM BP neural network. Journal of Dalian Ocean University 23(6), 221–224 (2008)
5. Lee, J.H.W., Huang, Y., Dickman, M., et al.: Neural network modeling of coastal algal Blooms. Ecological Modeling 159, 179–201 (2003)
6. Liang, G., Wang, P., Zhao, Y.: Water quality forecast through application of BP neural network at Sifangtai. Journal of Harbin Institute of Technology 41(6), 62–66 (2010)
7. Wang, X.-P., Sun, J.-Y., Jin, X.: Prediction of water quality index in Qiantang River based on BP neural network model. Journal of Zhejiang University (Engineering Science) 41(2), 361–364 (2007)
8. Shi, W.-R., Wang, Y.-X., Tang, Y.-J.: Water quality parameter forecast based on grey neural network modeling. Journal of Computer Applications 29(6), 1529–1531 (2009)
9. Sun, Z.-X., Sun, Y.-L.: Study of GM (1,1) model and its application in forecast of the water quality. Marine Science Bulletin 28(4), 116–120 (2009)
10. Yu, C.X.: Water Quality Early Warning System for Intensive Aquaculture of Paralichthys, China Agricultural University (2008) (in Chinese)

11. Palani, S., Liong, S.-Y., Tkalich, P.: Development of a neural network for dissolved oxygen in seawater. Indian Journal of Marine Sciences 38(2), 151–159 (2009)
12. Li, F.F.: Dissolved Oxygen Prediction in Apostichopus japonicas Aquaculture Ponds by BP Neural Network and AR model. Sensor Letters 8(1), 95–101 (2010)
13. Zhang, Q., Xu, Z.: Prediction of Data from Pollution Sources Based on Elman Neural Network. Journal of South ChinaUniversity of Technology, 135–138 (May 2009)
14. Wang, R., Fu, Z.: Dissolved Oxygen Fuzzy System Predicting Model in Aquaculture Pond Based on Neural Network. Journal of Anhui Agricultural Sciences, 18868–18870 (2010)
15. Elman, J.: Finding structure in time. Cognitive Science 14, 179–211 (1990)
16. Sastry, P.S., Santharam, G., Unnikrishnan, K.P.: Memory neuron networks for identification and control of dynamic systems. IEEE Transactions on Neural Networks 5, 306–319 (1994)
17. Ozcan, F., Atiş, C.D., Karahan, O., Uncuoğlu, E., Tanyildizi, H.: Comparison of artificial neural network and fuzzy logic models for prediction of long-term compressive strength of silica fume concrete. Advances in Engineering Software 40, 856–863 (2009)
18. Tarassenko, L.: A Guide to Neural Computing Applications. Arnold Publishers, London (1998)
19. van Leeuwen, J., Chow, C.W.K., Bursill, D., Drikas, M.: Empirical mathematical models and artificial neural networks for the determination of alum doses for treatment of southern Australian surface waters. J. Water SRT-Aqua 48(3), 115–127 (1999)
20. Maier, H.R., Dandy, G.C.: Neural networks for the prediction and forecasting of water resources variables: a review of modeling issues and applications. Environmental Modelling and Software 15(1), 101–124 (2000)
21. White, M.C., Thompson, J.D., Harrington, G.W., Singer, P.C.: Evaluating criteria for enhanced coagulation compliance. J. AWWA 89(5), 64–77 (1997)
22. Portegys, T.E.: A maze learning comparison of Elman, long short-term memory, and Mona neural networks. Neural Networks 23(2), 306–313 (2010)
23. Kashani, M., Mohammadi, M., Han, D., Piri, J.: Comparison of LLR, MLP, Elman, NNARX and ANFIS Models: with a case study in solar radiation estimation. Journal of Atmospheric and Solar-Terrestrial Physics 71(8-9), 975–982 (2009)
24. Lv, S.Y., Liu, Z.W., Wang, X.Y., Cui, L.F.: Short-term predicting model for water bloom based on Elman neural network. In: Control Conference, 27th Chinese, pp. 218–221 (2008) (in Chinese)
25. Ozcan, F., Atiş, C.D., Karahan, O., Uncuoğlu, E., Tanyildizi, H.: Comparison of artificial neural network and fuzzy logic models for prediction of long-term compressive strength of silica fume concrete. Advances in Engineering Software 40, 856–863 (2009)

Finite Element Analysis and Design Improvement of Film Picking Forks Roller Tooth in Field Cleaning Machine

Xufeng Wang[1,*], Yonghua Sun[1], Shaohui Ma[1],Wei Wang[1],
Jungang Wang[1], and Xuejun Zhang[2,*]

[1] College of Mechanical and Electronic Engineering, Tarim University,
Ala'er, Xinjiang 843300, China
[2] Mechanical and Traffic College, Xinjiang Agricultural University,
Urumuqi, Xinjiang 830052, China
wxfwyq@126.com
zhxjau@sina.com

Abstract. In this paper the mechanical analysis of the film picking forks roller tooth in field -cleaning machine was done. A finite element analysis model was built and used by the non-linear finite element analysis method. It is obtained from the result of post-processing calculation and analysis that according to the Fourth Strength Theory, the maximum equivalent stress on the pole tooth root under the uniform load. Root strength should be strengthened to ensure the evenly stress overall the pole tooth, because pole tooth root department would be deformed easily. And the largest stress is at the end of pole tooth and decreases gradually from end to root, and deformation is also the same. Based on the analysis of strength and rigidity, the bearing forces and deformation of the film picking forks roller tooth in work were predicted and validated. It was found that the finite element analysis and the result of test were well coincided. The reliable tool was provided for the design of the film picking forks roller tooth by the finite element analysis. The Roller tooth was designed and improved according to the requirement of deformation and operation.

Keywords: Field Cleaning Machine, Film Picking Forks Roller Tooth, Non-linear Finite Element.

1 Introduction

The pole tooth ought to have enough strength to provide a safe space because of the big propellers to the pole tooth by soil after it sowing into the layer when the field cleaning machine recycled the remnant film in the coated cultivated land. It needs a

---

* Fund Project: The Funded Projects of the National Scientific Research Plan (2005BA9O1A24); High & New Technology Research and Development Program of Xinjiang Production and Construction Corps (2006GJS20).
* Corresponding author. Professor, Engaged in agricultural machinery design theory research

D. Li and Y. Chen (Eds.): CCTA 2011, Part III, IFIP AICT 370, pp. 519–526, 2012.

long period using the traditional experience design method. In recent years, more and more techniques are used in simulating nonlinear reaction of agricultural machine's working parts under the static load from different directions. However, there is still less study of the deformation of agricultural machine's working parts under uniform loading of soil pressure [1-6].

There are three processes for picking up film of picking forks roller tooth, including push film, pick film and upward transportation. The stressed deformation of picking forks roller tooth in field cleaning machine in working process is simulated and studied by using finite element method in this paper. Finite element model was established in software ANSYS and the pole tooth's stress and deformation was got based on nonlinear finite element analysis[7-8]. The structure design was improved after the analysis that the variation was to meet the recovery requirements of remnant film as well. Reliable basis was provided for the design of picking film device in field cleaning machine according to accuracy test of finite element model in different speeds. The innovation of this paper is that, by the finite element analysis working with uniform load instead of the concentrated, the method simulated more accurately the actual force situation of picking forks roller tooth in field cleaning machine in operation.

2   Establishment of Mechanics Model for Picking Forks Roller Tooth

2.1   End Shovel Resistance of Picking Forks Roller Tooth

2.1.1   Cutting Resistance of Blade Positive
The cutting resistance expression[9] of blade positive was got by professor Dechao Zeng of China Agricultural University in soil cut process with ploughshare blade simulated by wire when he was researching curved-surface resistance of the body of bottom plow.

$$P = \frac{q_0}{S}[\frac{S}{2}\tan(\frac{\pi}{4} + \frac{\phi}{2}) + \frac{S}{2}\frac{1}{\tan(\frac{\pi}{4} - \frac{\phi}{2})}]^n \tag{1}$$

q_o ——Penetration resistance coefficient;

n ——Regression coefficient;

S ——Shovel blade thickness;

ϕ ——Soil internal friction angle.

Resistance expression for shovel blade inclined an angle γ:

$$\mathrm{Pr} = p\sin\gamma + fp\cos\gamma \tag{2}$$

f ——Friction coefficient between metal edges and soil.

2.1.2   Friction Resistance

It is kind of mixture composed of water film, colloid, pollutants, soil particles in the contact area between metal and soil. It is essentially a relative motion between contact area materials about the relative sliding between metal and soil. Stafford. J.V deems it a linear relationship [10] between friction stress and positive pressure when the sliding speed must.

$$pf = C_p + \tan \phi_a \delta_n \qquad (3)$$

C_p ——Sticky gathered force between metal and soil when the sliding speed of them must;

ϕ_a ——Vertical stress on metal surface;

δ_n —— The friction angle of soil and metal.

Friction resistance calculation formula of end shovel of picking forks roller tooth was quoted from the research of Dr. Yusu Yao:

$$pf = 0.8[C_1 + A\ln V_r][\frac{1}{2}(n_1 + n_2) w] + pv \tan \phi a \qquad (4)$$

2.2   The Stress of Up Film Device

Stress shown in figure 1 and the test point stress results shown in table 1 were got from testing the field cleaning machine in the field with the instruments as speed device, force measurement device, etc, after reasonable test design [11] .

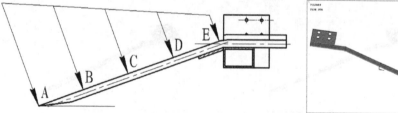

Fig. 1. Bearing forces of roller tooth

Fig. 2. Geometry model of roller tooth

2.3   Force Calculation of Up Film Device

Approximate the whole force on linear interpolation after mastering the point stress through the experiment above.

It is line integrals to point pressure for the whole rods. Set stress equation for A, B two point is $f(x)$, then get stress equation in A, B section for:

$$F = \int f(x)dx \tag{5}$$

Take torque to the supporting point from stress point in A, B section for:

$$\mathrm{M}_{A0} = M_{B0} \tag{6}$$

So the stress position of concentrated force can be concluded.

The only method can be used is approximate processing in linear interpolation because the approximate treatment can be done only by linear interpolation and it is impossible to analyze the whole stress.

3   Finite Element Analysis of Picking Forks Roller Tooth

3.1   Material and Finite Element Model

Take a single pole tooth of up film fork row of field clearing and ploughing machine for study object in order to reduce the complexity of computation and simplify the simulating process for computer. The connected steel of the pole tooth and the root is Q235, and the yield limit $\sigma_s = 235$Mpa. Define material performance in software of ANSYS, elastic modulus of the connected steel of pole tooth and root ⊞=200GPa, Poisson's ratio $\mu = 0.3$, density $\rho = 7.8 \times 103$kg/m3. Effective working length of pole tooth is 750mm, diameter is 20mm, acorns angle is 20°, and the thickness of the connected steel welding with pole tooth is 10mm.   Geometric model of the pole tooth is established as is shown in figure 2 by directing the pole tooth for the X axis.

Fig. 3. Entitative model after plotting mesh of roller tooth   **Fig. 4.** Surface freedom and force on poles of roller tooth

3.2   Network Division and Unit Selection

Create three-dimensional entity model with computer-assisted designing software Pro/E and then import it into ANSYS[12]. Define unit type respectively and divide pole tooth in free grid in grid division. The entity unit number of pole tooth is 11165,and the node number is 19723. Unit division of pole tooth is shown in Fig 3.

3.3   Processing of Constraint and Loading

Constraint processing: Constraint all displacement and rotation for the hole of connecting board and exert boundary conditions to pole tooth due to fixed connection of the fork platoon with frame, and pole tooth with fork platoon. It means that limiting all DOF except effective acorns part of pole tooth.

Loading processing: Work parts of the fork row pole tooth must be acorns and picking the remnant film. Soil mainly forces to the surface of pole tooth. Thrust of soil applied to the pole tooth surface is in uniform load. Corresponding parameter data was measured based on the testing of field cleaning machine in the field.   Average stress was got through calculating for measuring point. In Fig 1, A, B, C, D, and E imposed respectively forces as PA=432 N , PB=335 N , PC=254 N , PD=157 N , and PE=87 N . Shown in Fig 4 is the DOF constraint of pole tooth and forces on it.

3.4   Calculation and Analysis

Through the post-processing calculation and analysis, it is possible for reading the original data file in and restoring other data item, and also showing analysis results in many ways through postprocessor. It helps users to check for the influence of the model because of loading on it.

3.4.1   Stress Analysis

Equivalent stress distribution for pole tooth is shown as shown in Fig 5. It is obtained from the result of post-processing calculation and analysis that according to the Fourth Strength Theory, equivalent stress is $6633 \sim 6984 \, kPa$ in most areas pole tooth, and the maximum equivalent stress on the pole tooth root is $6984 \, kPa$ under the uniform load. So pole tooth root department would be deformed easily. Therefore, root strength should be strengthened to ensure the evenly stress overall the pole tooth, and that the static strength safety coefficient can meet the specified design of the field cleaning machine.

3.4.2   Deformation Analysis

The deformation of pole tooth after being loaded is shown in Fig 6. From analysis, the largest stress is at the end of pole tooth and decreases gradually from end to root. Deformation is also the same. The largest deformation in the Y direction is $11.713 \, mm$.

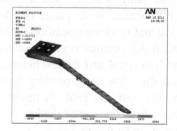   

Fig. 5. Distribution nephogram of roller tooth bearing force   **Fig. 6.** Anamorphic map of roller tooth

4   Designing Improvement for Structure

According to the results of finite element analysis, it would influence the operation quality if deformation of the pole tooth is too big because the ploughing layer of the field cleaning machine is 100~120mm. In order to meet operational requirements, the structures should be improved [13] as increasing the diameter of the pole tooth to 25mm, strengthening the thickness of the connection plate in root to 12mm.

Deal with the improved entity model of picking forks roller tooth improved and establish corresponding finite element model. Exert boundary conditions according to the actual force in working. The force imposed in place of A, B, C, D and E is consistent with Fig 4. Restarted the finite element analysis and got the result that the largest equivalent stress on the root of pole tooth was 220413 Pa and the largest deformation in the Y direction was 1.158 mm. So the deformation of improved pole tooth meets the operational requirements. The distribution of equivalent stress for pole tooth is shown in Fig 7. The deformation of pole tooth by the load effect is shown in figure 8. The deformation of other testing point is shown in table 1.

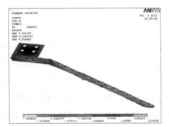   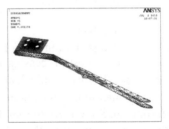

Fig. 7. Distribution nephogram of roller tooth bearing force   **Fig. 8.** Anamorphic map of roller tooth

5   Experimentally Verification

Conduct field experiment on the structure improved pole tooth with the field cleaning machine shown in figure 9 in plowed cotton land with sand soil whose moisture content is 28.9% in Southern Xinjiang. Connect resistance strain gauge into test to ensure the reliability of the test data and close to actual working condition. Influence on operation of its front-end deformation and torsion deformation is greater according to force analysis of Pole tooth. Point the pole tooth in equal and fix test points as A, B, C, D and E. Patch direction is the horizontal direction corresponding to the X direction of finite element model of pole tooth. The test and analysis results were shown in table 1. Determinate each testing points for five times and calculate average. The stress and deformation results of testing points were shown in Tab 1.

Fig. 9. Test in field

Table 1. Results about bearing forces and deformation of testing points

Items	Testing points				
	A	B	C	D	E
Average stress of each point for five tests / N	432	335	254	157	87
Average deformation of each point in test / mm	1.135	0.932	0.758	0.539	0.340
Deformation of each point in finite element analysis / mm	1.158	0.912	0.745	0.557	0.350
Error of deformation finite element analysis relative to test /%	2.0	2.2	1.7	3.2	2.8

Test out the deformation of picking forks roller tooth in actual working testing in field. It showed that the deformation of pole tooth decreases gradually from ends to root and the largest deformation 1.135 mm occurred at the end.

6   Conclusions

(1) Improved the structure of pole tooth and shorten the design cycle through nonlinear finite element analysis of picking forks roller tooth according to its working requirement.

(2) Compared the deformation in actual working with finite element simulation of the picking forks roller tooth and got the deformation error of each testing point. The largest one is 3.2%, which is less than 5%.

(3) By the nonlinear finite element analysis and actual test of remnant film picking-up of picking forks roller tooth with specific product examples, got the result from the data contrasting between ANSYS simulation and actual testing. The result verified the correctness of the finite element theory analysis and laid the foundation for the next step of structure optimization designing. Its method of analysis has certain practical value for enterprise product development.

References

1. Wang, X., Zhang, X., Ma, S., et al.: Finite element analysis of clod crushing rake tooth in field cleaning machine. Transactions of the Chinese Society for Agricultural Machinery (4) (2011) (in Chinese)

2. Zhang, X., Wu, C., Ma, S., et al.: Fuzzy optimization design of the Links mechanism with film rake of remnant plastic film collector. Transactions of the Chinese Society for Agricultural Machinery 38(9), 55–58 (2007) (in Chinese)
3. Ciark, B.J.: The Behaviour of roll over protective structures subjected to static and dynamic loading condition. Queensland University of Technology, Brisbane (2006)
4. Kim, T.H., Reid, S.R.: Multiaxial softening hinge model for tubular vehicle roll-over protective structure. Institternational Journal of Mechanical Sciences 43(9), 2147–2170 (2001)
5. Ciark, B.J., Thambiratnam, D.P., Perera, N.J.: Analytical & experimental investigation of a roll over protective structure. Institution of structural Engineers 84(1), 29–34 (2006)
6. Cheng, X., Wu, C.: Trial analysis on constitutive relation and finite element method analysis of unsa turated cultivatable soil. In: Proc. 1st Conf. ISTVS/Beijing, China, August 4-8, pp. 101–114 (1986)
7. Chi, L., Kuxhwaha, R.L.: Three dimensional finite element interaction between soil and tillage tool. ASAE Paper, No 88–1611
8. Zhang, X., Wu, C., Wang, W., et al.: Design and experiment on the zigzag scraper transportation device for remnant plastic film and stubble. Transactions of the Chinese Society for Agricultural Machinery 38(9), 55–58 (2007) (in Chinese)
9. Zhang, X., Wang, X., Ma, S., et al.: Design of a Field—clearing Machine. Journal of Tarim University of Agricultural Reclanetion 14(1), 1–4 (2002) (in Chinese with English abstract)
10. Ciark, B.J.: The Behaviour of roll over protective structures subjected to static and dynamic loading condition. Queensland University of Technology, Brisbane (2006)
11. Wang, X., Zhang, X., Li, Y.: Dynamic Simulation of Device about Film Uncovering and Clod Crushing of Field—Clearing Machinery Based on Pro/E. Journal of Agricultural Mechanization Research (2), 49–51 (2008) (in Chinese)
12. Fu, C., Wang, Y.: Research of 3D Finite Element Modelling on Wind Wheel Blade of Wind Power Generator. Journal of Machine Design 26(9), 50–53 (2009) (in Chinese)
13. Luo, M.J., Wang, W.L., Xu, G.X.: Finite element analysis and structural optimization of IOW stress frame. Machinery Design & Manufactur 32(8), 32–34 (2009) (in Chinese)

A Kind of Proxy Caching Program Based on Doubly Linked List in VOD System

Jianzhong Hou and Qiaolin Chai[*]

College of Computer Science and Technology,
Shandong University, 1500 Shunhua Road Jinan,
Shandong, P.R. China, 250100
Houjz2010@foxmail.com

Abstract. The VOD (Video-on-Demand) service has come to a reality because of the development of computer network technology and digital technology being more and more mature. But it demands high bandwidth requirement, high quantity data volume and strong real-time, these make the network bandwidth become the bottleneck of the VOD's development. So, an agent-based distributed VOD model appeared. We present a useful proxy caching scheme based on doubly linked list according to this model, it could settle the problem effectively which server load and network bandwidth base the current network equipment.

Keywords: VOD, Proxy caching, Doubly linked list.

1   Introduction

With the development of Internet technology, more and more user began to abandon the traditional passive reception and viewing of multimedia, which made video on demand services became a reality. VOD is a kind of streaming media player application system that users can get any type of multimedia data to the client end to be broadcast from the server at any time [1] .In view of the existing network infrastructure, server load and network bandwidth become the main limited factors in the widely using of video streaming. Set proxy, between the server and the user, is considered as a highly effective solution to reduce the bandwidth consumption. This system is called distributed VOD system [2]. Somebody proposed a variety of cache scenarios in accordance with different situations [2-7]. In these cache scenarios, the typical scenario is to proxy cache the initial part of the program (program head, Prefix) [2]. However, how to determine the size of the cache to effectively maximize the proxy role has become a very real problem.

1.1   Distributed VOD System Model

The system model includes the server, caching proxy, and user clusters.

---

[*] Corresponding author.

D. Li and Y. Chen (Eds.): CCTA 2011, Part III, IFIP AICT 370, pp. 527–531, 2012.

Fig. 1. Distributed VOD model

Server and caching proxy is connected through backbone net. Caching proxy and user clusters are connected through access network.

Users get video on demand service through proxy from the server. Assume that the user always wanted to watch the video from the beginning, after the proxy receives the user's request, if the video head was cached on the local proxy, then the proxy transfers it directly to the user; if the program was not fully cached in local proxy, then proxy requests the program end from the server, and then transfers to the user [7].

2   Program and Related Parameters

In response to these models and a variety of network conditions people have proposed a variety of programs, existing programs as follows:

2.1   Analysis of Existing Programs

Existing mainstream programs are as the followings

2.1.1   Batching Program and Patching Program

Batching program is initially proposed in response to server-based -demand system. It is based on the combined flow ideas, using the same media streaming to provide on-demand services for multiple users who request the same program. Its implementation is based on multicast technology. After the introduction of cache in the VOD system, batching scheme has been applied to proxy-based-demand systems and the use of proxy cache prefix program to provide timely services without delay.

Patching program is also based on the multicast merged flows idea. Server time generate entire length of the full broadcast program stream SR (called Regular Stream) for r_0 user request arrived at t_0. At t_1, r_1 user request arrives, and the server generates program fragment stream SP_1 (called Patching streams) which contains content [0, t_1-t_0]. User 1 receives these two program streams simultaneously, and immediately plays SP_1 stream data, and caches the SR stream data to disk. When finished playing SP_1 flow, the user 1 will play the SR stream data cached in the disk, and then the SR date that is receiving will continue to join the SR stream data disk buffer. Adoption of such technology, the program only requires a complete data stream and a very short clip streaming, you can satisfy both the user request r_0 and r_1. In t_2, r_2 user request arrives, similarly, the server program again generate a fragment containing [0, t_2-t_0] Patching stream of SP_2.The twice user finishes playing the SP_2 stream and then merge into the Regular stream SR generated for r_0.

Advantages: Ease the video server I / O bandwidth and network bandwidth limited by the using of multicast technology.

Disadvantages: does not consider on-demand strength. That is to say, all the programs stored in the proxy at the same length.

2.1.2   An Optimal Proxy Cache Allocation

Optimal Proxy Cache Allocation (referred to as the OPCA) is based on the global searching of excellent method to achieve the optimal program, which the proxy cache space is divided into a number of data units, and which distributes units one by one, until all data unit is distributed off, and the distribution of each unit are optimally allocated to a certain program.

Advantages: allocated the best local proxy cache space of each program to achieve the globally optimal allocation.

Disadvantages: initialization requires a lot of calculations. Each new program will also add a lot of calculations, especially when there are more programs. These two points lead to low proxy performance.

2.2   Programs Based on Double-Linked List and Related Parameters

Because these types of programs still have some shortcomings, for the network bandwidth bottleneck phenomenon, this paper proposes a proxy cache solution based on doubly linked list.

2.2.1   Doubly Linked List

Also known as Doubly Linked List, it's a kind of list. It has two pointers in each data node that point to the direct successor and direct predecessor. Next node in each node stores successor address, besides, each node adds a point which named prior which points to its direct predecessor. The doubly linked list is determined only by the head pointer.

2.2.2   Program and Ideas

The proxy storage space is divided into three parts: one is mainly used to maintain the normal operation of the system; another is used to cache the information requested from the server; another is used to store video information. Store some of the settings in the video space and maintain two overall control parameters: One is the total storage space S, the other is the free space L. Create several (refered as N) doubly linked list in the space which stores video information. The value of N can be selected according to the actual performance of the proxy (under normal circumstances we take 5-10). According to the video on demand strength, the video information is distributed to different doubly linked list. And then assign different size video space for each video information based on the function F (V_i, L_i, R_i).

2.2.3   Function and Relevant Parameters

Function F (V_i, L_i, R_i) = (V_i / L_i) * R_i: V_i stands for the video playback speed; L_i stands for the length of the video information; R_i stands for the video information on demand strength.

The first two parameters can be obtained from the video information itself. For R_i, set up a counter for each video information. Each time a user requests a video on demand, the video of the counter plus one: the counter value is considered as the strength of the video information on demand. That is the value of R_i.

In order to increase the flexibility of the function F (V$_i$, Li, R$_i$) to make it possible to adapt to a variety of network environments, we can take some improvements.

Function F '(V$_i$, L$_i$, R$_i$) = (p*V$_i$ / L$_i$) * (q*R$_i$) ,in which p, q are constants, p and q can take their value flexibility based on the actual bandwidth, the proxy performance and the storage space.

2.2.4   Program Implementation

Periodically check the counter value, record and then clear and after that, start count again. Then according to the recorded value of the counter, adjust the video to a different queue and calls the function F (V$_i$, L$_i$, R$_i$) to recalculate the space distributed for the video. If the new allocated space is less than the original space, then start to drop from the end of the video until it reaches the size of the new space, and the remaining space is for recycling. If the new allocated space is more than the original space, then request the end of the video information from the server, until fill the remaining space. When the re-allocated space is greater than the remaining space L, find the video information which has the smallest counter value from the minimum video-on-demand strength double-linked list, and then remove it. Recycle it space to the remaining space, and re-allocate it. If the re-allocated space is still larger than the remaining space L, then repeat the process of recycling space.

The time to check the value of this counter can't be set too short nor too long, if not it would cause the queue jitter or we will not achieve the proper adjustment.

At the proxy initialization, based on the actual situation, we can design video information on demand strength artificially, and allowed it to be added into the specified double-linked list, and then according to its following on-demand strength, dynamically adjust it periodically according to the program.

2.2.5   Program Benefits

Proxy-based distributed VOD cache model which adapt double-lists structure has the following advantages:

1) The management of the programs according to the on-demand strength meets the actual application;

2) Reduce the user's response time. When a user requests a video, you can search in several doubly linked lists simultaneously. It reduces the time spent to search the targeted video, thereby reduce user's response time;

3) The calculate amount is small, and it won't affect the proxy performance. Whether adding a new program or in the proxy cache initialization, simply compare the value of R$_i$ to determine the list, then call the function F (V$_i$, L$_i$, R$_i$) to compute the space. This calculation will be small and will not change with increasing number of larger programs;

4) The program is simple, easy to implement.

2.3   Applications and Developments

Above we only consider the case of only one server. However, in practical applications, since there are a large number of users in user clusters, to improve the video service loss rate [9], we need multiple servers to work together. In order to improve server efficiency, we introduced the load balancer.

All servers are connected with the load balancer, and send their load information in real-time to load balancer. After the load balancer receives a request for information send by the proxy, assign proper sever to carry out the appropriate request processing according to the load of each server.

3   Conclusions

VOD system has a huge potential market and application prospect in the long run. It represents the application and development trends of future all-function network and digital interactive information. The server load and main network bandwidth bottleneck problem have been effectively mitigated, if adopting double-linked list-based proxy caching scheme.

References

1. Little, T., Venkatesh, D.: Prospects for interactive video-on-demand. IEEE Multimedia 1(3), 14–24 (1994)
2. Sen, S., Rexford, J., Towsley, D.: Proxy prefix caching for multimedia streams. A. IEEEI NFOCOM, pp. 1310–1319. EEE Computer Society, New York (1999)
3. Guo, Y., Subhabrata, S., Towsley, D.: Prefix caching assisted periodic broadcast: framework and techniques to support streaming for popular videos. R. Tech Rep, UM- CS-2001-022. University of Massachusetts Amherst, Amherst (2001)
4. Wang, B., Sen, S., Adler, M., et al.: Proxy- based distribution of streaming video over unicast / multicast connections. R. Tech Rep, 01-05. University of Massachusetts Amherst, Amherst (2001)
5. Verscheure, O., Venkatramani, C., Frossard, P., et al.: Joint server scheduling and proxy caching for video delivery[EB/OL],
   http://www.citeseer.ist.psu.edu/verscheure01joint.html
6. Eager, D.L., Ferris, M.C., Vernon, M.: Optimized caching in systems with heterogeneous client populations. Performance Evaluation, Special Issue on Internet Performance Modeling 42(2), 163–185 (2000)
7. Yan, R.X., Hu, Y.G., Wang, H.J., et al.: Partitioned proxy: a new caching method for video-on-demand system. Journal of Northeastern University (Natural Science) 23(8), 742–745 (2002)
8. Hu, Y., Zang, H., Gao, Y.: Optimal Proxy Cache Allocation of VOD System. Journal of Northeastern University (Natural Science) 25(4), 341–344 (2004)
9. Peng, Y., Chen, F.: Video Data Storage of Distributed VOD System. Chinese Journal of Computers 23(6), 671–672 (2000)

Author Index